TELEVISION: THE CRITICAL VIEW

"TELEVISION

THE CRITICAL VIEW,,

Fourth Edition

EDITED BY

HORACE NEWCOMB

University of Texas at Austin

New York   Oxford
OXFORD UNIVERSITY PRESS
1987

Published by Oxford University Press, Inc.,
200 Madison Avenue, New York, New York 10016

Library of Congress Cataloging-in-Publication Data
Television : the critical view.
Includes bibliographical references.
1. Television broadcasting--United States.
I. Newcomb, Horace.
PN1992.3.U5T42 1986   791.45'0973   86-23548
ISBN 0-19-504175-5

3 5 7 9 8 6 4
Printed in the United States of America

For my colleagues
past and present
in the Department of Radio-Television-Film
The University of Texas-Austin
Artists, Critics, Scholars, Teachers

PREFACE TO THE FOURTH EDITION

It has now been more than ten years since the first edition of this collection appeared. In that time television studies and television criticism have flourished. There are now far more courses in colleges and universities that take the medium seriously as an object of study. And as some of the essays in this edition make evident, serious thinkers who may never teach a course in television have also turned their consideration to the medium. In this sense, I think we have begun to think of the medium in light of Moses Hadas's admonition quoted in the Introduction: "all who take education seriously in its larger sense—and not the professed critics alone—should talk and write about television as they do about books."

People concerned with general literacy, with the political role of mass entertainment, and with the imaginative life of the culture now deal thoughtfully with television. While most of the writers whose works are collected here are "professed critics," they write for all of us. And they are brought together here as part of a general cultural discussion, not an exchange among a small group. To the degree that we learn from them, and apply what we learn, the climate of television criticism may develop in even healthier ways.

The best indication of this is the range of concerns and methods gathered here. While some underlying matters run throughout these essays, they represent a rich diversity of approaches. This accounts for a comment I hear often about the book, that it is unsystematic and eclectic. Intended or not, I take that judgment as a compliment. Television is too big and too baggy to be easily or quickly explained. No single approach is sufficient to deal with it adequately. Multiplicity is what I am after, both as editor and teacher.

This should not be taken as an endorsement of casual or unsystematic criticism. Rather, the aim of the book is to provide a variety of models with which students and their teachers may create and adapt careful and systematic approaches of their own. Out of the exchange of ideas and critical questions, forms of writing and thinking, we are able to sharpen our best individual responses. If some of the essays here contradict one another, that simply means we will have to criticize the critics as well as the object of their study. The result should be a still more precise understanding of television. For the climate of television criticism to continue in its current vitality, that precision is ever necessary.

Austin   H. N.
April 1985

PREFACE TO THE FIRST EDITION

The essays in this collection were selected because they view television in broad rather than narrow perspectives. Newspaper columns have not been included. This is not to say that newspaper criticism is excluded by definition from a breadth of vision, but simply that the pieces included here all develop their point of view in the single essay rather than over a period of time, as is the case with the columnist.

The essays in the first section all deal with specific program types. They serve as excellent models for practical television criticism because they show us that there is a great deal of difference between watching television and "seeing" it. They are, of course, involved with critical interpretation and assertion. Other analyses of the same programs may be offered by other critics, and the audience, as critic, must learn to make its own decisions. These essays will help in that learning process.

The second section is comprised of essays that attempt to go beyond the specific meanings of specific programs or program types. They suggest that television has meaning in the culture because it is not an isolated, unique entity. These writers want to know what television means, for its producers, it audiences, its culture.

The essays in the final section are concerned with what television is. They seek to define television in terms of itself, to determine how it is like and how it is different from other media.

All the essays are seeking connections, trying to place television in its own proper, enlarged critical climate. Consequently, many of them use similar examples, ask similar questions, and rest on shared assumptions. Some of the connections are obvious. Others will occur to the reader using the book. In this way the reader too becomes a critic and the printed comments may serve to stimulate a new beginning, a new and richer viewpoint regarding television.

I would like to express my thanks to John Wright of Oxford University Press for his initial interest and continued support for this book. His suggestions have strengthened it throughout. A special note of thanks must go to all my friends and colleagues who have made suggestions about the book and who, in some cases, have offered their own fine work for inclusion. Thanks, too, goes to my family for the supportive world in which I work.

Baltimore   H. N.
November 1975

CONTENTS

Contents

TELEVISION: THE CRITICAL VIEW

HORACE NEWCOMB

INTRODUCTION
TELEVISION AND THE
CLIMATE OF CRITICISM

Writing in 1962, Moses Hadas suggested that television, already considered a nearly worthless pastime, be taken far more seriously by thinking persons.

> Because he is not directly determining profit and loss, because he is contemplating a range of subject matter almost unlimited in scope and has regard to an audience almost as large and varied, the critic of television is in effect dealing with universals and hence he must cultivate the philosophical approach. To have validity, universals must, of course, be solidly grounded in particulars, and our critic must obviously be expert in various relevant techniques; but these are ancillary to his larger aims. The larger aims are, in a word, educational. And education in its fullest sense, not schooling alone, is the single most important enterprise of civilized society.
>
> A truer analogy than drama, therefore, is literature, which has traditionally held the general educational mandate television has now come to share. In literature, too, the scope is vast, the audience coextensive with literacy, and the benefits need not involve cash expenditure. In literature, as we have observed, there is a tangible critical climate, guided and made articulate by professional critics, perhaps, but shaped by all who take books seriously and write and talk about them. The critical climate, in turn, determines what books are made available; no writer who wishes to be heard and no sane publisher will fly in the face of it. A similar critical climate must be created for television; all who take education seriously in its larger sense—and not the professed critics alone—should talk and write about television as they do about books.[1]

I take Hadas's phrase, "education in its larger sense," to mean something like "culture" in its most pervasive and all-inclusive form. What he is suggesting has little to do with the idea of formal instruction, or as he says, with "schooling." It has much to do with the ways in which members of a society are shaped, changed, directed, and influenced by their most pervasive forms of communication. It has to do with the ways in which the lives of people are reflected by the content of those communications forms. We are "educated," our culture is reflected by the stories that are told to us in literature or by way of television, by commentary on daily occurrences (the "news"), by the thorough explorations of important or unique events (documentary), by the personalities and stars who entertain us. This is the sort of education that goes on each day, unconsciously and largely without evaluation on the part of the audience. It is part of the texture of our lives.

This broad educational or cultural function of television has not, of course, been overlooked or denied. From the earliest development of the medium it has been of great concern to those who deal with television on a daily basis: newspaper critics of television, researchers, professional educators, and parents. Television producers and network officials have recognized the enormous power of their "business" and have issued statements denying the negative influence of TV almost at the same time as they have praised its positive effects. Governmental agencies such as the Federal Communications Commission, and professional organizations such as the National Association of Broadcasters have written professional regulations and codes designed to clarify the function of television and to protect the viewing public from possible harm. The most careful defenders of television, therefore, have often based their concerns in fears of television's educational function, an attitude which is, to some degree, well founded. If it is not always easy to accept the judgments of elitist critics who fear for the degradation of mass "taste"; it is quite simple to accept the concern of writers who remind their audiences that television is a complex financial system in which the viewers are consistently manipulated for profit. The realization that television demands no essential literacy forces us to see that among its available victims are children, an issue that forms the basis for extensive research into the effects of violence and aggression as seen on television. A similar concern for TV's political and economic power warns minority or special interest groups that their integrity must be protected and that other audiences must be forewarned about false stereotypes and negative portrayals.

Unfortunately, our fears about television, no matter how healthy or well founded, have restricted the development of a critical climate for television as called for by Hadas. Most serious television commentary, for example, has been directed toward the audience rather than to the content of the medium. The primary concerns have been with audience response as influenced by television. While this results in an extensive body of research literature, there are very few careful descriptions of television programs. Similarly, while we have several political and economic histories of broadcasting, there are no histories of television programming. Without such descriptions and histories, there is no sense of development in television and little awareness of differences in program type, in writing, in production. On the one hand, television is seen as new and unique, its behavioral influences unrelated to those of other communications media. On the other, it is denied qualities and properties of its own and is only judged comparatively. Usually the comparisons are invidious ones in which television is condemned for what it is not rather than for what it is or even for what it might become. Excellence in television is taken to be the exception with continual surprise, as if this were not also the case in literature and film. Television, then, has no heritage of its own, no place in the culture except as an intruder. And while it should be clear that more comprehensive critical approaches would not see television exclusively in virtuous terms, it should also be clear that an assumed negativism can effectively prevent thorough analysis.

Such analysis and its contribution to the creation of a true "critical climate," have been further restricted by the most prevalent forms of television commentary, journalism and research. Journalism, by its very daily nature, responds to the brutally immediate aspects of television, as Lawrence Laurent makes clear in his essay, "Wanted: The Complete Television Critic."

This complete television critic begins with a respect and a love for the excitement and the impact of the combination of sight and sound—pictures which can be viewed and words which can be heard, by millions of people at one time. This complete critic must be something of an electronics engineer, an expert on our governmental processes, and an esthetician. He must have a grasp of advertising and marketing principles. He should be able to evaluate all of the art forms; to comprehend each of the messages conveyed, on every subject under the sun, through television. And there's more.

He must be absolutely incorruptible, a firmly anchored man of

objectivity in a stormy world of special interests and pressure
groups. At the same time, he should stand above the boiling
turmoil while he plunges into every controversy as a social critic
and guardian of standards. While being both aloof and involved,
he must battle for the right, as his judgment and instincts guide
him toward that right.[2]

Laurent notes, of course, that the total fulfillment of all these
tasks is beyond the human capacity of a single individual. But it
is in the very attempts to complete the tasks that the real
failures of journalistic writing about television occur. The journalist feels and accepts the responsibilities that Laurent outlines, feels the responsibility to form judgments that will guide
the audience to some understanding of the issues. The journalist must "keep up" with the latest problem, whether that means
reviewing an important show, responding to the latest research
report, or writing about the most current political or financial
restrictions. His subject matter is, in this way, determined by
what is most important in a journalistic sense, by what should
go into a daily newspaper designed for a single, quick reading.
The journalist, then, is open to manipulation by the medium
about which he writes. The networks see that the "best" shows
occupy directly competing time slots. They bring out special
shows during essential "rating periods." Weeks of "good" or
"important" shows are run together, leaving the critic at the
mercy of consistently mediocre programming at other, leaner
times.

Frequently, the critic learns that he must develop some formula that will allow him to have something to say day after
day. Some resort to scorn, pouring out column after column of
satire. Television becomes a whipping boy, always available and
ultimately impervious to the blows delivered by the critic. Others resort to the easiest and handiest resource, passing along to
their readers condensed versions of the massive public relations
packets that arrive with each day's mail. When the critic
chooses to combine scorn with ready made publicity there results the gossip column, devoted more to amusement than to
commentary on television.

There are, on the other hand, truly responsible critics who
pursue courses designed to provide significant commentary on
the medium. Superior journalists—Laurent, Jack Gould, John
Crosby, Robert Lewis Shayon, John O'Connor, and others like
them—shape television with views as responsible as Laurent
would have them be. These critics often see their role as one
that allows the audience to have its own views corroborated or

challenged, and realize that such a process can aid both critic and audience in seeing television more clearly. Still, in most cases, there is time and space for the expression of only imme- diate response, and no matter how informed or responsible, such immediacy does not tend toward the development of a clear overview of television's complex role in culture and so- ciety. Over a period of months or years the faithful reader may see the growth of a set of critical principles for judgment and analysis, but he will see them only if the critic has been able by withstanding the pressures of his position to state them clearly. And because of the multiplicity of the journalist's concerns the reader must pick through comments on politics, economics, technology, aesthetics, and personality before he can discover consistency or its absence. Even when the journalist produces a book-length examination of television such as Martin Mayer's *About Television*, the essential concern is with bringing every aspect of television into the critic's purview. Instead of brief columns devoted to a range of immediate concerns we have lengthy chapters devoted to them. Ultimately, the journalist gives us small bits and pieces of ideas about a great many aspects of television. The business of the journalist is informa- tion, and we are informed with fragments.

The researcher too is concerned with fragments. He is con- cerned with individual programs or with parts of them, with particular portions of the audience under special circumstances. His primary questions have to do with the ways in which television affects the behavior of the audience. Most often his questions focus on the ways in which television *causes* certain types of behavior rather than with the broad and general sort of effect. Here, for example, is a statement describing in simple terms one method used by the researcher in establishing such links.

> The experimental method involves the manipulation of some experience (called the *independent* variable) and then the measure- ment of some aspect of behavior (the *dependent* variable). The major purpose is to determine if the changes in the independent variable produces changes in the dependent variable; that is, to determine whether there is a causal relationship between the two. An additional goal is to insure that *only* the independent variable could have caused the difference—to eliminate alterna- tive interpretations of the results.[3]

This use of experimental techniques to establish causal links between television and audience behavior is only one of many

sophisticated research techniques. To supplement this essentially laboratory procedure the researcher also uses field studies
in more natural settings. In order to be as accurate as possible
he will also modify and correct his findings with elaborate
statistical techniques. Nevertheless, if the fault of journalism is
that it gives us no systematic overview, the fault with research
is that we see such overviews built on statistical inference.
Critics of such methods are quick to point out that such inferential system building tells us little about individual behavior,
about single lives. Because the researcher, so far, has most
often been concerned with the possibility of harmful influences
on behavior he is able to reply that even a minimal significance,
if carefully established, is sufficient to call for reform, regulation, or continued monitoring.

Both the researcher and the journalist act most often out of a
deep concern for the meaning of television. Each in his own
way tells as much as possible about the medium. But because
their concerns are reportorial and fragmented on one hand and
narrowly defined on the other, neither can be properly termed
criticism in Hadas's sense. A far better example of that sort of
criticism is offered by Robert Warshow in his comments on
how the critic should examine another form of popular art, the
movies. Dissatisfied with both sociological and "art" criticism of
the movies, Warshow suggested that there is a more accurate
way to establish the critical relationship.

> This is the actual, immediate experience of seeing and respond-
> ing to the movies as most of us see them and respond to them. A
> critic may extend his frame of reference as far as it will bear
> extension, but it seems to me almost self-evident that he should
> start with the simple acknowledgment of his own relation to the
> object he criticizes; at the center of all truly successful criticism
> there is always a man reading a book, a man looking at a picture,
> a man watching a movie. Critics of the films, caught in the
> conflict between "high culture" and "popular culture," have too
> often sought to evade this confrontation.[4]

Or, putting the same view even more succinctly, he says, "A
man watches a movie, and the critic must acknowledge that he
is that man."[5]

With this sort of statement we are approaching Hadas's admonition that all who take education seriously in its larger
sense should think and write about television as they do about
books. But there is one more step that must be taken before
that is fully the case. We must acknowledge that Warshow's

"man watching the movie," is in some sense a special sort of man. That is, he is the man aware of what he is doing, aware of the relationship between himself and the movie, aware of the relationship between the movie and the cultural traditions that contribute to its production. Finally, he is aware of his own relationship with that same culture. Again, Warshow points the way for this sort of criticism.

> I have felt my work to be most successful when it has seemed to display the movies as an important element in my own cultural life, an element with its own qualities and interesting in its own terms, and neither esoteric nor alien. The movies are part of my culture, and it seems to me that their special power has something to do with their being a kind of "pure" culture, a little like fishing or drinking or playing baseball—a cultural fact, that is, which has not yet fallen altogether under the discipline of art. I have not brought Henry James to the movies or the movies to Henry James, but I hope I have shown that the man who goes to the movies is the same as the man who reads Henry James.[6]

The "man at the movies" then is a self-conscious man. He is a self-conscious critic. He is aware of the movies as he is aware of Henry James, and if he wishes to make distinctions between the two he must make them critically, on the basis of judgment and definition and not on the basis of snobbery and condescension.

The first task of this collection of essays, then, is to bring together some of the best writing about television. This writing goes beyond journalism and research. At times it goes beyond it by simple extension; the essays here are longer, more thorough, more reflective, even when they are written about topics that would interest the journalist in a brief comment. Most often, however, they go beyond the other forms of television commentary in that they seek to establish more carefully the cultural context of television. Some of that context forms the background from which television develops, other parts of it are caused by television. The essays prove that such thorough television criticism can and does exist, that the medium itself does not dictate the more superficial or the more narrowly defined comment. They also make painfully clear the fact that such excellent criticism has not been the dominant mode of discourse regarding television. Their scarcity indicates that Hadas's critical climate has not yet developed, but rather, that those who take education in its larger sense most seriously have too often been those who have left television out of their thought, even as it changed the world in which they lived.

There is another purpose of this collection. It is based in the assumption that people other than self-styled, self-conscious critics are seriously involved with "education in its larger sense." In our culture, even those who do not like books take them seriously. They may even take their dislike seriously. But at the very least they are introduced formally to books, they are required, at some stage of their lives, to think about them, to look at them. And they are required to look at them in particular ways. Books are considered the repository of cultural heritage and the agents by which that heritage is not only reserved and transmitted, but examined and amplified as well. Because television has not been given attention by those whose professed purpose is the serious concern for education in its full sense, it has developed no respected place in the culture. The end result of this chain of consequences is that the mass audience, sensing this general lack of concern, this pervasive attitude of fear and negativism, has little of the respect for television that it has for books, and is left without general critical guidance. Because it is uncritical the mass audience is left at the mercy of those willing to manipulate it. The old network excuse, "We give the audience what it wants," must finally be laid at the feet of those who would be first to state publicly their concern for education in its larger sense. Their lack of concern for this medium that has assumed "the general educational mandate" indicates ultimately a lack of concern for the audience rather than for the medium itself. They do not care for the people who watch television.

A true climate of criticism, then, will involve not only those who consider themselves to be professional critics, researchers, journalists. It will also involve most of the population, for most people do care in their own way about the general education of the culture. Such caring is at the heart of the critical enterprise and as Robert Lewis Shayon suggests, that enterprise is at the heart of what it means to be human. "The critical spirit is the supreme manifestation of human intelligence which sets man off from the animals. It is the world's best hope." His purpose in writing criticism, then, and the purpose of this collection, is "the making of critics":

> not only professional critics of the arts, of society, of the various departments of human affairs, but also and especially "people critics," alert, perspicacious individuals who know how to confront the assorted phenomena of their own lives, their own

worlds, and their own relationships, how to analyze them, to manage them dialectically, and to discover in the dialectic creative new possibilities for human dignity and mutuality.[7]

Surely it is not too much to ask that we turn this sort of critical intelligence toward television. Nor is it too much to ask that the climate of criticism so created by thoughtful writers be frankly and openly educational. Until the audience understands what it sees in larger contexts, until it develops its own critical facilities we will live in a world dominated by one-eyed monsters. When all of us participate in the critical climate we will live in a world more thoroughly humane than any other.

NOTES

1. Moses Hadas, "Climates of Criticism," in *The Eighth Art*, ed. by Robert Lewis Shayon (New York, 1962), p. 19.
2. In *The Eighth Art*, p. 156.
3. Robert M. Liebert, John M. Neale, and Emily S. Davidson, *The Early Window: Effects of Television on Children and Youth* (New York, 1973), p. 38.
4. Robert Warshow, *The Immediate Experience* (Garden City, N.Y., 1964), p. xxv.
5. *Ibid.*, p. xxvii.
6. *Ibid.*
7. Robert Lewis Shayon, *Open to Criticism* (Boston, 1971), p. ix.

PART I

SEEING TELEVISION

All of us watch a great deal of television. Whether or not we "see" it, in any critical sense, is another question. The essays in this section are concerned with how to do more than watch, absorb, react to, and forget the hours we spend before the set. They all represent ways of examining television more closely, more thoroughly, more analytically. They offer us different ways of seeing the medium. Most often they are focused on specific programs and program types, or on specific problems involved in studying television. Some depend on knowledge of history, others on knowledge of technique. Where that knowledge is missing, the essays fill in the gaps. Where it can be expanded, they point in new directions. All offer excellent models for practical criticism of television and any one of them can be used to study, analyze, or criticize programs other than those that are the subject of the essay.

James Chesebro's essay, for example, deals with many television shows that are no longer in current, prime-time programming. But the method he constructs to study those shows can be applied to shows familiar to all of us. We may disagree with Chesebro regarding the placement of specific programs, but that disagreement should serve as the source of a critical discussion, both of the programs and the method. And that discussion can range over the entire body of television works, historical and contemporary.

The essays by Jane Feuer, Thomas Schatz, and Michael Schudson make up a group, in that all of them deal with television created by Mary Tyler Moore Productions. These shows—*The Mary Tyler Moore Show*, *Rhoda*, *Newhart*, *Lou Grant*, *Hill Street Blues*, and *St. Elsewhere*, among others—are among the most famous and influential in the history of television. Feuer's overview of the "quality style" of the MTM productions traces interactions among producers, writers, forms, and meanings of many of those shows. Originally published as part of a larger

study of the MTM organization and its products, it is one of the
first studies of television to examine the entire production
process as it relates to the cultural status of the products.
Schatz focuses more specifically on one aspect common to these
shows, the use of the ensemble cast. This is not mere description of fictional technique, however, for what he is able to
demonstrate is that this technique is central to the sense of
realism, complex morality, and compassion that we find in
these programs. Schudson, affirming these qualities, raises an
issue not fully explored in the other essays—the relation of
fiction to specific political reality. What does it mean, he asks,
when we deal with large public issues as if they were private
troubles? What is the relation between the two? How do these
patterns relate to television at large? Again, these questions
can be applied to any of the programs studied in this entire
collection.

The next three essays discuss diverse program types. Susan
Horowitz traces changes in the depiction of women in situation
comedy. Focusing on *Kate and Allie* she reminds us of the distance we've come since early situation and domestic comedy
restricted the roles available to women and of the restrictions
and possibilities that remain. Horowitz's essay was written in a
brief period when it appeared that the situation comedy was a
form no longer central to television. The appearance of *The
Cosby Show* and other successful situation comedies has proven
that view wrong. Reading Horowitz now reminds us that the
situation comedy is a form taking many shapes, a form with a
life-force of its own. It also reminds us that any guess about
"trends" and "patterns" in television programming is hazard-
ous.

Christopher Anderson looks at *Magnum, P.I.* and explains
how it is more than a simplistic "hunk show," glorying in
action, adventure, fast cars, and shoot-outs. As Anderson demonstrates, this program reconstructs conventional television
narrative forms. By creating a powerful sense of memory it
brings us into closer proximity to our own social and cultural
history. Because other shows are adopting a similar strategy,
Anderson's observations can be aptly applied in other places.

Cathy Schwichtenberg analyzes the structure and form of
Love Boat in order to foreground its hidden ideological motives.
This sort of careful attention shows once again that programs
thought to be the most trivial are often powerful revelations of
social and cultural assumptions. As with Anderson's analysis of

Magnum, this approach can be used to study many other kinds of television.

Robert C. Allen turns our discussion to soap opera. The soaps, once the most despised examples of popular entertainment, have recently come to be among the most studied and, in some cases, the most praised. Their narrative innovations and stylized treatments of emotional strategies are often seen as true inventions. Allen examines the interaction of industry and story to explain the cultural place of these never-ending fictions. Bernard Timberg focuses more closely on the contribution of visual elements to the ways in which soap operas inform their audiences, shape responses, and contribute to other narrative elements.

David Barker asks similar questions about visual meaning in television. His close comparative analysis of *All in the Family* and *M*A*S*H* is built on a survey of general production techniques. We should note here that in spite of its status as our most widely shared visual medium, television's visual elements have not often been studied. Barker and Timberg are among a new generation of television analysts who are trained in production techniques and, at the same time, vitally concerned with critical questions. Their studies offer excellent models for application to other television series.

Douglas Gomery, Horace Newcomb, and Marsha Kinder examine some of television's most popular and successful forms and programs. Gomery's approach to the made-for-television movie combines historical, industrial, and aesthetic analysis. He reminds us that television is directly related to the film industry in many ways, and that the creation of new forms clearly builds on the old. Newcomb's discussion of *Dallas* raises similar questions by relating that popular show to the Western.

Kinder studies one of the newest versions of television, one that many people see as a link not only to music, but to experimental film and video as well: the music video. She explores the phenomenon in terms of its form and its audience, and most importantly, she raises questions about the interaction of the two. This question of audience relations to television returns in later sections as one of the most important problems now facing television studies.

With Hal Himmelstein, Jonathan Black, and Martin Esslin, we move to different kinds of television, though all three essays raise questions regarding the degree of difference. Himmelstein surveys television news and documentary. Black hones in on one of television's most popular programs, *60 Minutes*. Esslin takes a closer look than usual at the ever-present commercials. All three suggest that these forms, sometimes more closely related than television is to our common experiences, take on some elements of the fictional programs we've looked at earlier.

These concerns, of course, like many expressed in other essays in this section, extend far beyond their concern with single programs or even with program types. They are part of a general discussion of the role and significance of television in culture and society, and that discussion forms the center of the essays in Part II.

JAMES W. CHESEBRO

COMMUNICATION, VALUES, AND POPULAR TELEVISION SERIES— A FOUR-YEAR ASSESSMENT

Our attitudes and behaviors are typically a reflection of the values we have acquired. As we mature, our value orientations are subtly shaped by our parents, churches, and schools. However, researchers are less confident that the mass media— particularly television—decisively affect and control our value judgments. As Steven Chaffee, L. Scott Ward, and Leonard P. Tyston have observed, "There has been little evidence for mass communication as a causal element in a child's development. . . . Debate usually centers around the relative effects of processes initiated by the more primary agents."[1] Even though television viewing is now this nation's major activity, Jeffrey Schrank has accurately noted that, "Exactly how television has influenced our psychology we don't know."[2]

Yet, we clearly have reason to believe that television could be affecting our value judgments. Producers of popular television series admit, for example, that they selectively dramatize certain values rather than others. While entertaining their viewers, these producers also appear to be functioning as persuaders who intentionally emphasize certain values discriminantly. While each might promote a different value, virtually all of the major producers are overtly aware that their series dramatize certain values at the exclusion of others.[3] In producing *The Waltons*, for example, Lee Rich has reasoned that "the success of this series is because of what is going on in the country today, the loss of values. Many people see ethical qualities in this family that they hope they can get back to."[4] In this context, Richard D. Heffner has aptly argued that television series may appropriately be viewed as "subtle persuaders." As he has put it, "Television, the newest and far more prevalent form of fiction, is even more profoundly influential in our lives—not in terms of the stories it tells, but more importantly, the values it portrays."[5]

The relationships among communication, values, and popular television series are complex; no single study is likely to reveal all of the dynamic intricacies among these three systems. In this essay we can only begin the complex process of identifying the ways in which popular television series affect the values of viewers. This study is designed to identify the communication strategies employed on television series to convey and to reinforce selective values.

Four questions mold the analysis offered here:

1. *What patterns, types, or kinds of human relationships are portrayed in popular television series?*

2. *How are human problems and difficulties resolved in popular television series?*

3. *What images or character references are portrayed in popular television series?*

4. *How have popular television series changed, particularly in the last four years?*

In order to answer these questions, four lines of analysis are developed. First, a system is outlined for describing and interpreting popular television series as communication systems. Some fifty-seven different series appeared on the air during the 1977-78 season, each with a host of different plot lines, minor characters, and ideas expressed each week. A classification system was needed which could "make some coherent or logical sense" out of this barrage of messages. The formulation of such a system requires the presentation of what is called a "theory of logical types," which simply allows a critic to explain the symbol-using on popular television series in the context of a systematic framework. The theoretical system outlined here produces a framework which allows the critic to view a television series as essentially one of five communication strategies. This scheme is detailed in the first section of this essay. While this classification system was developed to explain symbol-using in popular television series, the basis for the system is also explicitly identified because it can account for major types or forms of communication in everyday situations. Second, these five types of communication are illustrated from television series in the

1977-78 season. Third, this theory is employed as a grid for classifying all television series in the 1977-78 season and for identifying changes in the nature of communication patterns in these series since the 1974-75 season. Fourth, image or character references portrayed in the 1977-78 season are specified and described.

A THEORY OF LOGICAL TYPES FOR CLASSIFYING COMMUNICATIVE ACTS

A theory of logical types for classifying communicative acts requires rules for the formulation of such a matrix. These concerns led Herbert W. Simons to propose that generic formulations proceed along certain methodological lines:

> First, there must be a class of genres into which a particular genre can be put. . . . A second requirement for generic identification is that the categorizer must have clear rules or criteria for identifying distinguishing characteristics of a genre. . . . Third, the necessary and sufficient distinguishing features of a genre must not only be nameable but operationalizable; the categorizer must be able to tell the observer or critic how to know a distinguishing feature when he sees it. Finally, if items of discourse are to be consistently identified as fitting within one genre or another, it follows that those items should be internally homogeneous across salient characteristics and clearly distinguishable from items comprising an alternative genre.[6]

These rules are used for the formulation of the communication matrix proposed here.

In order to generate a matrix, all communicative acts must first be examined on the same level of abstraction or be members of one "class of genres." Among communicologists, any number of approaches or classes may be selected to satisfy this first methodological requirement. Communicative acts may be selected to satisfy this first methodological requirement. Communicative acts may be viewed as manipulative *strategies* which has, for example, generated a matrix in which communicative acts were classified as either consensus, confrontation, apologia, or concession strategies.[7] Or communicative acts may be viewed as responses to various types of *situations*.[8] Communicative acts might also be grouped by the apparent *purpose* for initiating the act, and thus a set of categories might include acts as attempts to persuade, to entertain, or to inform.[9] Others might group communicative acts by their similarities and differences as policy recommendations, essentially an *act*-centered matrix.[10]

An *agent*-oriented criterion is employed here for the classification of communicative acts. An agent-centered approach reflects the image orientation of our popular culture. The notion of an *image* implies that there is a presentation or staging of the self to others. While an image may conceal or distort, there is also a sense in which every person must employ one role or posture rather than another, depending upon the time, circumstances, needs, and available means which emerge during an interaction. While less contrived or more spontaneous presentations of the self may be preferred, nonetheless image creation and image manipulation are now a focal point of all complex cultures. Whether these images are created with clothing, make-up, hair arrangements, or by carefully worded policies which compromise differences, *style* is now a "god-term" of our culture. In this context, Daniel Boorstin has observed that the number of "pseudo-events" or "planned, planted or incited" events have increased drastically.[11] Kenneth Boulding has likewise argued that there has been a "growth of images, both private and public, in individuals, in organizations, in society at large, and even with some trepidation, among the lower forms of life."[12] This constant bombardment of images may be created, for example, by magazines such as *Playboy* and *Playgirl* which suggest that a satisfactory lifestyle may emerge from a quasi-sexual and quasi-technological orientation, while other public forms such as television talk shows or *People* magazine may reinforce particular lifestyles by virtue of their coverage of such "popular images." In this regard, David M. Berg has noted that mass media, "particularly television," create "a higher incidence of exigencies than that reality which is experienced directly." He concluded that "media do more than merely reflect events; they also create them."[13] Thus, our decision to employ an agent-centered orientation in the formulation of a communication matrix appears appropriate, particularly given the centrality of image or character references which dominate popular television series.

Having selected an agent-centered matrix, Simon's second methodological requirement becomes relevant: "clear rules or criteria for identifying distinguishing characteristics of a genre" must be employed. Northrop Frye provides a convenient set of rules for distinguishing types of central characters in fiction.[14]

Because Frye's concern and the focal point of this analysis are similar, Frye's scheme is easily adapted as a mechanism for analyzing central characters on television series. In Frye's view, two variables generate and distinguish major kinds of communication systems: (1) the central character's apparent intelligence compared to that of the audience, and (2) the central character's ability to control circumstances compared to that of the audience.

These two variables produce five kinds of communication systems. In the *ironic communication system*, the central character is both intellectually inferior and less able to control circumstances than is the audience. In the ironic communication system, the person responsible for an act lacks both the scope and the appropriate kinds of interpretative concepts and categories for assessing reality as well as the skills necessary to mobilize or to generate the support required for concerted agreements and actions; a situation all of us have faced at one time or another. In the *mimetic communication system*, the central character is "one of us," equally intelligent and equally able to control circumstances. In mimetic communications systems, all are perceived, believed, or treated as equals: a common set of symbolic perceptions, descriptions, and interpretations of reality are shared by individuals if they are members of a mimetic system; moreover, members of such a system face and deal with similar problems and situations with equal skill. In the *leader-centered communication* system, the central character is superior in intelligence to others but only in degree by virtue of special training, personality conditioning, and so forth. However, the central character in the leader-centered communication system faces and deals with the same kinds of circumstances the audience confronts. Thus, the leader generates a configuration of symbols for acting that others find compelling, thereby creating the concerted actions necessary to deal with shared problems, situations, or questions. In the *romantic communication system*, the central character is superior to members of the audience in degree, both in terms of intelligence and in terms of the ability to control circumstances. In romantic communication systems, the central character thus possesses a symbol system which allows her or him to account for more environmental variables in more incisive ways than others (intelligence) and to create more effective programs for action upon these environmental factors than others (control of the environment). In the *mythical communication system*, the central character is superior in kind to others both in terms of intelligence and in terms of his or her ability to control circumstances. If we view Christianity as a communication system, for example, the "word of God" is presumed to stem from a kind of superior intelligence far beyond any kind of understanding humankind may ever possess as well as being capable of producing environmental changes which no mere mortal may ever achieve. While "mystical" in nature, such symbol systems should *not* be viewed as somehow less "real" than any other mode of communication, for such systems have profoundly altered the attitudes, beliefs, and actions of massive groups of people. These five communications systems thus constitute the basic distinguishing categories or framework for classifying television series.

However, our ability to distinguish these communication systems remains imcomplete, for the question emerges: How does the critic determine the relationship between the central character and the audience? Simons's third rule for matrix formulation provides a reponse to this question, for it posits that systems must be *operationally discrete* as well as conceptually distinct: "the categorizer must be able to tell the observer or critic how to know a distinguishing feature when he sees it."

In order to identify operationally and systematically the unique pattern of dramatic action which characterizes each communication system, Kenneth Burke's "dramatistic process" has been employed. Burke maintains that all human dramas are carried out in four discrete stages.[15] These four stages and their concomitant critical questions are : (1) *Pollution*—What norms are violated and cast as disruptive to the social system involved? (2) *Guilt*—Who or what is generally held responsible for the pollution? (3) *Purification*—What kinds of acts are generally initiated to eliminate the pollution and guilt? and (4) *Redemption*—What social system or order is created as a result of passing through the pollution, guilt, and purification stages? This *pollution-guilt-purification-redemption* framework can be used to describe systematically behavioral differences among each of the five communication systems at each key stage of a human drama. A series of very different behaviors develop each dramatic stage of each communication system identified here. Thus, the dramatistic process allows us to detect operational differences among the five communication systems.

Surveys of popular television series carried out by this researcher for the last four years have led to the conclusions that:

(1) the central characters in television series engage in varied behaviors when functioning in human relations or human dramas (conflict-resolution patterns); (2) this allows a critic to employ explicit behavioral standards when classifying each television series into one of the five communication systems; and (3) suggests that television series grouped together into one of the five communication systems display shared, common, or redundant patterns of conflict resolution. Figure 1 provides a complete conception of the behavioral matrix ultimately generated.

SYMBOLIC AND DRAMATIC PROGRESSIONS IN POPULAR TELEVISION SERIES

The dramatic progressions which distinguish the ironic, mimetic, leader-centered, romantic, and mythical communication systems can be illustrated by specific television series in the 1977-78 season. The ironic system is first examined and is appropriately revealed as a symbolic system by the character of Archie Bunker in *All in the Family*.

The Ironic Communication System

An ironic character may assume two forms. The ironic character may *intentionally* assume a pretense of ignorance or pretend to learn from others in order to reveal the false conceptions of others. Such ironic characters purposely use words which convey the opposite meaning of their literal meaning, typically producing an incongruity between the normal or expected results and the actual results of a sequence of events. Thus, the notion of *Socratic irony* has come to identify the agent who intentionally pretends to be stupid in order to inconspicuously force an answerer to reveal false conceptions.

However, the ironic character may also function in yet another form. The ironic character may *unintentionally* articulate and defend positions which are inconsistent with known events. In such cases, the character has unknowingly become ironic; only the audience is aware of the incongruity. Unintended ironic behaviors introduce a comic dimension into an interaction. Thus, the role of "expert," for example, is ironically portrayed if the actor mispronounces the technical terms of a field, misstates common understandings of a discipline, or em-

Figure 1: TYPES OF COMMUNICATION DRAMAS

Dramatistic Stages	Ironic	Mimetic	Leader-centered	Romantic	Mythical
Pollution	The central character violates major rules of the system.	Rules violated are minor and the result of accidents, the best of intentions, and/or circumstances.	Values of the central character are violated by others.	The central character identifies the significance and scope of the problem (a problem of mind, body, and spirit).	Universal problems beyond human control—unreasonable, overwhelming, and often religious/ideological—set off the drama.
Guilt	The central character is explicitly recognized as the cause of the pollution: scapegoat.	Guilt is easily admitted by agents because pollution is both insignificant and unintentional.	The central actor assumes responsibility for correcting the pollution: self-mortification.	The central character is the primary, if only, agent who identifies all of the dimensions of blame in a way that allows for correction.	Blame cannot be attached to any particular and individual agent—forces are to fault.

Purification	Characters beside the central character initiate acts to correct the pollution.	The accidents and/or circumstances are explicitly recognized; intentions are explained; forcing a reinterpretation and/or forgiveness for the pollution.	The leader mobilizes others to achieve the original ends through selective means chosen by the leader.	The more highly developed skills, intelligence, and sensitivity of the central character are combined in the unique fashion essential to produce the most desirable set or corrective acts.	Superhuman powers of the central character emerge during the corrective process.
Redemption	The central character is reestablished as the controlling force to reinitiate pollution.	The previous system can be reestablished with all characters "wiser" for the experience.	The leader's values are reestablished and explicitly recognized as controlling.	The central character is recognized overtly as the embodiment of all that's right.	A new social system is established due to unique powers of central character.

ploys nonverbal symbols which are inconsistent with the verbal symbols of the field of expertise. Thus, the intentions of the character, the environment in which the character exists, and the "universe of understanding" possessed by an audience, all determine the degree to which a given set of behaviors is perceived as ironic.

Typically portraying the latter of these two ironic postures, the character of Archie Bunker on *All in the Family* predisposes an audience to anticipate that he will function as an ironic character in a human drama. His faulty diction, misstatements of fact, and failure to interpret events as most would, all predispose most audience members to view Archie as an ironic character. Moreover, Archie is inconsistent with the environment in which he must function. He applauds the politics of Herbert Hoover, endorses outdated systems of discrimination, employs stereotypes as accurate barometers of reality, and unknowingly violates existing norms of propriety. Thus, Archie exists in a social context which he cannot appropriately respond to, adapt to, or control.

As human relationships and dramas unfold each week on *All in the Family*, the inciting incident or pollution is typically the result of Archie's actions. Archie's "sins"—after some five years of shows—are most unlimited now; he has lied to Edith, forged her signature, gambled, hurt the feelings of others, said the "unbelievable," and argued for the "impossible." At the same time, Archie is the "hero" of the series, and herein resides the irony. We anticipate that the hero of the drama will correct, not create, pollution. Yet, Archie is the breadwinner and the head of the family while simultaneously creating the pollution which generates the drama.

Others in the family attribute the responsibility for the pollution to Archie, or circumstances force Archie to admit that he has erred, or he slowly realizes that he has been mistaken. In a technical sense, Archie is a *scapegoat*, for others blame him for the disorder. The irony of the show is thereby extended, for again the hero is held to be a central causal agent for the pollution dominating the drama.

The pollution and guilt are typically resolved or "purified" by actions of characters other than Archie. When Archie plans to file a fraudulent insurance claim after a minor fire in the bathroom, for example, it is Edith who eliminates the basis for the false insurance claim and the foundation for any criminal action against Archie. Likewise, Archie detains a mentally retarded delivery man, knowingly jeopardizing the man's job. It is not Archie, but George the delivery man, who finds himself another job. Archie's patronizing attitude toward George and all mentally retarded persons is simultaneously "corrected," for George is employed in the same job on the same loading dock as Archie. In this case, the victim of the drama purifies the drama. The "hero" is again cast as ironic for the incongruity between common sense expectations of a hero and Archie's actions is reasserted.

In the final redemptive stage of the Bunker's drama, a closing scene typically reestablishes Archie as head of the family. The sensitivity of others, Archie's "basically good heart," and perhaps a begrudging act of atonement on Archie's part provide the warrant for reestablishing Archie's status. Thus, the show closes with a final touch of irony, for Archie is now able (next week) to set off an entirely new dramatic incident.

The Mimetic Communication System

Marcel Marceau has frequently been identified as the outstanding mime of the twentieth century. On an empty stage, in whiteface and dressed in black, he silently copies or imitates scenes from everyday life. The acts he portrays are intended to reflect what all of us do; the common, the ordinary, or those "slices of life" all of us experience are revealed. Thus, Marceau portrays a "man walking in the rain against the wind," a "man walking upstairs," or a "man trapped in a box." His mimetic acts closely resemble real life, but the resemblance is superficial and therefore a form of what is technically identified as "comic ridicule." While we may enjoy and laugh at the mime, the mimetic performer also allows us to prepare for those moments when others may find us in an embarrassing situation, and when we must admit the humor of our own everyday actions.

The mimetic form may also be employed to disarm us and make us view other persons or products as a normal part of our everyday lives when, in fact, such representations are persuasive efforts to make us endorse "foreign" agents or objects as part of us. Thus, the politician employs the mimetic form when he proclaims in the agricultural district: "I was once a farm boy myself."[16] Or the mimetic form is used to sell us papertowels or coffee: cast as "our next door neighbors," Rosie and Mrs. Olsen then proceed to reveal their overwhelming zeal and commitment to Bounty and Folgers. Such bandwagon techniques are grounded in the mimetic form—a dramatic imitation of life, usually but not always in a slightly exaggerated manner, designed to reinforce or to alter perceptions, attitudes, beliefs, and actions.

Moreover, the mimetic form can also be used to characterize entire patterns of human action. Such mimetic patterns attempt to cast both the "content" and the "manner" of dramas as everyday phenomena: the pattern thus minimizes the unusual and unique; it casts particular goals, values, beliefs, attitudes, concepts, actions, and manners as common or popular. Dramas operating within the constraints of this mimetic form, then, typically portray incidents as common: problems are conceived as accidents, a product of misunderstood intentions, or the results of unavoidable circumstances, all of which ultimately creates the view that the problems involved are relatively insignificant and unpremediated; once the accidental, unintentional, or circumstantial nature of the problem is confirmed, characters typically return to their previous and established modes of action, perhaps wiser for the experience.

Fish, the central character in the television series *Fish* is a retired police detective of no particular renown. We are led to believe, especially if we watched *Barney Miller* last season, that Fish was a rather typical, hard-working cop, who now faces with his wife Bernice the somewhat irritating but relatively common family difficulties as they function as foster parents for a group of "basically good" but formerly delinquent children. While such a setting appears uncommon, the constraints of the mimetic form transform the situation into an everyday experience. In one episode, for example, Jilly—one of Fish's children—reaches her sixteenth birthday and sets off a drama for Fish.

The pollution is initiated when Jilly confronts Bernice and explains that she wants Bernice to accompany her to a gynecologist to get the Pill. Jilly explains that she does not wish to contribute to the population explosion, that she is mature, and that she wishes to demonstrate that she is responsible. After some agony and a pointed order from Fish that Jilly is not to get the Pill, Bernice secretly and with some doubts accompanies Jilly to the doctor and obtains birth control pills for her. Bernice, then, is cautiously able to resolve this problem by assuming that Jilly is, in fact, a responsible adult.

However, for Fish, the pollution and guilt appear much more profound. At Jilly's sixteenth birthday party, Fish meets Jilly's boyfriends who, at eighteen years of age, appear fully grown and hardly "boys." Moreover, the number of boyfriends also worries Fish. When one of the boys kisses Jilly right in front of Fish and when he discovers she has the pills, the pollution and guilt appear extreme—immorality and promiscuity loom just around the corner in Fish's view.

At this juncture in the drama, Jilly initiates a series of acts which clearly transform the drama—her intentions make "all the difference." At the end of her party, she approaches Bernice and Fish and thanks them for the pills, for respecting her, and for treating her as a responsible adult. She then returns the pills to Bernice—"I won't need them." Thus, the drama has been transformed. The pollution perceived by Fish was, in fact, a question of misinterpreted intentions and circumstances. Jilly's guilt must also be reinterpreted by Fish, for her statement and behaviors have been clarified and they deny Fish's previous assumptions about Jilly. Thus, the pollution, guilt, and purification requirements of the mimetic drama have been revealed and satisfied.

Correspondingly, redemption involves the simple recognition that all has returned to normal. The norms of the family are reestablished. Fish, Bernice, and Jilly are wiser for the experience—they now understand, trust, and respect each other more.

However, some would question the kind of value employed to redeem such a drama: Is it desirable, likely, or normal for a sixteen-year-old woman to reject the pill for the reasons offered by Jilly? Perhaps not. However, in mimetic television series, certain types of value judgments may be expected. Of the twenty-five "shared cultural values" Redding and Steele identified as "premises for persuasion" most likely to be used in America,[17] ten of these value or moral standards repeatedly emerged in the mimetic dramas surveyed here. These values included puritan morality (particularly as reflected in its subthemes of honesty, simplicity, cooperation, orderliness, personal responsibility, humility, and self-discipline), achievement and success, effort and optimism, sociality and considerateness, external conformity, generosity, and patriotism. As noted four years ago when these five communication patterns were first employed, "As we considered series after series, we were ultimately able to predict the content of a show if we knew its form; if we had determined the form, we could make reasonable estimates about the kinds of principles that would be conveyed in the show."[18]

However, the central point observed here is that the mimetic form is used to rationalize any moral standard whenever that moral is cast as a normal part of everyday experience. While other critics have indirectly acknowledged the persuasiveness of the mimetic form on popular television series, they have viewed these series as accurate reflections of reality rather than as strategies which attempt to control how people respond to reality. Referring to shows such as *The Mary Tylor Moore Show*, *The Bob Newhart Show*, and *Rhoda*, for example, Sklar has argued that the new situation comedy deals with "how people really feel." He further observed that these characters are "as familiar as neighbors."[19] We are perhaps more cautious. It seems obvious that the mimetic form is used to create the *impression* that typical behaviors and values are being reflected, for this is the function of the mimetic form. It is less evident that the actual behaviors and values of "average" Americans have been captured in these dramas. As Lance Morrow has aptly put it, it may actually be that "TV humor, whether the players are black or white, now turns mostly on chaotic exaggeration."[20]

The Leader-Centered Communication System

As a point of departure, a common sense notion of a leader functions as an excellent description of the leader-centered communication system. Typically, leaders are believed to be those individuals who direct others, possess authority or influence, manage the affairs of a group, and possess some heroic characteristic. This conception of a leader corresponds nicely with our previous notion of a leader as one who possesses superiority in terms of intelligence by virtue of special training, personality conditioning, and so forth, but who must deal with the same circumstances others face. More particularly, from a communication perspective, leaders dominate others in the sense that they employ a set of symbols which mobilize the responses of others: they introduce and formulate goals, tasks, and procedures; they delegate or direct actions; they integrate or pull together the efforts of other individuals; they provide transitions or interconnections among events; and they appear confident of their values—others may, in fact, treat the value judgments of leaders as factual statements.

On the television series *Maude* we find a character who would initially seem to satisfy the requirements of a leader, for Maude is described in the theme song of the series as a "big bad wolf," a "slugger," the "tail end of the batting order," and "anything but tranquil." Moreover, a persistent theme of *Maude* is that a woman can be as strong and as powerful as *any* man. Insofar as Maude functions as a leader, then, we would expect her to define and to establish the goals and values which control the social system, to determine when these goals and values are violated, to assume responsibility for the rectification of these values, and to initiate those actions necessary to purify and to redeem the "original" goals and values. Indeed, Maude does seem to function as a central character might in a leader-centered communication system.

As one show opens, for example, we find Maude specifying, defining, and reinforcing a set of goals and values regarding one's "first love." Maude is talking on the telephone to her daughter Carol who must be out of town for two weeks. Maude is elated to tell her, as she puts it, "Carol—Phillip, your little boy, is in L-O-V-E. Yes, yes, he's in love for the first time. No, no, no, it's not Samantha. I don't know. It's some new girl. I haven't met her yet. Her name is Diane Harding. Yeah! Oh, Carol, it's so sweet." Later, Maude informs Walter (her husband) "He's crazy about her, and apparently she feels the same way about him. Phillip told me that she agreed to go steady with him. Oh, Walter, *fifteen years old*. What a beautiful time in life." Maude's tendency to control such a situation becomes even clearer when she says to Walter, "I want everything to go smoothly tonight. Phillip, my grandson, is in love for the first time. It is a very important night for him." Maude's decision to "want everything to go smoothly" initially involves only direct "recommendations" to Phillip, including the appropriate watch and shoes to wear: "Phillip, you can't go out on an important date wearing a Mickey Mouse watch. Only little boys wear Mickey Mouse watches"; moreover, Maude pleads, "Oh, Phillip, you're not wearing brown shoes. Phillip, young men wear black shoes in the evening."

However, pollution enters Maude's world, for Diane does not fit Maude's conception of what Phillip's first love should be— she is too old, too mature, too independent, and too sophisticated. Diane, indeed, is described as a "knockout college girl," who has just moved "into a new apartment with her girlfriend." When Maude is directly informed by Diane that she is nineteen, Maude's disapproval becomes overtly evident: "Are you familiar with the Mann Act?" After Diane and Phillip leave, again Maude's sense that something has gone wrong emerges: "Run after them! Save Phillip from that woman!" In a more thoughtful moment, Maude defines the problem for Walter and her two neighbors Vivian and Arthur: "Look, I don't think any of you really understands. Look, I can see where a young man might become interested in an older woman. That's normal. But, what does she see in Phillip? What's she getting out of this?"

The problem defined, Maude decides to assume full responsibility for "correcting" the pollution. Typically, we would expect the mother of the young man to handle such an issue, but when Carol telephones again, Maude decides that she will withhold the revelant information and any mention of the problem which exists. More directly, Vivian seems to sense that the problem is not Carol's, not Walter's, not Walter and Maude's, but solely Maude's: "Maude, we're just so sorry for you. Well, the minute Carol goes out of town and you're left in charge of your grandson, he starts running around with an older woman. You must feel just awful. I'd like to tell you not to blame yourself, but what good would that do? You've got to blame yourself when you can't even control your own grandson. Poor old grannie."

Having assumed and also been assigned the responsibility to purify the drama, Maude employs a dual strategy. She first approaches Phillip: "Phillip, how can I get through to you? Phillip, Phillip, I don't want to interfere in your life. I really don't, Phillip. But, your going around with Diane is wrong. Now, it is very difficult for me to explain why. Phillip, I just wish you'd trust me, and break off with her." Maude's appeal to Phillip is singularly unsuccessful, for Phillip ultimately rejects Maude's advice: "Grandma, if that's what you want, I'm glad you told me, because any advice you'd give me is always good advice. You know, I think I'm pretty lucky to have you as a grandmother, and if you weren't my grandmother, I'd want you for my friend. Well, I'd better go get ready for my date with Diane." Maude is forced to conclude that her strategy with Phillip was ineffective: "Phillip, you punk!" However, when Diane arrives to pick up Phillip, Maude employs her second strategy: "Look, Diane, I'll be blunt. I do not like your going out with Phillip. You're exploiting him. Look, admit it Diane, you should be spending your time with men of your own age." Diane responds and admits that she goes out with Phillip because she "feels safe" with him. With Maude's prodding, Diane further admits that she goes out with Phillip because she's "in control" when she's with him. Maude, then, intervenes, summarizes the matter, and draws the interconnections: "Diane, do you hear yourself? You go out with Phillip because he's safe." From upstairs, Phillip has overheard this conversation and he then enters the interaction: "Safe. You go out with me because I'm safe, sweet, and adorable. What a rotten thing to say about a guy. Look, Diane, if you feel like I'm safe, we're just going to have to stop dating. I have my reputation to think about.

The act done, Maude proceeds to redeem the drama and return to the original "order" of values. She notes to Diane that "you will find a wonderful boy your own age who won't put this pressure on you. But you have to keep looking." After Diane has said goodbye to Phillip, Maude suggests that Phillip give his old girlfriend Samantha the gold anklet he had planned to give to Diane. Things have thus returned to their proper places.

Maude typifies the behavior of the central character in the leader-centered communication system. She faces the same kinds of circumstances and situations that audience members can identify with. She can do no more with these circumstances than others. However, Maude is powerful, strong, and articulate. She is able to offer a symbolic conception of a situation which affects the perceptions, descriptions, and interpretations of others. She mobilizes the responses of others in such a way as to reestablish the goals and values which she had initially established. She is a leader. She is superior to others in intelligence only in degree, but she is equal to others in terms of the kinds of circumstances she faces and in terms of her ability to alter or change the nature of the circumstances. The drama of the leader-centered communication system is thus illustrated aptly by Maude.

The Romantic Communication System

In the romantic communication system, classical notions of romance are featured. The romantic hero or heroine is believed to be or is treated as if he or she had prodigious courage and endurance: the heroic are adventurous, idealized, and frequently mysterious; their tales are legendary, daring, and chivalrous. These classical conceptions of romance led us earlier to suggest that the central character in a romantic communication system would possess a symbol system which would allow the hero or heroine to account for more environmental variables in more incisive ways than others and to create more effective programs for acting upon those environmental factors. Thus, while romantic agents are superior to others only in degree, the situations they face seem to contain almost overwhelming elements of unknown danger and risk as well as requiring remarkable levels of human power, intensity, dedication, and capacity. We almost expect that the ordinary laws of nature must be suspended if these dramas are to be successfully resolved. Clearly, romantic agents must be intellectually superior to others and be capable of exercising superior control over their environment.

On the television series *Charlie's Angels*, three policewomen have left the police force because they were assigned only routine office work rather than dynamic detective work in the field. All three were at the top of their class in the police academy—they are expert shots, capable of executing crippling karate kicks and punches, extremely bright, creative, and, as we might expect in a romance, they are glamorous, slender, and beautiful. Affectionately called "his Angels," these three women are hired as private detectives by Charlie, a powerful, mysterious and wealthy figure who owns a detective agency designed to handle highly sensitive, complex, perilous, and demanding situations. Besides the subtle Cinderella transformation which is emphasized at the beginning of the series each week, the requirements of each show thus persistently call for a dynamic team of heroines capable of simultaneously resolving dramas laced with intricate psychological, explosive situational, and physically exacting dimensions.

In one show of the series, "Pretty Angels All in a Row," Kelly and Kris vie to be "Miss Chrysanthemum" while Sabrina and Bosley play television reporters when the Angels infiltrate a beauty contest being ravaged by terrorism. However, the necessity for all of these covert actions and even the existence of terrorism is unknown until the Angels begin their investigation.

Initially, the pollution detected by the coordinators of the beauty pageant is perceived only as an attempt to undermine and to destroy the pageant. Mr. Paul, master of ceremonies for the tournament, notes that the contestants are "dropping out right and left" and that the pageant starts "tomorrow and we only have nine girls left" out of the original fifty-six. However, during the Angels' briefing, Charlie sees the pollution as potentially more complex and dangerous, for he believes that the attempt to frighten a contestant with a tarantula constitutes a more serious issue. As the Angels investigate the situation, they confirm Charlie's speculation, and they find, in fact, that attempted murder, kidnapping, bribery, conspiracy, and blackmail are also part of the "problem." Thus, while others were unable to identify the "full" scope of the problem, the Angels were able to do so. In addition, only the Angels are able to determine that unsuspected psychological motivations also permeate the scene. Thus when an attempted gunshot misses Kris by three feet, only the Angels are able to determine that perhaps the gunmen "did not really want to kill her," especially given particular circumstantial evidence. Moreover, when a sandbag is intentionally cut from the ceiling of the pageant hall and just misses the contestants, Sabrina knowingly asks, "Was that sandbag supposed to scare someone or kill someone?" Moreover, after Millicent, one of the pageant judges, is assaulted and kidnapped, Kris pointedly alerts us that the scene has changed. "Up 'til now everything's been done only to scare everyone." Thus, the Angels reveal a controlling problem more profound and more extensive than anyone else had suspected. Not only are the kinds of crimes involved more extensive, but the psychological motivations for these crimes are understood and revealed only by the Angels.

Similarly, until the Angels enter the case, virtually no one connected with the pageant has any idea who is responsible for the terrorism or for what reasons. Sabrina, by virtue of her undercover role, is able to spot the most likely suspects, trail them to their car, sneak into the trunk of their car without the suspects' knowledge, overhear their telephone call to their boss C.J., and, before her hiding spot is detected, Sabrina is able to locate the suspects' hideout. Thus, at least one of the Angels is able to reveal the entire "web of guilt" which leads to a boss— C.J. is a millionaire stock broker who hopes to have his daughter Billy Jo crowned "Miss Chrysanthemum" so that she can model in his corporation's commercials on television. Prior to the Angel's investigation, no one within the drama had even been aware of C.J.'s existence.

Having identified the real pollution and guilt, the unique powers of the Angels enable them to purify the drama. They are able to function as undercover beauty contestants only because of their glamour and beauty, positions which allowed them to literally jump the suspects from the stage by surprise. Moreover, their karate experience allows the Angels to "make short work" of the suspects: they are "flattened in less than a minute." Likewise, from Sabrina's undercover role, she is able to trace as well as disarm the suspects because of her extensive knowledge of firearms acquired at the police academy.

Having purified the drama, the criminals are jailed, Billy Jo is disqualified from the contest, and C.J. is apprehended as an accessory to the crimes. Moreover, Kris and Kelly are redeemed as "beauties," for we are informed that Charlie had instructed the judges that they were only "substitute noncontestants" in the contest. The show closes with all of the Angels smiling. All conditions for the romantic drama have been satisfied.

The Mythical Communication System

A myth is a fabricated, invented, or imagined story of ostensibly historical events in which universal struggles concerning Truth, Beauty, and Patriotism are depicted. In an almost sacred or timeless order (ritual or dream), a hero or heroine embarks upon a long, unknown, and difficult journey in order to retrieve a "precious object" which is guarded by unusually powerful counteragents. In the process of completing the quest, the hero or heroine displays superhuman powers thereby creating a myth, fantasy, illusion, or vision. Thus, Jason's quest for the golden fleece and Superman's demand for law and order constitute myths. Both Jason and Superman face universal problems beyond the responsibility of any particular human force. The resolution of these problems requires "superhuman" powers employed toward the formulation of a new social system.

On *The Six Million Dollar Man*, Steve Austin, hero of the series, appears to meet the requirements of a mythical hero. Austin was a relatively successful astronaut until a nearly fatal accident forced him to lose an eye, an arm, and both legs. The government intervened; Steve was transformed into a bionic man at a cost of six million dollars. He can now run sixty miles an hour; he has x-ray and infrared vision; he can leap thirty feet into the air; and he has superhuman strength in his bionic legs and arm. An experiment in human imagination and technology has transformed Austin from a helpless cripple into a quasi-mechanical superman. In a mythical communication system, we would expect an agent like Steve Austin to function as a central character in such a drama. In fact, Austin passes through the pollution, guilt, purification, and redemption stages which we have attributed to the mythical communication system.

In one of the shows of the series, for example, Austin's counteragent is an indestructible, self-protecting computer set to initiate a nuclear war automatically in the context of tense Soviet-American relations. To complicate matters further, an earthquake has both disrupted the timing of the computer and closed off circuits essential to shutting down the computer. These circumstances generate a set of supernatural problems. Blame for these events cannot be placed on any human agent; guilt is beyond the limits of humans. Purification requires the strength, intelligence, and virtue of a mythical Hercules or Jason, willing to undertake a dangerous journey operating, at best, with the aid of a select few who complement the hero's power. No predictable set of purifying acts exists; the hero's power surfaces only during the struggle itself. To get to the computer, Austin must pass through an underground research center which has been designed to protect itself; this center has been blown up and all its mechanical devices are unpredictable. The hero alone controls the purification stage of the drama. Redemption occurs when the hero has accomplished the task and others are able to speak of the efforts employed to eliminate the pollution. Moreover, the act accomplished promises a new hope for a new social system. Thus, the mythical agent in a dramatic situation employs a set of symbolic tools—in this case, bionic—superior in kind to those possessed by other agents. Moreover, the mythical agents have affected the controlled circumstances in ways other humans cannot. Whenever agents are thus assumed, believed, or treated as if they possessed superior intelligence and a superior ability to control circumstances, the stage is set for a mythical symbolic progression in which others expect that universal problems are handled in superhuman ways as steps toward the creation of a new social system. While utopian in nature and therefore potentially unattainable, mythical communication systems are frequently employed to deal with, or perhaps to rationalize a decision not to deal with, a human condition. Nonetheless, the form is common enough and important enough to recognize as part of the human response to communication dramas.

POPULAR TELEVISION SERIES
AS COMMUNICATION SYSTEMS,
1977-78 AND 1974-75

Having defined and illustrated the communication matrix proposed here, the 1977-78 television series are now appropriately classified into this matrix. Figure 2 provides the results of such

Figure 2: TELEVISION SERIES—A FOUR YEAR COMPARISON*

Communication System	1974–75 Season	1977–78 Season
IRONIC	All in the Family The Texas Wheelers Sanford and Son	All in the Family The Jeffersons Sanford Arms
MIMETIC	The New Land Friends and Lovers The Mary Tyler Moore Show The Bob Newhart Show Apple's Way Rhoda Happy Days Good Times That's My Mama Little House on the Prairie The Odd Couple Paper Moon Chico and the Man	Fish Operation Petticoat The Love Boat The Bob Newhart Show We've Got Each Other The Tony Randall Show Rhoda On Our Own Alice The San Pedro Beach Bums Little House on the Prairie Happy Days Laverne and Shirley Three's Company The Fitzpatricks Busting Loose One Day at a Time Mulligan's Stew Eight is Enough Good Times Chico and the Man Welcome Back, Kotter What's Happening!! Barney Miller Carter Country Chips The Betty White Show
LEADER	Emergency Nakia The Rookies Maude Born Free Adam-12 Lucas Tanner Movin' On The Rockford Files	Maude M*A*S*H Young Dan'l Boone Family Lou Grant Police Woman

Figure 2: (*Continued*)

Communication System	1974–75 Season	1977–78 Season
	Mannix	The Life and Times of Grizzly Adams
	Gunsmoke	
	Cannon	The Oregon Trail
	Streets of San Francisco	Big Hawaii
	Kodiak	The Rockford Files
	Police Woman	Rosetti and Ryan
	Get Christie Love	Barnaby Jones
	M*A*S*H	
	Barnaby Jones	
	Kung Fu	Starsky and Hutch
	Kojak	Kojak
	Medical Center	Rafferty
	Marcus Welby, M.D.	Charlie's Angels
ROMANTIC	Hawaii Five-O	Baretta
	Manhunter	The Waltons
	Petrocelli	Hawaii Five-O
	Harry O	Logan's Run
	The Waltons	Switch
	Ironside	Quincy, M.E.
		Six Million Dollar Man
	Six Million Dollar Man	The Bionic Woman
MYTHICAL	The Night Stalker	The Man from Atlantis
	Planet of the Apes	The New Adventures of Wonder Woman

*A "television series" was defined as being: prime time (7–11 P.M. EST), national network productions of a dramatic nature (conflict-resolution patterns excluding sports, news specials, regularly scheduled news programs, and documentaries) in which a single character or team of central characters appear weekly (which would exclude variety shows, movies, made-for-TV movies, specials, and semidocumentaries). While 1974–75 season series seldom changed, the "data base" for the 1977–78 season changed continually. Some critics claimed that by the midpoint of the 1977–78 season, the equivalent of three different sets of "seasons" had already been created by the networks. Almost 50% of all new series had been replaced by "newer" series, and many of these replaced by the "newest" series. Consequently, I decided that seasons would be defined as those series listed by *TV Guide* for the first week of the season. The 1974–75 season was those series listed Sept. 14–20, 1974; the 1977–78 season those listed Sept. 10–16, 1977. Only episodic shows were included as the soap opera form does not necessarily resolve all of the issues in its open-ended time format.

a classification; the 1974–75 television series have also been similarly classified because this contrast plays a central role in the analysis which follows. Moreover, once the nature of this classification system is understood, there is reason to believe that others are likely to classify popular television series into the same categories of the matrix.[21]

During the last four years, popular television series have changed in their communicative emphasis. Figures 3 and 4 provide a compilation of these changes.

As Figure 3 indicates, the mimetic form has become the dominant mode of communication on popular television series. While controlling over one-quarter of the series four years ago, the mimetic form is now employed as a controlling mode of presentation on almost half of current television series. Moreover, as Figure 4 indicates, television series employing the mimetic form are also the most stable—the apparently small percentage of 1973 series in the 1977 season is deceptive and due only to the drastic increase in the use of the form.

The increasing use of the mimetic form coincides with national changes in popular self-conceptions among Americans. Gallup poll data gathered in 1974 indicated that approximately one-third of Americans expressed "high levels of satisfaction" with "life in the country." Three and a half years later, in 1978, Gallup reported that this percentage had doubled and that almost sixty percent of Americans were now highly satisfied with their personal life. In greater detail, *The New York Times* characterized the shift in these words:

Figure 3: CHANGES IN THE COMMUNICATION PATTERNS
OF TELEVISION SERIES

Communication System	1974–75 season		1977–78 season		
	N	%	N	%	% shift
Ironic	3	6	3	5	−1
Mimetic	13	28	27	48	+20
Leader	18	38	12	21	−17
Romantic	10	21	10	18	−3
Mythical	3	6	4	7	+1
TOTAL*	47	99	56	100	

*Rounding off accounts for differences above and below 100%.

Figure 4: CHANGE IN TELEVISION SERIES

Communication System	1973 series in 1974 season		1974 series in 1977 season	
	N	%	N	%
Ironic	1	33	1	33
Mimetic	6	46	6	22
Leader	5	27	5	41
Romantic	3	33	3	33
Mythical	1	33	1	25

Dr. Gallup's pulse-takers and head-counters have just produced the dazzling news that since the autumn of 1974 the number of Americans expressing a "high level of satisfaction" with life in this country has risen from only 35 to a striking 57 percent. . . . the Gallup breakdown shows the boom in satisfaction to be uniformly spread across age, educational and occupational groups, and among men and women. Even the number of highly satisfied blacks rose, though by less than half the increase in contented whites. Can life in the United States really be that much better than it was in '74?

Dr. Gallup's own interpretation of his findings is plausible— "the somber post-Watergate mood of the public has given way to an increase in national pride." In support of that, it seems reasonable to point out also that the Vietnam War, which had cast its shadow on the national spirit for more than a decade, flared and sputtered to its bloody end in 1975.

Even so, a three-year rise from only one-third to nearly two-thirds in the number of Americans well pleased with their lot seems extraordinary.[22]

In contrast, the leader-centered form has sharply declined as a mode of dramatic presentation (Fig. 3). Moreover, leader-centered dramatic television series have been the most unstable category of the five modes of communication (Fig. 4). These series have yet to find a consistent or stable viewing audience; audiences are, in fact, turning from such modes of communication (Fig. 3). In addition, insofar as romantic television series reflect the nation's tendency to endorse highly idealized conceptions of people and values, Figure 3 suggests that idealism itself—as a persuasive mode of appeal—may also be declining relatively even though the absolute number is stable.

The decline in leader-centered and romantic television series coincides with our understandings of the changes in the popular conception of the nation's leaders and its institutions. Gallup poll data has noted an increasing distrust of the nation's institutions during the last five years.[23] Moreover, a study by the research firm of Yankelovich, Skelly and White, which was based upon their national random sample of 1,931 adults and a smaller sample of judges, indicates, for example, that a "a profound difference" exists between the public's and a judge's view of "what courts do and should do." In addition, the Yankelovich study suggests that as citizens gain an increasing "extensive knowledge of (the) courts," they express "less confidence" in the courts.[24]

Ironic and mythical television series have remained relatively important (particularly when the ratings of these series are considered) and stable. As Figures 3 and 4 indicate, during the last four years the ironic and mythical forms have been successfully employed as modes of communication. Insofar as the ironic form reflects the "rhetoric of the loser," viewers apparently continue to find such modes of interaction significant, although the absolute number of such series is relatively small compared to other kinds of series. Similarly, the need to fantasize (perhaps a measure of the need to escape from life's realities) has seemingly remained relatively important as a mode of communication. While mythical series are less stable than mimetic series (Fig. 4), the fantastic nature of mythical series may require that changes in this mode of communication be constantly introduced in order to preserve the novelty of the category. Thus, while bionics have continued to be a stable and appropriate reflection of the technological nature of our popular culture, other popular myths have shifted from an interest in communicating with intelligent animals (*Planet of the Apes*) and from a consideration of the occult (*The Night Stalker*) to the possibility of living in the sea (*The Man from Atlantis*) to an exploration of the nature of different kinds of human species altogether (*The New Adventures of Wonder Woman* and more recently *The Incredible Hulk*).

IMAGES CONVEYED BY
POPULAR TELEVISION SERIES

The communication matrix outlined here has allowed us to identify the major patterns of symbolic identification which distinguish popular television series and to trace the changes in these patterns over time. Yet, there are times when we wish to assess popular television series *as a whole,* for the series possess common characteristics as well as distinguishing characteristics. These common characteristics emphasize one set of behaviors and values rather than others, and for this reason they function as one model of communication which dramatizes and reinforces one kind of life-style rather than others.

In order to identify the common characteristics of all television series, a mode of analysis is needed which cuts across all series. A set of sociological categories provides such a method. While not all of the sociological characteristics of the central characters of these series can be determined solely by viewing the series, nonetheless the *sex, race, city size,* and *occupation* of the central characters of the series can be determined rather easily, or if the characteristic is not obvious (such as the occupation), it may often be revealed by a verbal reference. Focusing upon these defining variables, initially we should note that popular television series may be compared to a profile of the American culture as it is. Figure 5 compares the nature of central characters of this season's series to a random sample of Americans.

As the data show, the typical central character of current television series is an urban white male professional. Consequently, the typical central television character does not reflect the American culture as it is. In particular, when the decision is made to feature a male or a female as the central character of a television series, males are selected three times more frequently than females. In this sense, popular television series may be considered de facto sexist. However, current television series are racially balanced when compared to a cross section of the American population.[25] On the other hand, rural life-styles are slighted for the more dramatic image of the transient constantly on the move. Moreover, if we consider detectives, government agents, and police to be professionals, popular television series drastically over-emphasize and dramatize the life-style of the professional, almost three times more frequently than would be expected. Concomitantly, the life and drama of the manual worker is underestimated, reflecting an elitist orientation. Finally, non-labor force members—particularly the "housewife" and the unemployed—receive little attention; one is led to believe that housewives and the unemployed are nonentities in the world created by evening television series.

Thus, while a sociological analysis allows us to examine all

Figure 5: PROFILES OF CENTRAL TELEVISION CHARACTERS AND A RANDOM SAMPLE OF AMERICANS*

| Characteristics | 1977–78 characters | | Gallup sample |
	N	%	%
SEX			
Male	34	61	50
Female	11	20	50
Both†	11	20	
RACE			
White	50	89	89
Nonwhite	6	11	11
SIZE OF CITY			
Urban	47	84	75
Rural	3	5	25
Transient	6	11	—
OCCUPATION			
Professional/Business	33	59	21
Clerical/Sales	4	7	11
Manual workers	4	7	43
Farmers	2	4	4
Non-labor force	3	5	20
Undeterminable	10	18	—

*Rounding off accounts for differences above and below 100%.
†Two or more people were considered central characters and possessed more than one of the traits involved as a team.

television series simultaneously, we are really more interested in the *image* conveyed by the central characters of these series. This image orientation takes on a decidedly communicative perspective when we ask the following kinds of questions: Are the networks indirectly fostering or reinforcing sexist and elitist attitudes? Do the networks misrepresent the American culture? Are the networks aware of this misrepresentation? Should the networks take steps to correct this distortion? These questions reveal issues beyond the scope of this study. However, the issues are crucial, for the way in which these issues are resolved may ultimately determine the kinds of communication images and models which are portrayed on television.

In this context, it is interesting to note how the networks have altered evening television series during the last four years. Figure 6 provides some indications of this evolution along six particular dimensions.

Television series have rather persistently emphasized the life-style of the single adult (Fig. 6). Seventy-six percent of the central characters in the 1977–1978 season were unmarried, and 63 percent had apparently never been married. While the percentage of characters who are married with children has increased in the last four years, they are still outnumbered three to one by the unmarried. Similarly, while there has been a 15 percent decline in the decision to feature only males as central characters in television series, men are still represented three times more frequently than females. On the other hand, television series were already relatively balanced racially four years ago, and if anything networks have corrected for the slight imbalance in the 1977–78 season. At the same time, "city living" continues to dominate as the setting for television series. Rural settings—currently represented one-fifth as frequently as a national cross-section would suggest—occupy even less importance on television today than they did four years ago. The "rural life-style" has now been displaced by the life-style of the transient. While the tendency to emphasize professional and business roles has declined in these series, professionalism continues to be twice as high as would be expected, and housewives and the unemployed remain nonentities in the world of television. Finally, living alone continues to be the dominant image portrayed on television series, although this living style has gradually declined during the last four years. While Figure 6 also indicates that the large household is making a comeback, it should also be noted that only half of the "large-family" series (*Fish* and *Eight Is Enough*) continue to be on the air at mid-season this year. *Overall, these data suggest that popular television series have changed very little during the last four years. Four years ago, television series disproportionately dramatized the life-style of the white single urban professional male who lives alone. The networks continue to highlight this life-style.*

Moreover, the networks are dramatizing and overemphasizing a life-style which implicitly endorses, rather than counteracts, destructive patterns of interpersonal interaction. While the networks emphasize the desirability and utility of single living, the Bureau of the Census informs us that a primary interpersonal unit in our culture—the family—continues to grow smaller, less stable, and more fragmented.[26] Issues here are complex. The networks may be correct: it may be that the

Figure 6: LIFE STYLES OF CENTRAL CHARACTERS
(1974–75 and 1977–78)*

Characteristics	1974–75		1977–78	
	N	%	N	%
MARITAL STATUS				
Married with children	6	13	12	21
Married and no children	3	7	1	2
Widowed with children	3	7	1	2
Divorced with children	0	0	3	5
Widowed and no children	0	0	1	2
Divorced and no children	1	2	2	4
Single	29	62	35	63
Extended family	1	2	1	2
Undeterminable	4	9	0	0
SEX				
Male	34	72	32	57
Female	6	13	11	20
Both†	7	15	13	23
RACE				
White	38	81	50	89
Nonwhite	6	13	6	11
Both	2	4	0	0
Animals (apes)	1	2	0	0
SIZE OF CITY				
Urban	35	74	47	84
Rural	7	15	3	5
Transient	4	9	6	11
Undeterminable	1	2	0	0
OCCUPATIONS				
Professional/Business	32	68	30	54
Clerical/Sales	1	2	4	7
Manual workers	5	11	4	7
Farmers	3	7	2	4
Non-labor force	2	4	1	2
Undeterminable	4	9	15	27
MEMBERS OF HOUSEHOLD				
One	23	49	18	32
Two	10	21	9	16
Three	1	2	4	7
Four	5	11	4	7
Five or more	2	4	9	16
Undeterminable	6	13	12	21

*Rounding off accounts for differences above and below 100%.
†Two central characters representing more than one subcategory.

most desirable end for the nuclear family is extinction as a universal model for all. If so, it becomes equally important to generate multiple kinds of models for different kinds of life-style needs. Discussions of such alternative life-styles have included childless couples, communal families, geriatric families, unmarried men as childrearers, homosexual families, polygamous families, aggregate or "super" families, serial marriages, and trial or probationary marriages. Regardless of the ultimate personal choice made among such alternatives, it seems clear that the range and forms of alternatives must be explored toward the end of identifying more meaningful, collective, stable, and integrated interpersonal units. At present, the networks ignore such explorations. If the last four years are any indication, the networks appear to be making negligible, if any, attempts to identify a viable range of interpersonal alternatives. While it may *not* have been the intention of the networks to assume responsibility for such explorations in their series, nonetheless, the networks' twenty-eight hours of prime-time series each week currently deemphasize and detract from such essential explorations by predominantly emphasizing only one life-style. Consequently, the networks have implicitly assumed a "public responsibility" in this area, for they are already functioning as a primary source of information regarding interpersonal life-styles. In addition, while the networks cast single living as an essentially dynamic and satisfying experience, the decision to live alone may actually entail an agonizing sense of loneliness, for as Suzanna Gordon has demonstrated, loneliness has now become a major social problem in our land.[27]

CONCLUSION OF THIS STUDY

The approach taken by this essay sets it apart from the concerns of most critics. Typically, the fine arts and major political events attract the notice of critics. From one perspective, however, such traditional critics operate from a *high culture bias*—the one-of-a-kind, rare, and unique receive attention. This essay has implicitly suggested that phenomena viewed daily by millions of people throughout the entire year should be of equal concern.

Moreover, television series are typically conceived as vehicles which foster and reinforce violence and undesirable sexual mores. Here, however, other equally important features may be detected in popular television series, and this alternative emphasis reveals a host of subtle communication patterns, images, and models. The attention devoted to communication patterns and communicative images here was thus selected as a rationale for deemphasizing the current tendency to examine only the isolated and esoteric content of television series.

In this context, popular television series do not reflect the American culture; they disproportionately dramatize particular lifestyles at the expense of others. Moreover, these series may be cast in at least five different communicative forms which function as yet another way in which television series emphasize certain behaviors and values rather than others. Thus, a theoretical foundation and a methodological procedure has been established which would allow researchers to explore the possibility that popular television series selectively reinforce certain kinds of preferences, objectives, behaviors, and attitudes which may function as models for Americans. It now appears appropriate to consider the possibility that everyday communication and interpersonal relations are patterned after the central characters in popular television series.

Moreover, critical assessments of television series no longer have to be "one-shot affairs." While four year comparisons are not conclusive, research designs may be structured so as to allow for "follow-up" or longitudinal results. Herbert J. Gans has aptly noted that "all the studies measure . . . short-range impact occurring weeks or months after media exposure, and do not report on the long-range effects of living in a society where media use takes up so much time. There are thus significant omissions in the available evidence, mainly because long-range effects are difficult to study empirically."[28]

Granted, such requests for longitudinal studies are filled with difficulties, especially given a medium such as television. For example, when this study began four years ago, television series were typically twenty-six weeks long. During the 1974–75 season, the issue was *not* if a show would be dropped *during* the season, but if, as Paul Klein put it in 1974, a series would "be renewed for a second season."[29] During the 1977–78 season, however, series were frequently contracted for only thirteen, four, or two weeks of shows. In addition, today series are frequently replaced temporarily by specials, made-for-TV-movies, or semidocumentaries. The miniseries has also emerged as a regular feature of television since the 1974–75 season. While *Roots* might have been appropriately classified within the mimetic category of our communication matrix, nonetheless the number of changes which occurred since 1974–75 would seem to make significant longitudinal studies difficult to carry out. However, as the methodological procedure employed here has suggested, sufficiently flexible categories may be designed for such longitudinal studies by emphasizing the patterns of symbolic interaction and the concomitant communicative images reinforced by the national networks during prime-time viewing.

Finally, this essay had led to a major reconceptualizational issue: *Has the popular culture undergone a profound change?* From a communication perspective, the popular culture has been conceived as a mass communication system and examined as a source of mass concepts and mass categories which ultimately generated common or shared perceptions, attitudes, beliefs, and actions.[30] The emergence of short-term series, one-of-a-kind specials, made-for-TV-movies, semidocumentaries, miniseries, and "regular" series have created new levels and new kinds of choices, both in content and form, which may suggest that specialization and diversity may be increasingly a product of a popular culture medium.

NOTES

1. "Mass Communication and Political Socialization," *Socialization to Politics*, ed. Jack Dennis (New York: John Wiley, 1973), p. 391.
2. *Snap, Crackle, and Popular Taste: The Illusion of Free Choice in America* (New York: Delta, 1977), p. 25.
3. For an overview of the intentions of these producers see: Bill Davidson, "Forecast for Fall; Warm and Human," *TV Guide*, 22 (February 16, 1974), 5–8; 10.
4. Quoted in Davidson, "Forecast for Fall," p. 8.
5. Richard D. Heffner, "Television: The Subtle Persuader," *TV Guide*, 21 (September 15, 1973), 25–26.
6. Herbert W. Simons, "A Conceptual Framework for Identifying Rhetorical Genres," Central States Speech Association convention paper, April 1975, p. 2. While Simon's guidelines control the formulation of this generic system, the specific method employed here is frequently identified as *content analysis*: the content of television series is examined and persistent or repeating patterns of symbol-using found in these series are isolated. However, the method of content analysis used here avoids the methodological criticism frequently leveled at content analyses, for it attempts to reflect the subtle behaviors and context which unfold on these series as well as the motives controlling the central characters.
7. James W. Chesebro and Caroline D. Hamsher, "The Concession Speech:

The MacArthur-Agnew Analog," *Speaker and Gavel*, 11 (January 1974), 39–51.

8. Lloyd F. Bitzer, "The Rhetorical Situation," *Philosophy & Rhetoric*, 1 (January 1968), 1–14.

9. John F. Wilson and Carroll C. Arnold, *Dimensions of Public Communication* (Boston: Allyn and Bacon, 1976), pp. 132–147.

10. Ernest J. Wrage, "Public Address: A Study in Social and Intellectual History," *Quarterly Journal of Speech*, 33 (December 1947), 451–457.

11. Daniel Boorstin, *The Image: A Guide to Pseudo-Events in America* (rpt. 1961; New York: Harper and Row, 1964), p. 11.

12. Kenneth B. Boulding, *The Image: Knowledge in Life and Society* (rpt. 1956; Ann Arbor, Michigan: Ann Arbor Paperbacks/University of Michigan Press, 1966), p. 18.

13. David M. Berg, "Rhetoric, Reality, and Mass Media," *Quarterly Journal of Speech*, 58 (October 1972), pp. 255–257.

14. Northrop Frye, *Anatomy of Criticism* (Princeton, New Jersey: Princeton University Press, 1957), especially pp. 33–34.

15. Kenneth Burke, *The Rhetoric of Religion: Studies in Logology* (rpt. 1961; Berkeley, California: University of California Press, 1970), especially pp. 4–5; adapted for the purposes of this essay.

16. See Kenneth Burke, *A Grammar of Motives and A Rhetoric of Motives* (rpt. 1945 and 1950; Cleveland, Ohio: Meridian/World, 1962) for an extension of the concept of "identification" as a theoretical foundation for this discussion.

17. Edward D. Steele and W. Charles Redding, "The American Value System: Premises for Persuasion," *Western Speech*, 26 (Spring 1962), pp. 83–91.

18. James W. Chesebro and Caroline D. Hamsher, "Communication, Values, and Popular Television Series," *Journal of Popular Culture*, 8 (Spring 1975), p. 16.

19. Robert Sklar, "TV: The Persuasive Medium," *Popular Culture* (Del Mar, Calif.: Printers Inc., 1977), p. 18.

20. Lance Morrow, "Blacks on TV: A Disturbing Image," *Time*, 111 (March 27, 1978), p. 101.

21. The reliability procedure employed in this study involved three steps. First, 10 Ph.D. students were asked to study Fig. 1. The figure was described to them; they were not allowed to see any other part of this essay. They were then asked to classify 9 specific television series broadcast during the week of April 1–7, 1978, based upon their understanding of Fig. 1 only. The series had been randomly selected from each of the 5 categories in Fig. 2. Only one series—*The Jeffersons*—could be selected from the ironic category. *All in the Family* had already been employed as an extended example in discussing Fig. 1 and was therefore excluded. *Sanford Arms* was also excluded because it was no longer on the air. Any series mentioned in the second section of this essay was also excluded because they had been discussed as examples. Third, after being instructed to watch as many of the 9 shows as possible, they independently classified each show under 1 of the 5 categories immediately after viewing them. The results were:

	Students agreeing	Students disagreeing	Percent agreeing
Ironic:			
The Jeffersons	5	0	100
Mimetic:			
Alice	3	0	100
Happy Days	5	1	83

Leader-Centered:

Lou Grant	4	2	66
The Rockford Files	2	1	66

Romantic:

Starsky & Hutch	4	0	100
Quincy, M.E.	3	3	50

Mythical:

The Bionic Woman	6	0	100
The New Adventures of Wonder Woman	6	0	100

22. Tom Wicker, "The Satisfaction Boom," New York Times, February 19, 1978, Section 4, p. 17.
23. A complete assessment of these Gallup findings are reported in James W. Chesebro, "The Language of the Political Elites in the 1976 Presidential Campaign," Speech Communication Association convention paper, December 1977.
24. Tom Goldstein, "Survey Finds Most People Uninformed on Courts," The New York Times, March 19, 1978, section 1, p. 20.
25. Several critics have noted that racism may exist on these television series for other reasons even if the races are accurately represented. See Morrow's essay, note 20 above.
26. Bureau of the Census, Some Recent Changes in American Families (Washington, D.C.: U.S. Government Printing Office, Special Studies Series P-23, No. 52).
27. Lonely in America (New York: Simon and Schuster, 1976).
28. "The Critiques of Mass Culture," in Mass Media and Mass Man, ed. Alan Casty, 2nd ed. (New York: Holt, Rinehart and Winston, 1973), pp. 55–56.
29. "Who Will Win the Ratings Race?" TV Guide, 22 (September 14, 1974), p. 9.
30. For an example of this approach see E. Katz, M. Gurevitch, and H. Haas, "On the Use of Mass Media for Important Things," American Sociological Review, 38 (1973). A more profitable alternative and an approach more consistent with the findings reported here is to be found in Gans (note 28 above), pp. 49–58. For studies using similar approaches see: Melvin L. DeFleur, "Occupational Roles as Portrayed on Television," Public Opinion Quarterly (1966), pp. 57–74; John F. Seggar and Penny Wheeler, "World of Work on TV: Ethnic and Sex Representation in TV Drama," Journal of Broadcasting, 17 (Spring 1973), pp. 201–214.

JANE FEUER

THE MTM STYLE

THE MTM IMAGE

The fact that MTM *has* a public image is significant in itself. Most TV production companies remain invisible to the public. When Norman Lear made an appearance on the last episode of the first season of *Mary Hartman, Mary Hartman*, it seemed to contradict ordinary U.S. television practice. In fact, Lear had been unable to sell the controversial serial to any network and was syndicating it directly to local stations. But when, in 1983, Steven Bochco put in a plug for the new *Bay City Blues* ("by the producers of *Hill Street Blues*") it was on the NBC television network. Indeed it was largely through Grant Tinker's scheduling of MTM and MTM-related programming that NBC attempted to change its image from that of the "losing" network to that of the "quality" network, despite the network's continued low ratings. NBC's ad campaign for fall 1983 was based on a notion of "quality" for which MTM programmers provided the model.

The image of MTM as the "quality" production company extends to features about the company in the popular press: according to the *New York Times Magazine*, "MTM has a reputation for fair dealing, and, by prime-time standards, high quality."[1] Articles in the trades and in popular magazines and newspapers have demonstrated that MTM would spare no expense in the visual style of its programmes, putting "quality" above financial considerations. Long after other sitcom producers had switched to videotape, MTM continued to seek the "quality" look of film. And MTM hired a different breed of television actor, actors trained in the new style of improvisational comedy, such as Paul Sand, Valerie Harper, and Howard Hessemen, all of whom had their roots in improv companies such as The Second City and The Committee rather than in mainstream television acting.

Perhaps the central component in MTM's public image is its reputation for giving its creative staff an unusual amount of freedom. Article after article on MTM details the way in which Grant Tinker ran interference between his writer-producers and the network bureaucracy. According to the *Los Angeles Times*, "sources in and out of MTM insist he gives producers the freest hand in the business." According to the *Washington Post*, "the consensus at MTM is that there's a 'Tinker touch,' it's this harmony among Tinker and his employees." James L. Brooks told *Time* magazine, "Grant gave us blanket approval of anything we wanted to do, not just autonomy but support." And Steven Bochco told the *New York Times Magazine*, "he leaves you alone and lets you do what you can do." Tinker himself, ever modest in interviews, has said, "I see my prime role as being able to attract the right combinations of creative people and then staying out of their way . . . what I do mostly is try to remove distractions which might interfere with their work."[2]

To the student of cinema history, all of this sounds familiar. Much of the rhetoric of creative freedom within a system of constraints is reminiscent of *auteur* historians' claims for certain flim directors. In particular, the notion of the producer as protector and organiser of creativity permeates accounts of the Freed Unit at MGM in the 1940s and 1950s.[3] In much the same manner as Tinker, Arthur Freed forged a unit of the best "creative" talent in musical comedy. Their films are regarded as "quality" commercial entertainment at its best. As did MTM, the Freed Unit operated under conditions of exceptional freedom in part because their concept of quality was not outside the boundaries of commercial success.

Indeed MTM might be conceptualised—as the Freed Unit has been—as a corporate "author" in two senses and at two levels:

1. Conditions of creative freedom enabled MTM to develop an individualised "quality" style.

2. A corporate "signature" may be deciphered from the texts themselves.

According to Michel Foucault, "the name of the author points to the existence of certain groups of discourse and refers to the status of this discourse within a society and culture . . . [it]

accompanies only certain texts to the exclusion of others."[4] MTM's image as the quality producer serves to differentiate its programmes from the anonymous flow of television's discourse and to classify its texts as a unified body of work, two of the functions Foucault says the author's name serves.

As a specialist "indie prod" MTM was both an exception to the operation of American television in the 1970s and typical of that operation: exceptional in that Grant Tinker fitted his company into the cracks in the system; typical in that MTM operated under the same economic constraints as everybody else. Regardless of quality, the kitten also had to serve the devil Nielsen. A narrative in the industry's own terms of absolute success (high ratings) and absolute failure (cancellation), amply demonstrates both the freedom and the constraints. But establishing such a context does not explain the structure and effectivity of the programmes themselves. The relationship between commodity production and textual production is a thorny one to theorise. The usual solution is to consider each level separately, or else to argue that one level (commodity production) determines the other (textual production) in a directly causal manner. In film theory, the "relative" autonomy of the text from its conditions of production is now taken for granted: it has become a truism that a knowledge of industry practice does not explain the conditions of reception of the texts, conditions that may not correspond to a diary of profits and losses, however meticulously detailed. But in stressing the "autonomy" part of relative autonomy, one misses the distinction between "relative" and "absolute." If the corporate structure of MTM does not directly *cause* the structure of the texts or determine their reception, neither is it true that there is *no* relationship between the two levels. There exist structural correspondences (homologies) between the two levels that may be encapsulated in the terms "quality TV" and "quality demographics." MTM is in the business of exchanging "quality TV" for "quality demographics" but we need not view this process as a functionalist correspondence without contradiction. Contradictions abound even in Tinker's dualistic image in the industry as both hard-nosed executive and "creative genius."

This essay will analyse the MTM style, a style which signifies "regular TV" and "quality TV" simultaneously. I will argue not so much that MTM should be *considered* an author as that MTM's authorial status in industry discourse bears a relationship to its concept of "quality."

THE STRUCTURE OF THE MTM SITCOM

MTM and Tandem are said to have transformed the situation comedy as a form. The MTM and Lear sitcoms, the story goes, took a mechanistic, simplistic framework for one-liners and sight gags and made it into something else: whether an instrument for social commentary (Lear) or a vehicle for "character comedy" (MTM). In the handful of commentaries that have been written on the sitcom, this has become the orthodox view. Horace Newcomb, for example, sees the sitcom as the most elementary of TV formulas. Using *I Love Lucy* as an example, Newcomb describes the "situation" as the funny thing that will happen this week, developing through complication and confusion without plot development or an exploration of ideas. The only movement he sees is toward the alleviation of the complication and the reduction of confusion. The audience, he says, is reassured by this problem/solution format, not challenged by choice or ambiguity or forced to examine its values. Newcomb goes so far as to put the MTM and Lear programmes outside the sitcom proper in the category of "domestic comedy." With domestic comedy, he says, we find a greater emphasis on persons than situations; the problems are mental and emotional; there is a deep sense of personal love among members of the family and belief in the family as a supportive group. The form may be expanded when, as in the Lear comedies, the problems encountered by families become socially or politically significant.[5]

The critical view on the MTM sitcom supports Newcomb's description of domestic comedy as a transformation of the basic sitcom structure. According to one TV critic:

> In sitcoms, MTM's approach has always been quite specific, but its influence has also been so pervasive that it may be hard to remember what an innovation the style originally was. Before *The Mary Tyler Moore Show*, no one believed that a sitcom's foundation *had* to be in character ensembles, and humor wasn't even necessarily linked to motivation: on even the best pre-MTM sitcoms, with few exceptions, the personalities and interplay were machine-designed mostly to generate the maximum number of generic jokes—or, on family sitcoms, of generic parables. . . . After MTM made likability the key, even the most mechanical sitcoms had to pay lip service to the idea of the sitcom as a set of little epiphanies.[6]

"Character ensembles," "motivation," "a set of little epiphanies," have transformed the problem/solution format of the sitcom into a far more psychological and episodic formula in which—in the hand of MTM—the situation itself becomes a pretext for the revelation of character. The relative insignificance of the situation itself contrasts sharply with the Lear sitcom's significant issues. And yet one could argue that *All In The Family* actually retains the simplistic, insult-ridden, joke-machine apparatus to a far greater extent than did *The Mary Tyler Moore Show*. From the perspective of narrative and character, the MTM sitcoms are the more complex. A comparison between Tandem's *Maude* and MTM's *Rhoda*—two sitcoms from the same period and with aggressive female stars—illustrates this.

Maude is far more politically astute than Rhoda; she deals with controversial issues such as alcoholism and abortion; she is far more the "liberated woman" than Rhoda aspires to be. Yet the show *Maude* is structurally simplistic: there is one important dilemma per week which is usually resolved at Maude's expense, the main comedy technique is the insult, and the characters are uni-dimensional and static. Even those episodes of *Maude* which announce their experimental quality—Maude's monologue to her therapist, Walter's bout with alcoholism— seem to thrust themselves upon the viewer. *Rhoda*, whose most controversial moment occurred when Rhoda divorced her husband, nevertheless took the sitcom in new directions, employing a variety of comic techniques, an evolving central character and, arguably, moving toward the comedy-drama blend that would become the MTM formula of the late 1970s. The MTM sitcoms inflected the form in the direction of "quality TV," of complex characters, sophisticated dialogue, and identification. "Character comedy" in the hands of MTM became synonymous with "quality comedy."

"Character" in Character Comedy

It is in its conception of character that MTM's central contribution to the sitcom form is said to have been made. If we employ the traditional literary distinction between "round" and "flat" characters, MTM emerges on the "round" side of the sitcom form. Of course, the comic effect of feeling superior to a character depends upon a certain amount of stereotyping and a certain lack of depth. When, for example, Rhoda's response to her husband's departure became too serious and too psychologically "realist" the programme departed the realm of comedy, if only for an instant, and entered into the genre referred to by the industry as "warmedy," that is, comedy overlayed with empathetic audience identification. When comic stereotyping occurred on *The Mary Tyler Moore Show* it was reserved for the secondary characters such as Ted and Sue Ann. Mary herself functioned as what Richard Corliss has called a "benign identification figure," not herself the object of much comic attention or ridicule.[7] For the generation of women who came of age with Mary and Rhoda, these characters seemed "real" in a way no other TV character ever had. Of course the "realism" of any fictional character is an illusion of sorts. A round character seems more "real" than a flat one simply because "roundness" is produced by multiplying the number of traits ascribed to the character. A flat character has only a few traits, a process often referred to as "stereotyping." But what many in the "quality" audience felt for Mary and Rhoda went beyond a mere quantitative depth. Their "roundness" was also a cultural construct. The MTM women caught the cultural moment for the emerging "new woman" in a way that provided a point of identification for the mass audience as well. The MTM women could be read as warm, lovable TV characters or as representations of a new kind of femininity. In retrospect, the fact that the early MTM sitcoms were popular successes seems astonishing, but MTM knew how to provide the right combination of warmth and sophistication.

It would appear that Brooks, Burns et al. arrived at the correct formula through a process of experimentation. The first episode of *The Mary Tyler Moore Show* ("Love is All Around," 1970), despite its sophisticated humour, has not advanced much beyond *The Dick Van Dyke Show* in its conception of character.[8] While Mary is already established as the nice but "spunky" figure we will come to know and love, the secondary characters are heavily stereotyped. Rhoda is the obnoxious New York Jew who will do anything to keep Mary out of "her" apartment. Lou is portrayed as the typical drunken newspaperman, even affecting slurred speech. (Wanna drink?" he asks Mary.) The first episode is instructive because in its as yet undeveloped conceptions of Lou and Rhoda we can see what the MTM view of character added to the sitcom formula. From the standpoint of quality TV, the charge levelled against stereotyped characters has always been that they lack psychological realism and the potential for identification from the "quality" audience. The sitcom remains forever on the far side of quality for this reason, since a certain amount of stereotyping is necessary to get laughs. Ted Baxter may have elicited this kind of comic laughter, but the MTM characters evoked another kind of laughter as well, which I will call "empathetic laughter." Empathetic laughter is what we feel for Rhoda when she takes a piece of candy and quips, "I don't know why I'm putting this in my mouth—I should just apply it directly to my hips." It's what we feel for middle-aged Lou Grant, bravely attempting to put on a happy face at his ex-wife's wedding.

Sometimes, we don't laugh at all. A supreme example of the ability of the MTM sitcom to skirt the boundary of melodrama occurred in an episode of *Rhoda* called "The Separation" (written by Charlotte Brown, 1976). This unorthodox *Rhoda* episode shows us the MTM sitcom style pushed to the limits of pathos, exhibiting in extreme form MTM's conception of "character comedy," and "warmedy." In typical MTM sitcom fashion, "The Separation" follows an episodic plot structure divided into segments which are separated by commercial pauses or scene changes or both. Although the plot appears "loose," a closer inspection reveals that it is actually tightly structured. We can divide the episode into segments and subsegments as follows:

1. *Rhoda's apartment*
a. Rhoda and Joe bargain for a house with a real estate agent. Joe subverts the offer.
b. Rhoda fights with Joe and locks him out on the balcony.
2. *Brenda's apartment*
a. Brenda and Ida Morgenstern discuss Ida's camping trip and her feeling that something is amiss with a family member.
b. Rhoda enters and fakes out Ida.
c. Rhoda discusses her marriage with Brenda.
3. *Rhoda's apartment*
a. Carlton the doorman hears Joe's screams and thinks it's the voice of God.
b. After a discussion, Joe leaves Rhoda.
4. *Brenda's apartment*
Rhoda discusses the separation with Brenda; Rhoda phones Joe.
5. *Joe's Wrecking Company*
Ida visits Joe at work and finds out the truth.
6. *Rhoda's apartment*
Ida and Rhoda talk.

The episode is structured around three scenes of unusual seriousness (segments 1b, 3b, and 6), evenly distributed throughout. Two of these segments are preceded by light comedy "shticks" (segments 1a and 3a) involving stereotyped characters, an insincere real estate lady and Carlton the doorman in one of his set pieces. The final segment between Rhoda and her mother, however, contains only light humour and ends on a "warm" moment. There is no comic "tag" at the end. Almost all U.S. sitcoms use the tag as a opportunity for one last laugh. Even some of the serious issue-oriented Lear episodes would use the tag to lighten things up before the final credits. The standard *Mary Tyler Moore Show* and *Rhoda* episode employed the tag to end on an "upbeat." For example, a quite sad episode of *The Mary Tyler Moore Show* features Jerry Van Dyke as the quintessential loser—a scriptwriter for Chuckles the Clown who aspires to be a standup comic. He is humiliated in front of the WJM family when it turns out that his first standup engagement is at a bowling alley lounge. After a touching scene between Mary and Lou (discussed below), we return for the tag to find the comedian standing at the mike in the deserted lounge, finishing up his routine for an appreciative Mary.[9] In "The Separation," the absence of the tag emphasises the melodramatic nature of the ending.

A third type of segment in the *Rhoda* episode includes scenes between Rhoda and her sister (2c and 4); and scenes between Ida and Brenda, and Ida and Joe (2a and 5), symmetrically balanced around the major scene in which Rhoda's marriage collapses. In the world of the MTM sitcom, a couple's problems become the concern of the entire family, and any disruption of the extended family relationship is treated as seriously as a divorce. A good example of this pattern is *The Mary Tyler Moore Show* episode in which a disagreement between Mary and Rhoda involves all their friends and is eventually mediated by Georgette. Marriage is never privileged above friendship. Indeed it is arguable that the true "epiphany" of the separation episode consists not in Joe's departure but in Ida's atypical understanding response to it. Joe, an outsider to the show's family structure, could be written out, but Ida and Brenda could not be removed without the entire edifice collapsing.

As the subdivision of the episode's neatly patterned narrative reveals, "The Separation" moves back and forth between "warm" and "funny" moments to the point where the two blend into "warmedy." For example, the opening scene with the real estate agent is a typical MTM comic reversal; she tells Joe:

> Mr. Girard, in all my years as a realtor, I have never been subjected to the shame, the humiliation, and the degradation that you put me through on that phone. Mr. Girard, I have nothing but contempt for you—(cut to reverse reaction shot of Joe)—and if you're ever in the market for a house (cut back to shot of realtor) again—here's my card.

This very funny scene is followed by the quite serious confrontation between Rhoda and Joe, ending on Rhoda's hostile but comic gesture of locking him out. The following scene between Brenda and Ida is full of snappy one-liners:

> *Ida:* Your father and I are gonna just keep going until we stop having a good time.
> *Brenda:* I don't think you'll make it through the Holland tunnel.

This exchange is set up in typical MTM three-camera fashion. There is a cut to Brenda for her joke line, a cut to Ida's reaction and a re-establishing full shot for the next routine. In addition, Brenda has her typical, self-deprecating lines, the kind of lines they used to write for Rhoda before she spun off. For example, when Rhoda tells Brenda that she and Joe haven't had sex for seven weeks, Brenda whines, "Please, don't make seven weeks sound like a long time to me." But there are also touching, even sentimental moments between the sisters, as when, in the same scene, Rhoda tells Brenda, "If it were nothing, you wouldn't have your arms around me."

The "big" scene between Rhoda and Joe has laugh lines too, but they are echoed by the nervous laughter of the studio audience. The scene shifts from anger to humour to pathos (as when Rhoda begs Joe, "Don't do this to me"). It may be funny that Rhoda refuses to let Joe take his underwear, but her "damn" at the end of the scene elicits empathy rather than laughter.

But the true "epiphany" comes in the final scene of "The Separation" as Ida Morgenstern confronts Rhoda with her knowledge. In her appearances on *The Mary Tyler Moore Show*, Ida functioned as a comic foil for Rhoda's neurotic behaviour. In the spin-off, however, she began to emerge as something other than a caricatured Jewish mother. In an early *Rhoda* episode, Ida went so far as to throw Rhoda out of her Bronx apartment when it became obvious that Rhoda was enjoying her reversion to dependency. This new concern for Rhoda's maturation culminates in a scene all the more touching for being many years in the making. "Rhoda, I love you," she says. "Don't shut me out." And Rhoda, herself coming of age, doesn't. In this final scene of "The Separation," the long-time viewer is reminded of Ida's very first appearance on the parent show ("Support Your Local Mother," 1970) when Rhoda was so unable to cope with Ida's "Bronx love" that she allowed her mother to spend three days in Mary's apartment. Now they move closer together. Ida offers to stay, then corrects herself, "That would have been good for me, but it's not good for you." She starts to leave. Rhoda, reduced to tears, has a reversal of her own. "Ma," she says, "stick around." They embrace, and the episode is over. There is no tag, no comic relief. The atypical poignancy of "The Separation" stems from playing Ida against type far more than from Joe's desertion. (Indeed the pragmatic reason behind the separation was that the writers had trouble coming up with plots for the happily married couple and lines for Joe's wooden character.)

The *Rhoda* episode contradicts a commonly held notion that the sitcom cannot allow for more than trivial character development. In fact, the MTM sitcom operates almost entirely at the level of character. It would be more accurate to say that the sitcom does not allow for complexity of *plot*. Watching MTM shows rerun, "stripped" daily in syndication, one can view within an hour episodes from the first and last seasons of *The Mary Tyler Moore Show*. The situations are remarkably similar, even identical: Mary asks for a raise, Mary is offered a job by a competing station. But Mary herself has changed: she is more the career woman, less the daughter. This movement toward an expansion of character is arguably more an MTM than a Lear contribution to the sitcom. "Character comedy" hinges upon the stability of the quasi-family structure, yet it permits individuals to grow within the family rather than by leaving home. Such growth should not be measured against traditional literary norms of "recognition" and "reversal," but rather in terms of the sitcom's internal history.

A look at MTM's approach to the opening credit sequence reveals the importance of character transformation to the MTM conception of character comedy. In the original *Rhoda* credits, a chronicle of Rhoda's life, she quips, "I decided to move out of the house at the age of 24. My mother still refers to this as the time I ran away from home." For the regular viewer, the change between this and Ida's incarnation in "The Separation" is immense. Similarly, the title song of the first season of *The Mary Tyler Moore Show* begins by posing the question, "How will you make it on your own?" In the ensuing seasons, the question has been dropped entirely. Presumably, Mary's survival on her own is no longer in question. Mary's evolution as a character represents an enormous change, not just for the static sitcom formula but for women historically as well. But critics whose conception of dramatic change can accommodate only earth-shattering moments of reversal are likely to overlook it entirely. Arguably, the viewer does not.

"Character comedy," with its emphasis on family ties (not coincidentally *Family Ties* is the title of a 1980s sitcom created by MTM alumnus Gary David Goldberg) and on identification with characters, also changed the nature of humour in the sitcom. If we accept the traditional notion that a comic effect is produced by *detachment* from character, what brand of comedy could the fetishisation of character produce?

"Comedy" in Character Comedy

Jim and Allan and I agree on the most important things. None of us would ever write in a gratuitous putdown just because it was funny or satirise something that was pathetic. The characters have a lot of affection for each other and we don't want to destroy that. (Treva Silverman, Senior Story Consultant, *The Mary Tyler Moore Show*)[10]

The MTM sitcom employs a range of comic devices to produce both laughter and the pathos of "warmedy." Although MTM might use similar comic techniques to Lear—the insult, a Lear staple, forms the basis for the interactions between Rhoda and Phyllis, Murray and Ted—they rarely have the same impact. The vast majority of laughs one the Lear sitcoms are produced by name-calling and shouting, or by the malapropisms for which Archie is famous. We laugh *at* Archie or Maude because they are self-deluded. The laugh track on Lear sitcoms is full of hoots, applause and condescending giggles, whereas the MTM audience produces little chuckles of identification more often than howls of derisive delight. Treva Silverman's remarks are clearly a slap at the Lear sitcom factory's attitude toward its characters.

In the MTM sitcom, laughter tends to be tempered by sympathy. Even the most stereotyped characters—Ted, Phyllis, or Sue Ann—have their little moments of self-revelation: Ted when he meets up with the father who abandoned him as a child; Phyllis when her husband Lars has an affair with the Happy Homemaker; and Sue Ann herself when she admits to Mary that she's not attractive to men. The most ridiculous MTM characters—the group members and Howard on *The Bob Newhart Show*, for example—are rendered pathetic rather than thoroughly risible. Infantile, narcissistic characters are never expelled from the family: Ted remains on the air; Mr Carlin stays in the group; Carlton is rehired at Rhoda's request despite an astonishing lapse of "professionalism" in his doorman duties (he has ushered in the burglars who strip Rhoda and Joe of their possessions). Yet the MTM sitcoms remain remarkably funny. This is because the comic devices employed produce the laughter of recognition, an identification that is especially acute for the "sophisticated" audience.

Empathetic laughter transforms even the most primitive of sitcom devices: the sight gag. Every episode of *I Love Lucy* had at least one set piece of physical comedy. But they were rarely tied to character psychology. Surprisingly the sight gag turns up rather frequently on MTM sitcoms as well. Perhaps the funniest moment in "The Separation" occurs when Ida visits Joe, unaware that he has left her daughter. After Ida insists that "she can take it," Joe announces, "Rhoda and I are separated." Ida proceeds to grab his face and pinch his cheeks with considerable force. "Does Rhoda know?" she asks. Joe is unable to break her grip, but when he finally does, Ida claims she can behave with maturity, and then, as a parting thrust, zaps him with her handbag. This is a typical MTM situation: a character claims to be able to behave maturely, then proceeds to act childishly. A classic instance occurs on *The Mary Tyler Moore Show* when Mary, having been fired by Lou for writing with Rhoda a tongue-in-cheek obituary in the wee hours of the morning which Ted accidentally reads on the air, returns for a visit to WJM and finds another woman in her chair. In the midst of a polite visit to Lou Grant's inner sanctum, she becomes hysterical and sobs repeatedly, "Oh Mr Grant, I want to come back." She regains control, apologises, then lapses back into the same childish plaint. In both examples, the gag involves a set piece for the character—Mary's famous crying scenes or Ida's moments of fierce maternal protectiveness. And in each case, the motivation is familial love.

Another classic Ida Morgenstern sight gag occurs in "Support Your Local Mother" when Ida and Mary race around

Mary's sofa trying to stuff money in each other's bathrobe pocket. This hilarious scene reverberates at a number of levels. There is the obvious Bergsonian notion that humour stems from the human body being transformed into a machine. But there is also character comedy: Mary has refused to believe Rhoda's promise that Ida will drive her crazy with guilt. When Ida attempts to pay Mary hotel costs for sleeping on her sofa, she reduces Mary to the neurotic acting-out that is displayed in the physical gag.

Our response to MTM sight gags can even stem from pathos. In the Jerry Van Dyke episode, a moment of supreme embarrassment occurs when the comic is humiliated by having to deliver his standup routine to an audience of bored bowlers. In keeping with the MTM attitude toward characters, the routine is actually quite clever, which only increases our pity for the character. This reduces Mary to tears, and she flees to the ladies' room. To this point, the scene is embarrassing rather than funny. But Lou Grant, with typical paternal protectiveness, follows Mary into the ladies' room, much to the surprise of a woman who emerges from one of the stalls. As Lou attempts awkwardly to comfort Mary (herself a victim of over-identification with a friend's pain), another woman attempts twice to enter. "Not now," Lou growls at her. The culmination to this bizarre moment occurs as a visual joke, when Lou, trying to help Mary dry her tears, pulls out a towel from the dispenser. But it's on one of those circular rolls, and he winds up yanking the entire length of towel across the room, as the laugh track explodes with hilarity. We laugh in part at the notion of a machine not serving its proper function, in part at this bear of a man's very presence in the ladies' room, and in part at the genuine concern it takes for Lou to so abandon his macho decorum. Without the narrative context, the gag would seem only moderately funny, whereas most of Lucy's sight gags work perfectly well on their own.

But the tradition of physical comedy is not the essence of MTM character comedy; comic reversals of expectations are. Typically, an MTM script will set us up for a sentimental moment and then puncture it by reversing the predictable sentimental response. On a *Mary Tyler Moore Show* episode, Sue Ann has lured the WJM family into her studio during a November blizzard to consume the food prepared for her "Christmas Around the World" edition of "The Happy Homemaker." Prior to this, Mary and Murray were reduced to stony hostility over a disagreement as to whether Ted's new salutation should go "news from around the corner and around the world" or "news from around the world and around the corner." Now they are trapped together by the blizzard. At the dinner table, Sue Ann has forced everyone to wear silly "international" hats and sing "A Partridge in a Pear Tree." There is a moment of hostile silence, whereupon Georgette, ever the innocent peace-maker, begins to sing "Silent Night" *a cappella*. This reduces Mary to sentimental guilt and she says "Can anyone remember why we were angry with each other?", setting us up for a sentimental family reconciliation. But the reversal occurs when Murray grunts "Yeah, I can remember" and Mary replies, "Yeah, well, me too," and the feud continues.

The most famous MTM comic reversal occurs in "Chuckles Bites the Dust."[11] Chuckles the Clown, dressed up as a peanut, comes to a tragic end when he is trampled by an elephant. Mary is outraged when Lou, Murray, and Sue Ann persist in making jokes about it. But at Chuckle's funeral, in an atmosphere of hushed silence, Mary bursts into peals of laughter during the eulogy. The minister consoles the mortified Mary by telling her Chuckles loved to make people laugh. Mary, of course, promptly bursts into tears. Once again we have the puncturing of potential sentimentality but also empathetic laughter, since we too laughed at the jokes about Chuckles and at the very funny eulogy.

The reversal may operate in conjuction with another kind of MTM humour, the self-deprecating "Jewish" humour of a Rhoda, a Brenda, or a Bob Hartley. Most of Rhoda's laugh lines fall into this category, but this author's favourite self-deprecating reversal occurs in the scene between Ida and Brenda in "The Separation." Ida tells Brenda that she "feels in her bones" that something is amiss with a family member. Brenda takes this as an opening and muses, "I woke up this morning feeling very alone with this fear I'd never find anybody to love me. I would just be—" We cut to a reverse shot of Ida who interrupts, "Oh, please, I don't mean the normal stuff." It gets a big laugh, but also sympathy for poor Brenda whose neuroses are dismissed so lightly.

"Character comedy" reinforces MTM's emphasis on the familial and the interpersonal. It frequently verges on "warmedy." Since "warmedy" itself frequently verges on senti-mentality, the comic reversal also has its self-mocking aspect. The same sentimental moments are often played "straight" in the MTM dramas later in the decade. However, overt satire and self-parody are rare in the early MTM sitcoms. To be sure, local TV news operations are made fun of repeatedly in the person of Ted Baxter; and Bob Hartley's therapy group reduced psychotherapy to psycho-comedy. But because of the sympathetic attitude toward character, the satire lacks bite. This begins to change in the mid-1970s. *The Betty White Show, Phyllis, Remington Steele*, and the MTM-style *Buffalo Bill* introduce self-satire into the MTM comic repertory. yet self-reflexivity may be interpreted as yet another mark of "quality."

SELF-REFLEXIVITY AS "QUALITY"

"Intertextuality," a literary term, refers in its broadest sense to the ways in which texts incorporate previous texts. Sometimes this takes the form of "self-reflexivity," when a text refers in self-conscious fashion back to itself. Both terms have been associated with "modernist" art: T. S. Eliot's *The Wasteland* operates intertextually, whereas Pirandello's *Six Characters in Search of an Author* exhibits self-reflexivity. It has been argued that these self-conscious strategies distinguish "high-art" from the unselfconscious popular arts—such as TV series—and that even within high art, self-reflexivity distinguishes "modernist" from "classical" forms. Yet many popular forms are highly intertextual without being in a modernist vein.[12] In fact, the idea that within a form new works are created by recombining elements from previous texts in the same or different genres is crucial to an understanding both of Hollywood genre films and of TV series. The oft-accused lack of "originality" of most TV series stems from this self-generating mode of construction. Intertextuality and self-reflexivity operate both as the normative way of creating new programmes *and* as a way of distinguishing the "quality" from the everyday product. In aligning itself with the modernist self-conscious mode, the MTM style makes yet another claim to quality status. Within the MTM style, intertextual and self-reflexive references have both constructive and deconstructive purposes. When used constructively, these techniques renew and validate the style itself, as when new programmes spin off from old ones. But the same techniques may also be used so as to critique or *de*construct their own genre and style, as I will argue *Buffalo Bill* does in its commentary on *The Mary Tyler Moore Show*.

MTM's use of what Todd Gitlin calls "recombination" places its style within the norms of textual construction in American television. As Gitlin and others have argued, even the "innovative" *Hill Street Blues* recombines the conventions of the continuing serial melodrama with those of the cop show, adding a bit of cinéma vérité in the visual style.[13] Recombination continues from *Hill Street* with *St. Elsewhere* and *Bay City Blues. St. Elsewhere,* when it was being developed, was referred to around the shop as "Hill Street in the hospital." Its style is wholly derivative: the large ensemble cast, the blending of melodrama and comedy with the more or less "realist" treatment of the medical series tradition and of controversial issues (AIDS, sex change operations), and in its use of the continuing serial narrative. *Bay City Blues* bore an even closer family resemblance to *Hill Street,* imitating even the dense image and sound track of the parent programme.

At a high enough level of abstraction, one could see the entire core of MTM programmes as a process of "begats," with *The Mary Tyler Moore Show* as Abraham. The original programme (itself not without roots in the sitcom tradition) pioneered the ensemble cast of co-workers which would become an MTM trademark; it merged farce with forms of comedy based on empathy; it incorporated a literate style of writing in its dialogue. The sitcom spin-offs continued in this tradition with *Phyllis* and *The Betty White Show,* adding the elements of acerbic wit that would culminate in the MTM-related *Buffalo Bill.* The transition to the dramas occurred with *Lou Grant,* a programme poised midway between the sitcoms and the serial dramas. *Lou Grant* took the work-family concept from the sitcoms, added a heavier strain of drama and an emphasis on public issues, and began to expand the narrative beyond the "series of little epiphanies" that had distinguished the sitcoms. The most issue-oriented of MTM programmes retained a focus on the personal dimension of public issues. Sometimes it seemed to stress the public dimension of personal issues as well, as when, in the final season, Billie Newman's agonised decision to remarry appeared to have cultural significance.

One can see in *Lou Grant* the beginnings of the multiple-plot line construction often claimed as one of *Hill Street*'s great innovations in prime-time drama. In an episode about child pornography, four different plots are interwoven. Already the TV convention of main plot and subplot is being deconstructed. In both the sitcom and drama, the subplot serves to "lighten" the main plot. The Lear sitcoms would use this strategy in instances where the main plot was seen as too "heavy." In the *Lou Grant* episode, the two major subplots are also lighter, but they serve to reinforce the seriousness of the main plot, which concerns a young black female reporter named Sharon who gives confidentiality to a source. The conflict arises because her source is the mother of a young daughter who has allowed her child to appear in porno movies. Meanwhile, Donovan, a regular character, breaks his ankle after skydiving from a helicopter while covering a story on a mountain search and rescue team, in consequence failing to cover an important story for Lou. Both Sharon's and Donovan's commitment to getting the story at all costs alienates them from the "Trib" family. In the end, both are accepted back into the family, with Donovan regretting his macho pride and Sharon feeling she would proceed differently in the future. In another comic subplot, a cub reporter named Lance finds out his ear problem will prevent him from achieving his goal of being the first reporter in space; this comic relief echoes the theme of risk-taking in the larger plotlines. Although the main plot/subplot division remains distinguishable, there is a thematic connection between them, and both take the form of the parable. The public issue of child pornography remains unresolved, but the familial conflicts are mediated. *Hill Street* would take the multiplication of plots one step further, reducing the sense of hierarchy to the point where the plot lines would take on nearly equal status, and rendering the sense of closure even more ambiguous.

The *Lou Grant* episode also moves toward the serial form in a discussion Sharon has with Rossi about the issue of confidentiality. Rossi refers to the time he went to jail for refusing to reveal a source. This had indeed occurred on an episode about pill pushers in a previous season. (Indeed Mary Richards had been the first MTM character to go to jail for refusing to reveal a source, so that there is a double level of historical reference operating.) Rossi recaps what had happened in the earlier episode but tells Sharon his case was different in that he wasn't protecting a criminal. The reference calls for the viewer to compare the issues involved. In this way, the series *Lou Grant* is seen as possessing a history, moving it away from the ahistorical sitcom genre and toward the continuing serial, as Rhoda's divorce had produced a series of interconnected episodes within the sitcom form. *Lou Grant*'s insistence on relating the private to the public sphere would continue in *The White Shadow* and in the serial dramas. Yet all would retain the MTM characteristic of focusing on the personal dimension of the public issue, never inverting that hierarchy as Lear had done, by using characters as stick figures in a political allegory.

In this way, intertextuality can be seen as the generator for the entire MTM output. Yet when self-referencing occurs, it tends to be constructive rather than critical of the MTM heritage. As an example of constructive reflexivity, no MTM programme is more significant than the company's excursion into musical-variety with the short-lived 1978 *Mary/The Mary Tyler Moore Hour*. The abysmal failure of Mary Tyler Moore's return to the small screen might make it appear that the programme was—like *The Texas Wheelers* or *Three for the Road*—foreign to the MTM style or aberrant in its generic uniqueness. Quite the contrary: the variety hour took the self-referencing of the MTM style to its furthest extreme in the constructive direction. A contemporary of *Lou Grant*, *The White Shadow*, *WKRP in Cincinnati*, and *Taxi*, *Mary* faced many of the same problems as the other shows attempting to compete in the Silverman era, and in attempting to extend the MTM sitcom bloodline at a point where the blood was getting a bit tired.

Would the public accept Mary as a dancer and sketch comedienne, or would the memory of Mary Richards prevent such an acceptance, was the question the writers had to ask. Their solution was one encountered many times before in the movies and in television series: rather than ignoring Mary's past incarnation, it would become the point of reference for her present one. In the first hour of *Mary*, Mary Tyler Moore addresses the live studio audience, asking them what they've been doing on Saturday nights. The first comedy routine has Mary looking back upon Ed Asner's audition for *The Mary Tyler Moore Show*. She then introduces the "Ed Asner" dancers, and an ensemble of fat balding middle-aged men in Lou Grant outfits emerges dancing to a disco beat. Mary then introduces the "family" of comedy players for the new programme by showing excerpts from their audition tapes, one of which consists of imitations of Mary's lines from the old show. Although it is primarily constructive, the new programme takes an ambivalent attitude towards the old show, on the one hand wanting to capitalise on its success and the audience's affection for Mary; on the other hand wanting to go off in a newer, more "modernist" direction, derived from the late-night improvisational comedy tradition that was then emerging. (The idea of a pure construction is of course a theoretical fiction; there can be no construction without some element of deconstruction and vice versa.) The first episode is *self*-reflexive to an extreme. In addition to the audition tapes, it features a satire on television's self-congratulatory tendencies in a recapitulation of "historic moments from the first 25 minutes of *Mary*." And in a segment at the end of the hour, the cast members gather at a restaurant across the street to discuss the programme we've just viewed. They decide they really like Mary, but trash David Letterman who has appeared as an obnoxious member of the ensemble.

After the ratings failure of *Mary*, the show went on hiatus and returned in a revamped version, *The Mary Tyler Moore Hour*. Far from having disappeared, the intertextual references and self-reflexive moments were once again central to the show's format. Now the programme took on a backstage musical plot structure whereby Mary Tyler Moore played "Mary McKinnon," a fictional character who just happened to have her own musical variety television show. Each week Mary McKinnon would deal with problems involving that week's guest star on the fictional programme. *The Mary Tyler Moore Hour* commenced with a re-arranged version of the old "Love is All Around" theme song, and continued the references to Moore's previous television roles. Mary McKinnon seemed familiar; she was nice, spunky, and a pushover for manipulators. In an episode centering around Mary's fear of dancing with guest star Gene Kelly, her assistant answers the phone saying, "She's exactly like she is on television," reinforcing our fondest desires about Mary Richards. Iris, Mary McKinnon's unglamorous female secretary, discusses Mary's weekend during which she attended a "little" testimonial dinner in her own honour. It does not take us long to realise that Iris is a Rhoda-substitute. "Iris, what do you want?" Mary inquires of her. "I want your life," Iris replies, in typical Rhoda fashion.

Not surprisingly, the new programme's only satirical comment on Mary's past involves not her sacred role of Mary Richards but her far more vulnerable stint as the featherbrained Laura Petrie on *The Dick Van Dyke Show*. Mary McKinnon's guest star is Dick Van Dyke, and the joke revolves around his never having met Mary McKinnon. The producer asks him, "Don't you think Mary looks like the girl who played Laura Petrie?" Dick Van Dyke ponders for a moment and replies, "No." He goes into a flashback on the old *Dick Van Dyke Show* set, in which Laura has become a feminist, Richie a gay, etc. The skit plays the audience's recollection of their mutual video past against Van Dyke's claim never to have met "Mary." Finally they meet at the end of the hour. "I auditioned for *The Dick Van Dyke Show*," Mary McKinnon tells him. "Rose Marie got the part."

Although the variety hour took self-referencing to an extreme, other MTM programmes of the period also referred back to the MTM past, either directly or indirectly. A direct reference occurred on an episode of *Taxi*, the first programme produced by the MTM creative team after they left the company. In the fall 1982 première, Marcia Wallace, who had played Bob Newhart's secretary, is the guest star. In an odd play on the fictional status of a television character, Jim, one of the regular fictional characters on *Taxi*, is portrayed as idolising Marcia Wallace in her role as Carol, the secretary on *The Bob Newhart Show*. But Marcia Wallace plays "herself." The episode makes numerous references to Jim's memories of the older programme, culminating in a scene with all the fictional *Taxi* characters and the "real" Marcia Wallace, in which Jim makes up a hymn of praise to the tune of the old Bob Newhart theme song. Although it is not unusual for actors to appear as "themselves" in a fictional TV series (after all Henry Kissinger appeared as "himself" on *Dynasty*), the complexity of the reference on *Taxi* puts it in a modernist vein, especially since the programme does not ordinarily use guest stars in this fashion. The *Taxi* episode plays on nostalgia for the earlier show, but also plays with the nature of the fictional enclosure, as does much modernist "high art." A similar play on the border between fiction and reality occurs in an uncharacteristic in-joke on a 1984 *St. Elsewhere*. Dr. Morrison goes on a tour of Boston, the locale for the hospital series, with his young son, Petey. Suddenly they pass by the "fictional" bar, Cheers, and Dr. Morrison asks Petey, "Do you want to eat where everybody knows your name?" One expected them to go inside and chat with Sam and Diane, but the fiction of *St. Elsewhere* was rapidly re-established. Nevertheless the MTM company family had asserted its intergenerational bonds, as well as acknowledging that the same "quality" audience would watch both programmes.

Another late MTM programme which continually asserts a continuity with the modernist tradition as a claim to "quality" is the detective show spoof, *Remington Steele*. The show displays its sophistication by having Steele solve crimes by reference to plots from old Hollywood movies. Steele's relationship to the detective genre is entirely fictional. In this way the show includes the audience in its sophisticated circle of allusions. In the pilot, Steele, an ex-jewel thief, uses his aliases character names from old Bogart movies. In the second episode, he watches *The Thin Man* and uses its plot to solve a crime. The second season of *Remington Steele* stakes a further claim to the modernist tradition. "Small Town Steele" alludes to the Frank Capra tradition of small town populism as Steele and Laura visit a tiny burg named "Da Nada." But the townspeople are inhospitable and corrupt, and Steele is disillusioned. The first year credits had featured a first-person narration by Laura Holt of how she'd become a detective and had to invent Remington Steele. But the second season credits show Laura and Steele in a cinema, watching scenes from the first season. This self-reflexive vein culminates in an episode structured around dream sequences that Laura and Steele have about each other. The final dream involves Steele looking over a balcony from which Laura has fallen in the actual plot. He screams her name, and we cut to Laura in a hospital bed, having returned to "reality." The source of the final dream is never revealed to the audience.

If these stylistic touches link *Remington Steele* to modern art, its many media allusions place it firmly within a television tradition. Many American and British television programmes base their jokes and parodies on media references. This in itself does not necessarily entail a critical stance toward the television tradition, although it does reveal an awareness of television's status as "low culture." Most often, an appeal is made to a common media culture and a shared "inside" knowledge among audience members. If you watch TV, you will get the joke; just as if you are an educated literary intellectual, you will "get" the references in modernist poetry. Many MTM programmes seem to take this normative TV practice a bit further by being set in media institutions. WJM was always trying to improve its ratings, and many episodes showed these futile attempts in a humorous light. In one such episode, the WJM news team decides to broadcast from a singles bar. Mary's research goes well, but in the actual live broadcast, their sources panic in front of the cameras, and clam up, leaving Lou with egg on his face and Ted back in the studio with a lot of empty air time on his hands. MTM programmes not about media professionals often featured the media in a subsidiary way. *We've Got Each Other* had the female lead working as a photographer's assistant. Phyllis also went to work in a photography studio, allowing for jokes about advertising such as "I backlit the sesame seeds." This line exhibits more sophistication than the usual TV references to other programmes and stars because in order to laugh at it, you have to know what backlighting is, and you have to take an irreverent attitude towards advertising. *Remington Steele* shows its sophistication in episodes where Remington Steele and Laura Holt investigate crimes occurring in media contexts. In one such episode, they visit the set of a frozen food commercial. "Ah, commercials, the lynchpin of the television industry," Laura observes. Although it is not uncommon for U.S. TV shows to mock the ads that enable them to exist, such a literate analysis is characteristic of quality TV, especially since Laura is also mocking Steele's elevated style of speech. "Television is so disillusioning," says Mildred Krebs in the same episode, after discovering that the romantic TV stars featured in the boeuf bourguignon commercial actually hate each other.

When media references occur on U.S. television, they rarely take up such a deconstructive position. Yet a number of MTM series episodes have tackled the nature of their own medium in a manner verging on the critical. Since presumably it's OK for the quality audience to hate TV, this practice should not be construed as subversive in any absolute sense. It does, however, exhibit MTM's "quality" mode of satire. Another episode of *Remington Steele* involves a sustained sendup of local TV news operations far less affectionate than *The Mary Tyler Moore Show* ever was. Various members of the news team are being murdered on the set of the evening news. After a lengthy exposé of the idiocies of producing "happy news," it is revealed that the culprit was a formerly respectable print journalist outraged at the way the news was being corrupted into entertainment. He delivers his confession on the air in the form of a *Network*-like diatribe against broadcast news.

The Betty White Show, the most brilliant and acerbic of the MTM "failures," also had a quite reflexive format. White's character was a toned-down version of her Sue Ann Nivens, another acid-tongued television performer. The pilot episode begins with a show-within-the-show, a TV cop show called *Undercover Woman*. The camera pulls back to reveal Betty White as Joyce, watching the female cop show on her TV. We then see the credits for *The Betty White Show* itself. This is perhaps the only recorded instance of a TV pilot within a TV pilot, setting the self-reflexive tone for the sitcom which follows. The episode revolves around whether the network (actually called

"CBS") will buy the series Joyce makes under the direction of her much-loathed ex-husband. Such a situation provides many opportunities for media-related jokes, although in typical MTM fashion another focus for humour is Joyce's relationship to her ex. The CBS liaison, Doug Porterfield, figures prominently in the pilot. His title is Vice-President in Charge of Prime-time Dramatic Development, but he tells Joyce, "Yesterday I was working in the mailroom." (This brand of satire is repeated in a later *Taxi* episode in which the spaced-out Jim reveals an uncanny ability to predict which network programmes will "score" in a given time slot, and becomes a consultant to a juvenile network programming executive.) At the script reading, Porterfield tries to censor a scene in which the undercover woman is disguised as a nun. "What do you suggest," the director says, "that we disguise her as an atheist?" Later Joyce asks her ex-husband director, "What is my motivation in the car chase?" Sight gags involve a burly stunt man emerging in Joyce's brief costume and a scene in which the entire set collapses when Joyce slams the door. At a cast party celebrating the network's acceptance of the programme, Doug Porterfield reads the network's report on the show: "Lurid, the mentality of an eight year old . . . they loved it." The parody of the television industry combines with the show-within-a-show device to place *The Betty White Show* in the quality reflexive style. In mocking ordinary television, *The Betty White Show* exempts itself and claims quality status.

An episode of *The White Shadow* appears even more critically reflexive in that it sets up pointed parallels between a TV show within the show and *The White Shadow* itself. *The White Shadow* revolves around a white former basketball player who becomes the coach for a Los Angeles ghetto high school basketball team. Typically, the programme dealt with interpersonal conflict and social issues among the largely black, youthful cast. Unlike other MTM programmes involving media professionals, the incorporation of a parallel television programme within the programme does not evolve naturally from *The White Shadow*'s premise; the commentary in this case appears all the more overt. As did the *Betty White Show* pilot, this episode of *The White Shadow* commences directly with the internal programme. We are shown a typical TV drama series about a black kid with a drug problem, and the camera pulls back to reveal the film crew on a Los Angeles-based location accessible to the regular cast. The kids are critical of the TV show for its portrayal of blacks and for its lack of realism (all criticisms which might be levelled at *The White Shadow* itself). In the school corridors, the team members discuss this "ridiculous" new TV show about a white principal in a black ghetto school who always gets involved in the kids' personal problems. "Sounds like a lotta bull to me," one of them says. At that point Reeves, the white coach, walks past and the kids do a double take, reminding us again of the parallels between the much-maligned internal show and the programme which contains it. While observing on the set, Warren Coolidge, a regular character, is invited to direct the TV episode, after he criticises its lack of realism. We then fade in to Coolidge *on* TV, in the role we saw at the beginning of the episode. He has just been cast in the lead, and the team is watching him at the coaches' home. (A third such pullback shot occurs later when it is revealed that the team is watching the internal show on a bank of TV monitors in a video shop; we always see the programme from their point of view as "real" spectators.)

The remainder of the episode involves the problems that occur when Coolidge "goes Hollywood," and his conflict with another team member, Hayward, who thinks the show puts black people down. The team visits Coolidge on the set and Hayward complains to the production staff that they are making blacks look like fools. Hayward's charges are corroborated in a scene in which the white director asks Coolidge to strut soulfully with a ghetto blaster. "You don't dress like that," Hayward tells him. "It ain't supposed to be real," Coolidge replies. A secondary satirical strain revolves around Coolidge's immersion in the Hollywood scene. He begins to pick up the lingo, saying that he and his girlfriend are "on hiatus." When they run into Ed Asner (playing himself) on the lot, Asner shakes hands with Coolidge and calls him by name. Both strains culminate when the team crashes a Hollywood party. Hayward argues with the white creative staff of "Downtown High" who are exposed as hypocritical and more than a little racist. When Coolidge evicts them from the party, Hayward tells him he's "developed a serious case of Oreo mentality." Ultimately, Coolidge comes around to this point of view. He refuses to do a comic scene in which he shines a white man's shoes; the producer gives him an ultimatum and Coolidge quits, returning to the team. From this description, the episode would seem to be a scathing critique of the portrayal of blacks on American television, and possibly a self-criticism as well. Yet this latter aspect

is never fully brought out. At the end, Coolidge tells the high
school drama teacher that there was some good and some bad
in his experience of the TV world. Moreover, the parodic exaggeration with which that world is portrayed tends to set up the
team members as "real blacks," in a sense congratulating *The
White Shadow* for doing a better job than the programme portrayed within. Ultimately, the episode sets us up for a genuine
self-criticism, then fails to deliver.

None of the examples discussed to this point has been wholly
subversive of dominant television practices, nor have they invoked the MTM tradition in a critical manner. Indeed it could
be argued that in their very "modernism" and their satire of
"regular TV," they are further distinguishing the MTM "quality" style. It took a non-MTM sitcom, yet one wholly within the
MTM style, to take the parodic strain in this style beyond a
mere "quality" reflexivity. *Buffalo Bill* is the most subversively
comic programme yet to emerge out of the MTM style. Earlier
MTM sitcoms, *Phyllis* and *The Betty White Show*, had featured
unpleasant lead figures and acerbic wit, but Bill Bittinger was as
far as one could go from the benign identification figure that
Mary Richards had epitomised. The programme received a lot
of publicity, centering around the unqualified nastiness of its
central character, which was seen as transgressive of television's "likeability factor," a normative strategy central to the
MTM style. The most subversive reading of *Buffalo Bill* would
see it as a complete inversion of *The Mary Tyler Moore Show*. Its
modernist style and use of the anti-hero makes it recuperable
to the quality tradition, but it does not take a "forced" reading
to see that *Buffalo Bill* also subverts that tradition.

The inversion is accomplished by incorporating all the MTM
traits and then playing them against themselves. Instead of the
sympathetic Mary, we have a Ted Baxter as the main character
but one without any of Ted's endearing child-like qualities nor
his familial acceptance. Like Ted, Bill is wholly a television
personality, a talk show host in Buffalo, New York. Unlike Ted,
Bill is clever and manipulative, giving his immersion in the
world of image-making a far less affectionate slant. He is a fool,
but not, like Ted, an innocent fool. Instead of the gruff but
kindly Lou Grant, we have Karl Schub, the ineffectual station
manager whose repeated failed attempts to stand up to Bill
render him a comic figure. In lieu of the naive Georgette, we
have the beauteous Wendy, the show's researcher who, although a bit naive, is nevertheless committed to liberal social

issues and aware of the exchange value of her good looks. The other characters are less obvious inversions of the old MTM show crew, but all lack the "warmth" of the old characters, and lack as well much familial feeling toward Bill Bittinger. Woody, played by the same actor who had portrayed the henpecked Mr. Petersen in Bob Newhart's therapy group, is Bill's devoted and self-effacing factotum and floor manager. He would thus seem to occupy the same comic space as his previous role. Yet Woody is allowed to comment on his persona in a way Mr. Petersen never could. In a moment of revelation, he tells another character that he considers Bill to be his mission in life, that Bill is so despicable that he needs Woody's faith if he is ever to be redeemed. Similarly, the two black characters, Tony, the assistant director, and the "uppity" make-up man, hold Bill to account for his racism, and make scathing comments on their boss's personality. The other major character is the female director of "The Buffalo Bill Show," JoJo, who is also Bill's sometime lover. But she is no Mary Richards, eternally respectful of "Mr. Grant." In a controversial two-part episode, JoJo even has an abortion, knowing that Bill could never be a suitable father.

The *Buffalo Bill* characters thus seem to serve as a commentary on the old *Mary Tyler Moore Show* Utopian family of co-workers. They are a family, but at best a neurotic and disturbed one, headed by a father who is also a child. This twist on the warmth of the MTM family is brought out in an episode in which an unctuous correspondent for the station's "View on Buffalo" does a spot on "The Buffalo Bill Show" staff. We see her interviewing the various family members, trying to get the dirt on Bill. Her interviews with the cast members are intercut with scenes of Bill in his dressing room, anxiously preparing for his own interview. In each of the staff interviews, Bill is damned with faint praise. "I don't hate Bill Bittinger," says Karl Schub, "occasionally he's selfish . . . he can be cruel and vicious." To JoJo the reporter says, "It probably helps having a personal, intimate relationship." She proceeds to read aloud a diary of Bill's sexist comments which JoJo is forced to corroborate. Even the benevolent Wendy is led to make unfavourable comments about Bill. "Bill can be cruel and hateful," she says, "but lately he hardly ever tries to get me into bed." Meanwhile, we view Bill alone in his dressing room, trying out different charming personae for the interview. As we keep returning to these monologues, Bill's narcissistic imagination runs wild. He becomes incensed by an imaginary scene in which the reporter seduces him and he tells her, "I'm offended by your lack of journalistic ethics." Bill proceeds to evict the "View on Buffalo" crew, pulling open the door and shouting "get out" only to return from his fantasy to discover they are waiting at the door to enter. In a typical face-saving manoeuvre, Bill has nothing but praise for his staff; as he tells them afterwards, "Liane tried to get me to knock you guys." He traps his guilty cohorts into coming to his flat to view the broadcast.

As everyone but Bill could have predicted, all of the scenes we have watched being taped are edited into a scathing exposé of Bill Bittinger. The staff's worst comments are selected and, with heavy irony, the segment ends with Bill himself speaking of "warmth, family and love." (A caustic echo of Mary Richard's speech on "The Last Show.") After the broadcast there is a deathly silence, with everyone looking for an escape hatch. Wendy begins to cry and Karl carries her out. JoJo tells Bill, "I said things like that to your face, but to say it on television is inexcusable." As the deeply ashamed group gathers in the corridor, Bill, isolated as ever, drags his immense TV set onto the balcony and starts to shove it over the edge. JoJo tries to stop him, at which point Bill delivers a speech about his relationship to the family which, although pathetic in its way, is a far cry from the typical MTM attitude of sentimental familial affection:

> Friendship happens to be a very overrated commodity . . . I believe in me . . . because I've been left too many times by too many people . . . starting with my father . . . friendship just slows me down . . . [to be and stay on TV] you'd better learn to live by yourself . . . for yourself . . . I like living alone . . . I may be the happiest person I know of . . .

JoJo responds, "Oh, Bill," and as she starts to embrace him, they knock the TV set over the ledge. This undercuts any sympathy we may have felt for Bill. We return for the tag. Bill is yelling "$800 cash" while JoJo expresses concern that it might have killed someone below. "Don't worry," Bill tells her, "nobody's down there . . . except Karl, Wendy, Tony, Woody . . ." and the episode ends. This is a far cry from the typical MTM pattern whereby family harmony is restored by the end of every episode. In the usual pattern, a violation of family harmony is seen as a breach that needs to be healed in order to restore the Utopian moment; in this case, the aberration is Bill's uncharacteristic moment of concern for the others, a moment which is itself rapidly undercut. As a character, Bill is compelling in his very narcissism and isolation, but he is not "benign" and he is not an identification figure. We are more likely to identify with the other staff members and to laugh at Bill's pain, an inversion of the MTM pattern which produces a dark rather than light mode of comedy. The Buffalo Bill family is the MTM family viewed through dark glasses instead of the usual rose-coloured ones.

Even more subversive than its treatment of the work-family, is *Buffalo Bill's* attitude toward television itself. *Buffalo Bill* directs its satire *at* television as an institution. Its critique of television does not occur on isolated episodes; it informs the very core of the programme's structure. The various broadcasts of "The Buffalo Bill Show" take up far more time than Ted's bloopers ever did, and these on-air sequences are played off against Bill's off-camera hypocrisy. In addition, our view of the show is frequently from the inside of the control booth, so that we watch Bill's show on the various monitors and from the viewpoint of the production staff. Much of the satire is achieved through the staff's outraged reactions to Bill's on-camera antics. The "inside" point of view is subversive as well as reflexive.

An especially blatant instance of *Buffalo Bill's* critique of television occurs in the episode in which Bill invites an octogenarian former tap dancer on the programme. Bill coerces the old man, who has long been retired, to do a few steps on the air, during which the man has a heart attack and dies. At this point Bill goes beserk and addresses the studio audience directly. Quite like the anchorman on the *Remington Steele* episode, Bill's speech is a condemnation of television. In this case, however, the message is complicated by the fact that it was Bill himself who brought on the man's death. Bill refuses to allow JoJo to cut to a commercial. "Television killed him," he tells the audience, referring to it as "the human sacrifice business." He asks the audience to quit watching TV. Of course Bill's hypocrisy is revealed when a woman in the audience goes into labour and Bill turns it into melodrama with a "miracle of life" speech. Then Bill runs out of steam with 51 minutes of air time left for the staff to fill. They go immediately to a pre-recorded "Best of Bittinger." In the tag, Bill has returned to normal, refusing to see the woman who has named her baby after him.

Buffalo Bill's critique of television is complex since the characters themselves have an ambivalent attitude toward the medium. "The Buffalo Bill Show" is no respected Los Angeles daily; it is not even the second-rate but sincere WJM local news. The internal show is unlikely to be perceived as having any redeeming virtues, even if the programme as a whole may be read as an "intelligent" criticism of the lowest form of television. If *The Mary Tyler Moore Show* was both regular TV and quality TV, *Buffalo Bill* was both "quality TV" and "radical TV." But the programme started no trend. *Buffalo Bill* was replaced in its time slot by Allan Burns' *The Duck Factory*, a virtual re-creation of *The Mary Tyler Moore Show* set in a cartoon factory, complete with warm, likeable characters and an identification figure even more benign than Mary Richards. It also failed in the ratings, indicating that even the orthodox MTM style of sitcom may have outlived its cultural moment.

CONCLUSION: THE POLITICS OF MTM

Quality TV is liberal TV. Given its institutional constraints and its entertainment function, one cannot expect American television to take self-criticism to the level of a Godard film. Yet both MTM and Godard gear their discourse to an assumed audience. Godard's extreme self-reflexivity appeals to the small audience of avant-garde intellectuals who pay to see his films. The appeal of an MTM programme must be double-edged. It must appeal both to the "quality" audience, a liberal, sophisticated group of upwardly mobile professionals; and it must capture a large segment of the mass audience as well. Thus MTM programmes must be readable at a number of levels, as is true of most U.S. television fare. MTM shows may be interpreted as warm, human comedies or dramas; or they may be interpreted as self-aware "quality" texts. In this sense also, the MTM style is both typical and atypical. Its politics are seldom overt, yet the very concept of "quality" is itself ideological. In interpreting an MTM programme as a quality programme, the quality audience is permitted to enjoy a form of television which is seen as more literate, more stylistically complex, and more psychologically "deep" than ordinary TV fare. The quality audience gets to separate itself from the mass audience and can watch TV without guilt, and without realising that the double-edged discourse they are getting is also ordinary TV. Perhaps the best example of a programme that triumphed through this process of multi-

ple readings is *Hill Street Blues*, the programme which marked
MTM's transition to the quality demographic strategy.

This does not mean that the MTM style lacks progressive
elements, only that, as with all forms of artistic production
under capitalism, the progressive elements may be recuperable
to an ideology of "quality." As an illustration of the politics of
quality, I will take as an extended example one of the crucial
innovations that MTM gave to the sitcom and the TV drama:
the idea of the family of co-workers.

Every genre of American television is based on some kind of
family structure. Even the personnel of the news programmes
are presented to us as a "family"; and until MTM came along,
the nuclear family was the subject of most TV genres, as it was
for the Lear sitcoms. At a time when the nuclear family was
under attack outside the institution of television, MTM pioneered a different kind of family, one that retained certain
residual ideologies of family life while doing away with the
more oppressive aspects of the nuclear family. The MTM
work-family both reproduces the wholesome norms of family
life on TV and presents us with a Utopian variation on the
nuclear family more palatable to a new generation and to the
quality audience.

Rhoda was the only successful MTM sitcom to centre on a
nuclear family rather than a family bonded by work and freely
chosen (even then, Rhoda didn't live at home and the Mor-
gensterns weren't very wholesome). *The Bob Newhart Show* featured a married couple, but the family unit included Bob's co-
workers and even his therapy group. Those MTM sitcoms
which featured a traditional family structure—*The Texas Wheelers*, *Doc*, *The Bob Crane Show*—tended to use an extended family
structure and, moreover, tended to be outside the MTM creative nucleus and outside the "quality" style. Eventually the idea
of the non-nuclear family became the television norm.

The MTM work-family is clearly a response to the breakdown of the nuclear family inside and outside of the television
institution. But how are we to interpret the politics of that
response? On the one hand, the work family can be seen as
Utopian in a reactionary direction. It presents a view of work as
a familial activity, a view far from a "realistic" representation of
the real world of work. And the work family portrayed may be
seen as a conservative force, valuing stasis over change. Many
episodes of *The Mary Tylor Moore Show* take for their situation an
eruption of disharmony within the WJM family: Rhoda and

Mary feud; Murray and Mary feud; Lou fires Mary; Mary is offered another job; Rhoda gets a chance to move back to New York (this last prior to her actual spinning-off). In every case and in traditional sitcom form, harmony is re-established by bringing the family back together at the cost of what, in another context, might be seen as change or growth. Nobody is ever permitted to leave home. As one critic has written, the MTM shows' "standard moment of epiphany" occurs with the discovery "that nothing ever changes and people always stay reassuringly the same."[14] This ideology of family harmony permeates the dramas as well, the difference being that in the continuing serial format, the moments of harmony are brief. Even *Buffalo Bill* represents the unity of the work family as a positive goal; it is just that Bill's presence makes that goal an impossible one.

Many MTM programmes make explicit references to the idea of the work family. In "The Last Show" of *The Mary Tylor Moore Show*, Mary makes a long, sentimental speech about having found a family in her friends at work. The idea of the work family as a reactionary concept is rendered explicit in an episode of *WKRP in Cincinnati*. The employees of WKRP were asked to join a union. When Travis, the "benign identification figure" of the programme, refuses to grant a pay raise, Johnny Fever calls him "a true crypto-fascist puppet of the managerial elite," thus exposing Travis' position seemingly on the side of the workers but really on the side of management. Yet the rest of the episode undercuts this explanation. Johnny only becomes interested in the union when he discovers he will be paid by seniority (he is the oldest living DJ). When he gets this information, he breaks into the song, "Look for the union label," and the others join in. This song comes from an unusually proletarian advertisement widely shown on U.S. TV in which members of the International Ladies Garment Workers Union stand in formation and sing for us to buy clothing with the union label. In invoking the advertisement, including its image of solidarity, WKRP mocks its message. After much discussion, the situation is resolved when Travis negotiates with the station owner. He forces her to give the employees a raise, and they "freely" vote against the union. In this way, an opposition is set up *between* the union and the family of workers (deductively, their interests might be seen as similar, but the MTM concept of the work family is an individualistic one). The owner's son, the timid Carlson, says, "We're a *family* here. I'm not going to have outsiders telling us what to do." Andy Travis says, "Don't let this union business split us up." Although management is portrayed unfavourably, the message is clear: the work family does not need to organise because it is already a democratic institution; all problems can be resolved within the family structure. A union would represent an intrusion from the real world of work into an already Utopian situation. This reading of the work family would view it as a reactionary force, in that it presents an unrealistically familial view of what we know to be an alienated labour process.

Yet such a reading of MTM's own discourse about the family of co-workers is only the most obvious interpretation of the Utopian dimension of the work family. For the MTM family also represents a positive alternative to the nuclear family that had for so long dominated representations of the family on American television. If nobody ever changes (a reading we have already shown to be dubious at best), if nobody ever has to leave home, perhaps it is because the MTM family is one in which it's possible to grow up. This more positive reading depends on the assumption that American network television never represents "realistic" solutions to "real" problems, but that, for this very reason, it is capable of showing us ideal solutions to mythicised versions of real problems. The work family is a solution to the problems of the nuclear family. It gives us a vision of that merger of work and love that Freud said was the ideal of mental, and that many would also see as the ideal of political, health. MTM shows us this ideal over and over again within what in reality are the most oppressive institutional contexts: the hospital, the police precinct, the TV station. Media institutions work especially well for an idealised vision of work, since we already have a mythology of "creative" work as an ideal.

The WJM family is what Mary Richards left home for, and it fulfilled her expectations and ours. For women especially, the alternatives presented were ideal ones, not depictions of the reality of work but images of a liberated existence that could be taken as a goal to strive towards. Mary and Rhoda came to represent an ideal of female friendship, a relationship that, due to the redundancy of the sitcom form, could never be torn asunder by the marriage of either woman. Mary's romances never represented a serious threat to either her relationship with Rhoda or her family at work. If the work-family concept proved pleasureable and reproducible, perhaps it was because it provided a positive alternative for the families who watched Mary and Rhoda on their TVs.

It must be stressed that neither of these readings of the work-family concept is "correct." Both are possible, but only the latter can explain the pleasure the concept must have provided in order for the programmes to be popular. That pleasure can encompass both progressive longings for an alternative to the nuclear family, and "reactionary" longings for a return to the presumed ideal family structures of the past. The liberal, quality structure of the programmes permits and encourages both kinds of pleasure.

NOTES

1. September 9, 1979.
2. July 16, 1974; November 2, 1975; July 13, 1981; September 9, 1979; *Los Angeles Times*, July 16, 1974.
3. See, for example, Donald Knox, *The Magic Factory* (New York: Praeger, 1973), and Hugh Fordin, *The World of Entertainment* (Garden City, N.Y.: Doubleday, 1975).
4. "What is an Author?" *Screen*, 20 (Spring 1979), p. 19.
5. *TV: The Most Popular Art* (New York: Anchor Books, 1974).
6. Tom Carson, "The Even Couple," *The Village Voice*, May 3, 1983, p. 59.
7. "Happy Days are Here Again," *Film Comment*, 15: 4(July/August 1979).
8. Described in detail in Rick Mitz, *The Great TV Sitcom Book* (New York: Richard Marek, 1980).
9. MTM also developed a "tag" ending that would trail off in such a way that the conversation appears to continue after the programme ends; this produces a "quality" effect by rendering the sense of closure less emphatic.
10. *New York Times Magazine*, April 7, 1974, p. 97.
11. Written by David Lloyd; Mitz, *TV Sitcom Book*.
12. I make this point at greater length in my book, *The Hollywood Musical* (London: Macmillan, 1982).
13. Todd Gitlin, *Inside Prime Time* (New York: Pantheon, 1983).
14. Tom Carson, "Lame Duck," *The Village Voice*, May 1, 1984.

THOMAS SCHATZ

ST. ELSEWHERE AND THE EVOLUTION OF THE ENSEMBLE SERIES

In the hermetic fictional world of series television, the change could be explained easily enough. Lou Grant, the cantankerous news director at Minneapolis' WJM-TV, suddenly faced a career crisis. Already mired in a middle-aged funk after his divorce, Lou now found himself out of work when WJM was sold and the entire news production staff fired. Undaunted, Lou followed Horace Greeley's advice and his career fix as well, heading west for a newspaper job as city editor for the *Los Angeles Tribune*. So instead of Mary Richards, Murray Slaughter, Ted Baxter, and the rest of WJM's working "family," Lou would play the hard-headed, soft-hearted patriarch for Joe Rossi, Billie Newman, Art Donovan, and the other employees of the *Trib*.

What we are considering here, quite obviously, is that inveterate television institution, the series spinoff—in this case the genesis of *Lou Grant* and the dramatic rationale governing its creation. Outside the series' fictional universe, however, the reasons behind that particular spinoff and its eventual impact on the industry are elements in a very different drama. In fact, *Lou Grant* stands as a major plot point in the ongoing story of network programming, marking two of the more significant series trends in recent TV history: the decline of the situation comedy and the rise of the hour-long ensemble drama.

The most obvious reason for creating *Lou Grant* was to sustain the momentum of *The Mary Tylor Moore Show* when its star decided to leave the series after seven successful seasons on CBS. In early September of 1977, *The Mary Tylor Moore Show* (hereafter *The MTM Show*) left prime time; *Lou Grant* premiered later that month. For MTM Enterprises, the independent television production company formed by Moore and husband-producer Grant Tinker back in 1970, putting *The MTM Show* to pasture via syndication (off-network reruns) eliminated the drudgery and expense of production and generated enormous revenues. MTM's other sitcom success from the early 1970s, *The Bob Newhart Show*, had left prime time for syndication a year before. Now that MTM was finally cashing in on those early successes (prime-time TV series rarely generate profits for their producers until they reach syndication), the company could afford to experiment. Veteran character actor Ed Asner had become an increasingly important and popular performer on *The MTM Show*, and both MTM and CBS were willing to test his capacity to carry a series as star.

Asner's character wasn't the first from *The MTM Show* to spin free of the show's ensemble constellation and become a star in his own narrative universe. In the 1974 season Mary's neighbor Rhoda Morgenstern left Minneapolis for New York City and a series of her own. And another neighbor, Phyllis Lindstrom, departed for San Francisco and her own series the following TV season. Both *Rhoda* and *Phyllis* were virtual clones of the original: they were half-hour sitcoms focusing on the domestic and professional concerns of semi-liberated, upbeat, insecure, and aggressive career women in a predominantly male world. Spinning off Lou Grant and building an hour-long dramatic series around him obviously marked a change in MTM's spinoff strategy, and one that involved more than simply a change in format. It represented an effort to adapt the very best qualities of the ensemble sitcoms—particularly *The MTM Show* and *M*A*S*H*—to an expanded dramatic and technical format. *Lou Grant* was less a clone of its predecessor than an experiment in generic recombination, with its unique blending of comedy and drama, of realism and stylization, of episodic and serial story lines, of social relevance and soap-opera melodramatics.

By the early 1980s this hybrid narrative form would reach maturity in two subsequent ensemble dramas, *Hill Street Blues* and *St. Elsewhere*. Back in 1977, though, MTM's segue from the half-hour sitcom format to the hour-long drama was decidedly unexpected. The company had staked its claim to industry dominance on the strength of its sitcoms, and the genre still dominated prime-time schedules at all three networks. But in fact MTM's sitcom savvy was waning in the late 1970s, due primarily to a loss of personnel and the recent surge of ABC's comedy programming. MTM's early-seventies sitcoms, along with other CBS series like *M*A*S*H* and Norman Lear's productions (*All in the Family, Maude, The Jeffersons*, etc.) had generated a virtual renaissance in prime-time television. But by the end of the decade the genre was suffering from its own version of Gresham's law: mediocre product was muscling quality comedy out of the mainstream and into the living museum of syndication.

The rise of ABC on the strength of what TV critic Gary Deeb disparaged as its "tits 'n' zits" comedies (*Three's Company, Laverne & Shirley, Happy Days, Mork & Mindy*) marked the beginning of the end not only for the CBS renaissance and the MTM-style sitcom, but for the genre itself as television's most enduring and successful programming form. By 1980 Deeb would be looking back on the early 1970s with the kind of lament that critics usually reserve for the 1950s. "It seems like an eternity," wrote Deeb, "but it wasn't all that long ago that Saturday night was the home of TV's golden age of comedy. CBS had put together the most soul-satisfying three-hour comedy block in history, . . . the murderer's row of *All in the Family, M*A*S*H,* the Mary Tylor Moore, Bob Newhart, and Carol Burnett shows." Unlike the adolescent sitcoms and comic-book adventure shows that carried ABC to ratings supremacy, Deeb found the earlier CBS comedies "witty, sophisticated, humanistic, and nearly always magnificently acted."[1]

Many of the renaissance sitcoms from CBS were still popular in the late 1970s, and in fact the genre's all-time peak came when CBS's sitcoms were accompanied atop the ratings by ABC's wave of adolescent comedies. In the 1978–79 season, nine of the top ten series on television were situation comedies. Within another few seasons, however, the public—that ultimate arbiter of TV values—would sense the sitcom's devaluation and begin turning away from the genre en masse. By the 1982–83 season, only *M*A*S*H* and *Three's Company* remained in the top ten. The following year, for the first time since *I Love Lucy* took to the airwaves in October of 1951, there was not a single situation comedy among television's top ten programs. And two of the three sitcoms that edged into the top twenty— *AfterMash* and *The Jeffersons*—were spinoffs of early-seventies successes, the residue of television's comedy renaissance.

By then MTM had moved almost exclusively into dramatic programming, although its roots were planted firmly in the early-seventies sitcom—and not only in the earlier MTM series but others as well, particularly *M*A*S*H.* In fact *Lou Grant,* the pivotal series in MTM's shift to hour-long drama, was created through a collaboration between the creators of *The MTM Show,*

James Brooks and Allan Burns, and *M*A*S*H*'s executive producer, Gene Reynolds. *Lou Grant* adapted from these and other
sitcoms the basic conventions of the ensemble cast and domesticated workplace; from *M*A*S*H* it also adapted a more aggressive cinematic technique and narrative structure, along
with a subtle undercurrent of self-righteous male superiority.
The elements adapted from *M*A*S*H* were vital to *Lou Grant*
and the evolving MTM style, but the essential feature of all
MTM's series has been the ensemble itself. Like the news team
at WJM-TV and the personnel of the army's 4077th, the staff in
the *Trib*'s city room—city editor Lou Grant, reporters Billie
Newman and Joe Rossi, assistant editor Art Donovan, and
photographer "Animal" Price, along with managing editor Charlie Hume and publisher/owner Mrs. Margaret Pynchon—represented a kinship system bonded by more than mere blood
ties. They coalesced into an integrated constellation of characters from disparate backgrounds, working together, whose commitment to their work and to one another had become the
governing force in their lives.

While the characters on *Lou Grant* were committed journalists, they were not reduced to one-dimensional narrative
agents. They were not mere plot functions in a news-story-of-
the-week strategy, nor were they idealized stereotypes. Instead, these characters were complex, vulnerable, humane, capable of growth and change, free to anguish over and learn
from their mistakes. Just as *The MTM Show* and *M*A*S*H* had
been more character comedies than situation comedies, *Lou
Grant* was essentially a character drama. The series did focus
each week on some relevant or fashionable social issue, but the
primary focus was invariably the lives and interrelationships of
the ensemble. That's not to say the social issues tackled on the
series were simply artificial narrative devices to advance and
complicate stories involving some character's personal life.
Those issues elicited genuine, deeply felt social concern of the
characters, and thus they served to reinforce the governing
subtext in the series—namely, that Lou and Billie and all the
Trib staff were married first to their jobs and one another, and
that their off-duty lives were secondary. What the series was
"about" on a fundamental level was the pain and sacrifice and
guilt that accompany professional and social commitment, and
how each of the characters dealt with it.

The effort to portray the characters' jobs and personal lives
more authentically and less heroically on *Lou Grant* contributed
to the oft-cited "realism" of the show. Equally important to its

realist esthetic were the visual and narrative techniques employed. Whereas the earlier MTM shows, like so many seventies sitcoms, had been shot before a live audience in a proscenium (stage-bound) environment, *Lou Grant* was filmed on a sound stage or on location, enabling its producers to develop a much different "look" and also a more complex method of structuring the series segments. If any single TV series anticipated this look and structure, it was *M*A*S*H*. While other renaissance sitcoms were following *The MTM Show* and *All in the Family* to a proscenium style and production context, Gene Reynolds and writer-producer Larry Gelbart developed *M*A*S*H*, according to Gelbart, as "a TV series with motion picture values."[2]

These values were evident in two general areas: the visual quality of the series (in terms of both set design and more formal aspects like lighting, camera movement, and editing), and also in the narrative construction (especially the tendency to develop multiple plots in a given segment which could be played out simultaneously in different locations and intercut for dramatic effect). This reliance on a more cinematic style in *Lou Grant* was scarcely innovative; all hour-long dramatic series utilized a similar technical approach. What was innovative, though, was the way that *M*A*S*H* and later *Lou Grant* applied this approach to an ensemble drama with multiple characters and plots set within a chaotic workplace. The camerawork and editing provided a means of weaving the various plot threads together into an integrated, apparently seamless narrative. These techniques also situated the viewer as a sort of participant-observer, drawing the audience "into" the drama without binding them to any single character or plot line, as most dramatic series tend to do.

Another quality that distinguished *Lou Grant* was socioeconomic rather than formal or dramatic. While the series was generally successful it never amassed a sufficient quantity of viewers to emerge as a genuine hit series. But still the series was renewed for several seasons largely because of the *quality* of viewers it attracted—namely, up-scale urbanites whose status as active consumers rendered them a desirable "target market" for TV advertisers. Thus *Lou Grant* was among the first prime-time series to elude the industry's dominant "least common denominator" and "least objectionable programming" mentality, a factor which certainly reinforced MTM's commitment to more literate, sophisticated, and socially complex drama.

By the early 1980s, the basic qualities that distinguished *Lou*

Grant—particularly its ensemble cast, domesticated workplace, multiple plots in a semi-serial format, aggressive cinematic technique, and "quality" viewer demographics—would coalesce into a virtual signature style of MTM Enterprises' productions. That style is most evident in MTM's successful hour-long dramas, *Hill Street Blues* and *St. Elsewhere*, although by then even the sitcom was exhibiting these qualities, particularly *Taxi* and *Cheers* (both produced by MTM alumni). *Hill Street Blues* has most often been cited as the "breakthrough" series in developing that style, which seems logical enough in that its advances over *Lou Grant* were so pronounced that it did appear to be a radical departure from even that MTM ensemble drama. To begin with, *Hill Street* doubled the size of the ensemble to fourteen series regulars, and it expanded the range of social, economic, ethnic, and ideological types within that ensemble. The series moved more directly into a multiple-plot, serialized orientation, exploiting its expanded ensemble and also the steady drift toward "ongoing" stories in other TV genres (especially the prime-time soaps like *Dallas*). The series was situated in an institution whose professional demands and social conditions were considerably heavier than in earlier ensemble series; on "the Hill" the issue was not only professional commitment and integrity, but human survival.

Hill Street Blues also developed a more aggressive visual style than either *M*A*S*H* or *Lou Grant*, a style that *St. Elsewhere* would adjust to its own dramatic needs. When Gelbart and Reynolds adapted *M*A*S*H* from Robert Altman's hit 1970 movie, they could push television's established "telefilm" values only so far. Altman's dense imagery, elaborate sets, overlapping dialogue, constant camera and character movement, and seemingly meandering narrative development were ideally suited to the movie's ensemble cast and multiple plots, but these techniques were far removed from the clean, well-lit images and straightforward linear plots of prime-time television. The TV version of *M*A*S*H* pushed telefilm conventions in the general direction of Altman's esthetic, and MTM would push them even further in each of its ensemble dramas. Todd Gitlin's description of the look and feel of *Hill Street* suggests how far MTM was indeed willing to push: "In *Hill Street* shop talk, the intercutting, which is characteristic of soap opera, was joined to a density of look and sound that was decidedly un-soap operatic. Quick cuts, a furious pace, a nervous camera made for complexity and congestion, a sense of entanglement and continuous crisis that matched the actual density and convolution of city life."[3]

Like earlier innovative series that started slowly before finding an audience—including *M*A*S*H* and *The MTM Show*—*Hill Street Blues* suffered a dismal reception but steadily built a following. By the 1982–83 season it was nearing top-ten status among network series, and its viewer demographics were such that many sponsors were paying NBC more to advertise on *Hill Street* than on other series with considerably larger audiences.[4] But by that 1982–83 season, the same season *Lou Grant* left CBS for syndication and *St. Elsewhere* debuted on NBC, *Hill Street* was beginning to show signs of wear. Both of its creators, Michael Kozoll and Steven Bochco, were channelling their energies in other directions: Kozoll writing movie scripts and Bochco developing yet another MTM ensemble series, the ill-fated *Bay City Blues*. Meanwhile, *Hill Street* was lapsing into a formulaic predictability, with its characters often reduced to caricature and its plots edging ever closer to the cop-show conventions that it had so carefully avoided in its earlier seasons.

Whatever its shortcomings, however, the overall success of *Hill Street* was reason enough for NBC's initial and sustained support of *St. Elsewhere*, which was as distinct a departure from previous medical series as *Hill Street* had been from the urban crime genre. But as much as *St. Elsewhere* owed *Hill Street*, it was scarcely the clone that the network and much of the audience had expected. In Paltrow's words, "If people wanted *Hill Street Blues* in a hospital, they were bound to be disappointed. The similarities are that both have ensemble casts and multiple plots. But we're more like *M*A*S*H* and *Lou Grant*."[5] Paltrow's point is instructive. The setting for *St. Elsewhere*—a social service institution in the decaying inner city of an Eastern industrial center—was indeed similar to "the Hill." But the characters in St. Eligius hospital were not subject to the same state-of-siege mentality and penchant for violence that dominated *Hill Street*. The Hill Street precinct house was itself a virtual war zone, a microcosm of its surrounding milieu. St. Eligius, a teaching hospital and haven for the less than affluent, was distinctly at odds with the inner-city environs beyond its massive brick facade. And although the writers for *St. Elsewhere* were encouraged by NBC's executives to exploit its setting as a source of "jeopardy" in the series (i.e., for action and violence), the heart of the series—like those of its characters—was much too soft for that kind of conflict.

The *St. Elsewhere* ensemble is indeed reminiscent of the staffs of the 4077th and the *Trib*'s city room. The hospital's chief administrators are Drs. Donald Westphall (Ed Flanders), the Director of Medicine, and Mark Craig (William Daniels), Chief of Surgery. The other dozen members of the regular cast are the staff doctors, the nurses (with Christina Pickles as head nurse Helen Rosenthal), and various first- and second-year residents. Much of the action in the series' first season centered on the initiate student-doctors, particularly Jack Morrison (David Morse), Wayne Fiscus (Howie Mandel), Peter White (Terrence Knox), and Victor Erlich (Ed Begley, Jr.). One character with a fairly peripheral role early on who would become quite important to the series was Dr. Daniel Auschlander (Norman Lloyd), an aging specialist in internal medicine suffering from terminal liver cancer.

As is altogether obvious from this roster of principal characters, the *St. Elsewhere* ensemble is predominantly male, reflecting conditions in the medical profession but also in the MTM ensemble dramas. Recalling *Lou Grant*, it is worth noting that one of the more telling but (at the time, anyway) less obvious aspects of MTM's shift from sitcom to drama was the related shift from a female to a male focus and world view. While *The MTM Show* and its sitcom spinoffs treated the vagaries of working women in male-oriented professions, *Lou Grant* and the other ensemble dramas moved steadily away from the feminine—and the vaguely feminist—orientation of the sitcoms. But paradoxically, the ensemble dramas sustained certain "feminine" narrative qualities, particularly in terms of social and interpersonal problem-solving and in the burgeoning soap-opera strategies of each series.

The authority figure and ideological touchstone in each of the ensemble dramas—*Trib* editor Lou Grant, Hill Street's precinct captain Frank Furillo, St. Eligius' Dr. Westphall—served as role models and patriarchs for their respective professional clans. Each figure favored conciliation over confrontation, negotiation over pontification, communication over authoritative administration. Yet there was never any doubt about where the buck stopped in each institutional hierarchy. Moreover, the problems (i.e., dramatic conflicts) that these men generally faced had less to do with the actual practices of the institution in relation to the outside world—reporting the news, apprehending criminals, treating the sick—than with creating the proper environment for their clan to practice its social function.

The patriarch's primary role, in other words, was to humanize a traditionally insensitive bureaucracy, to transform a group of disparate and potentially alienated wage slaves into a working family.

This domestication of the workplace is a key element in the ensemble series, and also an area where *St. Elsewhere* has been fairly unique. In *The MTM Show*, *M*A*S*H*, *Lou Grant*, and even *Hill Street*, the ensemble actually took on the structural features and individual roles of a surrogate family, complete with *pater familias*, matriarch, unruly kids, avuncular old pro, and so on, all pulling together against both the imperfect (if not malevolent) world "out there" and also the constant interference of less enlightened and sensitive bureaucrats within the same institution. (One of the more interesting aspects of *M*A*S*H*'s evolution, in fact, was the replacement of commanding officer Henry Blake with Sherman Potter, a considerably more paternal type, and the gradual transformation of Major Houlihan's character from "Hot Lips" to "Margaret." These and other factors during the series' life span might be read as a shift to a more overtly familial ensemble.)

St. Elsewhere, with its male authority figure, matriarchal head nurse (who was working on her fifth marriage), and array of initiate personnel, seemed destined at first to follow this pattern. But actually the series has moved gradually into another conception of domestication and kinship altogether. To really appreciate this movement, we need to trace the steady emergence of the hospital's patriarchal triumverate—Westphall, Craig, and Auschlander—over the past three seasons. Back in early 1983, the show's low ratings signalled its struggle to find not only an audience but its own formal and dramatic bearings as well. Like *Hill Street*, *St. Elsewhere* was caught between TV's traditional "franchise series" orientation (here an episodic disease-of-the-week strategy), and its quest for a more authentic and humanistic depiction of the hospital. In January of 1983, Joshua Brand suggested the possibility of a more conservative approach: "There will be less of what I call 'controlled messiness' in future episodes, and there will be fewer stories. I'm sorry to see this happen. But we've been in the bottom of the ratings because we are outside the conventions of television. I guess there have been too many deviations from the norm."[6]

At the time, the same kinds of "deviations" were working well enough for *Hill Street*—in fact that series' initial director of photography had instructed his camera operators to "make it look messy."[7] And this was a quality in both series that wasn't just a matter of the look but also the pace and plotting of the stories. Just as *Hill Street* had learned to integrate its episodic crime-solution dimension with a serial treatment of its characters' individual and interpersonal lives, so would *St. Elsewhere*, but not without objections from the network. A few months after Brand's comment, Bruce Paltrow was quoted as saying, "NBC also wants us to simplify our stories, making it a little easier for the audience."[8] The pacing, visual complexity, and multiple plotting of both *Hill Street* and *St. Elsewhere* did indeed make heavier demands on its viewers than did most prime-time series, especially considering how little time was spent in each with expositional rehashing of previous events and background information.

In its initial season, though, *St. Elsewhere* struck a compromise between these episodic and serial strategies. By way of example, consider the interwoven plot lines in a three-segment block spanning late January and early February in 1983. There were two dominant plot lines extending through the three segments, both of which involved "outside" characters whose medical conditions motivated their presence in St. Eligius, generating conflicts that were raised and resolved within the three-segment block. In one of the plots Mark Craig's college roommate, once a close friend but now estranged, arrives at the hospital for a sex-change operation. The other plot involves a teenage boy brought dead-on-arrival to the emergency room; the boy is saved, miraculously, but is then found to be suffering from amnesia and thus requires extensive psychotherapy.

Besides these extended-episodic storylines, there is one straight episodic plot in each of the segments as well. In the first segment, an Asian boy dying from a mysterious spinal disease is saved when his relatives enact an ancient Chinese ritual (providing a nice cultural contrast to the D.O.A. saved by more familiar techniques). In the second segment, the family of a just-deceased cancer victim is badgered into allowing an obnoxious medical examiner to perform a needless autopsy, severely disfiguring the corpse and further traumatizing the family. In the third segment, a crusty and aging orthodox Jew suffers from symptoms whose cause cannot be diagnosed until a second-rate resident finally connects the symptoms to a rare blood disease. In each of these episodes, interestingly enough, established medical practices are shown to be either inadequate or inhumane. *St. Elsewhere* clearly was not formulating a facile celebration of the medical status quo in the tradition of *Ben Casey, Marcus Welby,* and *Medical Center.*

Besides these short-term conflicts, there are four other plot lines extending into this three-segment block that already had been set up. These dealt with Dr. Auschlander's physical and emotional bout with cancer, a rekindled romance between two staff doctors, the deepening marital crisis of first-year resident Peter White, and the efforts of staff psychologist Hugh Bailey to treat a burnt-out prodigy who now thinks he's a bird. Of these four long-term conflicts, one (the romance) gradually dissolves by season's end. Two others (Auschlander's cancer bout and White's marital crisis) would be extended for at least two more seasons. Only the bird-man storyline would be resolved within this block, when the disturbed patient takes a suicidal flight from the hospital roof as Bailey and others look on helplessly.

Most of the screen time in these three segments is devoted to the amnesia victim and to Craig's friend's sex-change operation. A closer look at the latter storyline provides a useful illustration of *St. Elsewhere*'s early extended-episodic strategy, and also an idea of how that strategy would be modified as the series and its ensemble developed. In the first of the three segments, Craig is incredulous when he discovers his friend's situation, flatly refusing to discuss the issue or even face his former roommate. By the second segment, both the pending surgery and Craig's reaction to it have become an issue in the hospital, providing a pretext for discussing the nature of human sexuality and sex-roles within our society. Craig does come to terms with his friend's sex-change in the third series segment, though. He is counselled, despite his protestations, by his friend's male lover who has himself undergone a sex-change (he was formerly a woman) and is now a therapist for transsexuals. Later, Craig slips discretely into a pre-op area where his friend, now sedated, awaits surgery. Craig leans over him and says, "You were right—you can't make new old friends. I just wanted to say good luck, old buddy." Craig then kisses his unconscious ex-roomate, glances awkwardly at an orderly reading a newspaper nearby, and exits. We learn later that the surgery is a success, but this is the last we see of Craig's "old buddy."

This particular storyline seems to have served two distinct narrative functions. On the short term, it provided a context for addressing and re-examining sexual identity in contemporary society and the capacity of medical science to affect and transform that identity. On the long term, it served to flesh out Mark Craig's character, in terms of both his "backstory" (college days, early courtship of his wife, etc.) and also his essentially reactionary (although flexible) ideological bent. This is indicative of how "outside" characters would be utilized on *St. Elsewhere*, particularly in relation to the three patriarchs. But as the series evolved the writers have been less prone to simply jettison these characters once their storylines have been played out. In later segments, in fact, these "related" characters tend to be just that—for example, somehow *kin* to the ensemble character either professionally, personally, or biologically. Also, the introduction of these related characters would be motivated less often by some physical or psychological malady that warranted treatment at the hospital.

In this sense *St. Elsewhere* has been steadily outgrowing its earlier (and perhaps necessary) penchant for episodic plotting and expendable outside characters, developing a sort of centripetal narrative force that draws its external subplots into the dramatic maelstrom. As *St. Elsewhere* has evolved over the past two seasons, then, it has taken on the qualities of a cumulative text, quite literally accumulating peripheral characters—including rather important ones like Craig's son who very rarely actually appears "on-stage" but are referred to quite often. Equally important over the past two seasons has been the growing emphasis on the "patriarchal order" within St. Eligius. (The three patriarchs are, by the way, the only characters to elude the ensemble's alphabetically ordered presentation in the opening credits.) And a survey of each season's narrative development indicates that *St. Elsewhere*'s textual system is not only cumulative but seasonal as well, with the season finale from both 1984 and 1985 focusing directly on the complex network of father-son relationships within the constellation of characters.

The 1984 season-ending segment introduced Mark Craig's son, a medical student whose career is jeopardized by his dependence on amphetamines to get through his internship. That segment also treated the relationships between Westphall and his autistic son, Tommy, and between recently widowed resident Jack Morrison and his son, Peter. The segment ends with a poignant scene involving Westphall and his own mentor and surrogate father, Daniel Auschlander. The aging doctor's cancer has flared up, endangering his life and eliciting a visit from

Westphall in the dead of night. In the darkened hospital room, illuminated only by flashes of lightning from outside, Auschlander and Westphall drift into a reverie about their own fathers; we learn that Westphall had had a very positive relationship with his father and Auschlander a very difficult one. Auschlander describes a recurring dream in which he and his father are playmates, and he wonders whether their rapport might have been better outside the constraints and tensions of biological father-son bonding. Westphall then recalls his father's mental lapses as he neared death, including an incident when he mistook Westphall for his own father. The scene—and the season—ends with the two of them reaffirming their dependence and unspoken love for one another, with Westphall saying, "Don't die, Daniel," and Auschlander assuring him, "I have no intention of dying."

This interplay of biological and professional fatherhood would continue to dominate the series throughout the following (1984–85) season, to a point where a system of interlocking kinship would govern the series—particularly the relationships between Auschlander and Westphall, Westphall and Morrison, Westphall and Tommy, Craig and Erlich, and Craig and his own son. The 1985 season finale even carried this father-son motif onto a metaphysical plane via three Easter-related storylines: one involving a third-world messiah (a black with a Latin accent wearing flowing robes and long braided hair) who is crucified by street thugs and literally brought back from the dead in St. Eligius' emergency room; another tracing the preparations for a Passover service in the hospital which is later attended by Westphall and Auschlander; and finally an Easter-egg hunt for the children in the hospital, orchestrated by Auschlander's wife, Catherine (played by Jane Wyatt, once the matriarch of television's Anderson family on *Father Knows Best*). Catherine suffers from heart disease which requires surgery, an episodic maneuver with long-term implications: it forces Auschlander to re-examine his own "obsession with death." There are significant storylines involving the other two patriarchs as well. Westphall is suffering a lingering malaise over his son's autism and his decision to sell the home in which he'd raised his family. Mark Craig learns early in the episode that his son has eloped with a woman Craig has never met, and that she is expecting a child. Craig also learns that his mentor during his initiate years, a Dr. Dimidian, is visiting in Boston, so Craig decides to visit Dimidian and takes along Victor Erlich, his own student-initiate. As it happens, Dimidian has been ill and is in such a deteriorated mental state that he doesn't even recognize Craig—which is so disconcerting to Craig that he literally bolts out the door and back to St. Eligius.

The myriad father-son connections all surface in a scene in which the three patriarchs meet at a bar (at "Cheers," in fact, in a delightful bit of self-referential generic cross-breeding and comic relief) just after the Passover service. There the three men replay much of the conversation between Westphall and Auschlander from a season before, motivated by Craig's complaints about his son getting married without the requisite social and familial rituals. Craig goes on to lament the emotional distance between him and his father—a man who never told Craig that he loved him and only demonstrated his affection on one occasion, with an embrace on D-Day some four decades earlier. Westphall recalls how close he was to his dying father even after his father's mind had gone and he recognized no one. This ties directly into Tommy's autism, and also to Dr. Dimidian's deteriorated mental state—although Craig doesn't mention his meeting with Dimidian. Craig leaves, since he will be operating on Catherine early the next morning, and Westphall then confides to Auschlander that his commitment to medicine and to St. Eligius has somehow waned, and that he plans to leave the hospital.

The next morning, Easter Sunday, finds Catherine recovering from surgery. As she sleeps, Auschlander slips into her room and confides: "Catherine, I'm beginning to understand. I still don't want to die but the calm which we ourselves create comes from some secret place within—we together—and now we don't have to be afraid." This remarkable moment of resolution is followed by Auschlander's taking on Catherine's role, supervising the children's Easter-egg hunt. Craig, meanwhile, has returned to see Dimidian, motivated apparently by Westphall's description of his loving relationship with his dying father in a similarly deteriorated mental state. Craig's visit also provides a dramatic payoff: the oblivious old man is lost in a game with tissue paper, but when Craig adjusts his shawl there is a flash of recognition and Dimidian stutters, "Mark!"

Thus both Craig and Auschlander realize epiphanic moments in this season-ending segment, moments when their individual roles within the professional, interpersonal, and "natural" (biological) scheme of things are somehow clarified and resolved, even if only for a moment. It's interesting that these moments are shared with "significant others" (Dimidian and Catherine) who are unaware of their contributions to the patriarch's epiphany. The role of the father, finally, is a lonely one whose triumphs are intensely private. While Craig and Auschlander undergo a resurrection and reaffirmation of faith, however, Westphall's faith is shaken and his deliverance is not at hand. He too reaches a point of closure in his resolve to leave St. Eligius and all that it represents. The segment ends as Westphall, having cleared out his office, walks down an empty corridor. As he passes a fire extinguisher he spots something nestled in the folded fire hose: it's the golden egg, undiscovered by the children who'd been told by Auschlander that "whoever finds it will possess magical powers, go on exciting adventures, do wonderful new things." Westphall smiles grimly as he picks up the egg. The image freezes; the season ends.

This segment of *St. Elsewhere* strikes me as one of the richest and most rewarding hours of dramatic television in my viewing experience, and one so complex that it demands considerable reflection to be appreciated. Whatever producer Paltrow's earlier promises to the network, it scarcely seems that MTM has made it any "easier" on the series' viewers. The segment does contain the usual dose of comic relief: a huge black orderly in a white Easter-bunny outfit trying to use the bathroom, Erlich searching for a suitably laid-back religion, Craig badgering an Indian resident during surgery concerning his whereabouts "the day Indira Ghandi was shot," and so on. This brand of dark humor is itself complicated by the series' tendency to interweave the real with the surreal (as with the black messiah's crucifixion and resurrection), the everyday with the mythical (the Easter and Passover services, the mystical golden egg at segment's end).

What binds all of these plot threads into a seamless narrative fabric is *St. Elsewhere*'s governing kinship theme, qualified in this segment by the Easter-Passover motifs—which themselves invoke quite different conceptions of father-son relations and also of death, resurrection, and deliverance. At one point in the segment Westphall, discussing Tommy's autism with Craig and Auschlander, laments "the rites of passage I can't pass on to my own son." After a pause he concludes: "Living by the rules doesn't pay off, gentlemen." Auschlander is wise enough to let the crisis play itself out; he even provides his surrogate son with a talisman for his inevitable journey. Auschlander understands that if Westphall has lost faith in himself, he cannot fulfill his patriarchal mission not only to keep the faith but to live it, and thereby to pass it on to succeeding generations.

In a rather curious way, Westphall's midlife crisis takes us back to our point of departure with Lou Grant—and to the ensemble drama's point of departure as well. But Westphall's malaise is so much more genuine and deeply felt than Lou Grant's had been; and Westphall's journey is bound to be more spiritual and inner-directed. Heading west in search of a new job and another kinship system will not soothe Westphall's troubled soul. His fate is with St. Eligius, inexorably bound to a kinship system that penetrates his personal and professional being, that extends indefinitely into his past and future. The ultimate triumph and the essential paradox of *St. Elsewhere*, I think, is just this capacity: to reveal the nature of men whose lives are public and yet intensely private, to reveal the abiding spiritual faith that fuels the fires of their social and professional commitment.

NOTES

1. Gary Deeb, "The Man Who Destroyed Television," *Playboy*, vol. 21 (February 1980), p. 220.
2. Larry Gelbart, "Its Creator Says 'Hail and Farewell' to 'M*A*S*H,' " *The New York Times*, February 27, 1983, "Arts and Leisure Section," p. 1.
3. Todd Gitlin, *Inside Prime Time* (New York: Pantheon Books, 1983), p. 274.
4. See Michael J. Pollan, "Can 'Hill Street Blues' Rescue NBC?" *Channels*, vol. 2, #6 (March/April 1983).
5. Fred Rothenberg, "Death Rattle?" *Austin American-Statesman*, May 8, 1983.
6. Diane Holloway, " 'St. Elsewhere' Needs Intensive Care," *Austin American-Statesman*, January 21, 1983.
7. Gitlin, p. 291.
8. Holloway, " 'St. Elsewhere.' "

MICHAEL SCHUDSON

THE POLITICS OF LOU GRANT

Lou Grant began its third season this fall, a third round at providing "quality television." Always a critical success, the program has attained an enviable position in the ratings as well. It is avidly followed not only by the general public but by print journalists themselves, who seem to be pleased with TV's rendering of their world. A small-town editor in South Dakota even insists that he picks up editorial strategies from the program.

One *Lou Grant* episode drew fire over the summer from the American Health Care Association, a nursing home federation, which attacked the "distortions and lies" in an episode that dealt with nursing homes. While the AHCA persuaded Kellogg's, Oscar Mayer, and Prudential to withdraw their sponsorship of the August 27 rerun of the nursing home segment, the American Association of Retired Persons and the National Retired Teachers Association urged people to tune in, and newspapers editorialized in defense of *Lou Grant*.

Such public response raises unusual questions for a television series. What is its political perspective? Does it have one? Or does it, like most television handling political topics, check and balance every strong statement and neutralize any political impact? Is the program, like the character of Lou Grant himself, more nice than strong—or is there a strength in being nice?

Lou Grant does take a political stance. A show on Vietnam veterans left no doubt that they have been badly treated by society and by inadequate federal provisions. The nursing home episode left no doubt that nursing home regulation is inadequate, that at least some nursing home operators are heartless, and that American society has badly neglected the

Published by permission of Transaction, Inc. from *Society*, Vol. 17, No. 2, 1980. Copyright © 1980 by Transaction, Inc.

elderly. On many issues, *Lou Grant* takes a liberal, reforming stand.

There is a hitch in that stand, however. It has to do with the distinction C. Wright Mills made between "private troubles" and "public issues." Troubles, Mills wrote, have to do with the self and the limited areas of social life of which an individual is directly aware. The resolution of troubles, then, lies "within the individual as a biographical entity and within the scope of his immediate milieu." Issues, in contrast, concern matters transcending local environments and passing beyond the range of an individual's inner life. They concern the "larger structure of social and historical life." The task of what Mills called "the sociological imagination" is to understand the connections of private troubles and public issues, to see personal problems in relationship to social structure.

Lou Grant tries to do exactly that, to show how large structural issues impinge on personal troubles. In one program the staff photographer, Animal, takes a number of unnecessary risks on the job. Reporters Billy and Rossi worry about him. With Lou Grant, they discover that Animal is a Vietnam veteran and that the widow of one of his war buddies has been plaguing him recently, accusing him of responsibility for the buddy's death. Meanwhile, in a subplot, Lou meets a young black veteran named Sutton. Sutton wants to, but cannot, find work. Impressed with Sutton, Lou gets him an appointment with the *Tribune's* personnel manager. The personnel manager turns Sutton down, rather brusquely, because of his "bad paper" (discharge papers). When Lou finds out, he is furious and goes over the personnel manager's head to get Sutton hired. At the same time, Lou is counseling Animal to face up to the widow who keeps calling him and making accusations, while Billy and Rossi pursue a newspaper series on veterans. At the end of the show, Animal makes a reconciliation with the widow. Sutton—who does not know there is now a job waiting for him at the *Tribune*—disappears.

At the end of the program, a personal issue involving a regular on the show, Animal, has been fully resolved. The larger problem of dealing with the difficulties of Vietnam veterans, as represented by Sutton, is unresolved. In both cases, the connection between private troubles and public issues is drawn, and this is the notable advance that *Lou Grant* makes on most other television programs (including some of the news programs).

Lou Grant has another message, a much less happy one. The second message is that while private troubles and public issues are related, one has control over the troubles and little leverage with the issues.

An episode concerning illegal immigrants from Mexico highlights this. Rosa Ortega is an illegal immigrant working as a waitress in a restaurant where the *Tribune* staff regularly has lunch. While Lou and Rossi are eating one day, the immigration service raids the restaurant and Rosa is deported. The *Tribune* folks are worried about her two children. When they inquire after them in the Chicano community, they are rebuffed by Rosa's friends, who fear they work for immigration. However, the two children get lost and Rosa's sister comes to Billy for help. In the meantime, the *Tribune* begins work on a series about illegals. The television audience learns a lot about them—from their percentage in the total U.S. population to arguments for and against the notion that they take jobs away from Americans. Rossi goes on border patrol with immigration. With a patrol officer, he finds a woman dead, suffocated when a truck full of illegals was abandoned by smugglers with the illegals locked inside. At first, Rossi thought the woman was Rosa, and he was deeply shaken. Even when, at the end of the episode, Rosa has returned and her boys have been found, Rossi is unmoved by the good news. The image of the dead woman is still with him.

Again, the personal problem has been happily resolved. The larger issue of illegal immigrants is anything but resolved, and its lack of resolution is made abundantly clear to the viewer. Again, luck and the caring concern of the folks in the city room manage a private trouble and, again, their best intentions prove insufficient to control the larger disasters associated with the public issue.

An episode about a dictatorship in the mythical Latin country of "Malagua" follows the same logic. The personal trouble, in this case, is that of managing editor Charlie Hume, who confronts the dictator's wife on her visit to California and makes a scene which embarrasses publisher Mrs. Pynchon. Why did he do this? Because, we learn, Charlie had once been imprisoned and tortured in Malagua for five weeks, but never wrote about it. This private trouble is resolved: Charlie finally writes his story and the *Tribune* prints it, even though it is old news. Charlie and his colleagues are happy that they have stood up for human rights. Meanwhile, the implication is obvious that people continue to be tortured and killed in a Latin American dictatorship while prominent North Americans like Mrs. Pynchon wine and dine the dictators. The program leaves no doubt where it stands on Mrs. Pynchon's behavior. But what can be done about this larger question of dictatorship and torture? The dictator's wife is confronted in Mrs. Pynchon's office by Malaguan students, including her own nephew, who oppose her husband. The ending is ambiguous—we do not know how much she has been affected by this meeting and certainly do not know if she will be able to use her influence even if she wants to when she returns home.

This interpretation of *Lou Grant* is supported by an episode in which the situation seems to be inverted. The show begins with Rossi, his childhood friend Sam, and Sam's fiancée Carol walking through a tourist "Wild West" town. Sam, it turns out, works at a nuclear power plant: though a firm believer in nuclear energy, he is appalled at the poor safety conditions at the plant. He tries to get evidence on the safety violations for the *Tribune*. He is killed in an automobile "accident" on his way to give the materials to Rossi, obviously a fictional translation of the actual case of Karen Silkwood. So here the private trouble appears to end quickly and unhappily—the friend is dead. But by the show's end, a private trouble does get resolved for, in a fashion, the friend returns to life to help resolve it. Rossi needs to get a story to be faithful to Sam and to justify Sam's sacrifice for the *Tribune*. But Rossi keeps striking out until, in the last minute of the show, he is saved by Sam himself. An extra copy of all the materials Sam had gathered appears in Rossi's mail. Rossi's personal trouble is resolved—he will have his story and he will have kept faith with Sam. Indeed, in this last minute we see Sam keeping faith with Rossi. At the same time, while friendship triumphs over death itself, there is no suggestion that the larger issues of nuclear energy will be resolved or even greatly illuminated by Rossi's efforts.

Not every *Lou Grant* episode follows this formula. Many of the episodes focus first of all on an issue of journalism, not a topic covered by journalists. The episode "Murder" does not explore violence in black ghettos but concerns, instead, the strong tendency of the press to ignore murders among minorities. Billy raises one side of the question: why do we fail to report on blacks who are murdered while vain old rich women who defend themselves against burglars with a golf club (the story Rossi was covering) are splashed all over the page? Lou sympathizes but takes the city editor's stand: if you can make interesting the violent death of an anonymous black woman by an unidentified man where we have no clues and no witnesses, then we will run it, and not before. The issue is resolved—Billy humanizes the story, helps catch the murderer in the process, and her story displaces Rossi's follow-up on the nine-iron-swinging woman. Still, while this episode does tie things up neatly at the end, there is no pretense that the *Tribune's* policy has been altered or that the problems of journalism have been, in the larger sense, resolved.

"The art of writing popular entertainment," critic Robert Sklar has written, "is to create a structure that the casual viewer will accept as serious even while the serious themes are carefully balanced and hedged." He concludes that on *Lou Grant*, as on other programs, the result is "an intellectual muddle." But this is not the case. On *Lou Grant*, serious themes are frequently well presented. Occasionally the show feels like an adult "Sesame Street," with informative lessons in current events being rescued from documentary dreariness by a modest plotline and a familiar cast of attractive characters. The question is not one of balancing andd hedging. The political failure is one that shows well-meaning liberals ultimately helpless to affect large social problems even while they battle effectively with private troubles. I think that is a failure. But the failure of *Lou Grant* is also the failure of American journalism and American liberalism. It is not intellectually muddled but presents our intellectual muddles to us. And that is no small success.

SUSAN HOROWITZ

SITCOM DOMESTICUS— A SPECIES ENDANGERED BY SOCIAL CHANGE

Back in the 1950s, when television was young and the children of the Baby Boom still nestled in the embrace of the nuclear family, watching the domestic zaniness of *I Love Lucy* was a Monday-night ritual. Lucy's portrayal of housewife as clown/ child beset by familiar problems, surrounded by husband and friends, entranced millions of loyal viewers. (The birth of Little Ricky outdrew the Eisenhower Inauguration.)

In the decades that followed, dozens of sitcoms succeeded by playing lightly upon recognizable family situations. As families, and family problems, changed, so did the sitcoms: from *Ozzie and Harriet* to *The Mary Tyler Moore Show*, whose snug "family" consisted of co-workers and boss. Situation comedies dominated the airwaves to such an extent that ten years ago they constituted eight of the ten top-rated shows.

But now, in the 1980s, the popularity of the form is waning. In the 1982–83 season, there were only three situation comedies among the top ten shows. Last season, 1983–84, no situation comedy was consistently able to hold a place among the highest-rated shows—with the exception of CBS's *Kate and Allie*, a midseason entry whose good press and word of mouth helped land four of its first episodes in the weekly top twenty.

The decline of the sitcom—and perhaps the success of *Kate & Allie*—has much to do with changes that have occurred in family structure in our society. The half-hour domestic comedy, as a form, has barely survived the breakdown of the traditional nuclear family for which it was originally designed.

Reprinted from *Channels*, Vol. x, Sept./Oct. 1984, by permission. Copyright © 1984, *Channels* Magazine.

Kate & Allie, a show about two divorced women who live together along with their children, is as carefully crafted for the contemporary domestic mood and circumstance as *Lucy* and other successful comedies were for their times.

Network researchers are acutely aware of how changes in the structure of the audience have imperiled the sitcom. "In the early days, the whole family sat down to watch television together," says Marvin Mord, ABC marketing and research vice president. "Theory was that the woman controlled the dial in the evening, so others in the family who might not have made a sitcom their first choice came along for the ride." The concept of women as the choosers of programming for the family was of major importance to advertisers, and consequently to prime-time schedules.

Though no longer the choosers, women still contitute about 60 percent of prime-time viewers; when it comes to sitcoms the ratio is even higher. "Three out of every four advertising dollars in prime time are aimed at women," says David Poltrack, CBS research vice president.

How life has changed from the days when the family watched television together is reflected in the evolution of the sitcom. This longtime staple of television has gotten grittier in its style and bolder in its themes since the sweet, innocent days of *I Love Lucy*.

The divorce rate, relatively low in the 1950s, soared through the sixties and seventies and has continued high in the eighties. Grown children left home and often postponed parenthood and even marriage—trends that promoted the pursuit of entertainment outside the house.

In the days when most households had a single TV set, the sitcom flourished because it was, as CBS's Poltrack puts it, "the best example of a broad-based program. They would take a situation that everyone could identify with, such as a husband, wife, and kids trying to get through the normal toil of daily existence—the *Lucy* shows being the best example—and introduce exaggerated characters and a lot of physical humor that would add comedic elements to the show."

But the sitcom no longer has the natural constituency it once had. According to Poltrack, "there's no intensity of viewer loyalty. They're shows you watch because you're watching television—not shows you go out of your way to watch. This week's audience of a serial drama will generally be back next week; in sitcoms maybe only 33 percent will be back. So when there are more options, a sitcom is vulnerable."

The half-hour comedy of yesteryear was protected from this lack of viewer loyalty by a surrounding "comedy block" of similar programming, creating a mood that carried over from show to show. Today's sitcom, often adrift in a sea of unrelated programming, is forced to create its own viewer loyalty—and may very well fail in the attempt.

Thus the sitcom is more vulnerable than other television forms to today's competitive situation, in which broadcast television vies for attention alongside cable, video cassettes, and the like. "No one is doing 40 shares anymore," says Marvin Mord. "The average sitcom draws only 25 percent of all viewers tuned in at any one time. Performance of all network programs has declined 10 percent, and for sitcoms, it's down 32 percent."

"Sitcoms tended to run in the 8-to-9 period on network prime time," adds Poltrack. "But now, independent TV stations rerun the best of sitcoms, like *M*A*S*H, All in the Family, Barney Miller*, and *Taxi*, between 6 and 8 o'clock. The one thing the audience (particularly the children and teens who watch the early shows) is not ready for at 8 P.M. is an untried and perhaps inferior sitcom."

The influence of *M*A*S*H*'s seriocomic tone and multi-character format can be found in many of the shows that now outrank sitcoms in appeal, such as *Hill Street Blues*, a dramatic series with traces of black comedy about an inner-city police precinct. Another police show, *Cagney & Lacey*, has been able to incorporate much of the traditional female appeal of the sitcoms by providing two women as leads. Its mixed format allows the show to combine domestic life (one cop is single, the other married) and comedy with the action of the police show.

These and other, more lighthearted shows, such as *A-Team, Magnum, P.I.*, and *Simon and Simon*—what Poltrack calls "action/adventure with comedic overtones"—have usurped a good part of the sitcom audience. The adventure comedies pull in children, teens, and men (with the macho action), along with a fair number of women who tune in for the handsome, tough-yet-vulnerable heroes. The juiced-up plots of these shows are well served by the promotional spots used to attract viewers, among whom the flashiest package tends to win out. "A high-concept show like *A-Team* can attract more than a sitcom that depends on involvement with characters over a period of time," says Mord.

Even juicier—and more successful—is the recently evolved format of the night-time soaps: *Dallas, Dynasty, Falcon Crest,* and *Knots Landing.* The degree of titillation, violence, and cynicism in these shows would be completely incongruous in a family vehicle such as the sitcom. Their melodramatic style engages the crucial female viewers, while their obsession with power and action draws the men. The appeal of the night-time soaps lies mainly in their depiction of family life, exaggerated and disordered though it is. Almost all the serials feature fantastically wealthy, powerful, and corrupt extended families. The shows reflect the disruption of contemporary family life while providing fantasies of a glamorous alternative lifestyle.

But for the sitcom to break loose from the traditional family—the original source of its broad-based appeal—has been more difficult. Even *All in the Family,* for all the controversy it stirred, featured a close-knit group of mother, father, and child. So, despite its superficial provocativeness, does *The Jeffersons,* one of the few sitcoms surviving from the seventies. Even so, the same period saw the rise of such situation comedies as *Alice, The Mary Tyler Moore Show,* and *One Day at a Time,* in which single women tried to make it alone, often with the support of a surrogate family of co-workers. With these shows, the sitcom found a way of relating to the increasingly common reality of its viewers, as *Lucy* had in the fifties. That is the line of succession that led to such contemporary shows as *Kate & Allie.*

According to Sherry Coben, creator and principal writer of *Kate & Allie,* "Our show is really a personality comedy—*Mary Tyler Moore* style. The Mary and Rhoda friendship was only a little thing between other scenes, but that's the part I adored—I'd never seen it before. It's like most of the female friendships I've had, where we just talk on the phone or over lunch. And it's probably the strength of our show."

The viewer's identification with the character is the crux of it. This wasn't so vital before, when the viewer could consider Lucy an improbable lunatic and yet tune in to laugh at the physical comedy. Even if Archie Bunker seemed exaggerated and obnoxious, you could laugh at his one-liners or get caught up in the moral issues raised on the show. But *Kate & Allie* and its ilk demand that you like and believe in the characters.

Mary Tyler Moore was one of the first to depend in this way on audience identification—primarily with Mary Richards, the spunky heroine. To the extent that popular televison programs reflect contemporary audience concerns, one might loosely speculate that the largely middle-class, educated, female audience tuning in to *MTM* in the 1970s now identifies less with the single career woman trying to "make it after all"—as the theme song cheerfully advised us—and more with a somewhat older (mid-thirties to forty) divorcee, often with children.

This woman, as represented in *Kate & Allie*, is trying to balance domestic obligations with the need to make a living, and is overwhelmingly concerned with personal relationships. As Coben says, "There are so many issues—the woman without a career; the woman with a career, but not the one she wants; the woman alone with children; the woman looking for a man; the ex-husband who's still around.

"My phone number is listed, and I've gotten at least two calls a day from people I've never met—divorced women with children who say, 'It's about me. How did you know? I've never seen myself on television before.' You touch something that's real raw for a lot of people, and they love to laugh."

If *Lucy* was rooted in the certainty of marital devotion, the household of *Kate & Allie* is founded on the shakiness of marriage in the eighties. Kate (Susan Saint James) and Allie (Jane Curtin) are divorced women with children, who move in together to split expenses and lend each other emotional support. While Lucy's basic economic needs (though not her fantasies of a glamorous lifestyle) were supplied by her breadwinner spouse, Kate and Allie must support themselves—Kate by working her way up from an unsatisfying job, Allie by trying to develop some marketable skill.

The safety net of Lucy's domestic stability allowed her to bounce off into wildly improbable, comic antics. Getting a job meant conniving her way into a candy factory with sidekick Ethel, and coping with a speed-up on the assembly line by stuffing her uniform, chef's hat, and cheeks with sweets until her eyes bulged, fishlike. Home-baked bread was likely to burst out of the oven in a six-foot loaf, pinning Lucy to the wall.

In the most Lucy-like episode of *Kate & Allie*, Allies winds up on her own chocolate treadmill. Dumped by her husband, a doctor, and with no career of her own, Allie accepts Kate's advice to start a baking business. She works day and night to fill orders for a family-recipe chocolate cake, so as not to disappoint entrepreneurial-minded Kate. By the time Kate decides to close up shop, and Allie can toddle off to bed for desperately needed sleep, they have developed a deep aversion to chocolate. But never does a six-foot cake explode out of their stove, nor do they stuff their faces for laughs. Kate and Allie are grown-up (albeit quirky) women in a sometimes painful, sometimes amusing situation from which neither they nor their audience expect an absurd, farcical escape. Coben found even this episode a bit "slapsticky" for her taste. "The more reality humor we do," she observes, "the better off we'll be.

As the typical situation comedy founders in the ratings, network executives protest that they are baffled by the erosion of a genre that has nourished television from the beginning. "I don't know why the shows aren't better written," says CBS's Poltrack. "I have a hard time believing that the writers don't exist. It may just be this transitional period, where the writers are confused about what to do with the form."

Yet the success of earlier sitcoms—no less than that of *Kate & Allie*—should offer some guidelines to perplexed writers. The sitcoms of the *Lucy* era reflected to their viewers a common domestic ideal; those of the *All in the Family* period mirrored the social upheaval of the time. Today, with all the diverging lifestyles, and the splintering of both television audience and the nuclear family, the sitcom must adjust to the viewers' new realities. Certainly the genre is at a crossroads. Other once-popular television forms have faded from the screen, and the situation comedy may one day be as passé as the western or the variety show. But this year's sitcom rating slump may be only temporary, as in the 1970–71 season, when the only such program rated in the top ten was *Here's Lucy*—a temporary lull that was shortly to be exploded by *All in the Family* and *M*A*S*H*. When Lucille Ball was fêted at the Museum of Broadcasting last spring, we were honoring a great clown and expressing our nostalgia for a classic of a genre now more than thirty years old.

As the television marketplace becomes increasingly competitive, the success of new shows will determine whether the sitcom can be revamped to maintain viewers' interest, or whether the form will become a cult object seen, like *I Love Lucy*, only in reruns and museum retrospectives.

CHRISTOPHER ANDERSON

REFLECTIONS ON *MAGNUM, P.I.*

One of the great achievements of twentieth-century culture beams into our living rooms every Thursday night. Offered to us by the only household appliance that really cares about Western civilization, it has insinuated itself into the fabric of American society with a subtlety that would confound Iago. And Karl Marx. And Ronald Reagan. Its name is *Magnum, P.I.*

While untold copies of *Ulysses*, their pages yellowed and brittle, sit forgotten in the dark corners of bookshelves throughout the land, *Magnum, P.I.* surges through twenty million homes each week. While Godard's *La Chinoise* lures thirty-seven acolytes into a darkened, isolated chamber only to reinforce their faith, *Magnum, P.I.* addresses an impossibly disparate audience in the space where people live their lives and contest their beliefs daily. While so many texts and artifacts throughout our culture primp and preen before the mirror of art—trapped forever in a lost world in which culture is determined by Matthew Arnold, tenured faculty, and the personal ads in the *New York Review of Books*—*Magnum, P.I.* quietly forges onward through the culture as it actually exists—and changes—in the United States during the last decades of the twentieth century.

This has been a weak season (1983–84) for *Magnum, P.I.*, and still I can name at least six episodes which surpass in quality any movie nominated for an Academy Award this year. These episodes display all of the qualities that we seek in our finest motion pictures—ambiguity, attention to detail, thematic complexity, formal self-consciousness, a concern for their social and historical context. In the same season, however, *Magnum, P.I.* has dumped upon the airwaves a half-dozen miserable episodes that make *Fantasy Island* seem like Ibsen. This contradiction, which could never be accepted of high art, is exactly what makes television the most exciting form of popular culture. Only convention defines aesthetic quality. Only convention dictates that a work of uneven quality must be inferior. Television, like all great popular art, celebrates the expressive power of imperfection, the epiphany that lurks beneath an unraveled seam. An exploitation film like *Mandingo* may tell us more than a classic work like *Uncle Tom's Cabin* about slavery in the American South. *The A-Team* may come closer than *Apocalypse Now* to understanding America's role in Vietnam. As one who took keen interest in the development of twentieth-century culture, Walter Benjamin noted: "There are many people whose idea of a dialectician is a lover of subtleties. . . . Crude thoughts, on the contrary, should be part and parcel of dialectical thinking, because they are nothing but the referral of theory into practice. . . . A thought must be crude to come into its own in action."[1]

Television makes no guarantees. Each episode is an adventure. As the epitome of contemporary culture, television is an impure cultural form. Unlike forms of high art, television cannot isolate itself from the ebb and flow of social life. Produced at high speeds, without time to ensure the quality of each episode, television series prove that the so-called "culture industry" is not monolithic, but is subject to the capriciousness of human creativity. Without the luxury of time, television artists construct their work by collage, by pillaging the culture for the pieces of their construction. They exhibit their art—the television series—in our homes, not hung in stately repose on a museum wall, but unfolding within the rhythms of daily life. Television is isolated neither by space nor by time; it is inextricably woven into the environment of its reception. In many ways, the meaning of a TV series or episode emerges more as a product of its context than of any textual operations. For this reason, television is both the central cultural form of our society, transcendent in its banality, and a truly postmodernist apparition, heterogenous to a fault. Television is a sieve through which passes the best and worst of contemporary culture. Some elements of that culture become trapped within the mesh, while others slip away. The capriciousness of this process, in which the artwork develops as the unconscious residue of living culture, makes television an exciting, unpredictable force.

As a witty poet remarked so rightly, the mirror would do well to reflect a little more before returning our image to us.—Jacques Lacan[2]

When you look closely at the indignant stare of a blank television screen, you see yourself and your home reflected back. Although this mirror appears to act effortlessly, it reflects with shrewd calculation before returning our image to us. Despite our wishes, it never offers us the image that we expect. In many ways the traditional disdain for much of prime-time television occurs because television is imprudent. It refuses to deliver the image that we desire. In a medium that changes perpetually—even when the television set is switched off— nothing on television is precisely as we imagine, remember, or hope. Even series television, defined by repetition, forever plays havoc with our expectations.

The incredulity I face when I champion *Magnum, P.I.* arises from the fact that television programs depend so strongly upon their context for meaning. Both the uninitiated and the regular viewer define *Magnum, P.I.* by its relation to other television series as much as by the texts that bear its name. Since commercial television depends upon placing its texts within familiar contexts, this is an understandable phenomenon. Many people who reject the possibility that *Magnum, P.I.* is a great work immediately assume that it is simply another "beefcake" show like those that premiered in the early 1980s (*Vegas, Matt Houston*) to showcase attractive male heroes. Or they fail to distinguish the show from the remainder of television's unfailing supply of detective programs. Or they identify *Magnum, P.I.* with the great monolith of Hawaiian *policiers, Hawaii Five-0*. To be honest, in a medium that trades on the subtle balance of similarity and difference, *Magnum, P.I.* actually does resemble those shows. But with a difference.

At first glance, it may be difficult to distinguish the difference, because television rejects our crude attempts to apply traditional critical methods. Consequently, it raises our worst fears about popular culture and democracy. (Who actually watches *The Dukes of Hazzard*, anyway?) We refuse to admit that what appears to be the impoverishment of television programming may, in fact, arise from our misrecognition of the medium, from our attempts to identify it in accordance with previous cultural forms and to define it with critical methods developed for those forms. (If a misinformed taxonomist tosses a frog from a cliff and it crashes to the ground, must we blame the frog for failing to fly?) How simple it is to dismiss television programming to the tyranny of the masses, to corporate cynicism, to hegemonic forces, or to the decline of Western civilization. These interpretations have one common feature: a reactionary fear of a dynamic cultural process. Rather than recoil from a medium that does not reward our traditional aesthetic criteria, however, we should begin by admitting that we may be mistaken about television. In *Magnum, P.I.* we have seen the future of narrative artistry. And it exists on a nineteen-inch screen.

As the central cultural medium of our time, television enables our society to tell stories about itself. During the television age, our culture has shown a fascination for Hawaiian crime stories. Broadcast television has existed in this country for parts of five decades. In four of those decades, the medium has presented a popular Hawaiian crime series. Through close analysis of these series, we might begin to understand the elusive process of cultural change. We might see how television—as much as traditional folk tales or handicrafts—functions as expressive culture.

Hawaii, the ritual setting for each of these series, offers an American Paradise, the ultimate reward for America's obsessive westward journey. (Magnum often explicitly refers to the islands as Paradise.) But, like everything gained in the nation's western expansion, this promised land is tainted by the blood spilled to acquire and retain it. As Pearl Harbor taught us, Paradise comes only at great expense. Isolated, vulnerable, and yet unimaginably beautiful and bountiful, Hawaii is a powerful symbolic force, a perilous idyll. The image of tainted Paradise, a motif familiar to American culture, provides the motivation for setting crime stories on the islands. By emphasizing the vigilance required to sustain even an image of utopia, these series establish a complex, mythic setting that embodies the basic contradictions of our society. While all of the shows situate themselves within this symbolic arena, they, nevertheless, articulate the Hawaiian crime form according to the demands of their contemporary context.

Between 1959 and 1963, ABC broadcast *Hawaiian Eye*, a detective series spun off from the hit series, *77 Sunset Strip*. Starring Robert Conrad, Anthony Eisley, and the queen of hardware-convention variety shows, Connie Stevens, this series offered an image for its time: the Beat Generation meets *Dragnet* in Paradise (a combination which would be updated in the late sixties with *The Mod Squad*). *Hawaiian Eye* delivered many of the elements that make *Magnum, P.I.* a success—handsome detective, glamorous settings, beautiful women, loveable sidekicks, and crime melodrama.

From 1968 until 1980, CBS presented its version of crime in Hawaii, the longest continuously running show in television history, the redoubtable *Hawaii Five-0*. With his iconic Hawaiian-wave hairstyle, Jack Lord, along with sidekick James MacArthur, cleaned up the Hawaiian isles for twelve stern, law-and-order years. Weathering the countless social changes that occured over its run, the Five-0 team staved off all forces that threatened to contaminate our nation's Paradise.

When the *Hawaii Five-0* ratings-tide ebbed during the late 1970s, CBS gave the series an ocean burial. Less than one year later, the network launched *Magnum, P.I.* in its place. When it premiered in December 1980, *Magnum, P.I.* entered directly into the tradition established by its predecessors. CBS designed the series specifically to fill the gap left by the cancellation of *Hawaii Five-0*. *Magnum, P.I.* utilized the expensive Hawaiian production facilities constructed by the network for *Hawaii Five-0* in the mid-seventies and, of course, incorporated the rich landscape (both actual and symbolic) of the Hawaiian islands. Clearly, the network hoped to recover the once-enormous *Hawaii Five-0* audience by inserting *Magnum, P.I.* into the legacy established by the former show. This decision represents a clear example of television's function as a culturally expressive medium. At the same time that it hoped to engage the detective tradition, CBS planned to capture a rapidly changing audience by adding a new twist to the recognized form. For those who think that television programming is monolithic, unchanging, and unresponsive to its audience, this example provides a different perspective. In direct reaction to changes in the audience (comprehended through the decline in ratings for *Hawaii Five-0*), CBS developed a unique articulation of the Hawaiian *policier*.

Over the years, *Hawaii Five-0* had developed an unmistakable identity as a cultural monument. Understandably, therefore, *Magnum, P.I.* sought its own audience by immediately declaring its distance from its ancestor. Perhaps the most famous feature of the former series was the ritual conclusion that wrapped up nearly every episode. Case solved, McGarrett (Jack Lord), the police-detective patriarch, hands over the criminal to his assistant and barks, "Book 'em, Danno." In this series, the solution to the crime is both inevitable and final. Nothing escapes the detective's determinate will. During the twelve turbulent years that the series aired, however, McGarrett's potency—the ease with which it made sense of the world and triumphed over threats to the social order—had become increasingly disturbing, nearly anachronistic.

Magnum, by contrast, is often confused and vulnerable, a detective unable to protect himself from the impinging forces of a world which he often fails to understand or to affect. Also, he is not a *police* detective, an institutional agent of social order whose work keeps him at the center of society, but a *private* detective who often treads its margins. The clearest examples of Magnum's difference from a detective like McGarrett appear in the episodes which have inaugurated the series during each of its four full years (1981–84). Each scripted by executive producer Donald P. Bellisario, these episodes find Magnum in a series of crises which repeatedly demonstrate his inability to act as the traditionally authoritative detective-hero: through ignorance, he nearly provokes an international incident and the assassination of his wife; he inadvertently causes the death of a friend and, in retaliation, murders an unarmed Soviet agent; he spends an entire episode stranded in the ocean while his buddies rally to save him; he watches helplessly while his lover shoots herself. In these remarkable episodes—the showcase episode of each new season—*Magnum, P.I.* reminds us that the historical circumstances of modern life make it impossible for a lone individual, even a detective-hero, to force the chaos of experience to submit to his will.

> The history of every art form shows critical epochs in which a certain art form aspires to effects which could be fully obtained with a changed technical standard, that is to say, in a new art form. The extravagances and crudities of art which appear, particularly in the so-called decadent epochs, actually arise from the nucleus of its richest historical energies—Walter Benjamin[3]

Despite its apparent similarity to other art forms, television is a distinctly new form which has developed during the most intense and disorienting period of change in recorded history. *Magnum P.I.* represents the zenith of the new art form. Like any art, television has taken time to develop. Failing to realize this, the first mistake that most people make is to lump TV series into one unified mass, a never-ending episode of *I Married Joan*. Although *Magnum, P.I.* emerges from the detective series tradition, it is as different from *Dragnet* or *The Untouchables* as *Ulysses* is from *Moll Flanders*. While it occasionally demonstrates the worst of television's formulaic excesses (meaningless fistfights, needless automobile crashes), *Magnum, P.I.* exhibits a narrative sophistication, a knowledge of its tradition, and a field of references that can only emerge at an advanced stage of an art form's development.

As the consummate twentieth-century art form, television is a cultural junkyard. In response to the protestations of high art, the medium defiantly asserts that no artistic text is original, that all stories emerge from the dismantled pieces of other stories. By embedding itself in a field of allusions to its tradition, *Magnum P.I.* acknowledge its intertextuality, the fact that its stories are permeated by other stories. Throughout the series, *Magnum P.I.* has referred to McGarrett and the men from *Hawaii Five-0* as though these special police officers still roam the islands. This sort of cross-reference between series is a traditional marketing startegy for the networks. As long ago as *Hawaiian Eye*, Efrem Zimbalist, Jr., occasionally journeyed from the world of *77 Sunset Strip* to visit his spin-off comrades on the island. It is also common for a television series to refer to other programs. But no series before *Magnum, P.I.* has ever referred to a series that no longer exists as though its characters actually inhabit the same fictional world. By recalling the former series, this unique form of reference demonstrates *Magnum, P.I.*'s peculiar concern for the historical development of its tradition.

Often, *Magnum, P.I.* quietly borrows crucial plots from previous sources, as when Magnum's wife returns mysteriously (*Casablanca*) or when Soviet agents program Magnum's pal, T. C. (Roger E. Mosley), to become an assassin (*The Manchurian Candidate*). Just as frequently, however, the show makes explicit its cultural thievery—often by allusion to other fictional detectives. After watching four Agatha Christie movies on television one night, Magnum consciously attempts to solve his next case using the deductive methods of Poirot and Miss Marple. On another episode, Magnum arrives at a costume party dressed as Dashiell Hammett, only to be faced with a Hammettesque crime. One episode features a British gentleman who, convinced that he is Sherlock Holmes, repeatedly interferes with Magnum's case. The most delightful allusion, however, involves a number of episodes which feature Luther Gillis (Eugene Roche), a crusty old detective from Detroit who reluctantly joins forces with Magnum. In these episodes, Gillis shares the voice-over narration with Magnum, his terse, hard-boiled style providing a humorous counterpoint to Magnum's laid-back, self-revelatory musings. The humor that emerges from the clashing styles plays upon the viewer's recognition of the disparity between Magnum and the hard-boiled model. At the same time, the studied artificiality of Gillis' narration—its clichéd, anachronistic feel—reminds us that neither form of discourse is natural, that both are the manifestation of ever-changing narrative conventions.

Considering the monumental number of stories told on television, it is no wonder that these stories develop through formulaic repetition and the invocation of references, sterotypes, and clichés. This is necessarily the way in which popular culture works. Meaning develops according to a delicate operation of similarity and difference. In this process, a single story gains significance both through its identity with the stories that precede it and through its disruption of these stories. With such near-ritual repetition, televison defines its social role. *Magnum, P.I.* stands apart from most television series because it consistently examines its function in this system.

In a 1984 episode, "Dream a Little Dream," the narrative comes to a complete halt while Magnum tells the fairy tale "Goldilocks and the Three Bears" to a little girl. The girl has obviously heard the story so many times that she has memorized its every facet. Nevertheless, she hangs on each word of Magnum's version, alternately correcting his errors, applauding his variations, and prodding him along. And, although she knows the conventions well, the girl becomes genuinely frightened when the bears find Goldilocks sleeping in their beds. In this self-referential moment, the series marks its own place within the process of popular culture by identifying itself with a tradition of folk performance. It demonstrates the practice of these tales: the significance hidden within the narrator's limitless alterations, the listener's knowing suspension of disbelief toward a familiar tale. At the same time, it reminds us of the satisfaction provided by the ritual tale's ability to impose a sense of order on the world.

In *Magnum P.I.*, however, the recognizable story offers only fleeting satisfaction. In this episode, Magnum is interrupted before he can provide closure to the tale of Goldilocks. In voice-over narration, he elaborates with unselfconscious irony: 'Gold-ilocks and the Three Bears' wasn't the only story left unfin-ished in Karen's cabin. What was nagging about it was that I hadn't the slightest idea how either of [the two stories] wrapped up. At least, though, there's always more comfort to be derived from the stories that had been wrapped up. Because even though many, many things have changed, others have remained the same. And probably always will. It's the little constants in life that are comforting." Magnum's speech is wishful thinking, a dramatic misrecognition of the events of his life. In many ways, it parallels our naive misapprehension of series television. Because closure on *Magnum, P.I.* is nearly al-ways deferred or undermined (as in this story of Goldilocks), the sense of comfort that follows the "wrapping up" of a story forever slips away. Even though these neatly closed stories appear to be one of the reassuring "little constants in life," they are inevitably bound to "unwrap." Stories which once seemed comfortably resolved return with devastating force to unsettle the present.

By questioning the possibility of closure, *Magnum, P.I.* points toward the cultural significance of television's boundless com-pulsion to recycle familiar stories. The recognizable stories that permeate a series like *Magnum, P.I.*—stories coaxed from our culture—may appear stable, closed, and comforting. Their es-tablished cultural position may seem to have fixed their mean-ing once and for all. From this point of view, television's plund-ering of previous stories seems merely derivative; the series themselves appear repetitive and monotonous. They seem to be one of "the little constants in life." As Magnum's performance of "Goldilocks" reminds us, however, familiar stories are open to limitless variations—any of which may significantly alter the story's meaning. Similarly, the insertion of familiar stories into a new context—and here we return to the television's depen-dence upon context—often causes them to come "unwrapped." Stories that once seemed reassuringly familiar appear, on sec-ond thought, to be slightly bewildering. As they unravel, famil-iar stories gain new life, a new strength to provoke thought, argument, and action.

Distraction and concentration form polar opposites which may be stated as follows: A man who concentrates before a work of art is absorbed by it. He enters into this work of art the way legend tells of the Chinese painter when he viewed his finished painting. In contrast, the distracted mass absorbs the work of art—Walter Benjamin[4]

Benjamin characterized movies as the art form in which reception occurs in a state of distraction. Obviously, his description applies even more appropriately to television, a cultural form so banal that its narratives often unfold while we read the paper, wash the dishes, or feed the hamsters. Benjamin compares the movies to architecture, an art form that we inhabit and appreciate without awareness. Television, the art form of distraction, is a type of mental architecture. As it blends into our domestic environments and the rhythms of our lives, nearly unnoticeably providing our lives with a certain structure, it is the only narrative form that we inhabit.

Television does not desire rapt attention. Therefore, it has developed a narrative structure based heavily upon formulaic repetition, common cultural codes (including references, clichés, and stereotypes), and an emphasis upon narrative fragmentation rather than narrative unity. We may commonly conceive of narrative as a unified whole, but television narrative—constructed with cultural bric-a-brac and segmented by the structure of its presentation—requires that we alter these traditional notions. Composed of fragments, television narratives flash between brilliance and banality. Generally, they alternate unique passages of intense meaning with formulaic passages that require little attention, but which are necessary structurally (for instance, to bring closure at the end of an episode). The resulting text, a tempestuous collage, embodies Barthes' notion of tableau: "The tableau (pictorial, theatrical, literary) is a pure cut-out segment with clearly defined edges, irreversible and incorruptible; everything that surrounds it is banished into nothingness, remains unnamed, while everything that it admits within its field is promoted into essence, into light, into view."[5]

A *Magnum, P.I.* episode exhibits all of these characteristics but usually exalts them by stressing their fragmentation. The series often emphasizes the discord that it produces through its playful use of references. When faced with the clashing styles of Magnum and the hard-boiled Luther Gillis, the series takes away Magnum's role as the single, authoritative narrator and allows both characters to act as the narrative voice. The "Dream a Little Dream" episode moves this self-examination to

the structural level by developing an extremely complex narrative structure that moves rapidly between Magnum's first case
and his current case. This contrapuntal flashback structure,
often used on *Magnum, P.I.*, emphasizes the fragmentation of
the narrative. It stresses the disjunction of successive scenes,
rather than their continuity, and marks each scene as an isolat-
able expressive tableau. To appreciate *Magnum, P.I.*, then, we
must remain conscious of the ways in which the series acknowledges narrative fragmentation, a structure essential to
television, and transforms it into an important expressive characteristic.

When *Magnum, P.I.* introduces an extremely conventional
narrative fragment (especially when bringing closure to an
episode), it often emphasizes the absurdity of the convention.
During the "Dream a Little Dream" episode, a manic chase
scene suddenly interrupts the narrative. This is a purely formulaic scene, an element tossed into the story in order to hold
the attention of the *Dukes of Hazzard* fans (after all, this is an art
form that must appeal to a wide audience). At the end of the
chase, however, Magnum discovers that he has not had a reason to chase the man; it is a case of mistaken identity. This long
red-herring chase scene, an abrupt departure from the rest of
the story, may serve the narrative by demonstrating Magnum's
inadequacy as a detective, but, more than anything, it cries out
the absurdity of its own existence.

At the same time that *Magnum, P.I.* displays an impressive
formal self-consciousness, it is also a strikingly ambitious television series. Although each episode develops around some
type of detective case and makes movements toward closure,
Magnum spends exceptionally little time solving crimes. The
show's lack of concern for the detective formula enables it to
break out of television's eternal present tense. In the late seventies, with the advent of prime-time continuing dramas such
as *Dallas* and *Dynasty*, television narrative began to develop a
sense of process. Until that time, TV series narrative had been
enslaved to mindless repetition in which very little changed
from week to week. Programs such as *Father Knows Best* represent formula as a way of life. Following the example of daytime
soap opera, prime-time television at last realized that series
narrative could express a processual sense of past and future.
While series like *Hill Street Blues* and *St. Elsewhere* adopted the

serial format to genre television, *Magnum, P.I.* developed a unique hybrid by injecting a sense of history into a traditional series format. While each episode is a self-contained unit, many of its narrative developments continue to resonate throughout the series.

Slowly, over the course of four years' episodes, a sense of Magnum's past has emerged to reveal a man tortured by sadness and guilt. As the historical circumstances of modern life shatter any hope for a unity or wholeness of experience, the desire for unity finds its expression in an obsession with the past and with memory, precisely in the longing to re-member one's fragmented experience of self and surroundings. Magnum struggles to create a consistent sense of self from the anguish of his past, to find some continuity among past, present, and future. To master his life he must first master his memories. The return of a lost friend from the past becomes a recurrent motif in the series. Magnum has faith in the friend because he assumes that this person has not changed, that the past can be present. But in a world in which change is the only certainty, the friend inevitably turns out to have changed ineradicably—often to become a nemesis in the present. Magnum is not so much betrayed by his friends as by his desperate need to maintain the past.

Vietnam plays a crucial role in Magnum's memories. Initially, the Vietnam War might have seemed to be a topical gimmick, a novelty to distinguish the series. Over the course of time, however, it has become a vital symbolic force, and perhaps the most complex representation of the Vietnam War in popular culture. Nearly all of Magnum's most painful memories—in fact, most of his defining experiences—revolve around the war. While serving in Naval Intelligence in Vietnam, he gained his friends, Rick and T. C., and lost his wife, who was killed on the day they were to evacuate Saigon (later she returns, alive, to betray him). In fact, the memories of all the major characters affix themselves to crucial war or war-time experiences: for Magnum, Rick, and T. C., the Vietnam war; for Higgins, the British major domo, his decades of service in the British Army. The fact that the memories of these individuals are bound up within events central to social memory begins to suggest the symbolic function of the characters and the cultural function of the series. By identifying personal narratives of individual memory with social historical narratives, the series links its characters' efforts to resolve past and present with society's similar efforts. Individual memory becomes a metaphor for collective history.

The series has developed a camaraderie among the three men who shared the experience of Vietnam—including time spent in a North Vietnamese prisoner-of-war camp—that is reminiscent of the films of Howard Hawks. But *Magnum, P.I.* does not allow itself to romanticize the experience of Vietnam, nor does it take any simple position in relation to the war. Instead, the series constantly questions the dialogue of history, fiction, and memory that constructs—and limits—our experience of events.

The 1982 season-premiere episode, "Did You See The Sunrise?," begins with Magnum watching the 1953 World War II prisoner-of-war movie, *Stalag 17*, on television. This experience triggers Magnum's flashback memory of the Vietnamese prisoner-of-war camp. Coincidentally, Higgins is at the same time remembering his own experience as a World War II prisoner-of-war—in this case, by constructing a scale-model replica of the bridge on the River Kwai, the camp where he had been held. When Magnum confuses the historical events at the River Kwai camp with the 1956 movie, *Bridge on the River Kwai*, Higgins (for whom the events represent, neither fiction nor history, but memory) attempts to set the record straight. By this time, however, the episode has thrown into doubt the possibility of ever isolating memory, fiction, or history. Magnum's own memories of the prison camp no longer possess the authority of personal experience because the episode suggests that personal recollection cannot be separated from the potent cultural combination of history and fiction. In the attempt to apprehend reality, the independent existence of any of these three levels of discourse cannot be upheld. No single expression of the past takes precedence over the others; no single expression can stand alone. Among television series, only *Magnum, P.I.* has developed such a complex view of human understanding.

In effect, *Magnum, P.I.* has developed a Proustian fascination with the interaction of memory, history, and fiction. By refusing to privilege a solution to the detective's investigation, the show denies the validity of the explanations offered by itself and its predecessors. Instead, *Magnum, P.I.* suggests that solutions are merely stop-gap measures able only temporarily to control the fundamental chaos of life. Thomas Magnum himself is more generally concerned with sorting out his own past than with solving cases; in fact, he is an inept detective throughout the series. The overwhelming burden of his memory, combined with his struggle to master the past, make Magnum the first tragic character on prime-time television.

NOTES

1. Quoted in, Hannah Arendt, "Walter Benjamin: 1892–1940," in Walter Benjamin, *Illuminations*, translated by Harry Zohn (New York: Shocken Books, 1969), p. 15.
2. Jacques Lacan, "The Freudian Thing," in *Écrits* (New York: 1977), p. 138.
3. Walter Benjamin, "The Work of Art in The Age of Mechanical Reproduction," in *Illuminations*, (New York: Shocken Books, 1969), p. 237.
4. Ibid., p. 239.
5. Roland Barthes, "Diderot, Brecht, Eisenstein," in *Image-Music-Text*, (New York: Hill and Wang, 1977), p. 70.

CATHY SCHWICHTENBERG

THE LOVE BOAT: THE PACKAGING AND SELLING OF LOVE, HETEROSEXUAL ROMANCE, AND FAMILY

THE LOVE BOAT: AN EMPTY STRUCTURE INFLATED WITH BANALITY

According to many critics, *The Love Boat* is a situation-comedy that should have failed. For instance, Karl E. Meyer of the *Saturday Review* calls the show "a cruise ship afloat on pink lemonade and chartered in candyland" with "capsule plots . . . as in a paint-by-number set" (Meyer, 1978: 30); while *Newsweeks*'s television reviewer, Harry F. Waters, states that "if intelligence and taste ruled the airwaves, ABC's *The Love Boat* should have sunk quietly from view" (Waters, 1978: 65). *The Love Boat*, as a purely formulaic show, invites such critical barbs. Its plotline is repetitive and deals with the love problems of old and young, married and unmarried passengers (the featured guest stars), in three interwoven playlets which are parallel and alternate. Unifying the show are the crew of regulars: Captain Merrill Stubing (Gavin McLeod), Ship's Doctor Adam Bricker (Bernie Kopell), Yeoman-Purser Burl "Gopher" Smith (Fred Grandy), Bartender Isaac Washington (Ted Lange), and Cruise Director Julie McCoy (Lauren Tewes). Crewmembers either involve themselves directly in the "dramatic" action or help to mediate and resolve their passengers' love problems. By the end of the cruise, the passengers in all three playlets find their love problems resolved and leave the ship as a reunited family or as a couple which has "family potential."

Reprinted from *Media, Culture and Society* 1984 vol. 6. Used by permission of Sage Publications Ltd, London. Copyright © 1984 by *Sage Publications*.

Thus from an aesthetic point of view, *The Love Boat* presents an essentially empty tri-part structure unified by the ship and crew, and inflated with the problems of banal love situations. For instance, a typical plot summary from *TV Guide* (1981:A–B) reads:

> 1. Doc is leery about entertaining his friend's amorous wife. 2. A man will receive $10,000 if he can prove his friend holds a record for making love. 3. A social climber engaged to a man of means runs into an old friend.

The show is an adult *bildungsroman* of love in which resolutions are laced with didacticism and sacharrine—the perscription and prescription that "love conquers all." Hence, it is little wonder that critics interested in the aesthetic potential of television programs take a dim and often caustic view of *The Love Boat*. It *lacks* everything and anything which could be construed as artistic, inventive, or substantial, and it is for this reason that *The Love Boat*'s packaging is far more revealing than its banal content.

Both audiences and critics alike need to be more critical of a show such as *The Love Boat* which is usually designated as innocent, mindless entertainment, for a show of this type has the greatest ideological[1] power because it is made more palatable for mass consumption through its packaging. Thus, while superficially, *The Love Boat* sells "things," that is, cruises, clothes, exposure, star-following,[2] underlying these commodities, the show really sells an ideology based on the promise of personal transformation. Hence, the purpose of this paper is to examine this ideology by analyzing: (1) how love is transformed into a commodity as the central motivation for the "love boat" cruise, (2) the crewmembers' function, (3) the opening sequence which articulates a "personal" promise, and (4) a specific playlet from an episode which illustrates personal transformation.

LOVE AS COMMODITY

In *The Love Boat*, to purchase a ticket is to purchase the experience of love. *The Love Boat* is similar to a before-and-after advertisement which has been animated. Before the characters begin their "love boat" journey they are beset by problems such as lack of love, wrong love-partner, or loved based on mistaken identities. But by the end of the cruise, characters are coupled with their proper mates. The show, which illustrates this shift from lack to gain, from sad to happy, teaches viewers that they can buy happiness and love for the price of a ticket on a luxury cruise. Viewers are made to believe that their lives are unsatisfactory as they are. According to John Berger (1973:142) in *Ways of Seeing*:

> The purpose of publicity is to make the spectator marginally dissatisfied with his present way of life. Not with the way of life of society, but with his own within it. It suggests that if he buys what it is offering, his life will become better. It offers him an improved alternative to what he is.

Indeed, love, as advertised by *The Love Boat*, can be bought like any other product.

This bartering system of commodity-relations is discussed by Georg Lukács, who cites Marx's notion of the commodity-structure as "the central, structural problem of capitalist society in all its aspects." (Lukács, 1972: 83). The commodity-form, that is, "love" tangibly realized in a purchased product, is a building bloc in the construction of economic relations under advanced capitalism. What is subjective ("love") is objectified as a form which corresponds to the larger framework of commodity-structure:

> Its basis is that a relation between people takes on the character of a thing and thus acquires a "phantom objectivity," an autonomy that seems so strictly rational and all-embracing as to conceal every trace of its fundamental nature: the relation between people.

"Love" is a complex, abstract relation between persons. However, in *The Love Boat*, "love" as a floating signifier is transformed into a commodity when linked with "boat"—a "thing." Through the exchange of money for a cruise, love becomes the ultimate reward, the panacea for all ills. As the lyrics of the "Love Boat song" indicate, love is "life's sweetest reward." Hence, the cruise functions as the mediating term between money and love. Indeed, once the promise of love is bought via the cruise, the crew, which functions to unify couples, must do good on the promise.

THE CREW AS "FAMILY"

As a kind of "model family" the crew is able to bring together heterosexual couples to perpetuate the ideology of the nuclear

family. Lured on board by the promise of personal transformation in their romantic lives, the love-starved characters are
"coupled" with the aid of the crew. For instance, Isaac as bartender offers lover's advice to passengers who, dejectedly, find
their way to the bar, determined to drink away their impossible
love problems; while Julie as cruise director will actively encourage older women to be liberated in their coy pursuit of
older single men. Often Julie will go so far as to arrange meeting situations as part of her function as go-between.

"Gopher," Dr. Bricker, and even on occasion Captain Stubing
himself, will work over-time to unite troubled lovers who must
have the promise of love realized by the end of the voyage. The
passengers must get their money's worth. Indeed, in one episode when lonely bachelor Barney Briscoe asks Julie, "How do
you meet a lady?" Julie replies, "Well Mr. Briscoe, you've certainly come to the right place—we don't call this the 'love boat'
because we're crazy about tennis!"

Thus, the crew as "family" creates other families. Through
"love" as a commodity-form, characters buy into a circular
system. This system helps to construct the family unit as the
central socio-economic structure of production and consumption under capitalism. Using the lure of romantic love, the
crew/family works to create families, which will in turn create
other families and hence feed back into the commodity-structure where love is the reward for a "wise purchase." Thus, as
an institution in the service of ideology, the family reproduces
the relations of production. According to Rayna Rapp (1978:
91,87):

> Autonomy means escaping your childhood family to become an
> adult with your own nuclear family. But, of course, autonomy is
> illusive. The family is classically seen as an escape from produc-
> tion, but in fact it is what sends people into relations of produc-
> tion.

and:

> [T]he concept of family is a socially necessary illusion which
> simultaneously expresses and masks recruitment to relations of
> production, reproduction and consumption.

The Love Boat packages and sells love as a commodity-form which
creates the conditions for the heterosexual romance and consequently constructs the ideology of the family. Thus it is crucial
to analyze *how* the promise of this personal transformation,
which prepares viewers (and characters) for marriage, is articu-

lated in the show's opening sequence. For indeed, the opening sequence functions as a kind of rhetorical "hook" or interest-statement which provides the viewer with a context and a promise of what the show's narrative will fulfill.

THE ARTICULATION OF THE PERSONAL PROMISE

The opening sequence which uses the second person point of address can be understood as a promise for the benefit of the spectator/consumer. Since love can be purchased for the price of a cruise which leads to a change in one's life, this promise of love as "personally" transformative sets the narrative in motion. For instance, the opening lines from the "Love Boat song" are an invitation to "you" to enter the narrative by taking a cruise: "Love, exciting and new/come aboard, we're expecting you." The "love" which is promised as "life's sweetest reward" can transform any of life's dissatisfactions: "Love won't hurt anymore/It's an open smile on a friendly shore." Thus the personal promise of love is the narrative's point of departure. However, it is necessary to examine the specific attributes of the "you," the second person, to determine how this mode of address functions to lure the spectator into the narrative, for the "you" deceptively personalizes the message.

The Shifty Shifter and Ideology

In "Shifters, Verbal Categories, and the Russian Verb," Roman Jakobson (1971: 130–133) categorizes the second person "you" as a shifter. A shifter is distinguished from all other grammatical units in that it is a context-sensitive personal pronoun. This means that the "person" designated by the message is always determined by the message itself, which contains and specifies "person." Hence, shifters get their name for their referential ambiguity which can only be defined within, not only the context of the message itself, but the situation (the moment) in which the message is uttered.

Jacobson elaborates on both the context and moment of address by using Pierce's trichotomy of signs: icon, index, symbol. According to Jakobson, the shifter is an *indexical symbol* since it combines sign-functions of both symbol and index. For instance, the "you" is associated with a referent (a person) who is contextually represented as the addressee of the message through a conventional rule (the property of symbol, e.g., "you" refers to Mary); while "you" is also determined by an existential relation with the addressee (the property of index, e.g., I look or point to signify "you" as receiver of the message).

Further, Jakobson (1971: 132) cites Bertrand Russell who stated that "shifters are defined by the fact that they never apply to more than one thing at a time." While this formulation may apply to instances of direct address where there is no mediation, it does not apply to a mediated form of direct address such as that employed by television. As a medium of mass-mediation, television is able to split shifters to simultaneously indicate two levels of operation, that is, "you" as specific, as individual and "you" as general, as collective. Although it can be argued that professors, political candidates, preachers, and dictators employ the dual-level "you" in a similar fashion when addressing their audiences, it is important to note that in these cases, the suasory function of the "you" designed to move a *real* group to action is expected in the context of the speech situation. Moreover, the disparate group becomes unified as a "second person."

Conversely, television is not expected to be persuasive. The television set is situated in the private space of the livingroom where family members gather to watch for entertainment and information. Thus, in *The Love Boat* the effectivity of the dual-level "you" as individual/collective is heightened. In the private space of the home the "you" seems personal, individual, but is far more impersonal and removed in its general, collective articulation than in any lecture-type situation due to television's technological ability to address a mass audience.

This power of mass-audience transforms the referent as the real spectator/addressee into an interpretant (a sign which stands for another sign). A real spectator/addressee does not exist for the medium of television which mediates any direct form of address and attracts/creates types of audiences. Thus the hypothetical "Love Boat" viewer is both recruited by the show's second person mode of address and constructed and positioned by the show. This ideological power of address is perceived by Louis Althusser (1971:174) as interpellation or hailing, a primary function of ideology which transforms the individual into a subject and positions the subject within ideology:

> [I]deology "acts" or "functions" in such a way that it "recruits"
> subjects among the individuals (it recruits them all), or "trans-
> forms" the individuals into subjects (it transforms them all) by
> that very precise operation which I have called *interpellation* or

hailing, and which can be imagined along the line of the most commonplace everyday police (or other) hailing. "Hey, you there."

Although in "Ideology and Ideological State Apparatuses," Althusser's notion of subject interpellation is too general to accept wholly, his formulation is well suited to the mass-mediation of television, especially within the context of the split second person in *The Love Boat*. Here, although the "you" is dispersed to refer to a collective (a diverse TV-viewing audience comprised of various classes), membership in this collective is constructed as desirable and elite (those with money to buy love on a cruise ship) through the illusory personalization of the "you" in the form of an invitation in the opening sequence. Viewers are asked to identify themselves as the subjects of the second person point of address who comprise an elite group.

The Shifter in Action

A close analysis of the image-track in the opening sequence of *The Love Boat* graphically illustrates not only this "lie" of personalization, but also maps out the trajectory of this lie through the symbolic function of the credits and the indexical function of the crewmember's direct gaze. These two visual operations conjoin to construct a deceptively personal spectator position, as well as a hypothetical consumer desirous of upward mobility and a nuclear family.

The show opens with a long shot of the ship in the harbor followed by the words: "Guest Stars in Alphabetical Order." A porthole (with hearts around the border) containing quick, close-up shots of each guest star appears superimposed over a long shot of the ship. With each shift to the next guest star, the ship in the background gets closer until the porthole contains successive close-up, profile, and aerial shots of the ship itself. Thus viewers are given a porthole with which to look into the world of *The Love Boat*. The narrative is about the boat (as a place of love) and the boat contains the narrative. Viewers may be on the outside, but through the porthole they can project themselves into this self-contained universe. As Colleen McCullough has stated: "No matter where the cruise destination be, once out of port the ship becomes an enclosed and self-sufficient world" (McCullough, 1979: 22).

Suddenly the "Love Boat" logo appears over the long shot of the ship followed by the words: "Starring Your Love Boat

Crew." Thus the personal possessive pronoun "your" attached to "Love Boat Crew" names the crew as the viewers' mediation between the spectator space they occupy as prospective consumers and the *Pacific Princess* afloat in the harbor.

Next, a large stylized graphic representation of an anchor appears, and moves up and out of the top of the frame. Each time the anchor appears and moves upward, it replaces the previous long shot of the ship with a series of quick, individual medium shots of crewmembers positioned on the deck. For instance, the Captain faces viewers smiling followed by similar shots of the Doctor and the Yeoman-Purser. The Bartender points toward viewers and the Cruise Director looks up from her roster to smile directly. The credits which match each shot at the bottom of the frame read, respectively: "Gavin McLeod as Your Captain," "Bernie Kopell as Your Ship's Doctor," "Fred Grandy as Your Yeoman-Purser," and so on.

Thus within the context and through a conventional rule, the "you" symbolically names the spectators as the addressees who "possess" the crewmembers. Each direct gaze by a crewmember marks out the spectator space as near and intimate. This space is both indexically signified (through direct looking) and imaginary since the camera (not the crewmembers) is the true intermediary that undermines and disperses any personal forms of address into millions of homes. Thus narratively, the viewer's point of departure is articulated as a personal form of address which masks the impersonal. The promise of personalization articulated through a mediated form of second person direct address is the lure, the lie which draws viewers into the narrative.

The shots following the crew/credit sequence ease spectators into the narrative by generalizing identification. Since a shift from a "seemingly" direct address to the characters would be too abrupt, the opening sequence provides several transitional shots. These shots move from a long shot of the ship to a long shot of passengers waving to friends from the deck to another long shot of passengers boarding the ship. Thus similar to the referential ambiguity of shifters, which must be specified and placed within a context (as the "your" was in the credit sequence), so these vague, general group shots ask spectators to identify with a group that sails on luxury cruises in search of "love." The "you" which was initially personalized is extended to include a specific, privileged group.

Moreover, while these group shots differ from the previous

mode of address which seemed more "personal," they acquire
their own "personalization" through verisimilitude. The transitional group shots, unlike any other shots in *The Love Boat*
(except for aerial and long shots of the ship) are filmed on-
location, outdoors, and consequently possess a documentary,
grainy quality associated with non-fiction films. The viewer's
possession of the crew as indicated by the credits and affirmed
by the crew's "direct" gaze, situates him/her as one of the
passengers in the group shots embarking on a voyage that
offers "personal" transformation—love—as the reward.

For finally, in *The Love Boat*, the "seeming" directness of the
second person point of address explicitly "hooks" and situates
the viewer within the context of a situation he/she could identify with, that is, *You* could be on this cruise. While other
television programs may disguise this form of address, *The Love
Boat* foregrounds it because within the "real life" context of a
cruise, invitations, promises, and friendliness are expected by
passengers as inclusive in the price of the cruise. *The Love Boat*
easily links a viewers' romantic inflated sense of self and desire
for love and adventure with the opening sequence which explicitly promises these things. Indeed, the myth of the romance
which takes place on cruise ships is enacted in the narrative
section of the show. The narrative is presented as a concrete
illustration of personal transformation that results in love as
promised by the opening sequence. Indeed, the opening makes
promises which the narrative must act on.

PERSONAL TRANSFORMATION NARRATIVIZED

The opening sequence which lures spectators into the narrative
with the "personal promise" of love is complemented by the
narrative depiction of character transformation—a transformation ending with the family as the "proper" model. Indeed, the
narrative structure of *The Love Boat* is based on what Northrop
Frye has termed "the quest-romance pattern." The movement
of the *Pacific Princess* from port to its destination is analogous to
the character's personal growth towards a goal: love. This journey of personal transformation begins with the character's
quest for love and ends with the discovery and fulfillment of
love between couples within a potential family unit by the end
of the voyage. According to Frye (1957:193):

The quest-romance has analogies to both rituals and dreams, and the rituals examined by Frazer and the dreams examined by Jung show the remarkable similarity in form that we should expect of two symbolic structures analogous to the same thing. Translated into dream terms, the quest-romance is the search of the libido or desiring self for a fulfillment that will deliver it from the anxieties of reality but will still contain that reality. . . . Translated into ritual terms, the quest-romance is the victory of fertility over the wasteland. Fertility means food and drink, bread and wine, body and blood, the union of male and female.

Thus the love boat is a symbol, a commodity-form in a ritualistic journey, a love-quest from port to destination. The characters who participate in this mating ritual ("mating" and "ritual" as the terms of the cruise itself) are thus personally transformed as a consequence of their journey. Hence, the movement of the love boat provides a basis, a transformational structure, upon which each of the three personally transformative playlets rest.

Significantly, the love boat's journey charts a movement away from society at large, and onboard the social microcosm of the ship, large social problems are resolved at the personal level which makes possible a final integration with society. While each playlet is thematically linked to a love problem, each episode which contains the three playlets is thematically unified by a larger social problem which love, as the ultimate term, must resolve. Thus the love boat voyage guarantees that it can transform and resolve social problems, through a progression which leads to the family and social reintegration.

Each "Love Boat" episode usually deals with one, central social problem such as alienation, education, capitalism versus humanism, etc. One of the most ideologically significant episodes I have seen concerns the theme of violence and its subsequent transformation through love, the heterosexual romance, and the family within all three playlets. One playlet involves a man left with two children to care for after his wife has deserted him and the children for a career. Violence is illustrated through the children's vicious pranks against their nanny. This violence is finally quelled through a reconstruction of the family when a child-like woman, who loves the children, sacrifices her career as a singer to function as the children's maternal substitute: a family position that exceeds the duties of a nanny's job.

Another playlet deals with a young girl whose parents are afraid to tell her that she is dying of leukemia. Here violence consists of the ravaging of the body by disease. Even this type of violence is recuperated through the heterosexual romance and the family, for the girl meets a young man on board and decides to marry him even after her parents have informed her of her condition.

While the first two playlets dealt respectively with the resolutions of familial and internal violence, the final playlet in this episode is perhaps the most crucial, for it focuses on the literal representation and threat of violence. Since the character's personal transformation hinges on the working through of larger social problems, it would be most instructive to analyze closely the process by which the threat of physical violence against a woman is ideologically transformed through romance and excluded from the family structure. Briefly, through a case of mistaken identity, young hood Joey Delmar (Richard Kline) is instructed to beat up Toni Battachio (Lisa Hartman) whom he believes to be a man but is in actuality the woman he has fallen in love with.

At the outset, the threat of violence is transformed through romance. Joey predictably meets Toni at the poolside after his attempt to call "Toni," the "guy he's supposed to rough up for welching on a loan." When Toni attempts to tell him her name during their flirtatious exchange, he nicknames her "Peanuts." Thus the potential for violence is ellided in favor of sexism, which is represented as the favorable alternative. Joey defines Toni's position as that of sex-object through a name associatively linked with sexist slang such as "cupcake," "honey," and "cookie." Moreover, "Peanuts" lacks the gender ambiguity of "Toni" (upon which the narrative of mistaken identity is based). Thus, "Peanuts" (which refers to "cute woman") and "Toni" (which refers to "gambler on the lam") are mutually exclusive names that establish roles and behavioral expectations along the lines of gender-identity. Through this sexist split masked as "romance," violence is subsequently transformed.

Later, when Toni and Joey meet in the dining area, the threat of violence is symbolically represented. When Joey is unable to reach "Toni" by phone he double-checks the number with the operator. Lacking a paper or pencil to jot down the number, Joey uses Toni's lipstick to print the phone number on a portion of her back which is exposed. Thus Toni is physically marked, not by bruises, but by her own lipstick. Indeed, Joey unknowingly "marks her" as his victim, for the number supposedly belonging to a man is her number on her body. Thus a woman's body maps out man's domain which conflates sexual-objectification and violence under the auspices of romantic comedy.

At the end of the evening Joey kisses Toni goodnight at the door to her cabin and promises in the morning that they will go to Puerto Vallerta. Before Joey leaves, he retrieves the lipstick from his pocket and draws a heart around the number, "A206" on her door. Once again Toni is marked through the mediation of a number as both intended victim and intended lover. The violence Joey will inflict on the supposedly male "Toni" and the love he will lavish on his "Peanuts" are signified as the same thing through a symbolic convergence. As Joey leaves he meets Doc Bricker in the hallway and inquires where "Toni's" cabin "A206" is located. When Joey returns to the door marked by the heart, he suddenly realizes that he must "rough up" the woman he loves.

The following morning, Joey refuses to see Toni but later explains the situation to her at the poolside. In a moment of exasperation he exclaims: "Life would be much simpler if girls had girl names and boys had boy names." Indeed, the two mutually exclusive categories Joey had originally constructed as "Peanuts" and "Toni" merge. Joey is unable to resolve the dilemma which necessitates that he punish a woman for stereotypical male behavior: gambling. As Toni laments her bad luck at gambling, Joey instructs her to "bet on things you can control" and proposes that they play a game of poker.

Violence transformed by romance is finally portrayed as necessarily absent from the family. Later, in the bar, Toni wins the poker game and all of Joey's money. He retreats to the deck, upset. Seemingly, Toni has bet on something she can control; however, later, she appears on deck to show Joey his marked card, the king of hearts. Toni calls Joey her "king of hearts," for he has let her win all of his money so she could repay the loan. Thus Toni is "properly" placed as female and and not in control. As Toni turns to leave, refusing Joey's money, he says to her: "If we were married the money would belong to both of us. How can I marry you and kill you at the same time?" They kiss and she teasingly replies: "You are a killer."

Here, violence is represented as something outside the family when in real life, it is often actually contained and suppressed within it. Marriage and killing are not mutually exclusive and wife-beating and murder are very real manifestations of violence against women within the family structure. This playlet takes the problem of violence, transforms it through love as the ultimate "cure," and banishes it. Indeed, Toni has shifted from victim to sex-object only to find her proper definition as wife which denies the existence of the first two roles as potentially functional within the family. As Sheila Rowbotham has pointed out: "The family is thus in one sense the dummy ideal, the repository of ghostly substitutes, emotional fictions which dissolve into cloying sentimentality" (Rowbotham, 1973: 59). The family as a social institution is not immune to commodity-relations, sexual, social, economic or ideological pressures. Instead, the family ensures a continual recirculation of the very problems it would seek to eradicate through the smokescreen of love and the heterosexual romance—both of which can be bought.

THE IDEOLOGICAL CIRCLE: THE END OF THE CRUISE

In conclusion, in *The Love Boat*, the promise of personal transformation is neither personal nor transformative. Rather, it is a general reinforcement which, under the guise of personal transformation, operates to ensure, enforce, and perpetuate commodity-relations based on the structure of the nuclear family. Spectators/consumers buy ideology, and ideology assures them that they have made a wise purchase. These are the terms of the narrative voyage articulated and illustrated by *The Love Boat* which may be expressed succinctly in a line from the opening song: "Let love [it] flow, it floats back to you." Within the commodity-structure of capitalism, money floats out and what floats back is a packaged experience that reaffirms the correctness of existing social institutions. The overthrow of capitalism in the near future is highly unlikely, and such an overthrow would not *necessarily* transform bartering systems (i.e., an experience in exchange for goods or currency). We live in and through ideology (ideology is *not* false consciousness) and the nuclear family is an entrenched, solid social institution. Given this view, it might appear as if criticizing *The Love Boat* is an exercise in futility.

However, *The Love Boat* is a valuable object of study (as I believe all commercial television programs to be), in that it provides critics with an operational model. As a model which structurally foregrounds its method of operation through a promise in the opening sequence ("you" get love for money) which is acted upon in the narrative section (love for money begets marriage—the resolution of personality problems cures social ills), *The Love Boat* is representative of *commercial* television par excellence. Thus, by investigating those banal but popular shows which offend aesthetic sensibilities, we may better be able to understand how those shows gain their popularity if we study address and myth—indeed, *how* the audience is positioned by address, and gratified and reinforced through myth. What keeps audiences glued to their television sets is not Gavin McLeod, but rather the promise that love and marriage on a cruise ship *could* happen to them. A myth that is believed is real, and its method of operation should be investigated and criticized. No matter how we flinch, as critics we must prepare an answer to the invitation: "Welcome aboard, it's love," for only then can we think of ways to sink the ship.

NOTES

1. I am using Louis Althusser's definition of ideology as a system of representations such as images, myths, ideas or concepts which represent the imaginary relationship of individuals to their real conditions of existence, taken from Althusser (1970) and (1971).
2. References to the popularity of Princess Cruises (the Love Boat is real!) and how passengers are used as extras can be found in Riley (1979). A description of *The Love Boat* fashion show episode where Bob Mackie, Gloria Vanderbilt, Halston, and Geoffrey Beene originals were exposed to an audience of sixty-five million can be found in Kalter (1981).

REFERENCES

Althusser, L. (1971) "Ideology and ideological state apparatuses," pp. 127–186, in *Lenin and Philosophy and Other Essays*. New York: Monthly Review Press.
——. (1970) "Marxism and humanism," in *For Marx*. New York: Random House.
Berger, J. (1973) *Ways of Seeing*. New York: Viking Press.
Frye, N. (1957) *Anatomy of Criticism*. Princeton: Princeton University Press.
Jakobson, R. (1971) "Shifters, verbal categories and the Russian verb," pp. 219–247, in *Selected Writings: Word and Language*, vol. II. The Hague: Mouton.
Kalter, S. (1981) "'Love Boat' gets buoyed up with some titanic egos like Halston, Gloria and Beene." *People*. February 23.
Lukács, G. (1972) *History and Class Consciousness: Studies in Marxist Dialectics* (trans. by Rodney Livingstone). Cambridge: MIT Press.
McCullough, C. (1979) "In the wake of cruise ships." *Saturday Review*. August 4.
Meyer, K. E. (1978) "Television: Saturday night dead." *Saturday Review*. June 10.

Rapp, R. (1978) "Family and class in contemporary America; Notes toward an understanding of ideology." *Papers in Women's Studies.* May.

Riley, F. (1979) "The Love Boat love-in." *Saturday Review.* August 4.

Rowbotham, S. (1973) *Woman's Consciousness, Man's World.* London: Penguin Books.

TV Guide (1981) July 4–10: A–18.

Waters, H. F. (1978) "Television: the Leer boat." *Newsweek.* January 2.

ROBERT C. ALLEN

THE GUIDING LIGHT: SOAP OPERA AS ECONOMIC PRODUCT AND CULTURAL DOCUMENT

Soap opera? The very term has a pejorative connotation—as in, "That movie was nothing but a glorified soap opera." Viewed largely by women and relegated to the netherworld of daytime television, soap operas until recently have remained "hidden" from public and scholarly view, while reams of publicity and scholarly writing have been devoted to prime-time commercial television. As recently as 1972, Natan Katzman prefaced his analysis of soap opera content with the admission, "Despite the magnitude of the phenomenon, there has been no published research on television serials."[1]

Thanks in large measure to a broadening of the soap opera audience to include college students and a greater proportion of male viewers, soap operas have received considerably more attention both in the academic and general press since the mid-1970s. But this attention is still minuscule in light of the economic importance of soaps to the commercial broadcasting industry ($700 million in advertising revenue each year) and their audience appeal (10 million viewers daily).[2]

Focusing on one particular soap opera, *The Guiding Light*, this essay examines the role of the soap in the history of the commercial television industry and suggests a starting point for the study of soap operas as cultural phenomenon.

Each autumn the resources of the three major television networks are brought to bear on the new prime-time season. Program executives, advertisers, and stockholders anxiously await the "overnights" (Nielsen daily ratings data from selected

---

From *American History/American Television*, edited by John O'Connor. Copyright © 1983 by John O'Connor. Reprinted by permission of the Ungar Publishing Company.

cities) on shows to see which network "won" a particular time period. With hundreds of thousands of advertising dollars riding on each rating point, a hit series can mean millions in profits. As programming executives frequently discover, however, prime-time programming is a high-risk and high-cost undertaking—the "sure-fire" idea for a series, which the network spent millions to acquire, may disappear. The economic role of soap operas must be set against the turbulent, unpredictable, and risky nature of prime-time programming. By comparison, soap operas since the early 1950s have provided the three networks (particularly CBS and ABC) with a large and predictable profit base. While a single episode of a soap probably will never garner the prime-time ratings of *Roots*, *Dallas*, or the Super Bowl, far less must be spent to attract the soap audience. And, once a soap has established itself, the outlays for talent and production are almost sure to be recouped many times over.

What makes the soap opera so profitable is its ability to attract and hold what is, in advertising terms, a quality audience—women between the ages of eighteen and fifty-four. This group, particularly that portion of it under thirty-five, makes most of the American family's "soft"-goods purchases (consumable items as opposed to "durable" goods)—food, clothes, and, of course, cleaning products. This historical ability to sell products is evidenced by the fact that the soap opera is the only extant form of network television programming some of whose shows are still owned and produced by a sponsor and its advertising agency.[3] In prime time the television "series" brings audiences back week after week by presenting familiar characters in new, self-contained stories. The soap opera goes the series concept one better by presenting, on a daily basis, familiar characters in episodes that build one upon the other and in plot lines that can never (so long as the soap is on the air) be fully resolved.

Another reason soaps might be looked upon as the best solution yet devised to the networks' problem of the need for habitual viewing is that the costs of a soap opera are, relative to prime-time shows, low and, for the most part, predictable. As commentators have long pointed out, the soap opera world is an interior world. The mythical cities of "Springfield" and "Port Charles" are constructions in the minds of viewers built upon what little the audience actually sees of these "typical" American metropolises. The hospital nurses' stations, lawyers' offices, restaurants, and executive suites that form the visual iconography of the soap opera world are the products of the economic need for locales that can be suggested by small sets erected cheek by jowl in one or two television studios. Keeping the number of these sets to a minimum and shooting on videotape rather than film helps keep the per episode cost of a soap opera a fraction of that for a prime-time series.[4]

The development of self-contained, portable video recording equipment in the mid-1970s has enabled soap opera writers and producers to extend the landscape of the soap world to include such exotic exterior settings as Jamaica, Hong Kong, Bermuda, and the Canary Islands. Today characters are constantly flying off to these and other resorts—thanks to the assistance of national tourist boards, which provide transportation, production assistance, and sometimes even room and board for cast and crew in return for "plugs" added to the script and title credits. The cost to the production company for such location shoots is higher than that of shooting standard interior fare, but according to a *Guiding Light* producer, less than that of constructing even the most transparently bogus tropical island sets in the studio.[5]

Over the more than three decades of televised soap operas, elaborate systems of production control and division of labor have been devised both to maintain production schedules and to keep production costs low. Scripts are turned out on an assembly-line basis, dictated by the need to produce five hours of new material each week. The show's head writer determines long-term story developments and provides a written summary of the action to occur in each episode. This outline is then turned over to associate writers, who fill in the dialogue to be spoken.

Production control and production economy are also exercised through contractual relationships between soap operas and their actors. An actor is under contract to a soap for a period of a year or more, during which time he/she is obligated to appear. Built into each contract, however, are thirteen or twenty-six-week renewal periods at the end of which the actor's contract can be terminated by the production company. If viewer response to a new character fails to come up to expectations or if a plot line falters, the story line, character, *and* actor can be disposed of quickly and economically. Within this system of labor relations lies a fundamental difference between soaps and prime-time shows—even the recently successful "serialized" prime-time offerings such as *Dallas* or *Flamingo Road*. The basis of the soap opera is the community of characters and their relationships rather than the actions of any one particular character. Hence soaps are not star-oriented as are many prime-time shows. Over the summer of 1980, *Dallas* star Larry Hagman (J. R. Ewing) used his summer-hiatus deathbed limbo and the resultant "Who shot J.R.?" media hype as a position from which to negotiate a substantial salary increase and financial participation in the profits of the show itself. No similar situation has or, in my opinion, ever could arise in daytime soaps. Whereas Hagman's agents successfully argued that without Hagman there would be no viable *Dallas*, no daytime star could exert such leverage. It is not just the serial format of soaps, with ample opportunities to dispose of recalcitrant actor/characters in narratively convenient ways, but the multiplot and multicharacter orientation of the soaps that put power in the hands of the production company rather than the actors.

The televised soap opera is, of course, a direct descendant of the radio soap. *The Guiding Light* began on radio in 1937. The popular literature usually traces the origins of the radio soap to an Ohio schoolteacher, Irna Phillips (the creator of *The Guiding Light*), who was hired by Chicago station WGN in 1930 to create a dramatic program for women. The success of that show, *Painted Dreams*, sparked interest among other stations, and by 1933 the networks picked up on the idea—or so we are told.[6] Irna Phillips certainly was a major force in the development of the soap opera in America (the creator of several radio soaps as well as *The Guiding Light* and *As the World Turns* for TV), but it is unnecessary (not to mention historically misleading) to cast one person as the mother of soap operas. The soaps developed in the early 1930s as radio first searched for ways to attract and hold a national audience, and then discovered the profits to be made from programming directed specifically toward women. When Phillips arrived in Chicago in 1930, radio as a mass-advertising medium was but a few years old. Already, however, both the serial form and the dramatic form had been used as a means of generating both audience and advertiser interest in radio—most notably in the case of *Amos 'n' Andy*, a serialized comedy with a national following of some 40 million.[7] The local and, later, network soap operas adapted the serialized dramatic form (used also in newspaper comic strips) to appeal to women by focusing on "female" concerns: the family, homemaking, romance, and perhaps most importantly, interpersonal relationships in general. As in television decades later, radio soap operas worked splendidly as an enticement to regular, habitual viewing.

The tremendous economic success of soap operas on both radio and television has made the form one of the most enduring and prolific in the history of American commercial broadcasting. Soap operas have been a daily part of network broadcasting since 1933, and one show, *The Guiding Light*, has run continuously since January 1937. Katzman found the number of minutes of soap opera programming to have risen steadily between 1952 and 1970, from approximately 60 minutes to 510 minutes (8.5 hours).[8] In the decade since his study, several half-hour soaps have expanded to one hour, and by 1981 the total minutes per day of soaps had reached 660 (11 hours). No prime-time programs can match the longevity of *Search for Tomorrow*, *As the World Turns*, or *The Guiding Light*, (which together represent eighty-four years of continuous television programming). Nor can any prime-time programming form (situation comedy, talk show, variety, comedy variety, newsmagazine, action/adventure, etc.) match the soap opera quantitatively in terms of hours of programming per day, week, or year. At the time of this writing (late 1981) the twelve soap operas currently being broadcast generated fifty-five hours of programming each week, approximately twenty-eight hundred hours each year, or the equivalent of nearly two thousand ninety-minute feature films. In short, in terms of numbers of network broadcast hours per day the soap opera is and has been for years the predominant commercial television form, constituting at present 28 percent of the total network broadcast hours each weekday, 34 percent of the entertainment (nonnews) programming.

Finally, the soap opera's historical role in commercial broadcasting must be viewed in terms of the special relationship soaps enjoy with their viewers. Prime-time shows do develop strong viewer interest and loyalty, but none has engendered the long-term devotion that soaps have. In the case of some viewers, soap opera watching has been a part of their daily lives for decades, producing a relationship between soap and audience that Sari Thomas has characterized as "continuous intimacy."[9] When Pope John Paul II was wounded in Rome in May 1980, a St. Louis Television station reported to the Associated Press more than 100 calls from irate soap opera viewers complaining that their programs were being preempted by news coverage of an individual who, after all, "wasn't even an American." The loyalty of soap viewers combined with the size of the soap audience makes soap watching not a curious social anomaly, but a significant cultural phenomenon. In 1979, Arnold Becker, vice-president for research for CBS, estimated that 63 percent of all American women living in houses with television sets could be classified as soap opera viewers, making the audience for soaps 50 million persons. Over the summer of 1981, *General Hospital*, the highest-rated show in the history of daytime television, captured 14 million viewers daily.[10]

If soap viewing has been an important leisure activity for millions of Americans for decades, how can we get a handle on the social significance of soaps and soap opera viewing? What do soaps say about American society? That soaps might be important cultural documents has been recognized by scholars since the early 1940s, but studies of soap opera audiences have been relatively few. The predominant approach to the social meaning of soap operas has been content analysis—the quantitative analysis (counting) of various discrete categories of soap content. Scholars have tallied the number of marital infidelities, illegitimate births, alcoholics, criminal acts, and mental cases. Not surprisingly, scholars have been intrigued by what Natan Katzman has called the "almost reality" of soap operas: that fictional, parallel world that in so many ways seems to resemble the social world of the viewer, but that is also quite different from the world of the viewer's experience. Time in soap operas, unlike in prime-time shows, much more closely approximates real time. Characters on soaps do grow old, marry, bear children, and, sometimes, die. Their lives unfold over a period of years, if not decades. Bert Bauer, the character played by actress Charita Bauer on *The Guiding Light* for thirty years, has gone from feisty bride to consoling grandmother. Many of her viewers have, as she puts it, "grown old with her." But few viewers' lives can even begin to approach the traumatic eventfulness of most soap characters. Jo Anne Tate on *Search for Tomorrow* has been thrice widowed, tried for murder, kidnapped on the eve of her third marriage by her second husband (whom she believed dead), twice saved from murderers, stricken by psychosomatic blindness, and temporarily paralyzed by a gunshot wound—to name but some of her tribulations.

Most of the content analyses of soap operas have implicitly or explicitly presumed that soaps constitute a pseudoreality that can be measured against the "real" world. For example, in a study published in 1979, Cassata, Skill, and Boadu investigated "the occurrence and distribution of health-related conditions in the soap opera world" and compared these health conditions to their statistical occurrence in the American population in general. They discovered that soap characters are more likely to suffer accidental death, murder, and mental illness and less likely to contract cancer than people in the "real" world.[11]

In 1981, two separate studies examined the depiction of sexual activity on soap operas. Each coded the variety and frequency of intimate acts and references. One of the studies even produced a rank ordering of soap operas in terms of sexiness—*General Hospital* "was clearly the 'sexiest' of the soap operas, with 16.00 incidents per hour." The authors of this study concluded, "Soap operas can be assumed to be presenting a distorted picture of sexual behavior in America. . . . A steady viewing diet of role models who engage in fornication and adultery may influence or cultivate viewers' attitudes and values concerning what is 'normal' and 'proper' in society." [12]

In her study of conversation topics and styles on soap operas, Marlene G. Fine found that, on the whole, soap opera characters discussed what we would expect them to discuss: romantic couples talked about marriage and romance; friends talked about friendships; co-workers talked about work; and strangers engaged in smalltalk. However, she concluded, soap opera conversations differed from those in "the world we live in" in several respects. Most importantly, perhaps, men and women soap opera characters talk to each other far more than do real-life working-class married couples.[13]

One of the most useful findings of soap opera content analysis comes from an ongoing study of television content conducted by George Gerbner and colleagues. In 1981 his research team reported in *New England Journal of Medicine*: "It may well be that daytime serials are the largest source of medical advice in the United States."[14]

Content analysis as a method has two serious shortcomings, however, when applied to soap operas. First, while it can tell us how the social world of the soap opera is similar to or different from certain aspects of empirical reality, it cannot tell us *why* soaps represent reality the way they do. Second, content analysis presumes that the manner by which soap opera audiences derive meaning from their viewing activity is both known and unproblematical. For purposes of quantitative analysis, events must be pulled out of their context in the soap opera world and isolated as discrete units of meaning. For his content analysis of soap opera, Katzman chose observers who had never seen the serial they were coding. Cassata, Sill, and Boadu did not even find it necessary to view the soap opera content they studied; rather they relied on plot descriptions provided in *Soap Opera Digest*.

The question arises: Does a sexual reference, heart attack, or illegitimate pregnancy "mean" the same when it is pulled out of its aesthetic context? Put another way, is reading a soap opera the same as reading a newspaper? I would argue that content analyses will continue to be of limited explanatory value until we have a better understanding of the aesthetic processes that lie behind soap operas' representations of social reality. Creation of meaning and aesthetic pleasure in the soap opera is a much more complex process than is generally recognized. In addition, what a soap opera means in a social sense is inextricably tied up with how it creates meaning for its viewers.

Let us consider how meaning is produced in a single episode of a soap opera—in this case the August 18, 1981, episode of *The Guiding Light*, an example chosen more or less at random. On the basis of the content summary of this episode (provided at the end of this essay), several things stand out. First, except in the most superficial sense, there is very little meaning one can derive from this summary, or indeed from the actual episode itself, unless one has seen other episodes of *The Guiding Light*. Unless you catch the first episode of a new soap, you always join a soap's action *in medias res*. The meaning of the events in any one episode depends upon your knowledge of characters and events from previous ones.

This fact points to a fundamental problem in reading soap operas: what, for purposes of analysis, *is* a soap opera? This is a necessary question for two reasons: first, soap operas *do* create meaning differently than most other media forms, and second, if we desire to know the relationship between a phenomenon and its culture, we had better be able to define that phenomenon.

Clearly one episode of a soap opera cannot be said to "be" that soap any more than a page from the middle of a novel can be said to "be" that novel. But how can we define a soap? As a week's worth of episodes? A year's worth? Since any one episode of a soap is built on all the episodes that have preceded it— since soap operas accumulate meaning over time—then the only logical way to define a given soap opera is as the sum of all its episodes broadcast since its origination. Any more delimiting definition would of necessity be arbitrary. Hence with the soap opera we have a situation unique to broadcasting in which a program, *The Guiding Light*, for example, has taken shape over the course of thirty years (more than forty-five if we include the years it was broadcast on radio). But even this definition has not completely solved the problem of specifying the nature of a soap opera. Whereas soaps do have a definite beginning (even if thirty or more years in the past), they have no endings. They are, in narrative terms, open—resistant to closure. The soap opera is unique among broadcast programs in this respect as well; it is the only form whose very nature precludes its having an ending. Even when soaps are taken off the air because of poor ratings (as was *Love of Life* in 1980), they do not wind up their subplots and leave everyone living happily ever after, but rather expire into a sort of eternal limbo of unresolution. Thus in the case of *The Guiding Light*, we have thirty years of a program that if broadcast sequentially would take more than a month of continuous viewing, twenty-four hours a day, to watch. But even at the end of this marathon screening, we could still not claim to have "seen" *The Guiding Light*, since during our sleepless month in the screening room another sixteen hours of the show would have been produced!

One way around this awkward definitional problem might be to attempt to discover the underlying principles of a given soap. Can we discern the vocabulary and grammar of the soap opera form that any episode or group of episodes uses to create meaning?

Some of these underlying principles can be extrapolated from the episode of *The Guiding Light* under consideration. Upon viewing this episode one is struck by the fact that so little "happens" in it in terms of plot development or, indeed, in terms of action of any kind. No time is spent establishing locales, there are no exterior shots, no character walks more than twenty paces in any given scene—we simple see characters talking to each other.

In terms of plot, the viewer learns very little from this episode. A few future plot lines are hinted at: what is the Springfield Investment Company and what is Ross's involvement in it? What secret does Henry Chamberlain not want his daughter to discover? Will Noela make good her threat of vengeance against Kelly and Morgan? But far less time is spent posing these questions than in elaborating on situations about which the viewer is already familiar: specifically, the Kelly/Morgan and Noela/Floyd weddings and the effect of Andy Norris's blackmail schemes on his mother and girl friend.

Further, there is in this episode a great deal of what we might call intraepisodic redundancy: the reiteration several times during the course of a single episode of information already known to the viewer. Redundancy between episodes (interepisodic redundancy) can be explained by the need to accommodate viewers who are unable to watch a particular soap every day and hence need to be reminded of events from previous episodes. The same reasoning cannot be used to explain intraepisodic redundancy, however.

If so little "happens" in a single episode of a soap, then what accounts for its daily appeal? Traditional narrative and dramatic critical approaches are of little use in answering this question, since soap operas are not "traditional" narrative or dramatic works. Applying the same critical standards to the soap opera that one would to the novel is inappropriate in that the soap opera lacks the climactic event and subsequent denouement that are defining features of the classic novel form. Traditional dramatic criticism still relies on Aristotelian notions of dramatic unity and structure that are ignored by the soap opera. If we turn, however, to semiotics (the scientific study of sign systems), we find an analytical approach capable of dealing with the peculiarities of the soap opera form.[15] Semiotics is the application of principles of structural linguistics to phenomena that are not, strictly speaking, linguistic: film, circus acts, table manners, wrestling matches, and television are among the sign systems that have been investigated by semioticians.

One of the fundamental discoveries of structural linguistics was that verbal languages are "arbitrary." The word *door*, for example, bears no natural or necessary resemblance to a real door; we might just as well substitute the word *cow* to stand for a door. *Door* takes on its meaning by virtue of its participation in a system of words. This system is one of similarity and difference, by which we are able to distinguish *door* from *boor*. Furthermore, verbal language is a "conventional" system, in that linguistic elements take on meaning because of their place in the system rather than through any natural or necessary relationships to something outside that system. We understand the meaning of *door* because in the English language it is conventional to refer to a large portal as a door. In other words, we participate in the "code" that is English. By knowing the lexical, grammatical, and syntactic codes of English, we can generate an infinite variety of word combinations from a finite number of letters and words.

Semiotics attempts to uncover the codes or generative principles that enable us to make sense of other cultural phenomena. We might ask, for example, "What are the codes that enable the viewer to understand and derive pleasure from soap operas?" A list of the codes of soap operas would include (but would not be limited to):

1. *Video–cinematic codes.* This is the complex of codes of visual and auditory representation that television—and, by extension, the soap opera—has borrowed from Hollywood filmmaking style. It would include such devices as unobtrusive camera movements, "invisible" editing, and a naturalistic style of acting, among others—all designed to focus the viewer's attention on the story unfolding on the screen and away from the manner by which that story is being told.

2. *Codes of the soap opera form.* This set of codes is derived in large measure from the soap opera form itself; together these codes work to make the soap opera look and sound different from other forms of television. For example, in soap operas time and space are used differently than in other narrative forms of television. Time is prolonged rather than compressed. The spatial world of the soap opera is predominantly an interior one. Instead of a single, linear narrative drawn to a close within an hour, the soap opera features multiple, intersecting plot lines, each of which might last years. There is a great deal of redundancy in soap operas, both between episodes and within an individual episode.

3. *Textual codes.* Although the twelve soap operas currently being broadcast share all the above codes, each has its own distinguishing conventions that are easily recognized (although not as codes) by frequent viewers. The long-time soap viewer can immediately sense when something is "wrong" with his or her soap: a character is behaving in an uncharacteristic manner, for example. The frequent viewer can recognize not only appropriate and inappropriate behavior in a given character, but appropriate responses of a given character to another, based on the two characters' relationships in the show's past. Characters in soap operas have memories, and relationships might well stretch back for a decade or more.

4. *Intertextual codes.* All cultural products exist within networks of other texts, to which they inevitably refer. The soap opera

frequently includes references to other texts: a plot line "borrowed" from a popular novel or film, the appearance of a movie star or other show-business personality as him/herself. In each case a level of meaning is created by reference to another text or set of texts.

5. *Experiential codes.* Often in interpreting an action in a soap opera, the viewer will rely upon his or her own experience of the world. The viewer constantly compares soap opera actions with what "should" happen in such a situation—what is plausible, veristic, morally correct, etc., not in terms of the world of the soap but in terms of the viewer's own world of experience and values.

Let us return to the question, "If so little happens in a single episode of a soap, then what accounts for its daily appeal?" A further principle of semiotic analysis will enable us to deal with this question and, by doing so, to begin to see the complexity of the soap opera as a conveyor of meaning. All narrative works create meaning along two axes. The syntagmatic axis defines the temporal ordering of elements in the work (what follows what). The paradigmatic axis has to do with the arrangement of elements in terms of their similarity and difference (what goes with what), and would include relationships among characters. Hence if we read this episode of *The Guiding Light* syntagmatically, we find very little of importance. But there *is* a lot going on in this episode—not in the syntagmatic sense of cause-effect plot relationships, but paradigmatically in the system of correspondence and difference the scenes set up. Paradigmatically, this episode is "about" the relationship between two similar, anticipated events: the weddings of Floyd and Noela and of Kelly and Morgan. But while both weddings involve young, attractive, well-established characters, the regular viewer of *The Guiding Light* is immediately aware of the contrasts set up between the two events.

Kelly and Morgan's wedding will be the culmination of a relationship begun over a year ago, but thwarted for much of that time by the lies Noela told Morgan about Kelly. Morgan's belief, fostered by Noela, that Kelly had been unfaithful to her prompted Morgan to run away to Chicago, where she was nearly tricked into a life of drugs and prostitution. Noela's motive for this deceit was her desire to marry Kelly, whom, she believed, would become a wealthy doctor and boost her out of her family's working-class status. When she failed to entice Kelly into a romantic relationship, Noela tried to force him to marry her by making him believe that he had fathered her child one night when he was drunk. In reality, Floyd, with whom she had been carrying on a secret liaison for months, was the father and quite willing to marry Noela.

The difference—we might even say opposition—between the two weddings is established in this episode by the reactions of other members of *The Guiding Light* community upon learning of the two events. Most of the other characters had learned of Kelly and Morgan's wedding plans in previous episodes; only Carrie and Derek learn of the news in this one. Everyone, however, with the obvious exception of Noela, is delighted by the prospects of their marriage. A total of seven characters are informed of Floyd and Noela's wedding in this episode alone (Derek, Katy, Kelly, Morgan, Hilary, Ed, and Vanessa). Their reactions range from shock (Katy) to anger (Kelly, Morgan, Hilary), to consternation (Ed), to indifference (Vanessa). Only Derek can muster congratulations and he only because he is uninformed as to Noela's lies and failed scheme to trick Kelly.

This episode tells us that Kelly and Morgan's wedding will involve the entire community. The event will take place at idyllic Laurel Falls, where the two fell in love last summer. Thirty-seven members of Morgan's high-school graduating class (we are told twice) have volunteered to prepare the site. Mike Bauer will give the bride away. Ben McFarren loans the couple his rural retreat for their honeymoon. Ed Bauer has provided them with a place to live. Even Vanessa has already sent her wedding gift. Floyd and Noela, on the other hand, will be married in the office of a justice of the peace with only Noela's brother and mother and Floyd's sister Katy witnessing the event. Katy remarks sarcastically to Tony that she's glad *Floyd* will be allowed to attend.

But the system of similarity and difference created in this episode does not end here. As plans for Kelly and Morgan's wedding are being made in the living room, Katy stays in her bedroom recovering from the shock of the news that her boyfriend, Andy Norris, has been unmasked as the blackmailer who had been terrorizing the community for months. The eager planning is in ironic juxtaposition to the effects of the dissolution of a relationship Katy had hoped would lead to marriage. Also, Katy's plight is made implicitly to correspond to the possible future unhappiness of her brother, since both Andy and Noela have been untruthful and selfish in their romantic relationships.

In scene 2, Tony's reference to his girl friend Darlene serves to remind Noela and the viewer of the contrast between her family's view of marital relations and that she had held for herself. Tony remarks that while he was away the night before (preventing Noela from going through with an abortion), Darlene stayed behind at his apartment. When he returned at two in the morning he found her "on her hands and knees scrubbing the floor." Noela, whose mother runs a boarding house, desires above all else to be free from domestic drudgery. The life of social status, wealth, and leisure she had fantasized about with Kelly is not likely to materialize with Floyd, a hospital maintenance worker.

In scene 4, Jennifer, Morgan's mother, tells Ben of her other daughter Amanda's emotional response to the news of Morgan and Kelly's wedding. Amanda, who is married to but separated from Ben, has been emotionally distraught since she miscarried some months ago. She believes Ben left her for his first wife, Eve, and mistrusts all romantic relationships. To her the news of Kelly and Morgan's marriage is merely a reminder of her own painful experience with marriage.

In scene 1, Derek asks Hilary what she thinks of Kelly and Morgan's wedding plans. This question probably seems innocuous enough to the inexperienced viewer, but to regular viewers it is quite significant. They know that Hilary was once in love with Kelly, while he regarded her as only a friend. In fact, Hilary's residual feelings for Kelly have hampered the development of her relationship with Derek.

These are the most firmly established parallels and contrasts in this episode. But for the experienced viewer the paradigmatic network, of which the two weddings are but a part, extends much further. Because parentage, romance, marriage, and the dissolution of marriage are the foci of most plot lines in *The Guiding Light*, the first marriage (there will almost certainly be others for all of the four) of four young characters reverberates throughout almost the entire community, setting up implicitly or explicitly relationships between these weddings and the current marital/romantic status of other characters and reminding the experienced viewer of their past histories. At the time romance is being consummated for Kelly and Morgan, it is beginning for Ross and Carrie. Ross, the overly ambitious lawyer brother of Dr. Justin Marler, has recently become en-amored of Carrie Todd, a new employee of Spaulding Enter-prises. Carrie, who describes herself as "hopelessly romantic," has already had, as Ross puts it, "a profound effect" on curbing his less ethical tendencies. In this case, as in others in *The Guiding Light*, love is presented as a regenerating and transform-ing force. Ross and Carrie make mention of Alan Spaulding and Hope, his estranged wife. Ross comments that Alan, a some-times selfish and materialistic business magnate, seems to have changed since his marriage to Hope Bauer, to which Carrie replies, "Love changes people."

There is also a budding romance between Ed Bauer and Vanessa Chamberlain. Separated from his wife, Rita, following Rita's affair with Alan Spaulding, Ed is connected with Kelly and Morgan's wedding plans in that he is Kelly's godfather. Ed and Vanessa met when Vanessa was brought to Cedars Hospital after she had taken an overdose of sleeping pills in a pseudosui-cide ploy to evoke the pity of Ross Marler, with whom she was infatuated. Thus, the wedding of Kelly and Morgan set up an implicit comparison with Ed's own marital difficulties, while the parallels between Noela's romantic dissimulation and Vanessa's "secret" are obvious to the experienced viewer.

In short, even at the level of a single episode, meaning in a soap opera is created in large measure through the audience's familiarity with a complex network of character relationships and the history of this network as it recedes back toward the program's beginnings. The recognition of the paradigmatic com-plexity of the soap opera form is but a starting point in under-standing the working of soap operas, but it does enable us to make a few generalizations—however preliminary—regarding the social meaning of soaps.

First and most obviously, the world of the soap opera is a social world—a world in which a character is defined in terms of his or her relationships with other members of the soap opera community. One reason it is difficult to describe what happened in a soap opera episode is not that soap opera plots are so convoluted but that each character has multiple, shifting identities vis-à-vis other characters. Ed Bauer is Vanessa's love interest, Rita's husband, Kelly's godfather, Bert's son, Mike's brother, and so on. The importance of any soap opera plot development is not so much its effect on a given character but the consequences of an event on romantic, familial, and other interpersonal relationships. There is no single protagonist with whose fate audience interest is ultimately bound. Even central characters of long standing have been eliminated from a soap (Adam Drake from *The Edge of Night* and Nancy Hughes from *As the World Turns*, to name but two) without doing noticeable damage to its audience acceptance. Individual characters might die, move away, be sent to jail, sink into comas, but the community survives; the functions played by departed characters are assumed by new ones. Hence it is not surprising that most current soap operas began as kinship sagas—*Ryan's Hope*, *The Guiding Light*, *As the World Turns*, *All My Children*, *Another World*, *Days of Our Lives*, *One Life to Live*. Particularly in the older, more established soap operas, family ties are of paramount importance. Romances, friendships, marriages might crumble over time, but ties of kinship can never be dissolved. In *The Guiding Light*, a new character's integration into the community is often marked by his or her joining a family (through marriage, usually), or through the establishment of a quasi-familial relationship between the new character and a family group. Kelly Nelson, a young medical student, was introduced into the show as the godson of longtime character Dr. Ed Bauer. Jennifer Richards and daughter Morgan entered *The Guiding Light* when their car crashed in Springfield. Morgan promptly took up temporary residence at the home of matriarch Bert Bauer while her mother recuperated in the hospital.

It would be simplistic to conclude on the basis of the above that soap operas function to reinforce the values of the nuclear family at a time of that unit's disintegration in the society as a whole. Few families in soap operas are themselves free from fragmentation—the single-parent family is the norm rather than the exception in the world of soap operas. One reason for this state of affairs is clearly narrative: were everyone in soaps happily married, the possible relationships among characters would be severely diminished. But the premium placed on kinship in soap operas does act as a socially conservative force— almost everything in the social world of the soap opera is mutable, except for the bond between mother and child, brother and sister.

Despite some plot lines dealing with working-class characters and interracial romances, the world of the soap opera is overwhelmingly white and middle class. The problem of including blacks and other racial groups in soaps is not one of working them into plot lines, but dealing with the paradigmatic consequences of their entry into the community of the soap opera world. These are three major types of relationships among soap opera characters: kinship, romance, and social (friend/enemy). As we have seen, much of the appeal of soap operas resides in the complexity and overlap of actual and potential relationships among these categories with regard to any particular character. Unless a particular soap were to embrace interracial marriage and parentage as a community norm, the admission of a non-white character into full membership in the soap community would be impossible. As yet this is a step no soap opera has been willing to take.

The middle-class orientation of all soaps is a frequently noted characteristic. To a degree this class focus is an attempt to make the soap opera world parallel that of the presumed viewer. The most frequently depicted work places in soap operas are hospitals, law firms, bars, restaurants, and the executive offices of business concerns. Physical labor, assembly lines, and factory work are almost totally absent. Blue-collar characters might inhabit the world of the soap, but the work they perform is almost never represented. But the middle-class work places of the soap opera world are also conditioned by narrative concerns. Because of the importance of interpersonal relationships in soaps, work places must allow for frequent contacts with other people and an opportunity to discuss matters not directly related to one's work—hence the prevalence of hospital nursing stations, waiting rooms, executive suites, and nightclubs. These are places where work is relatively unsupervised and does not require extended periods of close attention to mechanical detail. But much more socially significant, I believe, than the presence of certain middle-class and professional work settings is the total absence of the industrial work place from the world of the soap. Factory work and blue-collar employment in general have a negative social value in soaps, because these jobs are presumed to preclude the type of interpersonal contact upon which the soap opera community is based.

Despite the fact that a great deal happens in the lives of individual characters—multiple marriages, pregnancies, amnesia, temporary blindness, disabling accidents, and so forth—very little happens to alter the nature of the community. The soap opera community is a self-perpetuating and self-preserving system—a system little affected by the turbulence experienced by its individual members and fate of any one character. The naive viewer might be dazzled by the implausible constant state of crisis experienced by individual characters, but the experienced viewer is watchful for the sometimes glacially slow but far more significant alterations in the network of character relationships that forms the very basis for the soap opera world.

CONTENTUAL SUMMARY

The Guiding Light—August 18, 1981

Scene 1

Setting: Hilary's apartment
Time: Early morning

Derek, Hilary's boyfriend, arrives, having returned from a business trip. They talk briefly about Andy Norris, his refusal to accept legal advice, and the effect of his arrest upon Katy.

Hilary tells Derek of Kelly and Morgan's wedding plans.

Kelly and Morgan arrive. The four talk of wedding plans. Trudy, Morgan's friend, has lined up thirty-seven volunteers to help plan the wedding.

Floyd arrives to tell Katy, his sister, the news of his impending marriage to Noela. He informs the four of his plans, revealing Noela to be the "mystery woman" in his life.

Scene 2

Setting: Bea Reardon's kitchen
Time: Breakfast

Bea tells Noela she is glad the latter did not go through with plans for an abortion. Tony, Noela's brother, enters and tells how his girl friend, Darlene, cleaned his apartment while he was out. Noela sarcastically notes that Tony probably regards that as a sign Darlene would make a good wife. There is talk of the wedding and of getting the marriage license so the ceremony can be conducted as soon as possible. Bea offers Noela the larger bedroom for her and Floyd.

Scene 3

Setting: Katy's bedroom
Time: Immediately following Scene I

Floyd enters. Katy is depressed that everyone in the other room is talking of wedding plans. Floyd breaks the news of his plans to marry Noela. Katy is shocked.

Scene 4

Setting: Alan Spaulding's office
Time: Unspecified

Ben and Jennifer are discussing Amanda's seeing a new doctor. Jennifer says Amanda was upset at the news of Kelly and Morgan's wedding. Ben expresses suspicion regarding a company set up by Ross in Amanda's name, the Springfield Investment Co.

Carrie enters. Jennifer informs her of Morgan's wedding.

Jennifer leaves.

Carrie asks Ben why Philip, Alan's son, is living with Justin and Jackie. Ben tells her.

Ross enters. Ross inquires about Amanda's health.

Ben leaves.

Carrie is pleased that Ross is trying to control his dislike for Ben.

Scene 5

Setting: Fourth floor nurses' desk, Cedars Hospital
Time: Unspecified

Hilary, Kelly, and Morgan are talking about Floyd and Noela's wedding. Kelly says he feels awkward knowing that Noela tried to trick him into marrying her by claiming the baby fathered by Floyd was really his.

Kelly leaves.

Noela and Tony arrive on the elevator.

Scene 6

Setting: Same as Scene 5
Time: Same as Scene 5

Tony and Noela run into Kelly as he is about to get on the elevator. Noela walks away, and Tony asks that Kelly keep Noela's scheme a secret from Floyd. Kelly agrees to do so.

Floyd arrives on the elevator and walks over to where Noela is standing. He says he's been "walking on air" since Noela agreed to marry him.

Scene 7

Setting: Mike's office
Time: Unspecified

Mike and Derek discuss Morgan's wedding. Mike is to "give the bride away." Mike's secretary informs him that Henry Chamberlain is waiting to see him.

Mike asks Derek to check up on the Springfield Investment Co.

Scene 8

Setting: Alan Spaulding's office.
Time: Unspecified

Ross is alone in the room making a telephone call to a stockholder of Spaulding Enterprises, offering to buy the person's stock. In the midst of his conversation there is a flashback to the previous evening when he dropped Carrie off at her apartment. In the flashback Carrie reminds Ross that ambition is not the most important thing in the world. After the flashback, Ross terminates his call before making an offer for the shares.

Scene 9

Setting: Mike's office
Time: Immediately following Scene 7

Henry expresses sympathy for Barbara, Andy Norris's mother, saying she reminds him of someone he was once very close to. He then says he wants to tell Mike of a confidential matter, which he doesn't want his daughter Vanessa to know. Henry asks Mike if he knows about Vanessa's faked suicide. Mike does. Henry says Vanessa is terrified that Mike's brother Ed will learn of the ruse.

Scene 10

Setting: Hospital
Time: Unspecified

Ed and Vanessa are talking. Morgan enters and talks about the wedding and the garage apartment behind Ed's house she and Kelly are to move into. Morgan leaves Ed and Vanessa, walking over to the nurses' station where Hilary is standing. Noela and Floyd walk by. Hilary tells Morgan not to get upset by Noela's presence. Floyd walks up to Ed and Vanessa and tells them of his marriage to Noela.

Scene 11

Setting: Alan's office
Time: Midday

Carrie and Ross are talking after lunch. Ross tells Carrie that her "philosophy" is having a profound effect on him. They talk of Alan and his separation from his wife, Hope. Ross says he believes Alan has changed since his marriage to Hope. Carrie expresses the opinion that "love changes people." Their conversation is interrupted by Vanessa, who asks where her father is. Ross and Carrie leave the room and Henry enters. Vanessa asks if Joe, the private investigator, has been able to come up with any damaging evidence about Diane's past. Henry says no. They talk of Stephanie Ryan, Henry's former secretary, who has recently died in Mexico. Henry tells Vanessa that Mike knows of her suicide fakery, but says Mike will not tell Ed.

Scene 12

Setting: Hospital
Time: Immediately following Scene 10

Ed, Kelly, and Hilary discuss Floyd and Noela's wedding and Kelly's plans. Floyd and Noela enter from the elevator. Floyd tells Noela that they can be married at the end of the week. Floyd leaves. Noela asks to speak with Kelly.

Scene 13

Setting: Same as Scene 12
Time: Immediately following Scene 12

Noela asks Kelly not to tell Floyd anything of her scheme. Kelly says he won't tell, but warns Noela to "stay away from Morgan and me." Kelly leaves; Noela, speaking to herself, says, "You're going to be sorry one day, Kelly; so will Morgan."

Scene 14

Setting: Elevator at hospital
Time: Immediately following Scene 13

Kelly tells Morgan not to worry about Noela: "She can't touch us now."

Scene 15

Setting: Katy's apartment
Time: Unspecified

Tony arrives to tell Katy of the wedding. Katy says she's going through a rough time. Tony tells Katy not to let Andy Norris get her down.

Scene 16

Setting: Derek's office
Time: Midday

Ross arrives to see Mike. Derek tells him he's in his office talking with Jennifer. Ross sits down to wait. Derek leaves for lunch.

Scene 17

Setting: Mike's office
Time: Immediately following Scene 16

Jennifer talks of Morgan's wedding, saying her own was not a very good example. She also asks Mike to check on Ross's involvement in the Springfield Investment Co. Cut to Ross listening outside the door.

NOTES

1. Natan Katzman, "Television Soap Operas: What's Been Going On Anyway," *Public Opinion Quarterly* 36 (Summer 1972), p. 200.
2. "Television's Hottest Show," *Newsweek* (September 28, 1981), pp. 60–66.
3. Procter and Gamble currently own four soaps produced through their advertising agency, Compton Advertising.
4. For a fascinating examination of television programming in general, see Les Brown, *Televi$ion: The Business behind the Box* (New York: Harcourt Brace Jovanovich, 1971).
5. Interview with Michael Laibson, associate producer, *The Guiding Light*, October 23, 1981.
6. See Robert LaGuardia, *The Wonderful World of TV Soap Operas* (New York: Ballantine Books, 1974), pp. 58–65.
7. Erik Barnouw discusses *Amos 'n' Andy* in *A Tower in Babel* (New York: Oxford University Press, 1966), pp. 226–229.
8. Katzman, p. 201.
9. Sari Thomas, "The Relationship between Daytime Serials and Their Viewers" (Ph.D diss., University of Pennsylvania, 1977), p. 2.
10. Becker is quoted in Robert Lindsay, "Soap Operas: Men Are Tuning In," *New York Times*, February 21, 1979, p. 3:1; *Newsweek* (September 28, 1981), p. 60.
11. Mary B. Cassata, Thomas D. Skill, and Samuel Osei Boadu, "In Sickness and Health," *Journal of Communication* (Autumn 1979), pp. 73–80.
12. Dennis T. Lowery, Gail Love, and Malcolm Kirby, "Sex on the Soap Operas: Patterns of Intimacy," *Journal of Communication* (Spring 1981), pp. 90–96. See also Bradley S. Greenberg, Robert Abelman, and Kimberly Neuendorf, "Sex on the Soap Operas: Afternoon Delight," *Journal of Communication* (Spring 1981), pp. 83–89.
13. Marlene C. Fine, "Soap Opera Conversations: The Talk That Binds," *Journal of Communication* (Spring 1981), pp. 97–107. Fine's work suggested that especially "lower-class couples" conversed less than their counterparts in the soaps.

14. George Gerbner, Larry Gross, Michael Morgan, Nancy Signorielli, "Health and Medicine on Television," *New England Journal of Medicine* (October 8, 1981), pp. 901–904.

15. See in particular Ronald Barthes, *S/Z* (New York: Hill and Wang, 1974), and Umberto Eco, *The Role of the Reader* (Bloomington: University of Indiana Press, 1979). The paradigmatic/syntagmatic axes of narratives are discussed in Charles F. Altman, "The American Film Musical: Paradigmatic Structure and Mediatory Function," *Wide Angle* 2 (November 1978), pp. 10–17.

BERNARD TIMBERG

THE RHETORIC OF THE CAMERA IN TELEVISION SOAP OPERA

I recently had an exhilarating experience. Tuning into a soap opera I had once watched regularly but had not seen for a year and a half, I felt a shock of recognition. There they were—all my old friends and acquaintances from Port Charles (the mythical kingdom of *General Hospital*) just as they had been eighteen months before. It is true that several important events had occurred since I last tuned in, but the people I had gotten to know (Scottie, Laura, Jeff, Heather, Rick, Leslie, Monica, et al.) had not changed in any fundamental way, and more importantly, the soap opera rite itself was exactly the same. The same fluid camera moves took me into and out of each scene, making me feel somehow complicit in the ebb and flow of relationships and emotions in the soap world I had come to know so well. Because of my previous knowledge of the plot, characters, and conflicting moral principles in this soap opera, I was able to catch up—within a single day—on all the important developments. Almost immediately I settled into my customary patterns of booing and cheering, analyzing and second-guessing my favorite characters.

Seeing *General Hospital* fresh after eighteen months, I realized I had developed a strong point of view about the characters, and I began to wonder how I had come to see them as I did. Dialogue was important, but I found that words alone were not forming my point of view. The reader of a novel sees characters and action through the language of a narrator or other characters; but in soap opera there is no narrator to establish a point of view, and language is only one way of communicating. I found my point of view shaped most powerfully not by words but by visual images and sound. I suspect that these nonverbal, nonliterary forms of communication have kept many critics from understanding the rhetoric of soap opera—a rhetoric based on specific camera and sound conventions that structure the viewer's experience of the soap opera world.

Scholars of rhetoric have been late in turning to television, including the daytime dramas that are viewed regularly by millions. But television certainly has a rhetorical dimension. It has been described as lying "at the boundary between poetics and rhetoric,"[1] and this is especially true of soap opera, which lies on the boundary between the informal daytime rhetorical forms of monologue, dialogue, and direct-address (forms that create what one writer has called "parasocial relationships" with the viewer[2]) and the framed narratives of prime time television. While many studies have examined the values promoted by television, few have attempted close structural analyses of the discourse patterns that present those values. The studies that have been done have generally concerned themselves with the "poetics" of prime time narrative programming (English teachers apply their training in literary narratives to westerns, cop shows, and comedies; sociologists analyze how narrative entertainment reflects attitudes and values). Despite the acknowledged power and influence of television to convey information, persuasion, and entertainment in our society, the distinctive rhetorical relationship that exists between television program and viewer has gone largely unexamined.

In soap opera this relationship centers on the way the camera presents the story to the viewer. Though we readily see the importance of cinematic codes in film (camera angles, lighting, setting, camera movement, and editing all clearly play important roles in film art), we neglect to notice the effects of formulaic camera moves in soap opera, and in so doing we succumb to the "realist illusion"; the idea that the camera simply records reality.[3] We assume the soap opera camera is a utilitarian tool, not an expressive one, and so we see this kind of cinematography as dull, routine, obvious—of no import. And that is what the makers of soap opera count on. Like the visibility of the purloined letter in Poe's short story, the very obviousness of the cinematic codes of soap opera keeps people from thinking about them and thus makes them more effective in doing their job: to shape and direct the audience's point of view.

The camera's central role is evident from the beginning of the show, when we plunge into the first scene directly out of a commercial break. Though the traditional narrator of radio and early television may remain vestigially—in an announcer's voice or in the soap opera's logo (the hand-embroidered memory book of *All My Children* or the slide of the massive institutional structure of *General Hospital*)—to all extents and purposes the true narrator has become the camera. Choreographed camera movements, not scene-setting verbal descriptions, bring the viewer into and out of the soap world and guide the viewer through that world.

In examining the significance of specific kinds of camera movement and framing, we break through the illusion of realism and explore the ways audiovisual codes tell soap stories. For example, when we compare soaps to other types of daytime programming, we are struck by their use of close-ups and extreme close-ups.[4] This shooting style is consistent with the kind of world soap opera portrays. As a narrative ritual that centers on intense, concentrated forms of emotion, soap opera requires an intense, intimate camera style. Combined with slow truck-ins of the camera and slow, elegiac movements into and out of the action, this close-up camera style has the effect of bringing the viewer closer and closer to the hidden emotional secrets soap opera explores: stylized expressions of pity, jealousy, rage, self-doubt. When the camera actually enters the mind of a soap character—in dream or memory sequences—the inward movement is even slower.

Just as evening news rites require stiff postures, formal dress, formal sentence structures, repression of emotion, and fixed camera angles and distances (generally medium shots and long shots, rarely a close-up or extreme close-up of the news announcer), soap opera ritual requires a camera style that circles its characters and brings us closer and closer to them, right up to their eyes and mouths so that we see their tears and hear their breathing. This is the kind of device that is so taken for granted it escapes our conscious notice while shaping our unconscious response.

The way the camera directs our point of view from one shot to the next becomes clear in a close analysis of actual episodes. My observations on soap opera rhetoric rely primarily on scenes from two taped programs: a May 1978 episode of ABC's *All My Children* and a February 1979 episode of *General Hospital*.[5] However, I have watched many more episodes than the ones I taped and analyzed in detail, and I feel that it would not have mattered which episodes I picked. Things do get a little more exciting on Fridays, when major cliffhangers are prepared, but the same forms appear repeatedly from one day and month to the next. In fact, my interrupted pattern of watching each of these soap operas—with gaps of a little over two years and eighteen months, respectively[6]—helped me see at a glance the permanence of narrative strategies, archetypes, and symbols that sustained viewing might have obscured. (The power of realist illusion is the same for regular fan and analyst alike!)

All My Children was, at the time I taped it, the top-rated ABC daytime soap opera. Thanks to the publicity flair of its creator, Agnes Nixon (one of the founders of radio soap opera in Chicago in the 1930s), and thanks also to a behind-the-scenes book by Dan Wakefield titled *All Her Children* and published by Doubleday in 1976, *All My Children* is one of television's best documented soap operas.[7] Without getting too involved with the intricacies of the plot, I will introduce the characters who play important roles in the scene I wish to discuss.

First and foremost—and the villainess, the bitch goddess of soap opera, often establishes herself as first and foremost—is PHOEBE TYLER. (Soap opera characters' names are often given in capitals, emphasizing their importance in representing characteristic attitudes and passions.) Phoebe, mother of ANNE TYLER MARTIN, lives in a world of her own making, full of bitter self-delusion. As a mother whose neglect and constant criticism have seriously harmed her daughter Anne, she denies the effects of her self-centeredness on her family and turns any possible criticism levied at herself against others. Her best defense is a devastating offense, and she bursts in on various family members and their friends and intimates at all times of the day and night to display her mastery of guilt-inducing invective. The stronger characters stand up to her, but all have felt her venom. PAUL MARTIN, a lawyer in Pine Valley, is married to Phoebe's daughter Anne. He is decent, upright, responsible—too responsible perhaps. He is, in the character typology worked out for *All My Children* by one analyst, a good-father professional.[8] Phoebe Tyler and Paul Martin have been in conflict with each other for years, with Anne Tyler Martin (who has had a breakdown and is currently recovering in a sanatorium) squarely in the middle. The scene I have chosen to explore illustrates the archetypal struggle that has developed between these two characters.

The Paul Martin-Phoebe Tyler confrontation scene begins with a transition from a previous scene involving a character

named TARA MARTIN BRENT and her son, little PHIL. The transition
is from close-up to close-up, face to face, troubled expression to
troubled expression, and takes place on a dramatic chord of
music. This climactic chord, a soap opera convention we know
quite well, signals the crystallization of one problem as we leave
it and the entrance to another. From Paul Martin's expression,
the chord of music, and the context of the transition, we are
alerted to a web of meaning about to emerge before a word is
said. Tara Martin Brent suffers from a love triangle whose
complications and pain never seem to cease. In the scene just
past, her small son's refusal to accept her new husband has
precipitated a new crisis. We know, therefore, by the rules of
soap opera parallelism, that Paul Martin in the next scene is
also likely to be involved in a triangle, that he too will be
confronted by someone who will exacerbate his deepest guilt
(Phoebe Tyler takes the place of little Phil here), and that he too
has a loved one, absent but very much present to mind, who
will be the focus of his spiritual and moral agony. We can intuit
all this before a single word is spoken simply by the juxtaposition of shots between these two scenes.

Although there is a strong resemblance between the close-
ups of Tara Martin Brent and Paul Martin, the close-ups reveal
an important element of contrast as well. Tara's expression is
troubled and diffuse; she looks past the camera but not into it.
It is as if she is looking into her self. This inward gaze of
troubled preoccupation, obliquely angled past the camera lens
and seemingly oblivious to its presence, is also a well-recog-
nized sign in soap opera. It comes primarily at the end of a
scene, when the implications, complications, and consequences
of what has just transpired come home with full force to the
character who has just experienced a conflict or taken a decisive
action. This moment, frozen at the end of a long truck-in or
close-up, accompanied often by a climactic chord of music, is
what I will call "the inner look." It entices us, the soap viewers,
to enter as deeply as we dare into the feelings we imagine the
character to have—though we also know that the moment will
fade, dissolving or cutting to the next scene or commercial
break.

The expression on the face of Paul Martin is quite different
from that of Tara Brent. It is an intense, concentrated look that
is directed toward a person directly across from him. If we have
been following the narrative in the past few days, we know that

on the other end of that gaze is Phoebe Tyler. Even if we have
not been following the story, we know from his expression that
Paul is engaged, wary, up against someone or something that
will require his utmost concentration. His lips move. "I beg
your pardon," he says. The enforced civility of his tone is
chilling and sets in motion a theme that will continue to play
through the scene: the thin structures of etiquette (etiquette is
one of Phoebe Tyler's strong suits) continually threatened by
volcanic emotions underneath the surface. The politeness of
conversation forms a bitter counterpoint to the undercurrent
of rage.

"Let's go back to the beginning," says Phoebe. "If you had
only insisted that Anne have an abortion . . ." She goes on to
make the outrageous assertion that Anne's mental breakdown
was Paul's fault. The camera switches on her words to an over-
the-shoulder shot from Paul's point of view. Phoebe's hand is
clenched into a fist. (Hand, face, body gestures and intonation
take on emblematic significance in soap opera. Phoebe's tone of
voice—bitter, carping, tremulous—is a well-known sign. So is
her erect, brittle posture, her mannered way of speaking, and
now, in the bottom right of the screen, at this point barely
visible, her fist—a small token of the repressed urge to attack
and defend that she carries with her everywhere.)

After these first two shots, the camera switches back to
another close-up of Paul. "You dare say that!" he says. In the
first seconds of the scene, through two reaction shots of Paul
and an over-the-shoulder shot of Phoebe Tyler, we have established Paul as the center of our attention and the key to our
point of view. Further, we know that Paul is a good guy (is, has
been, and will always be)—the kind of guy who can take over
our flow of feelings for that good but troubled woman, Tara
Martin Brent. We also know that we must watch Phoebe Tyler
like a hawk, the thunderbolts of her destruction being the
works of an unpredictable evil genius. We identify with Paul
Martin in his coming affliction. The camera guides us smoothly
into his identification. The fist we see clenched in Phoebe Tyler's lap is, in a sense, coming our way. When Paul responds to
Phoebe's threat ("You dare say that!") we say the same thing.
We are as shocked as he is! We knew she was bad, we knew she
was a guilt monger, but could she be that bad? (Paul: "I don't
believe what I'm hearing!") At this point the camera gets up and
travels with Paul as he walks around his desk in astonishment.

We travel with him as he circles this malignant creature until he has come full circle and stares down at Phoebe Tyler, standing over her, from screen right.

Just as the initial close-ups left us in little doubt that we were in the middle of a confrontation, the circling camera movement cues us to another basic unit of meaning in the intricate choreography of soap opera emotion. The camera *pas de deux* tells us we are in the preliminaries of a fighting dance, a circling of some major issue or theme that will pit two characters against each other until the issue is temporarily resolved or suspended and the circling stops. In the process, as the camera moves away from Paul Martin's point of view, our identification with him shifts, for we are now watching both characters. Most of the rest of the scene plays from objective angles and classic shot/reverse shot patterns.

We see both characters equally, then, as Phoebe Tyler continues her bitter assault on Paul Martin ("You left Anne alone to take care of that mentally defective child all by herself . . . while you—you went out having secret luncheon dates!"). Paul, under ordinary circumstances a paragon of self-control, becomes more and more enraged ("That is a lie!" "You don't know what the hell you're talking about!" "Now that is enough!"). The scene culminates with his command that his accuser return and sit down (she had been preparing to leave). Then Paul Martin does something that has rarely been done before or since to Phoebe Tyler—he tells her the truth about herself. The scene shifts into a decisive reversal of Phoebe Tyler's verbal onslaught, powered by Paul Martin's (and the viewer's) cumulative rage at the malign conspiracies Phoebe Tyler has fostered. Most of the shots in this part of the scene are again from Paul Martin's point of view. He has now returned to his desk and is standing behind it looking down at Phoebe Tyler in the chair in front of him. We not only see what Paul Martin sees but follow his hand and finger as it points and gesticulates. The speech is a powerful one. ("Maybe I failed Anne, but for a little while she had a baby to love . . . *You* failed her from the moment she was born! Oh yes, just because she was a little bit awkward in growing up, just because she wasn't quite beautiful enough to suit your stupid, snobbish pride—you ridiculed her! You made her feel small and ugly, you—you told her how ashamed you were of her—remember that? You also laughed at her because she didn't look particularly good in those idiotic, over-designed dresses that you forced her to wear. You were an unfit mother then and you are an unfit mother now!")

As Phoebe Tyler draws herself up to leave, stricken and outraged, he says: "Oh, that's right, good. Just get the hell out of here!" Paul Martin has never been angrier in his life, and he displays emotion that we have rarely, if ever, witnessed in him. Phoebe Tyler manages one parting shot ("Anne's never coming back to you. I'll see to that!") and leaves the scene. Paul sinks back exhausted into his chair, overcome by the outpouring of feeling that has just occurred. In the last shot we see that diffuse inner look that ends so many soap scenes, in this case from exhaustion and the self-questioning and doubt that Phoebe Tyler's attack, as unwarranted as it was, has begun to stir in him. Fade to black and a commercial.

Let us summarize our progressive involvement in this scene. We were already within the soap world when the Paul Martin–Phoebe Tyler scene began. We moved from a close-up of the troubled but appealing Tara Martin Brent to a close-up of Paul Martin. Then we began to see things in the scene very much the way Paul saw them. We witnessed (and in some sense participated in) an elaborately choreographed exchange of emotionally charged attack and counterattack. In the course of the confrontation, when Paul Martin bade Phoebe Tyler return to the room, we circled the characters with the camera as the characters circled each other in a sort of revolving theater in the round. At the end of the scene we came to see Phoebe Tyler from a particular point of view. As Paul Martin pointed his finger of judgment upon her from above, we too looked down upon her, judged her with him, and cheered his eloquent denunciation. The camera not only showed us what was happening (in a realist sense), it directed our feelings and engagement in the narrative in very specific ways.

In addition, we see in this scene features of narrative economy that are common to almost every soap opera. The first is what soap writers call "backstory."[9] It is a way of catching the viewer up on what has been happening over days, weeks, and even years, through condensed narratives spoken by the characters to each other. Like name-labeling (soap characters invariably address each other by their first names), backstories help us tune in quickly to who is who if we are new or have not seen the soap opera in a while. It is a courtesy not only to the viewer watching the show at the time but also to the chain of people who may rely on that viewer for updates and summaries of the plot. Backstories can occur audiovisually (in a flashback, for instance, or in an audio memory echo) as well as verbally. Some scenes are primarily devoted to backstory; in others it makes a more fleeting appearance.

In the Phoebe Tyler–Paul Martin scene the backstory is a very basic one, stretching years back and detailing what Phoebe Tyler had done to her daughter Anne at a very young age. We also have an allusion by Phoebe Tyler to something said to have occurred at an earlier time (a luncheon date of Paul Martin with another woman) but which, not knowing the incident directly, we assume to have been twisted by Phoebe, in her usual insinuating manner, into something it was not. Such an allusion might provoke a soap viewer who didn't know about this luncheon to ask another viewer for his or her own backstory explanation.

A second prominent feature of the Paul Martin–Phoebe Tyler scene—as well as the scene before with Tara and little Phil and most, if not all, soap opera situations—is what I call "the missing other." Soap opera is built on twos and threes. Its basic structure rests on two—generally two characters engaged in intimate dialogue (Tara and little Phil, Paul and Phoebe, and, in earlier scenes that day in *All My Children*, Benny Sago and Donna Beck, Erica Kane and Mark Dalton, Mona Kane and Nick Davis). Sometimes a third person will enter the scene via doorbell, door knock, telephone call, or simply by walking into the room. But whether or not a third person becomes physically present, a soap opera scene will more often than not revolve around a missing other. (In the case of little Phil and Tara, the missing other is big Phil, Tara's husband and little Phil's father. In the Paul Martin–Phoebe Tyler scene, the missing other is Anne, Phoebe's daughter and Paul's wife.) Certain objects in the soap world become emblematic of the missing other—the telephone or door, for instance, can remind us of the missing other and the possibility that he or she will call or knock or that news will be received of this other person. These emblems also call to mind a fundamental issue or recurrent problem associated with the missing person. (Who or what caused Anne's breakdown? Will Paul remain faithful to her throughout?) Fidelity to a missing other is often the issue at stake. The invisible but central participation of the missing other parallels in an interesting way the invisible participation of the soap opera viewer, for whose sake the soap opera rite is enacted.

A third feature of this scene that is common to soap operas generally is the eye-level camera angle. We may look up or down at a character, but almost always we will be looking from the eye level of another character. Extreme low or high angles are used on occasion, but they are rare. The effect of this eye-level view, combined with the shot/reverse shot patterns of "classical" Hollywood editing[10] and a predominance of over-the-shoulder shots and z-axis alignments (one character in the foreground, another set deeper in the background on a z-axis, with the camera relating the two) works to reinforce the realist illusion. We feel that we are right there. We pull back to a high angle or wide establishing shot only when we leave (literally pull out of) the soap opera world.

It is when this pullback occurs, or the scene dissolves or fades to black or cuts to a commercial break, that the viewer is likely to start considering the drama from a critical perspective. At this point the soap aficionado can marshal all the resources of prior knowledge and soap expertise that he or she possesses. If other viewers are present to exchange views, all the better. Solitary viewers may rehearse opinions for later discussion with those who have not seen this episode and need to be caught up. Thoughts about the story, characterization, acting, and writing are all grist for the mill of soap opera armchair analysts.

Turning now from *All My Children* to *General Hospital*, we encounter other techniques that are widely used in soap narrative. *General Hospital* was already gaining on *All My Children* when I taped the episode of February 2, 1979, and six months later the show was achieving number one ratings for daytime serials. This was due in part to the efforts of producer-director Gloria Monty, who had taken over the series the year before. *General Hospital* had been on the air sixteen years at this point, and some of its cast had been there from the beginning.

Being able to catch up on a year and a half of plot developments in *General Hospital* in a single day, when I watched it again in the summer of 1980, made me appreciate the efficient back-story mechanism on this soap opera. However, I missed the excitement of the topic that had been on everyone's mind in February of 1979 when I first watched: the deadly "Laza Fever" epidemic. I was intrigued at that time by the ways in which

General Hospital assimilated a major film genre: the disaster epic.
At one point in this episode, the hospital's general alarm went
off, warning the staff and patients that the hospital was under
quarantine, and we were treated to a rare high angle bird's-eye
view of the entire staff of General Hospital, frozen in postures
of shock and disbelief. It was this kind of experimentation with
the standard patterns that excited viewers, I think, and put
General Hospital in the number one position.

Camera and sound codes work together in highly integrated
fashion in *General Hospital*. In one scene, for instance, a character
named LEE BALDWIN is dying of Laza Fever as his lover, DR. GAIL
ADAMSON, whispers, "Lee's running out of time; he's got to
respond now!" Her words overlap with the rising sound of an
amplified heartbeat, a dramatic swell in the music, and a cut to
Lee's pale and drawn face against the pillow of his bed. We hear
an ambulance siren in the distance, and the picture dissolves to
the *General Hospital* logo scene of the hospital gates with an
ambulance rushing through. At this dramatic moment of suspended crisis, I counted eight levels of visual and auditory signs
superimposed one upon the other in the same frame:

Audio signs
1. the rising level of heartbeat
2. the gradual crescendo of music (the *General Hospital* theme)
3. the sound of the ambulance siren approaching from the distance

Visual signs
1. the curving white line of the plasma transfusion to Lee's arm
2. Lee's face, almost a death mask
3. the bars on the gates of General Hospital (they intersect
   diagonally the plasma transfusion line in the dissolve)
4. the ambulance racing through the gates
5. the hospital itself, rising in granite grandeur in the distance,
   blue skies and white clouds overhead

The camera work is clearly crucial to the meaning of these
·signs (the line of plasma transfusion has been consistently
juxtaposed in previous shots with the telephone, both lifelines
to the characters involved, and the iron bars of the hospital gate
are dissolved into the picture in such a way as to portend
entrapment and death). Just as significantly, camera and sound
are the means by which we experience a general "thickening" in
the scene, a condensation of picture and sound images. This
thickening in the flow of the narrative (rising music, truck-in of

camera, suspended movement and expression) characteristically occurs in the suspended denouement that ends soap scenes. In contrast to game shows, where the piling up of images and sounds (applause, cheers, bells, buzzers, and screaming mixed with quick cuts of audience, emcee, game paraphernalia, and contestants) speeds up the action to herald an opening fanfare or winning round, at these condensed moments in soap opera things get still. The images congeal into fixed tableaux. Meaning is suspended, deferred, until we return, several scenes later, to the point where the scene was frozen in time.

Why is the action suspended this way, with the accompanying distortion of time? It has been suggested that the convention of slowed time, speech, and action in soap opera developed in the thirties on radio soaps when scripts were thin and actors and actresses had to fill time.[11] According to this theory, soap opera readers had to become adept at long, meaningful pauses, and the practice simply continued into the television era of soap opera. Another explanation—what might be called the sexual theory—compares the pleasure of deferred narrative gratification in soap opera with the wham-bam-thank-you-ma'am action of prime time adventure and cop shows. Whatever its origins, the tableau style of presentation matches soap opera's camera style (close-ups are conducive to subtle movement and nuance-filled expression), and it also suits the primary content of soap opera: intense, concentrated emotion.

The hospital scene also demonstrates the importance of certain symbolic objects in soap opera. As Lee begins to show signs of recovery, Gail goes to the phone, overcome with emotion, to phone Lee's son SCOTTIE. The phone—an all-important object in soap operas, since the intercession of fate constantly rides on the telephone's ability to communicate with the missing other—rings in the living room where Scottie and his girlfriend LAURA wait anxiously for the news. The camera cuts to a close-up of the phone filling the lower right portion of the screen. Scottie and Laura are huddled together on a couch in the background, tiny objects before the phone that looms before them. They jump when the phone first rings, and slowly, painfully, Scottie approaches the receiver. But Laura must answer it for him, so great is his fear of bad news. The entire telephone conversation is further drawn out as Gail, choked with emotion, is unable to speak in the first thirty seconds of the call. The use of the telephone in this scene exploits to the fullest the tension between what we know and what the characters know,

between Scottie's fears and our certain knowledge of his father's recovery.

Six other times that day, the telephone played a crucial part
in the story. On the level of plot mechanics, telephones as well
as doorbells and sudden knocks on the door are useful for
transitions in soap operas—we have to move from character to
character, scene to scene, and telephone calls admirably accomplish that purpose. But the fetishism of their portrayal goes
far beyond that. The telephone is a symbol of communication,
of talk, and despite a new predilection for action,[12] talk is still
what soap operas are all about. The telephone is used for a
special kind of talk—communication with someone who is not
there in one sense, present and close in another. The telephone
is thus a perfect emblem of the recurrent problem of soap
characters: together yet alone (in their secret feelings,
thoughts, and fantasies), apart yet together (in their passions,
obsessions, and searches for the missing other). An analysis of
scenes in *General Hospital* shows the telephone placed in almost
every scene between characters and beside them, significantly
foregrounded or subtly worked into the background. And the
telephone *in potentia* (the call that might come, the missing
husband, friend, or daughter who may or may not pick up the
phone) is an even more powerful ritual object in soap opera
than the telephone in use.[13]

Other symbolic objects recur, including surgical masks in
medical scenes. They are perfect signs for the masks (the personae) all characters in the soap world are assumed to wear. We
must peer carefully into the eyes of the masked doctors and
nurses in these life-and-death hospital scenes to discover their
true identities, their true thoughts and feelings.

These conventional objects—telephone, doorbell, surgical
mask—become invested with magical significance, helping or
hindering the soap characters' quest. But such objects do not
become meaningful by themselves; it is the camera that gives
them their symbolic power. As filmmakers like Alfred Hitchcock so forcefully demonstrate, the significance of objects is
based on our filmic perception of them. We do not see these
objects in any pure sense, but only in the composition of the
frame and to the degree that they are brought to our attention
by the camera lens. This is true in soap opera at least as much as
it is in film.

Much more could be said about the role of camera techniques
and sound conventions in soap opera. The musical common-

places that key our emotions to certain characters and themes warrant attention, for instance, as does the relationship between camera styles and narrative strategies of particular soap operas. For example, chiaroscuro lighting and rich two-tone color motifs give a number of soap operas, including *The Young and the Restless*, a distinct visual style. Centering an archetypal dream and fantasy, these shows are quite different in character from soaps like *All My Children* and *General Hospital*, which take pride in grounding themselves in realistic portrayals of relationships and emotional experiences.

Without attempting to be comprehensive, I have examined here some ways that audiovisual codes shape our experience of soap opera. Analytic procedures that have been applied in the past to script and acting styles can help us understand the symbolic codes of camera and sound as well. Only when we understand these codes can we fully understand the rhetoric of soap opera.

NOTES

1. Bruce Gronbeck, "Television Criticism and the Classrooms," *Journal of the Illinois Speech and Theatre Association* 33 (1979), p. 10.
2. Donald Horton and R. Richard Wohl, "Mass Communication and Para-Social Interaction: Observations on Intimacy at a Distance," *Drama in Life: The Uses of Communication in Society* (New York: Hastings House, 1976), pp. 212–227.
3. For extensive discussions of the realist illusion in film and photography see Andre Bazin, *What is Cinema?*, vol. 1 (Berkeley: University of California Press, 1967), pp. 9–23, Siegfried Kracauer, *Theory of Film: The Redemption of Physical Reality* (New York: Oxford University Press, 1976 [1960]), pp. 27–74, and Roland Barthes, *Image-Music-Text* (New York: Hill and Wang, 1977), pp. 15–33. Television adds something special to the realist equation: the sense of immediacy that developed out of television's origins as a live medium and continues today in the kinds of programming that television does best: spontaneous encounters in talk shows, coverage of news events as they happen, and intimate family drama in soap opera that seems to evolve before our eyes.
4. Soap operas vary considerably in this regard. Some soaps have a visual style that is almost entirely close-up and extreme close-up (*The Young and the Restless*, for instance); others (such as *All My Children* and *General Hospital*) alternate between medium shots, close-ups, and extreme close-ups, saving the extreme close-ups for moments of dramatic intensity or revelation.
5. *All My Children*, taped May 30, 1978, and *General Hospital*, taped February 1, 1979. James L. Kinneavy of the Freshman English program at the University of Texas, the Batts Language Lab, and the Undergraduate Library at the University of Texas all provided assistance in this project.
6. July 24, 1980 was the next time I tuned in to these programs.
7. In an interview on NBC's *20/20* on May 24, 1980, Agnes Nixon mentioned

a forthcoming book that would chronicle the doings of the people in *All My Children* over all the years it has been on the air.

8. R. E. Johnson, Jr., "The Dialogue of Novelty and Repetition: Structure in 'All My Children,'" *Journal of Popular Culture* 10:3 (Winter 1976), pp. 560–570.

9. Dan Wakefield, *All Her Children* (New York: Avon Books, 1977).

10. For an interesting discussion of this kind of editing pattern see Daniel Dayan, "The Tutor-Code of Classical Cinema," in *Movie and Methods*, Bill Nichols, ed. (Berkeley: University of California Press, 1976), pp. 438–451.

11. "Soap Operas: Sex and Suffering in the Afternoon," *Time* (January 12, 1976), pp. 46–53.

12. One of many evidences of soap opera's borrowing from prime time narratives in the interchange that is occurring between daytime and evening drama on television.

13. Telephones have not always had this function in television soap opera. In an early 1950s soap opera out of Chicago that I watched recently (*Hawkins Falls*, 1952) there were no telephones at all, nor were the conventions of scene entry truck-ins, tableau freezes, sweeping circular camera movements, and intimate close-ups developed to any significant degree. (These observations were drawn from viewing cines in the J. Fred McDonald collection in Chicago.)

DAVID BARKER

TELEVISION PRODUCTION TECHNIQUES AS COMMUNICATION

Some scholars of mass communication have begun to approach the television message as a visual text and interpretation of this text as a process of "decoding" (Fiske & Hartley, 1978; Silverstone, 1981). Perhaps the foremost proponent of this approach is Stuart Hall, who identifies this process of "decoding" as a "determinate moment" in television discourse (1980:129). Yet, Hall makes it quite clear that the process of "encoding" is equally determinate:

> A "raw" historical event cannot, *in that form*, be transmitted by, say, a television newscast. Events can only be signified within the aural-visual forms of the television discourse. . . . The "message form" is the necessary "form of appearance" of the event in its passage from source to receiver. Thus, the transposition into and out of the "message form" is a determinate moment. (129)

Within the growing body of work based upon the encoding/decoding model, however (e.g., Brunsdon & Morley, 1978; Morley, 1980; Wren-Lewis, 1983), discussion has been restricted almost exclusively to only one of these "determinate moments": decoding. Indeed, the process of encoding, despite its homologous position in the model, has by comparison, been virtually ignored.[1]

The purpose of this study is to examine this process of encoding or, more specifically, the relationship between narrative structure and production techniques, as it is manifested in entertainment television. It is the thesis of this essay that the communicative ability of any television narrative is, in large part, a function of the production techniques utilized in its creation.[2]

The two programs chosen for this study were *All in the Family* (*AITF*) and *M*A*S*H*. The decision to examine these particular programs was based on two factors. First, both programs were pivotal to their own specific narrative traditions. *AITF* represents the tradition of domestic situation comedies that revolved around a single axial character—in this case Archie Bunker. Archie was axial inasmuch as plot lines were usually built directly upon his character, and most other characters in the program were usually defined not so much by their own idiosyncrasies as by their relationship with him. We can find many of the seeds of *AITF* in *The Life of Riley, Make Room for Daddy, The Honeymooners,* and *Father Knows Best.*

M*A*S*H, on the other hand, was pivotal to a tradition of what might be termed ensemble comedies in which each character had a persona of his or her own, distinct from the rest of the ensemble. Yet the interplay and conflict among such characters worked to strengthen the personalities of all concerned, making the ensemble comedy very much more than the sum of its parts. Foreshadowings of *M*A*S*H* can be found in *Burns and Allen, The Addams Family, Gilligan's Island,* and *Hogan's Heroes.*

Prior to *AITF*, network situation comedy in general had become entrenched in what could be called "1960s telefilm values," which were characterized by a highly utilitarian approach to the communicative abilities of even the most basic production techniques. As exemplified by such programs as *My Three Sons* or *Leave it to Beaver*, this was a production style based on a highly repetitive and predictable shooting pattern: an exterior establishing shot (e.g., the Cleaver home as Ward pulls into the driveway) followed by sequences of alternating medium shots as the narrative progresses (e.g., Ward comes in the front door to be greeted by June who proceeds to inform him of the daily crises; Ward then decides on a course of action and initiates it). This pattern was occasionally punctuated with a tighter shot, such as a medium close-up (bust shot), but close-ups were virtually never used. Similarly, performer movement (blocking) was utilized only as a way to move characters into and out of an environment: Beaver walks into his bedroom and throws himself on the bed or Wally walks into the kitchen and stands by the sink. As Millerson (1979:287) has pointed out, there is a great deal of meaning in such production variables as shot selection and performer blocking. Programs produced with these 1960s telefilm values suggest that reinforcing the structure of the program narrative (e.g., the ebb and flow of conflicts) with particular production techniques was not a fundamental concern for the producers.

With *AITF* and *M*A*S*H*, however, close analysis of a number of episodes indicated that, for these two series, the relationship between narrative structure and production techniques was quite different. Thus, the second reason for choosing these two programs was that both were also products of conscious decisions by their respective creators, Norman Lear and Larry Gelbart, to utilize specific production techniques in specific ways.

In preparation for this study, twenty episodes selected at random of each series were analyzed for their use of particular production techniques, and it soon became clear that a number of these techniques—among them, control of screen space, lighting and set design, layers of action, and parallel editing—were manipulated significantly for narrative as well as aesthetic reasons. This analysis made it possible to draw some general observations about the role each of these techniques played in the communication of the particular narrative structures of *AITF* and *M*A*S*H*. As a way of providing specific examples for these observations, one randomly chosen episode from each series was videotaped and subjected to a rigorous shot-by-shot analysis.[3]

Before moving to a discussion of the way these variables were manipulated in relation to the program narratives, it would be useful to explore the nature of the narratives themselves. In Archie Bunker, Lear had an axial character whose persona was often patriarchal in the sense he was myopic and tyrannical.[4] Lear has stated that Archie reminded him a great deal of his own father (Adler, 1979:xx) and that much of *AITF* was intended to portray the patriarch as buffoon.[5] Lear thus decided to shoot *AITF* in proscenium. This meant that the cameras (and thus the viewing audience) would maintain a distinct distance; they would not be allowed to move into the set—into Archie's domain—for reverse angles. This, and the fact that the program was produced live-on-tape in front of an audience, created a great sense of theatricality. There were practical economic reasons for such a decision (Adler, 1979:xxii), but there were equally important narrative reasons as well: shooting in proscenium helped maintain Archie not only as the axial character but as the buffoonish patriarch. By preventing the cameras from moving into the set for reverse angles, viewers were allowed only to look at Archie, not with him.

Lear's decision to shoot *AITF* in proscenium with multiple cameras pulled situation comedy back to its roots. He essentially employed an updated version of the Electronicam system, a multiple film camera system Jackie Gleason had employed successfully on *The Honeymooners* some twenty years earlier (Mitz, 1983:123). But if *AITF* pulled situation comedy back to its roots, *M*A*S*H* pushed it forward into the somewhat more complicated aesthetic realm of the contemporary cinema. When Gelbart first saw the movie version of *M*A*S*H*, he realized the intrinsic role director Robert Altman's reflexive shooting style played in the film's narrative (Gelbart, 1983). Altman was not dealing with the all-pervasive influence of a single axial character, but with the nuances of an ensemble of characters, and the apparent aimlessness of his camera movements, the sheer "busyness" of his shots, actually helped define the characters and their relationships.[6] Thus a shooting style similar to that employed by Altman would be important in maintaining the spirit of the ensemble: a single camera with multiple set-ups, unimpeded by spatial or psychological boundaries, able to capture visual patterns of great complexity. In short, one might say that a more "aggressive" use of the camera than had been the norm for situation comedies would be necessary; programs like *Leave it to Beaver* had employed a single camera, but little effort had been made to use the camera (or any production variable) to reinforce the narrative.

THEORETICAL APPROACH

Effective control and manipulation of screen space is one of the most crucial elements of television aesthetics. While there are many ways of delineating such control (Arnheim, 1974; Burch, 1973; Heath, 1981; Zettl, 1973), for the purposes of this study I distinguished between two broad categories: camera space and performer space.

Camera space is composed of two elements: horizontal field of view and what I have termed "camera proximity." Horizontal field of view is the type of shot: CU (close-up, head and shoulders), MCU (medium close-up, taken at the bustline), MS (medium shot, taken at the waist), WS (wide shot, which encompasses the entire body or set), etc. The importance of field of view is underscored by Wurtzel and Dominick (1971) who argue that much of the perceived effectiveness of a television program depends on the way the director chooses the shots the audience is to see:

> The viewer, as represented by the camera, does not remain in one viewing position. He sees the action from both close-range and at a distance. (104)

The second component of camera space, camera proximity, is the location of the camera in relation to the performer—in front of them, behind them, etc. In *AITF*, camera proximity and, to a somewhat lesser extent, field of view, worked together to establish definite "geographical" boundaries for the cameras that were rarely violated. As will soon become evident, each performer in *AITF* had his or her own space that the other performers (to a greater or lesser degree) could move into and out of freely. But the camera could do so only at the risk of making the viewer uncomfortable. Such movement could be used for dramatic effect or to change the meaning of the narrative (e.g., the episode in which Archie and Mike were trapped in the basement and a camera was pulled into the set for a tight 2-shot as their usual antagonism gave way to a momentary rapport). In *M*A*S*H*, on the other hand, geographical boundaries for the camera were loosely defined if at all. The camera was allowed to move at will without fear of the movement necessarily affecting a change in the narrative.

The second type of television space distinguished here is *performer space*. This is primarily a function of performer blocking (positioning and movement) along axes. These axes are defined in relation to the camera: the horizontal x-axis perpendicular to the camera's line of sight and the z-axis of depth toward and away from the camera or parallel with the camera's line of sight (Zettl, 1973:174). Each of the cameras in multiple camera shooting or each new set-up of the camera in film style shooting has its own x- and z-axis. The distinction to be made concerns the way these axes are utilized.

Axis utilization is perhaps best described in terms of vectors. Zettl defines vectors as "directional forces [within the screen] which lead our eyes from one point to another within, or even outside of, the picture field" (1973:140). Further, Zettl distinguishes among three types of vectors: graphic (created by stationary objects arranged in such a way that they lead the viewer's eyes in a particular direction (e.g., a row of smoke-stacks), index (something that points unquestionably in a specific direction, e.g., a person looking or pointing), and motion (created by an object that is actually moving or perceived as moving onscreen) (Zettl, 1973:140–142). In discussing performer blocking the most important of these vectors is, of course, the motion vector.

COMPARATIVE ANALYSIS

In *AITF*, performers were blocked almost exclusively along the x-axis as they moved from the front door through the living and dining rooms to the kitchen and back again. The only time there was a real potential for movement toward or away from the cameras occurred when a character moved upstage to the stairway or downstage to the television set. *M*A*S*H*, on the other hand, utilized a great deal of movement along z-axis motion vectors. Because the camera was free to move into the performers' space for shot-reverse shot sequences, performers could move toward and away from the camera as easily as they could move perpendicular to it. In the episode of *AITF*, the vast majority (92 percent) of performer blocking was along x-axes. In *M*A*S*H*, the majority (78 percent) of performer blocking was along z-axes.

It is significant how the two components of space—camera and performer—worked together to reinforce the communicative ability of their respective narrative structures. In terms of space, the proscenium technique such as the one utilized in *AITF* would seem to favor an axial, somewhat patriarchal narrative structure in that it allows the viewer to only look at a character rather than with them. This is especially true when the patriarchal status of a character is the object of derision, as was the case with Archie. Such a status would be undercut somewhat if viewers were allowed to encroach upon that character's space proximally. Befitting a proscenium approach, the cameras thus became a fourth wall, allowing viewers to approach Archie's space from essentially only one direction.

Viewers could, and did, encroach upon Archie, however, through field of view: close-ups of Archie were often used for dramatic or comedic effect. This was especially true for reaction shots. In the particular episode under discussion here, there were six reaction shots, all were of Archie. Much of Archie's patriarchal stance, and the humor derived from making fun of such a stance, was a result not so much of what Archie said as the way he reacted to the words and actions of others. He appeared as the long-suffering father figure enduring the ignorance of the "children" about him (e.g., his reaction to Edith's news that she had promised their house for Florence and Herbert's wedding or his reaction to Edith's piano playing and singing during the wedding). Indeed, such reactions almost became narrative conventions within the series itself, aided considerably by the somewhat plastic quality of Carroll O'Connor's face and his remarkable ability to use it to show numerous inflections. Significantly, too, such reaction shots just as often showed Archie losing face, as he once again became the buffoon.

Reaction shots on $M*A*S*H$, however, were rare—the selected episode had none at all. Arguably, this was due to the fact that, in an ensemble comedy, the emotional reaction of any one character is in large part defined by the corporate reaction of the entire cast (witness the fact that in those episodes where a facial reaction of some sort was necessary the camera often panned across the faces of the entire cast).

The use of screen space to define a character in AITF was perhaps most conspicuous with regard to Archie and his chair. It was no accident that this particular chair occupied the point in the set where the x-axis vectors intersected the only real z-axis vector, that running from the television to the staircase. The action of AITF for the most part revolved around this throne; in fact, the space it usually occupied was the exact spot where Florence and Herbert said their vows. Normally, this was space Archie guarded zealously. Thus, the audience was never allowed to circle his chair or sneak up on it from behind, assuming Archie's place through a POV (point-of-view) shot.

The use of camera and performer space to reinforce the narrative was equally evident in $M*A*S*H$, where a large proportion of performer movement was employed as a transition device, to move the story from one subplot to another. In the sample episode, this was evident from the opening scene, which took place in the operating room (OR). In this scene, all three of the plotlines for the episode were laid out in dialogue between Hawkeye, Charles, B.J., and Potter. As they talked, Father Mulcahy paced back and forth, establishing a motion vector between them, asking questions that stimulated necessary plot information. The camera panned with Mulcahy as he moved, his movement acting not only as a transition between the surgeons but between the plotlines as well. More typically, however, movement-as-transition was achieved by having two characters moving along converging vectors meet, converse, then move on. The camera would pan or truck to follow them until they converged with another couplet standing still or moving in the opposite direction. The first couplet would "hand off" the story to the second and the camera would begin a new sequence with the second couplet.

This type of transition was seen when the Canadian leaves the *M*A*S*H* compound. Klinger escorts him to his truck and tells him goodbye. Klinger then continues across the compound along a z-axis until he converges with Hawkeye moving along the z-axis from the opposite direction. They stop, converse, and move on. Similar movement was used earlier in the episode when a nurse who had been talking to Hawkeye rises from their table and starts across the mess tent on the x-axis. The camera panned to follow her and came to rest on Klinger and the Canadian moving through the chow line on the z-axis.

This performer movement occurred in several planes simultaneously, thereby layering the action between foreground, middleground, and background. People were constantly moving in and out of the frame, past doorways and windows, between the camera and the subject of the shot, behind the subject, crowding the screen with visual information. To a very great extent, this layering was a result of the extensive use of z-axis motion vectors. As Zettl points out, "By placing objects and people along the z-axis in a specific way . . . we can make the viewer distinguish between foreground, middleground, and background rather readily . . ." (1973:207). This can of course be compared with *AITF*, where extensive use of x-axis motion vectors resulted in the action usually being carried out on only one plane as opposed to three or four.

The use of performer movement as a transition device and the layering of that movement into multiple planes was obviously tailor-made for an ensemble comedy like *M*A*S*H* which utilized interweaving characters and plots. The movement itself acted very much as a needle and thread, sewing the narrative together. But the multiple-plot narrative structure of *M*A*S*H* also benefited from parallel editing (the intercutting of two activities occurring at roughly the same time in different locations) which was used to enhance the program narrative by playing the dialogue and actions in one subplot of the narrative off those in another. Put another way, parallel editing was used to help establish comedic relationships.

The comedic relationships in M*A*S*H were sometimes obvious. For example, there was a cut from Hawkeye berating Klinger for paying off a five dollar debt with a bottle of wine to Charles begging Hawkeye to tell him where he got the wine. In another example, there was a cut from Potter and Klinger pouring Charles' wine into their stranded jeep to Hawkeye pulling the cork from a wine bottle in preparation for his tryst with the winner of his essay contest. Other times, however, the relationships were far more subtle, as when Charles, who has been talking to Hawkeye and B.J., turns his head towards the door of the Swamp and we cut to a moment later that day as Hawkeye and B.J. leave the Swamp and walk outside. In either case, however, it was the preciseness with which these words and actions were matched through editing (and judicious shot selection) that allowed the viewer to not only jump across space and time with no loss of orientation but to likewise make the comedic connection between a stranded Potter and Klinger and an amorous Hawkeye. These techniques also enabled the divergent strains of an ensemble comedy like M*A*S*H to converge into a unified narrative structure rather than collapse into a series of isolated vignettes.

The establishment of comedic relationships also owed a great deal to timing. This was particularly true with regard to AITF. Inasmuch as AITF was shot live-on-tape with multiple cameras, most "editing" as such was done on the spot by switching between the cameras. Thus, postproduction editing, while usually necessary, was not the process of shot-by-shot assembly that an episode of M*A*S*H entailed. Nevertheless, in AITF the establishment of comedic relationships and the proper coordination of dialogue and movement were just as essential. Due to the factors of shooting in real time, comparatively fixed camera positions, and a lesser degree of postproduction editing, however, the comedy had to be played and the comedic relationships made clear by the performers themselves. This meant that split-second timing was paramount to the success of AITF (Lynch, 1973:267–271).

By contrast, the single-camera film-style technique utilized in M*A*S*H did not require the performers to say their lines in real time to the extent the multiple-camera live-on-tape technique utilized in AITF did. In a shot/reverse-shot sequence, for instance, since only one camera was used, one member of the couplet would say all their lines for that camera position; then the camera would have to be moved for the lines of the second member of the couplet. Timing, so very important to the proper execution of comedy, was thus partially suspended, and only completely restored again when the editor assembled the film itself. Thus, performers in an ensemble comedy shot film-style must learn to set up their timing somewhat differently than those performers in a comedy like *AITF* shot in real time.[7]

Since the matter of timing was so crucial in *AITF*, every character had to know his or her blocking precisely, but this was especially true in Archie's case; it was through Archie's blocking that his role as the axial character within the narrative structure of *AITF* manifested itself so visibly. During the wedding ceremony for Florence and Herbert, Archie was constantly in motion, pulling one character after another about the set from one group and comedic situation to the next. It begins with Archie pulling a reluctant Herbert down the stairs and through the guests. Leaving him, he crosses the room to Edith and pulls her to the Priest in an effort to get the ceremony started. He then pulls Edith to the piano, pushes her onto the bench and tells her to start playing, only to return once again to tell her to stop. Archie then goes up the stairs and returns with Florence, depositing her next to Herbert. He crosses back to the piano, picks up Edith, and pulls her over to Florence and Herbert. The scene continues in a similar manner, with Archie orchestrating virtually every movement.

While this particular episode was exceptional in the number of people involved in this last scene and the degree of their movement, it was an exception that illustrates the point. In a scene this involved, precise execution of blocking and dialogue—both matters of timing—was essential. Any lapse in this execution would have prevented the director from getting the necessary shot. Further, the degree to which the timing in the scene depended on Archie's blocking was reflective of his axial status within the series as a whole.

The control of screen space through field of view, camera proximity, performer blocking, parallel editing, and timing all move a great distance towards explaining why *AITF* and *M*A*S*H* "looked" the way they did. But much of the particular "look" of these two programs, especially with regard to the division of the visual field into planes and the articulation of depth, was also a function of lighting and set design.

LIGHTING AND SET DESIGN

As Millerson (1982) points out, television is inherently a two-dimensional medium and the careful control of light and shadow is essential for creating the illusion of a third dimension. Zettl (1973) distinguishes two types of television lighting techniques. The first, chiaroscuro, is lighting for light-dark contrast. "The basic aim is to articulate space," writes Zettl, "that is, to clarify and intensify the three-dimensional property of things and the space that surrounds them, to give the scene an expressive quality" (38). The second type of lighting, Notan, "is lighting for simple visibility. Flat lighting has no particular aesthetic function; its basic function is that of illumination. Flat lighting is emotionally flat, too. It lacks drama" (44).

Notan lighting was obviously utilized on *AITF*, where the set was lit flatly and evenly. There was no regard for time of day—it was as bright inside the Bunker house at night as it was during the day. Similarly, there was no regard for light source—when it was day there was no appreciable difference in the amount of light coming through the windows than when it was night. Most importantly, shadows were virtually nonexistent. Thus, the fact that action occurred on only one plane was reinforced by a lighting design that, through the absence of shadow, helped to create an environment of only one plane.

*M*A*S*H*, however, utilized chiaroscuro lighting, primarily in the form of source-directed lighting: during the day the sets were bright with "sunlight" streaming through windows while, at night, shadows increased markedly, the sets becoming dimmer, with darkened windows and light provided by lamps or overhead fixtures. Yet even during daylight hours, many depth clues were offered by shadows. As an example, in the mess tent, as Klinger glances at Hawkeye, there is a shot of Hawkeye sitting at his table. Even though there is nothing between the camera and Hawkeye to act as a point of reference, it is still obvious that Hawkeye is completely across the tent from Klinger. The fact that the shadows deepen as they move toward Hawkeye articulates the amount of space that exists between him and Klinger.

Set design can likewise articulate space and, through the use of depth clues, degrees of depth in the televisual image. Zettl (1973:179) suggests a number of these clues, but three are of particular importance to the discussion here: overlapping planes, relative size, and height in the plane.

M*A*S*H utilized sets of great depth, and these three depth clues were all conspicuously evident. Overlapping planes (in which one object partially covers another so that it appears to be lying in front) were used in numerous shots. For example, shooting across a bunk when Hawkeye and Charles were in the Swamp arguing over the wine or shooting through the jeep windshield as Potter and Klinger return with the curare. Relative size (guessing how large something is or how far away it is by the size of its screen image) was also used a great deal due to the placement of set pieces in relation to the set and the camera (e.g., in the mess tent, shooting across one table at Hawkeye sitting next to the window with Klinger and the Canadian sitting in the background) or movement in various planes (e.g., Hawkeye and B.J. leaving the Swamp and walking towards the camera with jeeps and trucks passing behind them and nurses walking between them and the camera). There were also several occasions when height in plane (the higher something is in the picture field the further away it is) was used (e.g., Klinger turning around as the Canadian leaves to see Hawkeye approaching from across the compound).

Another conspicuous characteristic of the set design on *M*A*S*H* was the almost constant presence of the outside world. In the mess tent or in the "swamp," flaps were tied back, allowing viewers to watch the external as well as the internal workings of the camp: people walking by, jeeps passing, conversations being carried on, ballgames being played. Yet this presence in no way de-emphasized the importance of interiors. The more ensemble nature of *M*A*S*H* necessarily required an environment of diversity, and despite the superficial similarity of green canvas and tent poles, each of the sets on *M*A*S*H* maintained the distinct personality of its occupant. Character traits were conspicuously evident: the World War I memorabilia in Potter's office, the draped nylons and lace doilies in Margaret Houlihan's tent, the teddy bear tucked in Radar's bunk. In this regard, the most diverse habitat of all was the "swamp," where a still for making homemade hooch squatted side-by-side a phonograph and recordings of Rachmaninoff. The diversity here was of course due to the diversity of the occupants: at various times Hawkeye, Trapper John, Frank, B.J., and Charles.

The great use of depth in the set designs for *M*A*S*H* stands in sharp contrast to the designs for *AITF*, where sets tended to be long and shallow. But because there was comparatively little movement toward or away from the camera, sets with any degree of real depth were unnecessary (this can also be seen on other situation comedies like *One Day At a Time, Maude, The Jeffersons,* and *Alice*). It should come as no surprise then, that the depth clues identified by Zettl were all missing from the particular episode of *AITF* under discussion here and were comparatively rare in any of the episodes analyzed in preparation for this essay. Indeed, the only time any of the depth clues even came close to utilization were the occasional instances of shooting across the television set.

In contrast to the efforts to include the outside world in *M*A*S*H*, in *AITF* curtains were usually drawn over windows or, were they opened (e.g., the window in the Bunker's dining-room), the only thing visible through them was light, creating a sense of what Zettl calls "negative space" (1973:177). Similarly, when front or back doors were opened, the audience saw painted backdrops and an occasional artificial bush or tree.

Up to a certain point, set design on *M*A*S*H* and *AITF* was a function of performer blocking. As Alan Wurtzel reminds us, sets physically define the limits of performer blocking (1983:424), and *M*A*S*H*'s orientation towards z-axis blocking necessitated sets of great depth as much as *AITF*'s orientation towards x-axis blocking necessitated sets that were long and shallow. But, as Horace Newcomb has pointed out, one must also consider the degree to which sets reinforce the program narrative by "delineating a great deal of formulaic meaning" (1974:28).

The two-dimensional treatment of the outside world in *AITF* led to little or no sense of space beyond the confines of the Bunker home. This sense was further compounded by the great degree of homogeneity from one *AITF* set to another. The living/dining area, the kitchen, Archie and Edith's bedroom, and Mike and Gloria's bedroom all looked very much alike. While movement from one of these environments to another sometimes occasioned rhetorical shifts in the narrative (e.g., Archie and Mike often seemed more vulnerable, less defensive when in their respective bedrooms), together these sets provided a dramatic gestalt, a sense of psychological closure.

Metallinos (1979) states that psychological closure is "one of the most crucial forces operating within the visual field" and recounts Zettl's definition of it as "the perceptual process by which we take a minimum number of visual or auditory cues and mentally fill in nonexisting information in order to arrive at an easily managed pattern" (211). The basically two-dimensional set design of *AITF*—drab and nondescript—and the minimal visual information provided concerning the outside world, encouraged the viewer to focus attention on those things inside the Bunker house that were three-dimensional: the characters and their confrontations.[8]

This focusing of attention had a narrative function as well as a physiognomic one, however. Inasmuch as *AITF* revolved about an axial character, the true essence of the program was that the world began and ended with Archie. It was essential, then, that *AITF* employ a narrative gestalt to a much greater degree than *M*A*S*H*, and a great part of that narrative gestalt was the creation through specific set design and lighting techniques of a physical environment that was itself a complete, self-contained unit, apart from the outside world.

The need for narrative gestalt in *AITF* made it very much a drama of interiors. But in *M*A*S*H*, as much of the outside world as possible was included. I would argue that this was due to the fact that, unlike those in *AITF*, the characters in *M*A*S*H* were very closely tied to the outside world. So much of what happened in their lives was dictated by the ebb and flow of conflicts beyond their compound and beyond their control. Thus, a narrative heavily dependent on external realities was reflected in set designs that were open and emphasized the outside world.

CONCLUSION

It has been the thesis of this essay that the communicative ability of any television narrative is, in large part, a function of the production techniques utilized in its creation. While I think it quite clear that *AITF* and *M*A*S*H* support this thesis, one must be careful not to overemphasize the role of production techniques in the communication of entertainment television narratives based only upon the experience of two series. It would, however, seem appropriate to conclude that, at least in the case of *AITF* and *M*A*S*H*, the creators of the two shows, faced with a number of options (including the standard "1960s telefilm values"), made some deliberate production choices that, while gambles of sorts, were obviously felicitous—witness the influence the two shows have had on subsequent programming. *AITF*'s proscenium style has dictated the course of situation comedy ever since, as the vast majority of sitcoms in the past decade have utilized multiple camera, live audience configurations. Similarly, *M*A*S*H* has exerted a tremendous influence but, unlike *AITF*, not on programming within its own genre. The visually complex influence of *M*A*S*H* can best be seen in recent hour-long comedy-dramas like *St. Elsewhere* and *Hill Street Blues*, an influence Robert Butler, who directed the pilot for *Hill Street Blues* called "making it look messy" (Gitlin, 1983:293). Indeed, this influence can first be seen somewhat earlier in *Lou Grant*, when *M*A*S*H* producer Gene Reynolds teamed up with James Brooks and Alan Burns of MTM, the production company later responsible for *St. Elsewhere* and *Hill Street Blues*.

This is not to say that other production techniques could not have been utilized on *AITF* or *M*A*S*H* as, in fact, they were (e.g., the episodes where Mike and Archie were locked in the basement, where Gloria was molested, where the members of the 4077 were interviewed by a newsreel crew, where a subjective camera was used to show the 4077 from the point of view of a wounded soldier, etc.). These, however, were the rare exceptions rather than the rule and it is significant that such changes in production technique were not just the result of changes in narrative structure but were in large part responsible for the dramatic and emotional impact of these particular episodes.

In assigning meaning to specific production techniques, one runs the risk of overstating the importance of the television apparatus itself. Nonetheless, as Stuart Hall concedes, the way a message is encoded into televisual discourse has a great impact on what the message becomes and the way it is decoded. Indeed, the acknowledgement that the techniques of television production themselves have meaning questions the validity of looking at the production process as a given or, due to its often assembly-line, commercialized nature, as an endeavor unworthy of scholarly consideration. It argues, instead, that this process is an important link in human communication.

NOTES

1. There is a body of research that, while not working from the perspective of the encoding/decoding model, nonetheless deals with various production techniques. It has tended to fall into two categories. The first of these has dealt with television as a medium for instruction or information (e.g.,

McCain, Chilberg, and Wakshlag, 1977; Schlater, 1969, 1970; Tiemens, 1970; Williams, 1965). The second category, on the other hand, has dealt more closely with television as a medium of entertainment, most often focusing on questions of aesthetics or semiotics (e.g., Herbener, Tubergen, and Whitlow, 1979; Metallinos, 1979; Metallinos and Tiemens, 1977; Porter, 1980, 1981, 1983). To varying degrees, the vast majority of this research—the current study included—owes a debt to the seminal work of Herbert Zettl, whose articulation of many of television's aesthetic tenets (1973, 1977, 1978) has provided it a foundation upon which to build.

2. In this context, I define "communicative ability" as the degree to which an encoded text determines its own decoding.

3. The episode of *AITF* concerned a conflict between Archie and Edith. Archie had planned a weekend fishing trip for himself and Edith along with Archie's friend Barney and his wife. Unbeknownst to Archie, Edith had agreed to have a wedding ceremony in their home for two octogenarians from the Sunshine Home, Florence and Herbert. The wedding was to take place the same day Archie wanted to leave on the fishing trip, the problem being how to schedule both to the detriment of neither.

   The episode of *M*A*S*H* interwove three plots: procuring a drug, curare, used as a muscle relaxer prior to surgery; Klinger exchanging fruit cocktail with a Canadian M*A*S*H unit for several bottles of French wine; and Hawkeye holding an essay contest for the nurses with himself as prize.

4. My use of the term "patriarchal" in this context should be qualified, inasmuch as the term has gained a number of connotations, perhaps chief among them that of an historical system of male domination, though recently it has taken on a more Marxist bent, particularly in feminist film criticism. My use of it in reference to *AITF* is based upon the fact that while Archie is indeed a character axial to the narrative, his centrality has a blatantly oppressive, vituperative component to it (exemplified by his treatment of his family, particularly Edith) not necessarily associated with characters just because they are axial. Beyond this, however, further connotations of patriarchy are not intended.

5. During much of *AITF*'s first few seasons a debate raged as to whether or not the program endorsed bigotry or defused it by making it the object of ridicule. For a selection of literature from both sides, see Adler (1979).

6. Diane Jacobs (1977) calls this aspect of Altman's style "actualism." For further discussion of Altman's *mise en scene* and camera movement, see Rosenbaum (1975) and Tarantino (1975).

7. For an interesting discussion of playing comedy for a single camera versus playing it for multiple cameras, see Kelly (1981), pp. 28–35.

8. Indeed, Lear had originally intended to shoot *AITF* in black-and-white. When CBS balked, he compromised and made the sets a drab brown and as nondescript as possible.

REFERENCES

Adler, R. (1979) *All in the Family: A Critical Appraisal*. New York: Praeger Publishers.

Arnheim, R. (1974) *Art and Visual Perception*. Berkeley: University of California Press.

Brunsdon, C. and J. Morley (1978) *Everyday Television: 'Nationwide'*. London: British Film Institute.

Burch, N. (1973) *Theory of Film Practice*. Princeton: Princeton University Press.

Fiske, J. and J. Hartley (1978) *Reading Television*. London: Methuen.

Gelbart, L. (1983) "Its creator says hail and farewell to *M*A*S*H*." *New York Times*. February 27.

Gitlin, T. (1983) *Inside Prime Time*. New York: Pantheon.

Hall, S. (1980) "Encoding/decoding," pp. 128–138, in S. Hall, D. Hobson, A. Lowe, and P. Willis (eds.) *Culture, Media, Language*. London: Hutchinson.

Heath, S. (1981) *Questions of Cinema*. Bloomington: Indiana University Press.

Herbener, G., G. Tubergen, and S. Whitlow (1979) "Dynamics of the frame in visual composition." *Educational Technology and Communications Journal*, 27 (Summer): 83–88.

Jacobs, D. (1977) *Hollywood Renaissance: Altman, Cassavetes, Coppola, Mazursky, Scorsese, and Others*. New York: A. S. Barnes.

Kelly, R. (1981) *The Andy Griffith Show*. Winston-Salem: John F. Blair.

Lynch, J. (1973) "Seven days with 'All in the Family': case study of the taped TV drama." *Journal of Broadcasting*, 17 (Summer): 259–274.

McCain, T., J. Chilberg, and J. Wakshlag (1977) "The effect of camera angle on source credibility and attraction." *Journal of Broadcasting*, 20 (Winter): 35–46.

Metallinos, N. (1979) "Composition of the TV picture: some hypotheses to test the forces operating within the television screen." *Educational Technology and Communications Journal*, 27 (Fall): 205–214.

Metallinos, N. and R. Tiemens (1977) "Asymmetry of the screen: the effect of left versus right placement of television images." *Journal of Broadcasting*, 20 (Winter): 21–33.

Millerson, G. (1979) *The Technique of Television Production* (10th ed.). London: Focal Press.

———. (1982) *The Technique of Lighting for Motion Pictures and Television* (2nd ed.). London: Focal Press.

Mitz, R. (1983) *The Great TV Sitcom Book*. New York: Perigee Books.

Morley, D. (1980) *The 'Nationwide' Audience*. London: British Film Institute.

Newcomb, H. (1974) *TV: The Most Popular Art*. Garden City, N.Y.: Anchor Books.

Porter, M. (1980) *Two studies of Lou Grant: montage style and the dominance of dialogue*. Unpublished paper.

———. (1981) *The montage structure of adventure and dramatic prime time programming*. Unpublished paper.

———. (1983) "Applying semiotics to the study of selected prime time television programs." *Journal of Broadcasting*, 27 (Spring): 63–69.

Rosenbaum, J. (1975) "Improvisations and interactions in Altmanville." *Sight and Sound*, 44 (Winter).

Schlater, R. (1969) "Effect of irrelevant visual cues on recall of television messages." *Journal of Broadcasting*, 14 (Winter): 63–69.

———. (1970) "Effect of speed of presentation on recall of television messages." *Journal of Broadcasting*, 14 (Spring): 207–214.

Silverstone, R. (1981) *The Message of Television: Myth and Narrative in Modern Society*. London: Heinemann.

Tarantino, M. (1975) "Movement as metaphor: the long goodbye." *Sight and Sound*, 44 (Spring).

Tiemens, R. (1970) "Some relationships of camera angle to communicator credibility." *Journal of Broadcasting*, 14 (Fall): 483–490.

Williams, R. (1965) "On the value of varying TV shots." *Journal of Broadcasting*, 10 (Winter): 33–43.

Wren-Lewis, J. (1983) "The encoding/decoding model: criticisms and redevelopments for research on decoding." *Media, Culture, and Society*, 5 (April): 179–197.

Wurtzel, A. and J. Dominick (1971) "Evaluation of television drama: interaction of acting styles and shot selection." *Journal of Broadcasting*, 15 (Winter): 103–111.

Wurtzel, A. (1983) *Television Production* (2nd ed.). New York: McGraw Hill.

Zettl, H. (1973) *Sight, Sound, Motion: Applied Media Aesthetics*. Belmont, Calif.: Wadsworth.

———. (1977) "Toward a multi-screen television aesthetic: some structural considerations." *Journal of Broadcasting*, 20 (Winter): 5–19.

———. (1978) "The rare case of television aesthetics." *Journal of the University Film Association*, XXX (Spring): 3–8.

DOUGLAS GOMERY

BRIAN'S SONG:
TELEVISION, HOLLYWOOD, AND
THE EVOLUTION OF THE MOVIE
MADE FOR TELEVISION

In November 1971 Richard Nixon reigned as president; the Vietnam War still needed to be unraveled; campus protesters still took to the streets; and Watergate lay in the future. What were Americans watching on television? *All in the Family* (CBS, Saturday, 8:00 P.M. EST) had surged to the number-one spot, far surpassing its closest competition: *The Flip Wilson Show* (NBC, Thursday, 8:00 P.M. EST), *Marcus Welby* (ABC, Tuesday, 10:00 P.M. EST) and *Gunsmoke* (CBS, Monday, 8:00 P.M. EST). Fifth in the overall ratings battle for that season (1971–72) was ABC's *Movie of the Week* (Tuesday, 8:30–10:00 P.M. EST). Movies had always been popular on U.S. television, but this was the first series of movies made for television to break into the top ten. These movies easily surpassed a long-running detective series, *Hawaii Five-O* (CBS), and two short-lived offerings on NBC, *Sarge* (with George Kennedy) and *The Funny Side* (with Gene Kelly as host) on Tuesday night. On November 30 ABC presented a little-publicized TV movie, *Brian's Song*. That showing achieved a 32.9 rating and a 48 share, the highest for any TV movie up to that date. More importantly for the profit-seeking networks, *Brian's Song* ranked tenth for *any* movie presentation ever on television. With *The Wizard of Oz* accounting for five of the top ten to that November night, *Brian's Song* rose to join *The Birds*, *Bridge over the River Kwai*, *Ben-Hur*, and *Born Free* to form television's elite top-ten movies. Quite an honor for a film with no stars or publicity hype.[1]

From *American History/American Television*, edited by John O'Connor. Copyright © 1983 by John O'Connor. Reprinted by permission of the Ungar Publishing Company.

But why? Here was a tale of friendship between two running backs who played for the Chicago Bears. Brian Piccolo was white, slow, and small. Gale Sayers was black, fast, and correctly built to become one of professional football's greatest runners. The film focused on their differences as people: Sayers quiet and introspective; Piccolo merry, effusive, ever the clown. Their friendship began at the Bears' training camp in 1965 and ended with Piccolo's death from cancer in 1970. At age twenty-six Piccolo left a wife and three daughters (the latter not seen in the film). Neither the film's undistinguished direction nor its open sentimentality seemed to diminish its popularity. The sum of the parts overcame any single drawback. This narrative situation, drawn from real events, seemed to have provoked—quite unexpectedly—a moment of memorable potency in the midst of the chaotic Vietnam-Nixon era.

The public's response to *Brian's Song* certainly caught television moguls by surprise. Quickly, awards and praise issued forth from all sides. *Brian's Song* won five Emmy awards, including outstanding single program for entertainment for the 1971–72 television season. The Director's Guild honored Buzz Kulik. From nonindustry sources came a George Foster Peabody award for outstanding achievement in entertainment, and citations from *Black Sports Magazine*, the American Cancer Society, the National Conference of Christians and Jews, and the NAACP.[2] Even President Richard Nixon jumped on board. "Believe me," proclaimed America's thirty-seventh president, "[*Brian's Song*] was one of the great motion pictures I have seen."[3]

With *Brian's Song* the made-for-television motion picture came of age as an entertainment genre. Here we have a significant turning point in the history of United States television programming. Why did *Brian's Song* (and other movies specifically made for television) overtake Hollywood features in the ratings war of 1971? The answer takes us back to the origins of the American television industry, to the development of its business and programming practices. Most Americans are familiar with *The Late Show*, *The Early Show*, *Sunday Night at the Movies*, and other series that have turned television homes into cinema museums displaying the best (and worst) of Hollywood's creations. Nearly every one of the current "film generation" embraced the magic (and genius) of the American cinema through television. And throughout this era the American television industry has prospered, becoming one of the more profitable of U.S. businesses. Consequently, we first of all need to examine the history and relations of two American businesses, one growing (television), one declining (theatrical motion pictures). Since we have precious little that qualifies as systematic history in this area, we should immediately begin to integrate the business history of television into a literature well synthesized by Alfred D. Chandler in his book *The Visible Hand: The Managerial Revolution in American Business.*[4]

The methods of business history alone cannot explain, however, the extraordinary popularity of *Brian's Song*. From a sociological perspective television movies seemed to serve the need for topical entertainment in an era of instability identical to Warner Brothers' social films of the Great Depression. But why *Brian's Song*? What intersection of ideological forces produced its unexpected overflow of popular interest? All television programs, not just news shows, deserve to be studied as indicators of significant shifts in dominant attitudes, beliefs, and values. Like motion pictures from earlier decades, popular television represents the merger of art and industry, a mass spectacle. Understanding how "hit" shows reflect and/or shape the dominant ideology is a difficult task. New work in film studies provides us with a start. Thus, this essay will address two fundamental problems of television and history (business history, and television and ideology) through the genre of movies made for television and one product in particular, *Brian's Song*.

On the surface, the historical relationship between the U.S. film and television industries seems clear enough: the leaders of the film industry unilaterally opposed any interchange with the television industry between 1945 and 1955. Only after the movies had clearly surrendered their mass audience to television did the movie moguls consent to deal with their poor visual cousin. Such claims portray the chieftains of the motion picture industry as narrow-minded dolts.[5] I argue they were not. On only one level did they refuse to do business with television. Until the mid-1950s the major Hollywood studios did withhold feature films from television presentation—but for quite sensible reasons. From 1945 to 1955 even the largest television networks could simply not afford rents competitive with even a declining theatrical box office. During that decade the chief operating officers of Hollywood's biggest concerns embraced (as it turned out incorrectly) the vast potential of revenues from theater and subscription television.

At first, Hollywood tried to purchase shares of major television properties. For example, Paramount Pictures owned parts

of the DuMont network, KTLA (Los Angeles), a subscription
television firm, and a theater television corporation. Fox also
owned a subscription television concern. On the exhibition side
the United Paramount Theater chain (900 theaters strong)
acquired the American Broadcasting Corporation. For a variety
of reasons, however (which would constitute another essay),
the film industry never was able to gain enough power to
challenge the radio, then television networks. All attempts at
subscription and theater television during the 1950s proved
unprofitable. But Hollywood was able to gain a foothold in the
production end. As early as 1951 Columbia established a subsidiary, Screen Gems, to produce filmed material for television.
Within four years the major studios plunged headfirst into
production. Warner Brothers, with *Cheyenne*, *77 Sunset Strip*, and
Maverick, led the way. Soon this relationship proved so profitable that Hollywood stuck to the business of supplying programs, and/or studio space, while exhibitors turned to alternative investments.[6]

As this jockeying for power was taking place, feature film
material was being shown on American television. Initially it
came from abroad. In particular, the Ealing, Rank, and Korda
organizations in Britain, which had never been able successfully to crack the U.S. market, supplied features as early as
1948. Undersized U.S. producers like Monogram and Republic
came on board next. Although these two concerns and a dozen
other competitors tendered more than four thousand titles,
their cheap production values in Westerns (Gene Autry and
Roy Rogers) and serials (Flash Gordon) only served to remind
early television viewers of the vast storehouse of treasures still
resting in the vaults of MGM and Paramount.[7]

To understand how and why the major Hollywood producers
finally agreed to rent and/or sell their backtitles to television,
we have to return to May 1948 when an eccentric millionaire,
Howard Hughes, purchased controlling interest in the weakest
of the major Hollywood companies, Radio Keith Orpheum
(RKO). In five years Hughes ran RKO into the ground. Debts
soared past $20 million; production fell by 50 percent; new
activity neared a standstill. To appease minority stockholders,
in 1954 Hughes purchased their shares for $23,489,478.16—in
cash. (He wrote a personal check.) He then controlled a studio
lot, stages, properties, films, and other assets. A year later
Hughes sold the whole package to General Tire & Rubber
Company for $25 million. At the time General Tire controlled

WOR-TV in New York and desired the RKO features for its proposed *Million Dollar Movie* series. Since General Tire did not want to enter the film production business, it quickly rid itself of all nonfilmic physical property. The studio lot, for example, went to a former RKO employee, then television's number-one attraction, Lucille Ball, for her Desilu operation. It also peddled limited rights to 704 features and 1,100 shorts to C&C Television, Inc., for $15 million. Consequently, in July 1956, C&C auctioned rights to the RKO package to one station per television market for cash and/or "bartered" advertising spots. General Tire retained exclusive rights for WOR and other stations it owned. By July 1957, *Variety* estimated that C&C had grossed $25 million in eighty markets alone.[8]

Such profit figures impressed even the most recalcitrant movie mogul. Within the space of twenty-four months all the remaining major Hollywood corporations released their pre-1948 titles to television. For the first time a nationwide audience was able to confront a broad crosssection of American sound films, and rediscover two decades of Hollywood pleasure production. All the companies were able to tap a new source of needed revenue at the nadir of their transition into the post-television era. Columbia, a minor studio, moved first. In January 1956, it announced a deal to rent pre-1958 features.[9] As a result, in fiscal 1955—an otherwise dismal year—Columbia was able to achieve a record $5 million profit. Instantly this minor had become a major. Two months later, in March 1956, Warner Brothers sold its pre-1948 library of 850 features and 1,500 shorts to PRM, a Canadian-American investment company, for $21 million. Suddenly it could record a $15 million profit. Twentieth Century-Fox upped the ante. It licensed its pre-1948 features for $30 million (plus a percentage) to National Telefilm Associates. In August 1956, MGM topped the Fox figure. By distributing through a wholly owned subsidiary, on one day alone it completed contracts with CBS's owned-and-operated stations and seven other stations for more than $20 million, the largest single day's business in MGM's history. More came through additional contracts.

Paramount held out the longest because it had large investments in subscription television. In February 1958—nearly two years after the deals of RKO, Columbia, Warner Brothers, Fox and MGM—Paramount sold, rather than leased, its pre-1948 library to MCA, then a talent agent. At the time the deal, worth $50 million, surpassed all others. But because Paramount *sold* rather than leased its library, MCA made out far better in the long run. By 1965, MCA had grossed more than $70 million and had not even tapped the network market. The excess profits MCA generated from leasing Paramount pre-1948 features enabled it to purchase Universal and join the ranks of giant media conglomerates.[10]

From 1955 on, pre-1948 feature films functioned as a mainstay of off-network schedules. The networks only booked feature films as specials, not regular programming. For example, during the 1956–57 season CBS initiated its annual airing of *The Wizard of Oz*. By 1960 all three networks reasoned that *post*-1948 Hollywood features could generate high ratings if offered in prime time. Before that could begin, the studios had to settle with Hollywood craft unions on residual payments. In a precedent-setting action the Screen Actors Guild, led by Ronald Reagan, struck and won guaranteed amounts. Consequently, on September 23, 1961, NBC premiered *Saturday Night at the Movies* with *How to Marry a Millionaire*. The thirty-one titles shown in the series, fifteen in color, all were post-1950 Fox productions. All had their television premiere on *Saturday Night at the Movies*. Color films helped spur sales of RCA sets; then, as now, RCA owned NBC. Moreover, feature-length movies enabled NBC effectively to counterprogram proven hits on CBS (*Have Gun, Will Travel; Gunsmoke*) and ABC (*Lawrence Welk*). As was generally the case during the 1960s, ABC quickly imitated NBC's effort. A midseason replacement, *Sunday Night Movies*, commenced in April 1962. CBS, the ratings leader, did not feel the need to join in until September 1965. By then, the race was on. As early as the fall of 1968, the networks presented recent Hollywood feature films seven nights a week. By the 1970s, overlapping permitted ten separate "movie nights." In the long run, programming innovator NBC retained the greatest commitment to this particular programming form, probably because of continued corporate investment in color-casting.[11]

This vast display of movie programming quickly depleted the stock of available first-run material. Although the total number of usable features had increased from three hundred in 1952 to more than ten thousand in 1964, growth then slowed to a trickle. Station managers began to wonder just how often they could repeat pre-1948 titles. The networks established a formula for post-1948 titles: show it twice on prime time and then release it into syndication. Not surprisingly, movie producers began to charge higher and higher fees for current theatrical product. Million-dollar price tags became commonplace. Soon network executives reasoned that costs had reached the point where it had become more profitable to produce and sell their own movies. Such a practice would reduce costs and provide a method for making pilot programs for projected series. Since at this time networks normally paid for part (or all) of the development of pilots, significant savings could be effected. And these made-for-TV features allowed the networks to test the rating power of proposed series in order better to forecast success.[12]

The first made-for-TV feature as part of a regular series was presented on Saturday, November 26, 1966, by NBC, *Fame Is the Name of the Game*.[13] This "World Premiere" resulted from NBC's contract with Universal to produce low-budget movies to be released first on television. These color films would, following network television airing, revert to Universal for domestic theatrical release (rare), and foreign theatrical and television release (common). In a short time the number of made-for-TV features increased rapidly. By the 1971-72 season, when *Brian's Song* premiered, the networks had scheduled for the first time more made-for-TV features than theatrical products new to television. Again relative network power dictated who followed NBC's lead. In 1967 ABC reached an agreement with MGM for production of ninety-minute features. (NBC's television movies ran two hours.) Ratings leader CBS again trailed by two years.[14]

The rapid transformation to made-for-television movie programming took place because profits were higher than anyone expected. On the supply side a television movie cost on average $750,000, about equal to the cost of four showings of a popular theatrical release. On the demand side, TV movies quickly proved they could attract sizeable audiences, and even at times surpass blockbuster features. Not surprisingly top network movie rating choices have included *Gone With the Wind*, *Love Story*, *The Godfather*, and *Ben Hur*. More startling is the fact that *Ladies of the Night* (ABC, Sunday, January 16, 1977) vaulted to fifteenth place for all movies of any type ever shown on television. Others on the all-time top 100 list include *Helter Skelter*, *Night Stalker*, *A Case of Rape*, *Women in Chains*, and *Jesus of Nazareth*. The only repeat case in the top 100 has been *Brian's Song*. Moreover, this remarkable sports film achieved this honor in 1971 and 1972, when the made-for-TV publicity mill was only beginning to be set in motion. In general, ABC, which telecast *Brian's Song*, produced through its *Movie of the Week* the best ratings results. In 1971–72, for example, ABC gathered thirteen of the top fifteen telefeature ratings of the season. Barry Diller, then head of ABC's movie programming, parlayed that position into the chairmanship of a major movie studio, Paramount Pictures.[15]

Brian's Song was an altogether typical made-for-television production. Producer Paul Junger Witt had a connection with ABC through *The Patridge Family* series, first aired in September 1970. He hired William Blinn to create a script from Gale Sayers's routine autobiography, *I Am Third*. Witt also secured Buzz Kulik, a veteran television director. Kulik, a football nut, knew the Sayers/Piccolo story from the sports pages, saw it in the tradition of Howard Hawks as a love story between two men. At first there was a problem of casting, since in Hollywood there were few young male black actors with experience. Billy Dee Williams, then thirty-three, had been kicking around Hollywood and Broadway since age seven. His fame from *Brian's Song* shot him into major roles in Hollywood feature films—*Lady Sings the Blues* (1972), *Mahogany* (1975), and *The Empire Strikes Back* (1980). The latter made him a household name. Indeed, *Brian's Song* advanced many of its contributors forward several significant steps in their careers. Producer Paul Junger Witt went on to form his own production company, which turned out the controversial ABC comedy *Soap*. William Blinn wrote part of *Roots*. Kulik amassed a string of important made-for-TV movie credits including *Babe* (1975), *The Lindbergh Kidnapping Case* (1976), and *Ziefeld* (1978). Composer Michel Le Grand earned an Oscar for *Summer of '42* six months after *Brian's Song*'s premiere. Jack Warden (who played George Halas) was nominated for an Oscar as best supporting actor in *Shampoo* (1975) and *Heaven Can Wait* (1978). But it was James Caan who benefited most. In 1971 his career seemed at a standstill. *Brian's Song* thrust him into the spotlight; *The Godfather* (1972) made him a star. Since then he has remained a major box-office attraction. Here was an early case of a television movie helping create a theatrical movie star. James Caan has not appeared in a made-for-television movie since *Brian's Song*.[16]

Brian's Song cost about $400,000 to produce. The made-for-TV movie in the early 1970s had become what the B film was to Hollywood in earlier eras. Contending with restrictions on budgets, language and sex, ratings-minded networks, and a format demanding an opening "teaser" and six climatic "act curtains" before commercial breaks, creators had to work quickly and efficiently. The networks covered production costs in exchange for two runs. The producers then received 100 percent from syndication and worldwide theatrical rights. Production costs were kept to a minimum. Consequently, studio shooting constituted the bulk in most TV films. In *Brian's Song* the considerable use of NFL film highlights of actual Chicago Bears games reduced costs. Shooting schedules averaged eleven days. With the air date known in advance, all preproduction work was completed in less than two weeks. That time included script revisions, selection of locations and crew, and any hassles over casting the stars. No time was set aside for rehearsals. The script served as the director's bible—"Shoot as written," as in Hollywood in the 1930s. Lighting was one parameter that clearly suffered, for it required too much time to light elaborate shots; all Hollywood agreed that the TV movie was a form for the close-up. Postproduction necessitated yet another week or two. In fact that step was merely mechanical because so few additional takes were allowed, and only shots noted in the script were covered.[17]

If *Brian's Song* was a typical production, the public response was unprecedented. It proved to be the media phenomenon of late 1971 and early 1972, akin to *Love Story* of a year earlier. Columbia Pictures for the first time ever released the film to theaters after it was shown on television. This experiment was tried only in Chicago. Perhaps too many had seen it already on television; and against major Christmas releases, *Diamonds Are Forever* and *The French Connection*, this TV movie could not even hold its own. The most unexpected success came in ancillary areas. Books dealing with Brian Piccolo became bestsellers. The original Sayers autobiography had been issued by Viking in November 1970. After the film's success, sales took off. The publisher, caught short, had to double the copies in print within one month. Meantime *Brian Piccolo: A Short Season* by Jeannie Morris, wife of a Piccolo/Sayers teammate, was published by a small Chicago house to take advantage of the TV exposure. More than one hundred thousand copies were quickly sold, and Dell purchased the paperback rights for $175,000, a sizable sum even by today's inflated prices. The phonograph record industry was also caught short. Michel Legrand's orchestral version shot into the Top 100. Other artists quickly covered. Peter Duchin and Peter Nero produced versions for middle-of-the-road audiences; Hank Crawford created a soul version. This media blitz lasted only three months because the Hollywood publicity mill, caught unprepared, turned to other products. Yet the phenomenon has never completely died off. Throughout the 1970s *Brian's Song* continued to be shown on television, in syndication, and in classrooms and other social gatherings in 16mm. Uncounted numbers have seen it; few do not know of its reputation.[18]

The *Brian's Song* phenomenon points up the fact that in twenty-five years, 1946 to 1971, movies on television had traversed through four unique stages. First, the Hollywood studios tried to withhold their best films, and pursue subscription and/or theater television. Then, needing the cash, they eventually agreed to sell and/or lease pre-1948 features and shorts to local stations. In 1961 the networks initiated stage three by beginning to broadcast post-1948 theatrical features in prime time. Such a strategy proved so successful that fees quickly escalated and inventories decreased to problematic levels. Thus in the late 1960s the networks began to commission their own films. These made-for-TV features proved to be so popular that they rivaled the ratings power of even the most expensive theatrical products. Miniseries, novels for television, and docudramas came next. The 1980s will initiate movies made for pay cable. In October 1981, Alan J. Hirschfield, chairman of Twentieth Century-Fox, announced a series of original pay-cable movies. Costing about one-third the price of an average theatrical feature, each would be shown first on pay cable, then on over-the-air network television. Next would come foreign theatrical release. Worldwide syndication would terminate the revenue cycle. That same month Home Box Office, a Time subsidiary, announced its first movie made for pay cable, *The Terry Fox Story*, the biography of another athlete who died young. And so the economic cycle continues.[19]

The made-for-TV movie has formed its own genre since 1966. This form seems to have fulfilled a particular cultural need: topical entertainment reaffirming basic values and beliefs. Here its function has resembled those Warner Brothers' features of the 1930s so often utilized by historians to understand transformations in ideas and beliefs during the Great Depression. During the 1930s Hollywood had to struggle in a moral and political straightjacket to produce acceptable social dramas like *I Am a Fugitive from a Chain Gang* (1932) and *Black Legion* (1936). Consider how historian Andrew Bergman described these "topicals":

> Throughout the thirties, the Warner studios produced a number of films which dealt explicitly with aspects of social and political life Hollywood usually shunned. . . . [These] remain, without exception, fascinating documents, demonstrating both a gritty feel for social realism, and a total inability to give any coherent reasons for social difficulties.[20]

A similar situation has existed for TV movies. Pressures from advertisers, the Moral Majority and the U.S. Congress have limited what networks would attempt to present. Yet every executive knew that bizarre, topical films could attract large audiences. Their problem became how to make controversial, noncontroversial TV movies—film that could titillate viewers without scandalizing them. Some public wrangling has always generated useful publicity. But too much could be disastrous. And always there had to be a modicum of stress on the positive. So for every *Roots*, there were dozens of films like *Can You Hear the Laughter? The Story of Freddie Prinze*, and *Dawn: Portrait of a Teenage Runaway*. Topical products *Helter Skelter, Dallas Cowboy Cheerleaders, The Feminist and the Fuzz*, and *Raid on Entebbe* all reached the list of top-100 highest-rated films shown on American television during the 1970s. All emerged straight from the pages of a daily newspaper, *The National Enquirer, People*, and/or various features in broadcast journalism. Indeed TV-movie production schedules were so swift they could "scoop" theatrical fare. Some made-for-TV movies had completed their second runs before their more famous theatrical cousins had come to town.[21]

TV movies have excelled in telling small stories. Even in attempted extravaganzas or docudramas, the familiar elements of tight character development, the close-up, frequent interior shots, and repetitive dialogue help construct a particular form of narrative logic and style. As with Hollywood features from the 1930s, viewing could be interrupted and still be enjoyed because everyone was so familiar with the characteristics of the form. Film scholars David Bordwell and Kristin Thompson have described this mode as the classic narrative cinema. This formulation of storytelling on film depends on the assumption that action should result from individual characters acting as causal agents. Of course there can exist problems of nature and society. But these factors serve as catalysts or preconditions for narrative action. The story invariably centers on the difficulties of a small group of persons, their decisions, choices, and given character traits. So the hero or heroine has positive values and in the end wins (or loses gracefully). The villain has negative characteristics and fails in the end (or at least does not triumph). The plot moves on in a cause-effect chain as characters seek desired goals. When those figures with positive traits finally win out, we have the "happy ending."

In this classical narrative mode, according to Bordwell and Thompson, visual style is subordinated to a goal of effectively telling the story. So plot time omits all insignificant chunks in order to emphasize only the "important" events. The plot orders the story chronologically to tender the action most strikingly. If a character acts strangely, we soon learn why from (1) dialogue, (2) action, and/or (3) a flashback. Appointments, meetings, and "chance" encounters guarantee efficient character interaction. Motivation should be as clear and complete as possible. And all narrative puzzles must be closed at the finish. Leaving no loose ends, classical narrative films clearly seal up all questions or enigmas. We learn the fate of each major character, the answer to each mystery, and the outcome of each conflict.[22]

Although any subject is a potential candidate for classical narrative treatment, the more familiar the "story concept," the better chance it has to sell. Appropriately, for its *Movies-of-the-Week* ABC sought seventy-five-minute tales that could be comprehended in thirty seconds. In industry jargon, these were dubbed "concept films." And of course this meant that these narratives could effectively be promoted in thirty-second commercials. In fact network "concept testing" involved interviewing target audience members (twenty-five- to forty-year-old white, urban Americans): "Would you watch the story of such and such?" If the answer was yes, then the narrative concept was considered. Sex and violence were euphemized while "social realism" was zealously touted. So controversies surface predictably each year, to be quickly forgotten by the next season. For example, today few remember that NBC's *Born Innocent* kicked off the 1974–75 season. That film, which chronicled the corruption of a teenager in prison, contained a graphic sequence depicting rape with a broom handle. Controversy was initiated; lawsuits were begun, ratings were high. And the studio developed a sequel, *Sara T.—Portrait of a Teenaged Alcoholic.* Indeed, for a time during the 1970s, treatments of rape and alcoholism provided the most popular controversial noncontroversial subjects.[23]

Brian's Song represents a classic narrative tale. *TV Guide* efficiently summarized its essential narrative traits:

> A drama that captures the warmth of deep friendship—and the
> horror of dying young. It's the true story of Chicago Bears
> running back Gale Sayers and his teammate Brian Piccolo, who
> died last year of cancer. Their training camp rivalries are traced
> and there's plenty of NFL footage, but football is incidental to
> the real story: a deeply moving account of the growing friend-
> ship between the Bears' first black and white roommates.[24]

Here, classic narrative cinema boils down the complex issue of
race relations to competition between two individuals. Violence
comes in an accepted form—professional football games. Sports
fans, principally young urban males, already knew the ending.
The concept of a friendship between men that is broken by
death goes back to the origins of the American film industry.
Indeed male "weepies" had been a staple of Hollywood's golden
age. Consider *The Pride of the Yankees* 1942) or *Knute Rockne—All
American* (1940). *Brian's Song* was a traditional story ripped from
page three of 1970s sports pages.

Brian's Song's two central characters presented a vivid contrast. One was talented; the other tried hard. One was black;
the other white. Football, as the *TV Guide* blurb indicated,
simply served as a catalyst, a precondition for action. When
both made the team and they became close friends, another
enigma was needed. A clear villain emerged—cancer. But Brian
Piccolo did not die in vain. Consider the final lines of voice-over
narration in the film:

> But, when they [his friends and family] think of him, it's not how
> he died that they remember but rather how he lived. . . . How he
> did live . . .[25]

The lesson seems clear. Those who try hard and do their best in
the face of adversity are life's true heroes. This is a "happy
ending" in an otherwise very sad conclusion.

All techniques of camera work, editing, mise-en-scène, and
sound were subordinated to the story. The plot, spreading over
several football seasons, was easy to follow, since it always
centered on the relationship between the two men. The film's
structure, punctuated by five commercial breaks (two minutes
each), conformed to an ABCC'B'A' structure. The opening (and
closing) segment focuses on how the two men relate as they
meet (and part). The contrast is vivid and striking. In the
second and fifth segments we learn how each handles adversity. First, Sayers helps Brian Piccolo simply make the team. Of
course, All-American Sayers is assured of a place. Later Sayers

learns to handle his friend's impending death, and the frustration of not being able to do anything about it. The two middle segments also mirror each other. First, Brian assists Gale with the rehabilitation of his knee injury; then Sayers tries to help Piccolo with his physical problems. This process of rhyming constitutes a classical cinematic ploy and unifies differences in the story elements. From beginning to end, *Brian's Song* ceaselessly repeats itself, making it easy to follow and fulfilling yet another characteristic of the classic narrative cinema.[26]

On the level of film genre *Brian's Song* sparked a resurgence of the sports biography. That category of narrative subjects had been important throughout the sound era. After *Brian's Song* came *Rocky* (1976), *Semi-Tough* (1977), *Slap Shot* (1977), and *Heaven Can Wait* (1978). In 1973 *Bang the Drum Slowly* earned sizeable box-office revenues. It too concerned a dying athlete (here a baseball player) befriended by a superior teammate.[27] Yet on the level of genre *Brian's Song*'s connections to the past were even more subtle than similarities in subject matter. Consider a long-standing character type film historian Russell Merritt has labeled "the bashful hero."[28] Since the 1930s one durable male figure has dominated American cinema. Whether essayed by Gary Cooper, Jimmy Stewart, or Henry Fonda, all moviegoers are familiar with the character of the easygoing, stalwart young fellow who was suddenly entrusted with great responsibility. Armed with homespun shrewdness and a laid-back, laconic attitude, he (never she) subsequently overcame formidable adversaries. He was likable, tall, lean, and soft-spoken. But when the situation demanded, he became eloquent in a simple, straightforward way. Fame seemed to seek him out. By any film's close he had emerged as the best at his calling. Success came to him, seemingly by chance.

The bashful hero was spawned in popular culture in the Progressive Era. The egalitarian philosophy of the Progressives precipitated as an article of faith the ineffable wisdom of the common man. Merritt locates its origins in the movies in a variety of genres created before World War I. The drawling cowboy, bashful in front of women yet stalwart in the face of danger; the rustic country boy; the shy but creative Chaplin tramp figure—all began in motion pictures made near the end of the Progressive Era. But this figure moved to the forefront in the 1930s with the emergence of sound films. Merritt points out the importance of the character this way:

[The bashful hero] reassures us that we too could have enjoyed the same success in his shoes, if we only had the opportunity he had. His creators want to assure us that we are heroic, attractive people in our natural state.[29]

In an interesting twist *Brian's Song* cast a black man in the bashful hero role. Gale Sayers is the easygoing, quiet young man who possesses homespun shrewdness. But he changes. When the film opens we learn of Sayers's inability to speak before large audiences. Brain Piccolo must coach Sayers for a speech at a rookie-of-the-year award banquet. Yet when it becomes necessary Sayers can speak directly and to the point. Consider his terse but effective advice to Piccolo during their first training camp:

Try it going to your left. They don't look for a right-handed guy to throw going to his left.[30]

All this changes when adversity strikes. Sayers takes charge. He *asks* to tell their Bear teammates of Piccolo's illness and presents a moving speech "from the heart." Later at another banquet he informs the world of Brian's real courage in a touching address. Generally the bashful hero seems to be a gentle, nonaggressive man. Yet he thrives on adversity, drawing on a seemingly unlimited pool of talent. He then easily moves others to tears and action. Gale Sayers in *Brian's Song* exemplifies this tradition with his new-found power of public address; as Merritt notes,

the conversion scene itself, in which the hero converts skeptics into true believers, is a constant feature in films of this kind.[31]

Sayers moves the audience in the film (and at home in front of the television set) to tears by telling the world of the true courage of Brian Piccolo. And many seemed to respond, signaling the film's extraordinary success.

Yet the figure of the bashful hero cannot completely explain *Brian's Song*'s popularity. Simply put, why did it touch such a wellspring of public sentiment on that Tuesday late in November 1971? What intersection of special themes produced such an outpouring of interest and praise? In short, the film reconstituted a potent mix of popular mythic material during an era when many Americans seemed confused about fundamental conceptions of race, sex, and economics.[32] Specifically *Brian's Song* reworked three basic thematic concerns: (1) relations between blacks and whites, (2) the proper roles for women, and (3) the image and trappings of big business in the U.S. economy. The techniques of mythologization in *Brian's Song* function in subtle and complex ways, even as the film's form and style remain simple and direct.

What was this era like? Historians are still working on that question. But at present certain generalizations do seem clear. The "seething sixties" still formed a part of viewers' memories. Richard Nixon had been in power for two years, trying to unite the country around new goals: "To a crisis of spirit, we need an answer of the spirit." Yet questions of race, the proper way to end the Vietnam War, protest, and law and order refused to go away. Who should run corporate America? Weren't all large cities falling apart? And the youth were on drugs and practicing free love. Religion seemed under attack, replaced by the new morality. The 1960s did not end on January 1, 1970. Questions and doubt seemed to plague Americans up and through the Watergate affair in 1974.[33]

All these uncertainties had seemed more pressing in the 1960s. Why? Partly because from 1963 to 1969 the United States experienced one of its longest periods of sustained prosperity. The 1970s changed all that. Depending on which economist or government expert one listened to, a recession or depression overtook the U.S. economy in mid-1970. Whatever the label, the situation became grave very quickly. Unemployment, especially for minorities and youth, surged upward. The overexpanded war industries were especially hard hit, reflecting the winding down of the American involvement in Indochina. Educated middle-class technicians and engineers suddenly found themselves out of work and competing in a glutted job market. Moreover since 1893 the United States had enjoyed a generally favorable balance of trade with foreign nations. In 1971 the dollars paid for international debt exceeded imports, adding to the domestic economic woes. Times were not good when *Brian's Song* was presented, and Nixon had chosen to do little to alleviate hard times until the 1972 election drew closer.[34]

A few sectors of the economy did continue to prosper. One was professional sports. The American Football League (AFL) and the National Football League (NFL) had just merged. Leagues in hockey, basketball, and tennis were created and/or expanded. By 1975 there were more than three times the number of professional teams as there had been a decade earlier. Sports truly became a big business. It rewarded its star performers as well as or better than some of the larger industrial corporations did their top executives. Teams annually mined new-found wealth from television. Far more people watched professional athletes on television than could have crowded into all of America's stadiums. For example, more than 65 million—the largest number ever to see a sporting event up to that time—looked on in 1967 as the Green Bay Packers beat the Kansas City Chiefs in football's first Super Bowl. Just about the time *Brian's Song* aired, the mania about pro sports was reaching the peak of its growth cycle.[35]

Yet *Brian's Song* was far more than a motion picture taking advantage of a popular fad. As recent work in film theory has demonstrated, it is far more interesting to learn what's systematically left unsaid in classical Hollywood films than to continue to probe for more surface themes. That is, ideas and beliefs more often are dealt with through what is left out, "structured absences." Seemingly, marginal assumptions can tell us much about what people took for granted, their "lived relationships."[36] A complete analysis of *Brian's Song* would stretch far beyond the limits of this essay, but we can see in three specific ways how the film structured and simplified complex issues without ever directly "sending a message."

Race relations continued to be a festering issue in 1971. In October 1970, the U.S. Commission on Civil Rights reported "a major breakdown" in enforcement of civil rights. Public opinion polls showed that 78 percent of all Americans opposed the idea of busing schoolchildren to effect racial integration. And the North was rapidly replacing the South as the focus of violent confrontations over school integration.[37] In *Brian's Song* direct presentation of these contradictions was glossed over. How? By reducing the issue to the most personal level. Could two players competing for the same job get along? Recognize that these were special men. Sayers was an All-American, not an "uppity nigger." Here the use of the bashful hero mythos effectively stripped the Sayers figure of the threatening quality often associated with black men. He was portrayed not as loud, demanding, or assertive, but as quiet and shy, simply wanting to fit into the system. Subtler touches underscored Sayers as a nonthreatening black. He was very well dressed. He showed up at the Bears' training camp in a spiffy blue blazer and a well-trimmed Afro haircut. No wild clothes or exaggerated hairstyle for this character. He looked white, even "higher class" than

Piccolo. Moreover he had a beautiful house in what was shown
to be an all-white neighborhood. Sayers's wife had straightened
her hair, and behaved appropriately "perky." She could be
white too. Black children (suggesting the busing issue) were
not seen, only referred to. In short, the Gale Sayers portrait fit
conveniently into the superblack mold established by Sidney
Poitier during the 1960s. He posed no problems. One can almost hear viewers saying: "If only all blacks could be like him,
then there would be no problems." Left unsaid is any consideration of the societal implications.[38]

Yet contradictions do exist. Consider the use of deep-focus
photography. Here, with a wide-angle lens and placement of
figures and decor, a motion picture director can create an image
in depth. It is not as frequently used in television as in theatrical
motion pictures because of video's limited screen size. But in a
confined space, there do exist a number of possibilities for
action on two levels, foreground and background. For example,
near the end of *Brian's Song*, Gale Sayers calls Brian Piccolo for
one last time. Behind Sayers, we see his new black roommate. It
would have been easier to frame a shot with no roommate, so
are we to believe that all other players at Sayers's position were
black? (A rule was laid down early in the film that players
should room together by position, hence Sayers and Piccolo.)
But we know from elsewhere in the movie and the history of
professional football that other whites were available. For example, Ralph Kurek, a white, was mentioned several times in
the film as the man Piccolo had to "beat out" for the job. Are we
then to assume that the interracial roommate scheme worked
only for Piccolo and Sayers? That would surely not contribute
to a happy ending. And such an interpretation undercuts the
otherwise optimistic portrait of race relations in the movie.

If race relations were presented in a simple but not always
straightforward fashion, so was the world of professional football. In 1971 professional football in the United States functioned as a prosperous, growing big business with enormous
player salaries, well-organized unions, and million-dollar television contracts. But in *Brian's Song* that world was categorically
denied. Football was reduced to a simple game, with just
coaches and players. For example, early in the film George
Halas, owner and coach of the Chicago Bears, is shown as a
single entrepreneur. He decorates his own office. Contract
negotiations are done man to man, without high-priced lawyers. Players have no union or long-term contracts. Here is a

world where all that counts is how one performs on the playing field. The best play; others warm the bench. *Brian's Song* omits all those characteristics sports fans have come to associate with professional football in its television era (post-1957). The George Halas figure states it directly in the film when he reminds Sayers that Piccolo cannot play:

> I've had a policy on this team from the very start—the best player plays, no exceptions. And right now Kurek is the best player.[39]

It's the outside world that is seen as unfair, either through racism (a societal problem) or cancer (a problem of nature). Cancer is the least fair because it is so random. There is no way one can compete against it. As such, cancer offers a counterweight to the film's portrayal of football.

Brian's Song portrays football as a Mom-and-Pop small-time business. But sometimes cracks show through. The producers made constant use of football replay films, some in slow motion, which visually reminded viewers of television's role in professional sports. Many sports contradictions are embodied in one character, JC. At first this black man seems to be a coach. He lectures the players about their playbooks; he instructs Gale Sayers on the difficulties of the new roommate policy. Quickly we sense he is merely a player, presumably the captain. (Knowledgeable football fans recognized the reference to J. C. Caroline, a famous Bears defensive halfback). But soon he is replaced by the "true leader," Gale Sayers. It is the latter who tells the team and the world of Brain Piccolo's death. Indeed by the end of the film JC has become just "one of the guys." Certainly it was too radical an idea for JC to be a coach. All coaches were white. Gale Sayers was as close to becoming a leader as is possible for a black. As a bashful hero, he took on many of the characteristics of the white mythos. Even in this simple portrait of big business, whites ran things, and blacks worked for them. Like Jefferson Smith in Frank Capra's *Mr. Smith Goes to Washington* (1939), Sayers only assumes temporary power, and in the end the institution remains unchanged.

The least complex mythic portrait involves the role of women. Although women's-rights groups had made some progress by 1971, their victories had been small. Along with teenagers, women continued to be less trained, lower paid, and the last hired and first fired. In the world of *Brian's Song*, women became nearly invisible. This was a man's love story in which

Sayers and Piccolo seem most comfortable together. So at the end Sayers held Piccolo's hand (we even got a close-up of that image), and comforted him while their wives, the only female characters in the fim, stood off-screen. The film closed with Sayers, not Piccolo's wife, Joy, declaring his love. *Brian's Song* is a throwback to the buddy films so common in the 1930s and 1940s.

The two principal female characters, wives Joy Piccolo and Linda Sayers, have been reduced to flat stereotypes. They literally appear first in the film as two-dimensional black-and-white images, faded photographs tacked on the walls of their husbands' common dormitory room. As extensions of their husbands, they quickly become best friends. They sit together at football games. They giggle in unison at their husbands' jokes. When "real" help is needed (Gale learning a speech, or needing rehabilitation), it is Brian who helps him. Characteristically, in the end Joy and Linda break down, unable to handle the situation. Even Brian Piccolo, as sick as he is, must confort his wife. In sum, women play limited and traditional roles in this modern "buddy" film. It is interesting to note that many traditional black groups like the NAACP and Urban League praised the film. At least blacks were visible on the screen. No women's groups lauded *Brian's Song*. In no way can it be seen as a positive portrait of women.

In general, *Brian's Song* represented a major turning point in the economics of U.S. television by confirming the popularity of made-for-TV movies as an approved, respectable genre, and thus breaking the ground necessary for *Roots, Shogun*, and other original works for television. Analysis of this particular film offers interesting examples of how social and cultural forces in the United States during the Nixon era were reflected in the mass media. Through TV movies Hollywood was able to tackle social issues of race and sex in a controversial yet noncontroversial way.

NOTES

1. Cobbett S. Steinberg, *TV Facts* (New York: Facts on File, 1980), pp. 172, 181; Alex McNeil, *Total Television* (New York: Penguin, 1980), p. 31; Tim Brooks and Earle Marsh, *The Complete Directory to Prime Time Network TV Shows, 1946-Present* (New York: Ballantine, 1979), pp. 419–420.
2. Other awards *Brian's Song* achieved include the following: Writers Guild of America Aware; Golden Globe nomination; Golden Reel nomination; an

"Eddie" nomination by the American Cinema Editors; National Conference of Christian and Jews Mass Media Brotherhood Award "For Outstanding Contributions to Better Human Relations and the Cause of Brotherhood"; Congressional Record commendation as "one of the truly moving television and screen achievements in recent years"; American Cancer Society Special Citation. As of 1981, all fines of the National Football League go to the Brian Piccolo Memorial Cancer Fund. See Craig T. Norback and Peter G. Norback, eds., *TV Guide Almanac* (New York: Ballantine, 1980), pp. 310–312.

3. *New York Times*, January 28, 1972, p. 91.

4. Alfred D. Chandler, *The Visible Hand: The Managerial Revolution in American Business* (Cambridge: Harvard University Press, 1977).

5. Gerald Mast, *A Short History of the Movies*, 3rd ed. (Indianapolis: Bobbs-Merrill, 1981), pp. 260–261; Robert Stanley, *The Celluloid Empire* (New York: Hastings House, 1978), pp. 126–127; Laurence Kardish, *Reel Plastic Magic* (Boston: Little, Brown, 1972), pp. 180–183.

6. Orton Hicks and Haven Falconer, MGM Television Survey: Interim Report, April 29, 1955, Dore Schary Collection, Wisconsin Center for Film and Theatre Research, Madison, Wisc., pp. 1–8; Charles Higham, *Hollywood at Sunset* (New York: Saturday Review Press, 1972), p. 149; Michael Conant, *Antitrust in the Motion Picture Industry* (Berkeley: University of California Press, 1960), pp. 109–110; Harvey J. Levin, *Broadcast Regulation and Joint Ownership of Media* (New York: New York University Press, 1960), pp. 62–63.

7. Hicks and Falconer, MGM Television Survey, pp. 8–11; Higham, *Sunset*, p. 107; *Broadcasting*, January 17, 1955, pp. 50–51; *Autry* v. *Republic Productions*, 213 F.2d 667 (1954), opinion; *Republic Productions* v. *Rogers*, 213 F.2d 662 (1954); Christopher H. Sterling and John M. Kitross, *Stay Tuned* (Belmont, Calif.: Wadsworth, 1978), pp. 345–346.

8. Hicks and Falconer, MGM Television Survey, Interim Report, pp. 14–25; *Broadcasting*, April 23, 1956, p. 96; Richard Austin Smith, *Corporations in Crisis* (Garden City, N.Y.: Doubleday, 1966), pp. 64–66; *Broadcasting*, March 15, 1954, p. 35; *Broadcasting*, December 19, 1955, p. 40; "Coup for Teleradio," *Time*, January 16, 1955, p. 86; *Variety*, May 1, 1957, p. 50; Conant, *Antitrust*, p. 132; Gertrude Jobes, *Motion Picture Empire* (Hamden, Conn.: Anchor Books, 1966), pp. 368–369; Donald L. Barlett and James B. Steele, *Empire* (New York: Norton, 1978), pp. 165–170, 210.

9. The preponderant number of titles were restricted to pre-1948 titles because of union agreements.

10. *Broadcasting*, January 2, 1956, p. 7; Bob Thomas, *King Cohn* (New York: Putnam, 1967), pp. 262–287; *Broadcasting*, April 23, 1956, p. 98; *Broadcasting*, August 27, 1956, p. 68; *Broadcasting*, May 21, 1956, p. 52; *Broadcasting*, November 5, 1956, p. 48; *Variety*, June 5, 1957, p. 27; *Broadcasting*, June 25, 1956, p. 48; *Business Week*, September 1, 1956, p. 63; *Variety*, March 6, 1957, p. 25; *Forbes*, December 15, 1957, p. 31; *Forbes*, November 15, 1965, pp. 24–28; Stanley Brown, "That Old Villain TV Comes to the Rescue and Hollywood Rides Again," *Fortune*, November 1966, pp. 270–272.

11. Hollis Alpert, "Now the Earlier, Earlier Show," *New York Times Magazine*, August 11, 1963, p. 22; "Over the Rainbow," *Time*, August 25, 1967, p. 60; Robert Rich, "Post '48 Features," *Radio-Television Daily*, July 29, 1960, p. 27; *Forbes*, August 1, 1960, p. 23; "Saturday Night at the Movies," *TV Guide*, September 23, 1961, pp. A–9; John B. Burns, "Feature Films on TV," *Radio-Television Daily*, July 30, 1962, p. 32; *Variety*, September 24, 1980, pp. 88–89;

Variety, June 21, 1972, p. 34; *Variety*, September 20, 1978, pp. 48, 66; McNeil, *Total Television*, p. 851; Cobbett Steinberg, *Reel Facts* (New York: Random House, 1978), pp. 355–357; Brooks and March, *The Complete Directory*, pp. 416–420; Harry Castleman and Walter J. Podrazik, *Watching TV* (New York: McGraw-Hill, 1982), p. 149.

12. Martin Quigley, Jr., "11,325 Features for TV," *Motion Picture Herald*, January 18, 1967, p. 1; Neil Hickey, "The Day the Movies Run Out," *TV Guide*, October 23, 1965, pp. 6–9; Avra Fliegelman, ed., *TV Feature Film Source Book* 13 (Autumn 1972): 10–15; Walt Spencer, "Now Playing at Your Neighborhood Movie House: The Networks," *Television* SSV, no. 1 (January 1968), p. 49; Ryland A. Taylor, "Television Movie Audiences and Movie Awards: A Statistical Study," *Journal of Broadcasting* 18 (Spring 1974): 181–182.

13. Several sources list Universal's *See How They Run* telecast October 7, 1964 as the first movie made for television. The distinction between that work and *Fame Is the Name of the Game* is that the latter was the first television movie broadcast as part of a regular series. *See How They Run*, *Scalplock* (1966), and *The Hanged Man* (1964) were more like filmed specials. See Alvin H. Marill, *Movies Made for Television* (Westport, Conn.: Arlington House, 1980), pp. 11–12, and Paul Michael and James Robert Parish, eds., *The American Movies Reference Book: The Sound Era* (Englewood Cliffs, N.J.: Prentice-Hall, 1969), p. 37.

14. Spencer, "Now Playing," p. 41; Henry Ehrlich, "Every Night at the Movies," *Look*, September 7, 1971, p. 63; Jack E. Nolan, "Films on TV," *Films in Review* 17 (December 1966): 655–657; *Variety*, August 18, 1971, p. 30; *Variety*, June 14, 1972, p. 29; *Broadcasting*, January 15, 1973, p. 37; Don Shirley, "Made-for-TV Movies: It's Coming of Age," *Washington Post*, October 6, 1974, pp. E:1–2; Douglas Stone, "TV Movies and How They Get That Way," *Journal of Popular Film and Television* 7 (1979): 147–149.

15. Dick Adler and Joseph Finnigan, "The Year America Stayed Home for the Movies," *TV Guide*, May 20, 1972, pp. 6–10; *Broadcasting*, January 15, 1973, p. 37; Roger G. Noll, Merton J. Peck, and John J. McGowan, *Economic Aspects of Television Regulation* (Washington, D.C.: The Brookings Institution, 1973), p. 67; Caroline Meyer, "The Rating Power of Network Movies," *Television* 25 (March 1968): 56, 84; Jack E. Nolan, "Films on TV," *Films in Review* 24 (June-July 1973): 359; Caroline Meyer, "Series Movies: New Headache for Programmers," *Television* 25 (January 1968): 44–60; Shirley, "Made-for-TV Movies," *Washington Post*, October 6, 1974, p. E:3; Herbert Gold, "Television's Little Dramas," *Harper's*, March 1977, pp. 88–89; *Broadcasting*, September 25, 1972, p. 61.

16. John W. Ravage, *Television: The Director's Viewpoint* (Boulder, Colo.: Westview Press, 1978), pp. 103–112; Ephraim Kataz, *The Film Encyclopedia* (New York: Crowell, 1979), pp. 191, 708, 1208, 1236, 673; Les Brown, *The New York Times Encyclopedia of Television* (New York: Times Books, 1977), pp. 477, 43; Christopher Wicking and Tise Vahimagi, *The American Vein: Directors and Directions in Television* (New York: Dutton, 1979), pp. 27–28; Leslie Halliwell, *The Filmgoers Companion* (New York: Avon, 1977), pp. 248, 548, 430, 410, 750, 771, 119; Arleen Keylin and Christine Bent, *The New York Times at the Movies* (New York: Arno Press, 1979), p. 89; Marill, *Movies*, p. 348; *Variety*, December 8, 1971, p. 34.

17. Martin Kasindorf, "Movies Made for Television," *Action* 9 (January/February 1974): 13–15; Eileen Lois Becker, "The Network Television Decision Making Process: A Descriptive Examination of the Process Within the

Framework of Prime Time Made-for-TV Movies" (Master's thesis, University of California-Los Angeles, 1976), pp. 19–56; *Variety,* December 8, 1971, p. 34; Gold, "Little Dramas," pp. 90–93; *Broadcasting,* January 27, 1975, p. 21; *Broadcasting,* January 15, 1973, p. 36; *Broadcasting,* August 7, 1972, pp. 23–25.

18. Kasindorf, "Movies," pp. 16–19; *New York Times,* January 28, 1972, p. 91; Gale Sayers with Al Silverman, *I Am Third* (New York: Viking, 1970); Jeannie Morris, *Brian Piccolo: A Short Season* (Chicago: Rand McNally, 1971); *Variety,* December 15, 1971, p. 29.

19. *Broadcasting,* October 19, 1981, p. 61.

20. Andrew Bergman, *We're in the Money: Depression America and Its Films* (New York: New York University Press, 1971).

21. Patrick McGilligan, "Movies Are Better Than Ever—On Television," *American Film* 5 (March 1980): 50–54; Becker, "Decision Making," pp. 41–54; Stone, "TV Movies," pp. 150–155; John M. Smith, "Making Do–Or Better? The American T.V. Movie," *Movie* 21 (Autumn 1975): 38–40; Bruce Cook, "Can Filmmakers Find Happiness on Television?" *AFI Report* 5 (Spring 1974): 38–40.

22. David Bordwell and Kristin Thompson, *Film Art: An Introduction* (Reading, Mass.: Addison-Wesley, 1979), pp. 50–59; Raymond Bellour, "To Analyze, to Segment," *Quarterly Review of Film Studies* 1 (August 1976): 331–354; Stephen Heath, "Film and System: Terms of Analysis," *Screen* 16 (Spring 1975): 7–77 and *Screen* (Summer 1975): 91–113.

23. Nancy Schwartz, "TV Movies," *Film Comment* 11 (March-April 1975): 36–39; Becker, "Decision Making," pp. 57–125; Gold, "Little Dramas," pp. 87–89; *Broadcasting,* January 27, 1975, p. 21; *Broadcasting,* January 15, 1973, pp. 40–45; Stone, "TV Movies," pp. 154–157; Smith, "Making Do," pp. 141–145; Cook, "Happiness," pp. 42–46.

24. *TV Guide,* November 27, 1971, pp. A–55.

25. William Blinn, *Brian's Song: Screenplay* (New York: Bantam, 1972), pp. 118–119. All dialogue quotations were double-checked against a 16mm copy of the film.

26. Other elements also help unify the story and develop its important themes. Obvious to all must be the theme music. The leitmotif is directly associated with death and dying. More subtle but just as effective is a motif of meeting and gesture. First we see Brian and Gale greet each other very formally by reluctantly shaking hands. As they become close friends, they "slap hands," a gesture of black origin. At the end the two men gesture awkwardly. When Gale first comes to see Brian in the hospital, they must shake hands left-handed because of Brian's infirmity. In the death scene they clasp hands for the first time. Here black and white are finally united, but only in death.

27. The theatrical film *Love Story* also influenced *Brian's Song.* Indeed young people dying through no fault of their own has been a popular narrative structure since the Romantic period. See also Steinberg, *TV Facts,* p. 334, and James Monaco, *American Film Now* (New York: Oxford University Press, 1979), pp. 7–10.

28. Russell L. Merritt, "The Bashful Hero in American Film of the Nineteen Forties," *Quarterly Journal of Speech* 61 (April 1975): 129–139.

29. Merritt, "Bashful Hero," p. 131.

30. Blinn, *Screenplay,* p. 25.

31. Merritt, "Bashful Hero," p. 134.

32. *Brian's Song*'s narrative and genre elements proved so powerful no commentators seemed to notice the liberty the film took with the story (the intercut football sequences contain errors in matching of costume and color) and fact (Piccolo and Sayers were not very good friends off the field; racism continued in their private lives).

33. John M. Blum, Edmund S. Morgan, Willie Lee Rose, Arthur M. Schlesinger, Jr., Kenneth M. Stampp, and C. Vann Woodward, *The National Experience*, part 2 (New York: Harcourt Brace Jovanovich, 1973), pp. 758–792; Richard Hofstader, William Miller, Daniel Aaron, Winthrop D. Jordon, and Leon F. Litwack, *The United States*, 4th ed. (Englewood Cliffs, N.J.: Prentice-Hall, 1976), pp. 678–705; Samuel Eliot Morison, Henry Steele Commager, and William E. Leuchtenburg, *A Concise History of the American Republic* (New York: Oxford University Press, 1977), pp. 715–745; Richard D. Current, T. Harry Williams, and Frank Freidel, *American History*, 5th ed. (New York: Knopf, 1979), pp. 768–799.

34. Blum et al., *National Experience*, pp. 804–805; Hofstader et al., *United States*, pp. 708–709; Current et al., *American History*, pp. 817–818; Howard Zinn, *A People's History of the United States* (New York: Harper & Row, 1980), pp. 529–569.

35. Roger G. Noll, ed., *Government and the Sports Business* (Washington, D.C.: The Brookings Institution, 1974), pp. 1–32, 275–324; Walter Adams, ed., *The Structure of American Industry*, 5th ed. (New York: Macmillan, 1977), pp. 365–400.

36. "John Ford's *Young Mr. Lincoln*" (a collective text by the editors of *Cabiers du Cinéma*), *Screen* 13 (Autumn 1972): 5–15; Nick Browne, "The Politics of Narrative Form: Capra's *Mr. Smith Goes to Washington*," *Wide Angle* 3 (1980): 4–11.

37. Morison et al., *Concise History*, pp. 740–744; Jerome H. Skolnick and Elliott Currie, *Crisis in American Institutions* (Boston: Little, Brown, 1970), pp. 70–123; Hofstader et al., *United States*, pp. 707–708; Current et al., *American History*, pp. 816–817.

38. The use of other filmic parameters reinforced this picture of race relations. Consider, for example, the use of camera work that created the motif of running. Sayers and Piccolo seemed always to be paired in training camp spring tests. Who was faster? Of course, Sayers, the superhero, always won, with Piccolo struggling close behind. But here the continuous use of a telephoto lens, squashing spatial depth, linked the two together as they ran. In one lyrical moment, coupled with slow motion, we see the two race through the park "for a beer." With a telephoto lens and slow-motion photography, they seem to run as one. Even though these two athletes compete, they are united.

39. Blinn, *Screenplay*, p. 52.

HORACE NEWCOMB

TEXAS:
A GIANT STATE OF MIND

One hundred and fifty years ago, people wrote "GTT" over the doorways of busted-out post-war rent farms in Mississippi, Alabama, and Georgia. That meant the family had "Gone to Texas." They piled everything worth taking onto a two-mule wagon and headed west. The people were after cotton and cattle. And land. The oil came later, much of it from under land that was fit for neither cows nor plows, land that had already changed hands more than once by the time it was drilled.

Today they come from Los Angeles and New York; they come in comfort, on the big jets, first class—high rollers, ready to buddy up with the down-home types. Taxiing into the gigantic horseshoes of Dallas-Fort Worth Regional Airport, they already sport the boots and hats, boutique items bought in little sidestreet shops in fashionable neighborhoods back home.

They've come to scout locations or to film some title sequences and "establishing shots." Or they've come just for the fun of it, to see what it's all about. They'll meet the rich folks with Hollywood connections, talk to the mayor, eat some barbecue. They'll hop in a pickup and wheel down to "Yewston" to see Gilley's and the Galleria, listen to a little music, cuss the heat, and head for home two days later. The very least the new travellers hope for is a good television pilot, something that blends stereotype and audience expectation, glamour and violence, high stakes and low-down loving.

It's residuals they're farming now, the gleam of syndication shining in the vice-presidential glance like hope in the eye of a forty-acre farmer. "GTT" still works. Now it means—"Get Texas Television."

From *Channels*, Vol. 1, No. 1, April–May 1981. Reprinted by permission of *Channels* Magazine. Copyright © 1981.

Because of the unexpected success of *Dallas*, Texas is hot. *Time* doesn't do covers on subjects that aren't. And while nobody in Los Angeles or New York knows how to start a trend, they certainly do know how to spot one. Quickly then, in every stage of production, come the copies. *Texas*, the daytime version of *Dallas*, brings the same soap-opera license to old topics of social intrigue, class strife, financial chicanery, and sexual confusion. With marvelous bravado this show moves into such topical areas as Middle Eastern revolution and petroleum politics, while keeping regional roots on the surface with such lines as, "If I had to move off this ranch I guess I would die." *Knots Landing* ties *Dallas* to Southern California with familial ropes, but little more than random accents remain. *Flamingo Road* leaves Texas for Florida, where flesh and sweat are supposed to be in equal supply.

What are we to make of this sudden run of "y'alls," these "ma'ams," and "Daddys"? These fanciful, often stereotypical, and sometimes exploitative images have seized the public's imagination—highbrow, lowbrow—in England and Nigeria, all around the world. We desperately needed to have J.R. live, and yet we knew so well that whoever shot him should be awarded a "Good Deed of the Week" prize. The audience's incredible involvement has a lot to do with the show's exquisitely fortuitous casting. Who could have planned the success of Larry Hagman's grin or of Victoria Principal's testy stride? Even greater contributions to the show's success were the spread of country music and the popularity of crossover performers like Dolly Parton and outlaws like Willie Nelson. Chicago wore boots and the Lone Star Cafe was a New York hit before we had the new television Texans. Even the Cowboys, called "America's Team," show striking similarities to *Dallas*. Like Miss Ellie waiting for a phone call, Tom Landry paces the sidelines in tense anticipation, and the Dallas Cowboy's bouncy, sexy cheerleaders give the younger Southfork women lessons in how to dress for breakfast.

"Trend" is too mild a way to explain television's country fixation. *Dallas* and the other shows—*Urban Cowboy* and the country music movies, Burt Reynolds as hero-hick, even Sheriff *Lobo*, *The Dukes of Hazzard*, and the cartoon characters who hang around *Flo's* café—tap a far deeper source in American entertainment. The West and the South, and now the new hybrid, the Sunbelt, have always served as a mirror on which the image-merchants project characters who never existed, the cowboys, hillbillies, bandits, and dumb sheriffs. Their actions are performed within the broad limits of the imagination, rarely bounded by the average person's experience. Still, they amuse and thrill us, *and* they seem familiar. We have heard it before but never in so appropriately contemporary a manner. These characters are talking to us about ourselves, and their words come from some of popular culture's most powerful and appealing language. What we get is a sense of place, of tradition, and of true character. And we like what we hear because such qualities are in very short supply these days.

For the most part television is as devoid of any real sense of place as a theme park. While most critics think that this is because everything is filmed in California, the visual aspects actually have little influence on our *sense* of place. Reference to a regional food, a touch of what the audience thinks of as an accurate accent, and the mood is set. A sense of place must be evoked, not duplicated visually. This is why *Kojak* was better at place than *The Mary Tyler Moore Show*. Jump-cut titles that take us around a city do little to evoke its mood if the immediate action doesn't follow through.

Southern shows have been best at developing this quality. *The Beverly Hillbillies* traded continually on the premise that the family had moved from *some*place to *no* place and that it was genuinely disturbed by the fact. *The Waltons* managed, with voice, theme, and historical reference, to plant itself in the minds of viewers as actually representing the mountain communities of Virginia.

Dallas and the new Sunbelt series are superb at creating this quality, weaving a texture of place that feels familiar. We've seen the huge swagger, the openness to stranger and friend alike. We've heard the loud, familiar voices, ringing as if everything is a celebration. But we've also seen the sinister threat that comes when the eyes narrow and the voices drop to a whispering intensity. We know all this from John Wayne's drawl, James Arness's stance, the soft thunder of "When you call me that, smile," even from Lyndon Johnson's remembered boasts.

These are the evocative cues. Their real importance is found in qualities that accompany them, telling us that this is a place of confrontation, of testing, of possible violence. The potential for failure is strong, matched only by the sense of possibility.

Men and women are measured here daily, and threatened frequently. It is an old and complex dream world in which one must gamble and fight repeatedly to hold on to what he has.

And when Texas is involved, there is always the lust for empire. In history and fiction the state has lured visionaries, politicians, scoundrels, outcasts, missionaries, and entrepreneurs. There was supposed to be enough for them all. But empires call for emperors, emperors become despots, and the dream curdles.

Played small, this is the plight of the gunfighter. Reputation established, he waits now for every puny fool who wants to bring him down. The best examples are in epics like *Red River*. John Wayne, as Tom Dunson, builds his vast ranch from nearly nothing, only to be defeated by a failure of nerve when he is threatened by financial ruin and the manhood of his figurative son. In a way this Texas story is a microcosm, not just for the West, but for the whole country. Cursed and blessed with grand dreams and vast land, we've spent decades trying to remain pure while making the big kill. From the very early westerns through the work of Ford and Hawks, to films like *Giant*, *Hud*, and *Urban Cowboy*, we live it out over and over again with our tainted heroes.

What *Dallas* has done—and it counts in large measure for the show's success—is to transfer these old western meanings to a new and different world, to the Dallas of express highways and sunning skyscrapers. The old shows began with the stagecoach topping the horizon. Now we swoop over the scurrying cars in a helicopter, carrying the horizon with us. We sense that the barbecues and lonesome music mask a deadly seriousness. The shootouts have merely been transferred to the boardrooms, and when we see the brothers W. Herbert and Nelson Bunker Hunt bluff Congress on the evening news we understand them better because we now know J.R.

But it would be a big mistake to define the new West or the success of *Dallas* solely in terms of these regional characteristics. Eventually tradition tamed the frontier and checked rampant opportunism.

In *Dallas*, tradition begins at home. Throughout the show we swing from office to ranch, restaurant to dining room, boardroom to den. Family is the second powerful attraction of the show. As we Texans sometimes say, "How's ya Mama'n'em?"

Thank goodness Miss Ellie didn't marry Digger Barnes. Despite his protestations to the contrary, not even the passionate love of this good woman would have kept him from becoming a whiny old drunk. In choosing Jock she chose the sunrise of a dynasty. She holds the family together with those crinkly-eyed smiles and bosomy embraces. Jock may not understand it all, but when one of the boys or girls offends his wife, or what she stands for, he comes down with both boots. Actually, like all good parents, Miss Ellie and Jock just want the best for their kids, and like most they spend a fair amount of time worrying about them. That's part of the tradition.

Again, the real genius of the show emerges in the tension of transferring those old values to the inhabitants of the new West. For all the younger Ewings, their spouses, friends, and assorted lovers, these traditions are the backdrop against which they play out their own frantic struggles for stability, happiness, and success. They believe in the old ways, but they don't know how to make them work in a time and place where money and power dominate. Tradition makes Pam feel inferior, but it also drives her to search for her own personal identity. For Sue Ellen and Lucy, tradition threatens freedom. Both are trapped, and to escape they must behave badly. To the old people, then, tradition is part of a rich existence and full of meaning. To the young ones it is merely part of the air they breathe. And to J.R. it is a tool.

Utterly realistic in the show's fictional world, J.R. at once embodies the sense of place and sneers at it. He believes in tradition and family, perhaps more than anyone else, and he uses them to keep Bobby in line and Sue Ellen on a string. Dynasty is what he wants and he will go to any length to obtain it. There is no contradiction in character when J.R. tenderly holds his infant son. He is holding his world together until his son can take over. That is J.R.'s one and only business, hobby, dream, and burden.

He is the third great feature of *Dallas*, made possible in part by the other two: sense of place and the idea of tradition. Without such texture he would be a caricature. Hagman also helps to prevent this with small actions. His face disintegrates when someone discovers one of his schemes; his anger pours out briefly before he regains control of Sue Ellen. He hurries from his call girl because he finds no real satisfaction.

As a result, television has its most developed character since Archie Bunker, and the two are much alike. Both are obstinate, intent on blundering through the world as if they were utterly

sure of their intentions and actions. All the while we know that
they remain on the verge of failure and defeat. They appeal to
us as much for their weaknesses as for their strengths. We like
to know that behind their facades our villains are touchy and
vulnerable.

J.R. blends the old West and new, inevitably winning battles
by using old ways. He pushes civility to the limits, strains every
family tie, every sign of love, overlooking basic morality, the
law, and business ethics. If there is something to grab, J.R.
grabs it.

In this way he is much like the prototypical "Good Old Boy."
What is marvelous about that term is that many of us truly
desire to be "Old" and to be a "Boy." We want to behave
rambunctiously and at the same time be taken seriously, getting adult responsibility in the arenas of money, sex, and
power. Therefore in his action, the Good Old Boy demands to
be honored, and pleads for approval.

More than anything else, more than money or even power,
J.R. longs for his father's approval. Without this he will have
nothing of true value to pass on to his own son. To receive the
nod from Jock, J.R. must be capable of some flamboyant act,
something truly worthy of his father's own exploits. Around
this theme all other Ewing narratives unfold. We wait and
watch as story after story develops and fades into another. We
wait as we waited in numberless westerns for the gunfight to
begin, held in suspense by our hope for the tarnished hero.
With its brilliant appropriation of soap opera form, *Dallas*, perhaps indefinitely, has postponed resolutions. In such an unending story there is always hope, for J.R. and for us.

The power of *Dallas* lies in this extraordinary accomplishment of the oldest pop-culture trick. It has recycled a cluster of
America's most basic images and polished them into a financial
success. Probably without knowing it, the show's creators
pump nourishment into audiences' veins. Their timing is perfect. As a nation we are actually growing older and developing
the caution that comes with age. It is a time of decline, of
recession and restriction, a time of real trouble. The grand old
cities of the East and the Midwest are burdened with financial
failure and bitter winters. Small wonder that the Sunbelt flour-
ishes and *Dallas* leads the ratings. Small wonder, too, that J.R.
has become a national symbol, replacing the mellower, resigned, saddened Archie Bunker.

A certain political resonance in all of this relates to our recent presidential elections. Carter's success was much like the initial success of *Dallas;* both were exotic. In the new South, the true southern romantic and the cavalier have long since been replaced by the efficient manager. There may have been little of J.R. in Jimmy Carter—but we usually go for the loner, the outsider from the hills that Carter represented. Four years ago he was the only one willing to face down the gang in town. The Sunbelt was promising its old salvation and, for a moment, when Carter's people walked down Constitution Avenue, it was as if the film hero Shane had come back. Now that all seems anachronistic. It didn't work, and like Cooper at the end of the film *High Noon*, Carter packed up his family and rode out. The Reagan Administration promises style and power, an understanding of boardroom politics, big money, and smooth deals. At the moment, J.R. and the glamour of high finance are more intriguing to us—offer more—than the gunfighter's purity of mission.

The paradox is obvious. The wheelers and dealers in *Dallas* are all hip-deep in booze, blackmail, and what some folks call illicit sex. Their world has a frightening callousness. It may sound rather offensive to many Reagan supporters, and no doubt the Moral Majority eschews *Dallas* as another example of crumbling values. But for them, as for many voters, the unpleasantness of tawdry glitter and soiled boots are overshadowed by what they see as the new Administration's sense of purpose and will. Maybe we should have anticipated the conservative sweep when J.R., acting on knowledge gained from his private intelligence sources, saved Ewing Oil from the clutch of greedy nationalists. In the face of utter disaster he took action and did what a man had to do. No negotiation. No fine ethical dilemma. That he sold friends out in the process might give momentary pause but for the ruthless clarity of intention. We had already heard of Lone Ranger diplomacy. No wonder "J.R. for President" bumper stickers appeared immediately.

What we see in J.R. is a refusal to give up. He holds on. The grand gestures count, as they always have in the romance of the West and the South. Why else would John Travolta in *Urban Cowboy* need so desperately to ride the bull and ride it better? Why would we thrill to Burt Reynolds' "bandit" character if it were not for his remarkable will?

This is why settlers came to Texas originally, and why

"GTT" never needed a translation. This is why we always have westerns in America although they are high-rise, glass-fronted, six-lane concrete westerns. Even if there are old Mercedes hubcaps lying beside the road instead of buffalo chips, we want the old dream. As usual, imagination exceeds experience.

Other shows will try to move in on the territory. Many of them will succeed in capturing one or two of the elements that have made *Dallas*. My hunch is that none of them will gather all of them into a single world as powerful and compelling as this one. *Dallas* got there first and claimed the water rights. If it comes to a showdown, we all know who to back.

MARSHA KINDER

MUSIC VIDEO AND THE SPECTATOR: TELEVISION, IDEOLOGY, AND DREAM

Music video is a protean form that has proven its magnetic power on MTV, a national 24-hour cable station devoted entirely to this programming on a continuous basis. It is now popping up on other cable stations, frequently appearing between movies the way cartoons and newsreels used to punctuate the spaces between features at movie theaters. It is also breaking into commercial television, where as many as 300 programs across the nation are devoted to music videos during carefully chosen hours.

Music video has even found its way into movies, providing the central creative energy for a subgenre launched by *Flashdance*—films that weave loose narratives around hot dance sequences created by montage and that generate fast-selling videos. The connection with film also proved lucrative in Michael Jackson's *Thriller*, the 14-minute video directed by feature filmmaker John Landis (*Animal House, American Werewolf in London, Twilight Zone*). According to *Newsweek* (August 6, 1984), the documentary film *Making Michael Jackson's Thriller*, though it's only a spin-off, has already sold 450,000 cassettes, making it the second-best-selling video in history. *Thriller*'s stunning commercial success, extended length, and conscious positioning within the horror film genre helped strengthen the link between music video and mainstream filmmaking. Respected auteurs like Nicholas Roeg, Bob Rafelson, Tobe Hooper, and Andy Warhol have entered the field, a trend that challenges the old unidirectional model which assumed *all* directors of commercials

Reprinted from *Film Quarterly*, Vol. 38, No. 1, Autumn, pp. 2–15 by permission of the Regents. Copyright © 1984 by the Regents of the University of California.

and television were fighting their way up from the boob tube to enter the celestial art of Cinema. Now, according to Warhol, "Everyone wants to make music videos!"[1]

What is the significance of this quicksilver phenomenon? Depending on which mass media reports you read, music video is a new means of extending the unique aesthetic possibilities of the avant-garde formerly restricted to independent filmmaking and video art, a new combination of music and images that redefines audiovisual relations in the mass media, a new means of marketing records and tapes that is saving the pop music industry, or a new source of violent sexist sadomasochistic images infecting the minds of our children.

While all of these perspectives may have validity, the underlying phenomenon that makes them all possible has been ignored: music video seems to be forging new codes of spectator relations, or more accurately, it is making the codes that were already operative in television more transparent. MTV provides a model that highlights through exaggeration the unique aspects of television, particularly those that distinguish the medium from cinema, and that have highly significant implications on two registers—television's relation to ideology and its relation to dream.

In the discussion of music video that follows, there will be no attempt to establish a canon or to create a pantheon of auteurs—projects that are already well under way.[2] I will not be examining the best works that the genre has produced, many of which have never been or are no longer being aired on MTV but are available in video stores and private collections. (Most songs have an even shorter life on MTV than they do on Top 40 radio stations.) Since I will be exploring MTV programming as a model of commercial television, I will limit my discussion to rock video, the station's main staple, though other forms of pop music such as jazz have also entered the field, and I will restrict my examples to those video clips being broadcast at the time I was writing this essay, choosing them almost at random to illustrate what is typical rather than what is most powerful aesthetically.

PRESENCE/ABSENCE OF THE VISUAL IMAGE

One of the most compelling aspects of rock video is its power to evoke specific visual images in the mind of the spectator every time one hears the music with which they have been juxtaposed on television. The experience of having watched and listened to a particular video clip on television establishes these connections in the brain circuitry; by repeating the experience very frequently within a short period of time (a situation guaranteed by the repetitive structure of MTV), the spectator strengthens these associations in the brain. Thus later when the spectator hears the song on the radio or in a different context in which the visuals are absent, the presence of the music is likely to draw these images from memory, accompanied by the desire to see them again. This process follows the basic patterns of conditioning well established in the field of cognitive learning.

In rock video it is not merely a matter of whether we hear and see the performer (as we do in live performance at a concert or nightclub). In many rock video clips the visuals do not focus *primarily* on the performer in the act of performing; those that do, risk appearing regressive for they are reverting to conventions used in rock film documentaries from the sixties and seventies like *Monterey Pop* and *Woodstock*. In most rock videos what we do see is a chain of disparate images, which may involve the musical performers, but which stress discontinuities in space and time—a structure that resembles the form of dreams. Though the pulsing kinetic rhythms of the visual montage are invariably accentuated by the musical beat, the continuous flow of the music and lyrics also imposes a unifying identity (sometimes augmented by a narrative component in the lyrics and/or visuals) onto the discontinuous visual track, distinguishing it from the chains of similar images in the video clips that precede and follow this particular musical text.

This structure insures that the visuals will be the primary source of pleasure, for it is the lush visual track that will be withdrawn, withheld or suspended, when the spectator is no longer watching television but *only listening* to the song on the radio or stereo. The reverse situation—the presence of the visuals and the absence of the audio—is not built into the system; it can be achieved only through technical breakdown or through the spectator's intervention (turning off the sound while watching the images). Pioneer plays with this irony in one of its commercials for laser disc players by having blind singer Ray Charles deliver their slogan: "Video for those who really care about audio." This music video structure tends to subordinate the audio component of television by linking it with radio. Although some critics have argued that this linkage enables television sound to act as a cue that draws the spectator's attention to certain video images, radio still remains the superseded medium which lacks the perceptual richness that television shares with cinema. In all television the visual component is privileged over the audio—a condition which is overdetermined by historical, cultural and psychological factors[3] and which is revealed in the very term used for TV spectators, *viewers*.

The complex structure of the visual chain of images in most rock videos makes the reliance on memory and the value of repeated viewings all the more essential. If a person hears the song first before seeing the video clip that combines sound and image, the complexity of the visual form makes it virtually impossible for this listener to predict how the video would look. The situation is very different from the way it was in the sixties or seventies when a rock fan might buy a new album or audio tape by the Stones and then while listening, sit back and imagine how Jagger might look while performing this particular number.[4] It probably would have been even more likely for such a listener to place her- or himself in an imaginary setting and fantasize erotic behavior evoked by the lyrics, or to use the music as a sound track for actual physical acts (sex, dancing, exercise, or what you will). In such instances, the very absence of the live performers (represented only by still images on album covers, which frequently featured suggestive scenes or fetishes instead of the performers) invited the listener to create a waking fantasy. In those days the rock fan was expected to generate his or her own images; the visual component of the fantasies elicited by pop music was not totally prefabricated.

I don't mean to imply that music video is incapable of stimulating viewers to dream up their own chains of images, perhaps in a different style and with new combinations. Yet the remembering of images one has already seen seems an essential first step—a process I have seen prepubescent and teenage viewers transform into a game of Who can remember the most details? This goal of memory retrieval or replication is fostered by some of the performers. When recently interviewed by a video jockey on MTV, Roger Waters assured his fans that those coming to his latest live concert would not be disappointed when they *heard* "5:05 AM, The Pros and Cons of Hitchhiking," for they would be *seeing* visual effects that equalled those they had seen in the video clip. Most concert promotions currently being aired on MTV stress the extravagance of the visual spectacle as much as the music—spectacle designed to match what is being seen on television.

Music video challenges the listener to play a hip *fort/da* game of Can you recall the absent visuals? Can you return to being a viewer and experiencing the original plenitude of sight and sound? This game is designed to drive all players back to the TV set to compulsively consume those prefabricated fantasy images on MTV (or wherever they can be found), knowing that all popular favorites will be repeated but rarely being able to predict more than a half hour in advance the precise time that any particular clip will be aired. (Didn't the followers of Pavlov and Skinner teach us that inconsistent patterns of reinforcement would intensify and prolong the compulsive repetition of the desired behavior?)

PERFORMANCE, NARRATIVE, AND DREAMLIKE VISUALS

Thus far I have been talking as if all music videos had equal visual complexity and were all characterized by one style, neither of which is the case. Yet virtually all rock videos *are* comprised of three distinct components, which are combined with different emphases to create considerable variety within the form. First, the performance of the singer or group identifies the form with the musical genre and with the historic pop tradition of recording live performances on tape or film. Second, a simple or complex narrative carried by the lyrics and/ or visual images, and sometimes featuring a guest star, turns the video into a minifilm with specific generic identification (e.g., horror, gangster film, screwball comedy, western, *noir*, melodrama, women's picture), making the visuals easier to remember and providing the spectator with a prefabricated daydream with varying degrees of space left for personal elaborations. Third, a series of incongruous visual images stressing spatial and temporal dislocations makes rock video closely resemble dreams—the primary medium that weaves loose narratives out of chains of incoherent images and that, despite its selective audio component, is predominantly a visual experience. Both performance and narrative work toward coherence, distinguishing the text from other rock video clips; in contrast, the dreamlike visuals work toward decentering and dissolution, revealing the deep structure of all television as an endless chain of images whose configuration into any structural unity or text is only a temporary, illusory by-product of secondary revision.

The musical performance always dominates the audio, but varies in the degree to which it controls or is even present in the visuals. The narrative element is variable both on the audio and visual registers, sometimes dominating one or both, other times virtually absent except for the tendency of the human brain to read a story into any series of consecutive images, particularly when accompanied by words. The chain of incongruous images is restricted primarily to the visuals, varying in the quantity and pacing of the spatial and temporal dislocations and in the degree to which special effects are employed, but at least minimally present in the form of rapid montage which is featured in virtually all rock videos and also characteristic of commercials. While many commentators have called these dreamlike visuals *surreal*, it is important to distinguish them from the historical surrealism represented in film by Buñuel, a modernist movement which used dream rhetoric as a radical strategy to undermine the power of bourgeois ideology, particularly as it was manifest in the fine arts. In contrast, this postmodernist pop surrealism uses dream images to cultivate a narcissism that promotes our submission to bourgeois consumerism.

Music video has adopted quite consciously the visual conventions of the TV commercial, which has provided many talented directors (like Tim Newman and Bob Giraldi) for the new form. When viewing MTV, it is difficult to distinguish the video clips from the commercials because of close similarities in visual style, background music, and short format. The same is true for the MTV news, which usually features three short items promoting commercial ventures, and for the station ID's, which sometimes include brief excerpts from clips of the most famous video stars—all presented in fast montage. These conventions from the commercial have been adopted because of their ability to capture and hold the spectator's attention, which is fundamental to their selling power. Research has shown that this kind of fast-paced visual style holds the attention even of the preschool viewer, which is one of the reasons why it has been incorporated into kiddie shows like "Sesame Street" and why rock video has such an hypnotic effect on young children. The fast pace of MTV's programming might also be connected with the rise of cocaine as the dominant drug in pop culture in place of acid and grass. In Michael Jackson's Pepsi generation full of Pepper-uppers, Coke is it.

Like all television, the primary function of MTV's rock video is to sell products. While this goal is explicit in the TV commercial and fairly visible on MTV, it is disguised in most conventional programming on commercial television. Nick Browne has argued that while the television program is presented as the primary text and the commercials that temporarily interrupt it as secondary, the opposite is true, for the main function of the program is to provide a suitable environment for the commercial message. The actual television text is "a 'supertext' that consists of the particular program and all the introductory and interstitial materials—chiefly announcements and ads . . ." and "advertising . . . the central mediating discursive institution."[5] MTV exposes the "supertext" by erasing the illusory boundaries within its continuous flow of uniform programming and reveals the central mediating position of advertising by adopting its formal conventions as the dominant stylistic. In fact, *everything* on MTV is a commercial—advertising spots, news, station ID's, interviews, and especially music video clips.

Whereas other TV stations usually have to pay for the programs which the commercials interrupt, MTV has no such overhead. No wonder their station ID's are so varied and spectacular; they are practically the only "programs" that MTV produces. This situation highlights the main business of every TV station—not to generate programs, but to deliver viewers (at the lowest cost per thousand) to advertisers who pay both for the commercials and for the time it takes to air them. The music industry is happy to provide the video clips as free programming for MTV because the air time for these thinly disguised commercials is also free. In this sweet business arrangement, as long as the viewers keep watching and buying, both station and advertiser not only profit, but get something for nothing.

All three components of rock video serve consumerist goals. The performance motivates the spectator specifically to buy a particular album on which the featured song is recorded. The name of the group, song, album, and record company appear at the beginning and end of every clip every time it is aired, implying that the spectator should be eager to note this information in order to facilitate the anticipated purchase.[6] More generally, the performance is also selling the performers, whose future commercial ventures (concerts, nightclub dates, and future recordings) the spectator will be expected to support. Both the narrative and dreamlike visuals motivate the spectator specifically to buy, not just the album, but the video

Monitored in Los Angeles
Sunday, July 15, 1984, 12 noon–1 P.M.
* = music videos

12:00   MTV station ID, leading
        into voice-over of VJ
        Mark Goodman announc-
        ing what clips and news
        items will be featured in
        the next half hour.

        *Scorpions: "Still Loving
        You." Performance rup-
        tured by fragmented visu-
        als and shifts of scene.

12:05   *Bette Midler: "Beast of
        Burden." Screwball
        comedy narrative co-star-
        ring Mick Jagger, incorpo-
        rating live performance
        by Midler, which Jagger
        eventually joins.

12:10   MTV promotion for
        stereo hook-up.

        Commercial for Thunder-
        bird cars, with fast mon-
        tage.

        Commercial for Little
        Steven album, including
        shots of live performance
        and concert schedule
        (usually included as news
        items).

        Commercial for Reese's
        Pieces candy, featuring
        comic narrative with E.T.
        lookalike.

        *Don Hartman (perfor-
        mance by the Sorels): "I
        Can Dream About You."
        Stage performance by
        black male singers, the
        Sorels, is framed by and
        intercut with romantic
        narrative about a white
        couple.

12:15   *The Alan Parsons Project:
        "Prime Time." Nightmare
        horror narrative featuring
        mannequins, some of
        whom come alive through
        the magic of special ef-
        fects. We never see the
        singer or musicians per-
        forming.

12:20   VJ Mark Goodman on
        screen, comments on clips
        just aired and then pre-
        sents the news, including
        3 items all promoting com-
        mercial ventures:
            Plasmatics singer
              Wendy O has done
              her first solo album;
              VJ presents a brief in-
              terview shown on a
              TV monitor.
            Grace Jones, who made
              her screen debut in
              the new Conan film
              now playing in the-
              aters, will have a new
              role in the next James
              Bond movie.
            Judas Priest concert
              dates.

        Commercial for the new
        Carpenters Album. The
        surviving brother talks
        about his dead sister
        Karen, who appears in
        brief excerpts singing
        their greatest hits.

12:25   *Stray Cats: "Stray Cats
        Strut." Comic narrative
        featuring the group per-
        forming in an alley, draw-
        ing female reactions from
        a real live puss, two grou-
        pies, and an old bitchy
        neighbor who throws

things at them and then switches channels on her TV set but keeps their performance or an animated cartoon starring other stray cats.

*Elton John: "Sad Songs (Say So Much)." Narrative involving another street performance, but featuring a catalogue of listeners in a vareity of contexts hearing those sad songs on radio, TV, stereo, etc., matched by multiple images of Elton performing in a variety of hats and styles.

12:30　MTV station ID

*Ratt: "Round and Round." Narrative that parodies the horror film, featuring an elegant formal dinner where two of the guests are played by Milton Berle. The dinner is disrupted by rock performers in the attic who transform one beautiful guest and the butler, not into vampires or werewolves, but punk groupies.

12:35　*Ultravox: "Vienna." Surreal visual images disguise narrative intrigue, as the lyrics keep telling us "this means nothing to me."

12:40　MTV promotion for appearance of Christine McVie.

Commercial for Mountain Dew soft drinks, with fast montage.

Commercial for Novabeam television, a large screen. "Once you see it, you'll never be able to watch a small screen again."

Commercial for Soft 'n Dri deodorant, featuring a narrative about a young black female newscaster making her TV debut.

MTV station ID

12:45　*Police: "Wrapped Around Your Finger." Performance disrupted by dreamlike visuals involving hundreds of long candles, constant camera movement with deep focus, cross dissolves, dynamic montage, and a flicker effect.

*Rick Springfield: "Don't Walk Away." Romantic narrative with dreamlike visuals that follow the singer to his apartment, where paintings provide settings for a series of inset narratives that tell the same story of a sad parting in a variety of scenes associated with different genres.

12:50　VJ Mark Goodman on screen to promote clips by Sam Hagar and Huey Lewis which will debut on MTV.

Commercial for Chrysler Laser XE—with fast montage.

Commercial for Fabergé body spray—with fast montage.

Commercial for "Electric Dreams," a new movie directed by the man who directed Michael Jackson's "Billy Jean" video (in some of the other commercials for this same movie we are told that it features music by the Culture Club and other MTV video stars).

Commercial for Scope mouthwash, with series of brief narratives.

MTV station ID—featuring brief excerpts from clips of some of the most famous video rock stars like Michael Jackson, Boy George, Billy Idol, etc.

12:55 *Van Halen: "Panama." Performance ruptured by fragmented visuals and brief scenes featuring bizarre or outrageous images, but which still tend to illustrate the lyrics.

1:00 MTV station ID, with voice over of VJ Mark Goodman announcing the clips that will be aired during the next half hour.

itself. If the viewer has no playback equipment, then he or she is motivated to purchase a VCR in order to make the purchase or rental of the video more feasible. The narrative and the visuals also strengthen the viewer's motivation to consume all products affiliated with the performers (other albums, tickets for live performances, T-shirts, and toys that diplay their name or image, soft drinks or other products that carry their endorsement). It is the narrative and dreamlike visuals, with their direct connection to private fantasy, that best define the unique features of rock video, distinguishing it from previous means of marketing pop music and supporting the infrastructure that insures the commercial success of the form.

At this point, it might be useful to examine some specific rock video clips to show the interaction among the three components.

VIDEOS DOMINATED BY PERFORMANCE

Performance dominates both the sound and image of many video clips, but usually with the intervention of a subordinate narrative or a visual fragmentation that disrupts the temporal and/or spatial unity. In those instances where such disruption is absent or minimal, as in the Pretenders' "It's a Thin Line be-

tween Love and Hate," the video seems old-fashioned and tedious. This judgment is supported by the fact that some vintage
songs have been released with historic footage of a live concert,
granting a place on MTV to dead veterans like Jim Morrison. In
such cases, the excitement is generated by the rarity of seeing
the "living" record of a great performer who was ahead of his
time but will be giving no more live concerts. But for live
performers who want to be on the cutting edge, something else
is needed.

In White Snake's "Slow 'n Easy," the sensuous, extravagant
performance of the singers is periodically interrupted by inserts
of a two-lane blacktop and by glimpses of a sexy blonde wearing
pearls tightened around her throat. Presumably the "supersti-
tious woman" mentioned in the lyrics, the blonde appears in
scenes that take place off stage—as if she is the woman the
singer has in mind while performing this song. Yet in some
shots she is positioned as a spectator, as if the masochism of her
response matches or is evoked by the aggression in the performance. We see a close-up of her throat that reveals the bruises
made by the pearls, and a long shot of her sitting in her flashy
car deciding whether to pick up the male singer (who stands
next to a smashed vehicle on a deserted highway) and then
speeding away leaving him stranded in the middle of the road.
These suggestive shots and lyrics encourage the spectator to
construct a sadomasochistic narrative in which either the man
or the woman is bound to be the object of desire and revenge.
The crosscutting between the narrative and the performance
gradually accelerates in pace, as do the tempo of the music and
the cutting rhythm with which the performance is fragmented
into close-ups of fetishistic details, an acceleration that renders
the song title ironic. Although this video clip is dominated by
performance, the fast pace of the montage makes it anything
but easy to recall the chain of visual images that accompany the
music.

In many videos the performance itself serves as the main
narrative event, whose spatial unity is broken by the disjunc-
tive visuals—either through special effects as in "Mental Hopscotch" by the Missing Persons or by shifts in setting as in
Nena's "99 Luftballoons." The lyrics in such video clips frequently comment reflexively on the cognitive process that the
visual style demands of the spectator (mental hopscotch) or on
the direct connection with dreams ("99 dreams I have had,
everyone a red balloon"). In "The Heart of Rock 'n Roll" the

performance of Huey Lewis and the News is fragmented spatially, as the settings for the singing shift from New York to
LA, and to other stops on the tour, and from concert halls, to
nightclubs, to the streets; and also temporally, as their performance is situated within the history of rock 'n roll. The inserts
of Elvis Presley and other historical precursors that are intercut
with present footage of Lewis and the News, are echoed in the
contrasting dance styles of different eras as well as in the two
historical TV formats of color and black-and-white, between
which the visuals constantly alternate. In this video, the self-
reflexive visuals narrativize the performance by positioning
within it the history of pop music and of television.

VIDEOS DOMINATED BY NARRATIVE

At its most extreme, narrative can dominate both words and
images—making the latter illustrate the former and moving the
song toward ballad and the visuals toward minifilm, as in the
case of Tony Carey's "A Fine, Fine Day." Opening with gritty
black-and-white images before shifting to color and relying
heavily on flashbacks, this minigangster film is presented with
low mimetic realism, except for the singing of the narrator
(who tells the story of his father released from prison and
rubbed out by gangsters all on one fine day) and by the incongruity, at a key dramatic moment, of having the Mafia boss
mouth Carey's words—an effect which is comically deflating,
to say the least.

Far more typical is the use of a thin narrative line, witty in
tone, which provides the basic situation for an erotic fantasy on
which the spectator can elaborate according to his/her sexual
tastes. The holes in the plot are usually filled by the lush
visuals—the exotic settings, costumes, hair styles, and make-up
as well as the fast cutting and effects. The narrative line makes
these visuals and their sequential arrangement easier to remember, for the order appears to make sense rather than being
random. Instead of performing on stage, the singer plays a
dramatic role within the story, which includes recitativo or a
singing narration.

As a case in point, Van Stephenson presents an explicit masochistic fantasy which transforms a hair stylist into a "Modern
Day Delilah." In a witty development of the conceit, the hairstyling equipment becomes elaborate sexual paraphernalia, the

beautician herself a feline predator with leonine tresses, and Stephenson the willing Samson. Despite the extravagance of the visuals, they are still limited to illustrating the lyrics. Though it is possible to identify either with Samson or Delilah in this fantasy, it is clearly the male masochist who controls the clip. While watching this video, the spectator is more likely to savor the wit at an emotional distance, storing the images for reprocessing in private fantasies to come.

Eddy Grant's "Romancing the Stone" pits sound against image to design a narrative (the raw material for a romantic daydream) that can be read from multiple points of view. While Grant, a black reggae singer, dominates the sound with his performance, the visuals focus on a white female magazine photographer working on chic shots so that she can afford to fly back to her romance-starved, machete wielding, hip-swinging third-world lover in vacation land. Each is a subject of the other's art and fantasies: from his humble shack, he sings to her about how much he misses her; in her urban studio his photograph is displayed like a trophy. He sends her a postcard that carries, not only the refrain from his lyrics, but also his moving image carefully packaged and framed. Later it appears in her studio next to his photograph—a moving audiovisual reminder, like a video clip displayed on an Advent, of his talent and appeal and a strong incentive for her to buy a plane ticket as soon as possible (in fact, her paycheck is magically transformed into a ticket by means of a dissolve). Depending on whether one focuses on the music or the photography, the fantasy could be interpreted as a product either of the man or the woman, the black or the white, the colonized third world which provides the raw talent and lush natural resources or the prosperous colonizer who develops and consumes them. Though at first we only hear him and see her, the visuals intercut between the white woman working in the city (coping with traffic and sexism) and the black man waiting in the tropics—a reversal of traditional sex roles, but a demystification of political-economic realities, particularly in the music industry (where black music is produced, packaged and sold by whites) and in the movies (where "Romancing the Stone" is the title song of a film that uses the third world as a background for romantic adventures of whites, a typical ploy of Hollywood thrillers). While the surface romance may evoke a daring fantasy of miscegenation and sexual reversals, the underlying politics tell the same old story of commercial exploitation. In this miniromance, the contrapuntal use of sound and image reveals an ideological subtext; yet by allowing more possibilities for spectator identification, it enhances rather than subverts the marketing strategy of selling reggae to American consumers.

VIDEOS DOMINATED BY DREAMLIKE VISUALS

Those rock videos that are dominated by dreamlike visuals seem to make the richest use of the medium—a judgment widely held by reviewers writing for pop magazines devoted to the art (*Record, Cream, Video, Optical Music,* etc.). Some video clips like Duran Duran's "Reflex," Peter Gabriel's "Shock the Monkey," and Depeche Mode's "Everything Counts" create effects that evoke works by some of the most advanced independent filmmakers, such as the rich multilayered imagery of Pat O'Neill. Such connections could presumably cultivate a more receptive audience for independent films, but it's also possible for those avant-garde conventions (that extend backward to Surrealism and Dada) to become co-opted.

The video clips that I find most revealing are those that comment self-reflexively on how rock video works, particularly in its relation to the spectator's private fantasies and dreams. Though we have already noted this tendency in performance-dominated videos like "Mental Hopscotch," "99 Luftballoons," and "The Heart of Rock 'n Roll," and in the narrative-centered "Romancing the Stone," it tends to be developed more fully in clips dominated by visuals and in those that make a balanced use of all three components.

One scene from Duran Duran's "Reflex" is particularly emblematic. We watch an audience watching a movie screen on which appears a giant wave. When it crashes, it breaks free from the screen and invades the audience's space, completely engulfing the spectators. This tidal wave, an archetype from nightmares and anxiety dreams, evokes rock video, whose images carried by the air waves break out of the television set to penetrate the private space of our consciousness and lives.

The process of internalizing media images from movies and television and combining them with private memories to generate new fantasies and dreams is dramatized in Cyndi Lauper's "Time after Time"—a process that is facilitated by repeated exposure, as the song title implies. The clip opens with Cyndi watching a Bette Davis movie on television while her lover sleeps beside her. Certain images from this woman's picture evoke personal associations from the singer's past, which are recombined to form a romantic fantasy that sharply contrasts in visual style and tone with the banal setting of the framing situation.

This same process—involving movies, fantasies and dreams, all mediated through video—is elaborated in Roger Waters's "5:01 AM, The Pros and Cons of Hitchhiking." Opening with movie images from *Shane*, the clip then turns to shots of a woman cruising in a convertible, picking up a handsome blonde hitchhiker. The lyrics reveal that she is an Encino housewife pursuing a romantic fantasy—one that was repressed in *Shane* (where the pioneer housewife never acted on her sexual attraction to the roving gunfighter played by blond Alan Ladd) but liberated in *The Wild One* (a film that is evoked in the clip, not through authentic footage, but through reprocessed lookalike images and whose rolling stone hero, clad in black leather, is associated with Jack Palance, the gunfighter villain whom we see blown away in one of the excerpts from *Shane*). Again, as in "Romancing the Stone," we are presented with a dual point of view—the male singer telling the story and the Encino housewife whose fantasies seem to control the visuals. Yet as the clip progresses, other dreamlike visuals disrupt the narrative—particularly images of a man flying across a cloudy sky. The dual perspective is revealed in the ending when we see a man and a woman asleep in bed, where they have both been reprocessing media images in their respective dreams.

OMNIPRESENCE OF THE SPECTATOR

This self-reflexive attention to the viewing process foregrounds another characteristic of television that is exaggerated on MTV—the omnipresence of the spectator. One video clip that plays with this dimension is "Tell Her About It," where performer Billy Joel is introduced by Ed Sullivan (really an impersonator) for his historic TV debut on "The Toast of the Town" while Rodney Dangerfield (the real comedian in a guest appearance) waits in the wings. The spectator is depicted not only through the live audience in the theater where Joel is singing, but also through diverse TV viewers who watch (or don't watch) his performance in a variety of period contexts, which provide settings for mininarratives eventually involving

Joel, whose live presence (like Duran Duran's tidal wave) invades their life space: a neighborhood bar, a family room, a sorority house, a TV studio, and even a Soviet spaceship. In contrast to "The Heart of Rock 'n Roll," here it is the TV spectator rather than the performer whose living continuity with the historic past is dramatized.

Through constant reminders that, at any moment of broadcasting, someone is watching, in television, unlike cinema, the spectator is made to seem omnipresent.[7] This sense is particularly strong in live television, where the omnipresence of the spectator is highlighted as a distinguishing feature of primary value. Live television departs from the basic filmmaking model (film crew and actors shooting on a closed set) by frequently granting a place for the spectator in the studio or on camera, as we see in game shows and comedy-variety programs like "The Johnny Carson Show" and "Saturday Night Live." The "live" component survives even in the reruns where we viewers are made to feel that we belong to a live audience responding to living legends like John Belushi. As with the historical footage of live concerts on MTV, "live" is redefined; no longer restricted to the recording or transmission, it becomes associated with whatever occupies the present consciousness of the spectator. It's as if by watching television, the spectator gains the divine power of granting life to whoever or whatever appears on screen. The viewer can extend the TV life of Phil Donahue and Joan Collins or kill them off in a season. Of course, it's really the networks and advertisers that decide what's on the screen, but the audience is constantly told that it is their viewing (and buying) habits that control those decisions.

This feeling of the spectator's omnipresence is cultivated even on shows that are taped or filmed. Canned laughter is used on situation comedy series, and viewers are directly addressed in the second person in commercials, on news and sports shows, on children's programs like "Sesame Street" and "Nickelodeon," and by virtually all video jockeys on MTV.

Instead of stressing the changeovers from one VJ to another, which would accentuate them as TV personalities and create the effect of separate programs (as occurs on some music radio stations), MTV makes the transitions subtle. The name of the next VJ is announced along with the upcoming performers and news for the next half-hour segment. Sometimes the new VJ is first heard in a voice-over at the end of a station ID before being seen on screen. Other times both VJ's chat together on

camera at the end of the connecting station break. Despite the
diversity in their age, sex, personality, and style, it's as if the
main function of these VJ's, who also double as newscasters, is
to maintain a continuous live presence that creates the illusion
of an on-going dialogue with the audience. On MTV the omnipresence of the VJ helps to strengthen the omnipresence of the
spectator.

When an audience is seen, heard, or addressed on screen, it
signifies for the individual spectator both the object of identification and the Other with whom he or she is temporarily
bonded. The TV spectator has a dual role: first, as an individual
viewer/listener absorbing images and sounds into one's own
consciousness and memory, usually in the privacy of one's own
home or bed; and second, as a member of a mass audience or
community (McLuhan's "global village") who share common
associations, desires, and ideological assumptions. In unifying
private and public identities, this dual role facilitates the integrated functioning of two complementary actions—both of
which are well illustrated in the specific video clips already
discussed: (1) the internalizing of TV images into one's own
fantasy life, incorporating them into a private reservoir of
dream images; (2) the positioning of the spectator in the public
marketplace where one becomes an active consumer purchasing products one has been trained by television to desire,
thereby contributing to the capitalist economy. Because of advertising's control over television, the private action is made to
serve the public goal of internalizing consumerist desires. Nowhere is this co-option more apparent than on MTV.

PRESENCE/ABSENCE OF THE TV RECEIVER

Since the TV spectator appears omnipresent, it is the presence
or absence of the TV set, the basic receiving apparatus, that is
all important. As a receiver, the TV set functions for the spectator in a dual capacity: both as an object of desire and as an
object of identification. If you don't have one, you are left out of
the community. If you don't have one, your dreams, fantasies,
and life will be impoverished. If you don't have one, you won't
recognize the names and faces of culture heroes that populate
mass-circulation magazines like *People* and *Star* and that pop up
in conversations. In order to enter the mass culture and its
marketing system, you must invest in this basic equipment that

promises, not merely temporary admittance to another world,
but a dramatic change in you and your world forever. Like
buying a Barbie doll, the purchase of a TV set begets other
purchases. Once you own and become the basic receiver, you
are trained to desire everything it has to offer—as big a screen
as possible, color as well as black-and-white, a stereo hook-up,
remote control, all of the commercial, PBS and cable stations
available, a VCR , and eventually 3-D, high definition and digital television. As in the automotive industry, obsolescence
and rapid technological improvement are made to seem inevitable.

Once you possess a TV set, you have unlimited access to the
images and sounds it receives. Yet the programming structure
with its varied repetitions is designed to create a withholding or
suspension that increases your viewing time by intensifying
desire. You find yourself waiting for your favorite clip on
MTV, waiting for a particular movie to appear on cable or
commercial stations, waiting for the particular guest you want
to see on the Johnny Carson show, waiting for the sports or
weather or whatever news feature will reveal the information
you seek, waiting for an instant replay of a dramatic moment in
sports, waiting for the reruns of a show that you missed,
waiting for the next episode in the soap or miniseries you're
faithfully following, waiting for the cable station to reach your
neighborhood, or even waiting for your favorite commercial
("Where's the beef?") to explicitly articulate the mechanism of
withholding.

When the spectator is not watching television, then he or
she, whether out in the world or at home, is still affected by the
TV images already internalized. That's when the *fort/da* game
really pays off for the sponsoring institution. In the public
marketplace, the spectator becomes a consumer looking for the
beef—following the cues of point-of-purchase advertising to
find and buy the videos, records, T-shirts, soft drinks, and toys
promoted on television. In private, the spectator becomes a
daydreamer, driving on the freeway listening to songs on the
radio or seeing billboards that trigger associations with TV
images already programmed into the brain; or by night, a
dreamer, reprocessing those TV images into visions of the
future. In order to understand the impact that television can
have on dreams, it's necessary to know more about the process
of dreaming.

SPECULATIONS ON THE DREAM CONNECTION

The most compelling dream models that have emerged from recent neurophysiological and psychological studies suggest that dreams are an evolutionary medium that mediates between biological programming and cultural imprinting. More specifically, the Hobson-McCarley Activation-Synthesis model assumes that the rapid firing of giant cells in the primitive brainstem activates the dream by generating signals within the brain; the rhythm, frequency and duration of the dream are biologically determined.[8] The forebrain then selects images from the memory to "fit" the internally generated random signals; this synthetic process (about which little is known) is probably a function of the right-brain hemisphere (that takes a synthetic or gestalt approach rather than an analytic one to problem solving) and also the site for the psychological level of the dream.[9] The images selected from the memory and recombined in new ways carry the cultural imprinting.

This model has significant implications for the study of television and movies since these two mass media play a key role in the imprinting process, supplementing the dreamer's ordinary experience with thousands of prefabricated moving visual images that are directly absorbed into the cultural dreampool and influencing both the form and content of dream texts. Since these two media have appeared fairly recently in the history of western civilization and since certain nations with advanced technology and imperialist tendencies (most predominantly the USA) have specialized in producing texts that could be exported (even via satellite) to other parts of the world, movies and television have the potential to render dreams more similar all over the planet, a tendency that could have far-reaching political and evolutionary implications. (This issue is brilliantly explored on film by Nicholas Roeg in *The Man Who Fell to Earth* and in literature by Manuel Puig in *Betrayed by Rita Hayworth* and *Kiss of Spider Woman*, which is now being made into a movie.)

The strong impact of the media on dreams is based partly on the phenomenological similarities between dreaming and the viewing of the movies and television: the visual primacy of these experiences; their spatial and temporal discontinuity; the double identity of the spectator as passive voyeur and active participant; the physical comfort and partial immobility of the spectator; the abrupt shift to a different physical and psychic

state and to the forgetting of most of the images when the
lights go on, the tube goes off, or one awakens from the dream;
the two-way process of adaptation, involving the use of dreams
as a creative source for artists generating movies and videos
and the incorporation of media images into the dreams of
viewers; the regressive nature of these fictions which arouse
pleasure by fulfilling repressed infantile wishes and needs; the
guilty feelings evoked by excessive indulgence in these idle
pastimes that substitute for constructive work; and the combination of private and communal roles in these experiences
which pass for personal pleasures while serving deeper cultural, ideological or evolutionary goals.

While considerable work has been done on dream and film,[10]
very little has been written on dream and television.[11] Yet this
relationship is particularly important since dreamers start
watching the tube from infancy and since television contributes
more images to the cultural dreampool than any other medium.
While I am in no way denying the important and unique connections between film and dream, I am interested here in exploring the unique similarities between dream and television.

What is particularly fascinating to me and central to my
argument is that the main similarities between dream and television which are *not* shared by film are precisely the same
characteristics that are exaggerated on MTV: unlimited access,
structural discontinuity, decentering, structural reliance on
memory retrieval, live transmission and the omnipresence of
the spectator. Most of these characteristics have been widely
written about by television historians and theorists; what I am
interested in briefly suggesting here is their connection with
MTV and dreams.

UNLIMITED ACCESS

While the frequency and length of dreams are biologically determined (a REM period occurs around every 90 minutes and
lasts about 20 minutes, making the daily average dreamtime
approximately 90 minutes), one can increase the amount of
time spent dreaming on any given night by extending the hours
of sleep or by taking catnaps throughout the day. The amount
of time that can be spent daydreaming is, of course, unlimited.

A similar unlimited access is offered, not by cinema, but by
"The tube of plenty," forcing the individual spectator to moni-

tor his or her own time devoted to TV viewing. This temptation is dramatized by the 24-hour availability of rock videos on
MTV—a feature that is prominently emphasized in all of the
promotional spots for the station.

STRUCTURAL DISCONTINUITY

All TV viewing is marked by a structural discontinuity caused
by frequent interruptions by commercials, station breaks, and
channel-switching. These frequent ruptures are exaggerated
on MTV where there is no long program to interrupt, merely a
chain of brief segments, all featuring spatial and temporal discontinuity.

Such structural discontinuity evokes a comparison with
dreams, which are similarly marked by abrupt scene shifts
which Allan Hobson has linked to the bursts of rapid eye
movements (REM's) and firings of brain cells that trigger and
accompany dreams.

> The rapid eye movements themselves appeared to be generated
> by the activity of a group of giant cells in the pontine brain stem
> whose bursting discharge preceded the eye movements during
> REM sleep. Thus the possibility was raised that specific visual
> information might actually be generated within the brain. The
> giant cells not only may drive the eye movements but also may
> send information into the visual relay nucleus and cortex about
> the direction and speed of the eye movements. Since this infor-
> mation is highly non-ordered with respect to the external visual
> world, *scene shifts and dramatic changes in visual dream content might
> possibly be a function of the generating system* [ital. mine] rather than a
> censor's attempt to disguise the ideational meaning of "dream
> thoughts."[12]

Both Hobson and Vlada Petrić have compared this structural
discontinuity of dreams to cinema: Hobson has charted structural analogies between film devices and dream processes,[13]
and Petrić has prescribed the four "most effective cinematic
techniques which can enhance the oneiric impact of a film and
stimulate the neural activities similar to those occurring during
dreaming": "camera movement through space (especially when
combined with deep focus)"; illogical and paradoxical combinations of objects, characters, and settings (while . . . preserving
the vivid representation of the photographed world); "dynamic
montage (with concentration on the close-up and subliminal

condensation of brief shots)"; and "dissolution of spatial and temporal continuity (especially by using 'jump-cuts')."[14] While these techniques can be used to single out certain film styles and auteurs for high praise, they are commonplace in music videos.

DECENTERING

The structural discontinuity of television creates a constant flow or decentered supertext. Viewers tend to watch television rather than specific programs. This decentering process is carried to an extreme on MTV, where the short commercial is the featured attraction. Though commercially determined, the sequencing of clips has a quality of randomness for the viewer; one sees whatever videos happen to appear on screen while one is watching.

One finds a similar decentering in dreaming, where all dreams on a single night tend to share the same themes, where the dreamer usually remembers specific images or scenes but no clear boundaries around individual dream texts, and where one never knows in advance which dreams or images will appear on the mindscreen. Individual texts of dream and television rarely receive the same degree of artistic status that is ordinarily attributed to film texts—a difference that is more a matter of structural presentation than of artistic merit.

One does not normally find decentering in film. It must be designed as a conscious artistic strategy as in the films of Godard, Makavejev and Alea, usually with the conscious political goal of breaking Hollywood's codes of representation to reveal and oppose the bourgeois ideology they carry. While bourgeois consumerism is also exposed in the decentering processes of television, it is not undermined, but, on the contrary, promoted.

STRUCTURAL RELIANCE ON MEMORY RETRIEVAL

The Hobson-McCarley activation-synthesis model posits that while dreaming, the forebrain selects sense images from memory to fit signals about eye movement that are internally generated by the dreamer's own brain and attempts unsuccessfully to render "the series of shots as a continuous narrative."[15] In elaborating on this model, Hobson frequently uses an analogy with film which sometimes becomes strained:

> During waking, the brain is 'taking pictures': images are accepted at a rate of about 10-20 per second. Owing to the operation of the afferent image-efferent signal comparator process and visual blanking, we perceive the visual world as continuous and the visual field remains constant in space. *Our brains shoot, develop, and edit instantaneously* [ital. mine]. The individual images or the fused image (we know not which) are stored in memory (by unknown mechanisms). They can be called up with difficulty and are weakly perceptible in waking fantasy, but are more easily accessible and vividly perceptible in dreams.[16]

In cinema it is impossible "to shoot, develop, and edit instantaneously," but these mental processes are ordinary practice in live video, which suggests that television might provide a better model than cinema for how the human brain processes images during waking hours.

Earlier I argued that one of the most powerful aspects of music video is its programming of viewers to retrieve specific visual images from memory every time they hear a particular song. Although the triggering sounds of the song usually come from external sources like radio or television (unlike the internally generated signals in dreams), the music video fan has been taught to identify with the external receiving apparatus, so some degree of internalization occurs. This process of retrieving the prefabricated video images from memory may help train viewers to retrieve them more readily during REM sleep. In other words, the structural reliance on memory retrieval shared by MTV and dreams may give these music video images a privileged position within the cultural dreampool. The fact that so many rock video artists cultivate the explicit connection with dreams in their song titles and lyrics, in the visual style and images of their video clips, in their narrative themes and situations, and even in the names of some of the groups (like R.E.M., or the Revolving Paint Dream) suggests that they are seeking this position of power.

LIVE TRANSMISSION AND
THE OMNIPRESENT SPECTATOR

As the most solipsistic of forms, the dream takes place inside the spectator, who is by necessity omnipresent. In the live transmission of dreams, the protean dreamer functions, not only as spectator, but also as writer, director, star, supporting players, location, and technical apparatus.

We have already seen how the television viewer is made to feel omnipresent, particularly through conventions associated with live transmission. It is this very quality that fosters the kind of delusional experiences depicted in Martin Scorsese's film *King of Comedy*[17] and in Hubert Selby's novel *Requiem for a Dream* in which isolated viewers lose the boundaries between television images and their private fantasy projections. In a sense these characters cannibalize the world of television, transformating it into a solipsistic medium like dream.

Unlike movies and dreams which suspend one's normal waking experience by functioning as an alternative reality, television, and radio, because they are not totally absorbing, only supplement one's ordinary life. Television viewers frequently do something else while watching. If that other activity happens to be daydreaming, a behavior stimulated by many programs and virtually all commercials, then it is easy for the two imaginary realms to be fused.

MTV tries to capture the best of both worlds. Like radio and ordinary television, it can provide a continuous sound track for partying, dancing, sex, or whatever you happen to be doing and brighten up a room with a flashy visual that can be glanced at whenever you get bored. Yet because of the visual intensity of most video clips, it also strives for the all-absorbing attention a spectator normally devotes to films and dreams. It's the omnipresent spectator, constantly addressed in the second person by the MTV VJ's, who decides which mode of viewing to adopt; but the very presence of both options makes it possible to watch the station for longer stretches at a time.

While exercising its powers of manipulation, MTV makes the spectator feel potent and decisive: he or she is the one who chooses which records, videos, and products to buy; who picks which styles and behaviors to imitate; who hums the tunes; who memorizes the visuals; who decides when to look and when to listen; who switches the station on or off. Like all television, it trains the spectator to focus on one's personal powers of choice and reception while ignoring the remote sources of transmission—the true Remote Control—whose ideological determinants and manipulative strategies remain mystified.

In this examination of MTV as a model for commercial television, I have focused on the medium's relationship both to ideology and to dream. The observations concerning ideology, for the most part, echo or lend support to arguments of others who have been writing on television. But the speculations on the connection with dreams open new paths that warrant further investigation. Perhaps most essential is the interaction between these two registers—the role of dream in internalizing and reprocessing the ideology transmitted through television, a process that is blatantly dramatized in music video on MTV. In the last sixty years we have witnessed how advertising has colonized the public airwaves, first on radio and then on television. Now, through the medium of music video, commercial interests may be extending their sway over the evolutionary medium of dreams.

NOTES

1. *Record* (July 1984), p. 41.
2. See, for example, "Rock Makers," *Video* (July 1984) by Noë Goldwasser, who writes: "The excitement in pop-music video is being generated by a handful of talented filmmakers working in the video-clip medium. People like Russell Mulcahy, Bob Giraldi, Tim Newman, and Tim Pope crank out clips by the hundreds and send them on their infectious way to MTV, *Night Tracks* and the like. This community of directors amounts to a video new wave which is forging the aesthetic basis of music video in much the same way as the French new wave in film—Godard, Resnais, Truffaut—changed our way of looking at movies 20 years ago. . . .

   "No one better personifies the music video *auteur* than Tim Pope. . . . He could be called the Jean-Luc Godard of the video age because of his frenetic pace and constantly flowing fountainhead of new visual images. . . . The skinny 28-year-old averages about two videos a week in his London studio, and is constantly turning down American groups who come over and throw money at him to make them stars on MTV Stateside." (pp. 81–82)
3. Such causes include the fact that television superseded the audio medium of radio, the neglect of sound and its potentialities both by filmmakers and film theorists, and the dominance of vision over all other senses in dreams.
4. One of the few precursors of the new relationship between music and image is the "Memo from T" sequence performed by Mick Jagger in Cammell and Roeg's *Performance* (1970), a visionary rock film that was far ahead of its time.
5. Nick Browne, "The Political Economy of the Television (Super) Text," *Quarterly Review of Film Studies*, 9, 3 (Summer 1984).
6. Unlike credits that appear at the end of a film, these data do not inform the viewer whom to credit for the artistic achievement (e.g., the name of the director never appears on the rock video clip); the information is provided solely to increase the likelihood of the sale.

7. Of course, there is also a place for the spectator in cinema, as current work on suture, spectators-in-the-text, and self-reflexiveness have shown; one can even find instances of direct address throughout the history of film. Yet these cinematic practices are not so direct as the on-screen presence of TV studio audiences nor as ubiquitous as the use of direct address on television.

8. J. A. Hobson and R. W. McCarley, "The brain as a dream state generator: An activation-synthesis hypothesis of the dream process," *American Journal of Psychiatry*, 134 (1977), 1335–1348. Hobson has also presented this model in relation to film studies in "Film and the Physiology of Dreaming Sleep: the Brain as Camera-Projector," *Dreamworks*, I, 1 (Spring 1980), 9–25; and in his reply to Raymond Durgnat's "The Hunting of the Dream Snark," *Dreamworks*, II, 1 (Fall 1981), 83–86; and in "Dream Image and Substrate: Bergman's Films and the Psychology of Sleep," in *Film and Dreams: An Approach to Bergman*, ed. Vlada Petrić (South Salem, N.Y.: Redgrave, 1981), 75–95.

9. An excellent survey of the issue of involvement of the right brain hemisphere is provided by Bruce Kawin in "Right-Hemisphere Processing in Dreams and Films," *Dreamworks*, II, 1 (Fall 1981), 13–17.

10. In the psychoanalytic context, the relationship between film and dream has received considerable attention in the line of discourse derived from Lacan and Metz, most prominently in *The Imaginary Signifier*. Still within the psychoanalytic context, but deviating from Metz on important issues are Robert Eberwein's *Film and the Dream Screen* (Princeton University Press, 1984) and Gay Lynn Studlar's *Visual Pleasure and the Masochistic Aesthetic: The Von Sternberg/Dietrich Paramount Cycle*, Unpublished dissertation, University of Southern California, 1984 (a selection from which will appear in Volume II of *Movies and Methods*, ed. Bill Nichols, University of California Press). Vlada Petrić's *Film and Dreams: An Approach to Bergman* is a collection of essays, some of which (including Petrić's work and mine) draw on the neurobiological models. This perspective is also represented in several essays (including ones by Petrić, Hobson, Durgnat, Kawin, and me) appearing in *Dreamworks*, an interdisciplinary quarterly on the relation between dream and the arts.

11. The two key works on this topic are Peter H. Wood's "Television as Dream" in *Television: The Critical View*, ed. Horace Newcomb, 2nd ed. (New York: Oxford University Press, 1979), 517–535, and "Reality and Television: an Interview with Dr. Edmund Carpenter," *Television Quarterly*, X, 1 (Fall 1972), 42–46. Works that have attempted a three-way comparison usually focus on cinema at the expense of television, arguing that the comparison between film and dream is more interesting (see Raymond Durgnat, "The Hunting of the Dream-Snark," *Dreamworks*, II, 1, Fall 1981, 76–82) or more fruitful in generating formal similarities (see Vlada Petrić's "A Theoretical-Historical Survey: Film and Dreams," in *Film and Dreams*, pp. 1–48.)

12. Hobson, "Film and the Physiology of Dreaming Sleep," p. 14.

13. Ibid., 23.

14. Petrić, "A Theoretical-Historical Survey," p. 23.

15. Hobson, ibid., p. 24.

16. Ibid., 23–24.

17. For an excellent analysis of what this film reveals about television, see Beverle Houston's "*King of Comedy*: A Crisis of Substitution," *Framework*, 24 (Spring 1984), 74–92.

HAL HIMMELSTEIN

TELEVISION NEWS AND
THE TELEVISION DOCUMENTARY

It would be both naive and presumptuous for the author to present an exhaustive overview of the development of television news and the television documentary in so limited a context as a single essay. Therefore, the author has chosen to limit his discussion on news and the documentary to an exploratory analysis of the myths that operate in both the newsgathering and the presentational apparatus itself and in the products of that apparatus—the stories which draw upon real events and people in the world.

There are many significant issues for current and future academic discussion of television news and the documentary, all deserving of careful consideration and detailed research, both critical and empirical. As these issues specifically impact on the discussion in this essay, they will be addressed within the context of myth analysis.

There is a continuing debate that has produced volumes of literature on such journalistic issues as the importance of organizational imperatives versus personal journalistic bias in news-content determination and presentation; and the relative importance of the so-called reality (or mirror) theory and the "collage" explanations for news determination (advanced by the news professionals themselves) as against the organizational and personal-bias explanations (advanced by critical sociologists).[1] There is the question as to how much of television news is "show," in which entertainment values predominate (especially at the local level as news consultants reorganize and standardize the presentational-packaging elements of the newscast), and how much is "substance."[2] Further, granted that there is, to a degree, substance in all news presentations—

First published in Himmelstein, *Television Myth and the American Mind* (Praeger Publishers, New York, NY, 1984), pp. 197–231. Copyright © 1984 by Praeger Publishers. Reprinted by permission.

including story content and packaging—if the substance is broadly defined as cultural information, the debate then moves to whether journalists are essentially objective in their journalistic practice (often defined as being fair and open to correction), or consciously adversarial (variously defined as being personal or polemical, depending on the politics of the definer). At a deeper level still, the question is raised as to whether so-called objectivity is possible in any case, given the ideological frames within which journalists must operate or against which they must rebel.[3] There are frequent debates regarding the ethicality of the television journalist's becoming involved in the story she is covering and thus either being forced or choosing to take an ideological stand by virtue of her involvement.

From various ethnographic observations of the network-television newsgathering process,[4] and from content analyses of news programs, it can be suggested that, to varying degrees, news organizations and the corporate chiefs to whom they must report have developed identifiable ideological perspectives that at least indirectly impact on the newsgathering process; that individual journalists have personal biases cultivated from years of experience in personal worlds that on the surface exhibit ethnic, racial, sexual, religious, economic, political, and geographic uniqueness, but underneath manifest a consistent motif of aggressiveness and achievement orientation tempered by a slight dissatisfaction with the monotony of the middle-class lifestyle and a certain skepticism that comes from an education that stresses the development of the critical faculties; and that both organizations and individuals operate in cultures which at any given moment provide certain dominant ideological frames that impact on reportage as they set limits to the journalistic discourse and determine the relationship of the journalistic apparatus to the government in power (e.g., which news organizations and reporters get access to the President of the United States, or which reporters are allowed scoops on breaking stories). The degrees to which each of these characteristics impacts on journalistic practice and in what combinations is the focus of important ongoing debate and research.

THE TELEVISION-NEWSGATHERING APPARATUS

The precise nature of the process of gathering and publishing news depends in large measure on one's definition of news. The assignment editor sends television reporters into the field to cover stories which may or may not make it to the air that day or evening, thus committing corporate funds to the process on what may seem like a speculative basis. But the odds are very good that, because of years of experience with the news formula, the news one went after will emerge. News is, at this simplest level, what the television-news department covers and airs on a given day. The screening out of that which is news from that which is clearly not news has already been accomplished before the raw remote videotaped footage and the reporter's or cameraperson's notes are relayed back to the newsroom (in the case of live news coverage, there are revealing moments when the newsgathering organization's selection process is publicly displayed and opened to a critique when the news doesn't materialize).

The frames within which news is defined are implicit and seem to become embedded in an undeclared yet commonly understood news-department agenda. This agenda, particularly on the local level, is often set by a combination of forces—of news executives at the local level responding to vague notions of the cultural composition, and the nature of the social interactions, within their coverage area, gathered in the past through periodic surveys of the community's opinion leaders (excluding more militant community forces), regarding important issues of local public concern, and by the group-station owners' reliance on news consultants who test and market formulas for successful news presentation. (The group-station owners are generally absentee managers who tend to resort to the same policies for all the stations in their group.) From this combination of perceived public interest, which is markedly centrist, and style, which is markedly entertaining, the news "package" emerges—it holds the news program together, giving it form and direction, and supposedly separates it from the competition. Beyond questions of form is the basic issue of the articulation of an overriding news philosophy. What do these various corporate enterprises consider "news?"

There is clearly no agreement among scholars and journalism critics as to a definition of news, yet the divergence of opinion is enlightening as we see the various definitions compete in the news packages we receive on our television screens. Let's first examine the competing definitions of news, then briefly look at the television-news frames that employ, whether explicitly or implicitly, these definitions.

University of Chicago sociologist Robert E. Park defined news as a part of our communications that calls for a change of attitudes concerning events of importance to a community—events whose significance is still under consideration and discussion. Journalism historian Frank Luther Mott defined news as an accurate, unbiased account of the significant facts of some timely happening. A synthesis of these definitional frames leads us to the definition of news as the provision of significant facts relevant to the formation of an opinion, or to the change of an attitude on some current public issue of importance to a community of persons. That community may be a group of workers, a neighborhood, city, county, state, region, nation, continent, or world. A public issue is one about which there already exists some division of opinion. Mott's call for an "accurate, unbiased account" is, of course, moot if one acknowledges the influence of ideology in the structuring of public discourse—accuracy and lack of bias will be claimed by different positions within the public debate in an effort to enforce or counteract an ideology. No journalist can divorce himself from the community of persons, and he thus cannot, in reality, stand apart from the world he covers. The resolution of debate is really a matter where whoever disseminates news either directly or indirectly determines its ideological slant.

In contrast to news, this traditional definitional scheme views human-interest content as that which describes, in a dramatic narrative style, some human experience in a manner that enables the reader, listener, or viewer to make a sympathetic personal identification with the subject. Facticity is not necessarily a requirement of the human-interest story, although the story should be grounded in real events and involve real people as subjects.

In such a contrived dichotomy between news and human-interest content, we find a verbal wall constructed between the truth of the accurate news report, which presents facts and lets us decide which side we will support, and the probing, interpretive psychological or biographical reportage that may be interesting but is subject to charges of sensationalism and questions regarding its veracity. Thus, public issues abstracted from everyday experience and presented by middle-class public officials within an aura of authority are treated with a certain reverence while the depiction of everyday experience, with its images of human suffering, frustration, and general despair, is open to question regarding reporters' motives. (ABC reporter/

muckraker Geraldo Rivera was frequently criticized for his overly liberal ideological bias as he reported on the disenfranchised and degraded minority cultures in American society, as if his work was something less than news.)

This definitional framework places the journalist in an essentially subservient role vis-à-vis the dominant political institutions—as "faithful messenger" of the political elites—whose task becomes, as Walter Lippmann described it, to simply "signalize" events about to unfold. Such a view of the newsgathering apparatus is by no means shared by all critics. Ron Powers, the Pulitzer prize-winning former television critic for the *Chicago Sun-Times* (who, as of this writing, was presenting critiques of television and television journalism on *CBS Sunday Morning*), takes a radically different view of the journalist's role in this process. Powers describes the function of news, which he admits he is narrowly defining, as monitoring and reporting "the conduct of public officials and others who exercise power over private citizens, toward the goal of assuring openness, accountability, and the intelligent administration of community life."[5] Powers, unlike Park and Mott in their more generalized definitions of news, sees the newsgathering apparatus operating to rebalance a system of social relations unbalanced by dominant-subordinate power relationships that are revealed in human experience. He adds that contemporary television newsgathering does not perform "the vigorous, adversary, check-on-government intervening role that American journalism has traditionally performed."[6] Far from the "signaling function," Powers concludes that the best American journalism "traditionally proceeded from the assumption that it is mining areas that the public did not even know existed."[7]

Journalism critic Edward Jay Epstein warned, however, of the inherent dangers of journalistic interventionism—of the journalist perceiving her role as public crusader, a role which can easily lead, wrote Epstein, to the myth of journalistic revelation of truth, in which the journalist, acting as "little David," punctures "the official veil of secrecy" and, in the height of melodrama, brings Goliath—monolithic government—to his knees.[8] Epstein believes that such a journalistic mythos conceals the actual relations of the process of revealing truth—a process in which the journalist, removed by at least one step from the context in which an actual event occurred, can best function honestly as a conduit for the release of information to publics.

With this debate unsettled regarding both the very definition of news and the proper role of journalistic practice in the conduct of human affairs, the activities of the television-news-gathering apparatus unfortunately become all too easily defensible.

Journalistic practice is significantly more complex than the tale of the "news hound" hot on the trail of an eye-popping story, although taken in by the contemporary mythology of the embattled star reporter seeking to blast through walls of governmental deception, duplicity, and euphemism, one might not recognize the competing pressures that delimit the journalistic endeavor. The reporter, whether print or broadcast, is, first of all, institutionalized by the very fact of his or her being hired to report for a particular organization, and by subservience to the needs of that organization as determined by the decisions of editors who assign the reporter stories and particular beats and thus determine at the outset the very quality of the relationship of the reporter to the subject matter (i.e., many reporters, especially electronic-media ones, have little or no special knowledge of their subject that insures that coverage will be limited to information from press handouts and that sources will not be seriously challenged; of course, the reporter can grow into the beat over time). Second, the ambitious young reporter is trying to make a name for himself or herself—to climb the middle-class ladder of achievement, success, and public recognition that has been firmly embedded in the reporter's subconscious following years of survival training administered through the culture's dominant educational apparatus, which, in journalism education, assumes the importance of the by-line as a token of professional existence and achievement. In the struggle which ensues, between the journalistic institution—which seeks to report news to fill the holes between ads and to avoid any major conflict with other institutions, especially those of the powerful, centralized executive branch of the federal government and large corporations—and the reporter, who seeks his distinctly middle-class spot in the community of publicly recognized journalism professionals, the institution often reaches a position of wary tolerance of the superstar, superego investigative journalist who will produce the Pulitzer Prize-winning or Columbia-Dupont Award-winning exposé of corruption. The prize is, of course, subsequently appropriated by the institution, which uses it as a mantle of prestige and respectability.

TELEVISION NEWS AND MYTH

The television medium is ideally suited to the transmission of the mythic world of news. Its combination of a simplified press, which fulfills needs for rudimentary political and economic information (e.g., how much the viewer can expect to pay for a loaf of bread, given the current international monetary crisis); the photograph, which presents the personal world of the community, the family, and personal life to the literate and the nonliterate alike; and the motion picture, which satisfies the need for curiosity and entertainment, establishes a readily accessible and understandable (and ultimately a palatable) context for the unfolding of our contemporary struggles.[9]

In television journalism much more than in print journalism, the symbol of truth becomes the image of the journalist himself—the aggressive advocate willing to challenge authority—rather than the story or editorial itself. Style predominates over content or context. The defender of the public's right to know satisfies the medium's insatiable demand for melodramatic personae who clearly and simplistically represent the just cause. These journalist-heroes allow viewers to vicariously watch the unapproachable bureaucrat or the arrogant general (who never answered letters of complaint or phone calls) brought to his knees by the crafty and efficient journalist—the modern-day personification of the Homeric epic hero who, like Odysseus, is condemned to a life of wandering, skepticism, and continual tests of his ability to outwit the dangerous adversary. The television audience revels in the myth of the individual in news, manifested in the reporter as "independent spirit," unafraid to take on the powerful on their own turf.

The mise-en-scène of the journalistic quest reveals first the reporter, standing alone in front of a backdrop, such as the immobile, ponderous architecture of the government building signifying stasis and impenetrability (or why would the reporter be standing outside?). The reporter then moves inside to the office of the interviewee, with its bookshelves lined with innumerable specialized reports that obviously were written to camouflage the clear and simple truth the reporter, and the viewer, are seeking. The reporter has now pierced the veil of secrecy, like Superman, who can see the enemy through concrete walls, and has brought us all closer to the correct solution to the investigative problem. At this point the reporter is "liv-

ing the myth" as Tom Wolfe once said regarding his own status
as star journalist.

One of the major characteristics of the myth of the individual
in television news is that heroes are more efficient than are
villains. The individual hero-correspondent, who has used his
craftiness and wit to outsmart the institution and to penetrate
the institutional barriers that hide the conspiracy or deception,
now reveals his efficiency by trapping the reluctant interviewee
into ostensible admissions of guilt or into internal contradictions in his answers (if the source refuses to appear on camera,
the journalist may implicate the institution in an implied cover-
up; he does this by orally berating the institution for its sphinx-
like failure to cooperate with the investigation while simultaneously flashing a picture of the institution's imposing
headquarters—the physical and intellectual barrier to the
truth—in the background). This aggressive journalistic dance,
when extended to its extreme, features, in the words of critic
Michael Arlen, the correspondent as "prosecutor" in a court-
room-style melodrama. Arlen discussed a CBS *60 Minutes* investigation of corruption in Wyoming as an example of the myth at
work.[10] Arlen saw television news and especially the news
magazine, of which *60 Minutes* is the most visible representative, as succumbing to the mystique of "the thrill of the chase,"
with the interview subjects serving as "quarry." The *60 Minutes*
correspondents were increasingly drawn into "prosecutorial
scenarios" in the 1970s, in which the reporter personified "judg-
mental righteousness." Here we find aggressive correspondents in search of a story upon which a moral judgment can be
passed. What becomes important in this realm of prosecutorial
journalism is "the *appearance* of a story: the dramatic texture of
televised confrontation."[11] By using a technique in which allegations of misconduct are framed as dramatic questions, *60
Minutes* reporter Dan Rather was able to "prove" that everyone,
from the Rock Springs, Wyoming, police chief to the state's
governor "knew about" prostitution in the energy boomtown
(and by implication were "guilty" of condoning prostitution).
Rather then attempted to demonstrate how the governor of
Wyoming might be linked to organized crime. Rather, as it
turned out, relied on a questionable source for evidence to
support this allegation (Rather set the source up as "a superb
investigator"). However, "facts" turned out to be, in Arlen's
subsequent personal investigation of the Wyoming reports,
"inaccurate, or incompletely presented or ambiguous."[12] The

newsgathering process was paramount here. Rather's inquisitorial style convinced the viewer that he was on top of the story so that his findings must be correct. The efficient, provocative interrogation of sources became the key part of the story, what Arlen termed "the seductive flow of the news-gathering drama."[13]

In another television-news context—the evening news report—the myth of the individual, of the larger-than-life journalist-hero, is further established in the persona of the anchorperson. The networks' public-relations campaigns promoting their anchorpersons project an image of the anchor as nearly omniscient and omnipresent. Before his death, Frank Reynolds was touted by ABC as "uniquely qualified to bring you the world"—Reynolds clearly operated on a plane considerably above that of the traditional newsreader or the contemporary print journalist, at least in the world of public relations.

In American television the news anchor, through his introductions to every story in the newscast, assumes a central role in all stories, usurping authority from the correspondent in the field (the anchor will go on location for the big story, e.g., the assassination of Egyptian President Anwar Sadat, or the Apollo moon launch, further relegating the correspondent to a minor position in the news operation by implication that he is not qualified to do the big stories). The anchor is the presence that connects the newscast, the voice that orders the chaos of the everyday world. The anchor is the loner of the myth of the individual. He stands outside the group of correspondents, sources, and viewers, secure in his lair—the television studio—diligently observing the world outside. He is above the fray, yet deeply involved in it. He does more than read us the news—he guides us through the world as his news organization has defined it that day. In the presentation of news, critic Raymond Williams noted, the anchorperson presents "a studied informality" with less emphasis on reading a script (a formal gesture) and more emphasis on "personal presentation" via eye contact through a teleprompter.[14] The personal gaze becomes the anchor's heroic signature as he confronts the world of danger and mystery. We live vicariously through his journey. Anchors become "arbiters of correct reactions to the news."[15] The anchor is detached one moment, cynical, amused, folksy, or self-righteous the next. After we are led through this range of emotional reactions to the world, we reach our final destination—the newscast's end, the drama's epilogue. The anchor-hero, having survived the dangerous world, signs off with a verbal coat of arms by which we identify his standing and worldly position. Walter Cronkite's famous "And that's the way it is," and Chet Huntley's and David Brinkley's "good night, David; good night, Chet" offer a note of finality and confident closure, a sign that they are still in control. In a nonnewscast context, Edward R. Murrow's "good night, and good luck" sign-off injected a more open-ended and cautious response to his world—his hero-character was not so self-assured as today's electronic journalists, perhaps because Murrow sensed, correctly, that the world of everyday experience was beyond the control of the journalistic apparatus. Murrow was the strong, worldly wise, tired hero of the traditional epic, not today's corporate hero for whom efficiency would always overcome ambiguity.

The anchor's sign-off leads us to a discussion of another myth revealed in the television-news presentation—the myth of the puritan ethic. The sign-off not only works to consolidate the anchor's position of power and control over news; it also leaves the viewer with the "illusion of hard work accomplished."[16] Reporters and news anchors must believe in this myth by the very nature of their occupation. Just as their work is to bring order to the world of dangerous events and personal confrontations, so too is the "work" of their news subjects celebrated in stories with such themes as "putting their lives back together after the disaster," or "a return to normal after the aborted coup d'état," or "a mother working two jobs to put her sons through college so they can have a better life than she." Work is rarely viewed for what it is in our society—by and large, an alienating experience to so many unskilled or semi-skilled laborers, and increasingly to the white-collar proletariat—the clerical-information workers of the computer age—as well. Rather, work is presented as evidence of the human will to survive and make a better life—a distinctly middle-class vision of the world. The stories are framed as highly individualized accounts of survival symbolic of the human condition and are thereby cut off from their more concrete and therefore more powerful social and ideological contexts. Rarely do we get an adequate exploration or analysis of the increased susceptibility of the lower socioeconomic classes to physical danger in the workplace or in inadequate housing, unsafe transportation, or lack of sufficient police protection outside the work environment; or of their desertion by the educational apparatus that teaches them at best how to cope in the technological world; at worst, how to fail. Instead, the sucess of those who have escaped these conditions through hard work is celebrated, while the basic structure of oppression is ignored.

The illusion of hard work is reinforced in the presentational elements of the newscasts themselves. In many newscasts, both local and national (e.g., the old CBS/Cronkite set and the *ABC World News Tonight* set), the working newsroom becomes the backdrop for the report. In the background of the establishing shots, we see people moving to and fro, seemingly preparing the news (the newscast, of course, is already prepared and very tightly scripted). At one particularly successful local news operation, CBS affiliate WBNS-TV in Columbus, Ohio, the newsroom becomes a special place to which the viewer is taken for a sneak preview of upcoming stories. Weatherperson Joe Holbrook is shown fiddling with a weather computer, the high-tech machine reinforcing the reporter's status as a hard-working expert in charge of his machinery. We cut to working-anchor Dave Kaylor in the bowels of the newsroom, shirt sleeves rolled up, preparing copy for the next half-hour's newscast. Here we are confronted with the old image of the hard-nosed reporter at his typewriter. All that's missing is the green eyeshade.

The calculated presentation of the journalist as a hard worker, a direct formatting change designed to counter the critical outrage over "happy-talk" and "tabloid" news, should not be taken as a total ruse; many journalists do work very hard. The issue is one of the nature of the work itself. With all that hard work done, why are television newscasts generally so stylized and devoid of cognitive substance?

An amazing spoof of the working newsroom was mounted by the Los Angeles Metromedia independent-television-station KTTV in the mid-1970s. Titled *Metronews, Metronews* (one surmises, after the *Mary Hartman, Mary Hartman* model of soap-opera spoof-celebration), the half-hour newscast featured two informal anchors—one in an army fatigue shirt, the other in a rumpled white shirt and tie with sleeves rolled up—who wise-cracked their way through the day's events in a mock-tabloid style using what appeared to be parodies of soft news features (one was never certain just how seriously the show took itself). The show's coup was its newsroom setting, which looked like a real newsroom with a water cooler, file cabinets, old desks, teletype machines, and messages scrawled on slips of paper and tacked up here and there. *Metronews* clearly confronted, through its style, the fake show-business world of the legitimate newscast. The informality of the *Metronews* anchors, who were really happy (and who seemed to border on being stoned), pointed to the contrived happy informality of "happy-talk" news. The telephone to the newsroom, a standard set piece, into which one anchor was seen talking as we returned from a commercial break, was dead—"nobody there," he exclaimed as he hung up.

The reward for the journalist's hard work is a combination of prestige and significant pecuniary compensation. At the highest levels of contemporary electronic journalism, the network news anchors, this reward is substantial. In television's early days, salaries were good, but not mind-boggling. In 1948, NBC paid John Cameron Swayze $25,000 a year to read news on the nightly *Camel News Caravan*, a 15-minute network newscast, while CBS paid Douglas Edwards $30,000 for his nightly news program. In contrast, in 1983, according to CBS's *60 Minutes*, ABC paid its anchor Peter Jennings about $1 million; NBC paid anchor Tom Brokaw $1.7 million; and CBS paid Dan Rather, the strong ratings leader in the competition, $2 million—some 67 times as much as fellow CBSer Douglas Edwards had earned some 35 years earlier.[17]

The anchors have developed their journalistic skills through many years of print- and electronic-news practice. They have made the right moves in the corporate news game, have been "team players." Now that they are millionaires, what impact do they have on news management? Have their years of hard work and newsgathering experience paid dividends in terms of personal control over the news apparatus? Both NBC's Brokaw and ABC's Jennings say they take an active role in their nightly newscasts. Brokaw, the "managing editor" of the *NBC Nightly News*, works with the program's executive producer to construct the newscast, and writes about 60 percent of the program; but, he noted, "it's not a big deal, . . . it's mostly lead-ins to the correspondents." Jennings, ABC *World News Tonight*'s "senior editor," says he has "an editorial presence." He helps determine the day's news coverage with his executive producer, and he writes the beginning and end of the broadcast and edits introductions to stories prepared by news-staff writers in New York.[18] Clearly, the pecuniary rewards seem linked less to current journalistic activities than to the anchorperson's presence, demeanor, and ability to attract and hold an audience in a fierce competitive battle wherein one rating point—

833,000 homes—is worth nearly $25 million in annual advertising revenue.[19]

In this world of high finance and prestige, there always exists a possibility that the network electronic journalist-superstar will fall out of touch with "the people" as he spends the preponderant amount of his working, and in many cases socializing, hours with national- and foreign-government officials. "The people," described by Brokaw as a "large mass, looking at us in a distracted way,"[20] are the true target audience for both the network and local evening-news programs. Audience studies have repeatedly found network and local news viewers to be below the national average educational level and generally older. The network news image makers, most likely unconsciously, work hard to project an atmosphere that is pure upscale suburban middle landscape—the mental landscape in which the majority of newspersons themselves dwell. Network reporters and anchors appear as highly successful, self-important personages, taking themselves too seriously. This image building does, however, serve a useful purpose in the larger world of network-affiliate relations, for the patronizing ambience of the national news, which exudes "responsibility," compensates for the tent-show atmosphere of so much local news, which gathers higher ratings than serious news but runs the risk of alienating government regulators. Local news generates carry-over for the network news that follows. What is therefore of primary importance is getting the "average Joe" to turn on the set for the fires, rapes, and murders, then keep him watching while the serious world events are presented in a truncated, easily digestible form by the serious people. The affiliates have made money and have kept the Federal Communications Commission off their case, the people have been entertained, and the networks have secured their carry-over into their prime-time shows.

The suburban middle landscape in network news is reflected in news values, dress, and presentational codes. This landscape is presented in news not as a geographic place (the suburb is exceedingly difficult to locate geographically any more, but it is there) but as a state of mind to which an appearance is correlated. Most of the spokespersons, both journalists and sources, seem to come from this place irrespective of their personal life histories or the nature of the story being reported. Their dress and their mannerisms point, above all, to their "belonging."

Values-and-lifestyle research would classify the successful

news anchor, male or female, as part achiever—a prosperous, middle-aged materialist—and part "belonger"—a patriotic, traditional, and stable person generally quite happy with his or her life. Critic Edwin Diamond provided his own version of the "anchor model": "middle-aged, mid-American, white males, . . . the men the old *Life* magazine used to refer to as 'the command generation.'"[21] They look and sound authoritative, but not too authoritative—the Walter Cronkite persona. Edward R. Murrow was too authoritative, too intense for the night-after-night presence of news anchoring, but his intensity was ideal for the clear focus and closure of documentary work. The anchors write and report well, but not too well; otherwise they sound erudite and are relegated to providing commentary, à la Eric Severeid and Bill Moyers. They are not too young, not too old (ABC's Peter Jennings spent four years as ABC anchor in the mid-1960s but was too young to command the necessary presence; ten years later, in 1978, now more mature, he returned to the anchor slot at ABC in their triple-anchor format, and in 1983 he took sole possession of ABC's anchor). They are good looking, but not too handsome. They are, above all, loyal to their corporation. And they have an "unceasing drive to win."[22] As CBS anchor Dan Rather said while being interviewed for a *60 Minutes* segment on network-television news anchors, part of his desire to be a network anchorperson was "to run something on your own." This entrepreneurial spirit is a prerequisite for the successful anchor, who is clearly now a corporate person, but one who also maintains his individual pride and the sense of skepticism that got him to this point in his career as a serious professional. He knows the limits to which he can bend the corporate apparatus and still maintain his professional integrity and personal status.

This perfect combination of fierce competitive drive, good looks, cool controlled informality, and substantial talent, which is nonetheless unthreatening to one's associates, is rare, and makes the ideal anchor a valuable commodity. Sociologist Orrin Klapp classified this classic American-hero character type as the "group servant"—a defender of the dominant order who, through tireless work, rights wrongs, and saves the weak from the strong. This hero is what Klapp terms a "compensatory type" helping people put up with a reality different from the ideal.[23] The television anchor, while he may not actually accomplish such feats, gives the appearance of such accomplishment. Compensation is particularly relevant, given the context of news, which so often presents to the viewer a vision of the urban frontier, which is, according to critic Tony Schwartz, "almost unbelievably grim," especially at the local, metropolitan level. This vision is "one dominated by film of burning buildings and smoke-blackened firemen; stretchers being loaded into ambulances and tight-lipped detectives pacing around cordoned-off crime scenes."[24] The same images are also prevalent in national and international news coverage as minor wars pop up all over the globe and American military forces and news correspondents are shipped off to become involved.

No longer the youthful independent spirit—the lone individual doing battle with the unyielding institution—but still personifying the myth of the individual in large measure, standing above the fray, guiding our view of the world, and teaching us how to react, the mature anchor now must also play a role of a reasonable arbiter of reality for millions of Americans; he must be strong and fair, decisive and warm. Above all, he must be trusted by tens of millions of average people. Dan Rather's warm, middle-class gentility is reminiscent of Steve Douglas, Ozzie Nelson, and Ward Cleaver, three famous denizens of television's suburban middle landscape. But Dan didn't exude such an aura until the sweater; before the sweater, we knew Dan as that tough White House correspondent who directly challenged Richard Nixon during the famous press conferences surrounding Watergate, and as the contentious, aggressive interrogator of *60 Minutes*. His image for millions of viewers was cool if not cold—a bit too hard-edged for the nightly exposure as news anchor. The sweater—a V-neck pullover—gave him, in the words of *Washington Post* critic Tom Shales, the "trust-me, you've-got-a-friend, hello-out-there-in-television-land sense."[25] *The CBS Evening News with Dan Rather*, which had lost much of its substantial ratings lead over NBC and ABC since Rather took over for Cronkite in March 1981, surged ahead once again, regaining Cronkite's commanding lead. Dan's sweater was Walter's pipe in disguise. The V-neck sweater became the talk of journalistic circles. Everywhere, anchors bought sweaters. Was the sweater a tremendous public-relations coup? Not to hear Rather tell the story, a story right out of *Leave It To Beaver*. It appears he had a cold in early winter and wore his V-neck sweater, which his wife had given him 11 years before, around the office. One night he kept it on for the newscast and his wife said it looked great on the air. The rest is history. What made the sweater so vital? One CBS executive hypothesized to Shales that Rather's handsomeness and perfection were putting some viewers off, making people feel inadequate by comparison. Rather, it is reported, went out and bought three new sleeveless sweaters and two long-sleeve sweaters, "off the rack."

The stories which reinforce this image of warm middle-class gentility are those which deal with culture and civility and act to set straight once again the world of bad news and human degradation. We see this clearly manifested in the lifestyle reports of *CBS Sunday Morning with Charles Kuralt* and occasionally on the tail end of the nightly newscast (PBS's new entry into the competition, *The MacNeil/Lehrer News Hour*, has adopted Kuralt's video-postcard motif as well as the "trip-to-the-art-gallery" report). The world of arts reportage, showing aficionados attending legitimate galleries or blockbuster museum retrospectives such as the 1983 Manet exhibit at the New York Metropolitan Museum of Art, serves to reinforce the power of corporate patronage under the illusion of democratic access to culture. As critic John Berger wrote, "The majority of the population do not visit art museums. . . . [They] take it as axiomatic that the museums are full of holy relics which refer to a mystery which excludes them, ... that original master-pieces belong to the preserve (both materially and spiritually) of the rich."[26] What is set straight in the world of news and of suburban-middle-landscape culture is the dominance of the corporate elite and the subservience of the people.

There can be no doubt that the news, especially local news and national network news in major markets, is a middle-class corporate venture. As critic George Comstock noted:

> News and public affairs programming, unlike entertainment, are the products of disseminators. . . . The daily selection and treatment of events are the responsibility of the news staff. These decisions are made autonomously of management. Yet news cannot escape the values of management, which reside in popularity. Journalists may manufacture the news, but management manufactures the newsmen and their tools. Formats and personnel are the creatures of management, as is the budget to do the job. Thus news, like entertainment, becomes honed to the exigencies of competition.[27]

When we involve management, the critique of news must include not only matters of style, but also related matters of technique, for management, not willing to trust its aesthetic or gut feel, and not prone to bold experimentation, turns to the

modern-day management tools—viewer surveys and news consultants—to generate information about news presentation.
Not even the sacrosanct anchor is spared such quantitative,
detached scrutiny. From the use of data on what viewers want
to see as their news, it is a small step to the concept of news
packaging—the employment of rigid formulas to structure and
order the presentation of each day's messy world according to
some notion of audience acceptability.

Technique operates on many levels in television news. As a
manifestation of the myth of eternal progress—of a technically
sophisticated America in charge of her destiny—technique is
most clearly visible in an ostensibly neutral technological context, represented by the progress of computer graphics on local
weather (which lend an air of authority to the performance of
the weatherperson via his association with sophisticated machinery); live minicam reports from the field on breaking stories (most of which seem yet to break or have already broken as
the correspondent tries desperately and, often on the local
level, comically, to inject his personality into the report to save
it from absurdity); computer-generated reports on battle tactics
(especially intriguing were the continual graphics displays during the 1982 Falkland Islands war between Britain and Argen-
tina—the viewer became engrossed in a real-life version of the
video game as little graphic Exorcet missiles were fired from
the graphic fighter planes, hit their targets, the graphic British
ships, and the ships exploded like so many images in an old
comic book); those incredible twirling graphics, in so many local
news openings, designed to give the cast a modern, "with-it"
look (one feels the world tumbling and swirling about until it
rights itself as the anchors appear on the screen and things
quickly settle down); and the promotional bumpers before the
commercials—graphics which provide teasers for upcoming stories. Viewers have generally reacted very favorably to such
technical improvements in news presentation, saying that
these technical feats enliven the show, making it more interesting to watch. This, of course, would be expected, given the
atmosphere of entertainment that pervades today's daily news
broadcasts.

Technique moves beyond simple fascinating electronic blips
and live reports. The "human technique" of which Jacques Ellul
has written is manifested in the pseudoscientism of war reportage, as war becomes body counts; of politics, as issues become
poll results; and of economics, as the economy becomes indexes

and graphs. The network newspersons try their best to balance numbers with stories about individuals who are included in those numbers. This "personal touch" obscures what is lost in the antinomy of data and living beings—namely, the intelligent discussion of issues related to existing social relations. The world of data-as-news is a world of "unassimilated facts"[28]—of "scenes," as critic Michael Arlen once described television generally. Closure in this world is structural, not conceptual. Each story, especially if it deals in relatively difficult abstractions, must be closed that night and filed away to be discussed again at some future time. Exceptions to this type of closure are voyeuristic journeys into violence, sex crimes, murder trials, and death-row watches, coverage of which continues in a serial format until the stories reach their conclusions.

Most local newscasts use technique in their story ordering within the news segment. It is predictable and, to the viewer, comfortable. The news generally moves from a description of the grave events of the day (fires, murders, auto accidents, natural disasters, and acts of terrorism are grist for the local news headlines whether they are local or not); to the description of more mundane affairs—the ones that really affect our lives, but to which few of us pay much attention because they are buried in the middle of the news and they lack exciting visuals—affairs such as the city council's resolution of the traffic signal dispute; and finally to the upbeat (from the pathos of the WCBS-TV "Our Block" motif, which often features hapless people, such as the elderly citizens of the South Bronx, struggling to hold their lives together—the-will-to-survive theme that tugs at so many middle-class and working-class heartstrings, to the contrived humor of "the story about the man with the winged cat").

Technique operates behind the scenes in television news as well, most notably in the activities of the audience survey and the regimes of the infamous news consultants. Here is where most of the damage is done, out of sight of viewers and critics. Networks have used Q-scales developed by market researchers to rate newspersons and television personalities generally according to a viewer's positive response to a performer's personality. According to the Q-scale, CBS anchor Dan Rather was found to be almost as warm, compassionate, and honest as Walter Cronkite (although not warm enough until the sweater) while Rather's major competition for the CBS anchor position, savvy veteran Washington correspondent Roger Mudd, scored "cold" in comparison. CBS executives denied the Q-scale played a role in their anchor decision. Local news operations have increasingly relied on news consultants such as Frank N. Magid Associates, and McHugh and Hoffman (the major competitors for consultancy supremacy in television news) to help them find ways to improve their news presentation. McHugh and Hoffman is generally credited with developing the lurid tabloid-news format featuring large doses of sex, violence, and corruption coverage, which transformed San Francisco station KGO from a loser to a striking news success in a very short time. Other news operations followed suit and San Francisco went from a town whose local news operations were nationally respected to the site of the nightly peep show. Generally, the formula for news success, the consultants determined, was reduction of the maximum length of a story to 90 seconds, regardless of the story's news value and relative importance to the community, and the attractive newsreader.[29] The revolving-door approach to news talent resulted, as Kansas City anchorwoman Christine Craft of KMBZ discovered to her dismay and anger in 1981 when she was demoted from anchor to reporter because she was not pretty enough and not deferential to her male colleagues. Ms. Craft sued the station and was awarded damages in a jury trial. News consultants poll viewers and tailor the news and the news personalities to fit viewers' desires. They fine-tune their clients' image through the use of technique. They are paid handsomely. Their clients, on the whole, realize increased profitability by following their advice.

As Jacques Ellul wrote, "Technique . . . clarifies, arranges, and rationalizes. . . . It is efficient and brings efficiency to everything."[30] Certainly television news is no exception. Here all is order, efficiency, and comfort as the familiar persona of the anchorperson night after night, aided by slick technical visualization and easily understood symbology, conjures up scenes of events from far and near via satellites, helicopters, microwave dishes, and minicams and entertains us while providing the barest hint of the day's happenings. That, after all, is what we have come to expect and what we have told the television news consultants we want. We have learned to march complacently in place in front of our television screens as the world out there muddles on.

The Clash of Myths in Television News

Beneath the smooth exterior of the television-news presentation are hints of the real conflicts that exist in contemporary
social relations, but seem somehow to escape the watchful eye
of the video camera and reporter. They are there nonetheless,
and can be discovered through an analysis of the complex clash
of myths that subtly pervades television-news content, despite
institutional attempts to present a world of clear-cut antago-
nisms dependent for their resolutions on the force and power
of the dominant culture.

As soon as television journalists announce their professional
status, namely, their objectivity, we discover perhaps the most
basic clash of myths in television news. As critic William Henry
wrote, "American TV news, like the rest of American journalism, is scrupulously 'objective'—which means it does not challenge the prevailing biases of a predominantly white, Judeo-
Christian, imperial, internationalist, capitalist society."[31]

Objectivity, which many journalists prefer to define as overall fairness in presenting various positions in a controversy of
immediate concern to a community or nation, and an openness
to correction, is in reality a subterfuge that conceals presentational inequities favoring the dominant cultural position in any
argument. This is most clearly evident in the clash of the myths
of the suburban middle landscape and the urban frontier as
represented in social conflict. Critic Jeff Greenfield described
the atmosphere in which these two myths collided as television
news was forced to deal with the social unrest of the 1960s: "A
largely unwilling participant, . . . the medium was communicating events over which *it had little or no control*—against its clear
institutional interests. . . . The cultural upheaval of fashion and
taste—rooted in the power of rock-and-roll music—was an
upheaval ignored on the national airwaves until its presence
was unavoidable."[32] [Italics mine.] Rock and roll, political assassinations, burning cities, police brutality, and violent demonstrations on college campuses and at a national political convention—all of these powerful symbolic images were
manifestations of the urban frontier. The news was certainly
incongruous in the context of the reassurance of the suburban
middle landscape of television comedy so popular during the
early years of the decade and of the rural middle landscape of
childlike escapism of the middle and late years of that same
decade. (Newscasts and live coverage of news events could thus

easily be considered by viewers to be staged or distorted because the predominant television-entertainment frames showed a much less troubled world.) One can argue with Greenfield's conclusion that television had "little or no control" over the events it was communicating. The television-news apparatus indeed worked hard, if subconsciously, to draw clear ideological lines between legitimate authority and anarchic protest. The voice of legitimate authority was heard resonating in the suburban middle landscape in the form of "reasoned responses of the arranged studio discussion," which had much greater persuasive power than "unreasoned, merely demonstrative, responses" of street confrontations.[33] The oppositional elements who were forced to resort to protest demonstrations to make their points took to the streets in the urban frontier. These political "happenings" often became violent, and the film crews provided millions of viewers with powerful scenes of the conflict shot from behind police lines. The point of view the images revealed showed us an unruly urban frontier in which young people wearing clown makeup, army fatigue shirts, torn blue jeans, and draped in American flags, threw rocks, bottles, and human feces at law-enforcement agents. When scenes of violent confrontation were presented, they provoked charges from news critics, such as Vice-President Spiro Agnew, that the television networks advocated radical change. On the contrary, as Edward Epstein pointed out, this bias toward change was "not ideologically motivated but an inevitable outcome of the search for a mass audience" through the construction of "highly simplified melodramas, built around conflict, and illustrated with visual action."[34] Clearly Epstein is closer to the truth in this debate, but he discounts use of the strong pull of the network news apparatus to balance coverage to the point that order inevitably predominates. Cronkite's liberal indignation at the thug tactics used by Chicago Mayor Richard Daley's police against CBS news correspondents, such as Rather, who covered the 1968 Democratic National Convention was clearly substantively motivated rather than some search for a mass audience. Cronkite's remarks set up a clear-cut conflict of ideas; yet it was quickly followed by Cronkite's invitation to the Chicago boss to appear in the CBS anchor booth to respond. Cronkite, the voice of reason, had backed down. The CBS news organization appeared to be apologizing, both to the mayor and to the American people, for Cronkite's justifiably passionate condemnation of the suppression of journalistic activity the night before. Daley appeared calm and authoritative. Everything was civilized. The confrontation was defused and the antiwar demonstrators protesting in front of the Conrad Hilton Hotel—the convention headquarters hotel—appeared by contrast to be overreacting. Cronkite's attempt at fairness and balance in the end confused the entire issue. As the protesters shouted that "the whole world is watching," the television news frames were pro-law and order. By emphasizing law-enforcement activities during the urban riots of 1965 and 1967 in Watts, Detroit, Newark, and other metropolitan areas, and by stressing interviews—many with whites in black neighborhoods—television news deflected substantive matters of blacks' "underlying grievances and tensions" and thereby failed to present a meaningful sociohistorical context for these confrontations.[35]

The myths of the individual and the puritan ethic lead the television news person ever closer to the status system that contains the politician. The ultimate fusion of journalism and politics comes at times like 1968, when the journalist whose reasoned voice seemed to rise above political demagoguery was touted as a potential presidential nominee: Walter Cronkite, the "most trusted man in America," seemed capable of running the country; indeed, on his February 27, 1968, evening newscast, Cronkite declared that the Vietnam War was lost and the only "rational" thing to do was to negotiate a settlement. He sounded more of a leader than our leaders.

Regardless of the journalist's sympathy with the cause of the underdog and tendency toward the more liberal stance, the status world of the hard-working achiever/belonger is far removed from the dirty nonstatus world of the street demonstrations. The urban frontier provides visual fuel for the nightly news report. The fire is put out by the boys from the suburban middle landscape. The technique embodied in the slick package and the instant report—the myth of eternal progress—reassures the viewer that the "radical messiness of reality" is under control.[36]

The myth of the individual as it operates in television news contains subtle internal contradictions. The basic operating frame of the myth is clear: An individual meets an institution in a confrontation. The results are far more complicated and hinge on characterization. When the individual is a superstar journalist, the likely outcome is that the individual will emerge victorious. When the individual is the common man, the likely outcome is that the individual will be wronged by the institution and rendered seemingly helpless, but will be saved through the intervention of the journalist as moral defender of the truth (thus demonstrating that democracy works; i.e., that a free and unfettered press protects men from abuses of power). If the institution in question is government, the institution is likely portrayed as unresponsive, anonymous, bureaucratic, and inefficient—in short, the institution is at fault. If the institution is a giant corporation, the wrong done to the individual is blamed not on the capitalist institution itself, hear .iess greed, or corruption, but rather, on individual mismanagement. If the bad manager is fired or if a more effective management strategy is initiated, the wrong will disappear. It is little wonder that the hard-working aggressive star journalist would implicitly view the problem as one of managerial ineptitude rather than as one of basic systemic structural deficiency, for his or her success had depended in large measure on his or her corporateness—a basic belief in efficient management and the value of creative entrepreneurial solutions to human problems. Entrepreneurial flair and style will inevitably produce the better mousetrap and the better social solution; bureaucratic hesitation, bungling, and lack of imagination will produce failed social programs. Admittedly this antinomy is presented here in broad brush strokes, but it can be argued that such a frame operates in television news in the broadest sense as well with particular exceptions now and then.

When things get so hot in the urban frontier that the men and women from the suburban middle landscape cannot seem to bring them under control, the television-news apparatus may invoke one of its most powerful myths—the myth of the rural middle landscape—to deflect attention from the chaos. This version of the myth is "Waltonesque"—the strong mature rural citizen coping with the evil world crashing all around him by maintaining pure country values, including the sanctity of the extended family and the value of hard work not for achievement, but for a higher moral purpose. The rural middle landscape speaks to a moral victory. Charles Kuralt's eloquent "On the Road" profiles of strong-willed, commonsensical country folks lent substantial credibility to the myth. In contrast to the rural middle landscape, the urban frontier, when it is New York City, may lose morally. But its portrayal in television news assures that it will win a cultural victory. The suburban-middle-landscape mind-set of the news packagers assures such victory by deflecting pressing questions of human degradation and social injustice in the name of the vibrancy of urban culture—the American melting-pot ideal which produces great authors from the slums. Howe ver, when the urban frontier is Los Angeles (the great television-entertainment capital), it pales in comparison with the rural middle landscape both morally (it is the epitome of the self-centered, egotistic "me generation" of which Tom Wolfe wrote) and culturally (it is inhabited by ostentatious kooks disguised as creative people; it has no urbanity in the New York sense, but rather, harbors Hollywood pretenders to the cultural throne of Broadway).

Network television news is a New York affair, with deference to the nation's political capital, which, unfortunately it would seem, was moved to Washington—that humid, rather uncultured marshland full of military personnel and glorified clerk-typists—nearly two centuries ago. While the roots of many of the anchors and correspondents are in southern or midwestern culture, those places have become merely origins from which occasionally a strong sense of morality will well up in condemnation of a generally uncivilized world. The world in which these people now live and work is at a far remove from those roots—it is a world of achievement, success, public prestige, and corporate control.

THE DOCUMENTARY: CONTROL AND DEMYSTIFICATION

The television documentary has taken on many forms in its three-decade history, including the television argument (Peter Davis's *The Selling of the Pentagon*, CBS, 1971); the personal television essay (*Bill Moyers Journal*); the television history (Allistair Cooke's *America: A Personal History of the United States*, NBC, early 1970s); television exposition (Dr. Jacob Bronowski's *The Ascent of Man*, BBC, aired on PBS, 1975); the television magazine (CBS's *60 Minutes*; NBC's *First Camera*; and ABC's *20/20*); and vérité (Frederick Wiseman's *Welfare*, WNET/PBS; Craig Gilbert's *An American Family*, PBS, 1973; and Peter Davis's *Middletown*, PBS, 1982).

Most television-documentary work has used a correspondent/narrator structure that packages various scenes into a clear linear presentation. The layer of external explanation is provided in both the on-camera speech and the voice-over nar-

ration of the correspondent or narrator, who generally follows
a script and an interview framework developed beforehand by
the documentary's producer/director/writer. The tone of the
documentary may be that of Edward R. Murrow's and producer
David Lowe's moral indignation in *Harvest of Shame* (CBS,
1960)—a powerful exposé of the terrible living and working
conditions of migrant farm laborers who feed the nation; that
of cynical distrust, as in producer Peter Davis's and correspondent Roger Mudd's *The Selling of the Pentagon* (CBS, 1971), which
focused on the highly questionable motives and fiscal waste of
the U.S. military's public-relations activities; or of irony, as in
the controversial 1970 PBS documentary *Banks and the Poor*,
which accused the banking industry of consciously perpetuating the miserable conditions in our urban ghettos, and which,
in a devastating indictment of governmental conflict of interests, superimposed a crawl listing 98 members of Congress,
who owned shares or were directors of banks, over a shot of
the capitol, while the "Battle Hymn of the Republic" played in
the background. These critically acclaimed efforts were a
needed antidote to the nightly scenes that passed as news on
the local and network newscasts. They attempted to transcend
the pattern of reassurance that had come to characterize the
"soft" evening news. The best work in the documentary form
was hard-edged, clear-cut, and provocative. The primary weakness with this narrative format, however, was the tendency for
viewers to feel that once these social injustices and institutional
excesses of power had been exposed and righteously condemned, the social problems would be resolved. (Such was obviously not the case as ten years after *Harvest of Shame*, NBC's
Martin Carr produced *Migrant*, which demonstrated that conditions for migrant workers hadn't changed despite Murrow's
exhortations.) The narrative closure encouraged such a feeling
of accomplishment.

Since 1959 the three commercial television networks have
packaged their documentary work in competing series, beginning with *CBS Reports*, and followed shortly by *NBC White Paper*
and *ABC Close-Up*. The forerunner to these efforts was the
provocative Edward R. Murrow-Fred Friendly documentary
series on CBS, *See It Now*, which began in 1951. PBS, founded in
1967, aired the *Realities* series (which was canceled after the
1970 season because of the congressional uproar over *Banks and
the Poor*). Ratings for these programs have always been considered failures by commercial television network executives. *The*

Selling of the Pentagon, which was aired February 23, 1971, and is considered by many as the hardest-hitting and most exciting investigative documentary of 1970s television, was seen by 5,350,000 homes, Like most documentaries, it came in last in the week's rating race. In contrast, its entertainment competition, *Marcus Welby, M.D.* was seen in 17,250,000 homes. *The Guns of Autumn* (CBS, 1975; Irv Drasnin, producer) was seen in 8,490,000 homes. It so angered the National Rifle Association that hate mail poured into CBS. Its ideological impact went far beyond its general popularity level. While these viewership figures are small compared to prime-time entertainment programs, they still reveal a significant national interest in such programming despite network executives' assertions to the contrary. Particularly low in the ratings are documentary works dealing with foreign affairs (e.g., the Communist party in Italy or the economic and social decline of Britain). Most viewers seem to be turned off by discussion of complex economic questions, especially in the international arena, where the immediate ramifications to the individual are more difficult to interpolate. More successful are documentaries which broadly survey domestic problems such as violence and crime.

In absolute numbers, documentaries on the commercial television networks have declined significantly in recent years. In 1975, for example, 61 documentaries were presented (28 on CBS, 18 on ABC, and 15 on NBC). In 1976, a presidential-election year, the total fell to 36 (15 on CBS, 13 on NBC, and eight on ABC). In the September-April period of the 1982–83 season, only 14 documentaries had been aired. These constituted 10.7 percent of all network specials. The average Nielsen rating for the documentary in the 1982–83 season was 8.0. The average share was 13.6 (about one in seven homes that were watching television at the time were tuned to a documentary—certainly not a negligible figure). A further analysis of the 1982–83 season's data reveals that nine of the 14 documentaries were aired in the 10:00–11:00 P.M. time slot (EST)—the last hour of prime-time, when audiences were beginning to decline. Two were aired in the early 7:00–8:00 P.M. time slot (EST) on Sunday. Thus, only three documentaries, or about one-fifth of the total, were aired in the heart of prime time. There were no documentaries aired between September 22, 1982, and December 4, 1982—the "new season."[37] Documentaries have been, and are more than ever, second-class citizens in the world dominated by melodramatic and comedic television entertainment.

In contrast to the typical documentary, the network news magazine, led by CBS's *60 Minutes*, has been a ratings success, and sometimes a huge success (*60 Minutes* has been in the top ten network programs since 1977). During the six-week period, April 7–May 12, 1983, *60 Minutes* averaged a 23.2 rating and 39.75 share—three times that of the average documentary aired during the 1982–83 season. ABC's *20/20* averaged a respectable 17.2 rating and 29 share during that six-week period (a level considered acceptable by network entertainment-program standards for renewal), or twice that of the average documentary. Especially revealing is the April 1983 reading for the *20/20* time slot (ABC, Thursday, 10:00–11:00 P.M., EST). On April 7, 14, and 29, *20/20* had a 29 share each night. On April 21, ABC substituted an *ABC Close-Up* documentary entitled "Banking." The *20/20* audience deserted in droves—the 29 share was nearly cut in half, down to 17. This suggests that viewers may watch the television news magazine more for the personalities of the correspondent-performers than for the substance, or that the substance of the magazine is less conceptually difficult and more entertainingly packaged than the traditional investigative documentary.[38] While *60 Minutes* and *20/20* demonstrate that audiences are not turned off by controversy, in which both magazines wallow, they may be turned off by the level of abstraction inherent in the serious discussion of economics, politics, and ideology.

The long-form, 60- or 90-minute documentary has suffered hard times in competition with the news magazine. CBS's vice-president for public-affairs broadcasts, John Sharnik, told critic John Culhane in 1977, "It's hard to drum up enthusiasm around here for some things when '60 Minutes' has taken off the cream."[39] By covering two or three stories in abbreviated form each week, the news magazine leaves the viewer with the feeling that all that need be said has been said on the subject (the same sense of closure one feels with traditional long-form narrative documentaries), while eating up potential topics at a rapid clip.

And when a long-form documentary project is undertaken, which may engage a producer and staff for a year and a half, the end result may be years of aggravation for the creative forces who worked hard to produce a meaningful piece. As one documentary producer told Culhane, "If the show is controversial enough . . . the producer finds that everything he did in the course of the film is subject to the minutest investigation. . . . The networks sometimes back you up and sometimes don't."[40]

The producer/director/writer and the correspondent of a highly controversial documentary may get pressure from outside their organization. While *The Selling of the Pentagon* was still on the air, CBS started getting angry telephone calls. CBS News President Richard Salant was called before the House Commerce Committee, and eventually the full House of Representatives, to answer questions about the documentary. CBS President Frank Stanton refused Representative Harley Staggers's subpoena for the outtakes of the documentary. The documentary was rebroadcast a month later with a 15-minute critical response from Vice-President Spiro Agnew, Secretary of Defense Melvin Laird, and Representative F. Edward Hebert, chairman of the House Armed Services Committee. Guards were placed at CBS studios in New York and Washington as a caller threatened to assassinate correspondent Mudd. In May 1971 Marine Colonel John MacNeil, who claimed CBS rearranged parts of a speech he had given in Peoria, Illinois, to publicly embarrass him on the documentary, filed a $2 million libel suit against CBS, Inc. and WTOP-TV in Washington, D.C., which carried the documentary. The same month, CBS won an Emmy Award for *The Selling of the Pentagon*. Clearly, the network backed its documentary workers in this case even though some questionable film-editing practices were employed, including the excision of qualifying phrases of some interviewees and the joining of statements, made in a number of different contexts, as the single answer to a question.

Eleven years later, CBS was faced with another libel suit over one of its investigative documentaries. This time the response was markedly different. Broadcast in January 1982 on CBS, *The Uncounted Enemy: A Vietnam Deception* featured a heated interview between CBS's Mike Wallace and retired U.S. Army General William Westmoreland. The 90-minute documentary's thesis was that in 1976, Westmoreland led a military conspiracy to sustain U.S. support for a faltering war by grossly underreporting enemy troop strength. *TV Guide* reporters investigated the documentary and questioned CBS's evidence. CBS News President Van Sauter conducted an internal investigation, upon receipt of which he publicly admitted that the broadcast contained factual errors. He labeled use of the word "conspiracy" as "inappropriate." CBS set up an ombudsman to hear complaints about future newsgathering practices. Although not mentioning him by name in the public admissions of guilt, Sauter found producer/director/writer George Crile negligent in "combining answers from several questions on the same subject into one answer," thus violating network guidelines. Sauter said the documentary should have included more remarks from officials who disputed the charge against the top-level military strategists. All this was not sufficient for Westmoreland, who filed a $120 million libel suit against CBS in September 1982. Claiming that CBS News "credibility" was at stake, Sauter had publicly called into question the techniques and, by implication, the ideological motives of the CBS documentary-production apparatus. The old balancing act had once again managed to divert attention from the issues at hand, namely, Westmoreland's conduct of the war in which over 50,000 Americans lost their lives. CBS News had apologized to city boss Richard Daley in 1968 before millions of Americans. Fourteen years later, CBS News was in essence apologizing to the man who drove us deeper into the morass of Southeast Asia. In both cases, the newsgathering apparatus had gotten so close to some real ideological questions (police as "thugs" and generals as "conspirators" in a lie that cost thousands of young men their lives) that a violent discourse ensued, but the network news operations, ever conscious of their status with their news sources in high places in government, hid behind the blind cloak of objectivity and balance. Clearly, different men in different political climates will react differently, regardless of the general tendency toward a particular type of behavior. News in general, and Salant and Stanton in particular, were more testy in the 1971 era of *The Selling of the Pentagon*—a time when Nixon's inherent distrust of all newsgatherers except those at the *Washington Star* and ABC produced a contentiousness among the press corps and press executives—than in 1982 when newsmen seemed strangely lulled by Reagan's public-relations posturing and his "sincere" warmongering.[41]

If the traditional network documentary, with its built-in layers of control through clear narrative structure, is exposed to charges of conscious manipulation from those whose ideological positions it challenges, the vérité documentary—a form in which the documentarian rejects external narration and instead ideally lets the subjects reveal themselves through their everyday activities, filmed or taped by the unobtrusive camera/observer—gives the appearance of objectivity. Of course, objectivity is impossible because the editing of thousands of feet of film or hours of videotape superimposes a structure on the work. The essential difference between the two forms is the latter's acceptance of life's complexity, ambiguity, and lack of closure. The vérité work ends, but the personal lives it revealed and the relationships among people and between people and institutions continue. Vérité thus seems to leave more room for viewer response and subsequent action because of the inherent continuation in the work itself. Vérité's weakness, however, is that the subsequent plan of action is often vague or nonexistent because the social relations explored in the work are not clearly explicated within a well-developed conceptual frame. While the traditional television narrative documentary may leave the viewer complacent, feeling the problem is under control because the network documentarian has discovered and properly framed the problem, the vérité documentary, with its very structure encouraging a nihilistic response, may leave the viewer cynical and frustrated. Neither response is optimal.

The vérité form is ideally suited to penetrating the veil of contemporary mythology, and herein lies its potential as a counterideological tool. By burrowing beneath the surface of the standardized public images of heroic character types presented in television entertainment, it can reveal the ugly blemishes which contextualize the myth. Whether focusing on social institutions, as Frederick Wiseman has done repeatedly and with powerful results, or focusing on individuals and intimate social groups such as families, as Craig Gilbert and Peter Davis have done in their work, the myths are opened up to the intense gaze of the unrelenting camera eye. Vérité can be a provocative tool since it cannot occur unless it is admitted into its subject's world and thereby becomes privy to the primary-source context of everyday experience—the place where mythology is manifested. Unlike news coverage or the tightly scripted traditional television documentary in which the correspondent enters the context for a brief moment, does a stand-upper or a few interviews, and leaves the scene, vérité is, at its best, cultural anthropology. While it could easily become voyeuristic, vérité's professed role is as a chronicler of and, by the very nature of its relationship with its subject, a participant in the social acts of the time.

Since the vérité form is synonymous with hand-held camera work, run-on scenes, and lengthy exposition, it is generally thought unsuited for commercial television network broadcast, with its time constraints and demand for careful narrative control. Most independent vérité work that has been aired has received its support from PBS, and especially from the New York flagship WNET. Two important examples of vérité's ability to unmask myth were aired nearly a decade apart on public television. Both explored, in vastly different ways, the reality behind the myth of the suburban middle landscape. The first, *An American Family*—a 12-part vérité series focusing on the Loud family of Santa Barbara, California—was produced by Craig Gilbert and aired in 1973. *An American Family* revealed the vacuousness in the anomic social relations of the suburban middle landscape. The second, the "Family Business" episode of *Middletown*, a six-part vérité series documenting life in Muncie, Indiana, was produced by Peter Davis, whose credits include *The Selling of the Pentagon* and the theatrical release *Hearts and Minds*, and directed by Tom Cohen. Aired in 1982, "Family Business" revealed the pathos of the Howie Snyder family as they struggled courageously to keep alive the great American Dream of the successful small entrepreneur, embodied in their suburban Shakey's Pizza Parlor franchise. They were deeply in debt to the central corporation and on the verge of foreclosure. The great American Dream was nothing but an empty slogan in the hollow lives of the Louds. In the lives of the Snyders, it was something to be cherished but its veracity was increasingly in doubt.

Conceived and produced by Gilbert, with cameraperson Alan Raymond and soundperson Susan Raymond (who were to produce *The Police Tapes* for PBS in 1976), *An American Family* documented the final stages of the disintegration of the 20-year marriage of William and Patricia Loud. The family was filmed from May 30, 1971, to January 1, 1972, in Santa Barbara and New York City. More than 300 hours of film were edited down. The serial cost over $1 million to make. The Louds and their five children were filmed in their lovely suburban house with its lovely swimming pool; 35 Wooddale Lane in Santa Barbara, California, became, for a few months, the stage upon which was acted out the promises and perils of the Great American Dream. It was the heart of the suburban middle landscape, a world right out of the film *The Graduate*, with heavy drinking, boredom, a twice-a-week Mexican maid, and gross materialism. When the scene shifted to New York City, 20-year-old homosexual son Lance was camped at the Hotel Chelsea on Twenty-third street—once a haven for some of America's great artists, now an overpriced boardinghouse for suburban avant-garde groupies. Lance constantly telephones home for money. The Louds' other children seem nondirected, bored—the forerunners of the "valley girls." Eighteen-year-old Kevin seems pleasant enough but vacuous. Seventeen-year-old Grant wants to be a rock star. Bill wants him to work at manual labor, but he would rather play. Fifteen-year-old Delilah tap dances in the third episode. She is going through adolescence. Thirteen-year-old Michele is shy, gentle—the warmest in the family. Admittedly, the children are frozen in time in the film. They will change and mature. But the scenes question the base upon which they will grow and mature.

Bill drinks too much, has numerous affairs with other women, and seems dissatisfied with his children. He blames Lance's failure on Pat for her allowing doctors to induce labor. Pat, a Stanford graduate, is interested in fashion, manners, and money. She blames Lance's failure on Bill for his not being closer to his son. Bill is busy trying to keep his strip-mining machinery business from going downhill. Rather than pursuing the great American Dream, he seems to be chased unrelentlessly by its ghost.

This is a far cry from Mayfield and *Leave It To Beaver*. The Louds' reality has order, but the order has nothing to do with mutual trust. Their order is that of routine. Love, which all of these people seem to desperately need, escapes their relationships. As Anne Roiphe wrote of the series, "The Louds have escaped the small-town mores of an earlier America" into a world with no central core of beliefs and little conscious understanding of work structures.[42]

But curiously, *An American Family* did share some of the attributes of *Beaver*. For during the filming, the Vietnam War raged on and Pakistan decimated Bangladesh, yet the Louds didn't notice. Theirs was a world, like that of Ward, June, Wally, and the Beaver, in which the view was cut off at the edge of town or at the perimeter of the front yard.

The Louds, who volunteered to be filmed and were paid no money for their participation, were bitter upon seeing the results. While critics generally were effusive in their praise of the work, Bill Loud accused Gilbert and the Raymonds of New York leftist leanings. Pat felt easterners lived too close together and seemed to be in an unending state of psychoanalysis.[43] Pat wrote an articulate and poignant "Letter to the Forum For

Contemporary History," dated February 23, 1973, thirteen months after the completion of filming. In it she stressed the horror of being constantly dissected, especially when "shows are being taped for replay in class, and . . . students are assigned to play one of the various roles within the family."

Reviews were generally scornful of the Louds. Pat felt critics treated her family as "objects and things instead of people." On one level, the Louds had become symbols, examples of contemporary bourgeois America. On a more personal level, Pat Loud wrote, "It has denuded us of such honor and dignity as we owned." The mirror, she felt, was distorted. Pat continued in her letter, "Like Kafka's prisoner, I am frightened, confused and saddened by what I see. I find myself shrinking in defense not only from critics and detractors, but from friends, sympathisers and finally, myself." The Louds didn't like what they saw. Pat concluded, "We have been ground through the big media machine, and are coming out entertainment . . . did we, *family and network alike*, serve up great slices of ourselves—irretrievable slices—that only serve to entertain briefly, to titillate, and diminish into nothing?"[44] [italics mine.] Fashion-conscious, status-conscious Patricia Loud seemed to have awakened from her suburban-middle-landscape dream. If so, the documentary effort was successful in human terms.

Following the airing of *An American Family*, Bill and Pat Loud became talk-show celebrities, their media "slices" not yet fully consumed.

If *An American Family* showed us all the warts of the myth of the suburban middle landscape in the era of the "me generation," Peter Davis's and Tom Cohen's *Family Business* showed us a moving personal struggle to hold onto the elusive great American Dream in an economic world that was constantly eating away at the outdated nineteenth-century promise of the independent entrepreneur. The protagonists, the Howie Snyder family, were part of the new entrepreneurial class—the franchisees. They operated a Shakey's Pizza Parlor in Muncie, Indiana—pure American middle landscape. The ma-and-pa-and-sons operation is characterized in the vérité piece by pride in their work, and the dream of sharing its financial rewards. Howie, a Marine Corps veteran is a natural-born entertainer, singing and clowning his way through the grueling work routine of long days and nights. Director Cohen captured the Snyders' despair in many moving scenes, including one in which Howie is talking on the telephone to the invisible parent-corporation's representative, asking, and almost begging for an extension on credit. The corporate operative on the other end of the line does not seem to be moved by Howie's personal stories of hard work and dedication to the company. Shakey's is threatening to foreclose. In the background Howie's wife is crying.

As the work at the pizza parlor drags on, we begin to feel its sweatshop atmosphere and both Howie's courage and, in a profound way, his naiveté emerge. At a family dinner, Howie discusses the possibility of giving up the business but decides he will continue. One son breaks down and sobs as he confronts the idea that his father might be a failure. It is powerful and revealing material, especially as it uncovers relationships between the traditional petit-bourgeois entrepreneur and the new middle-class corporate managers—an internal struggle for control within the suburban middle landscape. Howie Snyder, in the tradition of the small-shop owner, has roots and affiliations with the working class of which he is proud, and he is resentful of the efficient managerial system established in the pizza-franchising apparatus. He can't seem to understand, however, the extent to which he lacks control over his own business. He does not realize that in 1980, 25 percent of retail businesses were franchises and that their owners—businessmen such as himself—were accountable to the corporations who dictated to them how their businesses were to be run, the prices, and the look of the product and business establishment. He knows that on a personal level, Shakey's is threatening to foreclose. But on a social and macroeconomic level, he is overwhelmed by the abstraction. But while Howie has yet to clearly articulate his status in the context of Muncie and his pizza franchise, the viewer is able to see the economics in action.

Critics of vérité argue that the difficulty with the form is that social context is sacrificed in favor of the human, personal story; that the vérité works are little more than upper-West Side Manhattan liberal voyeurism. They argue that explanations of political economy require highly structured documentary work. *Family Business* demonstrates that vérité techniques can be effectively and profoundly used to reveal social processes by going into families' everyday experiences and by selecting families because they represent an idea. Such occasions are both memorable and rare in the world of television news and documentaries.

NOTES

1. For a full accounting of these approaches, see Michael J. Robinson, "Future Television News Research: Beyond Edward Jay Epstein," in *Television Network News: Issues in Content Research*, ed. William Adama and Fay Schreibman (Washington, D.C.: School of Public and International Affairs, George Washington University, 1978), pp. 197–211.

2. Daniel Menaker, "Art and Artifice in Network News," in *Television: The Critical View*, ed. Horace Newcomb, 3d. ed. (New York: Oxford University Press, 1982), p. 240 ff.

3. See John Fiske and John Hartely, *Reading Television* (London: Methuen, 1978), pp. 91–100, for a discussion of the ideological frames which impact on television news. Also see Raymond Williams, *Television: Technology and Cultural Form* (New York: Schocken Books, 1974), especially pp. 44–54.

4. Edward Jay Epstein, *News From Nowhere* (New York: Vantage Books, 1973) is the classic study of the organizational imperatives operating in the news-gathering process in television news, and is based on ethnographic observations of the process, with emphasis on NBC News, which provided Epstein with substantial access to their day-to-day news operations.

5. Ron Powers, "A Modest Proposal," in *The Newscasters* (New York: St. Martin's Press, 1978), p. 236.

6. Powers, "Vamping It," in *Newscasters*, p. 13. It must be noted that this "intervening role" is the exception in American journalistic history. Such journalists as James Franklin, with his editorial campaigns against the Massachusetts colonial government, and the heavy-handed theocracy of Mather in his *New England Courant* in 1721–26, and Horace Greely, with his prolabor and abolitionist editorials in his *New York Tribune* in the mid-nineteenth century, while examplary advocacy journalists, often stood alone in their eras as other journalists, more conservative, satisfied themselves with reprinting government and later corporate press releases.

7. Powers, "In the Palace of the Ice King," in *Newscasters*, p. 109.

8. Edward J. Epstein, *Between Fact and Fiction* (New York: Vantage Books, 1975), p. 19.

9. Williams, *Television*, pp. 22–23.

10. Michael Arlen, "The Prosecutor," in *The Camera Age* (New York: Penguin Books, 1981), pp. 158–79.

11. Ibid., p. 159.

12. Ibid., p. 172.

13. Ibid., p. 173. A Wyoming Grand Jury, dubbed "the 60 Minutes Grand Jury," met for a year on allegations of government corruption stemming from the *60 Minutes* telecasts, but returned no indictments of top officials, including the governor, the mayor, or the state's Democratic chairman, all linked to corruption by the two *60 Minutes* reports.

14. Williams, *Television*, p. 47.

15. Tom Smucker, "Control Factors: The Legacy of Lawrence Welk," *The Village Voice*, November 9, 1982, p. 56.

16. Menaker, "Art and Artifice," p. 233.

17. CBS, *60 Minutes*, September 26, 1983.

18. Sally Bedell Smith, "The Great Chase in Network News," *New York Times*, November 28, 1983, p. C21.

19. There can be little doubt that network news is a high-stakes enterprise. In 1983 it was estimated that the news budgets of the big-three networks were about $150 million each, and that of Cable News Network approximately $50 million. Each evening's 30-minute network newscast cost about $200,000 to produce and each 30-second spot sold for between $35,000 (NBC) and $44,000 (CBS). In view of these figures, an anchor's $2 million annual salary does not seem out of line if his presence nets the network an extra $25 million in revenue over the course of a year.

20. Smith, "The Great Chase," p. C21.

21. Edwin Diamond, "Television's 'Great Anchors'—And What Made Them Rate," *New York Times*, March 23, 1980, sec. 2, p. 35.

22. Ibid., p. 40.

23. Orrin E. Klapp, *Heroes, Villains, and Fools: The Changing American Character* (Englewood Cliffs, N.J.: Prentice-Hall, 1962), pp. 46–48.

24. Tony Schwartz, "What's Wrong With Local TV News?" *New York Times*, February 21, 1982, sec. 2, p. D1.

25. Tom Shales, "The Pull of the Pullover," *Washington Post*, February 8, 1982, p. C1.

26. John Berger, *Ways of Seeing* (London: British Broadcasting System, 1972), p. 24.

27. George Comstock, *Television in America* (Beverly Hills: Sage Publications, 1980), pp. 25–26.

28. William A. Henry III, "News as Entertainment: The Search for Dramatic Unity," in *What's News*, ed. Elie Abel (San Francisco: Institute for Contemporary Studies, 1981), p. 134.

29. Marvin Barrett, *Moments of Truth?* (New York: Thomas Y. Crowell, 1975), pp. 90, 94.

30. Jacques Ellul, *The Technological Society*, trans, John Wilkinson (New York: Vintage Books, 1964), p. 5.

31. Henry, "News as Entertainment," p. 135.

32. Jeff Greenfield, "Remembering the 1960's, as Seen on TV," *New York Times*, August 12, 1979, sec. 2, p. 25.

33. Williams, *Television*, p. 53.

34. Epstein, *Fact and Fiction*, pp. 204–5.

35. *Report of the National Advisory Commission on Civil Disorders* (New York: Bantam, 1968), pp. 369–73.

36. Menaker, "Art," p. 234.

37. On the local television level, very few individual independent stations or station groups bother to explore the serious long-form documentary as a way of fulfilling FCC public-interest obligations. The high cost and low return scare the local broadcast entrepreneur away. Even the well-intentioned Westinghouse Group-W documentary unit—the Urban America Unit—which did a series of 20 documentaries over a five-year period under executive producer Dick Hubert, could find very few commercial TV stations outside Group-W to take the works (exceptions were WMAL, Washington, D.C.; WHEC, Rochester, New York; WISN, Milwaukee, Wisconsin; and WCBW, Buffalo, New York). Out of 246 public-television outlets, only 13 put the UAU documentaries on, even when they were offered for free. See Barrett, *Moments of Truth?*, pp. 104–5.

38. Data for 1982–83 are interpolated from "Programming" reports of Petry, a station representative who distributes network ratings summaries to station clients.

39. John Culhane, "Where TV Documentaries Don't Dare to Tread," *New York Times*, February 20, 1977, sec. 2, p. D14.

40. Ibid., p. D15.

41. The libel suit is unsettled as of this writing. For background reports on the controversy, see Jonathan Friendly, "CBS Producer Defends Program on Vietnam," *New York Times*, July 17, 1982, p. 44; William A. Henry III, "Autopsy on a CBS 'Exposé,' " *Time*, July 26, 1982, p. 40; and John Corry, "Weighing the Facts in Westmoreland vs. CBS," *New York Times*, September 4, 1983, sec. 2, p. 19. [General Westmoreland withdrew his suit before any judgment was reached. ED.]

42. Anne Roiphe, "Things Are Keen But Could Be Keener," in *An American Family* (New York: Warner Paperback Library, 1973), p. 22.

43. Ibid.

44. *An American Family*, pp. 236–38.

JONATHAN BLACK

THE STUNG

Let there be no misunderstanding, *60 Minutes* has contributed great and wonderful moments to television journalism. There have been compelling interviews with the likes of Vladimir Horowitz and Fidel Castro, charming glimpses of faraway places, and exposés—the show's featured attraction—on subjects ranging from giant chemical companies to con-men, quacks, and charlatans. But in its twelve-year climb to Number One in the Nielsen ratings, *60 Minutes* has also evolved a style and method that occasionally erode the very trust and rigor at the heart of investigative journalism. Too often the show has impaired its own effectiveness with theatricality or slanted editing. The need to maintain the loyalty of forty million viewers can spawn an overwhelming desire to please. Were *60 Minutes* the subject of one of its own exposés, that compulsion might evoke some troubling questions.

A key problem lies in the misconstrued role played by *60 Minutes'* four correspondents, Dan Rather, Harry Reasoner, Morley Safer, and Mike Wallace.* Given our addiction to heroes—a habit bred in the glamor gossip of *People* magazine and on the talk-show circuit—it's inevitable perhaps that these on-screen stars should have become television's Four White Knights, indefatigable hounds of justice who pursue and nail the corrupt meat inspector, the Medicaid swindler, the mail-order minister. But, appearances notwithstanding, our heroes often play walk-on roles in the weekly Sunday drama. In fact, *60 Minutes* is largely the work of producers.

*Since this article first appeared Dan Rather has become anchorman for the *CBS Evening News*. Ed Bradley has replaced Rather on *60 Minutes* and Diane Sawyer has been added as a fourth Reporter-Investigator. ED.

From *Channels*, Vol. 1, No. 1, April–May 1981. Copyright © 1981, *Channels* Magazine. Reprinted by permission.

There are twenty producers at *60 Minutes*. Once a story idea is "blue-sheeted"—given the go-ahead—it's the producer who hits the field, prepares research, sets up interviews, and generally tailors a segment's focus. Then, and only then, does the correspondent arrive on-scene to be briefed for the interview segment. This division of labor places the correspondent at a dangerous remove from a story's development. It also makes his interview less a flexible probe for information than a mock trial with the verdict already determined by the producer's preset questions. Moreover, the producer decides in most instances who should, and who should *not*, be interviewed. And that decision may be influenced by a segment's predetermined slant.

On December 9, 1979, in a segment called "Garn Baum vs. the Mormons," Harry Reasoner reported on the travels of a Utah cherry processor, Garn Baum, who claimed the Mormon Church had conspired to drive him out of business. Not only had the church spearheaded a successful boycott among Utah cherry growers, Baum charged, but the church's all-pervasive influence made it virtually impossible for Baum to obtain lawyers in his subsequent antitrust suit against the church. "We have really had a hard time getting legal counsel," he told Reasoner, in an unrebutted statement that suggested Baum had had *no* lawyers. In truth, he'd been through five lawyers in four years, among them a top antitrust attorney, Dan Berman, who represented Baum for two years and ran up almost $8,000 in litigation costs alone. Berman was not interviewed for the segment because he had "checked first with the church on what line to take," according to producer Dick Clark. Berman vehemently denies this. But even if it were so—would that be sufficient reason to omit any mention of Berman, or of Baum's four other attorneys? In response to an irate 240-page complaint from the church-owned CBS affiliate in Salt Lake City, *60 Minutes* conducted an internal investigation and conceded the report "flawed . . . by the inadvertent omission of Baum's five lawyers." "Inadvertent" seems a diplomatic way of putting it. Allusion to Baum's attorneys clearly would have eroded the segment's thrust.

There was certainly nothing inadvertent in another producer's decision to censor vital data in a Reasoner report aired two weeks earlier. "Who Pays? You Do" reported on the shocking cost overruns at Illinois Power's (IP) nuclear reactor under construction at Clinton, Illinois. In painting his picture of waste and mismanagement, Reasoner interviewed several former IP employees—one, the "sharpest critic," as Reasoner described him, being cost engineer Steve Radcliff. There was only one problem: Radcliff had totally falsified his credentials. He'd never graduated from the Georgia Institute of Technology as he claimed he had, never received a PhD from Walden University, and was never a professor at Fairleigh Dickinson. These lies emerged long before broadcast, during testimony before the Illinois Power Commission, which was hearing IP's request for a consumer rate hike (and which refused to recognize Radcliff as an "expert witness"). The segment's producer, Paul Loewenwarter, knew of that testimony. CBS vice president Robert Chandler later admitted that "It was a very wrong decision. If I'd known, I would have insisted that be part of the story." One wonders. Had Radcliff's lies been made "part of the story," the case against IP would have been badly weakened.

In any case, the IP report was flawed by two *other* flagrant errors committed during that broadcast. Reasoner declared that IP requested a 14-percent rate hike. In fact, only one quarter of that amount was slated for the reactor at Clinton. And the Illinois Power Commission had *agreed to* IP's rate increase, not denied it, as Reasoner said.

"The IP story got by us, I'm not proud of that one," admits Don Hewitt, the show's executive producer, founder, and mastermind. Yet as with all segments where flaws are occasionally acknowledged, Hewitt and his colleagues insist the essence of the piece remains intact and accurate. Perhaps so. But an investigative news show risks its credibility when the errors accumulate. Nor is it reassuring when *60 Minutes'* correspondents minimize flaws by charging critics with what Dan Rather calls "misplaced attacks on the show's integrity." He says, "I plead for some perspective. When attention focuses on *our* mistakes, it's not whether Illinois Power did the job *they* should have done—it's whether *60 Minutes* did."

In a similar vein, Mike Wallace shrugs off the slipshod research in "Over the Speed Limit," a 1976 report on amphetamine abuse, because the man who eventually sued, a maligned diet doctor, was "not the proper subject of investigation." The report's prime target was Dr. Feridun Gunduy, who eventually lost his license thanks to Wallace's exposé.

It was only briefly and toward the end of the segment that Dr. Joseph Greenberg was put in the hot seat. Wallace interviewed Mrs. Barbara Goldstein, who claimed that the Long

Island endocrinologist had given her "eighty . . . eight-o" pills daily to reduce her weight, among them four to six amphetamine-type drugs. She then told Wallace that her complaints to Greenberg went unheeded, and that as a result of the medication she spent two years feeling utterly confused. Worse, she blamed Greenberg's pills for the birth defects of a daughter born later. Greenberg wasn't deterred by his brief moment of infamy. He slapped the show with a $30 million libel suit.

Though the files at *60 Minutes* are crammed with outraged, threatening letters, in its twelve-year history less than two dozen libel suits have been filed against the show, and not once has CBS lost. Few people stung by *60 Minutes* have the wherewithal, determination, or actionable complaint to sustain a long costly suit against CBS's crack attorneys. Dr. Joseph Greenberg, however, appeared to have money and outrage to spare, and as the trial progressed in a Long Island courtroom last spring, it seemed he might actually shatter *60 Minutes'* winning streak.

For starters, the doctor's sole on-air accuser, Mrs. Goldstein, had been a patient *ten years before* the segment ran. The "amphetamine-type" drugs were not strictly amphetamines as defined by the *Physicians Desk Reference*. The most damaging fact was that Wallace had never confronted Dr. Greenberg with Mrs. Goldstein's charges, never pressed Mrs. Goldstein for the exact names of her medication, and relied almost entirely on the tips of a former secretary and on the research of his producer, Grace Diekhaus. Mid-trial, however, as CBS was set to prepare its defense, Greenberg mysteriously dropped his suit and settled for an apology that was hardly an apology. "CBS regrets any embarrassment he *feels* [italics added] he sustained as a result of that broadcast," is the crux of the CBS statement. The statement was never aired and CBS cites the dropped charges as vindication—proof the doctor was guilty as charged (if not by Mrs. Goldstein, at least by several other witnesses CBS had ready to testify). Greenberg's attorney, Jonathan Weinstein, disagrees. The doctor achieved his aim, clearing his tarnished medical reputation.

Wherever the truth lies, Greenberg succeeded where most have failed. He aired his grievance in public. Usually, people burned by *60 Minutes* must nurse their outrage privately, because the show's most common infractions—the subtle distortion, the innuendo, the misleading statistic—neither warrant a day in court nor induce *60 Minutes* to issue one of its rare on-air "retractions."

In the course of a 1977 report on the hazards of excess sugar consumed by children, for instance, Dan Rather reported that General Foods' pre-sweetened breakfast cereal, Cocoa Pebbles, contained, astonishingly, "53 percent sugar." That charge was but one of a half-dozen slurs that prompted General Foods president Jim Ferguson to fire off an irate complaint, tagging the segment, "shallow, slanted . . . resorting to sensationalism." In fact, Rather was measuring Cocoa Pebbles' sugar content by *weight*—a misleading standard since sugar is so heavy. (General Foods also claims his figure was 8 percent too high.) The exact per-serving amount would be two rounded teaspoonfuls—somewhat less sugar than is found in a medium-sized apple or orange. During a three-hour interview with Rather, the General Foods spokesman had repeatedly pointed this out, but his protests got left in the editing room.

"But was 53 percent wrong?" asks Rather in defense. No, not exactly. Not grounds for libel. It was more a little white lie of ambiguity, not so different from an infraction Wallace committed that same year in a piece on Valium.

In building his case against the reckless marketing of the Hoffmann-La Roche drug, Wallace interviewed Dr. Bruce Medd, La Roche's "in-house medical expert," and asked him if he knew a Dr. Fritz Freyhan. "Reliable fellow as far as you know?"

"A knowledgeable person in psychiatry," answered Medd (thereby violating the first rule of combat with Wallace: Never attest to the credibility of a potentially hostile witness).

"A knowledgeable person in psychiatry," intoned Wallace, and proceeded to read from a Senate transcript: "Senator Gaylord Nelson asked him, 'If you were the editor of a medical journal, would you accept an ad like that?' He's talking about a Valium ad, and Dr. Freyhan says, 'I would not. As a matter of fact, I am editor-in-chief of a psychiatric journal, and my contract provides that I can accept or reject specific commercial advertisements.' He would not accept the ad," said Wallace.

As it stood, the statement was accurate. But a footnote would have revealed the following: Nelson's hearings on drug abuse were conducted in 1969, eight years before the broadcast. Furthermore, while the viewer might be left with the impression that Dr. Freyhan opposed Valium advertising, the truth was quite the opposite. The year of the Nelson hearings, as well as the year following, Freyhan ran Valium ads in every issue of his quarterly magazine, *Comprehensive Psychiatry*.

Misleading? Clearly. Just as the "cap" to the Garn Baum story gave viewers a false impression that nicely fit the segment's slant. "Garn Baum," read Wallace, "has now found a lawyer who will argue his case, but a federal judge in Utah says there isn't enough evidence for a trial. So Baum and his attorneys are appealing to a federal court in Colorado." What Wallace seemed to be suggesting was that even *judges* in Utah were so under the church's influence that poor Garn Baum had to seek impartial justice out-of-state. In fact, the Tenth Circuit Court of Appeals covering the Southwest region happens to be located in Denver and was merely Baum's next judicial recourse.

"Mistakes" like these are no doubt bred in that highly charged Nielsen atmosphere where, of necessity, subtlety is sacrificed for impact. There's no room at the top for dull shades of gray, a fact that slowly dawned on the "stung" as the show achieved its notoriety (at *their* expense). Increasingly then, potential interview subjects have grown wary of the predictable dangers that lie in wait at 7 P.M. on Sundays. And not a few have taken steps to protect themselves. Before its segment aired, Hoffmann-La Roche sent 400,000 physicians and pharmacists a brochure offering free copies of the entire, *unedited* transcript. Illinois Power had the wherewithal and cunning to counter-punch in a more unprecedented fashion. It decided to film *60 Minutes* while *60 Minutes* was filming IP, and just two months after the December 1979 broadcast, uncorked its own forty-five-minute tape—"60 Minutes/Our Reply"—styled and paced just like a slick Hewitt production, with Reasoner's on-air broadcast repeatedly interrupted to amplify, or correct and admonish, its accusers. To date, more than twenty-five hundred tapes of "Our Reply" have been dispatched to Kiwanis Clubs, utility companies, journalism schools, and members of Congress.

In the corporate community, there is now a trend toward hiring public relations consultants to avert a disaster on the tube. For years—even before Rather's report on sugar—General Foods has been sending vice presidents and employees to Dorothy Sarnoff, a New York consultant who specializes in grooming politicians and businessmen for jousts with the media. Not only does Sarnoff coach clients on poise and preparedness, but she

stresses their "rights" as interview subjects—such as controlling the interview site. General Foods, for instance, had selected the modest office of its on-air spokesman, although
Rather vetoed the office and maneuvered the company into its
giant wood-paneled boardroom. Finally, Sarnoff urges clients,
"Never do a show unless it's live and unedited." Clearly, if this
advice were followed it could seriously impair 60 Minutes' access
to future interview subjects.

A similar strategy prevails at Media Comm—an offshoot of
the giant public relations firm Carl Byoir Associates—that also
prepares naïfs for likely combat with the man whom Media
Comm president Virgil Scudder calls "Mike Malice." When a
large company embroiled in labor disputes was approached by
60 Minutes for an interview, its management went to Scudder
with the question, how do we wriggle out and not risk one of
those "refused to appear" charges? Scudder's strategy: "Tell
them you're willing to go on provided the interview runs intact
and unedited. Now I happen to know they just won't do that."
Sure enough, no interview was filmed.

"60 Minutes scares the hell out of my clients," says Scudder.
"It's the tremendous pressure to stay Number One. Everyone
knows the program's got to have a hanging each Sunday."

Yet despite the awaiting hangman's noose, 60 Minutes is still
surprisingly effective at enlisting the cooperation of even wary
interview subjects. Why, one wonders, have so many victims of
60 Minutes aided and abetted their own hoisting? "We don't
have subpoena powers and they don't have suicidal tendencies,"
says Wallace. "Something must persuade them it's in their own
self-interest."

The temptations of ego have led more than one innocent soul
to the gallows. Who, after all, can resist the macho challenge of
hand-to-hand combat with Wallace? Who doesn't secretly think
he can best the Grand Inquisitor at his own game? Then, too,
the journalists at 60 Minutes often disguise their motives. Richard Aszling, the General Foods vice president who supervised
the Rather interview, claims he was duped by producer Andrew
Lack's description—" 'A show on children's nutrition and what
they eat.' Of course it wasn't that at all."

In a celebrated interview with Daniel Schorr soon after the
House Ethics Committee cleared him of leaking a secret CIA
report to The Village Voice, Schorr claims Wallace lured him with
the line, "You're the champion of the First Amendment, you're
the hero of the week." Indeed, that was the topic of the first half

of the interview. But the second part—the part that aired—was a distinctly unworshipful grilling on Schorr's suspension from CBS and his rumored slurs at CBS colleagues.

Obtaining an interview under false pretenses lies at the crux of Billie Young's pending $25 million libel suit against *60 Minutes*. According to Young, she was asked to participate in a segment on "New Authors," and being the publisher of Ashley Books, a small Long Island press, she readily cooperated. In truth, the piece was an exposé of "vanity publishing"—"So You Want To Write a Book"—a fact that dawned on Young too late, well into her interview with Morley Safer. "What percentage of your authors' books are subsidized?" Safer suddenly asked. Ambushed, Young began protesting the interview was "dishonest" and "out of context." (Ashley Books publishes very few subsidized books, unlike Vantage Press, the segment's prime subject, which publishes any author willing to pay the costs.) She demanded, "Cut!" She tried to pull off her microphone. "I can't get it off, I don't know *how*," she wailed, and the interview continued, with Young a literal prisoner of her own naiveté.

But even those who are neither duped nor naive may be induced to cooperate after weighing the risks of non-appearance. Absence can look quite incriminating, especially with Dan, Mike, Morley, or Harry at center stage to point out that empty chair—"So and so, after repeated letters and queries . . ." In a Rather segment last spring—"The Kissinger-Shah Connection"—Henry Kissinger had considerable trouble weighing the pros and cons of appearing on the program. Granted an "equal time" interview after the piece, he agreed but later changed his mind. Whether he made the right decision will never be known. What is clear is that the piece prompted more outrage and criticism than any in the show's history.

The segment purported to document a "link" whereby Kissinger, during 1973 and 1974, acquiesced in the raising of Iran's oil prices so that the Shah could buy costly U.S. weaponry and serve as America's policeman in the Persian Gulf (recently abandoned by the British). The piece relied on four witnesses to connect Kissinger, the Shah, and "the price we're now paying for gasoline." By all accounts, the evidence was flimsy: Two of the four witnesses—former Undersecretary of State George Ball and James Akins, U.S. Ambassador to Saudi Arabia from 1973 to 1975—had openly hostile relations with Kissinger. Iran's Ambassador to the United Nations, Mansour Farhang, could only cite a "confluence of interests" between the Shah and Kissinger. William Simon, former Treasury Secretary, did little to confirm Rather's thesis, though he did concede. "Well, there could very well be some truth in that." (He later claimed his remark had been taken out of context.)

Critics, ranging from high-powered chums of Kissinger to newspaper columnists, lambasted the show for its biased witnesses and Rather's inadequate grasp of complex Mideast oil policies. "The argument made no sense," charged Thomas Bray, associate editor of the *Wall Street Journal*'s editorial page. "Supply and demand, not OPEC's or the Shah's blandishments, led to the quadrupling of prices in late 1973." Kissinger himself called the segment "malicious, ridiculous, and untrue" and, in an irate sixteen-page letter fired off to CBS News president William Leonard, charged, "The problem is that *all* your witnesses gave only one point of view, which was both tendentious and demonstrably erroneous, while *no* independent participants were presented to give a different view."

Apparently, Dr. Kissinger failed to grasp Hewitt's Nielsen-winning formula. A balanced in-depth probe on Mideast oil politics would have evoked a mighty yawn from *60 Minutes'* viewers, accustomed as they are to news presented as theater. And theater requires not only its stars—those heroic Knights—but an occasional villain. If Rather reduced a large, intricate topic to individual drama, the fault belongs largely to Hewitt's eagerness to personalize issues. Small wonder *60 Minutes* is often accused of squeezing the world into a hyped-up formula. Ideally, such topics belong to the networks' hour-long documentaries—*CBS Reports, NBC White Paper,* or *ABC Close-Up.* But ironically, the very success of *60 Minutes* has worked to weaken both the impact and frequency of those documentaries. "Has *60 Minutes* damaged other longer vehicles? Yes," concedes CBS's Chandler, "to a degree that's true." Meanwhile, every tick of that relentless stopwatch provides another confirmation of the viewer's narrowed attention span.

In dwelling on some *60 Minutes* flaws—the hype, the slant, the impulse to dramatize—there's always the danger of losing, as Rather says, "perspective." Debunking *60 Minutes* has become something of a popular sport. Why? Perhaps from the urge to shoot down any acclaimed success—the same temptation that lures *60 Minutes* into toppling a powerblock grown too strong, an idol verging on hubris. But then, just as one questions one's motives, there looms from the past that most troubling of stories: the seven-year-old, $22.5 million libel suit filed by Colonel Anthony Herbert.

Herbert was a Korean War hero and decorated battalion commander in Vietnam who was abruptly relieved of his command after he reported a My Lai-type massacre (six prisoners shot by American soldiers) that his commanding officer, Colonel Ross Franklin, allegedly ignored. Herbert's best-selling book, *Soldier*, recounted this shocking cover-up, as well as other atrocities, and landed Herbert on the Dick Cavett show, where he became an instant media celebrity. But Wallace and producer Barry Lando had their doubts. In twenty minutes they totally shattered the legend of Colonel Anthony Herbert by discrediting him as a fraud, a liar, and probably a brutal soldier prone to criminal acts of violence himself.

In this 1973 program, Wallace interviewed Herbert's commanding officer, Franklin, who claimed Herbert *never* reported the atrocity. Wallace produced receipts from the Hawaiian hotel that Franklin, recuperating on a brief R&R, seemingly left the day *after* the alleged report. General John Barnes, the man who had relieved Herbert of his command, described him to Wallace: "I thought he was a killer, enjoyed killing . . . " Barnes added that Herbert had never reported any war crimes or atrocities. In the interview with Herbert, Wallace showed him Franklin's canceled hotel check, and a flustered Herbert could only reply, "m-hmm. I can probably find you checks—I don't know. I can probably find you—I don't know about this check. I can probably find . . ."

The segment was tough and convincing and, if correct, gave its audience not just terrific drama but a worthy insight into the perils of blindly promoting media celebrities. However, during seven years of pre-trial discovery proceedings, and with a mass of data gathered by Herbert and his attorneys under the Freedom of Information Act, numerous disturbing facts have come to light. Among them:

—Franklin, during a *second* interview with producer Lando, admitted that Herbert said "such fantastic things sometimes . . . people could very easily disregard them, tune out, turn off." "Could you yourself have done that?" asked Lando. "Yeah," replied Franklin, "I have done that frequently with Herbert." That second interview was neither shown nor mentioned.
—During a Pentagon interview with Franklin and other Army officers, secretly taped by the Army, Wallace is heard pressing "Ideally, if we can get somebody on the film to say, 'I don't know

whether he reported but he is capable of doing that sort of thing himself [acts of brutality]." Wallace, searching for evidence to support the segment's thesis, seemed anxious to present Herbert as a brutal soldier.

—Franklin's canceled check—"made out to the exact amount," said Wallace—was, in fact, $25 short. Mistake? Confusion over a $25 deposit? Or could Franklin have returned to Vietnam one crucial day before he said he had?

Most important, numerous interviews and pieces of testimony were *omitted* by Wallace or Lando. "I do know for certain that Herbert reported the killing of six detainees," read the sworn statement of a certain Captain Jack Donovan—never aired. Another captain, Bill Hill, said he heard Herbert report the incident by radio to a superior—meaning either Franklin or Barnes. Interviews with men who served under Herbert, stressing his care for prisoners, were never mentioned or aired.

Ironically, Lando had first proposed a pro-Herbert piece "to take a look at the original charge of atrocities . . . whether the Army has tried to whitewash the whole affair." But with Herbert already a hot media item, neither Wallace nor Hewitt was interested. Then too, in 1971, CBS had aired its celebrated *The Selling of the Pentagon*, and perhaps a second military expose would not have delighted CBS president Frank Stanton—who had recently received a contempt citation for refusing to turn over *Pentagon* outtakes. In a lengthy *Atlantic* article, Lando himself summed up his abrupt about-face: "Something finally snapped. The inconsistencies, the evasions I had been so eager to overlook now took on a different hue."

Whatever the motives that launched the Herbert expose, Lando pursued his quarry with a zeal that, in hindsight, raises some serious questions about *60 Minutes'* commitment to fair, unbiased reporting (ones that may be resolved if *Herbert v. Lando* reaches trial later this year). In their eagerness to nail Herbert, the producer and Wallace may have calculatedly blindfolded themselves to contradictory data. Like the Mormons, like Illinois Power, like Dr. Joseph Greenberg and Daniel Schorr, Colonel Herbert may have been felled by Hewitt's all-consuming realpolitik: the desire for impact.

But the ultimate question is, has Hewitt performed an important public service by alerting countless millions to the dangers of sugar and Valium, to the hazards of church hegemony? Or has he not also further narrowed our vision of what to expect from the medium? Catering to our crudest entertainment reflexes, after all, risks demeaning the imagination, and thwarts the patient groping for reality that makes us not just informed but enlightened. To accept less turns us all into victims of *60 Minutes*.

MARTIN ESSLIN

ARISTOTLE AND THE ADVERTISERS: THE TELEVISION COMMERCIAL CONSIDERED AS A FORM OF DRAMA

We have all seen it a hundred times, and in dozens of variations: that short sequence of images in which a husband expresses disappointment and distress at his wife's inability to provide him with a decent cup of coffee and seems inclined to seek a better tasting potion outside the home, perhaps even on the bosom of another lady; the anxious consultation, which ensues, between the wife and her mother or an experienced and trusted friend, who counsels the use of another brand of coffee; and finally the idyllic tableau of the husband astonished and surprised by the excellence of his wife's new coffee, demanding a second—or even a third!—cup of the miraculously effective product.

A television commercial. And, doubtless, it includes elements of drama. . . . Yet: is it not too short, too trivial, too contemptible altogether to deserve serious consideration? That seems the generally accepted opinion. But in an age when through the newly discovered technologies of mechanical reproduction and dissemination drama has become one of the chief instruments of human expression, communication, and, indeed, thought, all uses of the dramatic form surely deserve study. If the television commercial could be shown to be drama, it would be among the most ubiquitous and the most influential of its forms and hence deserve the attention of the serious critics and theoreticians of that art, most of whom paradoxically still seem to be spellbound by types of drama (such as tragedy) which are hallowed by age and tradition, though practically extinct today. And surely, in a

This essay first appeared in *The Kenyon Review*, new series, Vol. 1, No. 4, Fall 1979. Reprinted by permission of the author.

civilization in which drama, through the mass media, has become an omnipresent, all-pervasive, continuously available, and unending stream of entertainment for the vast majority of individuals in the so-called developed world, a comprehensive theory, morphology, and typology of drama is urgently needed. Such a theory would have to take cognizance of the fact that the bulk of drama today is to be found not on the stage but in the mechanized mass media, the cinema, television, and, in most civilized countries, radio; that both on the stage and in the mass media drama exists in a multitude of new forms which might even deserve to be considered genres unknown to Aristotle—from mime to musicals, from police serials to science fiction, from Westerns to soap opera, from improvisational theater to happenings—and that among all these the television commercial might well be both unprecedented and highly significant.

The coffee commercial cited above, albeit a mere thirty to fifty seconds in length, certainly exhibits attributes of drama. Yet to what extent is it typical of the television commercial in general? Not all TV commercials use plot, character, and spoken dialogue to the same extent. Nevertheless, I think it can be shown that most, if not all, TV commercials are essentially dramatic, because basically they use mimetic action to produce a semblance of real life, and the basic ingredients of drama— character and story line—are present in the great majority of them, either manifestly or by implication.

Take another frequently occurring type: a beautiful girl who tells us that her hair used to be lifeless and stringy, while now, as she proudly displays, it is radiantly vital and fluffy. Is this not just a bare announcement, flat and undramatic? I should argue that, in fact, there is drama in it, implied in the clearly fictitious character who is telling us her story. What captures our interest and imagination is the radiant girl, and what she tells us is an event which marked a turning point in her life. Before she discovered the miraculous new shampoo she was destined to live in obscurity and neglect, but now she has become beautiful and radiant with bliss. Are we not, therefore, here in the presence of that traditional form of drama in which a seemingly static display of character and atmosphere evokes highly charged, decisive events of the past that are now implicit in the present—the type of drama, in fact, of which Ibsen's *Ghosts* is a frequently cited specimen?

What, though, if the lady in question is a well-known show

business or sporting personality and hence a *real* rather than a fictitious character? Do we not then enter the realm of reality rather than fictional drama? I feel that there are very strong grounds for arguing the opposite: for film stars, pop singers, and even famous sporting personalities project not their real selves but a carefully tailored fictional image. There has always, throughout the history of drama, been the great actor who essentially displayed no more than a single, continuous personality rather than a series of differing characters (witness the Harlequins and other permanent character types of the commedia dell'arte, great melodrama performers like Frédéric Lemaître, great comics like Chaplin, Buster Keaton, Laurel and Hardy, or the Marx Brothers, or indeed great film stars like Marilyn Monroe or John Wayne—to name but a very few). Such actors do not enact parts so much as lend their highly wrought and artistically crafted fictitious personality to a succession of roles that exist merely to display that splendid artifact. Hence if Bob Hope or John Wayne appear as spokesman for banking institutions, or Karl Malden as the advocate of a credit card, no one is seriously asked to believe that they are informing us of their real experience with these institutions; we all know that they are speaking a preestablished, carefully polished text which, however brief it may be, has been composed by a team of highly skilled professional writers and that they are merely lending them the charisma of their long-established—and fictional—urbanity, sturdiness, or sincerity.

There remains, admittedly, a residue of nondramatic TV commercials: those which are no more than newspaper advertisements displaying a text and a symbol, with a voice merely reading it out to the less literate members of the audience; and those in which the local car or carpet salesman more or less successfully tries to reel off a folksy appeal to his customers. But these commercials tend to be the local stations' fill-up material. The bulk of the major, nationally shown commercials are profoundly dramatic and exhibit, in their own peculiar way, in minimal length and maximum compression, the basic characteristics of the dramatic mode of expression in a state of particular purity—precisely because here it approaches the point of zero extension, as though the TV commercial were a kind of differential calculus of the aesthetics of drama.

Let us return to our initial example: the coffee playlet. Its three-beat basic structure can be found again and again. In the first beat the exposition is made and the problem posed. Always

disaster threatens: persistent headaches endanger the love relationship or success at work of the heroine or hero (or for
headaches read constipation, body odor, uncomfortable sani-
tary pads, ill-fitting dentures, hemorrhoids, lost credit cards,
inefficient detergents which bring disgrace on the housewife).
In the second beat a wise friend or confidant suggests a solution. And this invariably culminates in a moment of insight, of
conversion, in fact the classical anagnorisis that leads to dianoia
and thus to the peripeteia, the turning point of the action. The
third beat shows the happy conclusion to what was a potentially tragic situation. For it is always and invariably the hero's
or heroine's ultimate happiness that is at stake: his health or job
or domestic peace. In most cases there is even the equivalent of
the chorus of ancient tragedy in the form of an unseen voice, or
indeed, a choral song, summing up the moral lesson of the
action and generalizing it into a universally applicable principle.
And this is, almost invariably, accompanied by a visual epiphany of the product's symbol, container, trademark or logo—in
other words the allegorical or symbolic representation of the
beneficent power that has brought about the fortunate outcome and averted the ultimate disaster: the close analogy to the
deus ex machina of classical tragedy is inescapable.

All this is compressed into a span of from thirty to fifty
seconds. Moreover such a mini-drama contains distinctly
drawn characters, who, while representing easily recognizable
human types (as so many characters of traditional drama) are
yet individualized in subtle ways, through the personalities of
the actors portraying them, the way they are dressed, the way
they speak. The setting of the action, however briefly it may be
glimpsed, also greatly contributes to the solidity of characterization: the tasteful furnishings of the home, not too opulent,
but neat, tidy, and pretty enough to evoke admiring sympathy
and empathy; the suburban scene visible through the living
room or kitchen window, the breakfast table that bears witness
to the housewifely skills of the heroine—and all subtly underlined by mood music rising to a dramatic climax at the moment
of anagnorisis and swelling to a triumphant coda at the fortunate conclusion of the action. Of all the art forms only drama
can communicate such an immense amount of information on
so many levels simultaneously within the span of a few seconds. That all this has to be taken in instantaneously, moreover, ensures that most of the impact will be subliminal—
tremendously suggestive while hardly ever rising to the level of

full consciousness. It is this which explains the great effectiveness of the TV commercial and the inevitability of its increasing
employment of dramatic techniques. Drama does not simply
translate the abstract idea into concrete terms. It literally incarnates the abstract message by bringing it to life in a human
personality and a human situation. Thus it activates powerful
subconscious drives and the deep animal magnetisms which
dominate the lives of men and women who are always interested in and attracted by other human beings, their looks, their
charm, their mystery.

"A message translated into terms of personality"—that, certainly, is one of the focal points around which TV commercials
turn: the housewife, attractive but anonymous, who appears in
such a commercial, exudes all the hidden attraction and interest
she can command. Each of these mini-playlets stands by itself.
Each is analogous to a complete play in conventional drama. It
can be shown repeatedly, and can have a long run. But then the
characters in it are spent. There is another form, however,
even more characteristic of television drama—the serial. The
series of plays featuring a recurring set of characters is the
most successful dramatic format of television. No wonder,
then, that the TV commercial mini-drama also resorts to the
recurring personality, be he or she fictional; real-life-synthetic,
like the film stars or sporting heroes mentioned above; or
allegorical, like the sweet little lady who embodies the spirit of
relief from stomach acids and miraculously appears with her
pills to bring comfort to a succession of truck drivers, long-
shoremen, or crane operators suffering from upset tummies.

The free interchangeability of real and fictional experts in
this context once again underlines the essentially fictitious character even of the "real" people involved and shows clearly that
we are dealing with a form of drama. The kindly pharmacist
who recommends the headache powder, the thoughtful bespec-
tacled doctor who recounts the successes of a toothpaste, the
crusty small-town lady grocer who praised her coffee beans
with the air of experience based on decades of wise counseling
are manifestly actors, carefully type-cast; yet their authority is
not a whit less weighty than that of the rare actual experts who
may occasionally appear. The actor on the stage who plays
Faust or Hamlet does not, after all, have to be as wise as the one
or as noble as the other: it suffices that he can *appear* as wise or
as noble. And the same is true of the dramatized advertisement:
since illusion is the essence of drama, the illusion of authority is

far more valuable in the dramatized commercial than any real authority. The fact that an actor like Robert Young has established himself as a medical character in an evening series enables him to exude redoubled authority when he appears in a long series of commercials as a doctor recommending caffeine-free coffee. It need not even be mentioned any longer that he is playing a doctor. Everybody recognizes him as a doctor while also remaining completely aware that he is an actor. . . . (It is Genêt, among modern playwrights, who has recognized the role of illusion as a source of authority in our society. His play *The Balcony* deals with precisely that subject: the insignificant people who have merely assumed the trappings of Bishop, Judge, or General in that house of illusions, the brothel, can, in the hour of need, be used to convince the masses that those authorities are still present. Many TV commercials are, in fact, mini-versions of *The Balcony*.)

The creation of authority figures—in a world where they are conspicuously absent in reality—can thus be seen as one of the essential features, and endeavors, of the TV commercial. That these authority figures are essentially creations of fiction gives us another important indication as to the nature of the drama we are dealing with: for these authority figures, whether fictional or not, are perceived as real in a higher sense. Fictions, however, which embody the essential, lived reality of a culture and society, will readily be recognized as falling within the strict definition of *myth*. The TV commercial, no less than Greek tragedy, deals with the myths at the basis of a culture.

This allows us to see the authority figures that populate the world of the TV commercial as analogous to the characters of a mythical universe: they form an ascending series that starts with the wise confidant who imparts to the heroine the secret of better coffee (a Ulysses or Nestor) and leads via the all-knowing initiate (pharmacist, grocer, doctor, or crusty father figure—corresponding to a Tiresias, a Calchas, or the priestess of the Delphic oracle) into the realm of the great film stars and sporting personalities who are not less but even more mythical in their nature, being the true models for the emulation of the society, the incarnation of its ideals of success and the good life, and immensely rich and powerful to boot. The very fact that a bank, a cosmetics firm, or a manufacturer of breakfast foods has been able to buy their services is proof of that corporation's immense wealth and influence. These great figures —Bob Hope, John Wayne, John Travolta, Farrah Fawcett-

Majors—on the one hand lend their charisma to the businesses
with whom they have become identified, and on the other they
prove the power and effectiveness of those concerns. In exactly
the same way, a priest derives ¿restige from the greatness of
the deity he serves, while at the same time proving his own
potency by his ability to command the effective delivery of the
benefits his deity provides to the community. The great personalities of the TV commercial universe can thus be seen as
the demigods and mythical heroes of our society, conferring
the blessings of their archetypal fictional personality image
upon the products they endorse and through them upon mankind in general, so that John Wayne becomes, as it were, the
Hercules, Bob Hope the Ulysses, John Travolta the Dionysos,
and Farrah Fawcett-Majors the Aphrodite of our contemporary
Pantheon. Their presence in the TV commercial underlines its
basic character as ritual drama (however debased it may appear
in comparison to that of earlier civilizations).

From these still partially realistic demigods the next step up
the ladder of authority figures is only logical: we now enter the
realm of the wholly allegorical characters, either still invested
with human form, like the aforementioned Mother Tums, a
spirit assuming human shape to help humans as Athene does
when she appears as a shepherd or Wotan as the Wanderer; or
openly supernatural: the talking salad that longs to be eaten
with a certain salad dressing; the syrup bottle that sings the
praises of its contents; the little man of dough who incarnates
the power of baking powder; the tiny pink and naked figure
who projects the living image of the softness of a toilet tissue;
or the animated figures of the triumphant knights (drawing on
the imagery of St. George and the Dragon) who fight, re-
splendent in shining armor, endless but ever victorious battles
against the demons of disease, dirt, or engine corrosion—a
nasty crew of ugly devils with leering, malicious faces and cor-
rosive voices.

The superhuman is closely akin to the merely extra-human:
the talking and dancing animals who appear in the commercials
for dog and cat foods are clearly denizens of a realm of the
miraculous and thus also ingredients of myth; so, in a sense, are
the objects that merely lure us by their lusciousness and magnetic beauty: the car lit up by flashes of lightning which sym-
bolize its great power, the steaks and pizzas that visibly melt in
the mouth. They, too, are like those trees and flowers of mythical forests which lure the traveler ever deeper into their

thickets, because they are more splendid, more colorful, more magnetic than any object could ever be in real life.

Into this category, by extension, also fall the enlarged versions of the symbolic representation of products and corporations: those soft drink bottles the size of the Eiffel tower, those trademarks which suddenly assume gigantic three-dimensional shape so that they tower above the landscape and the people inhabiting it like mountain ranges, the long lines of dominoes that collapse in an immense chain reaction to form the logotype of a company. Here the drama of character has been reduced to a minimum and we are at the other end of the spectrum of theatrical expression, the one contained in the word itself— *theatron*—pure spectacle, the dominant element being the production of memorable images.

Like all drama, the TV commercial can be comprehended as lying between the two extremes of a spectrum: at one end the drama of character and at the other the drama of pure image. In traditional drama one extreme might be exemplified by the psychological drama-of-character of playwrights like Molière, Racine, Ibsen, or Chekhov; the other extreme by the drama of pure image like Ionesco's *Amedée*, Beckett's *Happy Days* or *Not I*. On a slightly less ambitious plane, these extremes are represented by the French bedroom comedy and the Broadway spectacular. At one extreme ideas and concepts are translated into personality, at the other the abstract idea itself is being made visible—and audible.

It is significant, in this context, that the more abstract the imagery of the TV commercial becomes the more extensively it relies on music: around the giant soft drink bottle revolves a chorus of dancing singers; the mountain range of a trademark is surrounded by a choir of devoted singing worshippers. The higher the degree of abstraction and pure symbolism, the nearer the spectacle approaches ritual forms. If the Eucharist can be seen as a ritual drama combining a high degree of abstraction in the visual sphere with an equally powerful element of music, this type of TV commercial approaches a secular act of worship: often, literally, a dance around the golden calf.

Between the extremes which represent the purest forms at the two ends of the spectrum are ranged, of course, innumerable combinations of both main elements. The character-based mini-drama of the coffee playlet includes important subliminal visual ingredients, and the crowd singing around the super-lifesize symbol contains an immense amount of instantaneous

characterization as the faces of the singers come into focus
when the camera sweeps over them: they will always be representative of the maximum number of different types—men,
women, children, blacks, Asians, the young and the old—and
their pleasant appearance will emphasize the desirable effects
of being a worshipper of that particular product.

The reliance on character and image as against the two other
main ingredients of drama—plot and dialogue—is clearly the
consequence of the TV commercial's ineluctable need for brevity. Both character and image are instantly perceived on a
multitude of levels, while dialogue and plot—even the simple
plot of the coffee-playlet—require time and a certain amount of
concentration. Yet the verbal element can never be entirely
dispensed with. Still, all possible ways of making it stick in the
memory must be employed: foremost among these is the jingle
which combines an easily memorized, rhymed, verbal component with a melody, which, if it fulfills its purpose, will fix the
words in the brain with compulsive power. Equally important is
the spoken catchphrase, which, always emanating from a memorable personality and authority figure, can be briefer than the
jingle and will achieve a growing impact by being repeated over
and over until the audience is actually conditioned to complete
it automatically whenever they see the character or hear the
first syllable spoken.

Brecht, the great theoretician of the didactic play (*Lehrstueck*),
was the first to emphasize the need for drama to be "quotable"
and to convey its messages by easily remembered and reproduced phrases, gestures, and images. His idea that the gist of
each scene should be summed up in one memorable *Grundgestus*
(a basic, gestural, and visual as well as verbal, instantly reproducible—quotable—compound of sound, vision, and gesture)
has found its ideal fulfillment in the dramaturgy of the TV
commercial. And no wonder: Brecht was a fervent adherent of
behaviorist psychology and the TV commercial is the only form
of drama which owes its actual practice to the systematic and
scientifically controlled application of the findings of precisely
that school of psychological thought. Compared with the TV
commercial, Brecht's own efforts to create a type of drama
which could effectively influence human behavior and contribute to the shaping of society must appear as highly amateurish
fumbling. Brecht wanted to turn drama into a powerful tool of
social engineering. In that sense the TV commercial, paradoxically and ironically, is the very culmination and triumphant
realization of his ideas.

From the point of view of its *form* the range of TV commercial drama can thus be seen as very large indeed: it extends from the chamber play to the grand spectacular musical; from the realistic to the utmost bounds of the allegorical, fantastical, and abstract. It is in the nature of things that as regards content its scope should be far more restricted. The main theme of this mini-species of drama—and I hope that by now the claim that it constitutes such will appear justified—is the attainment of happiness through the use or consumption of specific goods or services. The outcome (with the exception of a few noncommercial commercials, that is, public service commercials warning against the dangers of alcoholism or reckless driving) is always a happy one. But, as I suggested above, there is always an implied element of tragedy. For the absence of the advertised product or service is always seen as fatal to the attainment of peace of mind, well-being, or successful human relationships. The basic genre of TV commercial drama thus seems to be that of melodrama in which a potentially tragic situation is resolved by a last minute miraculous intervention from above. It may seem surprising that there is a relative scarcity of comedy in the world of the TV commercial. Occasionally comedy appears in the form of a witty catchphrase or a mini-drama concentrating on a faintly comic character, like that of the fisherman who urges his companions to abandon their breakfast cereal lest they miss the best hour for fishing, and who, when induced to taste the cereal, is so overwhelmed by its excellence that he forgets about the fishing altogether. But comedy requires concentration and a certain time span for its development and is thus less instantly perceivable than the simpler melodramatic situation, or the implied tragedy in the mere sight of a character who has already escaped disaster and can merely inform us of his newfound happiness, thus leaving the tragic situation wholly implicit in the past. The worshippers dancing around the gigantic symbol of the product clearly also belong in this category; they have reached a state of ecstatic happiness through the consumption of the drink, the use of the lipstick concerned, and their hymnic incantations show us the degree of tragic misfortune they have thus avoided or escaped. There is even an implication of tragedy in the straight exhortation uttered by one of the tutelary demigods simply to use the product or service in question. For the failure to obey the precepts uttered by mythic deities must inevitably have tragic results. Nonfulfillment of such commandments involves a grave risk of disaster.

And always, behind the action, there hovers the power that can bring it to its satisfactory conclusion, made manifest through its symbol, praised and hymned by unseen voices in prose or verse, speech or song. There can be no doubt about it: the TV commercial, exactly as the oldest known types of theater, is essentially a religious form of drama which shows us human beings as living in a world controlled by a multitude of powerful forces that shape our lives. We have free will, we can choose whether we follow their precepts or not, but woe betide those who make the wrong choice!

The moral universe, therefore, portrayed in what I for one regard as the most widespread and influential art form of our time, is essentially that of a polytheistic religion. It is a world dominated by a sheer numberless pantheon of powerful forces, which literally reside in every article of use or consumption, in every institution of daily life. If the winds and waters, the trees and brooks of ancient Greece were inhabited by a vast host of nymphs, dryads, satyrs, and other local and specific deities, so is the universe of the TV commercial. The polytheism that confronts us here is thus a fairly primitive one, closely akin to animistic and fetishistic beliefs.

We may not be conscious of it, but this *is* the religion by which most of us actually live, whatever our more consciously and explicitly held beliefs and religious persuasions may be. This is the actual religion that is being absorbed by our children from almost the day of their birth.

And no wonder—if Marshall McLuhan is right, as he surely is, that in the age of the mass media we have turned away from a civilization based on reading, linear rational thought, and chains of logical reasoning; if we have reverted to a nonverbal mode of perception, based on the simultaneous ingestion of subliminally perceived visual and aural images; if the abolition of space has made us live again in the electronic equivalent of the tribal settlement expanded into a global village—then the reversion to the form of animism is merely logical. Nor should we forget that the rational culture of the Gutenberg Galaxy never extended beyond the very narrow confines of an educated minority elite and that the vast majority of mankind, even in the developed countries, and even after the introduction of universal education and literacy, remained on a fairly primitive level of intellectual development. The limits of the rational culture are shown only too clearly in the reliance on pictorial material and highly simplified texts by the popular press that grew up in the period between the spread of literacy and the onset of the electronic mass media. Even the Christianity of more primitive people, relying as it did on a multitude of saints, each specializing in a particular field of rescue, was basically animistic. And so was—and is—the literalism of fundamentalist forms of puritan protestantism.

Television has not created this state of affairs, it has merely made it more visible. For here the operation of the market has, probably for the first time in human history, led to a vast scientific effort to establish, by intensive psychological research, the real reactions, and hence also the implicit mechanisms of belief, displayed by the overwhelming majority of the population. The TV commercial has evolved to its present dramaturgy through a process of empirical research, a constant dialectic of trial and error. Indeed, it would be wrong to blame the individuals who control and operate the advertising industry as wicked manipulators of mass psychology. Ultimately the dramaturgy and content of the TV commercial universe is the outcrop of the fantasies and implied beliefs of those masses themselves; it is they who create the scenarios of the commercials through the continuous feedback of reactions between the makers of the artifacts concerned and the viewers' responses.

It would be wholly erroneous to assume that the populations of countries without TV commercials exist on a higher level of implied religious beliefs. In the countries of the Communist world, for example, where commercials do not exist, the experience of the rulers with the techniques of political persuasion has led to the evolution of a propaganda which, in all details, replicates the universe of the TV commercials. There too the reliance is on incantation, short memorable catch-phrases endlessly repeated, the instant visual imagery of symbols and personality portraits (like the icons of Marx, Engels, and other demigods carried in processions; the red flags, the hammer-and-sickle symbolism) and a whole gamut of similarly structured devices that carry the hallmark of a wholly analogous primitive animism and fetishism. It is surely highly significant that a sophisticated philosophical system like Marxism should have had to be translated into the terms of a tribal religion in order to reach and influence the behavior of the mass populations of countries under the domination of parties which were originally, in a dim past, actuated by intellectuals who were able to comprehend such a complex philosophy. It is equally significant that citizens of those countries that are deprived of all commercials except political ones become literally mesmerized and addicted to the Western type of TV commercials when they have a chance to see them. There is a vast, unexpressed, subconscious yearning in these people, not only for the consumer goods concerned but also for the hidden forces and the miraculous action of the spirits inhabiting them.

In the light of the above considerations it appears that not only must the TV commercial be regarded as a species of drama but that, indeed, it comes very close to the most basic forms of the theater, near its very roots. For the connection between myth and its manifestation and collective incarnation in dramatized ritual has always been recognized as being both close and organic. The myth of a society is collectively experienced in its dramatic rituals. And the TV commercial, it seems to me, is the ritual manifestation of the basic myth of our society and as such not only its most ubiquitous but also its most significant form of folk drama.

What conclusions are we to draw from that insight (if it were granted that it amounts to one)? Can we manipulate the subconscious psyche of the population by trying to raise the level of commercials? Or should we ban them altogether?

Surely the collective subconscious that tends to operate on the level of animistic imagery cannot be transformed by any short-term measures, however drastic. For here we are dealing with the deepest levels of human nature itself that can change only on a secular time-scale—the time-scale of evolutionary progress itself. Nor would the banning of TV commercials contribute anything to such a type of change.

What we can do, however, is to become aware of the fact that we are here in the presence of a phenomenon that is by no means contemptible or unimportant, but, on the contrary, basic to an understanding of the true nature of our civilization and its problems. Awareness of subconscious urges is, in itself, a first step toward liberation or at least control. Education and the systematic cultivation of rational and conscious modes of perception and thought might, over the long run, change the reaction of audiences who have grown more sophisticated and thus raise the visual and conceptual level of this form of folk-drama. A recognition of the impact of such a powerful ritual force and its myths on children should lead to efforts to build an ability to deal with it into the educational process itself. That, at present, is almost wholly neglected.

And a recognition of the true nature of the phenomenon

might also lead to a more rational regulation of its application. In those countries where the frequency of use of TV commercials and their positioning in breaks between programs rather than within them is fairly strictly regulated (Germany, Britain, Scandinavia, for instance), TV commercials have lost none of their efficacy and impact but have become less all-pervasive, thus allowing alternative forms of drama—on a higher intellectual, artistic, and moral level—to exercise a counterbalancing impact. Higher forms of drama, which require greater length to develop more individualized character, more rationally devised story lines, more complex and profound imagery might, ultimately, produce a feedback into the world of the commercial. Once the commercial has ceased to be—as it is at present—the best produced, most lavishly financed, technically most perfect ingredient of the whole television package, once it has to compete with material that is more intelligent and more accomplished, it might well raise its own level of intelligence and rationality.

These, admittedly, may be no more than pious hopes, whistling in the dark. Of one thing, however, I am certain: awareness, consciousness, the ability to see a phenomenon for what it is must be an important first step toward solving any problem. Hence the neglect of the truly popular forms of drama—of which the TV commercial is the most obvious and most blatant example—by the serious critics and theoreticians of that immensely important form of human expression seems highly regrettable. The TV commercial—and all the other forms of dramatic mass entertainment and mass manipulation—not only deserve serious study; a theory of drama that neglects them seems to me elitist, pretentious, and out of touch with the reality of its subject matter.

PART II

THINKING ABOUT TELEVISION

The title of this section is hardly meant to suggest that other writers in other essays are *not* thinking about the subject. It merely indicates that with the critical study of television we are often involved in much larger issues. Some of them are historical. How, for example, have people related to other forms of entertainment in other times? Others are sociological. What are the industrial constraints on the production of art and entertainment? Still others are political. How does television shape, retard, restrict, enhance, and otherwise alter our perceptions of American society, its problems and promises.

David Marc's essay, for example, presents an overview history of American responses to television. In his view, any inherent simplicity in television as a medium, any attempt by television makers to present one-sided viewpoints, any inherent political, social, or cultural limitations in its forms of presentation, are subverted by the audience's resilience as individuals. He acknowledges television's power, but offers a Whitmanesque faith that users of television will remold it to their own purposes.

A different view is posed by Muriel Cantor. In her analysis the audience is relatively powerless, responsive only to network offerings. A major difference between her position and Marc's, a difference about which we must be constantly aware, has to do with their levels of analysis. Cantor sees the audience as a mass and would agree that individuals have more control, but that individual autonomy is undercut by what is made available to them, about which they have little to say. Marc finds far more diversity in television itself and thus sees it as the raw material for a much larger range of individual manipulation.

Wayne Booth is also concerned with audiences and their

interactions with television. His more philosophical analysis of how we relate to imaginative worlds also links television to other forms, primarily to literature. He presents a complex examination of the moral issues involved in giving ourselves over to different forms of fictional expression, and while he comes down in favor of more traditional forms, his reasons for that decision far exceed the common, knee-jerk reactions to television that are often couched in moralistic terms.

Still another approach to audience is offered by Elihu Katz and Tamar Liebes. Their project attempts to answer many of these same questions by going not to the medium, or the story form, or the social organization of television—but to the viewers themselves. They have developed ways to have audience members representing many cultures speak about their experiences with *Dallas*, and the results provide fascinating suggestions that all our speculation about such relationships are still quite incomplete.

Walter Karp approaches the cultural status of television in an entirely different way, though all the questions about audience addressed above come into play indirectly. He charges that various individuals and groups—with good will and intention—may have robbed child-television viewers of important pleasures and instructive fictions. He sees the move to use television to teach "pro-social values" as a simple-minded maneuver. The resulting cartoon entertainments lack moral and fictional sophistication in Karp's view. These same concerns, of course, can be applied to any sort of programming, and Karp's analysis of how some groups have moved to regulate fiction is most instructive.

Jimmie L. Reeves's essay on Mr. T does not deal specifically with regulation, but it raises issues growing directly out of Karp's observations. How are we to deal with "threatening" aspects of television? Reeves shows how a once-threatening social type literally muscles his way into the mainstream of American culture and asks what is gained and lost in the process. His analysis could be used to study other television stars, closely questioning their meaning and status in society.

For Horace Newcomb and Paul Hirsch, stars, children's programming, *Dallas*, and the rest of television's constant flow of fictional discourse make the medium into something like a forum. Issues central to American cultural development are offered there and "discussed" in the stories that we attend to night after night. It is not a forum in which everyone has an equal voice, however. And the constraints on the subsequent "discussion," the limited points of view, are topics for continued discussions.

These limitations and the ways around them are the focal points for Douglas Kellner's analysis of the political structures of television fiction. He, too, is concerned with what television offers its audiences, makes available to them as forms of thought and expression with which to view and act in the world. While he sees most television as drastically limited, he offers, in this essay, some suggestions as to how specific program types provide an emancipatory opportunity.

The central question here regards the degree to which television is an open or a closed system of expression. To understand the question even better, we must look with equal attention to the formal characteristics of television, to the ways in which it tells its stories. That concern forms the core of Section III.

DAVID MARC

BEGINNING TO BEGIN AGAIN

Never was there, perhaps, more hollowness at heart than at present, and here in the United States. Genuine belief seems to have left us. The underlying principles of the States are not honestly believed in (for all this hectic glow and these melodramatic screamings), nor is humanity itself believed in. What penetrating eye does not everywhere see through this mask?—Walt Whitman, *Democratic Vistas* (1871)

An unholy marriage of sociology and art—the shotgun is pointed at art—American television is a perplexing montage. The programs are conceived as stimuli for the masses, but it is left to the viewer to establish a text in a personal, even private, way. Whatever is exposed to television is under attack. Ideals are confounded by the depressing spectacle of astonishing technical acumen aimed at gross simplification. Belief is disappointed; the soul is not visible on the screen. Traditional political ideologies have been unable to respond coherently. The Left finds conspiracy snarling behind the pervasive promotion of consumer outlook even as it envies the industrial medium's ability to organize millions at the flick of a switch. On the Right, there is no less conflict. Television has become an integral factor in the processes of modern capitalism. Entrepreneurial success is largely based on effective use of it. As a consequence, however, what José Ortega y Gasset called "the bigotry of Culture" has itself become the victim of discrimination; the prerogatives of cultivated taste have become buried in an avalanche of processed styles. The achiever is awed by the material accomplishment of the national communications system but hates to waste time on the nonsense it delivers. The dreamer welcomes the continuous, coast-to-coast, willing sus-

Reprinted from *Demographic Vistas*, by David Marc, by permission of the University of Pennsylvania Press. Copyright © 1984.

pension of disbelief but is let down by the obsessive neatness of the narrative. The lover knows that all truths wait in all things.

In one of the few famous speeches given on the subject of television, Federal Communications Commission chairman Newton N. Minow shocked the 1961 Convention of the National Association of Broadcasters by summarily categorizing its membership's handiwork as "a vast wasteland."[1] The general acceptance of Minow's metaphor is outstripped only by the appeal of television itself. Americans look askance at television, but look at it nonetheless. Owners of thousand-dollar sets think nothing of calling them "idiot boxes." The home stereo system, regardless of what plays on it, is, by comparison, holy. While millions of dollars change hands daily on the assumption that 98 percent of American homes are equipped with sets and that these sets play an average of over six and a half hours each day,[2] a well-pronounced distaste for television has become a prerequisite to claims of intellectual and even ethical legitimacy. Social scientists, perhaps less concerned with these matters than others, have rushed to fill the critical gap. Denying the mysteries of teller, tale, and told, they have reduced the significance of this American storytelling medium to the study of the effect of stimuli on masses, producing volumes of data that in turn justify each season's network schedules. A disillusioned advertising executive, his fortune safely socked away, has even written a book entitled *Four Arguments for the Elimination of Television*. Hans Magnus Enzensberger preempted such criticism as early as 1962 when he wrote:

> The process is irreversible. Therefore, all criticism of the mind industry which is abolitionist in its essence is inept and beside the point, since the idea of arresting and liquidating industrialization (which such criticism implies) is suicidal. There is a macabre irony to any such proposal, for it is indeed no longer a technical problem for our civilization to destroy itself.[3]

Though Jerry Mander, the abolitionist critic, dutifully lists Enzensberger's *Consciousness Industry* in his bibliography, his zealous piety—the piety of the convert—could not be restrained. Masses of television viewers (Who else would read such a book?) scooped up the copies at $7.95 each (paperback). As Enzensberger points out, everyone works for the consciousness industry.

Despite the efforts of Erik Barnouw, Horace Newcomb, and a few others, the chilling fact is that the most effective purveyor of language, image, and narrative in American culture has failed to become a subject of lively humanistic discourse. It is laughed at, reviled, feared, and generally treated as persona non grata by university humanities departments and the "serious" journals they patronize. Whether this is the cause or merely a symptom of the precipitous decline of the influence of the humanities during recent years is difficult to say. In either case it is unfortunate that the scholars and teachers of *The Waste Land* have found "the vast wasteland" unworthy of their attention. Edward Shils spoke for many literary critics when he chastised "those who know better" but still give their attention to works of "mass culture" for indulging in "a continuation of childish pleasures."[4] Forgoing a defense of childish pleasures, I still cannot imagine a more destructive attitude in terms of the future of both humanistic inquiry and television. If the imagination is to play an epistemological role in a scientific age, it cannot be restricted to "safe" media. Shils teased pop culture critics for trying to be "folksy"; unfortunately, it is literature that is in danger of becoming a precious antique.

As the transcontinental industrial plant built since the Civil War was furiously at work meeting the new production quotas allowed by modern advertising techniques, President Calvin Coolidge observed that "the business of America is business." Since that time, television has become the art of business. The intensive specialization of skills called for by collaborative production technologies has forced most Americans to the marketplace for an exceptional range of goods and services. "Do-it-yourself" is itself something to buy. Necessities and trifles blur to indistinction. Everything is for sale to everybody. As James M. Cain wrote, the "whole goddamn country lives selling hot dogs to each other."[5] Choice, however, is greatly restricted. The permutation-bound structure of mass marketing theory has formalized taste into a multiple-choice question. Like the menu at McDonald's and the suits on the racks, the choices on the dial—and, thus far, the cable converter—are limited and guided. Yet even if the material in each TV show single-mindedly aims at the quality of quantity, too much happens along the way to cavalierly dispose of this body of dreams as a mere series of surface realizations of some master socioeconomic deep structure. If, as Enzensberger claims, we are stuck with television and nothing short of nuclear Armageddon will deliver us, then what choice is there but consciousness? Scripts are written. Sets, costumes, and camera angles are imagined and designed. Performances are rendered. No drama, not even melodrama, can be born of a void. Myths are recuperated, legends conjured. These acts are not yet carried out by computers, as much as network executives might prefer such a system.

When Marcel Duchamp signed a urinal "R. Mutt" and sent it to the Society of Independent Artists in 1917 for exhibition, he invited viewers to take advantage of the presentational structure of a show in order to look at what they live with. Television continually thanks us for inviting it into our homes and returns the invitation emphatically. A TV show or a commercial or any random moment of the broadcast day entreats the viewer to love it and live with it, and as even the programming executives must admit, the success or failure of the seduction, no matter how carefully and rationally ("scientifically") planned, is not predictable. Every television program that has been canceled for failing to capture an audience is the successful survivor of a battery of audience tests. But beyond the reams of Audience Research Reports stockpiled during these decades of agency billings, there is the living work of scores of television makers who accepted the marketable formats, found ways to satisfy both censors and the popular id, hawked the Alka-Seltzer beyond the limits of indigestion, and still managed to leave behind images that demand reimagining. The life of this work in American culture is a matter of taste, not test. It is ludicrous to crucify *Sgt. Bilko* for the sins of General Sarnoff. A fantastic, wavy, glowing procession of images hovers over the American antennascape, filling the air and millions of screens and minds with endless reruns. To accept a long-term relationship with a television program is to allow a vision to enter one's life. That vision is peopled with characters who speak a familiar idiosyncratic language, dress to purpose, worship God, fall in love, show élan and naiveté, become neurotic and psychotic, revenge themselves, and take it easy. While individual episodes—their plots and climaxes—are rarely memorable, though often remembered, cosmologies cannot fail to be rich for those viewers who have shared so many hours in their construction. The salient impact of television comes not from "special events," such as the coverage of the Kennedy assassinations or men on the moon playing golf, but from day-to-day exposure. The power of television resides in its normalcy; it is always there at the push of a button. Despite the frenzy of promotion that accompanies each new season, the debut of a series is not

much of an event. It rarely creates the will to view. The comedies uniformly promise nonstop laughter. The copshows dutifully guarantee fast-paced action. The melodramas will of
course be warm, human stories of contemporary life. There is
little significance in any of this. Why watch? Are the sex objects
compelling? Does the camera take me somewhere I like to be?
Is the time slot convenient? Should I make a "special effort" to
watch? It may take years to come to a show. If a show is a hit, if
the Nielsen families go for it, it is likely to become a Monday-
through-Friday "strip." The weekly series in stripped syndication is television's most potent oracle. Sitcoms, with their half-
hour formats, may air two or even three episodes a day on local
stations. Months become weeks, and years become months.
Mary accelerates through hairdos and hem lengths; Phyllis and
Rhoda disappear as Mary moves to her high-rise swinging-
singles apartment. Simple identification and suspense yield to
the subtler nuances of co-habitation. The threshold of expectation becomes fixed as daily viewing becomes an established
procedure or ritual. The ultimate suspension of disbelief occurs
when the drama—the realm of heightened artifice—becomes
normal. The aim of television is to be normal. The industry is
obsessed with the problem of norms, and this manifests itself in
both process and product. Whole new logics, usually accepted
under the general classification of "demographics," have been
imagined to create transformational models that explain the
perimeters of objectionability and attraction. A network sales
executive would not dare ask hundreds of thousands of dollars
for a prime-time ad on the basis of his high opinion of the show
that surrounds it. The sponsor is paying for "heads." What
guarantees, he demands, can be given for delivery? Personal
assurances—opinions—are not enough. The network must
show scientific evidence in the form of results of demographic
experiments. Each pilot episode is prescreened for test audiences who then fill out multiple-choice questionnaires to describe their reactions. Data are processed by age, income, race,
religion, or whatever cultural determinants the tester deems
relevant. Thus the dull annual autumn dialogue of popular
television criticism:

Why the same old junk every year? ask the smug, ironic
television critics after running down their witty lists of the
season's "winners and losers."

We know nothing of junk, cry the "value-free" social scientists of the industry research factories. The people have voted

with their number 2 pencils and tuners. We are merely the Board of Elections in a modern cultural democracy.[6]

But no one ever asked me what I thought, puzzles the viewer in a random burst from stupefaction.

Not to worry, the chart-and-graph *virtuosi* reassure. We have taken a biopsy from the body politic, and as you would know if this was your job, if you've seen one cell—or 1,200—you've seen them all.

But is demography democracy?

Walter Benjamin warned that ignoring such unquantifiable properties as creativity, genius, eternal value, and mystery as criteria for the creation and distribution of technologically reproduced art "would lead to a processing of data in the Fascist sense."[7] Though authoritarian use of the plebiscite can be well demonstrated from Napoleonic France to Khomeini's Iran, this need not be the case with American television. Television is capable of inspiring at least as much cynicism as docility. The viewer who can transform that cynicism into critical energy can declare the war with television over and instead savor the oracular quality of the medium. As Roland Barthes, Jean-Luc Godard, and the French devotees of Jerry Lewis have realized for years, television is American dada,[8] Charles Dickens on LSD, the greatest parody of European culture since *The Dunciad*.[9] Yahoos and Houyhnhnms battle it out nightly with submachine guns. Sex objects are stored in a box. Art or not art? This is largely a lexicographical quibble for the culturally insecure. Interesting? Only the hopelessly genteel could find such a phantasmagoria flat. Yesterday's trashy Hollywood movies have become recognized as the unheralded work of auteurs; they are screened at the ritziest "art houses" for connoisseurs of *le cinéma*. Shall we need the French once again to tell us what we have?

TELEVISION IS FUNNY

Comedy is the axis on which broadcasting revolves.—Gilbert Seldes, *The Public Arts*

Though network executives reserve public pride for the achievements of their news divisions and their dramatic specials, the fact remains that comedy—entertainment of a primarily humorous nature—has always been an essential, even dominant, ingredient of American commercial television programming. The little box, with its squared oblong screen, egregiously set in a piece of overpriced wood-grained furniture or cheap industrial plastic, has provoked a share of titters in its own right from a viewing public that casually calls it "boob tube." Television is America's jester. It has assumed the guise of an idiot while actually accruing the advantages of power and authority behind the smoke screen of its self-degradation. The Fool, of course, gets a kind word from no one: "Knee-jerk liberalism," cry the offended conservatives. "Corporate mass manipulation," scream the resentful liberals. Neo-Comstockians are aghast, righteously indignant at the orgiastic decay of morality invading their split-level homes. The avant-garde strikes a pose of smug terror before the empty, sterile images. Like the abused jester in Edgar Allan Poe's "Hop-Frog," however, the moguls of Television Row make monkeys out of their tormentors. Their deposit slips are drenched in crocodile tears; the show must go on.

In 1927, TV inventor Philo T. Farnsworth presented a dollar sign for sixty seconds in the first public demonstration of his television system.[10] The baggy-pants vaudevillians Farnsworth televised in 1935 have been joined by a host of modern cousins, including the sitcom character actor, the stand-up comedian, the sketch comic, and the gameshow host. No television genre is without what Robert Warshow called "the official euphoria which spreads over the culture like the broad smile of an idiot."[11] Police shows, family dramas, adventure series, and made-for-TV movies all rely heavily on humor to mitigate their bathos. Even The News is not immune to doggerel, as evidenced by the spread of "happy-talk" formats in TV journalism in recent years. While the industry experiments with new ways to package humor, television's most hilarious moments are often unintentional, or at least incidental. Reruns of ancient dramatic series display plot devices, dialogue, and camera techniques that are obviously dated. Styles materalize and vanish with astonishing speed. Series such as *Dragnet*, *The Mod Squad*, and *Ironside* surrender their credibility as "serious" police mysteries after only a few years in syndication. They self-destruct into ridiculous stereotypes and clichés, betraying their slick production values and achieving heights of comic ecstasy that dwarf their "serious" intentions. This is an intense comedy of obsolescence that grows richer with each passing television season. Starsky and Hutch render Jack Webb's Sgt. Joe Friday a messianic madman. The *Hill Street Blues* return the favor to *Starsky and Hutch*. The distinction between taking television on one's own terms and taking it the way it presents itself is of critical importance. It is the difference between passivity and activity. It is what saves television from becoming the homogenizing, monolithic, authoritarian tool that the doomsday critics claim it is. The self-proclaimed champions of "high art" who dismiss TV shows as barren imitations of the real article simply do not know how to watch. They are like freshmen thrust into survey courses and forced to read Fielding and Sterne; they lack both the background and the tough-skinned skepticism that can make television meaningful experience. In 1953 Dwight Macdonald was apparently not embarrassed to condemn all "mass culture" (including the new chief villain, TV) without offering any evidence that he had watched television. Not a single show is mentioned in his famous essay, "A Theory of Mass Culture."[12] Twenty-five years later it is possible to find English professors who will admit to watching *Masterpiece Theatre*. But American commercial shows? How could they possibly measure up to drama produced in Britain and tied in form and sensibility to the nineteenth-century novel? There is an important reply to this widespread English Department line: Television is culture. The more one watches, the more relationships develop among the shows and between the shows and the world. To rip the shows out of their context and compare them with the works of other media and cultural traditions is to deny their history—their American history—and misplace their identities.

The influence of other American media in the genesis of TV programming is obvious. Radio and movies immediately come to mind. In the early days of network telecast, however, viewers were treated to generous doses of "exhibition sports," such as professional wrestling and roller derby, phenomena that were new to electronic media. The outrageous antics of the performers on these shows were more in the realm of burlesque or the dance than sport. Wrestler Gorgeous George (the late George F. Wagner) was an early superstar of the genre who was capable of sending prespace-age viewers rolling off their couches. Borrowing a page from Max Fleischer's cartoon hero Popeye, he would struggle to his corner at the point of defeat, take a few hits from an oxygen tank marked "Florida Air," and, born again, return to the center of the squared circle to defeat his perennially wide-eyed opponent. The carnival-freak-show ambience of the program was enhanced by special matches featuring midgets and women. Wrestling was television's first original comedy, a grotesque comedy of violence. Not only did the performers have to be excellent acrobats possessing numerous circus skills in order to execute their complex ballets of flying dropkicks, atomic skullcrushers, and airplane spins, but they were also called upon to prove their mettle as character actors and stand-up comedians during the "interview" segments of the show, which can take up as much as half of a wrestling telecast. Playing various archetypal American figures, including ethnic stereotypes that date back to minstrelsy and the vaudeville stage, such characters as Killer Kowalski, Baron Fritz von Erich, and "Country Boy" Haystacks Calhoun would rant and rave, threaten their opponents' lives, and make promises to their fans, never for a moment stepping out of character. Roland Barthes has compared the technique of wrestling with that of the *commedia dell'arte*.[13]

The early tone that wrestling set in television comedy is in direct opposition, however, to the comic framework that eventually won commercial favor. As television strove to legitimize itself as a medium worthy of the attention of a middle-class sensibility (circa 1950s, U.S.A.), programming came packaged in more identifiably respectable wrappings. The "play area" or stage of the wrestling show was vague and undefined; the viewer could not automatically distinguish between stage and world. Was that wrestler leaving the arena on a stretcher truly unconscious? Was the blood on his face real? Were those women actually tearing chunks of hair out of each other's heads? The ring announcer said yes. Many viewers had their doubts. Could television lie? Was this any way to sell a Chevrolet? Previous to 1955, all four networks (including the now defunct DuMont Network) had offered coast-to-coast wrestling telecasts during the heart of prime time.[14] Though wrestling continues to be locally produced in many U.S. markets and has even reappeared nationally on superstations, it has disappeared from the network programming taxonomy. The only wrestling matches carried by the networks today are occasional telecasts of amateur wrestling on such shows as *The Wide World of Sports* and *Sportsworld*. Barthes likens the experience of watching this "respectable" sport to attending a suburban cinema; it is devoid of the spectacular distension of the professional variety.[15] The present-day descendants of professional wrestling

on television are such shows as *Real People* and *That's Incredible!*
These schlockumentary magazines (*TV Guide* calls them "sit-life
shows")[16] perhaps fill the void left by the cancelation of the
wrestling spectacle. Just as wrestling played on its superficial
resemblance to the relatively respectable sport of boxing in
order to establish a framework of legitimacy for outrageous
spectacle, the schlockumentaries borrow their form from the
respectable TV newsmagazine (notably *60 Minutes*).[17] These
shows stage phony sporting events (e.g., man in tug-of-war
with the Goodyear Blimp; daredevil attached to giant rubber
band leaping off bridge), and freaks are gratuitously displayed
(two-headed man; child savant, etc.); all is presented by a
straight-faced ersatz newsman, the successor to wrestling's
ersatz sports announcer.

ENTER THE PROSCENIUM

The forms that came to dominate television comedy (and therefore television) were video approximations of theater: the situation comedy (representational) and the variety show (presentational). The illusion of theater is a structural feature of both.
It is created primarily by the implicit attendance of an audience
that laughs and applauds at appropriate moments and thus
assures the viewer that the telecast is originating within the
safely specified walls of the proscenium stage. Normal responses are thus defined. The "audience" may be actual or an
electronic sound effect, but this is a small matter. The consequence is the same; the jokes are underlined. The ambiguities
of wrestling are thus avoided.

The situation comedy has proved to be the most durable of all
commercial television genres. Other types of programming
that have appeared to be staples of prime-time fare at various
junctures in TV history have seen their heyday and faded (the
Western, the comedy-variety show, and the big-money quiz-
show among them). The sitcom, however, has remained a consistent and ubiquitous feature of prime-time network schedules since the premiere of *Mary Kay and Johnny* on DuMont in
1947. The TV sitcom obviously derives from its radio predecessor. Radio hits such as *I Remember Mama*, *The Burns and Allen Show*,
The Goldbergs, and *Amos 'n Andy* made the transition to television
overnight. Then, as now, familiarity was a prized commodity in
the industry. In terms of preelectronic art forms, the sitcom

bears a certain physical resemblance to the British comedy of manners, especially in terms of its parlor setting. A more direct ancestor, as Jack Gladden has shown, may be the serialized family comedy adventures that were popular in nineteenth-century American newspapers.[18] Perhaps because of the nature of its serial continuity, the sitcom had no substantial presence in the movies.[19] Though *Andy Hardy* and *Ma and Pa Kettle* films deal with sitcomic themes, their feature length, lack of audience response tracks, and relatively panoramic settings make them very different viewing experiences. Serial narratives in the movies were usually action-oriented. *Flash Gordon*, for example, was constructed so that each episode built to a breathless, unfulfilled climax designed to bring the patrons back to the theater for next Saturday's resolution. The action of the sitcom is far too psychological for this. Urgent continuity rarely exists between episodes. Instead, climaxes occur within episodes (though these are not satisfying in any traditional sense). In the movie serial (or a modern television soap opera) the rescue of characters from torture, death, or even seemingly hopeless anxiety is used to call attention to serialization. The sitcom differs in that its central tensions—embarrassment and guilt— are almost always alleviated before the end of an episode. Each episode may appear to resemble a short, self-contained play; its rigid confinement to an electronic approximation of a prosce-nium-arch theater, complete with laughter and applause, em-phasizes this link. Unlike a stage play, however, no single epi-sode of a sitcom is likely to be of much interest; it may not even be intelligible. The attraction of an episode is the strength of its contribution to the broader cosmology of the series. The claus-trophobia of the miniature proscenium, especially for an au-dience that has grown casual toward Cinemascope, can be re-lieved only by the exquisiteness of its minutiae. Trivia is the most salient form of sitcom appreciation, perhaps the richest form of appreciation of any television series. Though television is at the center of American culture—it is the stage upon which our national drama/history is enacted—its texts are generally unavailable upon demand. The audience must share reminis-cences to conjure the ever-fleeting text. Giving this the format of a game, players try not so much to stump each other as to overpower each other with increasingly minute, banal bits of information that bring the emotional satisfaction of experience recovered through memory. The increased availability of all-rerun stations being brought about by cable services can only

serve to intensify and broaden this form of grass-roots television appreciation. Plot resolutions, which so often come in the
form of trite didactic "morals" in the sitcom, are not very
evocative. The lessons that Lucy Ricardo learned on vanity,
economy, and female propriety are forgotten by both Lucy and
the viewer. A description of Lucy's living room furniture (or
her new living room furniture) is far more interesting. The
climactic ethical pronouncements of Ward Cleaver conjure and
explore the essence of *Leave It to Beaver* less successfully than a
well-rendered impersonation of Eddie Haskell does. From about
the time a viewer reaches puberty, sitcom plot is painfully
predictable. After the tinkering of the first season or two, few
new characters, settings, or situations can be expected. Why
watch, if not for a visit to the sitcosmos?

The sitcom is a representational form, and its subject is
American culture: it dramatizes national types, styles, customs,
issues, and language. Because sitcoms are and have always been
under the censorship of corporate patronage, the genre has
yielded a conservative body of drama that is diachronically
retarded by the precautions of mass marketing procedure. For
example, *All in the Family* can appropriately be thought of as a
sixties sitcom, though the show did not appear on television
until 1971. CBS waited until some neat red, white, and blue
ribbons could be tied around the turmoil of that extraordinarily
self-conscious decade before presenting it as a comedy. When
the dust had cleared and the radical ideas being proposed during
that era could be represented as stylistic changes, the sixties
could be absorbed into a model of acceptability, a basic necessity
of mass marketing procedure. During the historical sixties,
while network news programs were offering footage of student riots, civil rights demonstrations, police riots, and militant
revolutionaries advocating radical changes in the American status quo, the networks were airing such sitcoms as *The Andy
Griffith Show, Petticoat Junction, Here's Lucy,* and *I Dream of Jeannie.*
The political issues polarizing communities and families were
almost completely avoided in a genre of representational
comedy that always had focused on American family and community. Hippies occasionally would appear as guest characters
on sitcoms, but they were universally portrayed as harmless
buffoons possessing neither worthwhile ideas nor the power to
act, which might make them dangerous. After radical sentiment crested and began to recede, especially after the repeal of
universal male conscription in 1970, the challenge of incorpo-

rating changes into the sitcom model finally was met. The dialogue that took place in the Bunker home was unthinkable during the American Celebration that had lingered so long on the sitcom. But if the sitcom was to retain its credibility as a chronicler and salesman of American family life, these new styles, types, customs, manners, issues, and linguistic constructions had to be added to its mimetic agenda.

The dynamics of this problem are perhaps better explained in marketing terms. Five age categories are generally used in demographic analysis: (1) 0–11; (2) 12–17; (3) 18–34; (4) 35–55; (5) 55+.[20] Prime-time programmers pay little attention to groups 1 and 5; viewing is so prevalent among the very young and old that, as the joke goes on Madison Avenue, these groups will watch the test pattern. Prime-time television programs are created primarily to assemble members of groups 3 and 4 for commercials. While members of group 4 tend to have the most disposable income, group 3 spends more money. Younger adults, presumably building their households, make more purchases of expensive "hard goods" (refigerators, microwave ovens, automobiles, etc.). This situation was profoundly exacerbated in the late sixties and early seventies by the coming of age of the Baby Boom generation. The top-rated sitcoms of the 1969–70 season included *Mayberry, R.F.D., Family Affair, Here's Lucy,* and *The Doris Day Show.* Though all four of these programs were in Nielson's Top 10 that season, their audience was concentrated in groups 1, 4, and 5. How could the networks deliver the new primary consumer group to the ad agencies and their clients? Norman Lear provided the networks with a new model that realistically addressed itself to this problem. In *Tube of Plenty,* Erik Barnouw shows how the timidity of television narrative can be traced directly to the medium's birth during the McCarthy Era. If the sixties had accomplished nothing else, it had ended the McCarthy scare. The consensus imagery that had dominated the sitcom since the birth of television simply could not deliver the new audience as well as the new consensus imagery Norman Lear developed for the seventies. This break in the twenty-year-old style of the genre self-consciously defined itself as "hip." The historian Daniel Czitrom has called this phenomenon "Lifestyle."[21]

In the fifties and sixties, the sitcom had offered the Depression-born post–World War II adult group a vision of peaceful, prosperous suburban life centered on the stable nuclear family. A generation that had grown up during hard times, and that had fought what Herbert T. Gillis always referred to as "The Big One," had seen its desires fulfilled on the sitcom. The economic, political, and social travail of the thirties and forties had been left behind by the brave new teleworld. Instead, there was a family: a husband and wife raising children. This family was white and had a name that bespoke Anglo-Saxon ancestry and Protestant religious affiliation. Surprisingly enough, the darnedest things happened to them. Each week a family member—usually a child—would encounter some ethical crisis or moral dilemma in the course of this relentlessly normal state of affairs. Dennis (the Menace) Mitchell hits a line drive through Mr. Wilson's kitchen window after being warned not to take batting practice in the backyard. Beaver unwittingly discovers a copy of tomorrow's history test, which Miss Landers has dropped in the school corridor. The man of her dreams finally asks Patty Duke out for an evening; should she send her twin cousin Cathy to keep her regular date with Richard? These families were all above the pressures usually associated with financial uncertainty. The father was comfortably placed in the professions—lawyer, doctor, insurance executive—or sometimes just amorphously well fixed (e.g., Ozzie Nelson). Furthermore, Dad was never in short supply of moral provisos, bromides, and panaceas to alleviate the anxiety of his little citizens-in-training. Mom, who worked for love not wages, though she was rarely shown doing any household tasks more demanding than serving dinner, managed to keep the family's spacious quarters in a state that can be best described as ready for military inspection; she could do it in formal attire to boot.

In these shows—*Father Knows Best, Ozzie and Harriet, The Donna Reed Show, The Trouble with Father, Make Room for Daddy*, et al.—actual humor (jokes or shticks) is always a subordinate concern to the proper solution of ethical crises. They are comedies not so much in the popular sense as in Northrop Frye's sense of the word: no one gets killed, and they end with the restoration of order and happiness.[22] What humor there is derives largely from the "cuteness" displayed by the children in their abortive attempts to deal with problems in other than correct (adult) ways. Sometimes an extra element of humor becomes the task of marginal characters from outside the nuclear family. Eddie Haskell (Ken Osmond) is among the best remembered of these domestic antiheroes. A quintessential wiseguy, Eddie's deviation from the straight and narrow—as walked by Wally Cleaver—is implicitly blamed on his parents. The fact that

Eddie is uniformly punished by the scriptwriters makes his rebellion all the more heroic.

A transformation on this model is the single-parent sitcom. Here the same moral universe remains intact. Instead of the traditional mom-and-dad, however, a widow, widower, aunt, or uncle is raising the children (divorce would not come to this subgenre until Norman Lear's *One Day at a Time* [1975]). This narrative format, pioneered in such shows as *My Little Margie* and *Bachelor Father*, makes it possible to augment the cuteness of the children's moral educations with situations involving romantic possibilities for the adult. Though Hays Office standards are rigorously adhered to, some relief is offered from the sexless picture of married life that otherwise prevailed in the genre.

Beneath the stylistic variances of *Father Knows Best* and *All in the Family* (and *Bachelor Father*/*One Day at a Time*), these shows are bound together by their unwavering commitment to didactic allegory. Lear indeed updated the conversation in the sitcom living room, but his sitcoms were actually quite conservative in terms of their form. Like the sitcoms of the fifties, Lear's shows reinforce what Dorothy Rabinowitz calls "our most fashionable pieties."[23] "Fashionable" is the key term. As Roger Rosenblatt has pointed out, the greatest difference between *Father Knows Best*'s Jim Anderson and Archie Bunker is that Jim, the father, is the source of all wisdom for the Anderson family while Archie is more likely to be the recipient of lessons from Mike, Gloria, and Edith.[24] In marketing terms, the representation of the higher spending power is consistently heroic.

Though didacticism may be a structural feature of the sitcom (and all storytelling), a strain of situation comedy has developed that is less emphatically moralistic and more concerned with being funny. *I Love Lucy* is one such sitcom; it is the prototype of the "zany" variety. Here, father still knows best, but his task is not so much to preach sermons to the children as to restrain his wife from doing "crazy" things that threaten middle-class order. Lucy is in no way the imperturbable wife and mother embodied in her contemporary, Margaret Anderson. She overspends her budget, acts on impulse, and does not hesitate to drop Little Ricky with Mrs. Trumble at the slightest hint that her dream of something more than a hausfrau existence might be satisfied by an audition for a show at the Tropicana. Lucy refuses to allow bourgeois role destiny to stifle her organic desires, no matter how often she is repressed. Her attempts to escape from what Ricky and society define for her as "her place in the home" turn her into a buffoon, and this is the center of the show. By the end of each episode she has been whipped back into middle-class-housewife shape. Her weekly lapse into "childish" behavior, however, makes her into a freak whose comic talents are far more compelling than the dismal authoritarian morality that controls her.[25]

Though Lucy was copied in such shows as *I Married Joan* and *Pete and Gladys*, the imitators could not easily come by the comic talents of Lucille Ball. To compensate for Lucy's personal magic, they frequently turned to the supernatural. In shows such as *Bewitched, I Dream of Jeannie, Mr. Ed,* and *My Favorite Martian,* an otherwise realistic (or at least scientifically feasible) vision of middle-class life is invaded not by a mere madcap but by a character (woman, animal, or alien) possessed of supernatural powers. Magic is both the cause of and the antidote to the much-feared curse of zaniness. The relatively naturalistic Lucy often becomes the victim of her own harebrained scheming and has to own up to Ricky in humiliation before the final credits. On the other hand, Samantha Stevens, a witch, can set things right with a twitch of her nose—with husband Darren often none the wiser. In each case the wife possesses energies and desires that tempt her to rebel against the constraints of middle-class-housewife status. The husbands, both the immigrant striver Ricky Ricardo and the Madison Avenue executive Darren Stevens, are determined to keep their contractual slaves/lovers locked safely away at home. Though a bandleader himself, Ricky simply forbids Lucy from pursuing a show business career. Darren is an even crueler sexist. He constantly expects Samantha to entertain his business contacts at home but forbids her to use her magical powers. Though she can prepare an elegant banquet with a spell (usually one heroic couplet) and a twitch of her nose, he forces her to slave over a hot stove all day for no other reason than to satisfy his incorrigibly puritanical "principles."

The domestic sitcom has strayed from its compelling middle-class center upon occasion. Though the conventions of teleculture define the middle class as a vast amalgamation of all those Americans who neither depend on welfare payments nor have live-in servants, there have been self-consciously proletarian sitcoms, including such early shows as *The Life of Riley* and *The Honeymooners*. As the titles suggest, there is little of Clifford Odets in them, though the Kramdens' stark two-room flat is notable. Interestingly enough, the working-class sitcom was virtually absent from the networks during most of the sixties. It was Lear who revived the idea with *All in the Family*. The black sitcom has a similar history. It appeared in TV's pioneer days (e.g., *Amos 'n Andy*, *Beulah*), only to disappear from view during the sixties and then make a comeback under Lear's tutelage. In acknowledgment of the protests of civil rights organizations against the lily-whiteness of the sitcosmos, NBC premiered its *Julia* series in 1968. This was a single-parent situation starring Diahann Carroll as a widowed, professional, middle-class mom; the tokenism of the series was as obvious as its resemblance to *The Doris Day Show*, which made its debut that same season. Lear and his Tandem Productions restyled and resurrected the black sitcom in *Sanford and Son*, which premiered in 1972. Other black sitcoms, such as *The Jeffersons* and *Good Times*, followed.

Faced with the problem of seeming fresh and different without upsetting expectations of the familiar formula, sitcom-makers have attempted to bring the form to various settings. In addition to the ubiquitous contemporary middle-class living room, sitcoms have taken place in military barracks, prehistoric caves, tenement flats, mansions, extraterrestrial space, junk-yards, offices, police stations, and high school and college class-rooms; in New York, Los Angeles, Minneapolis, Mayberry, Bedrock, Indianapolis, Moscow, Milwaukee, a Nazi prison camp, and Anytown U.S.A. The military sitcom has been a strong subgenre. *Sgt. Bilko*, *McHale's Navy*, *F Troop*, *Gomer Pyle, U.S.M.C.*, *I Dream of Jeannie*, *Hogan's Heroes*, *C.P.O. Sharkey*, *M*A*S*H*, and *Private Benjamin* (to name just a few) have extended the military setting through war and peace, present and past, and every branch of the U.S. armed services, save the Coast Guard. Deviation from "normal" (that is, nuclear family) life also occurs in a subgenre of the sitcom that focuses on single career girls. Early examples include *Our Miss Brooks* and *Private Secretary* (also known as *The Ann Sothern Show*). Like the blue-collar and black sitcoms, the career-girl sitcom faded from the homescreen during the halcyon days of the middle-class domesticom, only to resurface in the late sixties. *That Girl* (1966) was at the crest of the revival. Marlo Thomas starred as Ann Marie, a young woman who leaves her parents' suburban New York home to move to Manhattan and pursue a career as an actress. Ann's ties to her family, however, were emphasized. Both her father and mother were series regulars who kept a close watch on their daughter's fortunes in Sin City. Her thoroughly innocuous steady boyfriend stood between Ann and promiscuity. It was *The Mary Tyler Moore Show* and the MTM Enterprises spin-offs that finally presented a picture of women out in the world on their own. The career-woman sitcom became a staple of the seventies. The heroine, freed at last from her role as chief cook and bottle washer, as well as from the moral authority of a husband or father, entered the pantheon of telemythology.[26]

For all the stylistic variations on a theme that have characterized sitcom history, the comic success of a show ultimately has depended on the talents of its actors and their collaborative success as a troupe. As performers as diverse as Don Rickles and Jimmy Stewart have learned, the sitcom simply does not work as a one-star vehicle; the laughs—and usually the ratings—have gone to the well-formed ensemble. Andy Griffith's "stardom" fades from memory if isolated from Don Knotts's woefully neurotic Deputy Barney Fife, Howard McNear's apoplectic Floyd the Barber, and the other citizens of Mayberry. Compare the brilliant kabuki-like choreography of the original *Honeymooners* to the awkward, misplayed revival in the sixties; Audrey Meadows and Joyce Randolph were never quite replaced. Though Lucille Ball was able to stay atop the ratings throughout her sitcom career, she would never again attain the comic heights she had achieved with Desi Arnaz, Vivian Vance, and William Frawley. Lucy's artistic demise was due not only to the inferior comic technique of her later efforts (*The Lucy Show* and *Here's Lucy*), which can be explained in show business terms as "inferior timing," but more importantly to the absence of the mythological syntheses of *I Love Lucy*: male and female (Ricky/ Fred vs. Lucy/Ethel); native-born and immigrant (Lucy/Ethel/ Fred vs. Ricky); old and young (the Ricardos vs. the Mertzes); and organic genteel (Lucy vs. the middle-class world she lived in). These paradigms tightened the interstices of the field of American comedy. The later shows invested all comic tensions in the conflicts between Lucy and the hyperbolically genteel Gale Gordon; they pale in comparison.

Perhaps the reason that the sitcom has been looked down upon by critics as a hopelessly "low" or "masscult" form is that a search for "the best which has been thought and said" is wild-goose chase as far as the genre is concerned. R. P. Blackmur, though certainly no TV fan, commented germanely that the critic "will impose the excellence of something he understands upon something he does not understand. Then all the richness of actual performance is gone. It is worth taking precautions to prevent that loss, or at any rate to keep us aware of the risk."[27] Television is not yet a library with shelves; it is a flow of dreams, many remembered, many submerged. How can we create a bibliography of dreams? Blackmur also wrote that "the critic's job is to put us into maximum relation to the burden of our momentum."[28] As a culture, television is the engine of our momentum. It has heaped thousands upon thousands of images upon the national imagination:

Gleason rearing back a fist and threatening to send Alice to the moon.

Phil Silvers's bullet-mouthed Sgt. Bilko conning his platoon out of its paychecks.

Jack Benny and Rochester guiding an IRS man across the crocodile-infested moat to the vault.

Dobie Gillis standing in front of "The Thinker" and pining for Tuesday Weld.

Carrol O'Connor giving Meathead and modern philanthropic liberalism the raspberries.

Jerry Van Dyke settling down in the driver's seat of a Model T Ford for a heart-to-heart talk with *My Mother, the Car.*

Whitman, in *Democratic Vistas*, called for a new homegrown American literary art whose subject would be "the average, the bodily, the concrete, the democratic, the popular."[29] The sitcom is an ironic twentieth-century fulfillment of this dream. The "average" has been computed and dramatized as archetype; the consumer world has been made "concrete"; the "bodily" is fetishized as the unabashed object of envy and voyeurism; all of this is nothing if not "popular." The procession of images that was Whitman's own art, and which he hoped would become the nation's, is lacking in the sitcom in but one respect: its technique is not democratic but demographic. The producers, directors, writers, camera operators, set designers, and other artists of the medium are not, as Whitman had hoped, "breathing into it a new breath of 'life."[30] Instead, for the sake of industrial science, they have contractually agreed to create the hallucinations of what Allen Ginsberg called "the narcotic . . . haze of capitalism."[31] The drug indeed is on the air and in the air. Fortunately, the integrity of the individual resides in the autonomy of the imagination, and therefore it is not doomed by this system. The television set plays on and on in the mental hospital; the patient can sit in his chair, spaced-out and hopeless, or get up and push at the doors of consciousness. This is the happy ending for the sitcom.

IN FRONT OF THE CURTAIN

"The virtue of all-in wrestling," wrote Roland Barthes in 1957, "is that it is the spectacle of excess."[32] I have tried to show that the sitcom, on the other hand, is a spectacle of subtleties, an incremental construction of substitute universe laid upon the foundation of a linear, didactic teletheater. Even the occasional insertion of the *mirabile* or supernatural is underlined by the genre's broader commitment to naturalistic imitation. Presentational comedy, which shared the prime-time limelight with the sitcom during the early years of television, vacillates between these poles. The comedy-variety show has been the great showcase for presentational teleforms: stand-up comedy, impersonation, and the blackout sketch. This genre is similar to wrestling in that it too strives for the spectacle of excess. Its preelectronic ancestors can be found on the vaudeville and burlesque stages: the distensions of the seltzer bottle and the bannana peel; the fantastic transformations of mimicry; the titillations of the physical, psychological, and cultural disorders that abounded in frankly self-conscious art forms. But the comedy-variety show does not go to the ultimate excesses of wrestling. Like the sitcom, it is framed by the proscenium arch and accepts the badge of artifice.

While the representational drama of the sitcom and its cousins, the action/adventure series and the made-for-TV movie has flourished to the point that these genres consume almost all of the "most-watched" hours, the comedy-variety show has been in steady decline since the 1950s, when it was a dominant genre of prime-time television. Since the self-imposed cancelation of *The Carol Burnett Show* in 1978, the few presentational variety hours that have appeared in prime-time have been hosted by singers (Barbara Mandrell, Marie Osmond), and comedy has been relegated to a rather pathetic secondary concern on these programs. The demise of the genre has deprived prime time of some of television's most promising possibilities. Stand-up comedy, as developed in the American nightclub, is one of the most intense and compelling of modern performance arts. Eschewing the protection of narrative superstructure and continuity, the stand-up comedian nakedly faces the audience. He truly works in the first person, making no distinction between persona and self. When successful, the monologist offers an awesome display of charismatic power: the lone individual controlling the imaginative and physical responses of millions. By the same token, nowhere is failure more pathetic or painful. The rhythm of the stand-up monologue demands the punctuation of the audience's response; when it is missing, the spectacle of impotence is shattering. The stand-up comedian laying an egg is one of the few phenomena on television or in mass entertainment in general where the visible pressure to produce the desired effect emerges through even the slickest production values. That pressure is unrelenting. Like the wrestler who must continue to play his role during "interviews" outside the ring, the television stand-up comic is expected to remain in character at all times. After doing "five minutes," he must join Johnny and his guests as "himself," a clown, a wit, a funnyman. The ability to do this often provides satisfying performance art. Failure cracks apart the smooth veneer of TV "normalcy."

Television as a medium is particularly well suited to the presentation of stand-up comedy. The comedian is easily framed on the small screen. Perspective can be spontaneously shifted by the director from the full body portrait, which gives the comic the authority of a public speaker, to close-ups that are advantageous to mimicry and face-making. The intermediary teletheater is devoid of drunken hecklers and clattering dishes, making it a propitious showcase for the carefully rehearsed, well-timed routine (though admittedly, for some stylists, this loss of spontaneous give-and-take is regrettable). The structure of the show business industry, however, has inhibited stand-up comedy as a television art. Comedians, even the handful who employ writing staffs, must beware the plaque of overexposure. A powerful nightclub monologue can become worthless in Las Vagas and Atlantic City after even a single television appearance. Furthermore, the fetishization of "dirty words" on television puts severe limits on stand-up text. It is perhaps principally for these reasons that the stand-up comedian has been largely squeezed out of prime time into what the industry terms "marginal hours." On daytime television, for example, stand-up performers abound as players on gameshows and as guests on *Merv* and *Mike*. Gameshows such as *The*

Hollywood Squares and *Battlestars* have even been tailored as stand-up vehicles. The real stronghold for presentational comedy on television, however, has become the late-night spot.

In May of 1950, NBC premiered *Broadway Open House* in a late-night time period (i.e., 11:30, eastern time), and ever since, this segment of the NBC schedule has been reserved for presentational comedy. It has even become a relatively safe zone for artistic freedom (or at least TV's equivalent of "blue" material). Alex McNeil describes *Broadway Open House* as "a heavy-handed mixture of vaudeville routines, songs, dances and sight gags."[33] The cohosts were vaudeville veterans Jerry Lester and Morey Amsterdam, and much of the humor derived from their interplay with the Dolly Parton of early television, "a buxom blonde named Jennie Lewis, better known as Dagmar, who played it dumb."[34] By the midfifties, the program had evolved a more sedate format: a 105-minute, Monday-through-Friday, "desk-and-sofa" talk show known as *The Tonight Show*. It was hosted by *bon mot* comedians such as Steven Allen, Ernie Kovacs, and Jack Paar. The opening monologue became an institution, television's only daily comic paratext to The News. In 1981 Johnny Carson continues to deliver the only regularly scheduled comedy monologue on national television, but Jonny's ever-expanding vacation schedule has made even that an iffy proposition; the show has dwindled to a mere one hour due to Johnny's seemingly unquenchable thirst for recreation. The *Tonight Show* sofa, once filled with guests, including two or three comics a show, is relatively empty these days.

Weekly late-night comedy shows, such as *Saturday Night Live* and *SCTV*, have taken up some of the stand-up slack, but the great work of these shows has been to grandly resuscitate TV blackout. The blackout sketch, or short skirt, was pioneered as a distinctive teleform in the early days of TV. Before two-hour television movies ate up such a large chunk of network prime time, the viewer did not have to wait for the wee hours of the weekend to see sketch comedy. Milton Berle, Jimmy Durante, Jackie Gleason, Sid Caesar, Ernie Kovacs, Martha Raye, and Ed Wynn were just a few of the comedians who hosted their own weekly comedy hours. These stars were the pampered children of Television Row. Jackie Gleason was able to get CBS to build him a Hudson River mansion during the fifties; later, when he got Sunbelt Fever, CBS chairman William Paley granted him a complete new production facility in Miami Beach. Milton Berle, "Mr. Television," was signed to a thirty-one-year contract by

NBC in 1951. The role of Uncle Miltie in the early proliferation of the medium itself is, of course, legendary. His subsequent fall from Nielsen grace parallels the decline of the genre. From 1948 to 1956, the Berle show was a Tuesday night ritual. The first official ratings season was 1950–51, and A. C. Nielsen ranked Berle's *Texaco Star Theater* as the Number One attraction on television.[35] General Sarnoff's multimillion-dollar investment seemed to be paying off as the show consistently finished among the Top 5 for the next three seasons. However, in 1954–55, it slipped to Number Thirteen, and in 1955–56 it dropped out of the Top 20 altogether.[36] It is too easy to dismiss the Berle phenomenon as merely a case of the public's fickle favor. Not a single comedy-variety hour made the Top 10 in 1955–56.[37] Few variety shows hosted by comedians would finish in the Top 10 ever again. At the end of the 1955–56 season, the unthinkable happened—Berle was yanked off the air. After a two-year layoff, NBC tried him again, this time in a reduced half-hour format; the new show was not renewed for a second season. By 1960, stuck with an expensive long-term contract, Sarnoff was using Milton Berle as the host of *Jackpot Bowling*. Finally, with over fifteen years remaining on his contract, Berle and NBC came to an agreement, and the once indomitable star was let go. Last-place ABC promptly signed him for a comedy-variety comeback, but *The Milton Berle Show* could not survive six months in 1966.

The early rush to sign the stars for eternity ended as the networks entered the age of entropy.

The reasons for the failure of Berle and his "hellzapoppin'" burlesque style of presentation are not obvious. What can be said with some assurance is that this failure took place amid increasing demand for a "product" as opposed to a "show" in the growing television industry. As the prime-time stakes rocketed upward, sponsors, agencies, and networks became less tolerant of the inevitable ups and downs of a star-centered presentational drama offer the long-term rigidities of shooting scripts, which make "quality control" easier to impose. Positive demographic responses to dramatic "concepts" are dependable barometers. Performance comedy is only as good as an individual performance; the human element looms too large. Furthermore, the dreaded extremes of presentational comedy can be avoided. Kinescopes of *The Texaco Star Theater* reveal Berle in transvestite sketches whose gratuitous lewdness rivals wrestling at its most intense. The passionate vulgarity of these sketches could not have been wholly predictable from their scripts. Instead, it derives directly from Berle's confrontation with the camera—his performance. Censorship of such material presents complex editing problems, which are easily preempted in representational drama by script changes. It is my own feeling that the high-tech mystique of television itself—the sterile promise of the machine—is what kept the show from crossing the border from "family fun" to pornography in the early days of television. Gilbert Seldes described Berle's comedy as "good clean dirt."[38] Seldes called the early Berle a "stag entertainer," offering this observation: "The basic material of the stag entertainer, whether he dresses in women's clothes, pretends to be homosexual, or develops some other specialty, is still the off-color story, and the basic style is always the public one of maximum projection."[39] Perhaps the blinding gloss of the "modern miracle" of television was becoming subdued during television's second decade. Time, boredom, and the further technicization of the American household were making the future banal enough to generate a critical response. Were the full implications of burlesque beaming into the home becoming a bit too clear for Berle's family audience? Brooks and Marsh have indeed attributed the undoing of Uncle Miltie to increasing "sophistication" among the viewing public: "By 1956 the steam had run out for 'Mr. Television.' TV was by then becoming dominated by dramatic-anthology shows, Westerns, and private eyes, and the sight of a grinning comic jumping around in crazy costumes [i.e., women's clothing] no longer had the appeal it did in 1948."[40] When NBC gave Berle his second chance in 1958, the show was considerably toned down:

> Two years after his departure from the Tuesday line-up, Berle returned to prime time with a half-hour variety series for NBC. He was a more restrained performer this time—no slapstick or outrageous costumes—attempting to function more as a host than the central focus of the show.[41]

The consequence was clear: Berlesque, like wrestling, had been blackballed from television's increasingly genteel prime-time circle. The late fifties, of course, was the heyday of *Playhouse 90*, *The U.S. Steel Hour*, and *The Armstrong Circle Theater*, the "Golden Age" of respectable drama. Television then, as now and always, was on the verge of becoming sophisticated. The NBC late-night spot had passed from the wacky vaudevillian Jerry Lester to the neurotically urbane Jack Paar. Berle was certainly neurotic; he simply could not be urbane.

A survey cited by Sterling and Kitross shows the number of "Evening Network Television" hours given to comedy-variety shows declining from a high of 21.5 hours in 1951 to 5 hours in 1973.[42] The censorship problems I have mentioned have checkered the history of the genre. The case of the Smothers Brothers provides an example. Tom and Dick won their network wings with an innocuous sitcom in the 1965–66 season. When CBS gave them their own comedy-variety show, *The Smothers Brothers Comedy Hour*, the network suddenly found itself with a severe Standards and Practices crisis. As Brooks and Marsh have written, the show "poked fun at virtually all the hallowed institutions of American society—motherhood, church, politics, government, etc."[43] Controversial guests, such as folk singer Pete Seeger and Dr. Benjamin Spock (after his conviction for aiding draft evaders), were invited to appear on the show. Many segments were severely censored or deleted. An embarrassed CBS canceled the series on a technicality: a tape was delivered past the usual deadline. That tape contained a sequence in which Joan Baez dedicated a song to her husband, David Harris, who was serving a sentence in federal prison for draft evasion.[44] In 1981 the Smothers Brothers were back on the air, the stars of a short-lived representational drama series, *Fitz and Bones*.

Nat King Cole was a singer, not a comedian, but the peculiar case of his ill-fated variety series makes a stark point about the qualitative distinctions between presentation and representation on network television. Black actors and actresses were not complete strangers to television in the 1950s, Ethel Waters had played the title role in *Beulah* (ABC, 1950–53), and Tim Moore, Spencer Williams, Ernestine Wade, and the rest of the cast of *Amos 'n Andy* (CBS, 1951–53) were of course black (the radio cast had been white). Amanda Randolph played the part of Louise (the maid) on *The Danny Thomas Show* from 1953 to 1964. But when Nat King Cole was given his own variety show in 1956, not a single sponsor could be found. NBC affiliates in the North as well as the South declined to carry the program.[45] Even the appearances on the show of such mainstream white stars of the day as Tony Bennett, Frankie Laine, and Peggy Lee could not dissuade affiliates from their boycott. To its credit, NBC continued to air *The Nat King Cole Show* as a sustaining program for more than a year, juggling its time slot twice in an attempt to find a place for it. But a black entertainer stripped of the representational mask would not be successful in prime time until *The Flip Wilson Show* (NBC, 1970–74).

The comedy-variety genre never completely died off in prime time. A handful of hits such as *The Carol Burnett Show*, *The Flip Wilson Show*, and George Schlatter's innovative *Rowan and Martin's Laugh-In* managed to keep it alive. But pop singers, including Sonny and Cher, Tom Jones, Englebert Humperdinck, Tony Orlando and Dawn, the Captain and Tenille, and Donnie and Marie, took over the lion's share of the dwindling hours given to vaudeville-style presentation in the sixties and seventies. A later full-fledged attempt to revive the comedy-variety hour was *The Richard Pryor Show*, which premiered on the NBC fall schedule in 1977. It was destroyed by the old comedy-variety devil—censorship—after only five airings.

Generally speaking, the comedian has had to step back from in front of the curtain, cross the proscenium arch, and don the mask of a representational character to find a place in prime-time television. The networks have thus provided themselves with a modicum of protection from the unreliability of individual personalities. Presentational comedy—performance art—may simply be too dangerous a gamble for the high stakes of today's market.

Interestingly, the disappearance from television of the clown who faces the audience without a story line has occurred more or less stimultaneously with rising interest in and appreciation of performance art in avant-garde circles. In "Performances as News: Notes on an Intermedia Guerrilla Group," Cheryl Bernstein writes:

> In performance art, the artist is more exposed than ever before. The literal identification of artistic risk with the act of risking one's body or one's civil rights has become familiar in the work of such artists as Chris Burden, Rudolf Schwarzkogler, Tony Schafranzi and Jean Toche.[46]

Burden, for example, invites an audience into a performance space where spectators sit atop wooden ladders. He then floods the room with water and drops a live electrical wire into the giant puddle. The closest thing television offers to a spectacle of this kind is Don Rickles, who evokes audience terror by throwing the live wire of his insult humor into the swamp of American racial and ethnic fears. Rickles, for the most part, has been prohibited from performing his intense theater of humiliation in prime time. Twice NBC has attempted to contain him in sitcom proscenia, but these frames have constricted his effect and turned his insults into dull banter. In recent years he has been unleashed upon a live studio audience only during his infrequent appearances as a guest host on *The Tonight Show*. The erratic quality of Rickles's performance on *Tonight* offers a clue to the networks' reluctance to invest heavily in the presentational comedy form.

Bernstein points to The News as the great source of modern performance art on television. She deconstructs "The Kidnapping of Patty Hearst" by the Symbionese Liberation Army as a performance work. The SLA was a troupe that was formed to create a multimedia work—the kidnapping—principally for television. The mass distribution of food in poor neighborhoods in the San Francisco Bay area (one of the SLA's demands), as well as the shoot-outs and police chases that occurred, were all part of a modern theatrical art that can take place only on television. Perhaps the proliferation of The News on television can be tied to the decline of presentational comedy; the two have seemed to occur in direct proportion to each other. The sit-life schlockumentary is the point at which the two genres meet. Furthermore, the bombardment of the homescreen with direct presentations from every corner of the earth has created a kind of vaudeville show of history. The tensions of the nuclear Sword of Damocles create a more compelling package than even Ed Sullivan could have hoped to assemble. The nations of the world have become a troupe of baggy-pants clowns on television. They are trotted out dozens of ti.nes each day in a low sketch comedy of hostility, violence, and affectation. The main show, of course, is the network evening news. Climb the World Trade Center. Fly an airplane through the Arc de Triomphe. Plant a bomb in a department store in the name of justice. Invade a preindustrial nation with tanks in the name of peace. Can Ted Mack compare with this?

THE THEATER COLLAPSES

Random House, a subsidiary of RCA, publishes a dictionary that defines the verb "entertain" as follows:

1. to hold the attention of agreeably; divert; amuse
2. to treat as a guest; show hospitality to
3. to admit into or hold in the mind; consider
4. *Archaic.* to maintain or keep up
5. *obs.* to give admittance or reception to; receive

6. *v.i.* to exercise hospitality; entertain company
Late Middle English: *entertene*, to hold mutually[47]

The television industry is at the forefront of a vast entertainment complex that oversees the process of coordinating consumption and culture. "Entertainment" has been established as
a buzz word for narratives and other imaginative presentations
that make money. It is used as a rhetorical ploy to specialize
popular arts and isolate them from aesthetic and political scrutiny; such scrutiny is reserved for "art." An important implication of the definition of "entertain" is the intimate social relationship it implies between the entertainer and the entertained.
In 1956 Gunther Anders wrote that "the television viewer,
although living in an alienated world, is made to believe that he
is on a footing of the greatest intimacy with everything and
everybody."[48] The technological means to produce this illusion
have since been greatly enhanced. Anders describes this illusion
as "chumminess." Television offers itself to the viewer as a
hospitable friend: Welcome to *The Wonderful World of Disney*.
Good evening, folks. We'll be right back. See you next week.
Y'all come back now. As technology synthesizes more and more
previously human functions, there is a proliferation of anthro-
pomorphic metaphor: Automatic Teller Machines ask us how
much money we need. Computers send us bills. Channel 7 is
predicting snow. The car won't start. It is in this context that
television entertains. There is an odd sensation of titillation in
all this service. Whitman and other nineteenth-century opti-
mists foresaw an elevation of the common man to a proud
master in the technoworld. Machines would take care of life's
dirty work; this created the prospect of slavery without guilt.
Television enthusiastically smiles and shuffles for the viewer's
favor. Even bad television programs contribute to the illusion
(i.e., "We are not amused"). In Faulkner's *Absalom, Absalom!*
Sutpen comes down out of the classless *Gemeinschaft* of frontier
Appalachia and discovers his low station in *Kultur* when the
slave butler of a Piedmont plantation refuses him entry at the
front door of the mansion and sends him around back for a
handout. Determined never to suffer such an indignity again,
he does not return to Appalachia but works single-mindedly
until he can buy a gang of his own slaves. These slaves build
him a mansion and he becomes a colonel. It was of course cost
efficient to buy female slaves and impregnate them personally.
One of his mulatto sons finally shoots him. Similarly, the tele-

American emerges from the innocence of childhood into his or her first apartment. Success in life is measured largely by the quantity of machines in the quarters. Are all the household chores mechanized? Do you have HBO? Work is minimized. Leisure is maximized. There is more time to watch television— that is, to live like a king.

Backstage of this public drama, quite a different set of relationships is at work. In a demography, the marketing apparatus becomes synonymous with the state itself. As the quality of goods takes a backseat to the quantity of services, the most valued good of all—the measure of truth—becomes information on the consuming preferences of the hundreds of millions of consumer-kings. Every ticket to the cinema, every book, every tube of toothpaste purchased is a vote. The shelves of the supermarkets are stocked with referenda. Watching television is an act of citizenship, participation in culture. The networks entertain the viewer; in return, the viewer entertains thousands of notions on what to buy (that is, how to live). The democrat Whitman wrote that "the average man of a land at last is only important."[49] The demographer Nielsen cannot agree more:

> While the average household viewed over 49 hours of television [per week] in the fall of 1980, certain types viewed considerably more hours. Households with 3 or more people and those with non-adults watched over 60 hours a week. Cable subscribing households viewed about 7 hours a week more than non-cable households.[50]

Paul Klein, chief programmer at NBC for many years, characterized his programming philosophy as based on what he called the Least Objectionable Program (LOP) Theory.[51] This theory, expounded by Klein in the seventies, downplays the importance of viewer loyalty to specific programs. Instead, it asserts that television watching is more often dependent on a formal decision. The viewer does not turn on the set so much to view this or that program as to fulfill a desire "to watch television." R. D. Percy and Company, an audience research firm, has come to a conclusion that supports Klein's thesis. David Chagall, summarizing Percy's two-year experiment with 200 Seattle television families, wrote: "Most of us simply snap on the set rather than select a show. The first five minutes are spent *prospecting* channels, looking for gripping images."[52] Faced with the impulse (compulsion?) to view, the viewer then turns to the secondary consideration of choosing a program. In evolved cable markets this can mean dozens of possibilities. The low social prestige of TV watching, even among heavy viewers, coupled with the remarkably narrow range of what is usually available, inhibits the viewer from expressing enthusiasm for any given show. The viewer or viewers (TV, it must not be forgotten, is one of the chief social activities of the culture) must therefore LOP about, looking for the least bad, least embarrassing, or least objectionable program. While I am ill prepared to speculate on the demographic truth of this picture of the "average man," two things are worth noting: anyone who watches television has surely experienced this; and NBC fell into last place in the ratings under Klein's stewardship.

I cite Klein (and Nielsen) to demonstrate the character of demographic thought, the ideological template that ultimately produce most television programs and always is employed to authorize or censor their exhibition on the distribution system. The optimistic democratic view of man as a self-perfecting individual, limited only by superimposed circumstance, is turned on its head. Man is defined as a prisoner of limitations seeking the path of least resistance. This is an industrial nightmare, the gray dream of Fritz Lang's *Metropolis* reshot in glossy technicolor. Workers return from their multicollared tasks, drained of all taste and personality. They seek nothing more than merciful release from the day's production pressures; they want only to "escape." "Escapism" is a much used but puzzling term. Its ambiguities illustrate the overall bankruptcy of the criticism of television that uses it as a flag. The television industry is only too happy to accept "escapism" as the definition of its work; it constitutes a carte blanche release from responsibility for what is presented. Escapist critics seem to believe that the value of art should be measured only by rigorously naturalistic standards. Television programs are viewed as worthless or destructive because they divert consciousness from "reality" to fantasy. However, all art, even social realism, does this. Brecht was certainly mindful of this fact when he found it necessary to attach intrusionary Marxist sermons to the fringes of social realist stage plays. Is metaphor possible at all without "escapism"? Presumably, the mechanism of metaphor is to call a thing something it is not in order to demonstrate emphatically what it is. When the network voice of control says, "NBC is proud as a peacock," it is forcing the perceiver of this message to "escape" from all realistic data about the corporate institution

NBC into a fantastic image of a bird displaying its colorful feathers in a grand and striking manner. This is done on the assumption that the perceiver will be able to sort the shared features of the two entities from the irrelevant features and "return" to a clearer picture of the corporation. Representational television programs work in much the same way. If there are no recognizable features of family life in *The Waltons*, if there are no shared features of lifestyle in *Three's Company*, if there are no credible features of urban paranoia in *Baretta*, then watching these shows would truly be "escapism." But if those features are there—and I believe they are—the viewer is engaging in an act that does not differ qualitatively from reading a Zola novel (though the latter may be more successful in creating a "clearer picture" of society). The escapist argument makes a better point in relation to the structure of narrative in the television series. In the world of the series all problems are not only solvable but usually solved. To accept this as "realistic" is indeed an escape from the planet Earth. But how many viewers accept a TV series as realistic in this sense? John Cawelti has convincingly demonstrated that the success of popular formula narrative is not based on fooling a dull audience.[53] Interestingly, it is the soap opera—the one genre of series television that is committed to an anticlimactic, existential narrative structure—that has created the most compelling illusion of realism for the viewing audience.[54] The survival and triumph of an action series hero are neither convincing nor surprising but merely a convention of the medium. Like the theater audience that attends *The Tragedy of Hamlet*, the TV audience knows what the outcome will be before the curtain goes up. The seduction is not "What?" but "How?"

Thus far, I have limited my discussion to rather traditional ways of looking at television. However, television—as both a medium and an industry—has made a commitment to relentless technological innovation. The act of viewing cannot remain static in the face of this. The cable converter has already made the twelve-channel VHF tuner obsolete. From a comfortable vantage point anywhere in the room, the viewer can scan dozens of channels with a fingertip. From the decadent splendor of a divan, the viewer is less committed to the inertia of program choice. It is possible to watch half a dozen shows more or less simultaneously, fixing on an image for the duration of its allure, dismissing it as its force disintegrates, and returning to the scan mode. Unscheduled programming emerges as the

viewer assumes control of montage. It is also clear that program choice is expanding. The grass-roots public-access movement is still in its infancy, but the network mise-en-scène has
been at least somewhat augmented by new corporate cousins
such as the superstations and the premium services. Cheap
home recording and editing equipment may turn the television
receiver into a bottomless pit of "footage" for any artist who
dares.

Michael Smith, the Chicago-born New York grantee/come-
dian, is perhaps pointing the way in this respect. Whether
dancing with *Donnie and Marie* in front of a giant videoscreen at
the Whitney or performing rap songs at the Institute for Contemporary Art in Boston, Smith offers an unabashed display of
embarrassments and highlights in the day of a life with television. Mike (Smith's master persona) is the star of his own
videotapes (i.e., TV shows). In "It Starts at Home," Mike gets
cable and learns the true meaning of public access. In "Secret
Horror," reception is plagued by ghosts. The passive viewer—
that well-known zombie who has been blamed for every American problem from the Vietnam War to Japanese technological
hegemony—becomes do-it-yourself artist in Smith. If "interpretation is the revenge of the intellect upon art,"[55] parody is
the special revenge of the TV viewer.

Whatever the so called blue-sky technologies bring, there can
be no doubt that the enormous body of video text generated
during the decades of the Network Era will make itself felt in
whatever follows. The shows and commercials and systems of
signs and gestures that the networks have presented for the
last thirty-five years constitute the television we know how to
watch. There won't be a future without a past.

In *Popular Culture and High Culture*, Herbert Gans takes the
position that all human beings have aesthetic urges and are
receptive to symbolic expressions of their wishes and fears.[56]
As simple and obvious as Gans's assertion seems, it is the wild
card in the otherwise stacked deck of demographic culture.
Buhle and Czitrom have written:

> We believe that the population at large shares a definite history
> in modern popular culture and is, on some levels, increasingly
> aware of that history. We do not think that the masses of
> television viewers, radio listeners, movie-goers, and magazine
> readers are numbed and insensible, incapable of understanding
> their fate or historical condition until a group of "advanced
> revolutionaries" explains it to them.[57]

Evidence of this shared, definite history, in the form of self-reflexive parody, is already finding its way to the air. The television babies are beginning to make television shows. In the signatory montage that introduces SCTV each week, there is a shot of a large apartment house with dozens of televisions flying out the windows and crashing to the ground. As the viewer learns, this does not mean the end of television in Mander's sense but signifies the end of television as it has been officially experienced. SCTV is television beginning to begin again. The traditional theatrical notions of representation and presentation that have guided the development of programming genres are ground to fine dust in the crucible of a satire that draws its inspiration directly from the experience of watching television. SCTV was the first commercial network television program that absolutely demanded of its viewers a knowledge of a tradition, a self-conscious awareness of cultural history. In such a context, viewing at last becomes an active process. Without a well-developed knowledge of and sensitivity to the taxonomic framework and individual texts of the first thirty-five years of television, SCTV is meaningless—and probably not even funny. In 1953 Dwight Macdonald described "Mass Culture" as "a parasitic, a cancerous growth on High Culture."[58] By this, I take it, he meant that mass-consumed cultural items such as television programs "steal" the forms of "High Culture," reduce their complexity, and substitute infantile or worthless content. The relationship of mass culture to high culture, Macdonald tells us, "is not that of the leaf and branch but rather that of the caterpillar and leaf."[59] SCTV bears no such relationship to any so-called high culture. It is a work that emerges out of the culture of television itself, a fully realized work where history and art synthesize the conditions for a new consciousness of both. Other media—theater, film, radio, music—do not bend the show to televised renderings of their own forms but instead are forced to become television. The viewer is not pandered to with the apologetic overdefining of linear development that denies much of television its potential force. Presentation and representation merge into a seamless whole. The ersatz proscenium theater used by the networks to create marketing genres is smashed; the true montage beaming into the television home refuses to cover itself with superficial framing devices. The pseudo-Marxist supposition that SCTV is still guilty of selling the products is boring—the show is not.

I mention *SCTV* now because it is among the first tangible responses born of a critical stance of TV viewing that is more widespread than a reading of the TV critics would indicate. Television was born a bastard art of mass-marketing theory and recognizable forms of popular culture. Thirty-five years later, a generation finds this dubious pedigree its identity and heritage. The poverty of TV drama in all traditional senses is not as important as the richness of the montage in the cubist sense. For the TV-lifer, a rerun of *Leave It to Beaver* or *I Love Lucy* or *The Twilight Zone* offers the sensation of traveling through time in one's own life and cultural history. The recognizable, formulaic narrative releases the viewer from what becomes the superficial concerns of suspense and character development. The greater imaginative adventures of movement through time, space, and culture take precedence over the flimsy mimesis that seems to be the intention of the scripts. The whole fast-food smorgasbord of American culture is laid out for consumption. This is not merely kitsch. Clement Greenberg wrote that "the precondition of *kitsch* (a German term for 'Mass Culture') is the availability close at hand of a fully matured cultural tradition, whose discoveries, acquisitions, and perfected self-conscious *kitsch* can take advantage of for its own ends."[60] In fact, this process is reversed in television appreciation. The referent culture has become the mass or kitsch culture. Instead of mass-cult ripping off highcult, we have art being fashioned from the junkpile. The banal hysteria of the supermarket is capable of elegant clarity in Andy Warhol's "Campbell's Soup Can." Experience is reformed and recontextualized, reclaimed from chaos. Television offers no few opportunities in this regard.

The networks and ad agencies care little about these particulars of culture and criticism. The networks promise to deliver heads in front of sets and no more. But, as will happen in any hierarchical or "downstream" system, there is a personal space that will at least allow the subject of institutional power to maintain personal dignity. In the television demography this stance gains its sustenance from the act of recontextualization. If there is no exit from the demographic theater, each viewer will have to pull down the rafters from within. What will remote control "SOUND: OFF" buttons mean to the future of American retailing? What images are filling the imaginations of people as they "listen" to television on the TV bands of transistor radios while walking the streets of the cities wearing headphones? Why are silent TV screens playing at social gatherings? When will the average household using television (HUT) be equipped with split-screen, multichannel capability? What is interesting about a gameshow? The suspense of who will win, or the spectacle of people brought frothing to the point of hysteria at the prospect of a new microwave oven? What is interesting about a copshow? The "catharsis" of witnessing the punishment of the criminal for his misdeeds, or the attitude of the cop toward evil? What is interesting about a sitcom? The funniness of the jokes, or the underlining of the jokes on the laugh track? The plausibility of the plot, or the portrayal of a particular style of living as "normal"? What is interesting about Suzanne Somers and Erik Estrada? Their acting, or their bodies? Television is made to sell products but is used for quite different purposes by lonely, alienated people, families, marijuana smokers, born-again Christians, alcoholics, Hasidic Jews, destitute people, millionaires, jocks, shut-ins, illiterates, hang-gliding enthusiasts, intellectuals, and all of the members of the vast heterogeneous procession that continues to be American culture in spite of all demographic odds. If demography is an attack on the individual, then the resilience of the human spirit must welcome the test.

"To be a voter with the rest is not so much," Whitman warned in his *Democratic Vistas* of 1871.[61] The shopper/citizen of the demography ought to know this only too well. Whitman recognized that no political system could ever summarily grant its citizens freedom. Government is a system of power; freedom is a function of personality. "What have we here [in America]," he asked, "if not, towering above all talk and argument, the plentifully-supplied, last-needed proof of democracy, in its personalities?"[62] Television is the Rorschach test of the American personality. I hope the social psychologists will not find our responses lacking.

NOTES

1. As cited by Christopher H. Sterling and John M. Kitross, *Stay Tuned: A Concise History of American Broadcasting* (Belmont, Calif.: Wadsworth Publishing Company, 1978), p. 372. Minow coined the phrase in this passage: "I invite you to sit down in front of your television set when your station goes on the air and stay there without a book, newspaper, profit-and-loss sheet or rating book to distract you—and keep your eyes glued to that set until the station signs off. I can assure you will observe a vast wasteland."

2. *Nielsen Report on Television, 1981* (New York: A. C. Nielsen Company, 1981), pp. 3, 6.

3. Hans Magnus Enzensberger, *The Consciousness Industry* (New York: Seabury Press, 1974), p. 9.

4. Edward Shils, "Daydreams and Nightmares: Reflections on the Criticism of Mass Culture," *Sewanee Review* 65 (1957): 568–69.

5. James M. Cain, *The Postman Always Rings Twice* (1934; rpt., New York: Vintage Books, 1978), p. 96.

6. "A mass medium can only achieve its great audience by practicing . . . cultural democracy . . . by giving a majority of the people what they want"; Dr. Frank Stanton, the president of CBS, as cited by Gilbert Seldes, *The New Mass Media: Challenge to a Free Society* (Washington, D.C.: Public Affairs Press, 1968), p. 17.

7. Walter Benjamin, "The Work of Art in the Age of Mechanical Reproduction," in *Illuminations*, ed. Hannah Arendt (New York: Schocken Books, 1969), p. 218.

8. In *Skyscraper Primitives* (Middletown, Conn.: Wesleyan University Press, 1975), Dickran Tashjian writes, "While Waldo Frank's despair that America is Dada may have been exaggerated, the chaos of Dada illumines America's essential conflict with tradition and may even lend intelligibility, if not significance, to our contemporary chaos in the arts." See also Waldo Frank, "Seriousness and Dada," *1925*, 3 (1924).

9. See Marshall McLuhan, *The Gutenberg Galaxy: The Making of Typographic Man* (Toronto: University of Toronto Press, 1962), esp. pp. 255–63.

10. Sterling and Kitross, *Stay Tuned*, p. 147.

11. Robert Warshow, *The Immediate Experience* (Garden City, N.Y.: Doubleday, 1962), p. 128.

12. Dwight Macdonald, "A Theory of Mass Culture," *Diogenes*, no. 3 (1953), pp. 1–17; reprinted in *Mass Culture: The Popular Arts in America*, ed. Bernard Rosenberg and David Manning White (New York: Free Press, 1957), pp. 59–73.

13. Roland Barthes, *Mythologies*, trans. Annette Lavers (New York: Hill and Wang, 1972), p. 17.

14. Tim Brooks and Earle Marsh, *The Complete Directory to Prime Time Network TV Shows, 1946–Present*, rev. ed. (New York: Ballantine Books, 1981); see "Prime Time Schedules."

15. Barthes, *Mythologies*, p. 15.

16. David Chagall, "Reading the Viewer's Mind," *TV Guide*, Nov. 7, 1981, p. 48.

17. Barthes comments on this subject: "The public knows very well the distinction between wrestling and boxing; it knows that boxing is a Jansenist sport, based on a demonstration of excellence. . . . A boxing-match is a story which is constructed before the eyes of the spectator; in wrestling on the contrary, it is each moment which is intelligible, not the passage of time. The logical conclusion of the contest does not interest the wrestling-fan, while on the contrary a boxing-match always implies a science of the future;" *Mythologies*, pp. 15–16.

18. Jack Gladden, "Archie Bunker Meets Mr. Spoopendyke: Nineteenth Century Prototypes for Domestic Situation Comedy," *Journal of Popular Culture* 10, no. 1 (1976): 167–80.

19. A notable exception to this is the silent "Mr. and Mrs. Jones" series made by D. W. Griffith for Biograph in 1908–9. Robert Sklar describes these films as "situation comedies" in *Movie-made America*, p. 106.

20. Groups 4 and 5 are sometimes constituted as "35-49" and "49+"; in recent years, "35-55" and "55+" have been increasingly in use.
21. Daniel Cztirom, *Media and the American Mind: From Morse to McLuhan* (Chapel Hill: University of North Carolina Press, 1982), p. 190.
22. See Northrop Frye, *Anatomy of Criticism: Four Essays* (Princeton, N.J.: Princeton University Press, 1957).
23. Dorothy Rabinowitz, "Watching the Sitcoms," in *Television: The Critical View*, ed. Horace Newcomb (New York: Oxford University Press, 1979), p. 55.
24. Roger Rosenblatt, "Growing Up on Television," in Newcomb, *Television*, p. 351.
25. In 1961 Saudi Arabian State Television refused to show *I Love Lucy* on the grounds that Lucy dominated her husband. This misinterpretation of the text was later revised, and *I Love Lucy* was shown on Saudi Arabian television in the seventies. See Bart Andrews, *Lucy and Ricky and Fred and Ethel: The Story of "I Love Lucy"* (New York: Fawcett Popular Library, 1977), p. 13.
26. For a review of the changes in the image of the American woman signaled by the popularity of *The Mary Tyler Moore Show*, see Carol Traynor Williams, "It's Not So Much 'You've Come a Long Way, Baby'—As 'You're Gonna Make It after All,'" in Newcomb, *Television*, pp. 64-73.
27. R. P. Blackmur, "A Burden for Critics," in *Lectures in Criticism*, ed. Elliot Coleman (New York: Harper and Brothers, 1949), p. 189.
28. Ibid., p. 188.
29. Walt Whitman, *Democratic Vistas* (1871; rpt., London: Walter Scott, 1888), p. 83.
30. Ibid., p. 5.
31. Allen Ginsberg, "Howl," *Howl and Other Poems* (San Francisco: City Lights Books, 1956), p. 11.
32. Barthes, *Mythologies*, p. 15.
33. Alex McNeil, *Total Television: A Comprehensive Guide to Programming from 1948 to 1980* (New York: Penguin Books, 1980), p. 112.
34. Ibid.
35. "Ratings," in *TV Guide Almanac*, ed. Craig T. Norback and Peter Norback (New York: Ballantine Books, 1980), p. 546.
36. Ibid., pp. 547-48.
37. I am including neither *The Ed Sullivan Show*, which was a "straight variety" show, nor *The Jack Benny Show*, which was an eccentric self-reflexive sitcom, in the comedy-variety category.
38. Seldes, *New Mass Media*, p. 143.
39. Ibid.
40. Brooks and Marsh, *Complete Directory*, p. 496.
41. Ibid.
42. Sterling and Kitross, *Stay Tuned*, pp. 528-29.
43. Brooks and Marsh, *Complete Directory*, pp. 692-93.
44. McNeil, *Total Television*, p. 647.
45. Ibid., p. 502.
46. Cheryl Bernstein, "Performance as News: Notes on an Intermedia Guerrilla Group," in *Performance in Postmodern Culture*, ed. Michel Benamou and Charles Caramello (Madison, Wisc.: Coda Press, 1977), p. 79.
47. *The Random House College Dictionary*, 1975 ed., p. 441.
48. Gunther Anders, "The Phantom World of TV," in Rosenberg and White, *Mass Culture*, p. 365.
49. Whitman, *Democratic Vistas*, p. 33.

50. *Nielsen Report, 1981*, p. 7.
51. A concise description of Klein's "LOP Theory" is given by Les Brown, *The New York Times Encyclopedia of Television* (New York: Times Books/Quadrangle, 1977), p. 228. For an example of how Klein applies the theory himself, see Paul Klein, "Why You Watch, What You Watch, When You Watch," *TV Guide*, July 24, 1971, pp. 6–10.
52. Chagall, "Reading the Viewer's Mind," p. 48.
53. See John G. Cawelti, *Adventure, Mystery, and Romance* (Chicago: University of Chicago Press, 1976), esp. chap. 1, "The Study of Literary Formulas," pp. 5–36.
54. When I worked at NBC Television corporate headquarters in New York during 1976–77, I was shocked to learn of the kind of mail and telephone calls received by the Audience Response Department from soap opera viewers. Fans would ask for automobile directions to mythical soap opera towns. Letters were often addressed to characters, not actors, and these letters routinely offered advice concerning "decisions" the character was facing in the story line. Soap opera villains have been physically assaulted on the streets of New York and Los Angeles. For a catalog of some of these bizarre events, see David Johnson, "The Real and the Unreal," *Daytimers*, Nov. 1981, p. 17. For a more comprehensive analysis of art/life confusion among Americans, see George Gerbner and Lawrence Gross, "The Scary World of TV's Heavy Viewer," *Psychology Today*, Apr. 1976, p. 74.
55. Susan Sontag, *Against Interpretation* (New York: Delta, 1966), p. 7.
56. Herbert Gans, *Popular Culture and High Culture* (New York: Basic Books, 1975), p. 65.
57. Paul Buhle and Daniel Czitrom, Editorial, *Cultural Correspondence* 4 (1977): 1.
58. Macdonald, "Theory and Mass Culture," p. 59.
59. Ibid.
60. As cited by Macdonald, ibid., pp. 59–60.
61. Whitman, *Democratic Vistas*, p. 25.
62. Ibid., p. 23.

MURIEL CANTOR

AUDIENCE CONTROL

Whereas it is relatively simple to describe the nature of production, it is quite problematic to discuss the relationship of the audience to the production process. Not only do scholars and critics disagree on the nature of the audience, they also disagree fundamentally on the impact of the audience on the content. These disagreements are essentially the same as those critics and theorists have concerning the nature of society and human behavior. In this [essay], the discussion will be somewhat different from the preceding [sections of *Prime Time Television*]. The question being posed is: How does the audience influence content? Because the answer to the question is problematic, several important but varying perspectives on how the audience has been conceptualized will be presented. It will be shown that these varying perspectives are fundamental to how people view the audience's power in the production process. As one might surmise, some people believe the audience is very powerful, some think the audience is only moderately powerful, and some believe the audience is powerless. In addition, within each perspective there are variations and conflicts.

The first part of the [essay] will be devoted to what is being termed here the "demand" model. Adherents of this perspective believe that the market determines content. Most broadcasters, some producers, and others (such as market researchers) consider the audience very influential in determining content—in fact, the most powerful influence on content. In contrast, social scientists and other scholars are less convinced about the audience's power to determine content. At one extreme are the mass society theorists and some Marxist scholars who believe that the audience is helpless. Although

Reprinted from *Prime Time TV: Content and Control*, pp. 97–115, by Muriel Cantor, with permission of the publisher, Sage Publications, Beverly Hills and the author.

these theorists may vary when explaining the audience's lack of power, both mass society theorists and Marxists agree that demand is created by those who control the marketplace. The similarities and differences between the two approaches will be discussed in the second section of this [essay].

Mass society theorists generally believe the audience is help-less and that technology and industrialization are responsible for popular culture. Marxists and neo-Marxists, although dif-fering in several respects, have at least one commonality: they both believe that content is the result of the capitalist system. Proletariats (workers) are usually seen as passive recipients of the content, and those who control the means of production and dissemination are either consciously or unconsciously using popular culture, such as drama, as a means of social control to maintain the status quo.

In the third section of this [essay] those who hold a middle position about the influence of the audience will be discussed. Most people who present either a functional or systems analy-sis see the audience as having an indirect but active input into the creation of content. This section is labeled the sociological approach.

The material available on the audience is vast. However, most studies of the audience address questions relating to the effects of the content on viewers, the uses and gratification the content has for viewers, or descriptions of the audience. Essen-tially, this [essay] focuses on what impact the audience has on the communicators, defined as both decision-makers (such as network officials), producers and advertisers, and creators (such as writers, actors, and directors). Because there are al-most no studies addressing this question that specifically relate to television drama, the discussion often will go beyond prime-time drama and consider television, popular culture, and mass media generally. Whenever possible, however, the problems relating to the creation of television drama in particular will be examined. The study of mass media has been separated by some from the study of popular culture. Because prime-time drama is one kind of content that can be defined as both televi-sion content and a popular art form, I will draw from both traditions where relevant.

Content is produced by people who work in organizations and who are limited or enhanced by government and industrial policies. To study the impact of television it is necessary to know how the content gets on the air and how the content

changes (Comstock et al., 1978; Gans, 1974). Yet, most investigators, even those who advocate studying creators and the
decision-making process, find it difficult to include the audience
as one element of the total system. Based on a realistic assessment of the production process, the political milieu in which
television is programmed, and the size of the viewing audience
for successful shows, it is difficult to decide how to measure
"feedback" from the audience. Not only is the audience very
large for most dramatic programs (anywhere from 20,000,000
to 50,000,000 or more), but the production of television drama
takes place months before it is viewed nationally. Under these
circumstances it is difficult to conceive of how the audience
might have direct input into the creative process. Textbooks on
communications present models of how the communication
process takes place. The most simple formulation is one in
which the communication information flows in a reciprocal
fashion from the initiating source to the receiver, who in turn
becomes an initiator who sends feedback in some fashion to the
communicator (see Schramm, 1973). This model clearly works
for face-to-face communicators, but must be modified to be
applicable for television viewers. There is little opportunity for
those in front of the television sets to send simultaneous feedback to the source.[1]

The way the production of drama has been organized since
the early nineteenth century has made simultaneous feedback
difficult even when the audience is viewing a live theater production. Writers create plays which are financed by entrepreneurs. Plays are presented after many rehearsals. A theater
play, because of its costs, must be written and produced long
before an audience sits in a theater. There is some direct feedback at tryouts before the main run of a play, but changes at
that time can be only minor. Plays either succeed or fail after
they are created. Most drama produced in industrial societies is
written by those who hope the critics and paying audience will
like it. Although drama critics have exceptional power in live
theater, they, along with the paying audience, can only veto or
vote for a production. With the advent of the film, even the
tryout is almost impossible. Thus, for the film shown in the
theater there is even less opportunity for direct feedback than
there is for a live dramatic production. Hollywood films are
often premiered before they are widely distributed to the
general public. Occasionally two different endings will be tried
out before audiences to see which one has the most appeal.[2]

However, generally it is the box office where the public decides whether a film is a success or failure. Again, the audience only has veto power. For television drama, even those filmed or taped before a live audience, there are few second chances for changes in script or ideas. A pilot film storyline can be changed before it becomes an episodic series. However, because films are produced months before they are shown on the air, the only power the audience has is to turn off the sets.

THE DEMAND MODEL

Given that broadcasters and advertisers understand the reality that direct feedback is almost impossible, the question might be asked: Why do some believe the audience is the main directing force responsible for the content of drama? The answer to that question is very simple, and can be considered a tautology.

Because television is a marketing medium, it must present programs which appeal to a large number of viewers. The argument is made that television drama represents the desires of the viewers. This is justified by reiterating what the networks, the rating services, and the local broadcasters insist is true: Ratings are indices of audiences' wishes. This view of the audience is not necessarily one in which the audience is active and seeks entertainment with certain content; rather, the audience is simply a market for products. Content is seen as "mere entertainment" which is presented by an industry that is competitive, an open marketplace where those who sell the most receive the greatest rewards. What television is selling is not the drama, but the audience. The market system is made up of those who are in staff positions and make decisions about how to appeal to viewers and those on the line who are making the drama. Decisions on what to produce are based on the sales of the previous season, on the results from marketing research, and often on intuition. In the case of television drama, those making the decisions are the network officials. Those on the line try to please the networks by making shows which will attract the most viewers with the right demographic characteristics. Behind all of this is the sponsor who will keep the drama on the air if and only if the drama reaches those people who are potential buyers of the products the sponsors manufacture. The audience in this formulation is not necessarily a mass (large, heterogeneous, and anonymous to the decision makers), but rather a buying public, consumers of a certain age, sex, and income.

Martin Seiden (1974:156) contends that ratings determine content because the structure of the television industry is such that maximum rewards are obtained when the largest numbers of people with the right demographic characteristics are tuned in. The ratings from this perspective are compared with votes. The system is defended by network officials and those who obtain the ratings as being democratic. A. C. Nielsen, for instance, has said,

> After all, what is a rating? In the final analysis it is simply a counting of the votes . . . a system of determining the types of programs that the people prefer to watch or hear. Those who attack this concept of counting the votes—or the decisions made in response to the voting results are saying in effect: "Never mind what the people want. Give them something else" [quoted in Sandman et al., 1972:208].

This formulation of the audience as the most powerful influence on dramatic content is relatively simplistic. Although most investigators agree that the process being described does approximate reality, most also believe that by simply saying the audience gets what it desires leaves many questions unanswered. How does content change? How do creators know what will be popular with the audience since there is so little feedback? Why have some programs which have had a relatively small audience when first broadcast been able to build audience interest? In addition, the demand formulation treats television drama only as a business. Several producers I interviewed suggested that television dramatic production could be compared with the manufacture of automobiles. Producers, network officials, and others involved in the selection and creation operate as entrepreneurs who are dependent on consumers to approve of their product. The fact that the product they are creating is an art form is simply ignored. Under the demand formulation, the content comes from the creators who, through knowledge gained either from mystical intuition or through rational processes (such as marketing research), are simply conduits for their audiences.

Most serious analysts of culture industries are aware that the number of available goods (drama, in this case) can exceed the number that can be successfully marketed (Hirsch, 1972). Subsequent to their production, dramas are processed by a selection system described previously. The actual filtering takes place in the production companies and through the networks. Neither of these organizations is able to decide with any certainty whether a drama will succeed with the "voting" public. However, a reality of this screening and selection is that producers and network officials make decisions with the ratings in mind. The perceived likes and dislikes of some audiences operate as one basis of selection. This notion of the audience being in the heads of the creators and disseminators will be brought up again when I discuss the sociological approach to the role of the audience in the production process. In the examination of factual material about selection and creation of drama, it is obvious that other factors beyond ratings must be considered. The creators and selectors of drama often do not know what the audience might desire. That is clear after examining the number of shows which fail each season (for example, see *Newsweek*, 1979). Also there is no way to know if shows which were passed over might have been very popular.

Nonetheless, the demand model has provided the rationale for the system as it now exists. Those who fail to capture the right audience do not remain in their respective positions, and those whose shows get high ratings are very successful.[3] Writers, actors, and producers must reach the target audience to remain in production. Network officials are fired when the shows they pick are not attractive to the right audience. Thus, the selection and creation of drama within the framework of an industrial model attribute great power to the consumer.

The system as it exists may be the most efficient for reaching the audience desired, but it allows little direct input from the audience into the creative process. Critics are not defined as part of the audience. Citizen groups are seen as pressure groups who hold minority viewpoints; they are rarely considered the target audience. Although citizen and other pressure groups are sometimes placated when they become very vocal, network officials and producers define them as different from viewers. Because critics and protesters are perceived as a minority, those who produce and select content consider their protests as both limiting free speech and as antidemocratic (*TV Guide*, 1977).

The demand model has been criticized from many perspectives. The conservative critics suggest that defining the audience as those who will buy the advertisers' products limits the creativity of the creators. Moreover, television drama is seen simply as the tool of merchandisers. Most of these critics believe that all popular culture, and television drama in particular, has negative effects on the viewers. The audience, under this formulation, may like the programs, but television brainwashes and controls. This brainwashing is either in the form of alienating psychological effects (Goldsen, 1977) or false consciousness or both. Radical critics also see the content as destructive, it is a means of social control whereby the ideology of the capitalist class is communicated to maintain the status quo, to stifle criticism of capitalism, and to generate complacency in the working classes. The conservative criticism grew out of mass society theory, and the radical criticism can be considered Marxist or neo-Marxist. There are other critics of the demand formulation as well, including the social scientists, educators, and pressure groups who see the system as pluralistic and believe the content of television drama is a public issue. Essentially, they consider themselves part of the audience which is denied access. . . .

THE POWERLESS AUDIENCE

Mass Society Theory

The most frequent criticism of television entertainment comes from those who are usually called mass society theorists. This criticism has existed in some form from the onset of industrialization and has been applied to all popular cultural forms. From the inception of the penny press in the nineteenth century there has been great interest in the relationship of the creators of popular art forms and their audiences. One version of the critique of this relationship has its origins in nineteenth-century mass society theory. Mass society theory is far more complex than is being presented here, and there are variations and several modern revisions. One of the most persistent elements in mass society theory has been concern with perceived undesirable, pathological, and threatening changes associated with industrialization and the uses of technology. Mass society theorists have argued that urbanization, industrialization, and the accompanying rise of mass communications have caused traditional communities to decline in importance. Rather than the individual being tied to the family, the church, and the community, he or she is isolated, alienated, and lacking central, unifying beliefs (Kornhauser, 1959:33; Bell, 1961:75). Mass society theorists generally believe that cultural disintegration accompanies social and political disorientation. According to Bell (1961:75), the cultural values and standards of the elite no longer control the mores and values of the mass, and thus these values are in constant flux. Important social thinkers of the nineteenth and early twentieth centuries, such as Henry Maine, Auguste Comte, Herbert Spencer, Max Weber, and Emile Durkheim (see DeFleur and Ball-Rokeach, 1975:133–161), have addressed the transition from a traditional, familial society to a rationalized, industrial society. Industrial societies are characterized as complex, heterogeneous, and differentiated compared with traditional societies which are simple, homogeneous, and undifferentiated (see Bramson, 1961:31). In societies where there is increased occupational specialization (differentiation) and where the population is heterogeneous, adequate linkages between individuals and the growing centralized state do not exist. The social structure disintegrates into two components, the elite, a "qualified," creative, and selective minority; and the mass, an essentially "unqualified," unintelligent, crude mob. This mass may be literate but, because of its lack of classical education, has tastes which are low-level and unselective. In the place of high culture there develops a mass culture which destroys or displaces both high culture and the folk culture of traditional societies. This mass culture "levels the taste of the people, encourages mediocrity, conformity, passivity and escapism" (Gans, 1974:19–64).

Bell and Bramson find that mass society theory springs from the romantic idealism of nineteenth-century Europe, and much of the theory is characterized by emotional attacks on the evils of modern society. Although the theory (or theories of mass society) has been criticized extensively (Gans, 1974; Swingewood, 1977), its influence on how the audience for television is conceptualized has been substantial and, in fact, accounts for the name "mass media of communication" associated with modern, technological means of disseminating information and entertainment.

Mass society theorists have been particularly influential in the way intellectuals have reacted to popular culture and to the popular art forms disseminated by modern technology. According to intellectual critics, mass culture is considered undesirable, in that, unlike high culture, it is mass produced by profit-minded entrepreneurs solely for the gratification of the paying audience. Mass society critics contend that for a cultural industry to be profitable, it must create a low-level, sensational, standardized product. This criticism has been applied to the dime novel, to the movies, to radio, comic books, and to popular music recordings and television drama. The argument states that the commercial system, because it must appeal to mass tastes, limits the freedom of the creators to innovate and express themselves; in addition, the commercial system attracts persons of questionable skills and integrity who use the medium for personal gain at the expense of a public (mass) which is inert and nonactive. This viewpoint is elitist. Although it might be interpreted anticapitalist, it is not. Nineteenth-century critics thought the solution to the problems generated by mass culture was a return to old forms of social relationships, a clear status system with social groups in their respective places. In the period since World War II, the critics have been advocating the elimination of television or possibly more government conrol. One thing they have in common with earlier critics is that they believe a cultural elite should decide what the audience should see.

Twentieth-century critics generally see the audience as a mass of individuals whose lives are meaningless, empty, and passionless (Ellul, 1964:378). For instance, Bernard Rosenberg (1957:7–8) writes:

> Contemporary man commonly finds his life has been emptied of meaning, that it has been trivialized. He is alienated from his past, from his work, from his community. . . . It is widely assumed that the anxiety generated by modern civilization can be allayed, as nerves are narcotized by historical novels, radio or television programs and all the other ooze of our mass media.

According to Rosenberg, neither democracy nor capitalism is responsible for this condition; rather, it is technology. He says, "If one can hazard a single positive formulation, it would be that modern technology is the necessary and sufficient cause of mass culture." The argument has been continued by recent critics of television. For example, Winn (1977), in her criticism of television in the United States, says that there are many aspects of modern life beyond our control. Because people feel increasingly helpless, they depend on television as a substitute for real experience. In turn, television is destructive because the ideas, images, and symbols transmitted through the television screen govern the audience (Goldsen, 1977; Mander, 1978). Television, by the simple process of removing images from immediate experience and passing them through a machine, causes human beings to lose one of the attributes that differentiate them from objects. Jerry Mander (1978), drawing from Jacque Ellul's arguments against technology, asserts that once rid of television, our information field would instantly widen to include aspects of life which have been discarded and forgotten. Human beings would revitalize facets of experience that they have permitted to lie dormant.

> Overall, chances are excellent that human beings, once outside the cloud of television images, would be happier than they have been of late, once again living in a reality which is less artificial, less *imposed*, and more responsive to personal action [Mander, 1978; emphasis added].

Marxist Perspectives

There is not one sociology of art and communications from the Marxist position, but several. Those I have called the mass society theorists perceive weak community ties, technology, and too much leisure for the masses as a threat to culture, art, and true human experience. Unlike this cultural critique of modern industrial capitalism, the Marxists are more concerned with the fate of the potentially revolutionary working class (the proletariat) which, according to Marxist theory, should be ripe for a socialist revolution. The communication media propagate ideology which represents the interests of the capitalist, inhibiting the development of class consciousness. According to Alan Swingewood (1977), "Ideology becomes of crucial importance for the values associated with mass production and consumption of comics, pulp fiction and newspaper combine with the effects of television, cinema and radio to corrupt the proletariat."

When discussing Marxist thought about the production of mass culture and the audience, two separate but related schools of thought are usually compared: The Frankfurt school and the new left critique prevalent throughout the 1970s. The Frankfurt school developed in Germany before the rise of Hitler. Theorists such as Theodor W. Adorno, Max Horkheimer, and Herbert Marcuse, who were trying to explain how fascism was able to flourish in Germany, examined the role of media and popular culture in society. Swingewood distinguishes the Frankfurt group from other contemporary Marxists, because he thinks that the former have lost confidence in the revolutionary role of the industrial working class. For Adorno and Horkheimer in particular, the central fact of capitalist civilization was the progressive collapse of the family as an adequate socializing agent and its mediating function has been passed on to the culture industries. The audience, according to this view, becomes one-dimensional and passive (Marcuse, 1964). The Frankfurt critics are similar to the mass society critics in several respects, especially in the way they both see the media operating to fill a vacuum caused by the way work is organized in capitalist societies. Both schools of thought assert that happiness is identified with material possessions and with the psychological and social integration of the individual into the social order (Swingewood, 1977:12). The difference between the Frankfurt school and variations of mass society theory is in how each views the responsibility for the content. For example, in the *Dialectic of Enlightenment* Horkheimer and Adorno (1973) argue that

> art renounces its own autonomy and proudly takes its place among consumption goods—marketable and interchangeable like an industrial product—aesthetic barbarity become the essence of modern capitalist art, demanding from its subjects "obedience" to the social hierarchy.

Under such a formulation both the creators and the audience have few degrees of freedom. Both are subjects of the system.

The question of why the working class is not revolutionary forms the basis for all Marxist formulations on the media. Basic to the Marxist sociology of art and literature is that all knowledge and art, including mass media content, are formed in the superstructure of society and that the superstructure is conditioned by the mode of production (the economic and material base). The quote from Marx that most often provides the basic rationale for all Marxists analyses on art and media is: "The mode of production of material life conditions the social, political and intellectual life processes in general. It is not the consciousness of men that determines their being, but on the contrary their being determines their consciousness" (Marx and Engels, 1962:363). One's class perspective conditions one's individual perspective. Patricia Clarke (1978), who has summarized the Marxist position on the role of art and knowledge, contends that Marx probed into the roles played by certain ideas in terms of their utility to a certain segment of society.

Marxists and neo-Marxists criticize the content of television as basically supporting the status quo. Although these critics recognize changes in drama since 1950, they agree that the basic messages and values presented on television support the capitalist system. The content is produced either deliberately or unconsciously by those who share the ideology of those who control the means of production and dissemination. The key element is that those in direct control of the drama are also in direct control of the ideas, values, and images that appear on the screen. Thus, in capitalist societies the content of drama reflects the ideology of the capitalists, and the audience is conceptualized as powerless in the selection process of the content to be created. Many who hold this view believe that conducting audience research is irrelevant, and to understand the relationship of the audience to the content, the unit of analysis should be the industrial structures responsible for the content (Janus, 1977; Tuchman, 1974).

However, the problem for present-day critics has changed slightly from the original question raised by Marx and Engels mentioned earlier. Rather than asking why the working class has not revolted, those concerned with American television try to explain the change in content. Several have revised Antonio Gramsci's (1971) concept of hegemony. This concept incorporates the Marxist position of the relationship of the audience to content and goes beyond it. Ideological hegemony refers to an order in which a certain way of life and thought is dominant and to the ways conceptions of reality diffuse throughout all of society's institutional and private manifestations. Hegemony is established by the dominant class (capitalists) who control the means of production and dissemination and becomes so diffused and accepted that it is equated with common-sense knowledge. Hegemony is established to the extent the world view of the rulers is also the world view of the ruled.

The difference between the positions of Gramsci and Marx is somewhat subtle. Marx and those following the classic Marxist position either imply or overtly state that ideology is imposed on the working class by overt control. Gramsci's concept of ideological hegemony suggests that ideology is a shared view and thereby makes direct controls unnecessary. Both the ruling class and the ruled perceive ruling-class ideology as simply "social values" and as the natural state of existence. Raymond Williams (1977), Todd Gitlin (1979), and others address the question: If ideology is imposed as some Marxists contend, why is television drama (and other popular culture) accepted with such enthusiasm by the audience? Although they note the ambiguities in Gramsci, these researchers consider the idea of hegemony a great advance in radical thought because it calls attention to the routine structures of everyday thought, down to common sense itself. This everyday thought works to sustain class domination and tyranny (Gitlin, 1979:252; also see Andrews, 1978).

Gitlin notes that the discussion on hegemony in the literature has been abstract. Rightly, he says that hegemony becomes the answer to all questions concerning the role of ideas and change. Observing that television dramatic content has changed while the interests of the dominant class have not, Gitlin tries to explain the change from the radical perspective and addresses the same questions raised in this [essay]. He says that commercial culture packages and focuses ideology that is constantly arising both from social elites and from active social groups and movement throughout the society, as well as within media organizations and practices. Thus, he advocates an approach to studying the media and television drama similiar to the one being presented here. He suggests, as do Sallach (1974) and Tuchman (1974), that ideological processes (hegemony) should be studied by looking both to the elites and to the audience.

According to Gitlin, bourgeois ideology is not uniform and there are some conflicts within the elite class. However, the ideological core remains essentially unchallenged and unchanged in television. The commercial system is such that can absorb and domesticate conflicting definitions of reality and demands. Gitlin does not see the audience as entirely passive. However, when changes in content do come about through pressure of social groups or through other kinds of demands, these changes are cosmetic rather than basic. The basic message of prime-time television, and especially the episodic series, continues to reaffirm bourgeois liberalism because of the focus on individualism and individual solutions to social problems.

The new criticism is somewhat different from the criticism of the Frankfurt school. The Frankfurt criticism was very close to mass society theory suggesting a passive and manipulative audience. The audience is "one dimensional" and the presentation of fantasy through a mechanical device provides the mechanisms for escape rather than action from the masses. In both mass society theory and the Frankfurt school, the audience is unimportant and simply inoculated with the content. The new left critics, possibly because of their own activism, suggest a more active role for the audience. Capitalists are motivated to maintain the audience as con umers and must recognize changes in the economic and material roles of the audience. Rather than negating the notion of demand, the radical view extends and reformulates it. It argues that content changes to reflect changes in social and material relations, but not in ways that would encourage revolutionary change. Rather, the content adapts in ways which continue to encourage consumerism to maintain capitalist control. Several of the new left critics explain this adaptation by showing how responsive corporate interests are to changes in consumer ideology. For example, Norene Janus (1977), in her criticism of traditional methodologies that have been used for studying both content and control, notes that the images of women on television have changed in the 1970s. She explains why this change has occurred:

> There have been major changes in the lives of women at both the level of production and ideology and that the material basis for women's oppression is rapidly shifting from the family to wage labor. At the ideological level, women have developed a sense of their own oppression and increasingly resist performing the traditional roles. Corporations, no longer able to ignore these changes in women's lives, have adapted their policies to changing times; the drive for profit has taken a different form in many cases.

In her analysis, Janus sees the profit motive as the single determinant of content. Thus, to sell to women, corporate interests must respond to changes in women's position in society. This formulation differs from the demand model presented earlier in the [essay] in one important respect: Women viewers are not getting the content they necessarily want, but the content is determined by others who try to keep women as consumers.

THE SOCIOLOGICAL PERSPECTIVE

Although few social scientists have considered the relationship of the audience to the content, those who have usually approach the subject from a social organizational perspective. Many researchers assume that the nature and significance of communications and popular art forms are determined in large part by the expectations of the communicators and the audience, which tend to be reciprocally related. Others consider economic forces and organizational strategies and present models where the audience and creators are part of the same system (see DiMaggio, 1977; Hirsch, 1978a; Lewis, 1978, for a review). In both cases the creators and audience are examined within an industry or for a particular kind of communication or art form. These analysts criticize both the radical approach and the mass society approach because they believe the core characteristics of any art form can be seen as attributes of the way the art is created, distributed, and marketed (see Gans, 1974; DiMaggio, 1977; Peterson, 1976). Although social scientists see similarities among the various forms of popular arts, they are essentially looking for differences.

Basic to the social organization perspective is the assumption that all creators are communicating to some audience. It is suggested that "writers, broadcasters and political speakers all select what they are going to say in terms of their *beliefs* about the audience" (Riley and Riley, 1959, emphasis added). Ithiel de Sola Pool and Irwin Shulman (1964) claim that the "audience, or at least those audiences about whom the communicator thinks, play more than a passive role in communications." Raymond Bauer (1958) goes one step further, claiming that the audience has much more control over what is communicated, since it is the audience that selects what to read, listen to, or watch. Essentially, Bauer views communication as a transactional process in which both the audience and communicator take important initiatives. Herbert Gans (1957) also has argued that there is active, although indirect, interaction between the audience and the creator and that both affect the final product. Both Gans and Bauer have claimed that their "general feedback hypothesis" is quite different from the theoretical approach that sees the audience as passively receiving what the communicators provide. One problem with this view of the interaction between communicators and audience is that it is difficult to test. It is not known whether feedback as defined by Gans and the Rileys has any effect at all on communicators. They define feedback as information about the outcome of previous messages which changes the definition somewhat from the one presented earlier. Using their definition, feedback does exist as already explained. The ratings and other kinds of audience surveys provide measures for audience preferences and the number of people viewing shows. Both Gans and the Rileys agree that this kind of feedback is indirect, but seem to disagree on whether it is active, as Gans believes, or "obscure and scant" as the Rileys suggest. However, all agree that the impact of information about audience preferences and viewing on the communicator rarely has been scrutinized systematically. Although they wrote over a decade ago, the above statement is still true.

Some explain the content as representing the demands of the audience; others apply a more sociological feedback hypothesis. The differences between these two approaches are qualitatively different. In the *Hollywood TV Producer* (Cantor, 1971), I have taken the position that writers and producers are creating for an audience, but that audience is not necessarily the ultimate audience. Rather, the shows are created for an audience composed of network officials, producers, other gatekeepers, as well as for the writers and producers themselves. Thus, those who write stories and produce the films primarily consider what the buyers and distributors want. This means, of course, that they are very much influenced by ratings and the demographics when they create television drama. Because network officials and others conceptualize their audiences primarily by age, sex, and income, so do the writers and producers. If the target audience was people with certain political or religious beliefs, the content of drama might be quite different. Under this formulation, changes in content come when advertisers and other financial supporters of drama want to reach different target audiences. Joseph Turow (1978) has suggested that when communicators think of their audiences they do so in terms of the rewards they might receive. They construct an audience in their heads which reflects organizational necessities. This description of the relationship of the audience and the communicator is similar to the one I presented in my study of producers. To work in television, writers and producers, unless very well known or successful, must conform to the norms and policies of the industry. Those writers, producers, and other creators acknowledge the conflicts that arise because they know the audience they must ultimately please may be different from the audience they would like to please.

Herbert Gans (1974) and I agree that creators of popular arts would like to impose their tastes and values on the audience. Gans conducted interviews with writers of popular television drama and found that the writers asserted they were always trying to insert their own values into their writing, particularly to make a moral or didactic point. If and when producers objected, the end result was a compromise. Anne Peters and I found the same was true for the on-the-line producers and those actors with some power in the production process. Gans argues, and I agree, that the one major reason for the conflicts that arise between creators and decision makers is because of the class and educational differences between popular culture creators and their audiences.

This conflict manifests itself in several ways: writers conflict with producers and the producers conflict with the production company and the networks over immediate content decisions for a particular show; and some writers, actors, and on-the-line producers have a more basic conflict with the networks concerning who should be the audience. In the first instance minor disagreements over content end in compromise, and major disagreements end with the writer or producer being forced out of the industry. The second kind of conflict is more fundamental but less influential. Several producers and actors have suggested that the networks are losing a potential audience because television drama is too simplistic. If the goal were to reach a different segment of the audience, television series and other drama as well would be different. However, they know that they do not have the power to redefine the audience.

All of the above provides a justification for understanding the system of how drama is created. Rather than simply discussing television or popular culture, system analysis or organizational set analysis has the advantage of discussing each culture industry. Those studies of other cultural production point out common areas in creating popular art forms, as well as the differences between various kinds of culture. The creation of popular drama is similar to the creation of phonograph records, novels, and theater movies: All are high-risk businesses. On the one hand there is a demand for new and possibly innovative drama each season, and on the other hand there is difficulty having new ideas accepted by decision makers. The networks and the sponsors are unable to predict with certainty what the audience will prefer each season. Most decisions seem to rest on a combination of the previous record of success of the production company and the actors involved when selecting a new show. The critics, pressure groups, and others, along with the target audience (the market), are considered as well. Two questions are usually asked: What would a certain group (or groups) do if a program is aired? Will the target audience watch the show? Thus, programs are selected not only to please the target audience, but also to avoid offending powerful pressure groups.

Throughout this [essay] the use of the term "audience" has been abstract. The ultimate audience is composed of those people who watch television drama. However, there are other audiences as well. Critics and pressure groups, network officials, advertisers, and others are important audiences. Thus, the audience for each program on the air may be different from the audience in the heads of the creators. Both radical critics and those who take a social organizational approach to studying the mass communication process and the creation of content have suggested that to understand the influence of the audience on content more complex and different approaches are necessary. To understand the role of the audience, several radical critics have suggested the audience should be studied through ethnography and phenomenology (Gitlin 1979; Sallach 1974). Charles R. Wright (1975), who is often cited as presenting the dominant paradigm, makes a similar suggestion. He asks: What are the folkways, mores, and laws that determine who should be members of a particular audience? How should they behave while playing the role of audience, and what are their rights and obligations in relation to others in the audience, to the performers, and to members of the society not in the audience?

CONCLUSION

. . . In this [essay] the question is raised of whether creators and decision makers are expressing their own values or those of their audiences. It has been argued that producers, writers, and perhaps actors as well are of a different social class from the target audience for television drama. Not only are their values different, but they are better educated, possibly more liberal, and claim to be more "high brow" than the viewers of television drama (Cantor, 1971:164–187).

The creators have few degrees of freedom if they wish to stay in the business; and the ultimate audience, too, is limited to what is presented, simply having veto power. Also, certain publics are clearly being denied programs they might want to view through commercial television. Martin Mayer (1979) has argued that television drama in the seventies was the result of how the audience is defined. Moreover, he suggests that if pay television which mostly presents movies and drama, eventually is utilized by one-half the audience, those who do not subscribe will be offered limited dramatic fare. Although the demand formulation only answers part of the question about control of prime-time television, it does provide one justification for the drama as it is. Others believe that it is not the audience, not the creators, but rather the networks followed by the sponsors and the affiliates which control television. However, regardless of how control is perceived, the content is clearly the result of continuing struggles and conflicts, not simply demand (Cantor, 1979a, 1979b). Although television drama would no doubt be different if it were not for the capitalist system as it has evolved in the United States, it must be recognized that the drama has a long tradition in western society. It not only changes, but also remains the same. And as Todd Gitlin has noted, tastes are not entirely manufactured. That the audience accepts the system as it is exists and that drama continues to be profitable cannot be denied. Although the critics, some social scientists, pressure groups, and others define television drama as a public issue, the majority audience for drama remains silent, only turning the dial when programs are no longer appealing.

The question of whether the audience is being manipulated or harmed politically or psychologically cannot be answered by the kind of analysis presented here. There is no question that popular drama provides entertainment, possibly escape, and enjoyment for millions of people in the United States and abroad. Also, it is clear that, regardless of one's opinion that the audience is manipulated, helpless, or very powerful, the industrial structures define the audience and in turn the audience has the power to accept or reject the product.

NOTES

1. Most presentations of how feedback occurs are focused on the communicators (sources) and not necessarily on the receivers. Later in the [essay] the concept of feedback will be discussed in more detail as it applies to television viewers.
2. A recent example of a movie which was previewed with two different endings before separate audiences is *Apocalypse Now*. In the heyday of Hollywood during the 1930s and 1940s, it was common practice to try out various endings before a film was released.

3. Fred Silverman, presently head of NBC television, has received much public attention for his success when he was in a similar position at ABC. He is considered to be responsible for ABC's position among the three networks. ABC for many years received the lowest ratings for its shows. After Silverman headed the network and was responsible for program selection, ABC became the top network.

REFERENCES

Andrews, B. W. (1978) *Fiction in the Unites States: An Ideological Medium Supporting Capitalism?* M.A. thesis, Department of Sociology, American University, Washington, D.C. (unpublished).

Bauer, R. (1958) "The communicator and the audience." *Conflict Resolution* 2:66–78.

Bell, D. (1961) *The End of Ideology.* New York: Collier Books.

Bramson, L. (1961) *The Political Context of Sociology.* Princeton: Princeton University Press.

Cantor, M. G. (1979a) "Our days and our nights on TV." *Journal of Communication* 29 (Autumn):66–72.

———. (1979b) "The politics of popular drama." *Communication Research* 6 (October):387–406.

———. (1971) *The Hollywood Television Producer: His Work and His Audience.* New York: Basic Books.

Clarke, P. (1978) "The sociology of literature: an historical introduction," pp. 237–258 in R. A. Jones (ed.) *Research in Sociology of Knowledge*, Sciences and Art, Vol. 1. Greenwich, CT: JAI Press.

Comstock, G., S. Chaffee, N. Katzman, M. McCombs, and D. Roberts (1978) *Television and Human Behavior.* New York: Columbia University Press.

DeFleur, M. L. and S. Ball-Rokeach (1975) *Theories of Mass Communication.* New York: David McCay.

de Sola Pool, I. and I. Shulman (1964) "Newsmen's fantasies, audiences, and newswriting," pp. 141–159 in L. A. Dexter and D. M. White (eds.) *People, Society, and Mass Communications.* New York: Free Press.

DiMaggio, P. (1977) "Market structure, the creative process, and popular culture: toward an organizational reinterpretation of mass culture theory." *Journal of Popular Culture* 11:436–467.

Ellul, J. (1964) *The Technological Society.* New York: Vintage Books.

Gans, H. (1974) *Popular Culture and High Culture.* New York: Basic Books.

———. (1957) "The creator-audience relationship in the mass media: an analysis of movie making," pp. 315–234 in B. Rosenberg and D. White (eds.) *Mass Culture: The Popular Arts in America.* New York: Free Press.

Gitlin, T. (1979) "Prime-time ideology: the hegemonic process in television entertainment." *Social Problems* 26 (February):251–266.

Goldsen, R. K. (1977) *The Show and Tell Machine: How Television Works and Works You Over.* New York: Dial Press.

Gramsci, A. (1971) *Selections from the Prison Notebooks* (ed. and trans. by Q. Hoare and G. N. Smith; written between 1929 and 1935). New York: International Publishers.

Hirsch, P. M. (1978a) "Occupational, organizational, and institutional models in mass media research," pp. 13–42 in P. Hirsch, P. Miller, and F. G. Kline (eds.) *Strategies for Mass Communication Research*. Beverly Hills: Sage.

———. (1972) "Processing fads and fashions: an organizational set analysis of culture industry systems." *American Journal of Sociology* 77 (January):639–659.

Horkheimer, M. and T. W. Adorno (1972) *Dialectic of Enlightenment*. New York: Herder and Herder.

Janus, N. (1977) "Research on sex-roles in the mass media: toward a critical approach." *The Insurgent Sociologist* 7 (Summer):19–32.

Kornhauser, W. (1959) *The Politics of Mass Society*. New York: Free Press.

Lewis, G. H. (1978) *The Sociology of Popular Culture*. *Current Sociology* 26 (Winter).

Mander, J. (1978) *Four Arguments for the Elimination of Television*. New York: Morrow Quill.

Marcuse, H. (1964) *One Dimensional Man: Studies in the Ideology of Advanced Industrial Society*. Boston: Beacon.

Marx, K. and F. Engels (1962) *Selected Works, Vol. 1*. Moscow: Foreign Languages Publishing House.

Mayer, M. (1979) "Summing up the seventies—television." *American Film* 3 (December):27, 53–55.

Newsweek (1979) "Producers in revolt." December 10:126–129.

Peterson, R. A. (1976) "The production of culture: a prologomenon." *American Behavioral Scientist* 19:669–685.

Riley, J. and M. Riley (1959) "Mass communication and the social system," pp. 537–578 in R. K. Merton, L. Broom, and L. S. Cottrell, Jr. (eds.) *Sociology Today*. New York: Basic Books.

Rosenberg, B. (1957) "Mass culture in America," pp. 3–11 in B. Rosenberg and D. M. White (eds.) *Mass Culture: The Popular Arts in America*. New York: Free Press.

Sallach, D. L. (1974) "Class domination and ideological hegemony," pp. 161–173 in G. Tuchman (ed.) *The TV Establishment*. Englewood Cliffs, N.J.: Prentice-Hall.

Sandman, P. M., D. M. Rubin, and D. B. Sachsman (1972) *Media*. Englewood Cliffs, N.J.: Prentice-Hall.

Schramm, W. (1973) *Men, Messages and Media: A Look at Human Communications*. New York: Harper and Row.

Seiden, M. H. (1974) *Who Controls the Mass Media? Popular Myths and Economic Realities*. New York: Basic Books.

Swingewood, A. (1977) *The Myth of Mass Culture*. London: McMillan.

Tuchman, G. (1974) "Introduction," pp. 1–40 in G. Tuchman (ed.) *The TV Establishment*. Englewood Cliffs, N.J.: Prentice-Hall.

Turow, J. (1978) "Personal correspondence." January 28.

TV Guide (1977) "Sex and violence: Hollywood fights back." August 27:4–18.

Williams, R. (1977) *Marxism and Literature*. Oxford, England: Oxford University Press.

Winn, M. (1977) *The Plug In Drug*. New York: Viking.

Wright, C. R. (1975) *Mass Communications: A Sociological Perspective*. New York: Random House.

WAYNE C. BOOTH

THE COMPANY WE KEEP: SELF-MAKING IN IMAGINATIVE ART, OLD AND NEW

A voice comes to one in the dark. Imagine.—Samuel Beckett, *Company*

How will literature survive the development of other media of communication? . . . The day when the Book ceases to be the principal vehicle of knowledge, will not literature have changed its meaning once again? Perhaps we are quite simply living through the last days of the Book.—Gérard Genette, "Structuralism and Literary Criticism"

It really is of importance, not only what men do, but also what manner of men they are that do it.—John Stuart Mill, *On Liberty*

THE MANY IMAGINATIVE WORLDS WE LIVE IN

When I was four or five years old, a salesman came to our door and somehow managed to talk my father into buying a set of books he could not afford: *My Book House*. Memory says that we shelved many volumes, perhaps ten or twelve—certainly it seemed to me that there were more than any human being could ever exhaust. All these wonderfully gilded books (I have recently discovered that there were only six), and all for creatures like me! The ones on the right were for little children; the ones on the left were for "when you get older and learn to read."

They were all profusely illustrated, in a style that I now suppose was vaguely Pre-Raphaelite. Splendid knights, on marvelous steeds with flaring nostrils, battled with ugly, but ob-

---

Reprinted from *Daedalus*, Vol. 111, No. 4, Fall 1982, by permission of the publisher. Copyright © 1982.

viously vulnerable, dragons, to rescue sinewy princesses. The princesses quickly became confused in my mind with various "girls of my dreams," creatures of an imagination set on fire by various popular songs then current. We did not hear those songs on any radio; there was no radio in our home in the twenties. The same mother who read to me from the books bought the sheet music and sang them to us, to her own accompaniment on the piano.

"Art," you see, was already doing its work, creating a kind of culture of the imagination. But it was a highly commercial kind, obviously, most of its work done by salesmen moving door-to-door in the pursuit of profit, culture be damned. And here I am, more than half a century later, able to remember more about the set of illustrated books and those popular songs than I can about anything my parents said or did at the time—except, of course, for negative moments when punishment was vigorous. I can remember making up songs of my own, no doubt borrowed from favorites like "Hello, Central, Give Me Heaven," "You Can't Holler Down My Rain Barrel," and one about the ancient story of a sweet little "babe in the woods" who lay down and died, with her brother.

I asked my mother, in a burst of creative egotism, why nobody ever learned to sing *my* songs, since after all I was more than willing to learn *theirs*. I can't remember her answer, and I can barely remember snatches of two of "my" songs. But I can remember dozens of theirs, and when I sing them, even now, I sometimes feel again the emotions, and see the images, that they aroused then. Thus who I am now—the very shape of my soul—was to a surprising degree molded by the works of "art" that came my way.

I set "art" in quotation marks, because much that I experienced in those early books and songs would not be classed as art according to most definitions. But for the purposes of appraising the effects of "art" on "life" or "culture," and especially for the purposes of thinking about the effects of the "media," we surely must include every kind of artificial experience that we provide for one another. What better word have we than "art" to cover every piece of imitation-life, every experience invented for the sake of supplementing or counteracting or criticizing or evading or enhancing "life"?

In this sense of the word, all of us are from the earliest years fed a steady diet of art, and the quality of our lives at any given moment will, to a surprising degree—some these days would

say to an appalling degree—depend on the quality of what we
ingest. But the metaphor of nourishment is misleading; it suggests that we are talking about health as some future value,
judging food (or poison) only as it might be tested empirically
by some medical team ten minutes or ten years later. When we
talk in that way about the future effects of art, and especially
about what print and video culture are likely to do to us, we
disregard the qualities met in the moment of eating, the quality
of the meal itself, and of what might be called the aftertaste,
the quality of the mind that is full of *this* kind of melody or verse
rather than *that* kind.

Was I enjoying a good childhood, as I listened or read, sang
"real" songs or imagined others? I would sit and dream of those
Pre-Raphaelite lords and ladies, sit quietly for hours, singing
my songs, dreaming of "my" adventures. I would charge up
glass mountains, tiptoe into the chambers of sleeping maidens,
their seductive forms—oh, yes!—chastely concealed under
"counterpanes" with flowery patterns, like those that illustrated *A Child's Garden of Verses*. Soon I was making my own
variations, transforming in imagination characters from my
daily round. I found to my delight that, by a simple decision to
daydream, I could rescue my current love, Virginia Shelley,
from a cloudburst; reaching down from my seat upon my
charger, I would touch her hand and we would at once float up
a kind of dry funnel in what was otherwise a terrifying thun-
derstorm. Out over the threatened streets we flew, just like the
magical people in the books, together at last, untouched by the
rain, unafraid of the thunder, marveled at by the soggy crowds
of weaklings who looked up at us from below.

By then I was able to read some of the stories in *My Book House*
on my own. I read them again and again—though some were
already almost memorized. I thumbed them forwards and backwards. I chanted them aloud, sitting and dreaming over one
page for as long as my dreams required. And sometimes, with
lots of time on my hands, I would just ramble from the middle
of one story to the next, wondering what would happen if
Cinderella got lost in "Puss in Boots."

All Americans of my generation will be able to summon their
own memories to dramatize how different our childhood experience was from that of children reared in later years on radio,
on movies, on television. During my hours of dreaming, in the
1920s, nobody from outside my own head ever imposed a
flashing series of scene changes on my "screen." Until I had my

first radiant "video" experience (not what people now generally call video, but the movie *Ramona*, when I was perhaps eight or nine), I experienced no work of "art" one tenth as exciting, visually, as *Sesame Street* or even the next commercial you will see on the screen. Compared with almost every child in America today, I had a mind that was sluggish and impoverished, awkward in its inferences from visual signs, uninformed about the possibilities for excitement in the world.

Sluggish, uninformed, impoverished. Or was it reflective, independent, uncluttered, tranquil? We are quickly tempted into heavy judgments in these matters, even when we attempt pure description. I must move, before I am done here, to some overt evaluating, but the truth is that we have no established ways of talking about the relative value, as nourishment for a growing child or fading adult, of the various foods offered us in the 1920s or 1980s. Before we explore any such language, it will be better to step tentatively into some more raw description.

On a recent vacation, my wife and I and two freinds talked a good deal about two movies of 1981, *Reds* and *My Dinner with André*. We also followed a daily schedule of reading a given short story, each of us privately, and then discussing it later in the day. Our third activity, during those aggressively cultural ten days, was reading aloud for an hour or so from *Ulysses*, and discussing as we read.

Our only plan had been to "do some reading aloud together, and maybe discuss a story or two." But by the time we were done, we had accumulated a complicated variety of experiences with art, none of them quite like those of my childhood.

There were, most obviously, three experiences that might be called direct or primary: the moments spent in direct contact with the work. With the movies, that had of course been a one-time affair, already for some weeks fading in memory. With the short stories, it was time spent alone, transforming words into images and events; but that primary experience was extended by the secondary experience of discussion, checking memory and refining first impressions. With *Ulysses*, a work that all of us had previously read, or read at, the primary experience was communal and complex. For the most part, it was inextricably combined with secondary artistic experience: analysis, debate, and reflection were intertwined with the reading. But there were also moments that were almost as unmediated by reflection as the most direct and engrossed moments had been when Beatty/Reed faced down the commissars.

About all of the works, then, we engaged in a kind of reflection and debate that had never disturbed my childhood reading. But discussion of the movies was seriously hampered by our fading memories. Reading and rereading the printed stories, alive there before us, we could let them grow under our hands. Thus there was a fundamental contrast between works that were still somehow in process as we discussed and works that offered us only a closed memory of direct experience. The two movies led to discussions that were generally the most animated. Nobody actually struck anyone in anger, as people are said to do about some TV characters, but it was clear that, despite our lifetime commitments to literature, we were more passionately committed to our opinions about those two average movies, weeks after viewing them, than to our contrasting views about *Ulysses* or the short stories we had before us. Two of us "liked" *Reds* much more than did the other two; two of us disliked *My Dinner with André* intensely, while the other two thought it a valuable experiment. "Wonderful that Malle should attempt such a *daring* violation of what makes a 'good movie.'" Because we were free, like my younger self, to "waste" whatever time we pleased, we could talk indefinitely about our reasons for liking or disliking. We agreed that Beatty didn't know how to combine the political and romantic lines of *Reds*; we disagreed about whether André was a pretentious bore or a fascinating, though troubled, pioneer of the spirit. We disagreed about whether anyone responsible had recognized just how superficial and cliché-ridden was the conversation between André and Wally.

But with all our leisure, we soon began to run out of topics derived from memory of the movies themselves, and we might have ground to a halt if we had depended on *their* motive power. The primary experience, after all, was further and further in the past. Even if we had been able to locate another showing somewhere, we could never really "consult the text," though we were aware that certain fortunate students of film have the equipment needed to do so. Again and again some one of us would mention details that the others had overlooked, but there was no way to verify any memory. "Well, I guess I'll just have to see it again," or "I don't *want* to see it again. All I want to see is whether, as you claim, the camera was making that ironic point against André."

With all our variety, there was one experience we did *not* have, sixty miles from the nearest television or movie theatre, and with no radio, newspaper, or magazines available: a one-time encounter, with no chance to look again at details, and with little chance for discussion or private reflection—that is to say, the most frequent artistic experience in America today. Television programming, the art that is shared more widely than any other, assumes that whatever critical thought occurs will be itself broadcast: an occasional critic on the "Today Show" telling us what to think, in language cleverer than we ourselves could manage; an occasional talk show about "issues" reduced for quick consumption. Any such intrusion of a reflective voice is followed quickly by a fresh visual sensation: primary experience of a kind so immediate as almost to be called un*media*ted. Whatever one may think about that kind of uncomplicated primacy, we knew none of it as we read and talked.

WHAT DIFFERENCE DOES IT MAKE?

The usual way of taking the media seriously is to talk about their consequences—most often, for the growth of children. We are flooded both with indictments of sex and violence on television, and with replies that either deny the adequacy of the evidence of bad consequences or that see television as only a symptom, not a cause. Such debate is not necessarily pointless. If we can finally prove that children who watch a great deal of television have indeed been maimed, then it is possible—remotely possible—that we may find ways of controlling the medium without sacrificing essential freedoms for all concerned. But studies of consequences suffer from the defects that plague all empirical studies of cause and effect in human behavior: they seem never to be decisive, nor can investigators agree on how to conduct them or on how to evaluate even the most decisive results once they are in. If a given number of children are more violent after watching a given number of programs, how are we to prove that getting their natural violence out of their systems is not a good thing, a kind of vaccination while they are so young that they can't do a lot of harm? If we then turn, in a kind of desperation, to longitudinal studies, we must wait for ten or twenty years to decide whether to act—and meanwhile, the harm, if any, continues to be perpetrated.[1]

But the most serious limitation of consequence talk is that it tells us nothing about the quality of the lives lived *during* a given artistic experience. It is one thing to show that an experience changes people's behavior; it is quite another thing, obviously more important even though more difficult, to show that an experience is desirable or undesirable in itself *as* experience.

Though the distinction tends to get lost in our future-oriented society,[2] we all recognize it when we are thinking, not about other people's development, but about what is for *us* worth doing. Nobody can believe that all ways of "spending time" have equal value. Indeed, it is a constant assumption of our society—of our advertising, of our book reviews and criticism of the arts, of our easy talk about the difference between good spectator sports and bad, good and lousy baseball games, good and bad days—that some hours justify or enhance life, others poison it. And today, as in the past, people talk about our various forms of "art" as more or less adequate ways of providing a "good time." Only when we set out to prove something about good or bad effects do we forget our assumption that, *regardless* of consequences, some moments spent with books and plays and television and movies are worth living, while others leave us wondering whether the best for man is never to be born.

What kind of "good time" was I leading during my days with fairy stories and folk tales? What is the quality of my life during my three hours and forty minutes attending the movie *Reds*, or my occasional half-hour with Johnny Carson, or my three hours with Agatha Christie's *Curtains*, or the weeks of life spent reading and rereading Jane Austen's *Emma*? If anything is obvious about each of us, it is that we are very different persons depending on the art we are living with or in. The lives we live *in the moment* of the living are more or less defensible according to whether the worlds we live in prove to be habitable. Difficult as talk about such matters is, surely nothing could be more important than keeping alive the great critical traditions of describing and appraising the quality of experience made possible by different works and different kinds of work. Let others measure consequences, then, as we consider for a while here the quality of induced life that is enjoyed as we surrender to the different media. We can return, in the last two sections of this essay, to talk about consequences in a way that will be somewhat different from asking whether, in a world in which everybody is already violent in one degree or another, more children bop each other after watching a given kind of television.

We have already begun on our task, merely by trying to describe a variety of experiences with different media. Suppose we push farther into this immensely threatening terrain (acknowledging from the beginning that we will overgeneralize), and ask four neglected questions—neglected in talk about *these* matters, though of course we refer to them a good deal in other contexts: *Where* are we—that is, what kind of world or space do we inhabit, as we experience a given medium? *Who* are we, as we read or listen or look? *Who* dwells there *with* us? And— moving slightly in the direction of future consequences again— *what* do we desire, what do we hope for, in the imagined world we have entered?

WHERE DO WE LIVE OUR IMAGINATIVE LIVES?[3]

To describe where we are might seem an easy task: we are placed into this or that locale—the Bronx, a space station on Aldebaran, a battlefield outside the walls of Troy, an eighteenth-century drawing room, the riot-filled streets of the Left Bank in 1968, the ruins of Beirut in 1982, a TV newsroom with weather maps on the walls. But difficulties arise as soon as we distinguish the incidental results of a particular program schedule or library shelf from what is essential to the medium. Our questions then become: Where are we *always* when watching television or a movie? Where are we *always* when reading a story? If we can answer such general questions, we shall be on our way to locating who we are made to be, since where we live is part of the definition of who we are.

Like all of our questions, this one is ambiguous and difficult. Suppose we take it as asking *where the action takes place*. With all of our immense critical outpouring about the various media, I can find hardly anything about this question put in the form that makes it interesting. And of course we find no experimental data to aid us: "mental experiments" of the kind this piece is built on are for now all we have.[4]

Perhaps it is different for those whose first imaginative experience was with video and not with Grimm, but for me, the action of all TV drama takes place somehow in a physical location behind, or in some sense *in*, the set. At the movies, the action takes place "back there" or "out there," sometimes even out there in Hollywood if I become slightly disengaged: I "see" a set, not a scene. In every case, even when most fully lost in the action, I am somehow outside of it, not responsible for it. It is true that I more easily and uncritically lose all awareness of the "real" world when watching a movie than when reading a book or watching a play on the stage. (I have heard it said that people brought up on legitimate theater "lose" themselves at a play more than at the movies, but it's hard for me to believe it.) And yet I am by no means as close to any screened action as I am to those actions that occur in my head as I read. The set and the screen are themselves always *located*, with the action taking place on the other side of it. In this sense, all of the screened actions occur *in the same place*, and they occur in total independence of anything I do.

This fixity of location, and the pace of events within a location, are especially striking when, watching television, I discover that the family and I can circle the set, leave it, tune it out, come back to it, talk to each other over it—and the action carries on, indifferent to us. When we come back, the events in that fixed scene (regardless of whether the imagined "country" is a spaceship or the servants' quarters in an English mansion) have continued inexorably in our absence (unless of course, it was commercial-time, and then it is the commercials that have ignored our absence). Nothing that might have happened to me in the interval could make the slightest difference. The weekly newspaper columns summarizing "What Happened on the Soaps"[5] testify to the radical independence of the box from our own activity; "they" carry on their restless lives, such as they are, hastening toward their predictable doom (death for the minor characters, and for the others, not death, but lowered ratings and final withdrawal), whether I attend or not.

Printed stories are not like that. Though it may sometimes seem that the general outlines of their plots are fixed for all time, in fact they depend on me. Most obviously, the book I read is not itself the physical location of anything that occurs "in" it. The action takes place in a country somehow in my head, yet freed to occur in a space *not* in my head, let alone confined to some box or screen. *I* make the streets, the buildings, the people, the clothing, in a space that is in my head yet is larger than any "set" could ever be. If I get up from my chair and move to the kitchen for a sandwich, that "country" goes with me. In one sense, the action stops until I continue my creative work, yet in another sense, the world "in there" goes on shifting and changing as I munch. The action is, in other words, internal, mine in a way that is not true of the action on, or in, a screen.

No controlled study will ever show whether the effects of this difference are good or bad, but there can be no question about their being immense and complicated. No doubt the very fixities that from my present viewpoint seem troublesome will prove to have values of a kind that now escape me. Anticipating the questions, Who dwells there with us, who addresses us? we might even speculate about the valuable comfort we all find—a comfort not to be found from the fluid narratives of print culture—from knowing that all those TV people, obviously in some sense alive and kicking, are out there going about their incredibly eventful lives, regardless of whether I attend. *Those lives carry on, no matter what happens to me today; I am not responsible there*, and the holiday from life they give me is what keeps me going. In their fixities is my peace. Perhaps we have here a new form of religious solace—not an eternal world to look forward to, but at least a world that will prove to be indestructible for my own time, and thus in a way timeless. It may even be that a steady diet of such reassurance will, for people living *fully* in our time, provide a necessary base for enduring the daily flux, while a steady diet of printed narratives, consumed in private and with a strong sense of personal responsibility, will produce either self-pitying introverts, suffering in elitist isolation from the crowd, or nervous ineffectual worrywarts, miserable about not solving the shifting, ambiguous problems that printed narratives often evoke.

But I am getting ahead of my story. Hard as it is to evaluate the differences, there can be no doubt that they are great. Regardless of what dwelling in the two locations leads me to *become*, I am obviously living a totally different kind of life as I take in or recreate these narratives *now*. And one can hardly make that kind of statement without at the same time worrying about consequences—again to leap ahead a bit—consequences of a kind far more profound than will result from this or that content of any narrative. Our society is in fact conducting, with the new media as with many other technological developments, an *uncontrolled* experiment of vast proportions, the results of which we will never fully know. After all, we experimenters who might evaluate the results are shifting our natures daily, as our imaginations are schooled to work *this* way rather than *that*. Our way of appraising the results will be itself determined by those results: another reason for speculating about qualities now, without waiting for social scientists to get their act together.

WHO ARE WE?

Tourists/Sojourners/Naturalized Citizens

I have already suggested that we have less opportunity to dwell for long with the movies and TV dramas we enjoy than with narratives in print. It is true that, by taking special effort, the studiously inclined can now turn video tapes into a kind of book, "thumbing the pages," reflecting on forms, discovering ever more profound themes. But by and large, a video drama, like traditional stage drama, expects us to pass the way only once, or at most to visit by chance once again at some future time.

As tourists, viewing everything from a distance as it happens "out there," we are of course not expected to participate in the affairs of state. We have no right and no opportunity to change anything, and no responsibility whatever for what goes on. We are expected to be, not participant observers, but rather sympathetic bystanders. Reading a story, in contrast, I must be engaged with it at every moment, or it simply stops. If I stop moving, I may gain or lose by my shift of attention, depending on what I attend to, but I do not lose any sequence that will have gone on past me, when I return. This country needs me.

Passive Receivers of Frozen Input/Active Creators

This radical difference in the degree of active control is most evident in the absolute control video exercises over our visual imagery. As the four of us talked on vacation, our images of a given character in the movies were much more precise and—so far as we could tell—much more alike than anything we had derived from our reading. John Reed was vividly and forever fixed as our image of Beatty; Zinoviev was forever Jerzy Kosinsky; André was forever Malle's André. We tourists had been shown the people of that land once and for all, and with no exercise of our capacity to imagine figures of our own. We could no more substitute a different appearance for Reed than we could imagine a different New York City or Polish-Russian border. Though we were all, as it turned out, quite puzzled about the moral and political intentions of *Reds*, its visual intentions were so powerful that none of us is ever likely to break entirely free of them, no matter how many books we may read about the historical characters. Yet we all knew that the historical Reed and Louise Bryant and Zinoviev must have been vastly different from what we were shown, that the movie made up whatever images it needed to ensure its effect of seeming like history, and that everyone and everything was thus permanently Beattyfied for us.

The experience with all of the printed narratives was in this respect entirely different. Our talk was not only less excited; it included many more moments of silence, and of course it allowed for something entirely excluded by the movies, an unimpassioned reference back to the text, which was, after all, right there in front of us. But in another sense, the story—the events experienced by characters "imagined in our heads"—was not there in front of us, not in the sense or to the degree that the movie had been when we first viewed it. Searching the text could never be a return to see directly what the image in fact *was*; it had to be a search for evidence about what it was still to *become*. Since we as readers had been required to make whatever images constituted our story—images of character, of scene, of sequence—as disputatious but reflective *re*readers we had to continue remaking those images as we discussed. Thus the stories were still in process of being "written," and still are in process now, in my head, as I write this essay; from beginning to end I am schooled in imagining.

This continuing process can affect every part of our "reading": tone of voice, facial expression, the lighting of scenes, the presumed inner feeling of all characters, the significance of what anyone does. On vacation, we were often shocked to discover that our fellow readers had made quite "indefensible" inferences about all of these matters, not only about how a character appeared physically, but about whether a character's experience was tragic or comic, pathetic or contemptible. A given gesture might be seen as angry and defiant by one reader and as pathetically resigned by another, the physical accompaniment entirely different for each. Again and again one of us would say something like, "Oh, the dress is not *that* shade of blue—the point in this story is surely that everything is faded out to pastels," or "But you've overlooked the repeated reference to the shadows. Don't you see that the room must be of a kind that will represent. . . ."

In these and other ways, the stories and their characters shifted under our scrutiny. We were, in short, prolonging the primary experience *as* we discussed. Most of the stories grew in stature as we talked; a couple of them shrank before our eyes; but none remained what they had been. The important point is that the change was not only in their "meanings" (shifts of meaning occurred in discussing the movies, too), but that we were steadily engaged in imaginative recreation. The primary experience shifted as we engaged in the secondary experience. The engagement was thus inherently more sustained and imaginatively active—not because we spent more time (in fact, we spent on no story as much time as we spent originally just viewing *Reds*), but because the different media offered different invitations.

I have heard it said that this striking fixity of image given by the visual media (and the resulting passivity in the receiver) is curable by some sort of "technological fix"—that there can be no theoretical limit to what the new media can do. Perhaps. No doubt technology will continue to improve our access to movies and television, so that energetic students will increasingly find it possible to do term papers on structure and themes. But even as they do so, the precision of image will be reinforced: whatever happens to other meanings, visual meanings will have been created, once and for all, by the originators. In short, it is hard to see how anyone can eliminate the fundamental difference between media in which some kind of physical reality has established a visual scene *before* the viewer starts to work on it, and those like radio and print that can use only language for description—language that is always no more than an invitation to thought and imagination, never a solid presentation of finished reality.

This point perhaps should be illustrated with a closer look at a printed description. Show me any man or woman on the screen, any screen, and that will *be* forever that man or woman. But what do I do if you tell me, as does E. M. Forster in *Howards End*, that a young man "seemed a gentleman. . . . To a feminine eye there was nothing amiss in the sharp depressions at the corners of his mouth, nor in the rather box-like construction of his forehead. He was dark, clean-shaven, and seemed accustomed to command"?[6] What I must do is to begin some hard work of the imagination. Again: if you show me, on any screen, a given London residential square, it will be forever *that* square. But what must I do if you tell me the following?

> Their house was in Wickham Place, and fairly quiet, for a lofty promontory of buildings separated it from the main thoroughfare. One had the sense of a backwater, or rather of an estuary, whose waters flowed in from the invisible sea. . . . Though the

promontory consisted of flats—expensive, with cavernous entrance halls . . .—it fulfilled its purpose, and gained for the older houses opposite a certain measure of peace. These, too, would be swept away in time, and another promontory would rise upon their site, as humanity piled itself higher and higher on the precious soil of London.[7]

What I am required to do by such a passage underlines a further difference in the qualities of mind and heart expected of us when we visit these contrasting kingdoms. The video arts tell us precisely what we should see, but their resources are thin and cumbersome for stimulating our moral and philosophical range. Those who enter Forster's world are expected to be interested in questions that would be almost impossible to raise with any precision in video. How could any screen portray as much moral and intellectual meaning as is packed into the sentence: "These, too, would be swept away in time, and another promontory would rise upon their site, as humanity piled itself higher and higher on the precious soil of London." As sheer thought, this is by no means uncharacteristically deep or rich for fiction, but the concentration of preferred ideas is intense indeed, as compared with any "information" that could be conveyed by mere visual sequences. Perhaps each of the four major overt ideas of the sentence could be suggested by sufficiently elaborate sequences. Even the notion that the soil is precious could perhaps be given by a series of frames, accompanied with commentary spoken by some character who has been established as speaking reliably for the values of the work. If we became really desperate, we could always fall back on "voice over." But even at best, the result would be relatively indefinite. And meanwhile, the other three claims made by the sentence would remain unspoken. By the time a filmmaker had worked to convey the meaning of this sentence, any movie would be half over, and most TV dramas would already have been replaced on the screen by three others.[8]

Unlimited Sensation/Focused Reflection

We visitors to the realms of gold discover a further curious presupposition about what we will be able and willing to attend to. A full photographic frame presents an unlimited range of points on which one *might* focus attention and from which one could derive "the meaning" of the frame. It is true that skillful

directors and cameramen know how to limit that potential
infinity. But do what they will, they leave us always with the
question, "Of the possible centers of attention here, which one
shall I take as significant, and which shall I simply ignore? Does
it *mean* something that the hero has a wart beneath his left
eye?" In any printed story, a wart under the left eye carries
some sort of weight: it has been chosen from thousands of
other possible details. Even in detective stories, which depend
on planting irrelevancies, the wart means something as a deliberate deflection of attention. But in video, innumerable warts
are simply *there*, accidents that even the most skillful director
cannot eliminate completely. The result is that we visitors are
habituated to a kind of looseness of attention; no detail can
mean very much, when some details can mean nothing. And
there is always an open invitation for the eye to wander to
some further sensation.

Thus reflective study and imaginative inventiveness are to
some degree against the grain of the medium. The producers
may hope to make the new media as "arty" in this respect as are
serious literature and the traditional graphic arts, but they can
never go all the way: we continue—even in the most gloomily
metaphysical of scenes by Bergman or Antonioni—to revel in
the precise and almost infinitely various and rapidly flowing
imaginative worlds they have cooked up for us. We do not sit
before the object and use it as a stimulus for our own invention
of new worlds of our own or reflections about events as they
occur[9]—not at least to the degree encountered in reading.

In reading, even of the shoddiest stuff, I am given one word,
one phrase, one sentence, one relatively unfixed image at a
time, just as the author wrote them—or rather, as the author
decided to place them after trying out various orders. Every
mentioned detail thus comes labeled: "Attend to *this*." Even the
most dramatic label is still visually vague, requiring imaginative
work to bring it to life. "Her dress, a bright red silk, was so
dazzling that he at first hardly noticed her face." Well, yes, I've
seen ladies like that in that kind of dress, so my imagination
works one or another of their characteristics into the scene.
The result may be quite inappropriate—a stereotyped bitch,
when the author means an angel or a woman who resists such
stereotyping? But my mistake may not ultimately matter, not
to the essential quality of my activity, because I have time,
sitting alone in the light, turning my own pages, to revise my

imaginings, to readjust my types, to reclothe the lady, as it were, to study her face, the face that I have myself made. And what I study, when the fiction is any good, is not her face, finally, but her character.

Comfortable Stereotyping/Resistance to Simplicities

A further expectation about *my* character as visitor to video seems to follow from all of these. I am expected to engage willingly in stereotyping. I am not given time, after all, to engage in anything else.

I stereotype morally: this world consists almost entirely of heroes and villains. It is true that all narrative requires some moral simplifying. But printed fiction has found ways of resisting it, and even stage and film can prod us a bit. But television, by all the evidence so far, subsists on moral stereotypes.

I stereotype intellectually; there simply is no time to do anything else. The highly particular images presented by particularized actors will be much too confusing to make a story line, unless the issues can be taken in at a glance or word. The screen thus reinforces a general trend in *all* media toward simplification and polarization of the unlimited complexities of our lives. As citizen of the country presented to me by television, whether that country is literally the United States or some imagined world, I learn quickly that all problems could be solved simply, if only other people would think about them the way I am being taught to do *now*. It is no news to say that anybody who has read a book—any book, even the most distorted—on any subject will be appalled by the simplifications of that subject in any movie or television program. There are simply no movies or television programs, regardless of the depth of the chosen subjects, that make intellectual demands of the kind expected of even the most watered-down philosophical or scholarly text, or of the printed fiction that critics take seriously.

It is hard to decide how much of this constriction of mind is inherent in the medium and how much simply in market conditions (the pitch, after all, must be made to the average viewer). We should learn soon, as home-chosen television becomes more widespread. But what is important here is that, even if the medium were someday to overcome this limitation and become as sustained in its thought as Aristotle, the limitations I am concerned with would remain: the passivity of imaginative engagement, with a resulting simplified emotional engagement.

No doubt there will be great consequences for our future selves from all of these controls over our characters as we enter and leave the video worlds. But we do not know, we cannot prove, what those consequences will be. What we do know, what we need no experimental proof for, is that our lives are lived in *these* ways, sitting now before the screen, and not in other possible ways. The selves, souls, persons, characters that we are likely to become as a result of living in a print or a video culture for decades will matter greatly, but they are unavailable as evidence in our debates. The selves that we *are* now as we live in these worlds are to some degree known—at first hand. We have met the victims, here in our living rooms.

WITH WHOM DO WE DWELL? WHO ADDRESSES US?

Who I *am*, in a given imaginative encounter, is inseparable from the question of the kind of people I'm living *with*. Voices come to me from these screens and from these printed stories. Who converses with me here? What kind of companionship is being offered? What company do I keep?

The voices of movies and television come to us as we sit in the dark or half-light, sometimes alone, but more often in company. In all emotional drama, whether comic or sad, the company becomes crucial. When those we are with laugh or weep, we are more inclined to laugh or weep. When they remain silent, groan, walk out of the theater or leave for a snack, we are forced, by the company we keep, to modify our listening. We watch differently. The members of the company *in* the screen-world know about all that, play to it, make the comedy or pathos work by "playing" on the audience. In comedy, they provide evidences of amused company in *that* world too: studio audiences or canned laughter. In tragedy and pathos, that won't work so well, and we are given instead shots of minor characters weeping.

The voices of literature come to us, usually, as we sit alone, in the light. (On vacation, the four of us did read aloud some to each other. But how many people do that these days?) Even if someone else is present in the room, we read alone, except for the company of the author.

The new media thus support me, reassure me, provide me with a more visible and lively company. Print puts me on the spot, whispers to me of something only the author and I will understand, threatens me, finally, with loneliness, unless the author is very good company indeed. In the literature I most admire, especially the modern literature, I sense that the author writes specifically to me—there may, at most, be one or two others in this world of mine qualified to catch all the nuances.

It is by no means self-evident that the essentially lone, private experience of reading is a better way to live than to join those new, lively companies provided by video. For me, the most magical transport comes in fact not when reading alone, but when I share art in company—as in classical theater, great music festivals, reading aloud together, playing chamber music. But of course movie audiences—and even more obviously TV companies—do not work quite like that. And when we look at the company we keep *behind* the screen, most particularly the company of producers, the differences become really striking.

As viewer, I am part of a vast company exercising remote control through the ratings, a company that demands an unlimited supply of entertainment. The tube, representing those most anonymous producers, will provide—must provide—what I demand of it. The tube will not die: the company I keep as I watch it will go on eternally. Reading any beloved author, in contrast, I know that I dwell with someone whose powers are finite; the "supply" of this precise kind of company will someday come to an end. Though I can return to the author after he or she dies, we share, in our private companionship, a deep knowledge of our precious and poignant limitations.

The tube implies, insofar as it can, that there are no limits. Though producers may give us a few bad programs this season, they cannot afford to let us down, because our company is their bread and butter. If we are to dwell together in a global village, sitting before the screen, it will be a village in which none of the elders ever dies. When death in fact occurs—President Kennedy dies almost before our eyes, Johnny Carson is aging and will someday surely die—it will not finally matter very much, because the tube has promised us that some other show will easily take over the top ratings.

But who are these immortal producers? The company offered to me by the screens is unlimited, immensely varied, and largely anonymous. It is more varied, potentially, than even my library shelves. In the first place, it can draw on the riches of those shelves. What is more, no book can offer me the sheer, joyful gift that a fine juggler, dancer, singer, or gymnast can: television and movie producers can purchase these gifts for me. No book can possibly duplicate the gift of energy and concentrated courage and abandon of the "performance" of a football or soccer game. The tube offers me, not in its dramatic efforts, but in its images of real people doing what they do best, an endless supply of that supreme gift—the drama of the best that is in one.

The best authors try to do that too, implying: "Here I give you my notion of what living can be—it can be what it is during these moments we spend together." It may seem, then, that we have only to compare the quantity and quality of gifts offered by two equally good companions. And once we say that, must we not recognize that the world is enriched more broadly and variously by the new media than could ever be done by print? Must we not add that print will never provide as much good company from as many cultures—all periods and climes and genres—as television can?

Something seems wrong in this judgment. The gifts do not really come to us unmediated, on TV or on the movie screen. They have been chosen by a team of directors and associates. The juggler I see on the *Tonight Show* has been *chosen* to entertain me; if I saw him on the street, collection hat in front of him, I would accept or reject this offer of his gift, unmediated. It must be better, for him, to be paid by Carson than to be on the street with only my interest or my charity to depend on. Yet I wonder. Is it only a cheap nostalgia that leads me to see more dignity in a street performer, living in poverty, offering a gift that too many passersby don't even notice, than in the same performance offered (as mediated by teams of organizers) on the screen? The juggler himself has not changed, essentially, but the gift now comes from someone else—the producers. I recently saw a young trapeze artist perform, for the first time ever, four somersaults in a midair pass. It was a marvelous thing to see, but it was packaged in the dulcet tones of one of those *60 Minutes* people, watered down to seem really quite ordinary, the drama of the first three unsuccessful tries reduced to something staged. The total "act" was easy, muffling the immense achievement of the artist himself.

Like all of the questions I have raised, this one about the quality of a proferred gift cannot be answered simply. But a simple distinction operates here that one finds implacably controlling our responses to gifts from friends in everyday affairs. If you offer me a gift of something that you would yourself like to receive, if it is something that you respect as a gift, I accept it with love. If you offer me something that expresses your contempt for my taste, if you would yourself feel contempt or loathing for what you offer me, I have a right to feel—indeed I cannot help feeling—that the gift is no gift at all. All the evidence shows that most producers of TV shows, unlike that trapeze artist, offer gifts of the second kind. Indeed, they fall all over themselves claiming that they do not themselves watch the kind of stuff they produce, and they claim that they would much prefer a world in which better shows were demanded by the public. Nobody who pays any attention to the public statements of executives can believe that anyone except perhaps the frontline performer is giving his or her best.

One might argue that this blight is not in the least inherent in the medium, but only to our present methods of financing it. After all, our culture seems to produce as much hack work in print as on television. The producers of a great proportion of our printed matter must surely view it with as much contempt as any TV producer feels for the day's offering. But all evidence so far suggests that the medium of television itself for some reason *builds in* a contempt for us and our life. When anything we care for passes through its hands, what comes out is a single statement: none of this matters very much.

WHAT IS MY HEART'S DESIRE?

Does Anything Matter?

There is a sense in which a steady diet of television, like the printed narratives that most resemble it in brevity and stereotyping, seems to say that nothing matters, really. Whether I like a show greatly or detest it, there are no great consequences for me or for the makers. Just as the news (on both TV and radio, as in their predecessors on the movie screen, e.g., *Time Marches On*) reduces every event to the same reductive "spot," so the dramatic fictions are reduced to a few moments in which nothing matters except whether I have not turned the dial.

Defenders of television can point to fronts of resistance—the various efforts at "in-depth" news, the solemn moments when great classics like *The Scarlet Letter* are given an hour or so of uninterrupted time. No doubt the producers of *60 Minutes* or

Brideshead Revisited think of themselves as offering matters that matter. Presumably they can sometimes even pass the "hack test": Would I watch this show if someone else had produced it? And they manage to persuade many viewers that serious issues are being addressed seriously, and significant theatre being produced artistically. But somehow they can never escape the effect of the medium, its short attention span, its sheer quantity of appeals, its easy fixations of vivid imagery. One emerges from any extended viewing period, whether of the "best" or the worst, in a state of floating indifference.

The most obvious exceptions are those momentous public events when we all have the wrenching illusion that we are there, as during the week following President Kennedy's assassination. That whole event mattered a great deal to every viewer. As Robert Stein says, "In my own memory, John Kennedy's funeral is as *real* as anything that happened to me in combat during World War II." Given the existence of such moments and our convictions about them, we can hardly say that "nothing matters" to us as we watch television. Indeed, the more deeply we consider the question, the more obvious it becomes that to the steady viewer, whether in times of crisis or during the innumerable crises in the dramas, a great deal matters. The interesting question is what and how it matters, considering the trivialization of subjects and the casual indifference of viewers about what they watch—provided they can watch *something*.

What Do We Desire in the News About "Real Life"

Print culture allows for, though by no means ensures, sustained attention to issues. Books, articles in *Daedalus*, presuppose readers willing to spend not just the time necessary to read a discussion but the impulse to compare contrasting and sustained views. Video culture is, by contrast, a culture of the superficially informed, the hasty, the indifferent.

Consider one of the more "serious" shows about issues, *60 Minutes*. It will each week present four or five melodramatic vignettes, of perhaps ten or twelve minutes each, all in a form requiring me to make up my mind on issues of world-shaking importance. Indeed, I find that I *do* make up my mind, all too easily. They have given me the stereotypes that I need in making up my mind: the villainous insurance executive, obviously cheating the sensitive victim in the wheelchair, suffering while holding the cute child in his lap; the snarling prime minister of the contemptuously treated little country down under; the helpless old woman facing the impersonal forces of the bureaucracy—all followed by a cheery little vignette, in the final few moments, about the surprisingly widespread use of horses still in our modern age. The result: since everything matters equally, nothing matters really. Or rather: what matters is narrowed to a range chosen from among the available favorable outcomes; what matters is to move fast to the reward waiting at the end.

And what is the reward? A sense that somebody out there, *in* there, is taking care of these issues in quick order. Though for some viewers the effect may be despair, as the melodramas pile up, supported as they are by the nightly picture of mayhem throughout the world, the general effect is to reassure me about quick fixes in the world, and to make me sick with desire for similar quick fixes in my own troubles. What I am taught to desire is *relief*, as instantaneous as that promised in the analgesic ads; I have been taught to expect it, as the images of trouble shift refreshingly and painlessly from moment to moment.

Lessons of Desire in Narrative

Like traditional ethical criticism of literature, conventional criticism of drama in the new media, from the earliest movies on, has usually focused on the overt content as decent or indecent, virtuous or vicious. Virtue presented and properly rewarded thus earns a favorable judgment, vice triumphant is anathema. (Note that even the most avant-garde critic is likely to work in the same scheme, simply substituting up-to-date terms for virtue and vice: a "mind-shattering, no-holds-barred, devastatingly mischievous exposé of bourgeois pieties" is of course virtuous.) Since the creation of mass culture, some critics have worked on a simple scheme of highbrow versus lowbrow. A production of *The Scarlet Letter* financed by the National Endowment for the Humanities is of course good, even if deadly boring and shorn of all the complexities that Hawthorne cared for; while anything pop is by definition to be rejected. Though most actual examples of such well-meant judgments are absurd, the reaction of some political liberals who, for fear of encouraging censorship, have rejected all ethical, moral, or political judgments, is equally absurd. Surely the trick is to find some way of talking about the ethical and political effects of art that will get beneath a given surface image; even the most "objectionable" image may or may not be hurtful even to a child, depending on what is done with it *in the whole formed experience of the work*. Though there may be some specific images that are good or bad in themselves, I can think of none. It is our experience of the form into which each image fits that determines the quality of our deepest habits of desire.

Such "aesthetic habits" (call them that, though to do so obscures their being simultaneously aesthetic and practical) are built out of two kinds of formal experience. The first is the experience of a pattern of desire played upon, inevitably, by any temporal story. You simply cannot make an interesting story without playing upon patterns of hope, fear, and anticipation. The typical fairy tale leads us to desire (and to expect) a happy outcome through a combination of the protagonist's efforts and some kind of fantastic intervention, the happiness consisting in the possession of some conventional good: gold, a prince or princess, revenge, security. The typical nineteenth-century popular novel teaches us in much the same way to desire, through many hours of trials and tribulations, a happy ending that is again defined in conventional terms: for the women in the story (and hence for us readers, male or female), it is marriage to the ideal male; for the men, it is such a marriage combined with some sort of public honor, defined as wealth or fame or power. The typical highbrow novel of the modern period teaches us that it is wickedness and folly to seek such conventional goods, and that what we should desire is some deeper quality like maturity, self-knowledge, artistic integrity, or moral courage. Though there is obviously a great range in the quality of the experience offered by different exemplars of all of these "plottings of desire"—ranging from the cheapest form of a Horatio Algerlike grab for success to the subtleties of Stephen Dedalus's struggle for artistic independence and power—the basic pattern of *reliance on future payoff* is reinforced by all.

The same values are of course reinforced by most dramas on television or movie screen. To build a successful plot, the most obvious requirement is that the designer create a strong desire for some payoff that is just barely conceivable as within reach, given the probable length of the work in hand. When I begin a 300-page book called a novel, I can expect a long series of variegated instabilities to be faced and overcome before the final chapter. When I go to a movie, I can expect two hours, more or less, of frustration of desire before reward comes. When I turn on a TV drama, my usual expectations are for at most an hour of seeming-pain before joy reigns. And finally, when I experience the little thirty-second dramas offered me in the commercials, my hopes and fears, scratched into almost instant irritation, must be assuaged (though only partially, or I will not go out and buy) with an almost instant image of happy reward. These patterns, I must repeat, are entirely independent of the content; the differences would remain even if the characters in the novel found their bliss in final possession of a Mercedes-Benz, while the stick-characters on the thirty-second sales pitch found *theirs* in learning how to live right by reading the complete works of Plato. What we are talking about is habits of desire, expectations about how desires and their fulfillment work.

One modern definition of "the aesthetic" consists of a simple—if not simple-minded—repudiation of the entire domain of desire. Whenever we seek some good in the future, we violate the domains of art, where pure aesthetic contemplation reigns supreme. The definition has done great harm in the critical world, by leading to a denigration of *all* appetites and satisfactions; the rapid impoverishment of the palette that has resulted, in all the arts—though not, praise God, for all artists in *any* of the arts—makes one of the weirdest instances in history of the triumph of abstract theory over the plain teachings of everyday experience. (Yes, I am thinking of the "interesting" and impoverished experiences offered by John Cage and his successors, and of most other minimalists I know.)

But we need not repudiate all habits of desire to recognize a great qualitative difference between those arts that work to make the journey as valuable as the destination and those that "have no time" for anything but increasing hope for final success. Though the typical nineteenth-century novel may have been excessively goal-oriented, helping to build generations of success-mongers, the form of the novel allowed, even encouraged, an entirely different message: it is not where you go that matters but how you get there. You have time, we are told by those mammoth novels that Henry James called "great fluid puddings," time to pause now, to savor, to elaborate, to look at your surroundings. Though you care, as I the novelist care, about achieving a final happiness for our Pip, our Dorothea Brooke, our Emma Woodhouse, our Richard Feverell, you and I both care even more about the quality of their souls, the quality of what they say and do as we travel with them. We are thus encouraged, as we read, to linger, to reread, to extract parts and reflect on them, just as we all were led to reflection by the stories of our childhood.

I have just finished reading Paul Theroux's *The Mosquito Coast*. A few months ago I read Russell Hoban's *Ridley Walker*, and a few weeks before that, Wright Morris's autobiographical account, *Will's Boy*. In each work, a preadolescent narrator-hero grapples with a decayed or decaying adult world, trying to understand people and impersonal forces that adults themselves do not understand. In all three accounts, everything en route matters as much or more than the outcome. Not only does every detail count in one's picture of the "worlds" presented; not only does each moment of the work build toward another moment that makes the first one matter more. In all three, we quickly learn that what happens to *this* boy should matter very much to everyone. After thirty pages I care more about the quality *now* of Ridley Walker and Charlie Fox and the young Wright Morris than I have ever cared about any imagined man, woman, or child on television.

I am not making the sentimental point that they all made me weep; they did not. For the most part they made me laugh, often in ways close to my laughter in *Huckleberry Finn*. No, the point is that they made me care, made me care about what they cared for: about making sense out of a baffling world, surviving the incomprehensions and cruelties of adults, moving through troubled youth to mature decision—and above all, discovering how to act well in the world. Even the "two-hour forms"—traditional drama, modern movies, and occasional drama on PBS—are to some degree able to resist, in a similar way, the mindless pursuit of quickly fulfilled desire. There is, after all, time enough, time for soliloquy, for experiment with camera angle, for exploring a secondary character, for moving into a beautiful setting with a deliberate savoring of detail.

But we are now in general repudiating all that. Our culture seems to have "decided" to specialize in short spans, dividing experience into breathless desire-fulfillment patterns lasting from less than fifteen minutes to under an hour. What the decision means, we all know at first hand. Most of us fight it as best we can, either by refusing to watch or by obtaining the new network-free devices that take us back to the time span of traditional drama. But meanwhile the dominant culture of most Americans, the art we live by (many of us for scores of hours each week), teaches not simply the short attention span that educators have long noticed in children who have been "boxed in" from birth, but an attention to quick (though of course future) gratification. Here is the image, "real," fixed, lacking in only one simple thing to complete its happiness: a mate, a promotion, a killing of the bad guys, *anything* that can stand for a happy outcome. The dramatic resources of video seem permanently suited to imaginations of desire that are relatively scrappy, relatively passive, relatively frozen by the preimaginings of the makers, relatively resistant to reflection and reconsideration. Such patterns can be used, obviously, in the service of any uncomplicated surface value whatever. Any Christian preacher can use them to tout a desire for a particular brand of salvation, as some sects have long since discovered (though their cheap vignettes of easy salvation do not get onto prime time: try early Sunday morning). Any political system, program, or candidate can use them to push a given sloganized ideology. Any moral majority or well-heeled minority can use them to combat any given wicked thought or action. What they cannot be used for is to celebrate the possibilities of life lived *now* or of leisurely reflection about life in all its complexities.

COMMERCE, CONSEQUENCES, REMEDIES

Though my main subject here has been those features of the media that are largely or entirely independent of differences in content, the subject of the quick fix requires a brief look at the effect of commercials and of commercial pressures on a content that might, in an ideal world, be radically different.

When I began this exercise in speculation, I was determined not to load the dice against television. Too many indictments seem to me to be conducted on a level that would condemn the sex and violence in the Bible or Shakespeare as much as anything found in the most blatant rip-off. But I have now arrived at what looks like a highly pessimistic judgment indeed—pessimistic because I see no way that we can effectively "go back"; no hope that we are going to decide, not that we know something about the effects of the grand experiment, to cancel it; no real chance that we can reverse the disastrous effects, on print culture itself, of the patterns of desire taught us by video culture. Even knowing how chancy all predictions about the future of various media have been in the past, I feel fairly confident that the dominance of video will increase, not diminish, and that its shattering effects on who we are will become more evident as the new forms of computer-video triumph. *They* are obviously even shallower than the older forms, which at least made gestures toward portraying people, while the new multibillion dollar art form, Pac-Man and its siblings, reduce our imaginative world to the precharted ravages of gaping mechanical maws and exploding metal.

In short, I suspect that the sheer visual excitement made available by video is too much for the race to resist. But there is one by-product of the discovery of this art-domain that we could modify if we decided that is was important to do so. Clearly, there is no absolute bond linking video and commercial corruptions. And it is equally clear that some of the worst ravages of scrappiness, frenzy, and greed result, not from anything inherent in video, but from how we have chosen use it. As we witness a growing separation of home viewing from the imposed choices of network programming and the studios' quest for blockbuster movies, it is important to recognize just how much is at stake. Though nothing we can do will enable either video or print to match each others' effects, it seems probable that if video artists could be freed from their present bonds the worst losses might still be reversed. Our best hope for that, obviously, and our chief defensive weapon, in a culture that promises, at least in the short run, to become increasingly "videotic," is a developed practice of ethical criticism—by which I mean, of course, not a criticism that pushes a given moral creed, but one in which critics, in a sense dwelling together "in company," reflect on how the media shape the "ethos" of selves and societies.

What direction might such criticism take, when turned upon those brilliant flashing commercials that fill our nights and days?

Most traditional narrative has relied on imitating the seemingly natural form: "roused appetite—fulfilled appetite." But one prominent subgroup of narratives has always rivaled this pattern, the kind that rouses appetites and refuses to gratify them *within the form*. Pornography is the most obvious example, but every sensual pleasure and every passion can be exploited in what could be called the "pornographic structure": maximizing the desire and then cutting short the form, leaving the reader or viewer to complete the cycle in the real world. Satiric works are always in this form: people or institutions taken from the real world are made as contemptible as possible, leading us to desire their punishment, comic or serious, and to express our scorn actively in the real world. Literary works in themselves can only properly punish types and images, not real persons, but they can lead us to desire or detest real persons of a similar type. Some verbal descriptions (and many video portrayals) of food express the same pattern, leading us toward the refrigerator rather than toward any formal resolution in the art work. These pornographic patterns all depend on the fact that words can never satisfy actual hungers, whether for sex, revenge, or food. They are thus all essentially in conflict with the central enterprise of this essay—the search for experiences so valuable *now* that consequent actions seem, let us say, inconsequential.

If we think about advertising in general as depending on this same pattern—an inherently half-completed form leading to extraformal modes of completion—then we can see more clearly the staggering scope of the revolution that we have all undergone in this century, first in print, then in radio, and now in video.[10] Except for underground works of sexual pornography and satire, prevideo narrative culture provided all who shared it (whether literate or not) with completed forms (printed advertisement, the obvious exception, lacked the resources of narrative). It is no doubt true that those forms were in one sense still not shut off from effects in the practical world. Their consumers could be left with a strong desire for "more of the same," or with fantasies about finding a real "girl of my dreams" to match the figures of romance. Still, nothing in preadvertising times, and nothing in printed advertising, came even close to the specialization in frustration that TV culture has achieved. It could be said, of course, that not just TV ads, but the whole of modern culture leads to the "I want, I want . . ." that Saul Bellow attributed to Henderson. But TV culture makes previous "want-makers" seem puny. Even those who in effect make their living by proving, with their criticism, that they are too smart to be taken in by such stuff, are in fact strongly influenced by it, both its content (though that is not our main concern) and its repetitive form.

It would be tedious, unnecessary, and in itself unpersuasive, to describe any chance sampling from the day's fare. Every viewer knows from experience that the essential form of these tidbits is what I am calling pornographic: unlike even the shoddiest TV drama or talk show, the commercial is obviously and blatantly organized to leave itself uncompleted, to make us desire something that by definition the present moment cannot supply. The activity that its imaginings would stimulate is not an activity of the imagination at all, but an activity of possession. If I imagine anything, it is only the steps I must take to go downtown and get my hands on that new possession.[11]

It would be flatly against the purposes of such an art to provide any sense that this experience in itself, or repetitions of it, or reflection about it, will be enough. Many commercials do indeed these days come perilously close to violating their own purpose; it may turn out to be more fun to sit and watch these clever little dramas than to go shopping. While waiting for the glorious day when television thus gives us everything we might conceivably want, suppose we look closely at the qualities of the primary experience of watching one of the most successful of these, the AT&T spot that Michael Arlen follows, brilliantly and relentlessly, in *Thirty Seconds*.[12] Arlen's interest is different from ours. With great patience and quiet irony, he traces an immensely painstaking and expensive path from conception through months of labor to thirty seconds of TV time, every second designed to make us want to "reach out and touch someone far away. Give 'em a call."

There is nothing subtle or disguised about the message, and its overt ethical content is quite unobjectionable. Each episode is designed to carry the same moral: telephone calls can bring joy to your life by enabling you to "reach out" to someone far away. (The company, Arlen tells us, originally stressed a theme of giving pleasure to others by calling them, but it soon caught onto the need to stress the pleasure taken by the caller.) "From the beginning, AT&T wanted us to overcome the negative emotions associated with long-distance," one of the advertisers tells Arlen. "For years, there has been a definitely *negative, uncasual* quality to a lot of long-distance calling. AT&T wanted us to emphasize the *casual, positive* aspect: long-distance is fun, it's easy, it's cheap." The ad is designed to move "the twenty-five-to-forty-nine age bracket, and the tilt is definitely toward the female, seeing that women initiate sixty percent of all residence long-distance phone calls."[13] Nothing wrong here, so far: surely the more long-distance calling among friends and relatives, the better. Here is how they design vicarious experience to increase our loving calls:

1. Open on older man in a "show-biz" setting. He's standing

while listening, perhaps with his eyes closed, on phone. [Note association with fun, vitality.]

2. Cut to living-room scene with the corner of the rug thrown back. Little girl is tap-dancing with shiny new tap shoes. Proud father holds phone down near tapping as mother beams proudly. [Continuity of generations; parental pride.]

3. Cut back to elderly man as he smiles more widely and begins to impulsively dance to the same step himself. [The phone makes you want to dance; it expresses your love for family.]

4. Cut to brand-new Army recruit with brand-new short haircut. He's rubbing his head [and phoning home about it: when lonely you can keep in touch].

5. Cut to barber friend or dad sitting in his own barber chair; laughing. [Troubles shared by phone give joy.]

6. Cut to gal standing on head in yoga position. She's on the phone. [Phone is useful in all positions, situations, ages. And it's fun because funny.]

7. Cut to another gal doing the same. [Share, share, share.]

8. Cut to young man in cowboy getup—hat, jeans, etc. He has just competed in a rodeo, still has number on back and chest and is a little the worse for wear. . . . He's on the phone and happy [because he's sharing news of his victory; the phone brings good news, not bad].

9. Cut to young woman in jockey outfit just fresh from the race. She's full of mud. She's talking very happily on the phone. [More victory, more joy.]

10. Cut to locker room with hockey player waiting on phone. Lots of bustling around him. [Victory? Slight suspense.]

11. Cut to toothless little boy on phone in same uniform, whooping it up [about his father's victory; more victory, more joy].

12. Cut back to locker room as champagne is poured over his head and he breaks into a big toothless smile. Freeze on smile [identical to his son's: the phone thus identified with father-son love, with triumph in life].[14]

The final version adds some features; it gets a baby and a black girl into the act. (Why did it take them so long to think of a baby?) But it is essentially still a cluster of sentimental moments associating the telephone with the viewer's desire for love and victory and laughter. The makers rightly assume that we all desire these things, and if we can be made to desire them even more, and then to associate the desire with the next telephone call as fulfillment, we will make more long-distance calls.

All this is perhaps obvious, and we might be tempted to say that such superficial dramas are not worth our attention; nobody takes them seriously, except perhaps some of the hundreds of "artists" who make each one, and the advertisers themselves. But it takes no very deep analysis to show that they are among the primary forces shaping modern American character, as we have defined character.

What are the qualities of the imaginative experience provided by such an intensely crafted piece as the AT&T ad?

1. Like all video, the ad is of course visually intense, requiring considerable quickness and sophistication of inference, not from verbal but from visual signs. It tends to deflect our attention from the words. Yet it is accessible to every experienced viewer, however "illiterate" in other media. Mastery of this language apparently comes as naturally as learning to talk. In this, such mastery is unlike learning to read, which is a highly artificial process that in one sense is never fully mastered.

2. It assumes a passive level of *mental* attention (if we can contrast the mental to what the mind does in processing visual imagery); redundancy is thus essential, redundancy about every point. Each episode must mean exactly the same thing.

3. It allows for no ambiguities, either of image or of meaning. Moral values are either suppressed entirely or taken for granted (i.e., it is a good thing to "reach out and touch someone").

4. It forbids reflection. Both within the ad and in the movement from ad to ad we see one immediate sensation replaced quickly by another immediate sensation. To study the sequence, to think about anything at all, may increase one's admiration for the maker's skill, but it will always be subversive of the "artist's" true intent.

5. It identifies our deepest human emotions—love of family, desire for success, enjoyment of laughter, joy in dancing—with a material acquisition. In doing so, it denies every possible context for such emotions except instant gratification.

6. It requires me to view all people as stereotypes. In the invention of quickly recognized types, it is more resourceful than any previous art form except perhaps the comic strip. Raw types can be the only sort of "persons" taken in at such speed.

7. It portrays the goal of life as victory at the end of the day, not as conducting an effective or proper life en route. There can *be* no route, only *want*, followed at once by gratification. In this world, the winners are the ones who use those phones. There are no losers. Nobody calls mother for comfort after loss; nobody calls to tell of unexpected death or the loss of a job. The phone company would, of course, refuse to sponsor an ad that appealed to losers; losers will not have the money to make long-distance calls. All pain and all sense of struggle must be eliminated from this world.

Of course, there is nothing inherent in the nature of brief spots that requires mindless good cheer; they could just as well convey a mindless repetition of despair and emptiness, like some modern fiction, or a mindless repetition of political slogans, as happens both at home and abroad. In a sense, these short forms are as ideologically neutral as a computer—except for the fundamental ideology of repeated desire. The primary experience will always be of the same general kind, whether the product advertised is a new edition of Shakespeare's works, to make your family cultured, a new form of meditation or exercise, to make you serene or healthy, or a new deodorant or pantyliner to keep you fresh all day.

8. The company I keep (not of course the stick figures in the stories but their creators) do not respect me; they are not companions, but manipulators. Insofar as I am inclined to admire them, I do not admire their human depth or warmth or wisdom but their raw skill. If I infer an "author" or team of authors responsible for the presentation, I cannot think of them as friends who are themselves captured by any message conveyed. Unlike the implied authors of great fiction, they are admirable at most as instructors in technique: I can learn from them how to do this clever stuff. Or I may envy them their pay. As everyone knows, the actor in the ads get paid more than the actors in the programs; it is evident to anyone who watches for a few hours at almost any time of day that more attention and money have gone into the ads than into the shows they *seem* to interrupt. Yet we also know, from the statements of those executives who write about their experience, that they do not themselves respect their art as art. No one of the creators has ever claimed that he (I've seen none by women) so admired a given ad that he could not resist going out at once to buy the product. At most, they will say that they admire what they know to be mastery of a set of tricks.

In commercials, then, we encounter primary experience that seems the antithesis, in every conceivable respect, of the kind of imaginative experience that children encounter in fairy stories, or that we adults find in reading what we call literature. *Thirty Seconds* is a relatively benign version of the creature: "Reach out and touch someone" is no doubt a more humanly defensible message than "Why do *you* use Preparation H?" or Steve Allen pretending that he can play a piano in a Ford. But the specific content, I must repeat, doesn't matter much as compared with the patterns of desire conveyed by the form: happiness is identified with something more or less costly, to be obtained in the immediate future; the makers are paid to portray this something, not to give us good company in an otherwise troubled world. The whole enterprise could not be better designed to produce a restlessness of spirit antithetical to reflection or thoughtful analysis. Whatever analysis we perform will be, like Arlen's book about this one advertising program, entirely divorced from, and ultimately hostile to, the ends sought by the work itself. The best printed narratives have always stimulated criticism that *appreciates* their value, in several senses of the word. The best TV criticism, and certainly the best criticism of the commercials, seems always to engage in *de*preciation.

To say all this is not quite the same thing as simply reviving McLuhan's slogan, "The medium is the message." It is to say that the effects of the medium in shaping the primary experience of the viewer, and thus the quality of the self during the viewing, are radically resistant to any elevation of quality in the program content: as viewer, I become *how* I view, more than *what* I view. And the gloomy conclusion must be that, unless we can change their present characteristic forms, the new media will surely corrupt whatever global village they create; you cannot build a world community out of misshapen souls.

A HINT AT CONCLUSION:
THE PROBLEM OF EVALUATION

Such speculation, much of it gong far beyond any conceivable testing with hard evidence, "raises more questions than it answers"—a bit of socialscientese that I detest when others resort to it. About the only point that is beyond question is the immense power of the new voices to shape us anew. Difficult as it is to evaluate the differences, we are differently shaped by "Rumpelstiltskin," by *Ulysses*, by Johnny Carson, by *Dallas*, by *Sesame Street*, and by those thirty seconds.

Unfortunately for my case, the question of whether a given change in our habits of self-making is to be judged for better or worse cannot be answered quite as simply as I may have suggested. It is not at all hard to think of complicating objections. There are, for example, surely as many threatening corruptions of the printed word these days as of video. Certainly the print culture that I see disappearing nevertheless spawns today about as much hackwork, contemptuous of me as company, as does video culture. Indeed, the characters in the average soap or commercial are treated with relative respect, as compared with the monstrous abuses that now fill the pages of magazines like *Penthouse* or of many a best-selling book. Second, it is by no means as easy as I have implied to decide whether a given quality in current offerings—in any medium, new or old—is inherent to the medium or an accident of our times and economies. Nothing I have said can settle the old controversy about whether the awfulness of television, and of the kinds of printed fiction that are now produced and distributed like toothpaste, are causes or effects of this or that social reality. What's more, print itself was never—as Plato pointed out—an unequivocal good for souls or cultures. And finally, it is not obvious that we ever had a print culture of the kind my comments tend to idealize; indeed it may well be that ours is really no less a print culture than was mine as a child. And even in that culture, was not my imagination being fixed, not only by the illustrations of those lovely books, but by romantic patterns as potentially harmful as those that poor Emma Bovary imbibes from what Flaubert considers the dreadfully destructive romantic novels read in her childhood?

Wherever we may come out when we face such complexities, we cannot doubt that each of us grapples daily with a barrage of "art" unmatched in quantity and (potentially) unequaled in range by anything known to previous generations. Whether our lives make sense, then, whether we can in any way offer a defense of our works and days within this culture, depends more than ever before on our developing two great traditional arts: the art of rigorous selection from the offerings of all comers, friends, hacks, and con men; and the art of engaging together in the kind of critical talk that alone can protect us from selections that are arbitrary and dogmatic. By sharing our grounds for selection, we can create moments that turn even the trashiest offering into a genuinely *good* time. In short, whether the time spent with any medium is redeemed or wasted is not entirely in the control of the masters; we still have some choice about who we are to be, exercised whenever we choose how to talk about our would-be pushers and shapers.

It is by no means fashionable to talk as if a person's choice of artistic company could make the difference between a good life and a bad one, *now*. Obviously I am saying something as offensive as that. But must we not recognize that to keep company with all the suitors our society sends to our door will be to ensure, as times are, a life of frenzy if not of despair?

NOTES

1. In May 1982 a study by the National Institute of Mental Health concluded that there is now "overwhelming evidence of a casual relationship between violence on television and later aggressive behavior." Letty Cottin Pogrebin, in *Growing Up Free: Raising Your Child in the 80's* (New York: McGraw Hill, 1980), gives a disturbing summary of the quantitative role of television in our children's lives. I quote here her scary extracts from various studies, but not the documentation she provides for each claim: "More American homes have television than have heat or indoor plumbing. The average TV set is turned on for 6½ hours per day. Most children begin watching television at 2.8 *months* of age. Three- to five-year-olds watch television 54 hours a week. By the time a child enters kindergarten, she or he has spent more time in the TV room than a four-year college student spends in the classroom. By the time a child graduates from high school, he or she will have spent less than 12,000 hours in front of a teacher and more than 22,000 hours in front of a television set. By age seventeen, each child has seen 350,000 commercials." She reports one survey that found 20 percent of children aged four to six preferring television to their mothers and 44 percent preferring it to their fathers. Junior high-school students, another study claims, "believe television" more than they believe their parents, teachers, friends, or books, radios, or newspapers (p. 393).
2. I find it curious that in our time one has to labor to explain this distinction. In the nineteenth century, even hard-headed utilitarians like John Stuart Mill took if for granted as fundamental in all deliberation about how a society should be run. In *On Liberty*, for example, Mill again and again distinguishes between the consequences that a policy might have for society and the quality of life that it might encourage or discourage in individuals. In arguing for the importance of allowing citizens to exercise free choice, he says, "It is impossible that he [the citizen] might be guided in some good path, and kept out of harm's way," without cultivating his personal qualities. "But what will be his comparative worth as a human being? It really is of importance, not only what men do, but also what manner of men they are that do it" (Chapter 3, "Of Individuality," par. 4).

3. Having defined "art" in the broadest possible way, I am here narrowing the definition of "imagination" somewhat, bringing it closer to its roots. In what follows, I am thinking for the most part of what is quite literally "imagined" in our minds, "imitations"—though not of a separately existing reality. The term necessarily expands outward from specific colored shapes to include those shapes *in action*, and finally, it spills over to the moral qualities of those shapes: *that* woman, dressed *that* way, is a sympathetic image, while that other one is hateful, or puzzling, or doomed.

4. Our best performers of such mental experiments have been Marshall McLuhan and Father Walter Ong. It is unfortunate that McLuhan's love of highjinks and his frequently absurd praise for television obscured the immensely imaginative way in which he opened up new domains for criticism of the media. Though I hope to say something more than that "the medium is the message," it is unlikely that I would be talking in this way if McLuhan had not written, again and again, sentences like this: "We still cannot free ourselves of the delusion that it is how a medium is used that counts, rather than what it does to us and with us. This is the zombie stance of the technological idiot." The other sharpest influence I am aware of is Lessing, though I only scratch the surface of what would follow from taking him seriously in matters like these.

5. Perhaps readers of *Daedalus* do not follow these weekly summaries with the assiduity they deserve, so I shall quote one of the fourteen that appeared in the *Chicago Tribune* on May 29, 1982: *All My Children*—7—noon—Erica returned to Brandon's arms, then was miffed that he had accepted a Hong Kong job offer. Cliff exploded when Nina hired Mrs. Gurney as a live-in nursemaid and when Nina also accepted the presidency of Courtland Computers. Palmer's fake medic, Dr. Bentley, warned Donna she would die if she continued her pregnancy. Jesse played up to Angie after she caught him smooching Vera, who he later dumped. Angie's ma was dismayed by Jesse's appearance and manner. Phoebe flaunted the fact that she prefers Melanie over Carrie for Chuck. Harry enticed Benny to continue gambling even though Benny did not have enough money to keep searching for Estelle." If you have doubts about some of the locutions here, do not blame me; the quotation is accurate.

6. (New York: Knopf, 1921), chapter 3.

7. Ibid., chapter 2.

8. I resist talking here about the many thematic connections—"only connect"—that this passage suggests with other parts of the novel; such patterns are equally accessible to any dramatized version, except, of course, for the implacable restrictions provided by the uninterrupted pace of the stage or screen.

9. At first sight, it might seem that traditional drama is precisely like the new scenic media in these respects. After all, plays are designed to be viewed once, with no conventional opportunity for any "reader" to slow the pace, return to reconsider earlier parts, or to sit and muse on what is meant. And the visual effect of theater seems as fixed by the director and actors as it is in a movie or TV drama.

But there is, as many critics have pointed out, a great difference between our experience of the visual reality in the theater and on the screen. In the theater, not even the most naive spectator ever loses a sense of living in a double world: the world of the stage and the world that the stage portrays. Olivier is both Olivier and Othello, and the pleasure of watching "them" interact, as it were, is an essential part of our primary experience. In contrast, photographic media, though obviously less "personal" or "human" in that the screen is imposed between spectators and flesh-and-blood human beings, just as obviously "mediate" less; directors have always known that we tend to identify screen roles with real life. When naive viewers send gifts and telegrams and long personal letters to the "good" characters portrayed on television, and threaten real violence to the villians, they are really responding precisely as the medium asks them to. The fullest success, for any TV series, is to have one or another character become so real to the viewers that their minds are as fully occupied by his or her troubles as they would be by troubles in real life. But the fullest success for a "legitimate" actor is to be known as capable of an impressive range of characters—and thus identifiable with none.

10. It is not generally remembered on what a high pitch of public service radio broadcasting was launched. Robert Stein summarizes the story in *Media Power: Who Is Shaping Your Picture of The World* (Boston: Houghton Mifflin, 1972): "The channels are owned by the people and licensed by the government. In return for using the public airwaves, broadcasters were pledged to 'serve the public interest, convenience or necessity.' At the start, serving and selling were not considered compatible. Addressing the first conference of broadcasters in 1922, Herbert Hoover, then Secretary of Commerce, declared: 'It is inconceivable that we should allow so great a possibility for service, for news, for entertainment, for education and for vital commercial purposes to be drowned in advertising chatter.' In 1930 William Paley of CBS told a Senate Committee that during a recent week on his network 'the actual time taken for advertising mention was seven-tenths of one per cent of all our time.' "

11. Many shows are plainly pornographic in another sense: the thing to be possessed is a stick-woman reduced to the mindless essentials of male gratification—the nicest toy in the display case. But to dwell on that kind of corruption would lead us back to the subject that I have been trying—with only limited success—to rule to one side for a while: the appalling *content* of too many current *artistic* experiences, whether in video or print.

12. (New York, Farrar, Straus & Giroux, 1980).

13. Ibid., pp. 12–13, 47.

14. Ibid., pp. 69–70.

ELIHU KATZ
and
TAMAR LIEBES

DECODING *DALLAS*: NOTES FROM A CROSS-CULTURAL STUDY

There seems to be growing support for that branch of communications research that asserts that television viewing is an active and social process. Viewing takes place at home, and, on the whole in the presence of family and friends. During and after a program, people discuss what they have seen, and come to collective understandings. It is via such understandings, we believe, that the messages of the media enter into culture. We are suggesting, in other words, that viewers see programs, not wallpaper; that programs do not impose themselves unequivocally on passive viewers; that the reading of a program is a process of negotiation between the story on the screen and the culture of the viewers; and that it takes place in interaction among the viewers themselves.[1]

This perspective raises a question about the apparent ease with which American television programs cross cultural and linguistic frontiers. Indeed, the phenomenon is so taken for granted that hardly any systematic research has been done to explain the reasons why these programs are so successful. One wonders how such quintessentially American products are understood at all. The often-heard assertion that this phenomenon is part of a process of cultural imperialism presumes, first, that there is an American message in the content or the form; second, that this message is somehow perceived by viewers; and third, that it is perceived in the same way by viewers in different cultures.

Reprinted from *Intermedia*, May 1984, Vol. 12, No. 3, with permission of the publisher. Copyright © 1984.

Consider the worldwide success of a program like *Dallas*. How do viewers from another culture understand it? A common sense reply might be that such programs are so superficial that they are immediately understood by all: they portray stereotyped characters, visualised conflict, and much repetition. But this cannot be the whole of it. One cannot so simply explain the diffusion of a program like *Dallas* by dismissing it as superficial or action-packed. In fact, at least as far as kinship structure is concerned, the story might be considered quite complex. Neither can it be understood without words; there is very little self-explanatory action. And there are American mores and cinematic conventions to grapple with.

Alternatively, perhaps the program is only little understood. In many countries, American television programs are aired as a by-product of the purchase of American television technology—equipment, spare parts, and programs all arrive in the same package—and viewers may be satisfied to watch the lavish productions without paying much attention to their meaning. But this is also unlikely. Even children who do not understand the meanings intended by the producer, understand *something*, and shape what they think they are seeing in the light of their experience with life and with the conventions of the medium.

We are suggesting, similarly, that people everywhere bring their experience to bear in the decoding process and seek the assistance and confirmation of others in doing so. Some of these experiences are universal: deep structures such as kinship relations or relations between id and superego. Other experiences are more culturally differentiated by society and community and constitute more selective frames for interpreting the program and, possibly, for incorporating it into their lives. Incorporation, we think, is filtered by group dynamics—in conversations with significant others—and can be done in a variety of ways: by affirmation or negation of the moral of a story, for example, or through identification with a character, or by some more critical judgment.

SOCIAL DYNAMICS OF MEANING-MAKING: AN EMPIRICAL APPROACH

To observe these processes in action, we have undertaken a program of empirical research. We assembled 50 groups of three couples each—an initial couple invites two others from among their friends—to view an episode from the second session of *Dallas*, and to discuss it with us afterwards. These focus groups were of lower-middle class, with high school education or less, and ethnically homogeneous. There were ten groups each of Israeli Arabs, new immigrants to Israel from Russia, first and second generation immigrants from Morocco, and kibbutz members. Taking these groups as a microcosm of the worldwide audience of *Dallas*, we are comparing their readings of the program with ten groups of matched Americans in Los Angeles. The discussion following the program takes approximately one hour and is guided by a rather open interview guide for focus groups. The discussion is recorded, and it is followed by a brief individual questionnaire that asks participants to indicate whether and with whom they normally view and discuss the program.

If we are correct in our assumption about the social process of reading *Dallas*, the method we have chosen enables us to simulate and "sample" the high moments of this process. The postdiscussion questionnaire, as well as a preliminary inspection of some of the protocols, provide evidence that the program is viewed in the company of others and is widely discussed; there are repeated allusions in the focus groups to such discussions. Of course, we cannot prove that interpretation is altogether dependent on such interaction, or precisely how pervasive every day television talk might be. Even if we have overstated the "necessary" and pervasive aspects of such interaction, the method of focus group discussion provides a very close look at the social dynamics of meaning-making. People seem to express themselves very freely.

Of course, it is true that the statement of any individual in a group may be influenced by the statements—even the presence—of the others, and may well be different from what it might have been in a personal interview. But that's the point: if our assumption about the normality of the social reading of television is correct, it is precisely these group-influenced thoughts and statements in which we are interested.

Two other caveats need to be mentined. This particular study cannot provide a conclusive answer to the question of whether American programs are read with greater ease than programs from other countries. Nor can we generalise easily from *Dallas*, or its genre, to other American genres. So we cannot say with certainty that *Kojak* or *I Love Lucy* are processed in similar ways, cognitively or socially. These questions require complex and costly comparative research for which we are not yet prepared.

What we are doing is complicated enough. We are attempting to sample the interaction of small groups of different languages and cultures during and after the viewing of a television program that has been imported from outside their own culture and language, in an effort to identify the ways in which meaning and possible relevance is ascribed to the program.

A different way of stating our problem is to say that we are interested in the critical apparatus marshalled by lower-middle-class groups of varying ethnicity while sitting in front of the television screen. Again, we find ourselves in the midst of an almost unspoken debate over the activity level of television viewers and their conceptual powers. Most scholars and critics don't seem to give the common viewer much credit; yet, occasional research and some theories suggest that there is a native critical ability possessed even by the most unschooled viewer. One recent empirical study dares to suggest that lower-class viewers may be *more* articulate than well-educated ones in analysing popular television programs.[2]

If we restate our basic concern in these terms, we are asking, in effect, how the viewer analyses content or performs his own structural analysis of a program like *Dallas*. The group discussion, then, may be analysed as ethno-semiological data, in which the readings of the viewers may be compared to those of critics and scholars who have analysed the program. Since the effects attributed to a TV program are often inferred from content analysis alone, it is of particular interest to examine the extent to which members of the audience absorb, explicitly or implicitly, the messages which critics and scholars allege that they are receiving.

However one approaches the problematics of the study, we are, in effect, asking two basic questions: how do viewers make sense of *Dallas*?; and does viewer understanding differ in different cultures? To translate these questions into research operations, we ask, first of all, what happened in the episode, inviting group members to address the narrative sequence and the topics, issues, and themes with which the program deals.[3]

We pay particular attention to the ways in which these issues are discussed. For example, *Dallas* raises value questions about family life, living by the rules, loyalty, money versus happiness, civilisation versus "the frontier," the invasion of the family by business, and vice versa. Which of these issues will be raised in the group discussion, and what concepts will be invoked to discuss them? Are these concepts taken from: universal forms (deep structures)? tradition? personal experience? television genres?

We are also interested in viewer's perceptions of the message of the program. Do they perceive that the program proposes a correlation—positive or negative—between money and happiness? Do they agree that business is destroying the family, or vice versa? Do they feel that the program takes sides between the id and the superego? Do they feel that the program is about American decadence or American ascendance?

In addition to the analysis of issues and messages, we ask a second sort of question: how much "critical distance" can be discerned between the group discussions and the television screen? Thus, some groups will "gossip" about the characters as if they were real people, analysing their motivations in everyday terms. At the other extreme, certain groups will discuss attributes and actions as "functions" in a dramatic formula, groping, as critics do, towards a definition of the genre to which *Dallas* belongs. At this level of how "real" the characters and situations are thought to be, we ask whether they apply equally to all or only to "them," or to who "they" are: Texans? Americans? First World?

Yet another level of analysis is embedded in the sequences of conversation. Can one perceive in the interchange among group members a direction—some "progress"—towards a shared reading? Are there identifiable "outcomes" in the course of mutual help in understanding a character or an episode? Is there agreement or disagreement over whether an action is justified? Is there debate over whether a certain character or situation "could happen here"? What are the patterns of such processes of consensus-building or meaning-making? It is too early for us to answer these questions definitively. Nevertheless, we wish to share some very preliminary observations about this social process of meaning-making based on impressions from preliminary analysis of the Israeli cases.

MUTUAL AID IN INTERPRETATION

First, let us look at an example of a statement which reflects the process of mutual aid in the making of meaning. During the viewing of the program itself, group members fill in information for friends who missed the previous episode, remind each other about the past performances of certain characters who have been absent, explain motivations for actions, and prepare each other for a coming "surprise" or "unpleasantness." Consider the case of an illiterate middle-aged Moroccan woman named Ziviah conversing with her fellow-group members, including her husband, her sister, her sister's husband and a friend:

> *Salah*: [about Dusty]. It's not clear whether or not he can have children.
> *Miriam*: They talked about it in court [in the last episode].
> *Salah*: Why does she [Sue Ellen] live with him? That's strange.
> *Miriam*: Why? Because she's suffered enough. What do you mean, 'why?'
> *Ziviah*: Where's their father? Why don't we ever see him?
> *Miriam*: I think the father is dead.
> *Ziviah*: That's what they say.
> *Zari*: He died a few weeks ago, and it hardly matters.
> *Ziviah*: [indicating the screen] That's Bobby's wife. She's dying to have a child.
> *Miriam*: No, she's in a mental hospital now.
> *Ziviah*: Oh yes, yes, that's right.
> *Yosef*: Really?
> *Ziviah*: Yes, yes.
> *Salah*: She's in a hospital now?
> *Miriam*: A mental hospital.

But groups can reinforce each other not only in accurate exegesis of a test; they can also contribute cumulatively to a misreading. This process is particularly interesting when the distorted interpretation derives, apparently, from the attempt to incorporate a segment of the story into a familiar pattern of culture. Thus, in the following exchange, an Arabic group finds it culturally compatible to assume that Sue Ellen, having run away with the baby from her husband, JR, has returned to her father's home rather than to the home of her former lover and *his* father:

> *George*: He's trying to monopolise all the oil in order to destroy Sue Ellen's father. He wants to use it to pressure . . .
> *William*: Sue Ellen's father.
> *Interviewer*: Sue Ellen's father? Is that right?
> *William*: Wasn't that Sue Ellen's father that was with him?
> *Hyam*: Yes, Sue Ellen's father; that's him.
> *Interviewer*: Where was Sue Ellen at the time?
> *Hyam*: She's staying at her father's.

The previous example deals less with meaning, perhaps, and more with simple information. Let us look at an example of the way in which social interaction clarifies meaning. This is from a group of new immigrants from Russia, who know only a little of the English of the original and only a little more of the Hebrew of the subtitles. Yet here they are conversing in Russian, about Americans in Texas, on Israeli television. The issue is why the court gave custody of the baby to the mother, Sue Ellen, rather than to JR.

Liuba: Justice has a lot to do with it.

Misha: What justice? It was the medical certificate [attesting to the impotence of the man with whom Sue Ellen is living] that helped, not justice.

Mile: No, it's justice, not the medical certificate, that helped her to win.

Sofia: It was proven that Sue Ellen left him not to go to another man but to a sick man whom she was going to help at a difficult moment, and that was the decisive factor in the court's decision.

Misha: Nothing would have helped without the certificate.

Mile: Misha, he's not potent, this new husband of hers.

Liuba: She didn't go to a lover, but to . . .

Mile: Remember, he can't have any more children. So it's justice.

Misha: What justice? It's the medical certificate.

Mile: You're wrong.

All: You're wrong. It's about justice.

MUTUAL AID IN EVALUATION

Additionally, there are arguments about how things *should* have turned out. Some members of the group think well of the outcome of an issue raised in the program, while others disagree. Thus the group also sits in judgment of the values of the program, or at least brings its own values into open debate. Here is an example of this process from a group of Moroccan Jews, most of whom are already rather well integrated into Israeli society. The subject of this conversation is why Miss Ellie refuses to be JR's accomplice in the kidnapping of the baby:

Zehava: She [Miss Ellie] knows how it feels to be a mother. If her own son were taken away how would she feel? She would feel it keenly. She doesn't want others to suffer that way.

Yossi: You're talking as a mother. How about talking like a father?

Zehava: That's my opinion, and that's what I said. Let me explain to my husband. He's saying, 'Why should the father be the only one to suffer? Why should we be defending only the mother?' My answer is that the mother gave birth to the child and suffered for him. She loves him better than the father because the child is of her flesh. A father is a father; ok, so he loves his child.

Machluf: And not of his flesh? Isn't the father a partner in the child?

Zehava: The child's from his seed, but not of his flesh.

Machluf: What do you mean his seed and not his flesh?

Zehava: It's not the same thing. She suffered at the time of birth, and not the father.

Machluf: Don't they have half and half in the child . . . ? In the government you [women, feminists] say you want 50 percent, but you really mean you want 75 percent.

Another episode from this same group goes even further in questioning the wisdom of social arrangements for allocating and administering justice. Some members of the group insist that justice is too narrow in its focus. If only the judge had taken account of the whole of Sue Ellen's questionable past or the fact of her running off with the child, instead of focussing on her purity of soul, he would have awarded custody of the child to JR:

> *Yossi:* The kind of justice we just saw is called dry law. It's a kind of impersonal law, without people. Who says that the court had to decide that the child should stay with its mother? It's only a coincidence that her friend can't go to bed with her or give her a child. She shouldn't have been unfaithful, and the court shouldn't have given her custody of the child.

Such arguments are not limited to taking sides over issues within the program. A theme in the program as a whole is sometimes interpreted or evaluated against an opposite position which is embedded in the culture of the viewing group. Thus, one of the members of this same Moroccan group spoke eloquently, in liturgical rhetoric, of how much he did not feel allied to the values of *Dallas:*

> *Machluf:* You see I'm a Jew who wears a skullcap and I learned from this series to say, 'Happy is our lot, goodly is our fate' (*Psalms*) that we're Jewish. Everything about JR and his baby, who has maybe four or five fathers, who knows? The mother is Sue Ellen, of course, and the brother of Pam left, maybe he's the father . . . I see that they're almost all bastards . . .

A similar sort of rejection of the perceived message of *Dallas* can be found in a kibbutz group:

Sarah A: When I see them, I only pity them.
Amaliah: I live better than they do.
Sarah A: And I tell myself, how terrible it would be if I were one of them.
Amaliah: With all that they have money, my life style is higher than theirs.

But rejection is by no means the universal reaction. The groups we have examined so far are not so quick as the two just cited to reject the material values in *Dallas*. Indeed, even the groups that do reject them at one point in the discussion may reconsider at some other point. More typical, perhaps, is the following exchange from a group of North Africans in a semi-rural cooperative settlement:

Miriam: Money will get you anything. That's why people view it. People sit at home and want to see how it looks.
Salah: These are special people. Somehow they get it all, and we don't.
Ziviah: Right.
Joseph: Everybody wants to be rich. Whatever he has, he wants more.
Zari: Who doesn't want to be rich? The whole world does.
Miriam: Wealth also makes an easy life.
Ziviah: It's the best thing.

PERSONALIZATION VS OBJECTIFICATION: DIMENSIONS OF CRITICAL DISTANCE

It is clear from these examples that people are discussing and evaluating not only the issues of the Ewing family but the issues in their own lives. Indeed, much of the discussion in groups focuses on problems of conflict between the sexes, normative versus anomic family relations, money versus happiness, loyalty versus opportunism, and the like. Some of the discussants clearly use the program to discuss themselves and their conficts. Others do so less freely. This may turn out to be one of the important differences between the ethnic groups; namely, how much critical distance is maintained throughout the discussion. Here is an example of personal soul-searching triggered by the program:

Sarah A: When they tried to kill him [JR], her behaviour was simply . . . I don't know what to call it. How could she, suddenly . . . ? It's true you feel guilty, so you worry about a person. But

suddenly to love him? . . . That seems put on. So what? Because
I feel guilty, I should suddenly sell myself? sell my personality?

Consider the following—from a Russian group—in comparison:

> *Sima*: I'm surprised by his [JR's] attitude to his father. He must
> be feeling that his father is superior to him financially, as a
> businessman. What we see in the course of the program is that
> he is constantly telling his father, 'Father don't worry, the boy
> will come home, don't worry, everything will be all right,' as if he
> were giving a report to his father, as if he were bowing down to
> him.
>
> *Marik*: In my opinion, he has inferiority feelings toward his
> father . . .
>
> *Misha*: He's a very complex person . . . He has many contrasts.
> One can't say that such a person is very positive, although he
> does have certain positive qualities. I can't say that business for
> such a person, and his ambitions for achieving his goals, are
> negative. Without such qualities he couldn't work and make
> money, and making money is his profession.
>
> *Marik*: Agree.
>
> *Sima*: For him, everything is divided according to priorities,
> according to their importance. In business, let's say everything
> has to be organised. In a family, there has to be an heir. Every-
> thing as it should be.
>
> *Interviewer*: Do you mean without emotion?
>
> *Sima*: I wouldn't say without emotion. Maybe yes. It seems to
> me that he wants his son not because he loves him; he's not so
> devoted to him. He simply knows that's the way it should be. He
> knows that he's his father's heir. I believe that he's living accord-
> ing to his father's code.

The more systematic analysis on which we are now engaged
suggests that the several ethnic groups do differ, as we suspected, in degree of critical distance. Certain groups use the
program "referentially," that is, they relate the narrative to real
life. Others speak much more analytically, or "poetically," relating to the dramatic construction of the story rather than to its
reality.[4] The groups that specialise in referential statements are
the Arabs and the Moroccan Jews; culturally, they are probably
most distant from *Dallas*. The most purely poetic is the Russian
group, who have much to say about genre, dramatic conflict,
and the like. While the Oriental groups and the Russians may
be said to specialise in one mode on account of the other—
talking either about life or about genre—the American kibbutz
groups seem to be more flexible, speaking both critically and
referentially.

While the groups differ in the extent of their use of poetic and referential statements, the form of referential statements also appears to distinguish among the groups. Thus, when discussing the relationship of the program to real life, the Russians exceed all the others in their use of abstract or universal categories such as "businessmen" or "women" or "Americans." The others talk much more in terms of we-groups. Moroccans and Arabs do this more seriously, while Americans and kibbutz members do so more playfully, as if they were "trying on" the roles of the different characters of *Dallas*, imagining how wonderful or awful it might feel to be in their place.

While poetic statements are surely more distant than referential ones, it is not immediately clear that referential statements about general categories such as "businessmen" or "Americans" are less involved than references to oneself or one's we-group. In other words, it is possible that relating the program to broad categories of persons may imply a belief in the reality and generalisability of the program that is not necessarily present in talking about the relation of the program to oneself. If more generalised is more distant, then the Russians are the most distanced group, leading both in the proportion of poetic statements and in the proportion of referential statements that allude to abstract categories of people. According to the same calculus, the Arabs would rank least distant, or most involved.

Yet, for all their differences, there are interesting similarities between the Russian and Arab groups. Not only are they more "specialised" (in the ratio of poetic to referential) than the other groups, and more "serious" (compared to the more playful role-takings of the Americans and kibbutzniks), they are also more "evaluative." Both groups tend to prefer the rhetorics of evaluation (good/bad) to the rhetorics of interpretation. The Arabs use evaluation in their referential statement, the Russians do so in their poetic statements.

Because we are still in the midst of analysing these very complex protocols of the focus group conversations—a mere sampling of which is reproduced here—it is too early to propose anything as pretentious as conclusions. Nevertheless,

1. We are impressed by the sophisticated ways in which very common people discuss these stories. Clearly, they understand the broad outlines of the narrative; clearly they know the structure of the relations among the characters, their emotions and motivations, and are able to articulate at least some of the central themes.

2. There is evident selectivity in what is discussed. The importance of family far outweighs the importance of business, as we expected. Less sophisticated groups sometimes use kinship terms to identify the characters.

3. Issues discussed include success, loyalty, honour, money and happiness, sex-roles, the functions of children, and many others. Topics raised in the program are generalised in the discussions so that they refer to generic human problems or immediate personal issues. The feeling of intimacy with the characters, expressed in many of the groups, has a "gossipy" quality which seems to facilitate an easy transition to discussion of oneself and one's close associates. It is likely that the continuous and indeterminate flow of the program, from week to week, in the family salon invites viewers to invest themselves in fantasy, thought, and discussion. The social distance between the Ewing family and the rest of the world seems far less important than one might have thought. Unhappiness is the great leveller.[5]

4. Altogether, we feel strongly supported in our hypotheses that the viewing process is active and social—perhaps even among those who vigorously deny it. The discussion frequently alludes to what discussants said last week or last month. This social process surely contributes to the ease of understanding (and sometimes to misunderstanding) and to the making of meaning and evaluation. Anthropologists agree, even when survey statistics do not.[6]

5. The focus group method has proved very satisfactory. Discussions of television programs, as simulated in these groups, appear to constitute a forum for the discussion of basic social issues and themes. They liberate people to say playfully— among their peers—what they might say seriously only in situations of crisis or conflict. It seems unlikely that these statements would be evoked in reply to an individual questionnaire or interview.

6. Groups appear to differ in what we call "critical distance," that is, the extent to which characters and issues are generalised or personalised, and the extent to which statements about the program refer to the structure of the story or to "life." Certain ethnic groups switch easily from discussing the story to discussing life; others keep their distance. Certain groups generalise the program to abstract social categories such as "women" or "Americans"; others implicate themselves more directly.

7. What seems clear from the analysis, even at this stage, is that the non-Americans consider the story more real than the Americans. The non-Americans have little doubt that the story is about "America"; the Americans are less sure, and are altogether more playful in their attitudes toward the program.

8. Hegemonic theorists will find it easy to interpret the reactions of both acceptors and rejectors of the values in *Dallas* as establishment messages. If the money and muscle of the Ewings is an invitation to the fantasies of social mobility and the supposed "American way," then identification with the *Dallas* characters will serve the purpose. But what about those who see in *Dallas* only a reminder of how much better off they are without power? It takes only the slightest agility to see that this is even more hegemonic. It is a message to stay down, and enjoy the better of the possible worlds, letting the unhappy few take care of the rest.

NOTES

1. Here we are in disagreement with others who believe that the unit of television viewing is better conceptualised as background, or as a "strip" that cuts through an evening's viewing or as a pervasive barrage of messages about society that is embedded in all of prime time. Our argument is simply that certain programs—some more than others—are identified by viewers as discrete stories, and that such viewing entails attention, interpretation, evaluation, and perhaps social and psychological consequences. For recent, relevant writings on the "active" audience, see Philip Palmgreen, "The Uses and Gratifications Approach: A Theoretical Paradigm," in Robert Bostrom, ed., *Communication Yearbook* VIII (Beverly Hills, CA: Sage, 1984); Dave Morley, *The Nationwide Audience* (London: British Film Institute, 1980); and W. Anthony Collins, "Cognitive Processing and Television Viewing," in Ellen Wartella and J. Whitney, eds., *Mass Communication Review Yearbook* 4 (Beverly Hills, CA: Sage, 1983).

2. W. Russell Neuman, "TV and American Culture: The Mass Medium and the Pluralistic Audience," *Public Opinion Quarterly* 46 (1982), 471–487.

3. In their paper, "Television as a Cultural Forum: Implications for Research," *Quarterly Review of Film Studies* 8 (1983), 48–55, Horace Newcomb and Paul Hirsch argue that television is a "forum," presenting viewers with issues that need to be resolved. Their content analysis identifies three levels: topics, issues, and themes. [This paper appears as a selection in Part II of this volume. ED.]

4. See Roman Jacobson, "Linguistics and Poetics," in R. and F. de George, eds., *The Structuralists from Marx to Lévi-Strauss* (New York: Anchor Books, 1980). Larry Gross makes a similar distinction between "attributional" and "inferential" readings. The first connects the program to parallels in real life, and the second (realising the constructedness of the event) infers the producer's intentions. See "Life vs Art: The Interpretation of Visual Narratives," a

lecture on US-Hungarian Interaction in Literature. Hungarian Academy of Sciences, 1983. The classic statement, of course, is Roman Jakobson.

5. Content analysis finds that American prime-time family programs consistently offer this message of consolation for those who can't make it up. See Sari Thomas and Brian P. Callahan, "Allocating Happiness: Television Families and Social Class," *Journal of Communication* 32 (1982), 67–77.

6. Anthropologists are trying to show that survey research on the frequency of television talk is missing the active but subtle interpretations of programs and applications to relevant issues that go on during and after viewing. See Jennifer Bryce and Hope Jensen Leichter, "The Family and Television: Forms of Mediation," *Journal of Family Issues* 4 (1983), 309–328.

WALTER KARP

WHERE THE DO-GOODERS
WENT WRONG

There is something distinctly sinister about the world of children's television. I discovered this quite by accident while trying to resolve a difference of opinion: my children like Saturday-morning children's television; the critics loathe it. "A monstrous mess," Gary Grossman calls it in his 1981 study, *Saturday Morning TV.* "An animated world of meanness and mayhem," is how it appears to Peggy Charren, founder and head of Action of Children's Television. The critics especially deplore "outdated" cartoons such as *Bugs Bunny.* My children like Bugs Bunny best of all.

Intrigued by a difference of opinion so sharp, I decided to spend a few Saturday mornings judging for myself the merits and defects of children's television. Here I made the first of many curious discoveries. I thought judging the merits of children's television would be comparatively easy. Instead I found it virtually impossible. I simply had no standard for judging what I saw. One episode of the *Smurfs*, a blue-skinned race of dwarflets, convinced me of that.

In the episode, a trumpet-playing Smurf, feeling spurned by his fellows, blows a loud blast on his trumpet, unwittingly disclosing to the evil wizard the whereabouts of the Smurf village. What, if anything, did the plot signify? I certainly didn't know. The wizard looked to me far more comical than menacing, but was he? How can an adult know what a child will find fearsome? The wizard chases the tiny Smurf up hill and down dale, but in vain. His back aches, he gasps for breath. He is an *out-of-shape* wizard. A witty idea, I thought, but I wondered whether it was not perhaps too adult an idea. Do children really

think big hulking adults are too weak to harm them? I suspected not, but what did it signify one way or the other?

Ultimately the exhausted wizard winds up hanging from a
log slung over a ravine. Instead of shoving him to his doom, the
Smurf decides that vengeance is "un-Smurflike" and mercifully
spares the wicked wizard. When the Grimm brothers' Gretel
had the witch at her mercy, she shoved her into a hot oven.
Was Smurf mercy "better" for children than Hansel and Gretel's grisly justice? Again, I simply did not know, and I think
most people don't know. My own knowledge of children is
exactly the common knowledge: once I was one of them, now I
have two of them. The common knowledge does not suffice.
That leaves a vacuum and a politically perilous one, for the
ignorance of a free people endangers their freedom.

Trying hard to fill that vacuum are the various critics of
children's television. They include organized parents, educators, enlightened (usually public) broadcasters, pediatricians,
child psychologists, and professors of human development.
They have also included a few powerful politicians, but that I
did not know until much later.

The critics (whom I now began to read in earnest) have
evolved a stringent standard of judgment. They believe that
good children's television teaches children to be cooperative,
hard-working, and peace-loving members of society. Programs
that carry such lessons are praised as "pro-social." The critics
regard as defective those programs that appear to encourage
selfishness, self-assertiveness, and aggression. After an experimental group of young children watched *Superman* and *Batman*,
which are deemed to be "aggressive" shows, they demonstrated
a heightening of aggressive tendencies, according to two professors of human development at the University of Pennsylvania. After watching *Mr. Rogers' Neighborhood*, a much-lauded
"prosocial" program, young children reportedly demonstrated
greater "observance of the rules, tolerance of delays, and persistence in tasks."

In order to serve the pro-social ideal of peaceful, unselfish,
cooperative behavior, pro-social programming would feature,
for example, "television characters who solve problems in nonaggressive ways" and "television characters who cooperate
with each other, who openly express their feelings, who devote
their energies to helping other people." Pro-social programming would alter, often drastically, traditional storytelling de-

vices. In the *ACT Guide to Children's Television*, which was written "with the cooperation of the American Academy of Pediatrics," Evelyn Kaye points out that "constructive" children's stories would show superior evil forces overcome by means of "thoughtfulness, cooperation, or reason," rather than by "magic, cunning, or cheating"—traditional modes of besting giants and wizards who violate the pro-social rules.

Group-minded, industrious, and self-effacing, the pro-social child envisioned by the critics of children's television bears a curious resemblance to those Japanese workers so much admired of late by American businessmen.

Determined to "socialize" children and provide them with "strategies for coping with an increasingly complex world," the critics of children's television also prefer factuality to fantasy and realism to rowdy comedy. Slapstick, for one thing, is excessively aggressive, while fantasy the critics tend to regard as deceiving. As Peggy Charren puts it in *Changing Channels*: "Children need to understand that many of the things they see on TV do not happen in real life. Real people do not fly or disappear or walk through walls." The critics prefer programs that "reflect our own reality"—programs, for example, that would make children more aware of the people "who carry out the basic tasks of American society," such as blue-collar workers and sales personnel. They also prefer stories that show black and Hispanic characters in positions of leadership.

This kind of sanitized "realism" bears a striking resemblance to what was taught in the "progressive" schools of the 1940s, described by David Reisman in his celebrated work *The Lonely Crowd* as "agencies for the destruction of fantasy," where "fairy tales are replaced by stories about trains, telephones, and grocery stores and later by material on race relations or the United Nations or 'our Latin-American neighbors.'"

Lastly, the critics of children's television have taken great pains to demonstrate to the nation's parents that whatever is not pro-social is physically and mentally *harmful* to their children. Working closely with pediatricians and child psychologists, the critics contend that frightening stories and fearsome villains make children "anxious" and give them nightmares. Citing studies that show "some children" cannot distinguish an animated cartoon from real life, the critics demand the elimination of any rowdy or unreal actions that a deluded child might imitate at his peril, as in the extreme instance of children jumping off roofs thinking they are Superman. In this way the critics can demand on the grounds of safety the curtailment of "aggressive" actions that they disfavor, in any case, on pro-social grounds.

More persistently, the critics of children's television have tried to marshal incontrovertible scientific proof that viewing violent action on television incites violent behavior in children. The proof has not been forthcoming. The most positive conclusions are hedged and cautious, as in the assertion that "there is evidence to support the theory that watching destructive cartoons leads to destructive play." Other studies give exactly the opposite results. As Cecily Truett, a former PBS official, ruefully noted in *Television & Children*, "Studies on the effects of violence on children's behavior are inconsistent and inconclusive." Completely undaunted by these disappointing results, the critics of children's television remain determined to root out televised violence and destruction.

In their hostility to violent deeds and powerful emotions, the critics of children's television bear a remarkable resemblance to those bowdlerizing turn-of-the-century schoolmarms who used to march through Grimms' fairy tales snipping out cruelty and cutting down ogres in the name of "mental hygiene."

That resemblance, more than anything, made me suspicious of the pro-social standard. In defending the fairy tales from the censorious schoolmarms, England's G. K. Chesterton offered a memorable insight into the psychology of children and of the ancient children's stories. "Fairy tales," wrote Chesterdon, "do not give the child the idea of the evil or the ugly; that is in the child already because it is in the world already. Fairy tales do not give the child his first idea of bogey. What fairy tales give the child is his first clear idea of the possible defeat of bogey." Instead of protecting children from unhealthy fears, the bowdlerizers of the fairy tales were depriving them of much-needed hope, the hope that the ghouls beneath their beds and the monsters in their closets have forms and faces, and that there is a champion who can best them, if not by "thoughtfulness, cooperation, or reason," then somehow or other—perhaps with a sword. The fairy tales, as Chesterton understood them, exposed the schoolmarms as the children's false friends. I strongly suspected that they might shed the same merciless light on today's pro-social critics and, more important, on the real merits and defects of children's television.

I thought I knew where such light could be found. In 1976

Bruno Bettelheim, an eminent child psychologist and one of the shining spirits of our time, published a book entitled *The Uses of Enchantment: The Meaning and Importance of Fairy Tales*. It is a rich and difficult work (especially after reading the banalities of the pro-social), the fruit of high intelligence, long reflection, and deep compassion for children—the work of an "informed heart," to borrow the title of Dr. Bettelheim's own account of what he learned about himself and his fellow man in the hellhole of a Nazi concentration camp.

In *The Uses of Enchantment*, Bettelheim shows how irrelevant to the real needs of children the pro-social enterprise turns out to be. "Since the child at every moment of his life is exposed to the society in which he lives, he will certainly learn to cope with its conditions, provided his inner resources permit him to do so." In concentrating on mere outward behavior (cooperating, helping others), proponents of the pro-social neglect the child himself—the fearful, struggling child "with his immense anxieties about what will happen to him and his aspirations." The difficulties a child faces seem to him so great, his fears so immense, his sense of failure so complete, says Bettelheim, that without encouragement of the most powerful kind he is in constant danger of falling prey to despair, "of completely withdrawing into himself, away from the world." What children urgently need from children's stories are not lessons in cooperative living but the life-saving "assurance that one can succeed"—that monsters can be slain, injustice remedied, and all obstacles overcome on the hard road to adulthood.

Fairy tales can help provide the inner strength to grow up, notes Bettelheim, only because they are fantasies. The menace of despair weighs so heavily on a child that "only exaggerated hopes and fantasies of future achievement can balance the scales so that the child can go on living and striving." "Realistic" stories, he says, cannot give children inner strength because they can offer only pedestrian hopes and mundane triumphs. They inform without nourishing, like the "educational reports" and "social studies" that the pro-social critics demand of children's television as part of their curious campaign to make blissful Saturday a sixth day of school.

Fairy tales can "come to the rescue" of children, moreover, only because their fearsome, fantastic dangers are rooted in a child's real fears—the fear of being lost or abandoned; the dread of monsters, which represent to the child, says Bettelheim, the monstrous side of himself, the side he must learn how to master. Fairy tales, in a word, are meant to be scary. If they do not frighten, they do not work, for overcoming a flimsy danger gives a child no real assurance.

In the fairy tales, the hero of the story struggles alone. This, too, is an essential feature, for without it the fairy tales could not fulfill their task of helping the child "go on living and striving." The lonely hero offers the child "the image of the isolated man who is nevertheless capable of meaningful achievement." His isolation mirrors the isolation every child feels in the face of his real terrors. The hero's ultimate triumph provides the heartswelling promise that the child, too, will find inner strength when he ventures forth on his own.

Lastly, the fairy tales help rescue the child from despair with their triumphantly happy endings—gaining a kingdom, winning a peerless spouse, vanquishing all foes. "Without such encouraging conclusions, the child, after listening to the story, will feel that there is indeed no hope of extricating himself from the despairs of life." No happy ending is complete, moreover, unless the wicked are severely punished. To a child, says Bettelheim, only severe punishment truly fits the terrible crimes he believes are committed against *him*—which, in his own view, go utterly unpunished. The punishment of the wicked is welcome proof to the child that he, too, will find justice one day; the great world will not let him down. "The more severely those bad ones are dealt with, the more secure the child feels." Thus, the fairy tales (speaking through Bettelheim's deep, tender analysis) answered my question about the significance of mercy in a children's story. Quite simply, it is adulteration: something adults foist upon children at the children's expense.

By conjuring up fearful dangers, lonely trials, and justice triumphant, the fairy tales give children strength for their arduous journey to the kingdom of adulthood. Like wise and loving parents, these ancient, universal tales serve the true interests of children as distinct from the interests of society, which cares nothing about the inner strength of its members, but only about their outward conformity. The fairy tales are not pro-social. What they are is pro-child. They stand guard against the adulteration of childhood by society's overzealous agents.

How pro-child would children's television turn out to be, I wondered, when at last I felt ready to return to the animated cartoon world of Saturday-morning television? With eyes sharpened by *The Uses of Enchantment*, I discovered the astonishing answer quickly enough. Every essential element that makes it possible for fairy tales to give children inner strength, hope, and security is absent today from children's television.

The hero of children's television is not a person at all. It is the ubiquitous group. The group is five dogs roaming the world; two frogs and a turtle solving crimes; two teenagers and two dogs unmasking villains; a team of young gymnasts and their ghetto-smart leader; three chipmunks; an explorer, his niece, and a cowardly lion; a village of minuscule dwarfs; an island of minuscule monkeys; a team of tree-dwelling elves.

In this group-dominated world, deeds are group deeds, and motives, group motives. It is the group that faces the dangers and the group that emerges triumphant, demonstrating its invincible strength. The sources of group strength are constantly made clear through social backchat among the group members. Their discussions of tolerance, teamwork, and the evils of vanity and selfishness often rival, and sometimes overwhelm, the action. The sources of group weakness are also made clear. In Saturday's group-minded world, the nonconformist is an obnoxious complainer. In the *Smurfs*, he is Grouchy. In *Dungeons and Dragons*, he is Eric, the sneering sourpuss who constantly derides the group's judgment. In every conceivable way, children are taught the pro-social virtues of cooperation, self-effacement, and subservience to the group.

The "image of the isolated man who is nonetheless capable of meaningful achievement"—so important to the child, so useless to society—rarely crosses the screen on Saturday morning. Even when the group must split up to perform special tasks, nobody goes forth alone. Like an army unit, the group, when it splits, divides into squads. That an isolated being may be capable of meaningful achievement is an idea kept from the children as though it were a secret of state. If, as the fairy tales tell us, a child learns to have faith in his own inner strength through fantastic tales of lone heroes, then children's television systematically deprives children of that faith.

What is even worse, it actively subverts a child's faith in his own inner strength. On Saturday-morning television, practically the only thing a lone being can do is fall prey to wizards, wicked adults, and master criminals. On Saturday-morning television, the most vivid "image of the isolated man" is that of a hapless victim whom the group decides to rescue. The group-rescue motif is one of the main devices of children's television, and its primary message is perfectly plain: the lone individual is weak and helpless; the group is strong and kind. Several programs dramatize this seductive message by making one of the group's members a slightly comical coward whom the group treats with bemused toleration; the group has strength enough for all.

This kind of reassurance is sweet consolation to children (including my own), but it is treacherous and baseless, the most insidious kind of false comfort. In real life, no gang can help a child master the deep anxieties that beset him. In real life, cowardice is not in the least comical, for every child knows in his heart how desperately he needs courage. Like the sugary cereals the pro-social critics are forever assailing, this kind of sugary, pro-social reassurance sweetens subservience and weakens the child.

Children's television doles out equally poisonous comfort with its treatment of danger. Whereas the fairy tales confront the terrors of childhood by showing great perils overcome, children's television deals with those terrors by making light of them. The out-of-shape wizard who had puzzled me at first proved to be merely one example of television's massive falsifying of children's fears. With the consistent exception of two programs, *Dungeons and Dragons* and *The Littles*, the bogeys and perils of Saturday-morning television have little or no power to frighten.

Often the villains are deliberately portrayed as inept clowns. The Grumplins are manifestly too silly to do the Monchichis any harm. Dragons are drawn with goofy faces, or they trip over their tails as soon as they breathe fire. "Isn't danger funny!" these shows seem to say.

On the more "realistic" programs, children's fears are mocked outright: a disguised villain, seemingly scary and phantasmal, is unmasked at the end, revealing a run-of-the-mill crook. The two teenagers and two dogs on *Scooby-Doo* reveal that the "Hound of the Bakervilles" is only the caretaker disguised. Richie Rich reveals that the "Phantom of TV" is merely a security guard at the broadcasting studio. This kind of unmasking is petty rationalism at its worst. It does no good whatever to call a child's fears groundless. It only makes his demons all the more terrible, since the child sees no way to overcome them.

These cartoons seldom present the kinds of dangers that spring from the real fears of childhood. Bank robbers and master criminals are not rooted in children's primordial fears. They are merely cartoon copies of adult television. Wicked witches and evil stepmothers *do* rise up from childhood's primordial depths, but during many, many hours of watching Saturday television, I saw not a one of them. Rooted in the child's passionate life in the family, these mother figures (as Dr. Bettelheim shows) are much too potent, it seems, for the antiseptic world of children's television. In the great majority of children's shows, the family does not exist at all, perhaps because it is the only group that deeply matters to the child. The characters in most children's television shows dwell in a kinless, bloodless limbo drained of all real emotion.

Even the pro-social campaign against "aggression" and "violence" ends by betraying the real interests of children. Out of fear of encouraging "aggressive" behavior, it deprives children of the very promise of justice itself. In the sanitized world of children's television, the wicked are merely foiled, the scene quickly changes, and they are left scot-free, presumably because punishment would be too "violent." So children's television, which gives children no faith in their own inner strength, which gives them no hope that their demons will be bested, robs them of the precious assurance that justice will be theirs when they, too, venture into the great world. You must put no faith in yourself, says children's television: you must put no faith in an unjust world; the group alone can save you. This is a very strange lesson to teach a free people's children.

When I first read the pro-social critics, I assumed that they were lonely voices in the video wilderness. Yet nothing could be further from the truth. The pro-social standard dominates children's television. As one veteran children's show producer, David de Patie, put it four years ago: "The greatest changes [in children's television] are because of the ladies in Boston—Action for Children's Television. I think they have exerted a great influence." Rigid network codes, I learned, rigorously enforce the pro-social standard by eliminating "aggression" and emasculating danger. "Today, networks red-pencil any prolonged action that would so much as make a palm sweat," notes Gary Grossman in *Saturday Morning TV*. One network code rules that if a building is damaged in the course of an episode it must be repaired by the episode's end. The networks' "program practices" departments—the censors—also enforce with rigor the pro-social stricture against dangerously "imitable" behavior.

One network cut out a scene showing a pussy-cat character hiding from a monster in a dish of spaghetti on the grounds that some child might dunk his cat into pasta as well. "I can't even have a character throw a pie in somebody's face anymore," says Joseph Barbera, the most prolific producer of children's cartoon shows. "The reason is simple. It's imitable, and the networks say we can't do anything bad that a child might imitate. It's gone that far."

The pro-social may not be esteemed, but it is certainly feared. When I interviewed a children's programming executive, she quickly assured me (supposing me to be a snoop from pro-social headquarters) that her network was dedicated to promoting "positive values" such as "cooperation as a group," "teamwork," and "working together," and that it dutifully showed characters "resolving conflicts within the group" while scrupulously putting "selfishness" and "bellyaching" in a "negative" light. Only when I hinted that my preferences lay elsewhere did she feel free to tell me how "browbeaten" by the codes the scriptwriters felt and how hard it was, under the rules, to establish "emotional contact with the child." The pro-social has become a despotic little orthodoxy.

Interestingly enough, you would never know this from reading the pro-social literature. When a leading critic assails Saturday-morning television in 1982 as an "animated world of meanness and mayhem," who would ever suspect that the networks had paid the pro-social any heed whatever?

This, too, struck me as a little strange, because it cuts off a question that would arise naturally in people's minds if they knew how thoroughly the pro-social forces have triumphed. The question is: How did a band of pedagogues, "ladies in Boston," and professors of human development manage to wield so much power? The question would open up interesting lines of inquiry. It would lead back from the pro-social critics to the real wielders of power who have promoted the pro-social cause. It would lead, as I discovered, to powerful federal officials such as the Federal Communications Commission member who, in 1968, invited parents to *sue* the networks if they thought television had harmed their children—an invitation to the most overwrought, irresponsible, and censorious parents to help the government bowdlerize children's television. It would lead back to still more powerful political figures, such as Senator John Pastore of Rhode Island, a former chairman of the Senate Commerce Committee's powerful communications sub-

committee. In 1972 Senator Pastore put the frightened networks on notice that he and his senatorial colleagues would no
longer tolerate television's "endless repetition of the message
that conflict may be resolved by aggression." It was behind
Pastore's well-organized assault on televised aggression, begun
in 1968, that the pro-social critics gathered their forces. His
victory became their victory.

Interestingly enough, while Senator Pastore was forcing the
networks to cut down on "aggression" for the sake of the
children, he remained a diehard supporter of the Vietnam War.
Here was a powerful public man who approved of B-52
bombers blowing women and children to bits while frowning
on Bugs Bunny as an incitement to violence. Nor was Pastore
the first bellicose senator to campaign against televised violence. His predecessor in this work was the infamous Thomas
Dodd of Connecticut, who was as determined to rid television
of "aggression" as he was to see America girded for war in
every corner of the globe.

That those two senators should have worried so greatly
about televised violence struck me, I confess, as a very odd
coincidence. Pondering that coincidence brought dark suspi-
cions to my mind. I wondered whether the Dodds and the
Pastores were really worried about televised "aggression" at all,
or whether, perhaps, they harbored concerns of a very different kind. Their timing alone was worth considering. While
these two war-minded worthies were fretting over fisticuffs on
Wagon Train, a vast rebellion against official violence and official
aggression was taking place in America, a vast protest in the
cause of peace, a vast uprising against the war policies that the
Dodds and the Pastores had so ardently supported for so many
long years. For the first time in more than half a century,
private citizens in America were demonstrating that they still
had the inner strength to think for themselves, to judge for
themselves, and to act for themselves. That demonstration
profoundly shocked the established political leaders of the country, especially old-line machine politicians like Senator Pastore.

Entrenched in power for fifty years, unchallenged by a people
grown pliant and credulous, the nation's startled leaders suddenly found themselves facing a great democratic revolt against
their power and prerogatives. It was plain enough that the
nation's leaders needed to put their challenged power on a more
secure and lasting basis. They needed a citizenry more prone to

obedience and less prone to act for themselves than young Americans so surprisingly had turned out to be. It was clear, too, that the traditional anarchy of children's television, with its knockabout comedy, irreverent clowns, and headstrong heroes, had done nothing to aid and abet the nation's leaders. It seemed to me, therefore, that when Pastore struck his decisive blow for pro-social children's television, what he was really asking the networks to do was make a more positive contribution to the indoctrination of America's children, to play a more systematic role in modeling a more docile and subservient people.

Such was my suspicion, and it seems to me far from groundless, for this is precisely what pro-social television attempts to accomplish. It is systematic training for personal weakness and social subservience. It promotes conformity and saps inner strength. It teaches the children of a free people (whose ignorance thus menaces their liberty) to look to the group for their opinions and to despise those who do not do the same. Out of a pretended fear of "aggressiveness," it would deprive a free people of the very inner force and self-assurance they need to stand up and fight for their rights.

Is this not a little sinister?

JIMMIE REEVES

TELEVISION STARS:
THE CASE OF MR. T

> . . . Only people that are *really for real* will really get next to
> Mr. T. The woman that is *really for real* will get my heart. These
> that come around with, with, with big breasts and flashy smile
> and big behind and say, "Oh, you're on TV, I like you, and this
> and that." That don't move me, you know. They hollar about
> Mr. T now, but in a couple, uh, maybe less than a year ago, they
> were saying "look at that wild lookin' nigger with that funny
> haircut with that junk around his neck." Now, [*mimicking*] "How
> you doin', Mr. T, duh, duh, duh." You know, who are they
> foolin'? Don't ask me how I'm doin'! Don't ask me, "Hey, Mr. T,
> how 'bout goin' to lunch?" I can buy the whole restaurant, now.
> When I needed a lunch, they wouldn't take me out . . . [Author's
> emphasis.].   —Mr. T[1]

His has been a sudden stardom. First surfacing in a novelty
sporting event, then in a supporting role in *Rocky III*, in just one
year Mr. T became a houshold word—there was no doubt that
he was the most visible and controversial television star of the
1983–84 season. However, Mr. T's acting performance has not
placed him in the pantheon of permanent stars, and given the
fate of other star figures whose appearances suddenly saturated the flow of television, his stardom will probably not be an
enduring one.

Yet, should he prove to be a fad star, of short-term relevance,
the temporary symbolic power of his now familiar figure cannot be dismissed. What, after all, are we to make of this fad?
Might his performance contribute to the maintenance of hori-
zons and repair of gaps in our culture? We might suggest his
character on *The A Team* succeeds because it gives stark expression to a racial stereotype: the big, bad, "nigger" buffoon. Or

we could argue that the popularity of his figure and the ratings success of *The A Team* indicate a major shift in cultural attitudes, that his person has legitimated a once threatening ethnic type in the culture. If this is the case, his figure is repairing a racial gap in the "real" world.

There is evidence for both interpretations in the text of *The A Team*. However, if we consider his many performances outside the frame of *The A Team*, there is more evidence suggesting that he represents the legitimation of a once inappropriate social type than evidence suggesting that he is merely an ethnic fool. Consequently, this critical analysis will treat his stardom as a legitimation, while admitting that there are social agenda that would list his figure as the reworking of a stereotype.

If such a legitimation is true, it has been a long time coming. Ten years ago, Mr. T would not have been an appropriate hero-figure on prime-time television. He would have been too threatening to common sensibilities: his open belligerence, his unruly aggressiveness, and his unadulterated *blackness* too unsettling and disturbing to prime-time audiences, as well as to national advertisers. Even though his unique figure seems to have appeared from nowhere, the prime-time recognition of his individuality has resulted from a gradual social process, which can be studied by comparing Mr. T to black male figures appearing previously on television. And several relevant antecedents to Mr. T have surfaced in the flow of television, some in the series stories, but most in sports.

The multiracial professional team, of course, is nothing new to television: *I Spy, Mission Impossible, The Mod Squad*, and *Barney Miller* featured black male members of professional groups. Bill Cosby, as Alexander Scott in *I Spy*, broke a color barrier by becoming the first black performer to have a starring role in a regular dramatic series on American commercial television. Teamed with Robert Culp in portraying an American spy team, his character was an educated upper-middle class type: graduate of Temple, Rhodes scholar, and language expert. His cover during their missions in the show was athletic trainer to Culp's character, a top-seeded tennis player who traversed the globe for tournaments. Although Cosby's role represented a broadening of the parameters of the appropriate in prime-time television, his character only really legitimated sophisticated members of the black race—educated, expert types. An electronics wizard, Greg Morris's Barney Collier on *Mission Impossible*, was also an expert type, but his character was stripped of all ethnicity. Speaking, dressing, and performing like a middle-class white man, Morris was a "token" representative of the black race. Clarence Williams III's Linc Hayes on *The Mod Squad* was also clearly a token black, but his character did display some of the ethnic codes of the day: most notably an "afro" hair style. Even with the afro, Linc Hayes represented a relevant youth type of the period (the hippie) more than a relevant black type. On *Barney Miller*, Ron Glass's Detective Ron Harris was an ambitious and upwardly mobile black professional. His ethnicity became an issue in several episodes because Harris's character was racially aware, conscious of his blackness, and not just a token figure. However, like Cosby's Alexander Scott, he was also a convert to the values of white, middle-class America and his character did not pose a physical or sexual threat to common sensibilities. Both Cosby's Scott and Glass's Harris represented intelligent black men who, failing to lick them, had joined them.

The characters on *The A Team* are quite different from those on these other shows. Where the others are on teams connected to legitimate law enforcement and intelligence agencies, B. A. Baracus and company are a bunch of renegades. Clearly operating outside what is presented as the corrupt and ineffectual institutions of American society, the team members are, according to the opening montage of *The A Team*, fugitives from the army justice system: having been convicted of a crime they didn't commit, they escaped from a "maximum security stockade," and live in the "Los Angeles underground" surviving as "soldiers of fortune." Unlike Cosby's Alexander Scott and Glass's Detective Harris, Mr. T's character is not a convert to the values of middle-class America. The "B. A." at the front of his character's name standing for "Bad Attitude," Mr. T has not been allowed to join us, but he hasn't been licked by us, either.

But Mr. T's performance in *The A Team* also resonates with the performances of Cosby, Morris, Williams, and Glass. Like Morris's character on *Mission Impossible*, B. A. Baracus is an expert type. A mechanical wizard, he often supervises the customizing of civilian vehicles at hand, making them battle-ready with armor plating and improvised weapon systems. As with Williams's character in *The Mod Squad*, Mr. T's clothing and physical appearance set him off from the other team members. He never wears the suit and tie of white society. However, his costume on *The A Team* is his costume in everyday public life—a costume that is charged with meanings associated with his stardom. Where Morris and Williams were token figures in their respective series, B. A. Baracus is far from a token figure on *The A Team*. Instead, his ethnicity, his blackness are to the fore, grounded in his appearance, his language, and his actions.

But the black media figures who are most relevant to our discussion of Mr. T are from a different discourse system—the sports arena. Indeed, on the *The Barbara Walters Special* connected with ABC's coverage of the 1984 Winter Olympics, dedicated to individuals who, in Walter's introductory words, "had carved niches in the world of sports,"[2] Mr. T shared billing with Howard Cosell and Esther Williams. As Walters pointed out, Mr. T's figure first surfaced on the edge of television's sports arena before exploding onto the scene of serial television.

In high school, Mr. T was accomplished enough at football to receive an athletic scholarship at Prairie View A & M, but he abandoned the scholarship and returned home to Chicago after only one year. In the 1970s, he came into close contact with major sports figures by hiring out as a bodyguard to boxing champions Muhammad Ali and Leon Spinks. And Mr. T's first major national television exposure was on a sports program, of sorts: In 1979, Mr. T competed in and won the "World's Toughest Bouncer" contest, a contest staged by NBC for its short-lived novelty sports program, *Games People Play*. D. Keith Mano, in *Playboy*, describes Mr. T's performance in the contest and explains how important it was to his later career:

> . . . That contest fit him, ummm, to a T. He threw this 120-pound stunt man 17 feet, which was farther than I would trust him. He jumped a bar and broke through four inches of door without knocking. Then, as his *coup de gross*, he outboxed his nearest competitor. And he did it in 1979, when the casting director for *Rocky III* was watching. The rest is Hollywood.[3]

Rocky III marked Mr. T's first appearance as an actor-performer. Playing a heavyweight contender named Clubber Lang, Mr. T's role was definitely *not* heroic. Lang was mean, ugly, crude, and not redeemed at the end of the movie. Aside from being a physical threat, Lang was a *sexual* threat. Early in the movie, in a verbal confrontation, Lang insults Rocky's manhood and suggests Rocky's wife come make love with a "real man."

Of course, to be a prime-time hero, Mr. T's discourse in *Rocky III* would have to be revised. The made-for-TV Mr. T of *The A Team* is physically threatening, to be sure, but in making the transition to television he was stripped of his sexuality. Although in one episode B. A. Baracus encounters a romantic interest in the person of a young black woman, Mr. T's character is fundamentally an asexual creature, desexed before being released into the flow of television.

Safely neutered, Mr. T has been the subject of a great deal of media attention outside the serial frame of *The A Team*. During the 1983–84 season, he replaced the peacock as NBC's mascot, directly addressing the camera in the intimidating style of a professional wrestler and ordering the audience to "Be there!" He has made guest appearances on NBC's *Saturday Night Live* and *Diff'rent Strokes*. And, significantly, a Saturday morning cartoon on NBC titled *Mr. T* featured his heroic sexless figure protecting children from bullies and bad guys.

But NBC is not his only turf: he has appeared on Christian Broadcasting Network's *700 Club* with Pat Robinson, he was NBC's great black hope in ABC's annual airing of *Battle of the Network Stars*, and he has even become legitimate enough, safe enough, to play Santa for the Reagans at the White House, with First Lady Nancy Reagan sitting on his lap and kissing him on his shiny scalp.

If the week of March 11–17, 1984, is any indication, Mr. T's figure literally saturated the medium. That week, he made major prime-time appearances on three consecutive nights: Tuesday, he performed in the *The A Team;* Wednesday, again on NBC, he was roasted on *Dean Martin's Celebrity Roast;* and Thursday, he made a lengthy acceptance speech during CBS's coverage of *The People's Choice Awards* ceremony.

All this television coverage brings up a second issue that should be addressed in television star studies: over-exposure. Stardom requires the candidate to be visible in the flow of television. But being elected to stardom is not simply a matter of media exposure. The notion of over-exposure, seems to be tied up in this question: at what point can too much exposure cause an over-familiarity that robs the star of his or her specialness? It's a complicated issue. On the one hand, Johnny Carson and Walter Cronkite have become permanent stars despite making nightly television appearances. On the other hand, Mr. T seems perilously close to being over-exposed on the medium—a situation that will probably speed his recession into the realm of celebrityhood.

If Mr. T's stardom constitutes the prime-time legitimation of a once-threatening social type, then it is most evident in his appearances outside the frame of *The A Team*. This suggests still another issue, the relationship between the meanings assigned to the star in performance and the subsidiary public knowledge arising from the star's discourse outside his or her primary performance arena. Put another way, how do Carson's highly publicized divorces, salary, and arrest for drunken driving affect his role as stand-up comedian and an interviewer? And how does John Belushi's death by drug overdose re-accentuate a rerun of his performance in an old *Saturday Night Live*?

In these subsidiary appearances the meaning of Mr. T's performance most closely corresponds with that of black sports star performances. There can be no doubt that Mr. T's public self-presentation has been strongly influenced by the most hostile, threatening, and powerful sports star of the age of television: Muhammad Ali. After all, as Ali's bodyguard, Mr. T had the opportunity to witness first hand "The Greatest" in performance. And, indeed, the similarities between Ali's outrageous performances outside the ring and Mr. T's performances on the interview circuit are remarkable, both in terms of delivery and content.

Ali's and Mr. T's discourses both reconcile a violent way of life with deep religious commitments. Both men seem to gleefully bait and intimidate interviewers. Refusing to be manipulated by the interviewer's questions or diverted from their routines, they both enter every interview situation with a clear sense of self, an opinion about white oppression, and a social agenda that guides their dialogue. Mano comments on these similarities, as well as Mr. T's complete dominance of an interview situation:

> He [Mr. T] has started talking in this no-period, all-comma Muhammad Ali-sound-alike flume ride of a monolog. It'd be easier for me to knit a suit from mozzarella strands than to get any questions past him. His nose is flaring. The wild eyeballs stonewash my head. His mouth is snappish, like someone biting off one cigar tip after another . . .
>
> T is rapping off: about Christian commitment, about Mother, particularly about his positive effect on the ghetto youth of America. I'd get a more responsive interview from Mr. Coffee . . .[4]

In Mr. T's words, "everything I do, I make a statement."[5] His interview routine is premeditated, obviously rehearsed, and predictable. Although the following quotes are all from his performance on *The Barbara Walters Special* mentioned earlier, whether the other party be Barbara Walters, D. Keith Mano, David Letterman, Pat Robinson, or clones from *Entertainment Tonight* and *People*, Mr. T cannot be diverted from his agenda nor his routine:

1. Discussing the symbolism of his name, jewelry, haircut, and worn-out combat boots:

    a. *The name*. Born Lawrence Tero, he changed his name to Mr. T in 1970 at age 18 or 19. According to Mr. T, he did this "for respect":

> See in this world, in this society where a lot of white people have a problem calling a black man, "man" . . . I self-ordained myself Mr. T . . . when I was old enough to go in the army and fight and die for my country. So I changed my name to Mr. T so the first word out of everybody's mouth would be "mister." Nobody that's close to me call me T. My mother even calls me Mr. T.

    b. *The jewelry*. He wears a hundred gold chains around his neck, weighing a total of twenty-three pounds, which symbolize the bondage of his slave ancestors.

    c. *The haircut*. The traditional hair style of the Mandinka tribe, he wears it out of pride for his African heritage.

    d. *The combat boots*. The boots once belonged to his father. Even though the father abandoned the family after producing twelve children, Mr. T wears the boots out of respect for his father. And Mr. T is quite adamant about this respect, explaining that the father left for the good of the family:

> I still love my father and I say to the world that if somebody think for one moment that I don't love my father [then] disrespect him in any way and I will personally find you and break every bone in your body. I think that the reason my father left was because he understood how this system works. See society, white society would rather put a family on welfare than to give a black man a job because they want to keep him down, they want to keep him suppressed. So, my father knew that it would be easier, that the government would take care of his family, if he would leave. So that was his strategy.

2. Discussing the shallowness of stardom/celebrity/fame in conjunction with his commitment to a particular brand of "born again" Christianity:

    a. *On stardom*. Mr. T is often contemptuous of the celebrity treatment. See the quote at the beginning of this essay for his opinion of "groupies." Another example of his attitude toward the rituals surrounding fame are his thoughts on signing autographs:

I remember at first when this fame thing caught on. A lot of people wanted Mr. T's autograph. And earlier, I wouldn't sign the autograph because I said, and still say this even though I sign 'em now, I say the autograph have a tendency to make people think they're really greater than what they really are. Nobody asked Jesus for his autograph.

b. *On Christianity.* Mr. T often declares he wants to follow Jesus' example and feed 5000 hungry people. But there are some of Jesus' examples that he admits he isn't willing to follow. When Mr. T hints that he and his brothers murdered three men who robbed his mother of her welfare check ("I'm not saying we killed those guys, but no one will ever see them again"), Walters asks how he can reconcile that with his faith. Mr. T explains:

> I am a born again Christian. I do serve God. But I also point out, I'm not Jesus. So, if you hit me, Mr. T will not turn the other cheek.

3. Discussing the importance of family and the importance of education in connection with the plight of the black race in white society:

a. *On family.* Mr. T professes a devotion to his mother that rivals Earl Campbell's. The eighth son and the tenth born in a family of twelve children, Mr. T credits his mother's honesty and love for his high moral standards: "If a lot of kids had the opportunity to be brought up with a mother like mine, they wouldn't be in jail, they wouldn't be on drugs and all that, you know."

b. *On education.* Although scornful of black history ("When I'm hurtin', I don't want to go to a dentist and all he know is black history"), Mr. T values education as a solution to many of the social problems confronting young blacks. He believes blacks should spend as much time developing their minds as they do building their bodies:

> I spoke in a jail and a guy said, "Mr. T, the next time you come back, I want to challenge you to a weight lifting contest." I said, "I'll work out with you, brother, if you'll meet me in the library." That our problem. We got muscle-bound bodies, but we got malnutritioned brains, you know. Can the average black kid read a sentence? Can he multiply eight times seven and give a correct answer? No, he can't do that. Why? We spend too much time in the gym building up our biceps, our triceps, our deltoids, our calf muscles. But he say, "I'm tough, I'm tough." They so tough, but they can't get a job. Their muscles can't run a computer.

In many respects, then, Mr. T's discourse shares the same cultural space as the discourse of Muhammad Ali. Like Ali's performance, Mr. T's cannot be reduced to a single, essential meaning—in Mr. T's words, "People love and hate me for the same reasons." Accepting some central components of the dominant white ideology (anti-welfare, pro-education), while condemning other aspects of that ideology (white supremacy), his discourse animates a clash of conflicting meanings, depending on what aspect one chooses to emphasize. Mr. T's figure can be said to exhibit all the complexities of social types: his former life as a "no-nonsense" bodyguard and club bouncer coupled with his intended future life as an evangelist mark him as a star who gains notoriety by resisting being typed; like Ali before him, many have condemned Mr. T as a variation on the "uppity nigger" stereotype. Still others see his figure as a full-blown type, the incarnation of what Barbara Walters terms "Sheer Power . . . Toughness . . . Brute Force." Given the dullness of Ali's successors in the boxing ring—Leon Spinks and Larry Holmes—Mr. T's sudden popularity may, in fact, be filling a cultural void left by the sad decline of Ali's physical, mental, and spiritual presence.

But is Mr. T "really for real"? Although there's certainly no way to provide an answer to this question based solely on his media appearances, his public front is so carefully constructed and self-consciously presented that Mr. T is obviously a character of his own creation. He is not at all deceptive about the artificial aspect of his figure, often speaking of himself in mixed first and third person, as if Mr. T were a separate entity from the speaking "I" and "me." For example, when he says, "If you hit me, Mr. T will not turn the other cheek," the "me" is somehow detached and not responsible for the actions of the "Mr. T." He even openly describes his public front in terms of character and social type. Consider this interchange with Barbara Walters:

> *Barbara Walters*: Does it bother you that your looks frighten people? That you do look so strong and tough? Or . . .
> *Mr. T*: Well, that's all Mr. T's *character*. You got to understand that. My *reputation* preceded me. Here I am, a guy come straight from body-guarding. That's a no-nonsense *type of job*. [Emphasis mine.]

Of course, this all leads to a larger question: to what extent are we all self-constructed characters in our social relations with others? Paraphrasing Mr. T: everything we do, we make a statement. We all have reputations that precede us. And our sense of self, our identities, are influenced by the type of job we perform in our everyday lives. Some of us have no-nonsense occupations like bodyguarding; others have nonsense occupations like hosting a celebrity interview show, writing for *Playboy*, or selecting china for the White House. Mr. T is certainly as "real" as the figures surrounding him in the flow of television: Barbara Walters, David Letterman, George Peppard, Nancy Reagan. Ultimately, that Mr. T is self-conscious about his character—and that in individualizing and legitimating a social type he has encountered wealth and fame—does not make him any less *real* than those of us who are satisfied and comfortable with the anonymity of being normal.

NOTES

1. *Barbara Walters Special*, ABC, February 6, 1984.
2. Ibid.
3. D. Keith Mano, "Eye to Eye with Mr. T," *Playboy*, vol. 30, no. 9 (September 1983), p. 86.
4. Ibid., p. 84.
5. *Barbara Walters Special*.

HORACE NEWCOMB
AND PAUL M. HIRSCH

TELEVISION AS A CULTURAL FORUM*

A cultural basis for the analysis and criticism of television is, for us, the bridge between a concern for television as a communications medium, central to contemporary society, and television as aesthetic object, the expressive medium that, through its storytelling functions, unites and examines a culture. The shortcomings of each of these approaches taken alone are manifold.

The first is based primarily in a concern for understanding specific messages that may have specific effects, and grounds its analysis in "communication" narrowly defined. Complexities of image, style, resonance, narrativity, history, metaphor, and so on are reduced in favor of that content that can be more precisely, some say more objectively, described. The content categories are not allowed to emerge from the text, as is the case in naturalistic observation and in textual analysis. Rather they are predefined in order to be measured more easily. The incidence of certain content categories may be cited as significant, or their "effects" more clearly correlated with some behavior. This concern for measuring is, of course, the result of conceiving television in one way rather than another, as "communication" rather than as "art."

*The authors would like to express their appreciation to the John and Mary R. Markle Foundation for support in the preparation of this paper and their ongoing study of the role of television as a cultural forum in American society. The ideas in this paper were first presented, in different form, at the seminar on "The Mass Production of Mythology," New York Institute for the Humanities, New York University, February, 1981. Mary Douglas, Seminar Director.

The narrowest versions of this form of analysis need not concern us here. It is to the best versions that we must look, to those that do admit to a range of aesthetic expression and something of a variety of reception. Even when we examine these closely, however, we see that they often assume a monolithic "meaning" in television content. The concern is for "dominant" messages embedded in the pleasant disguise of fictional entertainment, and the concern of the researcher is often that the control of these messages is, more than anything else, a complex sort of political control. The critique that emerges, then, is consciously or unconsciously a critique of the society that is transmitting and maintaining the dominant ideology with the assistance, again conscious or unconscious, of those who control communications technologies and businesses. (Ironically, this perspective does not depend on political perspective or persuasion. It is held by groups on the "right" who see American values being subverted, as well as by those on the "left" who see American values being imposed.)

Such a position assumes that the audience shares or "gets" the same messages and their meanings as the researcher finds. At times, like the literary critic, the researcher assumes this on the basis of superior insight, technique, or sensibility. In a more "scientific" manner the researcher may seek to establish a correlation between the discovered messages and the understanding of the audience. Rarely, however, does the message analyst allow for the possibility that the audience, while sharing this one meaning, may create many others that have not been examined, asked about, or controlled for.

The television "critic" on the other hand, often basing his work on the analysis of literature or film, succeeds in calling attention to the distinctive qualities of the medium, to the special nature of television fiction. But this approach all too often ignores important questions of production and reception. Intent on correcting what it takes to be a skewed interest in such matters, it often avoids the "business" of television and its "technology." These critics, much like their counterparts in the social sciences, usually assume that viewers should understand programs in the way the critic does, or that the audience is incapable of properly evaluating the entertaining work and should accept the critic's superior judgment.

The differences between the two views of what television is and does rest, in part, on the now familiar distinction between transportation and ritual views of communication processes.

The social scientific, or communication theory model outlined above (and we do not claim that it is an exhaustive description) rests most thoroughly on the transportation view. As articulated by James Carey, this model holds that communication is a "process of transmitting messages at a distance for the purpose of control. The archetypal case of communication then is persuasion, attitude change, behavior modification, socialization through the transmission of information, influence, or conditioning."[1]

The more "literary" or "aesthetically based" approach leans toward, but hardly comes to terms with, ritual models of communication. As put by Carey, the ritual view sees communication "not directed toward the extension of messages in space but the maintenance of society in time; not the act of imparting information but the representation of shared beliefs."[2]

Carey also cuts through the middle of these definitions with a more succinct one of his own: "Communication is a symbolic process whereby reality is produced, maintained, repaired, and transformed."[3] It is in the attempt to amplify this basic observation that we present a cultural basis for the analysis of television. We hardly suggest that such an approach is entirely new, or that others are unaware of or do not share many of our assumptions. On the contrary, we find a growing awareness in many disciplines of the nature of symbolic thought, communication, and action, and we see attempts to understand television emerging rapidly from this body of shared concerns.[4]

Our own model for television is grounded in an examination of the cultural role of entertainment and parallels this with a close analysis of television program content in all its various textual levels and forms. We focus on the collective, cultural view of the social construction and negotiation of reality, on the creation of what Carey refers to as "public thought."[5] It is not difficult to see television as central to this process of public thinking. As Hirsch has pointed out,[6] it is now our national medium, replacing those media—film, radio, picture magazines, newspapers—that once served a similar function. Those who create for such media are, in the words of anthropologist Marshall Sahlins, "hucksters of the symbol."[7] They are cultural bricoleurs, seeking and creating new meaning in the combination of cultural elements with embedded significance. They respond to real events, changes in social structure and organization, and to shifts in attitude and value. They also respond to technological shift, the coming of cable or the use of videotape recorders. We think it is clear that the television producer should be added to Sahlins's list of "hucksters." They work in precisely the manner he describes, as do television writers and, to a lesser extent, directors and actors. So too do programmers and network executives who must make decisions about the programs they purchase, develop, and air. At each step of this complicated process they function as cultural interpreters.

Similar notions have often been outlined by scholars of popular culture focusing on the formal characteristics of popular entertainment.[8] To those insights cultural theory adds the possibility of matching formal analysis with cultural and social practice. The best theoretical explanation for this link is suggested to us in the continuing work of anthropologist Victor Turner. This work focuses on cultural ritual and reminds us that ritual must be seen as process rather than as product, a notion not often applied to the study of television, yet crucial to an adequate understanding of the medium.

Specifically we make use of one aspect of Turner's analysis, his view of the *liminal* stage of the ritual process. This is the "in-between" stage, when one is neither totally in nor out of society. It is a stage of license, when rules may be broken or bent, when roles may be reversed, when categories may be overturned. Its essence, suggests Turner,

> is to be found in its release from normal constraints, making possible the deconstruction of the "uninteresting" constructions of common sense, the "meaningfulness of ordinary life," . . . into cultural units which may then be reconstructed in novel ways, some of them bizarre to the point of monstrosity. . . . Liminality is the domain of the "interesting" or of "uncommon sense."[9]

Turner does not limit this observation to traditional societies engaged in the *practice* of ritual. He also applies his views to postindustrial, complex societies. In doing so he finds the liminal domain in the arts—all of them.[10] "The dismemberment of ritual has . . . provided the opportunity of theatre in the high culture and carnival at the folk level. A multiplicity of desacralized performative genres have assumed, prismatically, the task of plural cultural reflexivity."[11] In short, contemporary cultures examine themselves through their arts, much as traditional societies do via the experience of ritual. Ritual and the arts offer a metalanguage, a way of understanding who and what we are, how values and attitudes are adjusted, how meaning shifts.

In contributing to this process, particularly in American society, where its role is central, television fulfills what Fiske and Hartley refer to as the "bardic function" of contemporary societies.[12] In its role as central cultural medium it presents a multiplicity of meanings rather than a monolithic dominant point of view. It often focuses on our most prevalent concerns, our deepest dilemmas. Our most traditional views, those that are repressive and reactionary, as well as those that are subversive and emancipatory, are upheld, examined, maintained, and transformed. The emphasis is on process rather than product, on discussion rather than indoctrination, on contradiction and confusion rather than coherence. It is with this view that we turn to an analysis of the texts of television that demonstrates and supports the conception of television as a cultural forum.

This new perspective requires that we revise some of our notions regarding television analysis, criticism, and research. The function of the creator as bricoleur, taken from Sahlins, is again indicated and clarified. The focus on "uncommon sense," on the freedom afforded by the idea of television as a liminal realm helps us to understand the reliance on and interest in forms, plots, and character types that are not at all familiar in our lived experience. The skewed demography of the world of television is not quite so bizarre and repressive once we admit that it is the realm in which we allow our monsters to come out and play, our dreams to be wrought into pictures, our fantasies transformed into plot structures. Cowboys, detectives, bionic men and great green hulks; fatherly physicians, glamorous female detectives, and tightly knit families living out the pain of the Great Depression; all these become part of the dramatic logic of public thought.

Shows such as *Fantasy Island* and *Love Boat*, difficult to account for within traditional critical systems except as examples of trivia and romance, are easily understood. Islands and boats are among the most fitting liminal metaphors, as Homer, Bacon, Shakespeare, and Melville, among others, have recognized. So, too, are the worlds of the Western and the detective story. With this view we can see the "bizarre" world of situation comedy as a means of deconstructing the world of "common sense" in which all, or most, of us live and work. It also enables us to explain such strange phenomena as game shows and late night talk fests. In short, almost any version of the television text functions as a forum in which important cultural topics may be considered. We illustrate this not with a contemporary program where problems almost always appear on the surface of the show, but with an episode of *Father Knows Best* from the early 1960s. We begin by noting that *FKB* is often cited as an innocuous series, constructed around unstinting paeans to American middle-class virtues and blissfully ignorant of social conflict. In short, it is precisely the sort of television program that reproduces dominant ideology by lulling its audience into a dream world where the status quo is the only status.

In the episode in question Betty Anderson, the older daughter in the family, breaks a great many rules by deciding that she will become an engineer. Over great protest, she is given an internship with a surveying crew as part of a high school "career education" program. But the head of the surveying crew, a young college student, drives her away with taunts and insensitivity. She walks off the job on the first day. Later in the week the young man comes to the Anderson home where Jim Anderson chides him with fatherly anger. The young man apologizes and Betty, overhearing him from the other room, runs upstairs, changes clothes, and comes down. The show ends with their flirtation underway.

Traditional ideological criticism, conducted from the communications or the textual analysis perspective, would remark on the way in which social conflict is ultimately subordinated in this dramatic structure to the personal, the emotional. Commentary would focus on the way in which the questioning of the role structure is shifted away from the world of work to the domestic arena. The emphasis would be on the conclusion of the episode in which Betty's real problem of identity and sex-role, and society's problem of sex-role discrimination, is bound by a more traditional conflict and thereby defused, contained, and redirected. Such a reading is possible, indeed accurate.

We would point out, however, that our emotional sympathy is with Betty throughout this episode. Nowhere does the text instruct the viewer that her concerns are unnatural, no matter how unnaturally they may be framed by other members of the cast. Every argument that can be made for a strong feminist perspective is condensed into the brief, half-hour presentation. The concept of the cultural forum, then, offers a different interpretation. We suggest that in popular culture generally, in television specifically, the raising of questions is as important as the answering of them. That is, it is equally important that an audience be introduced to the problems surrounding sex-role discrimination as it is to conclude the episode in a traditional manner. Indeed, it would be startling to think that mainstream texts in mass society would overtly challenge dominant ideas. But this hardly prevents the oppositional ideas from appearing. Put another way, we argue that television does not present firm ideological conclusions—despite its *formal* conclusions—so much as it *comments on* ideological problems. The conflicts we see in television drama, embedded in familiar and nonthreatening frames, are conflicts ongoing in American social experience and cultural history. In a few cases we might see strong perspectives that argue for the absolute correctness of one point of view or another. But for the most part the rhetoric of television drama is a rhetoric of discussion. Shows such as *All in the Family*, or *The Defenders*, or *Gunsmoke*, which raise the forum/discussion to an intense and obvious level, often make best use of the medium and become highly successful. We see statements *about* the issues and it should be clear that ideological positions can be balanced within the forum by others from a different perspective.

We recognize, of course, that this variety works for the most part within the limits of American monopoly-capitalism and within the range of American pluralism. It is an effective pluralistic forum only insofar as American political pluralism is or can be.[13] We also note, however, that one of the primary functions of the popular culture forum, the television forum, is to monitor the limits and the effectiveness of this pluralism, perhaps the only "public" forum in which this role is performed. As content shifts and attracts the attention of groups and individuals, criticism and reform can be initiated. We will have more to say on this topic shortly.

Our intention here is hardly to argue for the richness of *Father Knows Best* as a television text or as social commentary. Indeed, in our view, any emphasis on individual episodes, series, or even genres, misses the central point of the forum concept. While each of these units can and does present its audiences with incredibly mixed ideas, it is television as a whole system that presents a mass audience with the range and variety of ideas and ideologies inherent in American culture. In order to fully understand the role of television in that culture, we must examine a variety of analytical foci and, finally, see them as parts of a greater whole.

We can, for instance, concentrate on a single episode of television content, as we have done in our example. In our view most television shows offer something of this range of complexity. Not every one of them treats social problems of such immediacy, but submerged in any episode are assumptions about who and what we are. Conflicting viewpoints of social issues are, in fact, the elements that structure most television programs.

At the series level this complexity is heightened. In spite of notions to the contrary, most television shows do change over time. Stanley Cavell has recently suggested that this serial nature of television is perhaps its defining characteristic.[14] By contrast we see that feature only as a primary aspect of the rhetoric of television, one that shifts meaning and shades ideology as series develop. Even a series such as *The Brady Bunch* dealt with ever more complex issues merely because the children, on whom the show focused, grew older. In other cases, shows such as *The Waltons* shifted in content and meaning because they represented shifts in historical time. As the series moved out of the period of the Great Depression, through World War II, and into the postwar period, its tone and emphasis shifted too. In some cases, of course, this sort of change is structured into the show from the beginning, even when the appearance is that of static, undeveloping nature. In *All in the Family* the possibility of change and Archie's resistance to it form the central dramatic problem and offer the central opportunity for dramatic richness, a richness that has developed over many years until the character we now see bears little resemblance to the one we met in the beginning. This is also true of *M*A*S*H*, although there the structured conflicts have more to do with framing than with character development. In *M*A*S*H* we are caught in an anti-war rhetoric that cannot end a war. A truly radical alternative, a desertion or an insurrection, would end the series. But it would also end the "discussion" of this issue. We remain trapped, like American culture in its historical reality, with a dream and the rhetoric of peace and with a bitter experience that denies them.

The model of the forum extends beyond the use of the series with attention to genre. One tendency of genre studies has been to focus on similarities within forms, to indicate the ways in which all Westerns, situation comedies, detective shows and so on are alike. Clearly, however, it is in the economic interests of producers to build on audience familiarity with generic patterns and instill novelty into those generically based presentations. Truly innovative forms that use the generic base as a foundation are likely to be among the more successful shows. This also means that the shows, despite generic similarity, will carry individual rhetorical slants. As a result, while shows like M*A*S*H, *The Mary Tyler Moore Show*, and *All in the Family* may all treat similar issues, those issues will have different meanings because of the variations in character, tone, history, style, and so on, despite a general "liberal" tone. Other shows, minus that tone, will clash in varying degrees. The notion that they are all, in some sense, "situation comedies" does not adequately explain the treatment of ideas within them.

This hardly diminishes the strength of generic variation as yet another version of differences within the forum. The rhetoric of the soap opera *pattern* is different from that of the situation comedy and that of the detective show. Thus, when similar topics are treated within different generic frames another level of "discussion" is at work.

It is for this reason that we find it important to examine strips of television programming, "flow" as Raymond Williams refers to it.[15] Within these flow strips we may find opposing ideas abutting one another. We may find opposing treatments of the same ideas. And we will certainly find a viewing behavior that is more akin to actual experience than that found when concentrating on the individual show, the series, or the genre. The forum model, then, has led us into a new exploration of the definition of the television text. We are now examining the "viewing strip" as a potential text and are discovering that in the range of options offered by any given evening's television, the forum is indeed a more accurate model of what goes on *within* television than any other that we know of. By taping entire weeks of television content, and tracing various potential strips in the body of that week, we can construct a huge range of potential "texts" that may have been seen by individual viewers.

Each level of text—the strip as text, the television week, the television day—is compounded yet again by the history of the medium. Our hypothesis is that we might track the history of America's social discussions of the past three decades by examining the multiple rhetorics of television during that period.

Given the problematic state of television archiving, a careful study of that hypothesis presents an enormous difficulty. It is, nevertheless, an exciting prospect.

Clearly, our emphasis is on the treatment of issues, on rhetoric. We recognize the validity of analytical structures that emphasize television's skewed demographic patterns, its particular social aberrations, or other "unrealistic distortions" of the world of experience. But we also recognize that in order to make sense of those structures and patterns researchers return again and again to the "meaning" of that television world, to the processes and problems of interpretation. In our view this practice is hardly limited to those of us who study television. It is also open to audiences who view it each evening and to professionals who create for the medium.

The goal of every producer is to create the difference that makes a difference, to maintain an audience with sufficient reference to the known and recognized, but to move ahead into something that distinguishes his show for the program buyer, the scheduler, and most importantly, for the mass audience. As recent work by Newcomb and Alley shows,[16] the goal of many producers, the most successful and powerful ones, is also to include personal ideas in their work, to use television as all artists use their media, as means of personal expression. Given this goal it is possible to examine the work of individual producers as other units of analysis and to compare the work of different producers as expressions within the forum. We need only think of the work of Quinn Martin and Jack Webb, or to contrast their work with that of Norman Lear or Gary Marshall, to recognize the individuality at work within television making. Choices by producers to work in certain generic forms, to express certain political, moral, and ethical attitudes, to explore certain sociocultural topics, all affect the nature of the ultimate "flow text" of television seen by viewers and assure a range of variations within that text.

The existence of this variation is borne out by varying responses among those who view television. A degree of this variance occurs among professional television critics who like and dislike shows for different reasons. But because television critics, certainly in American journalistic situations, are more alike than different in many ways, a more important indicator of the range of responses is that found among "ordinary" viewers, or the disagreements implied by audience acceptance and enthusiasm for program material soundly disavowed by professional critics. Work by Himmleweit in England[17] and Neuman in America[18] indicates that individual viewers do function as "critics," do make important distinctions, and are able, under certain circumstances, to articulate the bases for their judgments. While this work is just beginning, it is still possible to suggest from anecdotal evidence that people agree and disagree with television for a variety of reasons. They find in television texts representations of and challenges to their own ideas, and must somehow come to terms with what is there.

If disagreements cut too deeply into the value structure of the individual, if television threatens the sense of cultural security, the individual may take steps to engage the medium at the level of personal action. Most often this occurs in the form of letters to the network or to local stations, and again, the pattern is not new to television. It has occurred with every other mass medium in modern industrial society.

Nor is it merely the formation of groups or the expression of personal points of view that indicates the working of a forum. It is the *range* of response, the directly contradictory readings of the medium, that cue us to its multiple meanings. Groups may object to the same programs, for example, for entirely opposing reasons. In *Charlie's Angels* feminists may find yet another example of sexist repression, while fundamentalist religious groups may find examples of moral decay expressed in the sexual freedom, the personal appearance, or the "unfeminine" behavior of the protagonists. Other viewers doubtless find the expression of meaningful liberation of women. At this level, the point is hardly that one group is "right" and another "wrong," much less that one is "right" while the other is "left." Individuals and groups are, for many reasons, involved in making their own meanings from the television text.

This variation in interpretive strategies can be related to suggestions made by Stuart Hall in his influential essay, "Encoding and Decoding in the Television Discourse."[19] There he suggests three basic modes of interpretation, corresponding to the interpreter's political stance within the social structure. The interpetation may be "dominant," accepting the prevailing ideological structure. It may be "oppositional," rejecting the basic aspects of the structure. Or it may be "negotiated," creating a sort of personal synthesis. As later work by some of Hall's colleagues suggests, however, it quickly becomes necessary to expand the range of possible interpretations.[20] Following these suggestions to a radical extreme it might be possible to argue that every individual interpretation of television content could, in some way, be "different." Clearly, however, communication is dependent on a greater degree of shared meanings, and expressions of popular entertainment are perhaps even more dependent on the shared level than many other forms of discourse. Our concern then is for the ways in which interpretation is negotiated in society. Special interest groups that focus, at times, on television provide us with readily available resources for the study of interpretive practices.

We see these groups as representative of metaphoric "fault lines" in American society. Television is the terrain in which the faults are expressed and worked out. In studying the groups, their rhetoric, the issues on which they focus, their tactics, their forms of organization, we hope to demonstrate that the idea of the "forum" is more than a metaphor in its own right. In forming special interest groups, or in using such groups to speak about television, citizens actually enter the forum. Television shoves them toward action, toward expression of ideas and values. At this level the model of "television as a cultural forum" enables us to examine "the sociology of interpretation."

Here much attention needs to be given to the historical aspects of this form of activity. How has the definition of issues changed over time? How has that change correlated with change in the television texts? These are important questions which, while difficult to study, are crucial to a full understanding of the role of television in culture. It is primarily through this sort of study that we will be able to define much more precisely the limits of the forum, for groups form monitoring devices that alert us to shortcomings not only in the world of television representation, but to the world of political experience as well. We know, for example, that because of heightened concern on the part of special interest groups, and responses from the creative and institutional communities of television industries, the "fictional" population of black citizens now roughly equals that of the actual population. Regardless of whether such a match is "good" or "necessary," regardless of the nature of the depiction of blacks on television, this indicates that the forum extends beyond the screen. The issue of violence, also deserving close study, is more mixed, varying from year to year. The influence of groups, of individuals, of studies, of the terrible consequences of murder and assassination, however, cannot be denied. Television does not exist in a realm of its own, cut off from the influence of citizens. Our aim is to discover, as precisely as possible, the ways in which the varied worlds interact.

Throughout this kind of analysis, then, it is necessary to cite a range of varied responses to the texts of television. Using the viewing "strip" as the appropriate text of television, and recognizing that it is filled with varied topics and approaches to those topics, we begin to think of the television viewer as a bricoleur who matches the creator in the making of meanings. Bringing values and attitudes, a universe of personal experiences and concerns, to the texts, the viewer selects, examines, acknowledges, and makes texts of his or her own.[21] If we conceive of special interest groups as representatives of *patterns* of cultural attitude and response, we have a potent source of study.

On the production end of this process, in addition to the work of individual producers, we must examine the role of network executives who must purchase and program television content. They, too, are cultural interpreters, intent on "reading" the culture through its relation to the "market." Executives who head and staff the internal censor agencies of each network, the offices of Broadcast Standards or Standards and Practices, are in a similar position. Perhaps as much as any individual or group they present us with a source of rich material for analysis. They are actively engaged in gauging cultural values. Their own research, the assumptions and the findings, needs to be re-analyzed for cultural implications, as does the work of the programmers. In determining who is doing what, with whom, at what times, they are interpreting social behavior in America and assigning it meaning. They are using television as a cultural litmus that can be applied in defining such problematic concepts as "childhood," "family," "maturity," and "appropriate." With the Standards and Practices offices, they interpret *and* define the permissible and the "normal." But their interpretations of behavior open to us as many questions as answers, and an appropriate overview, a new model of television is necessary in order to best understand their work and ours.

This new model of "television as a cultural forum" fits the experience of television more accurately than others we have seen applied. Our assumption is that it opens a range of new questions and calls for re-analysis of older findings from both

the textual-critical approach and the mass communications research perspective. Ultimately the new model is a simple one. It
recognizes the range of interpretation of television content
that is now admitted even by those analysts most concerned
with television's presentation and maintenance of dominant
ideological messages and meanings. But it differs from those
perspectives because it does not see this as surprising or unusual. For the most part, that is what central storytelling systems do in all societies. We are far more concerned with the
ways in which television contributes to change than with map-
ping the obvious ways in which it maintains dominant viewpoints. Most research on television, most textual analysis, has
assumed that the medium is thin, repetitive, similar, nearly
identical in textual formation, easily defined, described, and
explained. The variety of response on the part of audiences has
been received, as a result of this view, as extraordinary, an
astonishing "discovery."

We begin with the observation, based on careful textual
analysis, that television is dense, rich, and complex rather than
impoverished. Any selection, any cut, any set of questions that
is extracted from that text must somehow account for that
density, must account for what is *not* studied or measured, for
the opposing meanings, for the answering images and symbols.
Audiences appear to make meaning by selecting that which
touches experience and personal history. The range of responses then should be taken as commonplace rather than as
unexpected. But research and critical analysis cannot afford so
personal a view. Rather, they must somehow define and describe the inventory that makes possible the multiple meanings
extracted by audiences, creators, and network decision makers.

Our model is based on the assumption and observation that
only so rich a text could attract a mass audience in a complex
culture. The forum offers a perspective that is as complex, as
contradictory and confused, as much in process as American
culture is in experience. Its texture matches that of our daily
experiences. If we can understand it better, than perhaps we
will better understand the world we live in, the actions that we
must take in order to live there.

NOTES

1. James Carey, "A Cultural Approach to Communications," *Communications* 2
   (December 1975).
2. Ibid.

3. James Carey, "Culture and Communications," *Communications Research* (April 1975).

4. See Roger Silverstone, *The Message of Television: Myth and Narrative in Contemporary Culture* (London: Heinemann, 1981) on structural and narrative analysis; John Fiske and John Hartley, *Reading Television* (London: Methuen, 1978) on the semiotic and cultural bases for the analysis of television; David Thorburn, *The Story Machine* (Oxford University Press: forthcoming) on the aesthetics of television; Himmleweit, Hilda, et al., "The Audience as Critic: An Approach to the Study of Entertainment," in *The Entertainment Functions of Television*, ed. Percy Tannenbaum (New York: Lawrence Erlbaum Associates, 1980) and W. Russel Neuman, "Television and American Culture: The Mass Medium and the Pluralist Audience," *Public Opinion Quarterly*, 46:4 (Winter 1982) pp. 471-487, on the role of the audience as critic; Todd Gitlin, "Prime Time Ideology: The Hegemonic Process in Television Entertainment," *Social Problems* 26: 3 (1979) and Douglas Kellner, "TV, Ideology, and Emancipatory Popular Culture," *Socialist Review* 45 (May–June, 1979) on hegemony and new applications of critical theory; James T. Lull, "The Social Uses of Television," *Human Communications Research* 7: 3 (1980) and "Family Communication Patterns and the Social Uses of Television," *Communications Research* 7: 3 (1979), and Tim Meyer, Paul Taudt, and James Anderson, "Non-Traditional Mass Communication Research Methods: Observational Case Studies of Media Use in Natural Settings, *Communication Yearbook IV*, ed. Dan Nimmo (New Brunswick, N.J.: Transaction Books) on audience ethnography and symbolic interactionism; and, most importantly, the ongoing work of The Center for Contemporary Cultural Studies at Birmingham University, England, most recently published in *Culture, Media, Language*, ed. Stuart Hall, et al. (London: Hutchinson, in association with The Center for Contemporary Cultural Studies, 1980) on the interaction of culture and textual analysis from a thoughtful political perspective.

5. Carey, 1976.

6. Paul Hirsch, "The Role of Popular Culture and Television in Contemporary Society," *Television: The Critical View*, ed. Horace Newcomb (New York: Oxford University Press, 1979, 1982).

7. Marshall Sahlins, *Culture and Practical Reason* (Chicago: University of Chicago Press, 1976), 217.

8. John Cawelti, *Adventure, Mystery, and Romance* (Chicago: University of Chicago Press, 1976), and David Thorburn, "Television Melodrama," *Television: The Critical View* (New York: Oxford University Press, 1979, 1982).

9. Victor Turner, "Process, System, and Symbol: A New Anthropological Synthesis," *Daedalus* (Summer 1977), p. 68.

10. In various works Turner uses both the terms "liminal" and "liminoid" to refer to works of imagination and entertainment in contemporary culture. The latter term is used to clearly mark the distinction between events that have distinct behavioral consequences and those that do not. As Turner suggests, the consequences of entertainment in contemporary culture are hardly as profound as those of the liminal stage of ritual in traditional culture. We are aware of this basic distinction but use the former term in order to avoid a fuller explanation of the neologism. See Turner, "Afterword," to *The Reversible World*, Barbara Babcock, ed. (Ithaca: Cornel University Press, 1979) and "Liminal to Liminoid, in Play, Flow, and Ritual: An Essay in Comparative Symbology," *Rice University Studies*, Vol. 60, No. 3 (1974).

11. Turner, 1977, p. 73.

12. Fiske and Hartley, 1978, p. 85.
13. We are indebted to Prof. Mary Douglas for encouraging this observation. At the presentation of these ideas at the New York Institute for the Humanities seminar on "The Mass Production of Mythology," she checked our enthusiasm for a pluralistic model of television by stating accurately and succinctly, "there are pluralisms and pluralisms." This comment led us to consider more thoroughly the means by which the forum and responses to it function as a tool with which to monitor the quality of pluralism in American social life, including its entertainments. The observation added a much needed component to our planned historical analysis.
14. Stanley Cavell, "The Fact of Television," *Daedalus* III: 4 (Fall, 1982).
15. Raymond Williams, *Television, Technology and Cultural Form* (New York: Schocken, 1971), p. 86 ff.
16. Horace Newcomb and Robert Alley, *The Television Producer as Artist in American Commercial Television* (New York: Oxford University Press, 1983).
17. Ibid.
18. Ibid.
19. Stuart Hall, "Encoding and Decoding in the Television Discourse," *Culture, Media, Language* (London: Hutchinson, in association with The Center for Contemporary Cultural Studies, 1980).
20. See Dave Morley and Charlotte Brunsdon, *Everyday Television: "Nationwide"* (London: British Film Institute, 1978) and Morley, "Subjects, Readers, Texts," in *Culture, Media, Language.*
21. We are indebted to Louis Black and Eric Michaels of the Radio-TV-Film department of the University of Texas-Austin for calling this aspect of televiewing to Newcomb's attention. It creates a much desired balance to Sahlin's view of the creator as *bricoleur* and indicates yet another matter in which the forum model enhances our ability to account for more aspects of the television experience. See, especially, Eric Michaels, *TV Tribes*, unpublished Ph.D. dissertation, University of Texas-Austin, 1982.

DOUGLAS KELLNER

TV, IDEOLOGY, AND EMANCIPATORY POPULAR CULTURE

The central cultural role of the broadcast media in advanced capitalist society has changed the nature and social function of ideology. This essay explores some of the changes in ideology under the impact of the communications revolution. In an earlier paper, I suggested that when "ism-ideologies" such as liberalism and Marxism were institutionalized in capitalist and socialist societies, there was a decline of rationality and ideology became increasingly fragmented, mythic, and imagistic.* Although hegemonic ideology tends to legitimate dominant institutions, values, and ways of life, nonetheless it is not monolithic. Instead, in advanced capitalist societies, hegemonic ideology tends to be fractured into various regions (the economy, politics, culture, etc.). There is no one unifying, comprehensive, "bourgeois ideology": hegemonic ideology is saturated with contradictions.

Many radical theories of ideology have neglected the role of mass-media images and messages in the production and transmission of ideology. Although Alvin Gouldner, for instance, is aware of the importance of television and devotes many interesting pages in *The Dialectic of Ideology and Technology* to analyzing both print and electronic media, he does not want to include the images and messages broadcast by the electronic media in the

*See my article "Ideology, Marxism, and Advanced Capitalism" in *Socialist Review*, 42, November-December 1978. Again, I am indebted for criticisms and comments on earlier drafts to the editors of SR, especially David Plotke, and to the Austin Television Group, especially to Jack Schierenbeck, who suggested many ideas which were incorporated into this article. I would also like to thank Carolyn Appleton and Marc Silberman for helpful comments and aid in preparing this manuscript.

Reprinted from *Socialist Review*, No. 45 (May-June 1979), by permission of the publisher.

domain of ideology.[1] Louis Althusser highlights the role of the educational system as the primary site of ideology, while ignoring the mass media.[2] These and many other discussions of ideology rely on an overly linguistic paradigm of ideology that cannot account for the impact of recent developments in the electronic media in shaping a new configuration of ideology in advanced capitalism.

To overcome the deficiencies of earlier theories of ideology, I propose that we view ideology as a synthesis of concepts, images, theories, stories, and myths that can take rational systematic form (in Adam Smith, Locke, Marx, Lenin, etc.), or imagistic, symbolic, and mythical form (in religion, the culture industries, etc.). Ideology is often conveyed through images (of country and race, class and clan, virginity and chastity, salvation and redemption, individuality and solidarity). The combination of rational theory with images and slogans makes ideology compelling and powerful. Ideology roots its myths in theories while its theories generate myths and supply a rationale for social domination (if the ideology attains hegemony).[3] Thus ideologies have both "rational" and "irrational" appeal, as they combine rhetoric and logic, concepts and symbols, clear argumentation and manipulation.[4]

Most theories of ideology have failed to analyze properly the apparatus that produces and transmits ideology.[5] For most of the history of capitalism, the ideological apparatus transmitted ideology through an elaborate set of rituals: military and patriotic pomp and parades, judicial ceremonies and trappings, religious rites, university lecture halls which invested professors with a priestlike aura, political speeches and campaigns, etc.

Ideology in bourgeois society has always been bound up with mythologies and rituals; the central role of the broadcast media in advanced capitalism, however, has endowed television and popular culture with the function of ritualistically producing and transmitting mythologies and hegemonic ideology. Hence, there is an increase of the imagistic, symbolic, and mythical components of ideology in advanced capitalism, and a decrease in rationality from earlier print-media forms of ideology.

TV AND HEGEMONIC IDEOLOGY

Conventional wisdom holds that television and the electronic media have provided a new kind of cultural experience and symbolic environment that increases the importance of images and decreases the importance of words. Many argue that television experience is more passive and receptive than print reading—that through American television people passively receive ideologies that legitimate and naturalize American society. Such a strategy of image production-consumption and cultural domination follows the logic of advanced capitalism as a system of commodity production, manipulated consumption, administration, and social conformity. In the words of Susan Sontag:

> A capitalist society requires a culture based on images. It needs to furnish vast amounts of entertainment in order to stimulate buying and anaesthetize the injuries of class, race, and sex. And it needs to gather unlimited amounts of information, the better to exploit natural resources, increase productivity, keep order, make war, give jobs to bureaucrats. The camera's twin capacities, to subjectivize reality and to objectify it, ideally serve these needs and strengthen them. Cameras define reality in the two ways essential to the workings of an advanced industrial society: as a spectacle (for masses) and as an object of surveillance (for rulers). The production of images also furnishes a ruling ideology. Social change is replaced by a change in images. The freedom to consume a plurality of images and goods is equated with freedom itself. The narrowing of free political choice to free economic consumption requires the unlimited production and consumption of images.[6]

Undoubtedly, American television plays an important role as an instrument of enculturation and social control. What is not yet clear is *how* television constructs and conveys hegemonic ideology and induces consent to advanced capitalism. The following analyses suggest how television images, narrative codes, and mythologies convey hegemonic ideology and legitimate American society; but I also want to show how the images and narratives of American television contain contradictory messages, reproducing the conflicts of advanced capitalist society and ideology. Against leftist manipulation theories which solely stress television's role as a purveyor of bourgeois ideology, I will argue that the images and messages of American television are contradictory both in their content and in their effects. Accordingly, after discussing how television functions as a vehicle of hegemonic ideology, some exploratory analyses of what forms emancipatory popular culture might take will be proposed.

TELEVISION IMAGES, SYMBOLS, AND
PALEOSYMBOLIC SCENES

Television contains a wealth of symbolic imagery, building on traditional symbolism but also creating symbols: the totality of Jack Webb's staccato interrogation procedures, authoritarian personality, and crisp recitation of the facts forms a symbol of law and order; the immaculate homes on the situation comedies or soap operas become symbols of domesticity; Ben Cartwright and Walter Cronkite become father symbols; Mary Tyler Moore provides a symbol of the independent working woman; and the soap operas generate symbols of stoic endurance through suffering.

Symbolic images endow certain characters or actions with positive moral features and other characters or actions with negative features, providing positive and negative models of identification. Symbols have a historically specific content; when television symbols become familiar and accepted, they become effective agents of enculturation. For instance, Kojak symbolized triumphant authority, law and order, and a stable set of values in an era of political upheaval and cultural conflict. His forceful advocacy of traditional values invested him with significance such that his features crystallized into a symbolic structure, linking his macho personality and authoritarian law and order.

Today television is the dominant producer of cultural symbolism. Its imagery is prescriptive as well as descriptive, and not only pictures what is happening in society, but also shows how one adjusts to the social order. Further, it demonstrates the pain and punishment suffered by not adjusting. The endless repetition of the same images produces a television world where the conventional is the norm and conformity the rule.

Some television symbols have powerful effects on consciousness and behavior but are not always readily identifiable or conventionally defined. Building upon Freud's notion of scenic understanding and the concept of paleosymbolism proposed by Habermas and Gouldner, I call these sets of imagery *paleosymbolic*.[7] The prefix "paleo" signifies a sort of "before symbolism" or "underneath symbolism." Paleosymbols are tied to particular scenes that are charged with drama and emotion. The paleosymbol does not provide or integrate holistic constructs such as the cross, the hammer and sickle, or aesthetic images that crystallize a wealth of meaning and significance; rather, the paleosymbol requires a whole scene where a positive or negative situation occurs. Freud found that certain scenic images, such as a child being beaten for masturbation, have profound impact on subsequent behavior. The images of these scenes remain as paleosymbols which control behavior, for instance, prohibiting masturbation or producing guilt and perhaps sexual inhibition. Paleosymbols are not subject to conscious scrutiny or control; they are often repressed, closed off from reflection, and can produce compulsive behavior. Thus Freud believed that scenic understanding was necessary to master scenic images, and, in turn, this mastery could help to understand what the scenic images signified (resymbolization) and how they influenced behavior.[8]

It is possible that television's paleosymbolic scenes function analogously to the sort of scenic drama described by Freud. Television scenes are charged with emotion, and the empathetic viewer becomes heavily involved in the actions presented. An episode on a television adaptation of Arthur Haley's novel *The Moneychangers* may illustrate this point. An up-and-coming junior executive is appealing portrayed by Timothy Bottoms. It is easy to identify with this charming and seemingly honest and courageous figure; he is shown, for example, vigorously defending a Puerto Rican woman accused of embezzling money. It turns out, however, that the young man stole the money himself to support a life style, including gambling, that far outstripped his income. He is apprehended by the tough black security officer, tries to get away, and is caught and beaten. There are repeated episodes where we may identify with the young man trying to escape, and then feel the pain and defeat when he is caught and beaten. Further, to white viewers the fact that the pursuer is black might add to the power of the imagery, building on socially inculcated fear of blacks. The multidimensional and multifunctional paleosymbolism in this example carries the message that crime does not pay and that one should not transcend the bounds of one's income or position. What will happen if one transgresses these bounds is shown dramatically. In case the moral does not sink in during the pursuit scenes, our young embezzler is brutally raped on his first day in prison, in a remarkably explicit scene. Although one may forget the story, or even the experience of having watched the program, a strong paleosymbolic image may remain. The paleosymbolic images in this program are multiplied and reinforced by other programs and thus become even more powerful.

Paleosymbolic scenes may shape attitudes and behavior in ways that encourage racism and sexism. In the first decades of film, for example, blacks were stereotyped as comical—eye-rolling, foot-shuffling, drawling, usually in the role of servant or clown—precisely the image fitting the white power structure's fantasy of keeping blacks in their place. Then, during the intense struggles over civil rights, blacks began appearing both as cultural neuters integrated into the system and as evil, violent criminals—a stereotype prevalent in television crime dramas featuring black dope dealers, prostitutes, and killers. These negative images were presented in highly charged dramatic scenes which conveyed paleosymbolic images of blacks as evil and dangerous. The viewer is likely to have a stronger paleosymbolic image of the black junkie shooting up dope and killing a white person to feed his habit than of the good black cop who finally apprehends him, since the scenes with the evil black are more charged with intense emotion.

Likewise, paleosymbolic images have portrayed women as foolish housewives, evil schemers, or voluptuous sex-objects. Images of women as scatterbrained (Lucy, Gracie Allen) or as adulterous, destructive, or greedy (in soaps, crime dramas, melodramas, etc.) are intensified by paleosymbolic scenes on television. Although these negative images of women are certainly countered by more positive images, it could be that the negative image remains most forcefully in the viewer's mind because of its place in the narrative.

In a crime drama, for example, in which the dramatic climax exposes a woman's murder, the evil act makes a particularly strong impression. In a soap opera, the paleosymbolic image of adultery and subsequent distress endows the characters and their actions with moral opprobrium that might evoke active dislike. Endlessly multiplied paleosymbolic scenic images of women committing adultery and wreaking havoc through their sexuality help create and sustain stereotypes of woman-as-evil, building on and reinforcing previous mythical images. These paleosymbolic images may overpower more positive soap-opera images of women and create consciousness of women per se as evil. Likewise, in a situation comedy, although the women often manifest admirable traits, such traits are frequently overshadowed by slapstick crescendos in which the woman star (Edith Bunker or Alice, for example) is involved in a particularly ludicrous situation.

Television commercials also utilize paleosymbolic scenes that associate desirable objects or situations with a product. For instance, Catherine Deneuve caresses an auto in one paleosymbolic extravaganza, linking the car with sexuality, beauty, etc. Other commercials create negative paleosymbolic scenes with ring-around-the-collar, bad breath, an upset stomach, a headache, or tired blood, creating anxiety or pain—which of course can be relieved through the products offered. TV commercials contain in an extremely compressed form the paleosymbolic drama which attempts to invest images with negative or positive qualities in order to influence behavior. The recent proliferation of commercials that sell no particular product but argue the merits of a generic item (milk, or chemicals) or even a way of life, as in corporate ads, whose content consists entirely in praise of the free enterprise system, suggests that the symbolic and socializing aspect of commercials is increasing. And it is possible that the definition of television as entertainment makes television images more easily accepted, or at least not resisted, than might be the case in other contexts.

The television world neither consists of "pap," nor is it a "vast wasteland"; it is teeming with images conveying an "impression of reality," values, ideologies, and messages. These images are bonded into narratives which form a set of American morality plays.

SITUATION COMEDY AND MELODRAMA AS AMERICAN MORALITY PLAYS

Television situation comedies center on a conflict or problem that is resolved neatly within a preconceived time period. This conflict/resolution model suggests that all problems can be solved within the existing society. For example, a 1976 episode of *Happy Days* saw the teen hero Fonzie out with an attractive older woman. He learns she is married, and a set of jokes punctuate his moral dilemma. Finally, he sits down with the woman, tells her he hears she's married, and when she says, "Yes, but it's an open marriage," he responds: "No dice. I've got my rules I live by. My values. And they don't include taking what's not mine. You're married. You're someone else's." He gets up, shakes her away, and is immediately surrounded by a flock of attractive (unmarried) girls—a typical comical resolution of an everyday moral conflict that reinforces conventional morality. In a 1977 episode of *Happy Days*, dealing with the high school graduation of the series' main characters, Fonzie moralizes, "It's not cool to drop out of school." In a 1978 episode, when his friend Richie is seriously injured in a motorcycle wreck, the Fonz "reveals his compassion in an emotional prayer for his friend" (*TV Guide* description), praying with eyes to heaven, "Hey Sir. He's my best friend. . . . Listen, you help him out and I'll owe you one." Here ideologies of religion and exchange reinforce each other; television attempts to be not the "opiate of the people" but their active instructor and educator.

Interestingly, the working-class character Fonzie, here used as the spokesman for middle-class morality, represents a domestication of the James Dean/Marlon Brando 1950s rebel. Whereas Dean in movies like *Rebel Without a Cause* was a hopeless misfit who often exploded with rage against the stifling conformity and insensitivity of those around him, Fonzie quits his gang (the Falcons) and comes to live in the garage apartment of the middle-class Cunninghams. Fonzie's defense of the dominant morality creates a melting-pot effect, where all good people seem to share similar values and aspirations. Hence, *Happy Days* provides a replay of *Ozzie and Harriet* and earlier TV family morality plays, with Richie Cunningham starring as David Nelson, the all-American good boy, and Fonzie as the irrepressible Ricky Nelson, whose "hipness" made him an effective salesman for the middle-class way of life.

Television melodrama also contains a variety of TV morality plays, full of conflict, suffering, and evil.[9] Not only is there an intense conflict between good and evil, but there are also clearly defined codes to depict moral and immoral characteristics. In most television series, the regular characters are good and intruders are evil, thus promoting fear of the "outsider" while teaching that conventional morality is good and its transgression is evil. After a highly emotional conflict, good triumphs and order is restored. The heated discussions of television violence and sex fail to note that they are the core of melodrama, since they heighten emotional impact and dramatize the moralities portrayed. Moralistic opponents of television sex and violence fail to note that it is precisely these features that actually help to reinforce the moral codes they themselves subscribe to, for transgressors of the established norms are always punished. For instance, the TV miniseries *Loose Change* portrayed the fate in the 1970s of three women who went to Berkeley in the 1960s trying to "make it" and "be free." It reduced the explosive politics of the 1960s to melodrama, emphasizing the pain and punishment inflicted for not conforming and the rewards for adjusting to the existing order. It presented the 1960s as a disorderly, chaotic period to be eschewed for the order and stability of the present.

Television morality plays present rituals that produce and transmit hegemonic ideology. The soap operas ritualize the suffering brought about by violating social norms. Situation comedies celebrate the triumphs of the norms, values, and good will that enable one to resolve conflicts successfully. Each program has its own formulas and conventions. For example, the comedy hit *Three's Company* (which has often been number one in the ratings during the 1977–79 seasons) celebrates the sexual attractions of two single women and a single man who live together. Every episode deals with suggestions of sexual temptation among the three, or their dates, and eventual frustration and renunciation. Every episode portrays the sexual advances and frustrations of the landlord's wife and her husband's lack of sexual interest in her. The young man pretends to be a homosexual in order to placate the moralistic landlords, and episodes of feigned homosexuality are repeated. These diverse rituals permit the audience to play out fantasies of tabooed sexual desire—and renunciation of such desires. Despite the sexy facade, the program conveys traditional, more puritanical ideologies of sexuality.* Yet it would be too simple to imagine that the viewers simply submit to these traditional ideologies, that the effort to express and contain sexuality works smoothly.

Other situation comedies allow the audience to experience dramatizations of their own problems with interpersonal relations, work, the family, sexuality, and conflicts of values: they offer opportunities to experience solutions to everyday problems that take the form of rites of submission to one's lot and resignation (*Laverne and Shirley*, *Rhoda*, and *Alice*), or rites of problem-solving through correct activity and change or adjustment (*Happy Days*, *All in the Family*, *Maude*, and most Norman

---

*The women on *Charlie's Angels* and similar shows rarely, if ever, have lovers or erotic relationships. Despite the increasing sexual references, jokes, and innuendos, there is very little real eroticism on TV.

Lear sitcoms). Rites of submission often utilize individual self-assertion to promote conformity and resignation. For instance, *Laverne and Shirley* provides narratives that inculcate acceptance of miserable working-class labor and social conditions. Although Laverne and Shirley occasionally rebel and assert themselves against bosses and men, they generally adjust and try to pull through with humor and good-natured resignation. The *Laverne and Shirley* theme song boasts, "We'll do it our way . . . we'll make all our dreams come true . . . we're going to make it anyway," but poor Laverne and Shirley simply espouse middle-class values and dreams, and do it the system's way. They usually fail to realize their dreams and every episode ends with acceptance of their jobs and social lives. The series tries, however, to make working-class life as appealing as possible for Laverne and Shirley and the audience, thus helping working-class people in similar situations to accept their fate with a smile and good cheer.

TELEVISION MYTHOLOGY

Television images and stories produce new mythologies for problems of everyday life. Myths are simply stories that explain, instruct, and justify practices and institutions; they are lived, and shape thought and action. Myths deal with the most significant phenomena in human life and enable people to come to terms with death, violence, love, sex, labor, and social conflict. Myths link together symbols, formula, plot, and characters in a pattern that is conventional, appealing, and gratifying. Joseph Campbell has shown how mythologies all over the world reproduce similar patterns, linking the tale of a hero's journey, quest, and triumphant return to rites of initiation into maturity.[10] It is a mistake to ascribe myth solely to a "primitive" form of thought that has supposedly been superseded by science, for the symbols, thematic patterns, and social functions of myth persist in our society, and are especially visible in television culture.

Jewett and Lawrence's fine book on American popular culture has described a recurrent pattern of an "American monomyth" which begins with an Edenic idyll, and is then interrupted by trouble or evil (Indians, rustlers, gangsters, war, monsters, communists, aliens, things from another world).[11] The community is powerless to deal with this threat and relies on a hero with superhuman powers (e.g., the Westerner, Superman, Supercop, Superscientist, the Bionic Man, Wonderwoman) to resolve the problem and to eliminate evil. In the ensuing battle between good and evil, the hero wins, often through macho violence (although redemption can take place through a character of moral purity like Heidi, Shirley Temple, or Mary Tyler Moore; a person of homey wisdom like the Wise Father, Dr. Welby, or Mary Worth; or even a magical animal like Lassie, Old Yeller, or Dumbo). Myths are tales of redemption that show how order is restored.

Jewett and Lawrence show in convincing detail that much American popular culture is structured by mythical patterns and heroes and that our supposedly "advanced" society has not transcended or abandoned traditional mythical culture. Their examinations of *Star Trek*, *Little House on the Prairie*, westerns, Walt Disney productions, *Jaws* and other disaster movies, and various superheroes demonstrate that mythical patterns and themes (e.g., retribution through blood violence, salvation through superheroes, redemption through mythic powers) are operative in many major works of popular culture, and that these are used to purvey American ideology and submission to social authority. *The American Monomyth* traces the rise of the myth of the American hero, shows its many manifestations in contemporary popular culture, and discusses the repertoire of heroes and mythologies that television provides.[12]

Television mythologies naturalize the dominant institutions and way of life. Roland Barthes' example in *Mythologies* of the picture of the black soldier saluting the French flag on the cover of *Paris Match* illustrates this point.[13] Barthes explains how the picture conveys ideologies of the French empire, the integration of blacks, the honor of the military, which in a single image convey an ideology of French imperialism. Likewise, the images of America on television election coverage propagate multiple political ideologies (the images of Carter in the 1976 presidential campaign communicated ideologies of the country, the small town, the family, and religion); TV sports transmits ideologies of macho heroism and competition; and the nightly crime and violence shows contain Hobbesian ideologies of human nature.

Television mythologies often attempt to resolve social contradictions. For instance, the cop show *Starsky and Hutch* deals with the fundamental American contradiction between the need for conformity and individual initiative, between working in a corporate hierarchy and being an individual. Starsky and Hutch are at once conventional and hip; they do police work *and* wear flashy clothes *and* have lots of good times. They show that it is possible to fit into society and not lose one's individuality. The series mythically resolves contradictions between the work ethic and the pleasure ethic, between duty and enjoyment. Television mythology speciously resolves conflicts to enable individuals to adjust.

CONTRADICTORY TELEVISION IMAGES AND MESSAGES

The forms of TV narratives and codes tend to be conservative. American television is divided into well-defined genres with their dominant conventions and formulas. Situation comedy, melodrama, and action-adventure series reproduce multiple ideologies of power and authority, law and order, professionalism and technocracy. But like all ideology in advanced capitalism, television ideology is full of contradictions. The regions of television ideology contain conflicting conceptions of such things as the family and sexuality, and power and authority; these conflicts express ideological and social changes in advanced capitalism.

In the 1950s, for example, a rather coherent dominant ideology of idealized family life permeated television situation comedies such as *Father Knows Best, Leave It to Beaver, Ozzie and Harriet,* etc. The middle-class family unit was idealized as the proper locus of sexuality, socialization, domesticity, and authority, even though in this period divorce rates began to soar and the family began to weaken as the dominant institution of everyday life. In the 1960s and 1970s, however, one-parent families began appearing on television, as did various other family forms, all symptomatic of the strains on the family and the fracturing of the dominant ideology of the family in American society. Contradictory portrayals of the family and sexuality appeared, showing changes in sexual relations and contradictory responses to social change.

Similarly, in the violent world of television crime and action-adventure drama, the prevalent ideologies in the first television decades were those of the "iron fist" authoritarianism of *Dragnet, The Untouchables,* or *The FBI.* (Although even here there were always some contradictions—a few of the most popular westerns of the 1950s and early 1960s, such as *Maverick, Gunsmoke*, and *Have Gun, Will Travel*, offered differing images of authority). By the late 1960s and early 1970s, the previously dominant forms were challenged by liberal morality plays like *Mod Squad, Dan August*, and *The Streets of San Francisco*—though older images of macho authority were resurrected in new form in such series as *Kojak*. In the 1970s, new ideologies of power appeared in the extreme individualism of *Starsky and Hutch, Baretta, Serpico*, and other series that featured passionately individualist cops who battled corrupt and inefficient authority figures. Other series, such as *Ironside, The Rookies*, and *S.W.A.T.*, stressed teamwork and the submission of the individual to hierarchy. The ideological region of power and authority is now saturated with competing and conflicting currents.

Ideology, moreover, is not monolithically imposed on a malleable subject as some Althusserians and manipulation theorists seem to assume. The process of individual decoding of television images and narratives contains the possibility of the production of contradictory messages and social effects. Individual television viewers are not passive receivers of encoded television, but rather tend to process television images according to their life situations and cultural experiences (of which social class is a determinant factor). Middle-class viewers of television violence tend to be scared into social conformity and fear of crime, making them susceptible to law and order political ideologies, whereas individuals prone to violent behavior may act out violent or criminal fantasies nurtured by heavy television watching. Likewise, although *Three's Company* and *Charlie's Angels* are encoded as vehicles of puritan sexual morality, they may be decoded as stimulants to promiscuity or sexual fantasy. Although *Laverne and Shirley, Alice*, and many situation comedies are coded as rituals of resignation and acceptance of the status quo, individual images or programs may be processed to promote dissatisfaction or rebellion. Even the most blatantly conservative-hegemonic images and messages may have contradictory social effects. Images of consumerism, money, and commodity happiness on commercials, game shows, and other programs may encourage expectations of happiness through affluence which if frustrated may breed discontent. Though news and documentaries on the whole attempt to legitimate the political-economic system, their images and messages may help lead the viewer to critical views of business, government, or the society. As long as individuals in advanced captialism are more than totally manipulable robots, they can process television images and messages in ways that may contradict the ideological encoding of the "mind managers."

The rather conservative effects of television codes may also be undermined by the introduction of new types of explicit content and new forms of symbolism. The insertion of more topical and controversial themes into the forms of situation comedy by Norman Lear and his associates helped produce a new type of popular television, as did the introduction of the miniseries and the docudrama form. Even within one of the most conservative forms, the crime drama, paleosymbolic scenes and images may contain subversive messages. For instance, *Baretta* and *Starsky and Hutch*, often criticized as among the most macho shows on television, often contain scenes that are antiauthoritarian and have broadcast frequent attacks on the FBI and CIA in recent years. Although paleosymbolic scenes often convey hegemonic ideologies, they too are full of conflicting meanings.

The contradictory images of popular culture produce the space for a discussion of emancipatory popular culture. The following discussion explores what images, scenes, and forms of television might be said to possess emancipatory potential, and is also intended to promote reflection on how the left can use television within advanced capitalism as a means of political and cultural development and enlightenment. . . . The following pages are animated by the belief that the central role of the electronic media in contemporary society makes it imperative for those who desire radical social change to explore the possibility of producing emancipatory culture and participating in media politics.

EMANCIPATORY POPULAR CULTURE

Popular culture per se is not manipulative, an instrument of class domination, nor a monolithic reproduction of capitalist ideology. Rather, in the historically specific form of popular culture produced by the culture industries controlled by corporate capital, popular culture has tended to reproduce hegemonic ideology. Traditionally, popular culture expressed people's experiences of oppression, struggle, and hopes for a better world, and served as an important part of oppositional cultures and political movements. In advanced capitalism, however, popular culture has lost many of its oppositional features and has become part of the apparatus of class domination. Nonetheless, the culture industries in America have never completely served as instruments of manipulation and class domination.

Radicals have often seen the production of an alternative, emancipatory culture as an important part of political struggle.[14] Today, since electronically transmitted culture in the broadcast media occupies so much of people's leisure time, the production of popular television, film, music, radio, and theater would seem to be a high priority on the agenda of cultural revolution. But the generally derogatory attitude of the left toward the broadcast media—especially toward television—has precluded much significant intervention in this area.* It would seem that as most people get much of their information and view of the world from the electronic media, and in particular from television, the left should make a serious commitment to these media. Sadly, there have been all too few attempts to present radical cultural productions within the electronic broadcast systems.

Furthermore, the most influential radical traditions in America have in recent years scorned the very idea of media politics and intervention in popular culture. The Frankfurt school analysis of the culture industries as mass deception has strongly influenced left views of popular culture in America and has helped to encourage an elitist and ultra-radical scorn for the productions of popular culture as debased, manipulative, and narcotizing.[16] Although the Communist Party pursued a popular-front policy for some time in the 1930s and 1940s, one that had a more complex (and occasionally uncritical) attitude toward popular culture, American radicals have generally tended to see the products of the culture industry as instruments of capitalist propaganda, and left cultural critics have usually preferred to investigate literature or "high culture" than to study the forms of popular culture. The new left largely followed this view of popular culture as manipulation, seeing the cultural industries as dominated by "mind managers" who served as instruments of corporate-capitalist rule.[17] This perspective has led to contempt for television and the broadcast media, and has

---

*Earlier, Bertolt Brecht, Walter Benjamin, and others saw the production of films and radio plays and the use of the new electronic and mass media for political ends as a crucial part of revolutionary practice, and Lenin said, "Of all the arts cinema is the most important for us."[15]

even evoked demands for "the elimination of television," a position that has found some sympathy on the left.[18]

Cultural criticism that works within this perspective is often able to state little more than the obvious: that television, and other media, is now dominated by various forms of capitalist ideology. Such an approach yields analyses of particular cultural productions that are banal and repetitive, and provides no way of taking seriously the rebellious, oppositional, and subversive moments in almost all forms of popular culture. Popular culture has traditionally contained at least elements of a protest against suffering and oppression. Oppositional moments in popular culture have taken the form of song and music, people's theater and festivals, and radical newspapers and literature. Blues, jazz, folk music, and union songs were a powerful voice which served to unite the oppressed in an oppositional culture. Socialists, the IWW, and anarchists had autonomous popular-oppositional cultures that bound together their members in a culture of protest and struggle. Early forms of mass-produced culture also had their popular and subversive moments: dime novels, nickelodeons, and popular magazines often undermined middle-class morality and expressed a rebellion against high-elitist culture, even though they often reproduced hegemonic ideologies.

What is crucial in this regard is to appreciate the ways in which these traditions of popular culture remain alive within the contemporary productions of the electronic media.* The left should not dismiss "mass culture" as an inferior form of culture that is counterposed to an "authentic" people's culture (which is usually confined in practice either to the culture of the left or to the margins of the society). Rather one should see the moments of protest and opposition within mainstream popular culture, and make these the focus of left cultural criticism and production (rather than restricting radical analysis to ritualistic denunciations of "bourgeois ideology" within popular culture). Even hegemonic ideology makes concessions to oppositional groups and people's experiences of oppression, injustice, and exploitation.[19] Careful analysis of American popular

---

*The oppositional and utopian moments of popular culture are developed in the theories of labor historians like E.P. Thompson and Herbert Gutman, the theories of Raymond Williams and Stanley Aronowitz, and the ongoing work of the *Cultural Correspondence* group.

culture shows a strong anti-capitalist and anti-business tradition that remains operative to this day.[20] In the muckraker tradition and in works of many of America's finest writers, there have been concerted attacks on business and businessmen. The novels of Theodore Dreiser, Frank Norris, Sinclair Lewis, Upton Sinclair, John Steinbeck, Norman Mailer, Gore Vidal, Joseph Heller, and other writers have depicted businesspeople as exploitative, mercenary, insensitive, and totally obsessed with the gods of mammon and profit. Far from idealizing business, many novels, films, and popular literature have been resolutely anti-business and even in network television there has been an increase in attacks on business.[21]

Opposition to the established society has expressed itself in satire and comedic attacks on authority, as well as in serious, realistic criticisms of the society. Comedy and satire have often been effective means of social criticism and enlightenment. The subversive tradition of comedy in the theater was early on incorporated in film, in the comedies of Chaplin and Keaton, which often depicted with sympathy the situation of the oppressed "little man," and still provide splendid examples of emancipatory comedy (as in the images of Chaplin on the assembly line in *Modern Times*). Emancipatory comedy provides insights into the nature of the society that break through ideological conceptions. Emancipatory laughter suspends the logic of everyday reality; it is surreal and helps one to rise above ideological preconceptions in order to recognize the workings of everyday life. It could foster critical awareness by enabling one to laugh at a miserable life—and to see that life could be different. Many of the films of Chaplin, Keaton, the Marx Brothers, Mae West, W.C. Fields, and "screwball comedy" contain moments of emancipatory comedy.

The contradictions of popular culture were reproduced in a particularly provocative way in American film. Although its genres and conventions were often vehicles for hegemonic American ideologies, sometimes film was satirical or sharply critical of the existing society. Early films were working-class/ immigrant oriented, and often opposed the values and institutions of the American system.[22] What was perceived as their immoral and subversive content led to ongoing censorship battles that finally produced the Hays Code as the industry's defensive maneuver to stem conservative outrage and avoid government regulation. Nonetheless, films continued to be perceived by conservatives and traditionalists as culturally and politically dangerous, and the film industry later became the subject of various inquisitions.

In the era of political and cultural repression in the 1950s, the oppositional voice of popular culture took many forms. The movies of James Dean and Marlon Brando, beatnik literature and poetry, and rock-and-roll music all contained moments of protest and subversion.[23] At a time when political opposition was extremely limited, popular culture often became a vehicle of social critique and protest. In the 1960s, popular culture became a more open vehicle of protest and opposition, particularly in music and film.

During this period of cultural upheaval and political struggle the most tightly controlled medium was television. It contained very few subversive elements in the 1960s, though such themes were never entirely absent. Earlier, in the 1950s, television had begun to develop a tradition of critical-realist dramas: plays adapted for television (such as Arthur Miller's *Death of a Salesman*) or original dramas by Paddy Chayefsky, Reginald Rose, and others, which took social-realist forms. But this tradition died off, as did much of early television comedy that could not readily be contained within the situation comedy format (Ernie Kovacs, etc.). Since television developed in ways so heavily dependent on corporate sponsorship, and since there was no tradition of critical or subversive works in the medium to which reference could be made, there was much in the actual history of American television that seemed to justify the versions of manipulation theory that are still dominant on the left.*

Yet in recent years a number of programs have shown, by their popularity, that more controversial realist drama and topical situation comedies are forms of popular culture that should be taken seriously by the left. For instance, the high ratings of *Roots* showed the networks that controversial political dramas

---

*Those television shows that did break taboos were often censored, or even eliminated, despite high ratings. For instance, *East Side/West Side*, a series with George C. Scott, was removed, though it gained high ratings, when the social workers on the show started talking about organizing the oppressed to deal more effectively with the problems of urban life, which the program realistically presented. Later, the Smothers Brothers show was also cancelled (again despite high ratings) when they escalated satirical attacks on the Nixon administration and the Vietnam war policy, and refused to submit scripts for prior censorship.

had popular appeal, as earlier the success of *All in the Family* had shown that more controversial and topical situation comedies could gain high ratings. These programs represent a real breakthrough in television and provide at least partial models for talking about emancipatory television culture.

Emancipatory popular culture challenges the institutions and way of life and advanced capitalist society. It generally has the quality of shock, forcing people to see aspects of the society that they had previously overlooked, or it focuses attention on the need for change. Emancipatory popular culture subverts ideological codes and stereotypes, and shows the inadequacy of rigid conceptions that prevent insight into the complexities and changes of social life. It rejects idealizations and rationalizations that apologize for the suffering in the present social system, and, at its best, suggests that another way of life is possible.

"Emancipatory" signifies emancipation *from* something that is restrictive or repressive, and *for* something that is conducive to an increase of freedom and well-being.* In this strong sense very little television, or any mass-produced popular culture, can count as "emancipatory." But certain forms do contain some emancipatory potential, forms that are present now in contemporary American society. No television program can be emancipatory per se, because the decoding by the audience can reject subversive messages or interpret them in a way that does not change anything. (Studies reveal that many bigots identified with Archie Bunker and that *All in the Family* strengthened their prejudices; other studies show that the strong condemnation of the military-industrial complex in the CBS documentary *The Selling of the Pentagon* confirmed—against the intentions of the producers—the belief of many that the Soviet Union is a dangerous threat and that a strong military establishment is vital.) Like the most conservative productions, more progressive efforts may have contradictory social effects.

Underlying this problem is the question of how people use TV, what its social effects are, and how television-watching relates to people's total experience. There is as yet no adequate answer to these questions—but it is clear that the passive spectator model is deficient. There are significant ideological contradictions in both the production and the experience of

---

*I am using "emancipatory" in its historical sense as signifying "enlightenment" which contains insight and awakening, leading to a transformation of thought and behavior.

watching television in this society, and many people are ready for more diverse, complex, and critical television than is now available on the networks.

Though no one television show or series can radically change consciousness or alter behavior, television can cause an individual to question previous beliefs, values, and actions. Such a process contains the potential for more significant subsequent changes. The following analyses search out the emancipatory potential in certain forms of popular culture. I am not suggesting that "emancipatory popular culture" is "revolutionary art"—the latter must be part of an actual revolutionary movement and should radically alter the forms, content, and means of cultural production. What is argued, however, is that judging contemporary forms of mass popular culture by the criteria of revolutionary art is likely only to perpetuate the cultural isolation of the left. We are not in a revolutionary situation in America (to put it mildly!) and the concept of emancipatory popular culture is a sort of transitional concept in a period of conservatism and diffuse discontent.

I will first discuss some TV documentaries and miniseries that fit into earlier muckraking and critical realist traditions, and that have employed conventional realist and melodrama narrative forms to present a more accurate picture of American life than was previously presented on television. Here I argue for rejecting the anti-realist stance that has informed much radical cultural criticism.[24] Then I discuss how certain Norman Lear comedies fit into a tradition of comedy as subversion and emancipation.

REALISM AS SUBVERSION

Although many consider "realism" a form of bourgeois narrative that simply reproduces the current form of society as "natural," in the falsely idealized television universe certain forms of realism are actually subversive. A more "realistic" picture could subvert the image of American society perpetrated by the television world, where society's chronic problems and worst failures have generally been repressed. Documentaries can call attention to problems and mobilize public opinion for social change. The CBS documentary *Hunger in America* helped win support for Johnson's war on poverty; *Harvest of Shame* called attention to the plight of farm workers; and

Vietnam documentaries and news footage helped mobilize public opinion against the war. Many other documentaries and *60 Minutes* studies have exposed business malpractice and economic-political corruption, the failures and crimes of the CIA and American foreign policy, and the problems of poverty, the cities, and oppressed minorities. Although network and PBS documentaries rarely analyze the roots of the problems, and even more rarely propose radical solutions and alternatives, nonetheless they have provided insights into American society that are usually excluded from the TV world.

Documentaries could be an important tool of political education. There is a long radical documentary tradition in America and some radical documentaries have even been aired on public television. *Hearts and Minds, Harlan County USA*, Emile de Antonio's documentaries on McCarthyism, Vietnam, Nixon, and the Weather underground, and many other radical documentaries represent an important resource which, if broadcast regularly on public, network, or cable-satellite television, could serve as important means of public enlightenment. Historical documentaries could create a better sense of the radical American heritage. There is also potential in the recent "docudrama" form to provide both a better sense of history and a clearer understanding of what is happening to us now. Docudramas on the Cuban missile crisis, the *Pueblo* incident, the Kennedy assassination, McCarthyism, and other topics, despite their distortions and exclusions, contain provocative accounts of recent American history which could prompt serious reflection on the need for change.

Recent network miniseries have used the forms of television melodrama and literary "critical realism" following the example of the British Broadcasting Corporation's presentation of dramas in a limited series form. The miniseries break from the series form, and have treated issues hitherto excluded from American television. Miniseries like *Roots, Holocaust, Captains and Kings, Second Avenue, The Moneychangers*, and *Wheels* have dealt with class conflict, racism and antisemitism, imperialism, and the oppression of the working class and blacks. They have often sympathetically portrayed the oppressed, poor, minorities, and workers, and presented capitalists and right-wingers as oppressors and exploiters. Docudramas like *Tailgunner Joe, Fear on Trial*, and *King* have criticized John McCarthy, J. Edgar Hoover, and the FBI, and vindicated Martin Luther King as well as victims of

McCarthyism and FBI persecution in the entertainment industry. *Kill Me If You Can* sympathetically depicted the plight of a victim of capital punishment, Caryl Chessman, while presenting as strong a case against capital punishment as ever appeared on television.

These programs represent an important revision of idealized images of history, and a reversal of conventional good guy/bad guy roles. Formerly, in a series like *The FBI* and numerous police and spy series, the FBI, CIA, and police were pictured as heroic saviors, whereas radicals or anyone failing to conform to the rules of the system were pictured as the incarnation of evil. The economic and political systems, and social institutions such as the family, were almost always idealized in television culture. From the mid-1970s, however, television dramas have exposed brutal racism (*Roots, King,* and *Roll of Thunder, Hear My Cry*); have shown the corruption of the political system (*Washington: Behind Closed Doors*); displayed the evils of McCarthyism and 1950s blacklisting (*Fear on Trial, Tailgunner Joe,* and the movie *The Front*); revealed class conflict; and in *The Moneychangers* and *Wheels* attacked two venerable institutions of corporate capitalism, the banks and the automobile industry. In all these programs the oppressed were portrayed in positive images and the oppressors in negative ones, reversing the usual content of television codes.

The phenomenal popularity of *Roots*—which broke all previous television viewing records—indicates that the American audience is receptive to historical drama that deals with oppression and struggle.[25] Whatever its failings, *Roots* offered a vivid picture of the effects of slavery and racism. Its images of the kidnapping of blacks from Africa and their suffering called attention dramatically to the unspeakable atrocities practiced by individuals driven by the profit motive. *Roots* showed how the slave system subjected anyone who came in contact with it to degraded forms of behavior and how it inflicted misery on both the oppressed and their oppressors. The series resolutely took the point of view of the oppressed and for almost the first time in television history attempted in a dramatic forum to present blacks as complex human beings. The reversal of codes in *Roots* and its tremendous popularity shows the potential for broadcasting forms of popular culture that evoke sympathy for the oppressed and favorably present their struggles.

Although *Roots* distorted some historical facts and used stereotypes to portray, in particular, white racists, the series none-

theless presented the most realistic account of slavery ever shown on network television. It encouraged millions of people to reflect on slavery and the evils of racism.[26] *Roots* was not a documentary and its historical distortions did not detract from its powerful and realistic picture of slavery. It used melodrama codes of clashes between good and evil to convey moral messages to audiences conditioned to such cultural forms. The recent Cuban film *The Other Francisco* is superior aesthetically and politically to *Roots* because it unmasks the codes of bourgeois melodrama and uses a variety of documentary and dramatic devices to depict the situation of slaves in Cuba. Nonetheless, *Roots* has its emancipatory moments for American culture by breaking down some stereotypes of blacks and slavery and by bringing to awareness usually repressed topics.*
Wheels, a television miniseries shown in May 1978, and generally ignored by the American left in its periodicals, is a more complex example of subversive television. *Wheels* was based on a novel by Arthur Hailey about the Detroit automobile industry. The series opens with a corporate executive, played by Rock Hudson, visiting a Detroit ghetto in flames. He was trying to understand the blacks' problems and what could be done. Shortly thereafter we meet some of the children of the corporate executives: one young woman is an activist involved with a black man, and other children are in varying degrees of conflict with their parents. The series details the problems of black workers, the assembly line, worker sabotage, union internal conflicts, and management-labor struggles. It realistically pictures intense conflicts within management and destructive corporate infighting (one executive, to advance his own position, sabotages the new car model Rock Hudson was working on). *Wheels* repeatedly makes the point that Detroit automobiles are unreliable, stressing that cars produced on Mondays or Fridays are often shoddy because of absenteeism, inexperienced

The Other Francisco, directed by Sergio Giral, Cuba 1975 (distributed by Tricontinental Film Center). This remarkable film opens with a melodramatic scene of a black Cuban slave's death, and then uses documentary to discuss a nineteenth-century anti-slavery novel (*Francisco*) by a progressive bourgeois liberal. The film reconstructs the melodrama form of the novel and stops to analyze the codes of melodrama narrative and the historical distortion in the novel. *The Other Francisco* next attempts to provide a more realistic cinematic reconstruction of the life of the Cuban slave. Such an attempt to provide new socialist cinematic codes and forms is very difficult within the dominant television practice of advanced capitalism, which first requires subversion of dominant codes and/or the use of traditional forms to convey subversive content.

replacements, or worker frustration expressed in sabotage or poor work. (A subplot shows in fascinating detail how car dealers rip off car buyers.)

The focus on corporate capitalism is critical and realistic, and the picture of Detroit and the automobile industry is devastating. All significant problems are left unresolved: the situation of the blacks remains bleak, and no reform of the industry is depicted. Rock Hudson's decision to remain in the industry is stoic resignation at best, leavened with the hopes of love from his mistress, after the disintegration of his family following the suicide of his wife. Redemption through love is presented as the alternative to an alienated world of labor and a disintegrating family and social scene. Capitalism appears as a system permeated with greed, exploitation, and waste. The series was anticapitalist to the core and can be interpreted as popular revenge against the automobile industry.

The picture of the Vietnam War is especially interesting. From the beginning, there are intimations that Rock Hudson's youngest son may be drafted. He is, and the Vietnam War is portrayed as an unrelieved nightmare, culminating in some remarkable footage of the son being bombed by his own troops (i.e., "friendly fire"). The war was portrayed as irredeemable evil perpetrated on the American people and the Vietnamese.

This miniseries often descended into soap-opera melodrama. Yet it is probably the appeal of the melodrama that makes this program an efficacious vehicle for its social critique. *Wheels* used melodrama conventions to convey social critique and to deal with real problems.*

POPULAR CULTURE AS POPULAR REVENGE

The previous analyses suggest that the conventions and genres of popular culture can convey social and cultural criticism and communicate radical political content. In fact, these TV miniseries contain a form of popular culture as popular revenge. The blacks are avenged against their oppressors in *Roots, King,* and other series that portray racists as evil and the struggles of

---

*In this sense, *Wheels* follows the melodramatic practice of the left filmmaker Douglas Sirk, who used lush color, intense passion, and conventional melodrama to engage his audience, while attempting to subvert bourgeois ideology.[27]

blacks as legitimate. *Holocaust* provides popular revenge against Nazi oppression in its harsh portrayal of fascism and sympathetic portrayal of Jewish victims and resistance. *Fear on Trial* and other TV portrayals of McCarthyism and blacklisting gained a retrospective cultural victory for the victims of political oppression by portraying the injustice, irrationality, and pettiness of right-wing oppression. Victims of FBI persecution gained revenge against J. Edgar Hoover in the portrayals of Hoover and the FBI in *King, Washington: Behind Closed Doors*, and the film *The Private Files of J. Edgar Hoover*.

Popular culture in all these examples—and there are many more—takes the point of view of the victims and attacks the oppressors, thus providing images that vindicate struggles against oppression. These images subvert more conservative, idealized images of American history and society which have tried to erase the memory of oppression and struggle from the popular consciousness. Moreover, as Jeremy Brecher suggests, "The very memory of revolt is a subversive force."[28]

The fact that many recent instances of television culture can be interpreted as forms of popular revenge indicates that the potential exists for using the electronic media for production of emancipatory popular culture. It may be that at present radical cultural production within advanced capitalism may have to use traditional forms to communicate subversive content. Since we are far from being in a revolutionary situation, it is counterproductive to limit what we count as emancipatory popular culture to the demands of avant-garde "radicalism" or "revolutionary art." Therefore, as part of a transitional cultural strategy, we should be aware of the usefulness of traditional dramatic forms for popular culture that seek to reach large audiences, and should be prepared to use and defend them in a strategy of left cultural intervention in popular culture.

None of the TV productions I have mentioned is free from distortion; nonetheless, they represent significant changes within television culture. Previously, for television, there was almost no treatment of the oppression of working people, blacks, or women. Whenever workers or the oppressed were dealt with in television culture, they were stereotypically portrayed, and rarely presented even as sympathetic characters. For the most part, television has systematically excluded the element of protest and attacks upon the oppressors from popular culture. During the cold-war era of the 1950s and 1960s, there was concerted ideological censorship and avoidance of

controversial material, out of anticommunism and as an attempt to attract a large audience. There was tight control of
programming by sponsors, network censors, and executives.
But in recent years the tremendous cultural and economic
success of television gives the networks the power to show
more controversial programs. In the drive for higher ratings
and profits, they will occasionally show controversial material
if they believe it will help attain these goals. Consequently, the
miniseries have been allowed to break previous taboos, as have
a number of comedy programs. The relations between those
who run the networks and the television audience are much
more complex than the usual versions of manipulation theory
allow. While it is easy to dismiss the apologists for the networks
who claim that what is run simply reflects popular tastes, the
response of the audience(s) does make a difference.

COMEDY AS SUBVERSION AND EMANCIPATION

Comedy provides the potential for subverting and discrediting
dominant cultural and social forms—yet it can also deride deviance and teach the renunciation of desire.[29] These "emancipatory" and "conciliatory" forms of laughter often coexist uneas-
ily within the same series or even the same program. In some
cases, the conciliatory aspects of comedy are clearly primary, as
in such ABC situation comedies as *Happy Days, Laverne and Shirley*,
and *Three's Company*. Conciliatory laughter binds together television's social role model-types into an idealized universe of good
times and comfortable conformity. Such laughter also involves
laughing at the renunciation of desire and at oneself for conforming, and encodes rites of renunciation.

The best work of Norman Lear, on the other hand, contains
moments of emancipatory laughter. Television's history has
seen few genuine innovations, but Lear's introduction of topical and controversial issues into situation comedy represents an
important development. His best work, *Mary Hartman, Mary
Hartman*, was on one level a subversion of the forms of the soap
opera and situation comedy, while on another level it engaged
in social critique and satire. Whereas soap opera generally triv-
ializes serious problems through pathos, sentimentality, and
pseudo-realism, *Mary Hartman* approached some of the same
problems more fully, often starting with apparently common
everyday problems, and using humor and self-reflective irony

to suggest that something is profoundly wrong with the current society. Whereas situation comedy uses a conflict/resolution model in which problems are humorously resolved in thirty or sixty minutes, the problems on *Mary Hartman* endlessly multiplied and were insoluble within the present way of life. In the process, authority figures of all types were ruthlessly satirized. Such reversal of codes and stereotypes could provoke reflection on social institutions and their workings. Further, more than any previous television show, *Mary Hartman* constantly reflected on television, the television view of the world, and its impact on American life. It confronted TV ideology with contradictory experiences and showed at once the false idealizations and distortions of the TV world and the failings of the social world. (That this view of TV and American society corresponded in many ways to radical perceptions helps explain the fascination of the left with this series.)[30]

Mary Hartman dealt with topics previously taboo: impotence, venereal disease, union corruption, alienated industrial labor, religious fraud, and many other issues were introduced that were either completely repressed or gingerly approached by previous television series. In fact, most Norman Lear series presented subjects previously eliminated from the television world. Whatever the failings of Lear's series, programs in *All in the Family* confronted bigotry and generational conflict more powerfully than ever before on television; *Maude* treated women's liberation and middle-class malaise in a provocative manner; *The Jeffersons* and *Good Times* dealt with middle-class and working-class blacks more interestingly than on previous series; *All's Fair* had more political debates (between the conservative male and liberal woman) than any previous TV comedy; and Lear's syndicated comedies *All That Glitters, Fernwood Tonight, America Tonight,* and *Fernwood Forever* were imaginative shows that contained some of the most striking satires of television and American society ever broadcast.

Lear's situation comedies have had their problems. *Mary Hartman* collapsed into cynicism and despair as the series ended after two years with Mary back in the kitchen, reproducing her former way of life with her new lover. The show was not really able to offer emancipatory alternatives. Most of Lear's other situation comedies are structured by the standard conflict/resolution model that manages to resolve the problems and issues confronted without serious change. *All in the Family* usually suggests that all problems can be settled within the family

(after all, "it's all in the family") and established way of life.
Though Lear's programs present real problems never before
portrayed in the television world, they never offer solutions
that transcend the limits of the current society.

Yet Lear's situation comedies do show that it is possible to
engage in social satire and critique in TV series. There have
been other efforts in this direction such as *Ernie Kovacs*, *The
Smothers Brothers*, and episodes of *Laugh-In* and *Saturday Night Live*.
Most such programs have sooner or later encountered problems with the networks, often over censorship. This is to be
expected, but should not obscure the changes that have taken
place since *Leave It to Beaver* and the *Dick Van Dyke Show* were the
exemplary television comedies.

Emancipatory comedy's ability to use generic subversion and
satire to provide critical insights suggests the inadequacy of
championing either formalism or realism as exclusive models
of emancipatory popular culture. *Mary Hartman* used formal-
generic subversion and surrealism to convey a critical picture of
the life of the "typical American housewife and consumer." In
one unforgettable scene, Mary is in the kitchen in the middle of
the night, unable to sleep. Her husband Tom wanders in, and
they discuss an article Mary is reading about the differing
sexual cycles of the male and female. Tom is experiencing
impotence problems and he flares up at Mary, asking what is
wrong with her. He demands to know what more she could
possibly want, noting that he's given her a home, family, modern appliances, and even a four-piece toaster. "I don't know,"
Mary answers, "I just want something more." Tom huffily
leaves the room, and Mary calls the telephone operator to see if
a Mary Hartman is listed, or a Mrs. Tom Hartman. She isn't,
and in a bizarre scene Mary crawls under the kitchen sink. Soon
her sister Cathy and neighbor Loretta arrive. They extricate
Mary, and the three women sit at the table, while Cathy and
Loretta talk about their orgasms. Mary, evidently ignorant of
what an orgasm is and extremely uncomfortable about the
issue, asks them to leave. Her grandfather then comes in and
tells her that she's right not to be satisfied with her present
existence and to want "something more."

This remarkable episode combines formal innovation with
thematic novelty, humor with serious drama. Perhaps the most
effective emancipatory popular culture combines, as does *Mary
Hartman*, formal and thematic innovation, following Brecht's

prescription that radical art must concern itself with innovations of form and content, as well as the apparatus of production.[31] But within the TV world, it is sometimes an advance even to use traditional forms as vehicles for controversial or subversive themes, as Lear has managed to do in some of his other situation comedies. This raises the difficult question of whether radical cultural production and criticism should demand that emancipatory popular culture meet the strict requirements of revolutionizing both form and content. It may be that given the current state of American television, radical cultural production might as a transitional strategy use traditional forms as vehicles of innovative, provocative, and politically challenging content. The problem with this approach, of course, is that it does not allow sufficient importance to the task of trying to create new cultural forms, subverting the codes of the dominant television genres and thus producing a new type of television experience.

Such questions can only be answered through the acquisition of a larger body of direct experience in these areas than the left now has. It is not necessary to make an exclusive choice for one or the other strategy at this point. What is most important is to appreciate the ways in which it is now possible to produce emancipatory popular culture within television. This possibility is opened up not only by changes in the television audience, but by contradictions within the American television system and the emerging cable-satellite technology. There is first the contradiction between public and network television. Public television, to legitimate itself and gain the viewer contributions it needs to survive, must show a variety of programming which sometimes includes critical-realist documentaries, provocative political discussion shows, and social satire. Even within network television, there are differences between the "mind managers" and the employees of the "cultural apparatus"—the producers, writers, actors, and technicians who may have ideas and interests very different from those of their corporate managers.[32] Today the networks will show just about anything that will increase their profits and competitive position in the ratings. Hence, if the audience responds to critical realism, subversive programs, or any type of potentially emancipatory culture, the networks will, within certain limits, probably play it.

Given this situation and the new opportunities that will be opened by the new communications technology . . . the left should consider how to produce, or how to participate in the production of, popular television, as well as documentaries, news commentaries and programs, and political discussions suitable for broadcast media. Yet if genuinely emancipatory productions are to be broadcast, there must be a cultural-media politics that will ensure public access and open new channels of communication. This would require radical transformation of the present communcations and television system. Can we begin talking of the liberation of television?

NOTES

1. See Alvin W. Gouldner, *The Dialectic of Ideology and Technology* (New York: Seabury, 1976). Gouldner argues that the major symbolic vehicle for ideology was print technology, which was primarily conceptual and relatively rational (p. 167ff.): "In contrast to the conventional printed objects central to ideologies, the modern communication media have greatly intensified the nonlinguistic and iconic component and hence the *multimodal* character of public communication" (p. 168). I reject Gouldner's identification of ideology with print media and electronic media with non-ideological symbolic imagery. The electronic communications revolution has provided powerful new means for the production and transmission of ideology. Gouldner tends to equate print media with rational discourse, and electronic media with the "irrationality" of symbolic imagery. This view exaggerates the rationality of print media, and also fails to discern the relative rationality of the ideologies centered in the electronic media. Gouldner suggests that the shift from a "newspaper to a television-centered system of communications" leads to "altogether differently structured symbol systems: of analogic rather than digital, of synthetic rather than analytic systems, of occult belief systems, new religious myths" (p. 170). He fails, however, to draw appropriate conclusions, arguing, "In this, however, there is no 'end' to ideology, for it continues among some groups, in some sites, and at some semiotic level, but it ceases to be as important a mode of consciousness of masses: remaining a dominant form of consciousness among *some* elites, ideology loses ground among the masses and lower strata" (p. 179). Against this position, I am arguing that ideology has had a remarkable new impact on individuals in advanced capitalist societies, through the effects of the technology of the communications revolution.
2. Louis Althusser, "Ideology and Ideological State Apparatuses," in *Lenin and Philosophy* (New York: Monthly Review Press, 1971).
3. On the relation between ideology, myth, and revolution, see Georges Sorel, *Reflections on Violence* (New York: Free Press, 1950), and Lewis S. Feuer, *Ideology and the Ideologists* (New York: Harper & Row, 1975), who has written probably the worst book on ideology in recent history. Feuer is wrong to claim that ideology is essentially mythical. Against Feuer, Gouldner's emphasis on the relative rationality of ideological discourse is clearly correct. Feuer's strategy is to claim that all ideological discourse is a form of cognitive pathology in order to debunk, above all, Marxism. Feuer neglects to discuss ideology as hegemony, and fails to see that the "science" that he counterposes to ideology itself takes ideological forms.

4. In a fine analysis, "The Metaphoricality of Marxism," Alvin Gouldner suggests that much of Marxism's appeal, power, and success lies in the attractiveness of its metaphors: socialism and the proletariat, bondage and revolt, alienation and its overcoming, class struggle and community. *Theory and Society*, vol. 1, no. 1 (1974), pp. 387–414. Extending this line of analysis, one could show that all ideologies owe much of their appeal to their symbols and images.

5. Althusser, "Ideology." Althusser really doesn't analyze the "ideological apparatus" here and falsely assumes a monolithic "state ideological apparatus," whereas in fact the ideological apparatuses are not all state-controlled, and are full of contradictions. For a critique of Althusser's analysis of ideology, see Douglas Kellner, "Ideology, Marxism, and Advanced Capitalism," *Socialist Review* 42 (1978).

6. Susan Sontag, *On Photography* (New York: Farrar, Straus & Giroux, 1977), pp. 178–79.

7. On the concept of paleosymbolism see Jürgen Habermas, "Toward a Theory of Communicative Competence," *Recent Sociology* no. 2, ed. Hans Dreitzel (New York: Macmillan, 1970), and Gouldner, *Dialectic*. Habermas and Gouldner claim that the concept of paleosymbolism derives from Freud but they provide no source references and I have not been able to find it in Freud's writings. In any case, the concept is rooted in Freud's notion of "scenic understanding" (see the Habermas source above) and is consistent with Freud's use of archaeological metaphors for the topological structures of the mind. See, for example, Freud's *Civilization and Its Discontents* (New York: Norton, 1962), pp. 16ff.

8. See Habermas, "Communicative Competence"; Freud, *The Interpretation of Dreams*; and Alfred Lorenzer, "Symbol and Stereotypes," in Paul Connerton, ed., *Critical Sociology* (New York: Penguin Books, 1976).

9. On the historical background of the concept of melodrama, see James L. Smith, *Melodrama* (London: Methuen & Co., 1973).

10. Joseph Campbell, *Hero with a Thousand Faces* (New York: Meridian, 1956).

11. Robert Jewett and John Lawrence, *The American Monomyth* (Garden City: Doubleday, 1977).

12. Ibid.

13. Roland Barthes, *Mythologies* (New York: Hill & Wang, 1972), pp. 109ff.

14. See the issue on left culture in America, *The Origins of Left Culture in the U.S., 1880–1940. Cultural Correspondence/Green Mountain Irregulars*, Spring 1978.

15. See Walter Benjamin, "The Author as Producer," *New Left Review* 62 (1970), and Douglas Kellner, "Brecht's Marxist Aesthetic—The Korsch Connection," in Betty Weber and Hubert Heinin, eds., *Bertolt Brecht: Literary Theory and Political Practice* (Athens: University of Georgia Press, 1980). The Lenin quote is often cited, but I have not been able to locate it in Lenin's *Collected Works*.

16. For the classical Frankfurt School theory of popular culture as "mass deception," see T. W. Adorno and Max Horkheimer, "The Culture Industry," in *Dialectic of Enlightenment* (New York: Seabury, 1972). The essays of Dwight Macdonald and other articles on popular culture in the radical journal *Politics* took the Frankfurt School position that popular culture was a manipulative instrument of social control and adulteration of high culture. See Macdonald's "Notes on Popular Culture," *Politics*, vol. 1, no. 1 (February 1944). The most influential anthology on popular culture in America, *Mass Culture* (Glencoe, Ill. Free Press, 1957) was strongly influ-

enced by the Frankfurt School view. See the introduction by the editor, Bernard Rosenberg, who contributed to *Dissent*, and the articles by Lowenthal, Macdonald, Greenberg, Kracauer, Anders, Adorno, Howe, and van der Haag.

17. Many American leftists accept the manipulation thesis expressed by Herbert Schiller, *The Mind Managers* (Boston: Beacon Press, 1973). For a critique of the manipulation thesis, see Daniel Ben-Horin, "Television without Tears," *Socialist Revolution* 35 (1977).

18. See Jerry Mander, *Four Arguments for the Elimination of Television* (New York: William Morrow, 1978).

19. "The transformations of ideology take place within a process of class stuggle, and hegemonic ideology is formed as a *set of negotiated settlements* between classes . . . hegemonic ideology is full of contradictions, shifts, and adjustments, and is constantly challenged by oppositional ideologies. . . . Hegemonic ideologies are not simply imposed on people. Ideology is not effective or credible unless it achieves resonance with people's experience. And to remain credible it must continually incorporate the new, responding to changes in people's lives and social conditions." Kellner, "Ideology," pp. 52–53.

20. See John Leonard, "What Have American Writers Got against Businessmen?" *Forbes*, 15 May 1977, pp. 117ff., and Jerry Flint, "The Banker in Poem and Prose," *New York Times*, Sunday, 14 March 1976, f3. I am grateful to Jack Schierenback for calling my attention to these articles; we are collaborating on a forthcoming study of the ambivalences within Marxian traditions in analyzing culture, and he is working on a study of relations among business, the state, and media.

21. Ben Stein in *The View from Sunset Boulevard* (New York: Basic Books, 1979) has documented many negative images of business and businessmen on network tv—these sections were reprinted in the *New York Times* and *Wall Street Journal*.

22. On the radical and democratic elements in the American film, see Robert Sklar, *Movie-Made America* (New York: Random House, 1976), and Garth Jowett, *Film: The Democratic Art* (Boston: Little, Brown, 1976). On leftist activity within the industry see David Talbor and Barbara Zheutlin, *Creative Differences* (Boston: South End Press, 1978).

23. See Stanley Aronwitz, "The Unsilent Fifties," in *False Promises* (New York: McGraw-Hill, 1973).

24. For a sharp critique of the sort of cultural radicalism that takes an antirealist stance and would reject all traditional "realist" or "melodrama" forms as inherently conservative or bourgeois, see Gerald Graff, "The Politics of Anti-Realism," *Salmagundi*, 42 (Summer-Fall 1978).

25. It is estimated that 130 million viewers saw *Roots* when it was first run in January 1977, and that 80 million viewers watched all or part of the rerun of *Roots* in September 1978. *TV Guide*, 23 September 1978, p. A-4.

26. For typical criticisms of the historical distortions in *Roots* see "Shrunken and Distorted Version of *Roots* on tv," *In These Times*, 16–22 February 1977, and the articles in "How Deep Did *Roots* Dig," ibid., 23 February–1 March 1977.

27. On the subversive aspects of Sirk's films, see the article by Rainer Fassbinder, "Six Films by Douglas Sirk," *New Left Review* 91 (May–June 1975); Michael Stern, "Patterns of Power and Potency, Repression and Violence: Sirk's Films of the 1950's," *The Velvet Light Trap* 16 (Fall 1976); and the articles on Sirk in *Screen*, vol. 12, no. 2 (Summer 1971).

28. Jeremy Brecher, *Strike!* (San Francisco: Straight Arrow Books, 1972), p. 314.

29. On "conciliatory laughter" see Adorno and Horkheimer, "Culture Industry."

30. See Elayne Rapping, "I've Got a Crush on Mary Hartman," *American Movement*, May 1976; Stephanie Harrington, "Mary Hartman: The Unedited, All American Unconscious," *Ms*, May 1976; Liz and Stu Ewen, "Mary Hartman: An All-Consuming Interest," *Seven Days*, 26 July 1976; and Barbara Ehrenreich, "Mary Hartman: A World Out of Control," *Socialist Revolution* 30 (October–December 1976).

31. Bertolt Brecht, *Brecht on Theater*, ed. John Willet (New York: Hill & Wang, 1971), discussed in Kellner, "Brecht's Marxist Aesthetic."

32. Gouldner, *Dialectic*, ch 7.

PART III

DEFINING TELEVISION

Todd Gitlin begins this section with an essay directly related to Douglas Kellner's in Section II. He explains the concept of *hegemony* and relates it to television. His aim is to show how the very structures of the medium—programming as well as narrative structures—work together to limit television's capacity for critical disclosure. In his view, television is central to the maintenance of the status quo in political experience. Though it may offer some forms of change, they, too, will be acceptable to the political establishment.

While he agrees with Gitlin's analysis of television form and content, Farrel Corcoran raises an interesting question that modifies Gitlin's sense of television's power. He suggests that television does not have the capacity to engage its audience in a compelling manner. If this is so, he argues, we will have to reconsider our notions of television's role in social life.

John Ellis and Rick Altman look very closely at various formal characteristics of television. Ellis is concerned with patterns of storytelling, Altman with the role of sound. Ellis examines visual elements from a somewhat different perspective than that offered by Bernard Timberg and David Barker in Section I and relates them to larger questions of how stories are told. Altman's analysis focuses on a little noticed but powerful aspect of television and provides a partial answer to some of the questions raised by Corcoran. He argues that the medium addresses us the audience as much with sound techniques as with visual techniques. In this way it "calls for" our attention at crucial moments and alerts us even if we are not attending to it.

From these close analyses of specific elements, Nick Browne moves to the macro level of television. Though he would find individual programs significant, he suggests that it is not programs that inform us best about the medium's significance. He encourages us instead to look at large patterns of programming, at the schedule itself, as a text for analysis. And he also

pushes toward an economic analysis of that text rather than
an aesthetic one, reminding us that television is fundamentally rooted in its relation to large-scale American economic
practices.

John Fiske and John Hartley look for another sort of relation.
They tie television to other forms of expression and other
times. They argue that television is often misunderstood by
those who link it to literature, the stage, even to film. For them,
television is an oral medium, more like the songs and poems
sung by medieval bards than like the novel or the newspaper.
To properly understand the medium, then, they suggest a reconsideration of its centrality to contemporary culture.

Horace Newcomb, in an essay more than ten years old, is
concerned with defining some specific properties of television.
While the notions of intimacy, continuity, and history may not
be applicable in all instances of contemporary television programming, they can be profitably used in examining shows
such as *Hill Street Blues* and *Cagney and Lacey*.

David Thorburn's project is similar and goes far beyond Newcomb in re-examining aspects of television that we often cite as
its worst qualities. He shows how even the commercials may
become elements useful to artists working in this medium. And
his notion of "the multiplicity principle" may be among the
most powerful insights into the way television actually works.

No single essay in this section, or in this collection, explains
television. Each of them offers observations that can be criticized, analyzed, applied, and reconsidered. With the techniques
of analysis offered in these essays we can better understand
television in its varied forms. And with that better understanding we should be able to consider the place of the medium in
our individual experience, our social and political lives, and our
shared culture.

TODD GITLIN

PRIME TIME IDEOLOGY:
THE HEGEMONIC PROCESS
IN TELEVISION ENTERTAINMENT

Every society works to reproduce itself—and its internal conflicts—within its cultural order, the structure of practices and
meanings around which the society takes shape. So much is
tautology. In this paper I look at contemporary mass media in
the United States as one cultural system promoting that reproduction. I try to show how ideology is relayed through various
features of American television, and how television programs
register larger ideological structures and changes. The question
here is not, What is the impact of these programs? but rather a
prior one, What do these programs mean? For only after thinking through their possible meanings as cultural objects and as
signs of cultural interactions among producers and audiences
may we begin intelligibly to ask about their "effects."

The attempt to understand the sources and transformations
of ideology in American society has been leading social theorists not only to social-psychological investigations, but to a
long overdue interest in Antonio Gramsci's (1971) notion of
ideological hegemony. It was Gramsci who, in the late twenties
and thirties, with the rise of Fascism and the failure of the
Western European working-class movements, began to consider why the working class was not necessarily revolutionary;
why it could, in fact, yield to Fascism. Condemned to a Fascist
prison precisely because the insurrectionary workers' move-

From *Social Problems*, Vol. 26, #3, February 1979. Reprinted with the permission of the Society of Social Problems and the author.

An earlier version of this paper was delivered to the 73rd Annual Meeting of
the American Sociological Association, San Francisco, Sept, 1978. Thanks to
Victoria Bonnell, Bruce Dancis, Wally Goldfrank, Karen Shapiro and several
anonymous reviewers for stimulating comments on earlier drafts.

ment in Northern Italy just after World War I failed, Gramsci spent years trying to account for the defeat, resorting in large measure to the concept of hegemony: bourgeois domination of the thought, the common sense, the life-ways and everyday assumptions of the working class. Gramsci counterposed "hegemony" to "coercion"; these were two analytically distinct processes through which ruling classes secure the consent of the dominated. Gramsci did not always make plain where to draw the line between hegemony and coercion; or rather, as Perry Anderson shows convincingly (1976),[1] he drew the line differently at different times. Nonetheless, ambiguities aside, Gramsci's distinction was a great advance for radical thought, for it called attention to the routine structures of everyday thought—down to "common sense" itself—which worked to sustain class domination and tyranny. That is to say, paradoxically, it took the working class seriously enough as a potential agent of revolution to hold it accountable for its failures.

Because Leninism failed abysmally throughout the West, Western Marxists and non-Marxist radicals have both been drawn back to Gramsci, hoping to address the evident fact that the Western working classes are not predestined toward socialist revolution.[2] In Europe this fact could be taken as strategic rather than normative wisdom on the part of the working class; but in America the working class is not only hostile to revolutionary *strategy*, it seems to disdain the socialist *goal* as well. At the very least, although a recent Peter Hart opinion poll showed that Americans abstractly "favor" workers' control, Americans do not seem to care enough about it to organize very widely in its behalf. While there are abundant "contradictions" throughout American society, they are played out substantially in the realm of "culture" or "ideology," which orthodox Marxism had consigned to the secondary category of "superstructure." Meanwhile, critical theory—especially in the work of T. W. Adorno and Max Horkheimer—had argued with great force that the dominant forms of commercial ("mass") culture were crystallizations of authoritarian ideology; yet despite the ingenuity and brilliance of particular feats of critical exegesis (Adorno, 1954, 1974; Adorno and Horkheimer, 1972), they seemed to be arguing that the "culture industry" was not only meretricious but wholly and statically complete. In the seventies, some of their approaches along with Gramsci's have been elaborated and furthered by Alvin W. Gouldner (1976; see also Kellner, 1978) and Raymond Williams (1973), in distinctly provocative ways.

In this paper I wish to contribute to the process of bringing the discussion of cultural hegemony down to earth. For much of the discussion so far remains abstract, almost as if cultural hegemony were a substance with a life of its own, a sort of immutable fog that has settled over the whole public life of capitalist societies to confound the truth of the proletarian telos. Thus to the questions, "Why are radical ideas suppressed in the schools?", "Why do workers oppose socialism?" and so on, comes the single Delphic answer: hegemony. "Hegemony" becomes the magical explanation of last resort. And as such it is useful neither as explanation nor as guide to action. If "hegemony" explains everything in the sphere of culture, it explains nothing.

Concurrent with the theoretical discussion, but on a different plane, looms an entire sub-industry criticizing and explicating specific mass-cultural products and straining to find "emancipatory" if not "revolutionary", meanings in them. Thus in 1977 there was cacophony about the TV version of *Roots*; this year the trend-setter seems to be TV's handling of violence. Mass media criticism becomes mass-mediated, an auxiliary sideshow serving cultural producers as well as the wider public of the cultural spectacle. Piece by piece we see fast and furious analysis of this movie, that TV show, that book, that spectator sport. Many of these pieces have merit one by one, but as a whole they do not accumulate toward a more general theory of how the cultural forms are managed and reproduced—and how they change. Without analytic point, item-by-item analyses of the standard fare of mass culture run the risk of degenerating into high-toned gossip, even a kind of critical groupie-ism. Unaware of the ambiguity of their own motives and strategies, the partial critics may be yielding to a displaced envy, where criticism covertly asks to be taken into the spotlight along with the celebrity culture ostensibly under criticism. Yet another trouble is that partial critiques in the mass-culture tradition don't help us understand the *hold* and the *limits* of cultural products, the degree to which people do and do not incorporate mass-cultural forms, sing the jingles, wear the corporate T-shirts, and most important, permit their life-worlds to be demarcated by them.

My task in what follows is to propose some features of a

lexicon for discussing the forms of hegemony in the concrete. Elsewhere I have described some of the operations of cultural hegemony in the sphere of television news, especially in the news's framing procedures for opposition movements (Gitlin, 1977a,b).[3] Here I wish to speak of the realm of entertainment: about television entertainment in particular—as the pervasive and (in the living room sense) *familiar* of our cultural sites—and about movies secondarily. How do the *formal* devices of TV prime-time programs encourage viewers to experience themselves as anti-political, privately accumulating individuals (also see Gitlin, 1977c)? And how do these forms express social conflict, containing and diverting the images of contrary social possibilities? I want to isolate a few of the routine devices, though of course in reality they do not operate in isolation; rather, they work in combination, where their force is often enough magnified (though they can also work in contradictory ways). And, crucially, it must be borne in mind throughout this discussion that the forms of mass-cultural production do not either spring up or operate independently of the rest of social life. Commercial culture does not *manufacture* ideology; it *relays* and *reproduces* and *processes* and *packages* and *focuses* ideology that is constantly arising both from social elites and from active social groups and movements throughout the society (as well as within media organizations and practices).

A more complete analysis of ideological process in a commercial society would look both above and below, to elites and to audiences. Above, it would take a long look at the economics and politics of broadcasting, at its relation to the FCC, the Congress, the President, the courts; in case studies and with a developing theory of ideology it would study media's peculiar combination and refraction of corporate, political, bureaucratic and professional interests, giving the media a sort of limited independence—or what Marxists are calling "relative autonomy"—in the upper reaches of the political-economic system. Below, as Raymond Williams has insisted, cultural hegemony operates within a whole social life-pattern; the people who consume mass-mediated products are also the people who work, reside, compete, go to school, live in families. And there are a good many traditional and material interests at stake for audiences: the political inertia of the American population now, for example, certainly has something to do with the continuing productivity of the goods-producing and -distributing industries, not simply with the force of mass culture. Let me try to avoid misunderstanding at the outset by insisting that *I will not be arguing that the forms of hegemonic entertainment superimpose themselves automatically and finally onto the consciousness or behavior of all audiences at all times*: it remains for sociologists to generate what Dave Morley (1974)[4] has called "an ethnography of audiences," and to study what Ronald Abramson (1978) calls "the phenomenology of audiences" if we are to have anything like a satisfactory account of how audiences consciously and unconsciously process, transform, and are transformed by the contents of television. For many years the subject of media effects was severely narrowed by a behaviorist definition of the problem (see Gitlin, 1978a); more recently, the "agenda-setting function" of mass media has been usefully studied in news media, but not in entertainment. (On the other hand, the very pervasiveness of TV entertainment makes laboratory study of its "effects" almost inconceivable.) It remains to incorporate occasional sociological insights into the actual behavior of TV audiences[5] into a more general theory of the interaction—a theory which avoids both the mechanical assumptions of behaviorism and the trivialities of the "uses and gratifications" approach.

But alas, that more general theory of the interaction is not on the horizon. My more modest attempt in this extremely preliminary essay is to sketch an approach to the hegemonic thrust of some TV forms, not to address the deflection, resistance, and reinterpretation achieved by audiences. I will show that hegemonic ideology is systematically preferred by certain features of TV programs, and that at the same time alternative and oppositional values are brought into the cultural system, and domesticated into hegemonic forms at times, by the routine workings of the market. Hegemony is reasserted in different ways at different times, even by different logics; if this variety is analytically messy, the messiness corresponds to a disordered ideological order, a contradictory society. This said, I proceed to some of the forms in which ideological hegemony is embedded: *format and formula; genre; setting and character type; slant; and solution*. Then these particulars will suggest a somewhat more fully developed theory of hegemony.

Format and Formula

Until recently at least, the TV schedule has been dominated by standard lengths and cadences, standardized packages of TV entertainment appearing, as the announcers used to say, "same

time, same station." This week-to-weekness—or, in the case of
soap operas, day-to-dayness—obstructed the development of
characters; at least the primary characters had to be preserved
intact for next week's show. Perry Mason was Perry Mason,
once and for all; if you watched the reruns, you couldn't know
from character or set whether you were watching the first or
the last in the series. For commercial and production reasons
which are in practice inseparable—and this is why ideological
hegemony is not reducible to the economic interests of elites—
the regular schedule prefers the repeatable formula: it is far
easier for production companies to hire writers to write for
standardized, static characters than for characters who develop. Assembly-line production works through regularity of
time slot, of duration, and of character to convey images of
social steadiness: come what may, *Gunsmoke* or *Kojak* will check
in to your mind at a certain time on a certain evening. Should
they lose ratings (at least at the "upscale" reaches of the "demographics," where ratings translate into disposable dollars),[6]
their replacements would be—for a time, at least!—equally
reliable. Moreover, the standard curve of narrative action—
stock characters encounter new version of stock situation; the
plot thickens, allowing stock characters to show their standard
stuff; the plot resolves—over twenty-two or fifty minutes is
itself a source of rigidity and forced regularity.

In these ways, the usual programs are performances that
rehearse social fixity: they express and cement the obduracy of
a social world impervious to substantial change. Yet at the same
time there are signs of routine obsolescence, as hunks of last
year's regular schedule drop from sight only to be supplanted
by this season's attractions. Standardization and the threat of
evanescence are curiously linked: they match the intertwined
processes of commodity production, predictability and obsolescence, in a high-consumption society. I speculate that they help
instruct audiences in the rightness and naturalness of a world
that, in only apparent paradox, regularly requires an irregular-
ity, an unreliability which it calls progress. In this way, the
regular changes in TV programs, like the regular elections of
public officials, seem to affirm the sovereignty of the audience
while keeping deep alternatives off the agenda. Elite authority
and consumer choice are affirmed at once—this is one of the
central operations of the hegemonic liberal capitalist ideology.

Then too, by organizing the "free time" of persons into end-
to-end interchangeable units, broadcasting extends, and har-

monizes with, the industrialization of time. Media time and
school time, with their equivalent units and curves of action,
mirror the time of clocked labor and reinforce the seeming
naturalness of clock time. Anyone who reads Harry Braverman's *Labor and Monopoly Capital* can trace the steady degradation
of the work process, both white and blue collar, through the
twentieth century, even if Braverman has exaggerated the extent of the process by focusing on managerial *strategies* more
than on actual work *processes*. Something similar has happened
in other life-sectors.[7] Leisure is industrialized, duration is ho-
mogenized, even excitement is routinized, and the standard
repeated TV format is an important component of the processs.
And typically, too, capitalism provides relief from these confines for its more favored citizens, those who can afford to buy
their way out of the standardized social reality which capitalism
produces. Thus Sony and RCA now sell home video recorders,
enabling customers to tape programs they'd otherwise miss.
The widely felt need to overcome assembly-line "leisure" time
becomes the source of a new market—to sell the means for
private, commoditized solutions to the time-jam.

Commercials, of course, are also major features of the regular TV format. There can be no question but that commercials
have a good deal to do with shaping and maintaining markets—
no advertiser dreams of cutting advertising costs as long as the
competition is still on the air. But commercials also have important *indirect* consequences on the contours of consciousness
overall: they get us accustomed to thinking of ourselves and
behaving as a *market* rather than a *public*, as consumers rather
than citizens. Public problems (like air pollution) are pro-
pounded as susceptible to private commodity solutions (like
eyedrops). In the process, commercials acculturate us to interruption through the rest of our lives. Time and attention are
not one's own; the established social powers have the capacity
to colonize consciousness, and unconsciousness, as they see fit.
By watching, the audience one by one consents. Regardless of
the commercial's "effect" on our behavior, we are consenting to
its domination of the public space. Yet we should note that this
colonizing process does not actually require commercials, as
long as it can form discrete packages of ideological content that
call forth discontinuous responses in the audience. Even public
broadcasting's children's shows take over the commercial forms
to their own educational ends—and supplant narrative forms
by herky-jerky bustle. The producers of *Sesame Street*, in likening

knowledge to commercial products ("and now a message from the letter B"), may well be legitimizing the commercial form in its discontinuity and in its invasiveness. Again, regularity and discontinuity, superficially discrepant, may be linked at a deep level of meaning. And perhaps the deepest privatizing function of television, its most powerful impact on public life, may lie in the most obvious thing about it: we receive the images in the privacy of our living rooms, making public discourse and response difficult. At the same time, the paradox is that at any given time many viewers are receiving images discrepant with many of their beliefs, challenging their received opinions.

TV routines have been built into the broadcast schedule since its inception. But arguably their regularity has been waning since Norman Lear's first comedy, *All in the Family*, made its network debut in 1971. Lear's contribution to TV content was obvious: where previous shows might have made passing reference to social conflict, Lear brought wrenching social issues into the very mainspring of his series, uniting his characters, as Michael Arlen once pointed out, in a harshly funny *ressentiment* peculiarly appealing to audiences of the Nixon era and its cynical, disabused sequel.[8] As I'll argue below, the hegemonic ideology is maintained in the seventies by *domesticating* divisive issues where in the fifties it would have simply *ignored* them.

Lear also let his characters develop. Edith Bunker grew less sappy and more feminist and commonsensical; Gloria and Mike moved next door, and finally to California. On the threshold of this generational rupture, Mike broke through his stereotype by expressing affection for Archie, and Archie, oh-so-reluctantly but definitely for all that, hugged back and broke through his own. And of course other Lear characters, the Jeffersons and Maude, had earlier been spun off into their own shows, as *The Mary Tyler Moore Show* had spawned *Rhoda* and *Phyllis*. These changes resulted from commercial decisions; they were built on intelligent business perceptions that an audience existed for situation comedies directly addressing racism, sexism, and the decomposition of conventional families. But there is no such thing as a strictly economic "explanation" for production choice, since the success of a show—despite market research—is not foreordained. In the context of my argument, the importance of such developments lies in their partial break with the established, static formulae of prime time television.

Evidently daytime soap operas have also been sliding into

character development and a direct exploitation of divisive social issues, rather than going on constructing a race-free, class-free, feminism-free world. And more conspicuously, the "miniseries" has now disrupted the taken-for-granted repetitiveness of the prime time format. Both content and form mattered to the commercial success of *Roots*; certainly the industry, speaking through trade journals, was convinced that the phenomenon was rooted in the series' break with the week-to-week format. When the programming wizards at ABC decided to put the show on for eight straight nights, they were also, inadvertently, making it possible for characters to *develop* within the bounds of a single show. And of course they were rendering the whole sequence immensely more powerful than if it had been diffused over eight weeks. The very format was testimony to the fact that history takes place as a continuing process in which people grow up, have children, die; that people experience their lives within the domain of social institutions. This is no small achievement in a country that routinely denies the rich texture of history.

In any event, the first thing that industry seems to have learned from its success with *Roots* is that they had a new hot formula, the night-after-night series with some claim to historical verisimilitude. So, according to *Broadcasting*, they began preparing a number of "docu-drama" series, of which 1977's products included NBC's three-part series *Loose Change* and *King*, and its four-part *Holocaust*, this latter evidently planned before the *Roots* broadcast. How many of those first announced as in progress will actually be broadcast is something else again—one awaits the networks' domestication and trivializing of the radicalism of *All God's Children: The Life of Nate Shaw*, announced in early 1977. *Roots'* financial success—ABC sold its commercial minutes for $120,000, compared to that season's usual $85,000 to $90,000—might not be repeatable. Perhaps the network could not expect audiences to tune in more than once every few years to a series that began one night at eight o'clock, the next night at nine, and the next at eight again. In summary it is hard to say to what extent these format changes signify an acceleration of the networks' competition for advertising dollars, and to what extent they reveal the networks' responses to the restiveness and boredom of the mass audience, or the emergence of new potential audiences. But in any case the shifts are there, and constitute a fruitful territory for any thinking about the course of popular culture.

Genre[9]

The networks try to finance and choose programs that will likely attract the largest conceivable audiences of spenders; this imperative requires that the broadcasting elites have in mind some notion of popular taste from moment to moment. Genre, in other words, is necessarily somewhat sensitive; in its rough outlines, if not in detail, it tells us something about popular moods. Indeed, since there are only three networks, there is something of an oversensitivity to a given success; the pendulum tends to swing hard to replicate a winner. Thus *Charlie's Angels* engenders *Flying High* and *American Girls*, about stewardesses and female reporters respectively, each on a long leash under male authority.

Here I suggest only a few signs of this sensitivity to shifting moods and group identities in the audience. The adult western of the middle and late fifties, with its drama of solitary righteousness and suppressed libidinousness, for example, can be seen in retrospect to have played on the quiet malaise under the surface of the complacency of the Eisenhower years, even in contradictory ways. Some lone heroes were identified with traditionally frontier-American informal and individualistic relations to authority (Paladin in *Have Gun, Will Travel*, Bart Maverick in *Maverick*), standing for sturdy individualism struggling for hedonistic values and taking law-and-order wryly. Meanwhile, other heroes were decent officials like *Gunsmoke's* Matt Dillon, affirming the decency of paternalistic law and order against the temptations of worldly pleasure. With the rise of the Camelot mystique, and the vigorous "long twilight struggle" that John F. Kennedy personified, spy stories like *Mission: Impossible* and *The Man From Uncle* were well suited to capitalize on the macho CIA aura. More recently, police stories, with cops surmounting humanist illusions to draw thin blue lines against anarcho-criminal barbarism, afford a variety of official ways of coping with "the social issue," ranging from *Starsky and Hutch's* muted homoeroticism to *Barney Miller's* team pluralism. The single-women shows following from *Mary Tyler Moore* acknowledge in their privatized ways that some sort of feminism is here to stay, and work to contain it with hilarious versions of "new life styles" for single career women. Such shows probably appeal to the market of "upscale" singles with relatively large disposable incomes, women who are disaffected from the traditional imagery of housewife and helpmeet. In the current wave of "jiggle" or "T&A" shows patterned on *Charlie's Angels* (the terms are widely used in the industry), the attempt is to appeal to the prurience of the male audience by keeping the "girls" free of romance, thus catering to male (and female?) backlash against feminism. The black sitcoms probably reflect the rise of a black middle class with the purchasing power to bring forth advertisers, while also appealing *as comedies*—for conflicting reasons, perhaps—to important parts of the white audience. (Serious black drama would be far more threatening to the majority audience.)

Whenever possible it is illuminating to trace the transformations in a genre over a longer period of time. For example, the shows of technological prowess have metamorphosed over four decades as hegemonic ideology has been contested by alternative cultural forms. In work not yet published, Tom Andrae of the Political Science Department at the University of California, Berkeley, shows how the Superman archetype began in 1933 as a menace to society; then became something of a New Dealing, anti-Establishmentarian individualist casting his lot with the oppressed and, at times, against the State; and only in the forties metamorphosed into the current incarnation who prosecutes criminals in the name of "the American way." Then the straight-arrow Superman of the forties and fifties was supplemented by the whimsical, self-satirical Batman and the Marvel Comics series of the sixties and seventies, symbols of power gone silly, no longer prepossessing. In playing against the conventions, their producers seem to have been exhibiting the self-consciousness of genre so popular among "high arts" too, as with Pop and minimal art. Thus shifts in genre presuppose the changing mentality of critical masses of writers and cultural producers; yet these changes would not take root commercially without corresponding changes in the dispositions (even the self-consciousness) of large audiences. In other words, changes in cultural ideals and in audience sensibilities must be harmonized to make for shifts in genre or formula.

Finally, the latest form of technological hero corresponds to an authoritarian turn in hegemonic ideology, as well as to a shift in popular (at least children's) mentality. The seventies generation of physically augmented, obedient, patriotic superheroes (*The Six Million Dollar Man* and *The Bionic Woman*) differ from the earlier waves in being organizational products through and through; these team players have no private lives from which they are recruited task by task, as in *Mission: Impossi-*

ble, but they are actually *invented* by the State, to whom they owe their lives.

Televised sports too is best understood as an entertainment genre, one of the most powerful.[10] What we know as professional sports today is inseparably intertwined with the networks' development of the sports market. TV sports is rather consistently framed to reproduce dominant American values. First, although TV is ostensibly a medium for the eyes, the sound is often decisive in taking the action off the field. The audience is not trusted to come to its own conclusions. The announcers are not simply describing events ("Reggie Jackson hits a ground ball to shortstop"), but interpreting them ("World Series 1978! It's great to be here"). One may see here a process equivalent to advertising's project of taking human qualities out of the consumer and removing them to the product: sexy perfume, zesty beer.

In televised sports, the hegemonic impositions have, if anything, probably become more intense over the last twenty years. One technique for interpreting the event is to regale the audience with bits of information in the form of "stats." "A lot of people forget they won eleven out of their last twelve games. . . ." "There was an extraordinary game in last year's World Series. . . ." "Rick Barry hasn't missed two free throws in a row for 72 games. . . ." "The last time the Warriors were in Milwaukee Clifford Ray *also* blocked two shots in the second quarter." How *about* that? The announcers can't shut up; they're constantly chattering. And the stat flashed on the screen further removes the action from the field. What is one to make of all this? Why would anyone want to know a player's free throw percentage not only during the regular season but during the playoffs?

But the trivialities have their reason: they amount to an interpretation that flatters and disdains the audience at the same time. It flatters in small ways, giving you the chance to be the one person on the block who already possessed this tidbit of fact. At the same time, symbolically, it treats you as someone who really knows what's going on in the world. Out of control of social reality, you may flatter yourself that the substitute world of sports is a corner of the world you can really grasp. Indeed, throughout modern society, the availability of statistics is often mistaken for the availability of knowledge and deep meaning. To know the number of megatons in the nuclear arsenal is not to grasp its horror; but we are tempted to bury our fear in the possession of comforting fact. To have made "body counts" in Vietnam was not to be in control of the countryside, but the U.S. Army flattered itself that the stats looked good. TV sports shows, encouraging the audience to value stats, harmonize with a stat-happy society. Not that TV operates independently of the sports event itself; in fact, the event is increasingly organized to fit the structure of the broadcast. There are extra time-outs to permit the network to sell more commercial time. Michael Real of San Diego State University used a stopwatch to calculate that during the 1974 Super Bowl, the football was actually moving for—seven minutes (Real, 1977). Meanwhile, electronic billboards transplant the stats into the stadium itself.

Another framing practice is the reduction of the sports experience to a sequence of individual achievements. In a fusion of populist and capitalist dogma, everyone is somehow the best. This one has "great hands," this one has "a great slam dunk," that one's "great on defense." This indiscriminate commendation raises the premium on personal competition, and at the same time undermines the meaning of personal achievement: everyone is excellent at something, as at a child's birthday party. I was most struck by the force of this sort of framing during the NBA basketball playoffs of 1975, when, after a season of hearing Bill King announce the games over local KTVU, I found myself watching and hearing the network version. King's Warriors were not CBS's. A fine irony: King with his weird mustache and San Francisco panache was talking about team relations and team strategy; CBS, with its organization-man team of announcers, could talk of little besides the personal records of the players. Again, at one point during the 1977 basketball playoffs, CBS's Brent Musburger gushed: "I've got one of the greatest players of all time [Rick Barry] and one of the greatest referees of all time [Mendy Rudolph] sitting next to me! . . . I'm surrounded by experts!" All in all, the network exalts statistics, personal competition, expertise. The message is: The way to understand things is by storing up statistics and tracing their trajectories. This is training in observation without comprehension.

Everything is technique and know-how; nothing is purpose. Likewise, the instant replay generates the thrill of recreating the play, even second-guessing the referee. The appeal is to the American tradition of exalting means over ends: this is the same spirit that animates popular science magazines and do-it-yourself. It's a complicated and contradictory spirit, one that lends itself to the preservation of craft values in a time of assembly-line production, and at the same time distracts interest from any desire to control the goals of the central work process.

The significance of this fetishism of means is hard to decipher. Though the network version appeals to technical thinking, the announcers are not only small-minded but incompetent to boot. No sooner have they dutifully complimented a new acquisition as "a fine addition to the club" than often enough he flubs a play. But still they function as cheerleaders, revving up the razzle-dazzle rhetoric and reminding us how uniquely favored we are by the spectacle. By staying tuned in, somehow we're "participating" in sports history—indeed, by proxy, in history itself. The pulsing theme music and electronic logo reinforce this sense of hot-shot glamor. The breathlessness never lets up, and it has its pecuniary motives: if we can be convinced that the game really is fascinating (even if it's a dog), we're more likely to stay tuned for the commercials for which Miller Lite and Goodyear have paid $100,000 a minute to rent our attention.

On the other hand, the network version does not inevitably succeed in forcing itself upon our consciousness and defining our reception of the event. TV audiences don't necessarily succumb to the announcers' hype. In semi-public situations like barrooms, audiences are more likely to see through the trivialization and ignorance and—in "para-social interaction"—to tell the announcers off. But in the privacy of living rooms, the announcers' framing probably penetrates farther into the collective definition of the event. It should not be surprising that one fairly common counter-hegemonic practice is to watch the broadcast picture without the network sound, listening to the local announcer on the radio.

Setting and Character Type

Closely related to genre and its changes are setting and character type. And here again we see shifting market tolerances making for certain changes in content, while the core of hegemonic values remains virtually impervious.

In the fifties, when the TV forms were first devised, the standard TV series presented—in Herbert Gold's phrase— happy people with happy problems. In the seventies it is more complicated: there are unhappy people with happy ways of coping. But the set itself propounds a vision of consumer happiness. Living rooms and kitchens usually display the standard package of consumer goods. Even where the set is ratty, as in *Sanford and Son*, or working-class, as in *All in the Family*, the bright color of the TV tube almost always glamorizes the surroundings so that there will be no sharp break between the glorious color of the program and the glorious color of the commercial. In the more primitive fifties, by contrast, it was still possible for a series like *The Honeymooners* or *The Phil Silvers Show* (Sergeant Bilko) to get by with one or two simple sets per show: the life of a good skit was in its accomplished *acting*. But that series, in its sympathetic treatment of working-class mores, was exceptional. Color broadcasting accomplishes the glamorous ideal willy-nilly.

Permissible character types have evolved, partly because of changes in the structure of broadcasting power. In the fifties, before the quiz show scandal, advertising agencies contracted directly with production companies to produce TV series (Barnouw, 1970). They ordered up exactly what they wanted, as if by the yard; and with some important but occasional exceptions—I'll mention some in a moment—what they wanted was glamor and fun, a showcase for commercials. In 1954, for example, one agency wrote to the playwright Elmer Rice explaining why his *Street Scene*, with its "lower class social level," would be unsuitable for telecasting:

> We know of no advertiser or advertising agency of any importance in this country who would knowingly allow the products which he is trying to advertise to the public to become associated with the squalor . . . and general "down" character . . . of *Street Scene*. . . .
>
> On the contrary it is the general policy of advertisers to glamorize their products, the people who buy them, and the whole American social and economic scene. . . . The American consuming public as presented by the advertising industry today is middle class, not lower class; happy in general, not miserable and frustrated. . . . (Barnouw, 1970:33).

Later in the fifties, comedies were able to represent discrepant settings, permitting viewers both to identify and to indulge their sense of superiority through comic distance: *The Honeymooners* and *Bilko*, which capitalized on Jackie Gleason's and Phil Silvers' enormous personal popularity (a personality cult can always perform wonders and break rules), were able to extend dignity to working-class characters in anti-glamorous situations (see Czitrom, 1977).

Beginning in 1960, the networks took direct control of production away from advertisers. And since the networks are less provincial than particular advertisers, since they are more closely attuned to general tolerances in the population, and since they are firmly in charge of a buyer's market for advertising (as long as they produce shows that *some* corporation will sponsor), it now became possible—if by no means easy—for independent production companies to get somewhat distinct cultural forms, like Norman Lear's comedies, on the air. The near-universality of television set ownership, at the same time, creates the possibility of a wider range of audiences, including minority-group, working-class and age-segmented audiences, than existed in the fifties, and thus makes possible a wider range of fictional characters. Thus changes in the organization of TV production, as well as new market pressures, have helped to change the prevalent settings and character types on television.

But the power of corporate ideology over character types remains very strong, and sets limits on the permissible; the changes from the fifties through the sixties and seventies should be understood in the context of essential cultural features that have *not* changed. To show the quality of deliberate choice that is often operating, consider a book called *The Youth Market*, by two admen, published in 1970, counseling companies on ways to pick "the right character for your product":

> But in our opinion, if you want to create your own hardhitting spokesman to children, the most effective route is the super-hero-miracle worker. He certainly can demonstrate food products, drug items, many kinds of toys, and innumerable household items. . . . The character should be adventurous. And he should be on the right side of the law. A child must be able to mimic his hero, whether he is James Bond, Superman or Dick Tracy; to be able to fight and shoot to kill without punishment or guilt feelings (Helitzer and Heyel, 1970).

If this sort of thinking is resisted within the industry itself, it's not so much because of commitments to artistry in television as such, but more because there are other markets that are not "penetrated" by these hard-hitting heroes. The industry is noticing, for example, that *Roots* brought to the tube an audience who don't normally watch TV. The homes-using-television levels during the week of *Roots* were up between six and twelve percent over the programs of the previous year (*Broadcasting*, Jan. 31, 1977). Untapped markets—often composed of people who have, or wish to have, somewhat alternative views of the world—can only be brought in by unusual sorts of programming. There is room in the schedule for rebellious human slaves just as there is room for hard-hitting patriotic-technological heroes. In other words—and contrary to a simplistic argument against television manipulation by network elites— the receptivity of enormous parts of the population is an important limiting factor affecting what gets on television. On the other hand, network elites do not risk investing in *regular* heroes who will challenge the core values of corporate capitalist society: who are, say, explicit socialists, or union organizers, or for that matter born-again evangelists. But like the dramatic series *Playhouse 90* in the fifties, TV movies permit a somewhat wider range of choice than weekly series. It is apparently easier for producers to sell exceptional material for one-shot showings—whether sympathetic to lesbian mothers, critical of the 1950s blacklist or of Senator Joseph McCarthy. Most likely these important exceptions have prestige value for the networks.

Slant

Within the formula of a program, a specific slant often pushes through, registering a certain position on a particular public issue. When issues are politically charged, when there is overt social conflict, programs capitalize on the currency. ("Capitalize" is an interesting word, referring both to use and to profit.) In the program's brief compass, only the most stereotyped characters are deemed to "register" on the audience, and therefore slant, embedded in character, is almost always simplistic and thin. The specific slant is sometimes mistaken for the whole of ideological tilt or "bias," as if the bias dissolves when no position is taken on a topical issue. But the week-after-week angle of the show is more basic, a hardened definition of a routine situation *within which* the specific topical slant emerges. The occasional topical slant then seems to anchor the program's general meanings. For instance, a 1977 show of *The Six Million Dollar Man* told the story of a Russian-East German plot to stop the testing of the new B-1 bomber; by implication, it linked the domestic movement against the B-1 to the foreign Red menace. Likewise, in the late sixties and seventies, police and spy dramas

have commonly clucked over violent terrorists and heavily
armed "anarchist" maniacs, labeled as "radicals" or "revolutionaries," giving the cops a chance to justify their heavy armament
and crude machismo. But the other common variety of slant is
sympathetic to forms of deviance which are either private (the
lesbian mother shown to be a good mother to her children) or
quietly reformist (the brief vogue for *Storefront Lawyers* and the
like in the early seventies). The usual slants, then, fall into two
categories: either (a) a legitimation of depoliticized forms of
deviance, usually ethnic or sexual; or (b) a delegitimation of the
dangerous, the violent, the out-of-bounds.

The slants that find their way into network programs, in
short, are not uniform. Can we say anything systematic about
them? Whereas in the fifties family dramas and sit-coms
usually ignored—or indirectly sublimated—the existence of
deep social problems in the world outside the set, programs of
the seventies much more often domesticate them. From *Ozzie
and Harriet* or *Father Knows Best* to *All in the Family* or *The Jeffersons*
marks a distinct shift for formula, character, and slant: a shift,
among other things, in the image of how a family copes with
the world outside. Again, changes in content have in large part
to be referred back to changes in social values and sensibilities,
particularly the values of writers, actors, and other practitioners: there is a large audience now that prefers acknowledging
and domesticating social problems directly rather than ignoring
them or treating them only indirectly and in a sublimated way;
there are also media practitioners who have some roots in the
rebellions of the sixties. Whether hegemonic style will operate
more by exclusion (fifties) than by domestication (seventies)
will depend on the level of public dissensus as well as on internal factors of media organization (the fifties blacklist of TV
writers probably exercised a chilling effect on subject matter
and slant; so did the fact that sponsors directly developed their
own shows).

Solution

Finally, cultural hegemony operates through the solutions proposed to difficult problems. However grave the problems
posed, however rich the imbroglio, the episodes regularly end
with the click of a solution: an arrest, a defiant smile, an I-told-
you-so explanation. The characters we have been asked to care
about are alive and well, ready for next week. Such a world is
not so much fictional as fake. However deeply the problem is

located within society, it will be solved among a few persons: the heroes must attain a solution that leaves the rest of the society untouched. The self-enclosed world of the TV drama justifies itself, and its exclusions, by "wrapping it all up." Occasional exceptions are either short-lived, like *East Side, West Side*, or independently syndicated outside the networks, like Lear's *Mary Hartman, Mary Hartman*. On the networks, *All in the Family* has been unusual in sometimes ending obliquely, softly or ironically, refusing to pretend to solve a social problem that cannot, in fact, be solved by the actions of the Bunkers alone. The Lou Grant show is also partial to downbeat, alienating endings.

Likewise, in mid-seventies mass-market films like *Chinatown, Rollerball, Network* and *King Kong*, we see an interesting form of closure: as befits the common cynicism and helplessness, society owns the victory. Reluctant heroes go up against vast impersonal forces, often multinational corporations like the same Gulf & Western (sent up as "Engulf & Devour" in Mel Brooks's *Silent Movie*) that, through its Paramount subsidiary, produces some of these films. Driven to anger or bitterness by the evident corruption, the rebels break loose—only to bring the whole structure crashing down on them. (In the case of *King Kong*, the great ape falls of his own weight—from the World Trade Center roof, no less—after the helicopter gunships "zap" him.) These popular films appeal to a kind of populism and rebelliousness, usually of a routine and vapid sort, but then close off the possibilities of effective opposition. The rich get richer and the incoherent rebels get bought and killed.

Often the sense of frustration funneled through these films is diffuse and ambiguous enough to encourage a variety of political responses. While many left-wing cultural critics raved about *Network*, for example, right-wing politicians in Southern California campaigned for Proposition 13 using the film's slogan, "I'm mad as hell and I'm not going to take it any more." Indeed, *the fact that the same film is subject to a variety of conflicting yet plausible interpretations may suggest a crisis in hegemonic ideology.* The economic system is demonstrably troubled, but the traditional liberal recourse, the State, is no longer widely enough trusted to provide reassurance. Articulate social groups do not know whom to blame; public opinion is fluid and volatile, and people at all levels in the society withdraw from public participation.[11] In this situation, commercial culture succeeds with diverse interest groups, as well as with the baffled and ambivalent, precisely by propounding ambiguous or even self-contradictory situations and solutions.

THE HEGEMONIC PROCESS IN LIBERAL CAPITALISM

Again it bears emphasizing that, for all these tricks of the entertainment trade, the mass-cultural system is not one-dimensional. High-consumption corporate capitalism implies a certain sensitivity to audience taste, taste which is never wholly manufactured. Shows are made by guessing at audience desires and tolerances, and finding ways to speak to them that perpetuate the going system.[12] (Addressing one set of needs entails scanting and distorting others, ordinarily the less mean, less invidious, less aggressive, less reducible to commodity forms.) The cultural hegemony system that results is not a closed system. It leaks. Its very structure leaks, at the least because it remains to some extent competitive. Networks sell the audience's attention to advertisers who want what they think will be a suitably big, suitably rich audience for their products; since the show is bait, advertisers will put up with—or rather buy into—a great many possible baits, as long as they seem likely to attract a buying audience. In the news, there are also traditions of real though limited journalistic independence, traditions whose modern extension causes businessmen, indeed, to loathe the press. In their 1976 book *Ethics and Profits*, Leonard Silk and David Vogel quote a number of big businessmen complaining about the raw deal they get from the press. A typical comment: "Even though the press is a business, it doesn't reflect business values." That is, it has a certain real interest in truth—partial, superficial, occasion- and celebrity-centered truth, but truth nevertheless.

Outside the news, the networks have no particular interest in truth as such, but they remain sensitive to currents of interest in the population, including the yank and haul and insistence of popular movements. With few ethical or strategic reasons not to absorb trends, they are adept at perpetuating them with new formats, new styles, tie-in commodities (dolls, posters, T-shirts, fan magazines) that fans love. In any case, it is in no small measure because of the economic drives themselves that *the hegemonic system itself amplifies legitimated forms of opposition*. In liberal capitalism, hegemonic ideology develops by domesticating opposition, absorbing it into forms compatible with the core ideological structure. Consent is managed by absorption as well as by exclusion. The hegemonic ideology changes in order to remain hegemonic; that is the peculiar nature of the dominant ideology of liberal capitalism.

Raymond Williams (1977) has insisted rightly on the difference between two types of non-hegemonic ideology: *alternative* forms, presenting a distinct but supplementary and containable view of the world, and *oppositional* forms, rarer and more tenuous within commercial culture, intimating an authentically different social order. Williams makes the useful distinction between *residual* forms, descending from declining social formations, and *emergent* forms, reflecting formations on the rise. Although it is easier to speak of these possibilities in the abstract than in the concrete, and although it is not clear what the emergent formations are (this is one of the major questions for social analysis now), these concepts may help organize an agenda for thought and research on popular culture. I would add to Williams' own carefully modulated remarks on the subject only that there is no reason *a priori* to expect that emergent forms will be expressed as the ideologies of rising *classes*, or as "proletarian ideology" in particular; currently in the United States the emergent forms have to do with racial minorities and other ethnic groups, with women, with singles, with homosexuals, with old-age subcultures, as well as with technocrats and with political interest groups (loosely but not inflexibly linked to corporate interests) with particular strategic goals (like the new militarists of the Committee on the Present Danger). Analysis of the hegemonic ideology and its rivals should not be allowed to lapse into some form of what C. Wright Mills (1948) called the "labor metaphysic."

One point should be clear: the hegemonic system is not cut-and-dried, not definitive. It has continually to be reproduced, continually superimposed, continually to be negotiated and managed, in order to override the alternative and, occasionally, the oppositional forms. To put it another way: major social conflicts are transported *into* the cultural system, where the hegemonic process frames them, form and content both, into compatibility with dominant systems of meaning. Alternative material is routinely *incorporated*: brought into the body of cultural production. Occasionally oppositional material may succeed in being indigestible; that material is excluded from the media discourse and returned to the cultural margins from which it came, while *elements* of it are incorporated into the dominant forms.

In these terms, *Roots* was an alternative form, representing slaves as unblinkable facts of American history, blacks as victimized humans and humans nonetheless. In the end, perhaps, the story is dominated by the chance for upward mobility; the upshot of travail is freedom. Where Alex Haley's book is subtitled "The Saga of an American Family," ABC's version carries the label—and the self-congratulation—"The *Triumph* of an American Family." It is hard to say categorically which story prevails; in any case there is a tension, a struggle, between the collective agony and the triumph of a single family. That struggle is the friction in the works of the hegemonic system.

And all the evident friction within television entertainment—as well as within the schools, the family, religion, sexuality, and the State—points back to a deeper truth about bourgeois culture. In the United States, at least, hegemonic ideology is extremely complex and absorptive; it is only by absorbing and domesticating conflicting definitions of reality and demands on it, in fact, that it remains hegemonic. In this way, the hegemonic ideology of liberal capitalism is dramatically different from the ideologies of pre-capitalist societies, and from the dominant ideology of authoritarian socialist or fascist regimes. What permits it to absorb and domesticate critique is not something accidental to capitalist ideology, but rather its core. *The hegemonic ideology of liberal capitalist society is deeply and essentially conflicted in a number of ways.* As Daniel Bell (1976) has argued, it urges people to work hard, but proposes that real satisfaction is to be found in leisure, which ostensibly embodies values opposed to work.[13] More profoundly, at the center of liberal capitalist ideology there is a tension between the affirmation of patriarchal authority—currently enshrined in the national security state—and the affirmation of individual worth and self-determination. Bourgeois ideology in all its incarnations has been from the first a contradiction in terms, affirming "life, liberty and the pursuit of happiness," or "liberty, equality, fraternity," as if these ideals are compatible, even mutually dependent, at all times in all places, as they were for one revolutionary group at one time in one place. But all anti-bourgeois movements wage their battles precisely in terms of liberty, equality, or fraternity (or, recently, sorority); they press on liberal capitalist ideology *in its own name.*

Thus we can understand something of the vulnerability of bourgeois ideology, as well as its persistence. In the twentieth century, the dominant ideology has shifted toward sanctifying consumer satisfaction as the premium definition of "the pursuit of happiness," in this way justifying corporate domination of the economy. What is hegemonic in consumer capitalist ideol-

ogy is precisely the notion that happiness, or liberty, or equality, or fraternity can be affirmed through the existing private
commodity forms, under the benign, protective eye of the national security state. This ideological core is what remains essentially unchanged and unchallenged in television entertainment, at the same time the inner tensions persist and are even
magnified.

NOTES

1. Anderson has read Gramsci closely to tease out this and other ambiguities
   in Gramsci's diffuse and at times Aesopian texts. (Gramsci was writing in a
   Fascist prison, he was concerned about passing censorship, and he was at
   times gravely ill.)
2. In my reading, the most thoughtful specific approach to this question since
   Gramsci, using comparative structural categories to explain the emergence
   or absence of socialist class consciousness, is Mann (1973). Mann's analysis
   takes us to structural features of American society that detract from
   revolutionary consciousness and organization. Although my paper does
   not discuss social-structural and historical features, I do not wish their
   absence to be interpreted as a belief that culture is all-determining. This
   paper discusses aspects of the hegemonic culture, and makes no claims to a
   more sweeping theory of American society.
3. In Part III of the latter, I discuss the theory of hegemony more extensively.
   Published in *The Whole World is Watching: Mass Media and the New Left, 1965-70*,
   Berkeley: University of California Press, 1980.
4. See also, Willis (n.d.) for an excellent discussion of the limits of both
   ideological analysis of cultural artifacts and the social meaning system of
   audiences, when each is taken by itself and isolated from the other.
5. Most strikingly, see Blum's (1964) findings on black viewers putting down
   TV shows while watching them. See also Willis' (n.d.) program for studying
   the substantive meanings of particular pop music records for distinct youth
   subcultures; but note that it is easier to study the active uses of music than
   TV, since music is more often heard publicly and because, there being so
   many choices, the preference for a particular set of songs or singers or
   beats expresses more about the mentality of the audience than is true
   for TV.
6. A few years ago, *Gunsmoke* was cancelled although it was still among the top
   ten shows in Nielsen ratings. The audience was primarily older and disproportionately rural, thus an audience less well sold to advertisers. So much
   for the networks' democratic rationale.
7. Borrowing "on time," over commensurable, arithmetically calculated
   lengths of time, is part of the same process: production, consumption and
   acculturation made compatible.
8. The time of the show is important to its success or failure. Lear's *All in the
   Family* was rejected by ABC before CBS bought it. An earlier attempt to
   bring problems of class, race and poverty into the heart of television series
   was *East Side, West Side* of 1964, in which George C. Scott played a caring
   social worker consistently unable to accomplish much for his clients. As

time went on, the Scott character came to the conclusion that politics might accomplish what social work could not, and changed jobs, going to work as the assistant to a liberal Congressman. It was rumored about that the hero was going to discover there, too, the limits of reformism—but the show was cancelled, presumably for low ratings. Perhaps Lear's shows, by contrast, have lasted in part *because they are comedies*: audiences will let their defenses down for some good laughs, even on themselves, at least when the characters are, like Archie Bunker himself, ambiguous normative symbols. At the same time, the comedy form allows white racists to indulge themselves in Archie's rationalizations without seeing that the joke is on them.

9. I use the term *loosely* to refer to general categories of TV entertainment, like "adult western," "cops and robbers," "black shows." Genre is not an objective feature of the cultural universe, but a conventional name for a convention, and should not be reified—as both cultural analysis and practice often do—into a cultural essence.

10. This discussion of televised sports was published in similar form (Gitlin, 1978b).

11. In another essay I will be arguing that forms of pseudo-participation (including cult movies like *Rocky Horror Picture Show* and *Animal House*, along with religious sects) are developing simultaneously to fill the vacuum left by the declining of credible radical politics, and to provide ritual forms of expression that alienated groups cannot find within the political culture.

12. See the careful, important and unfairly neglected discussion of the tricky needs issue in Leiss, 1976. Leiss cuts through the Frankfurt premise that commodity culture addresses false needs by arguing that audience needs for happiness, diversion, self-assertion and so on are ontologically real; what commercial culture does is not to invent needs (how could it do that?) but to insist upon the possibility of meeting them through the purchase of commodities. For Leiss, all specifically human needs are social; they develop within one social form or another. From this argument—and, less rigorously but more daringly from Ewen (1976)—flow powerful political implications I cannot develop here. On the early popularity of entertainment forms which cannot possibly be laid at the door of a modern "culture industry" and media-produced needs, see Altick (1978).

13. There is considerable truth in Bell's thesis. Then why do I say "ostensibly"? Bell exaggerates his case against "adversary culture" by emphasizing changes in avant-garde culture above all (Pop Art, happenings, John Cage, etc.); if he looked at *popular* culture, he would more likely find ways in which aspects of the culture of consumption *support* key aspects of the culture of production. I offer my discussion of sports as one instance. Morris Dickstein's (1977) affirmation of the critical culture of the sixties commits the counterpart error of overemphasizing the importance of *other* selected domains of literary and avant-garde culture.

REFERENCES

Abramson, Ronald (1978) Unpublished manuscript, notes on critical theory distributed at the West Coast Critical Communications Conference, Stanford University.

Adorno, Theodor W. (1954) "How to look at television." *Hollywood Quarterly of Film, Radio and Television.* Spring. Reprinted 1975: 474–488 in Bernard Rosenberg and David Manning White (eds.), *Mass Culture.* New York: The Free Press.

——. (1974) "The stars down to earth. The Los Angeles Times Astrology Column." *Telos* 19. Spring 1974: (1957) 13–90.

Adorno, Theodor W. and Max Horkheimer (1972) "The culture industry: Enlightenment as mass deception." Pp. 120–167 in Adorno and Horkheimer, *Dialectic of Enlightenment* (1944). New York: Seabury.

Altick, Richard (1978) *The Shows of London.* Cambridge: Harvard University Press.

Anderson, Perry (1976) "The antinomies of Antonio Gramsci." *New Left Review* 100 (November 1976–January 1977): 5–78.

Barnouw, Erik (1970) *The Image Empire.* New York: Oxford University Press.

Bell, Daniel (1976) *The Cultural Contradictions of Capitalism.* New York: Basic Books.

Blum, Alan F. (1964) "Lower-class Negro television spectators: The concept of pseudo-jovial scepticism." Pp. 429–435 in Arthur B. Shostak and William Gomberg (eds.), *Blue-Collar World.* Englewood Cliffs, N.J.: Prentice-Hall.

Braverman, Harry (1974) *Labor and Monopoly Capital: The Degradation of Work in the Twentieth Century.* New York: Monthly Review Press.

Czitrom, Danny (1977) "Bilko: A sitcom for all seasons." *Cultural Correspondence* 4:16–19.

Dickstein, Morris (1977) *Gates of Eden.* New York: Basic Books.

Ewen, Stuart (1976) *Captains of Consciousness.* New York: McGraw-Hill.

Gitlin, Todd (1977a) "Spotlights and shadows: Television and the culture of politics." *College English* April: 789–801.

——. (1977b) "'The whole world is watching': Mass media and the new left, 1965–70." Doctoral dissertation, University of California, Berkeley.

——. (1977c) "The televised professional." *Social Policy* (November/December): 94–99.

——. (1978a) "Media sociology: The dominant paradigm." *Theory and Society* 6:205–253.

——. (1978b) "Life as instant replay." *East Bay Voice* (November–December):14.

Gouldner, Alvin W. (1976) *The Dialectic of Ideology and Technology.* New York: Seabury.

Gramsci, Antonio (1971) *Selections From the Prison Notebooks.* Quintin Hoare and Geoffrey Nowell Smith (eds.), New York: International Publishers.

Helitzer, Melvin and Carl Heyel (1970) The Youth Market: Its Dimensions, Influence and Opportunities for You. Quoted pp. 62–63 in William Melody, *Children's Television* (1973). New Haven: Yale University Press.

Kellner, Douglas (1978) "Ideology, Marxism, and advanced capitalism." *Socialist Review* 42 (November–December): 37–66.

Leiss, William (1976) *The Limits to Satisfaction.* Toronto: University of Toronto Press.

Mann, Michael (1973) *Consciousness and Action Among the Western Working Class.* London: Macmillan.

Mills, C. Wright (1948) *The New Men of Power.* New York: Harcourt, Brace.

Morley, Dave (1974) "Reconceptualizing the media audience: Towards an ethnography of audiences." Mimeograph, Centre for Contemporary Cultural Studies, University of Birmingham.

Real, Michael R. (1977) *Mass-Mediated Culture.* Englewood Cliffs, N.J.: Prentice-Hall.

Silk, Leonard and David Vogel (1976) *Ethics and Profits.* New York: Simon and Schuster.

Williams, Raymond (1973) "Base and superstructure in Marxist cultural the-
    ory." *New Left Review* 82.
———. (1977) *Marxism and Literature*. New York: Oxford University Press.
Willis, Paul (n.d.) "Symbolism and practice: A theory for the social meaning of
    pop music." Mimeograph, Centre for Contemporary Cultural Studies,
    University of Birmingham.

FARREL CORCORAN

TELEVISION AS IDEOLOGICAL APPARATUS: THE POWER AND THE PLEASURE

Within the bounds of media theory in the English-speaking world in the last decade, there has emerged an important concentration of interest in ideological analysis which parallels contemporary currents in European thought. The result has been a major shift of interest away from the positivist emphasis of the dominant Anglo-American paradigm, towards a previously ignored set of problems: how mediated messages are structured (both as "texts" and as products of media organizations), how they function in the circulation and securing of hegemonic social definitions, and how communication can be analyzed as a process through which a particular world-view is represented and maintained. An essential component of this new textual, anti-empiricist paradigm is explication of the symbolic universe contained in the content of mass media. Modelled after a kind of literary and textual criticism, its vocation is the decipherment or unmasking of meanings in relation to the overall social formation in which they are encoded and decoded. It attempts to demonstrate the ways in which mass communication fulfills an ideological mission by legitimating this or that power structure. Central to this quest is Paul Ricoeur's (1970:27) concept of "hermeneutics" as a "manifestation and restoration of meaning addressed to me in the manner of a message, a proclamation, or, as is sometimes said, a kerygma . . . a demystification, a reduction of illusion." Cultural objects previously thought of as neutral depictions of reality, such as television programs or newsmagazine articles, are regarded as "texts" or "discourses" which were assembled in certain specifi-

Reprinted from *Critical Studies in Mass Communication*, Vol. 1, June 1984, with permission of the publisher and author. Copyright © 1984.

able ways and have certain discernible relationships to other cultural objects constituted in similar ways.

European "cultural studies," as Carey (1979:410) points out, have been "generally misunderstood, ignored or misrepresented in the United States" with the result that there has been a resounding absence of the notion of ideology in American media theory. The divergence characteristic of American and European communication theory in general since the 1960s has been slowed, however, if not reversed, by two recent factors: first, the introduction onto the American academic agenda of the critical media theories of such seminal thinkers as Jacques Ellul (Christians & Real, 1979) and Jürgen Habermas (Burleson & Kline, 1979); second, the growing awareness that rhetorical criticism in general needs to redefine its purpose in response to incessant and widespread awareness of global crisis: famine, destruction of the environment, open support of barbarous dictatorships by Western democracies, explosive superpower expenditures on war preparations, and fear of accidental destruction by ever more sophisticated nuclear weapons. "Criticism takes an ideological turn," Philip Wander (1983:18) suggests, "when it recognizes the existence of powerful vested interests benefiting from and consistently urging policies and technology that threaten life on this planet, when it realizes that we search for alternatives. . . . An ideological turn in modern criticism reflects the existence of crisis, acknowledges the influence of established interests and the reality of alternative world-views, and commends rhetorical analyses not only of the actions implied but also of the interests represented."

Television, in particular, has been slow to yield to ideological criticism, partly because of the traditionally elitist attitude of academics to the artifacts of mass media and partly because of the development of an academic professionalism which shunned sociopolitical controversy. A more subtle reason has been that the ideological process itself (a process which sets the bounds of what is reasonable and legitimate for the interests of a particular, dominant section of society) is achieved through television in a very indirect way. The claims on resources by corporate, political, and bureaucratic leaders are ideologically naturalized and universalized through a complex process of translation into professional norms guiding the work of journalists, writers, and producers. Since television production in general is rooted to business interests in the United States, these professionals are, as Muriel Cantor (1980:3) points out, "people who are either willing to suppress deep-seated dissident values, . . . or people who are fundamentally in agreement with the system." Although, as Kellner (1981) argues, the professional codes of the television community have helped place contradictory images on the screen, the day-to-day working principles with which professionals put together television programs construct social knowledge selectively. This is achieved by establishing classifying schemes which "actively rule in and rule out certain realities" in a consensual order "in which the direct and naked intervention of the real unities (of class, power, exploitation, and interest) are forever held somewhat at bay" (Hall, 1977:342). These principles of "good television," which shape actual events into televised meaning, are unconscious to those who make programs and to viewers alike. They appear, with all the self-evident force of "common-sense," as circumscribing the only set of possible meanings from which to choose. In an academic milieu where the empirical investigation of "effects" has been the privileged research trend, where the hermeneutic tradition of regarding television as a "text" to be "read" still seems radical, the very invisibility of television's professional norms (though passed on to students as the norms of "good television") has retarded the development of ideological analysis.

Nevertheless, a nascent trend of ideological criticism has taken root in Anglo-American media studies. The most obvious area of investigation is, of course, television news. A number of studies (e.g., Altheide, 1976; Chibnall, 1977; Clarke & Taylor, 1980; Fishman, 1978; Gans, 1979; Gitlin, 1980; Glasgow Media Group, 1976, 1980, 1982; Golding & Elliott, 1979; Hall, 1978; Hartley, 1982; Knight, 1982; Schlesinger, 1978; Tuchman, 1978; Tumber, 1982; Wren-Lewis, 1981) have examined how the journalistic commitment to "balance" and "objectivity," as well as the preoccupation with the disruption and restoration of social order, has structured news accounts in such a way that a certain view of the world is produced at the expense of alternatives. Television news constitutes a particular way of knowing the sociopolitical environment. It is offered as a fragmented inventory of decontextualized events given unity by the mediation of the anchorperson. Knight and Dean (1982) have suggested that alternative world-views are consistently ignored or devalued as comical, bizarre, or dangerous, thus mystifying social change as novelty. Gandy (1982) has investigated the mechanisms whereby bureaucratically supplied information comes to dominate mass media channels, which thus tend to reproduce the authority of dominant institutions and generally contribute to the hegemony of the corporate state.

Though not as well developed as the concentration on news, the ideological investigation of television drama has also been uncovering connections between fictional portrayals and the maintenance of the dominant social order. George Gerbner's Cultural Indicators project (Van Poecke, 1980), for example, has suggested that television has cultivated in heavy viewers a willingness to accept a reduction in civil liberties in exchange for increased protection from crime and violence. Gandy (1982) has explored connections between television drama, the cultivation of health anxiety, and the reinforcement of the dominant U.S. medical ideology. This ideology focuses on mechanistic views of health care, stresses cure by way of high-tech medicine rather than the less glamorous and challenging work of disease-prevention, and avoids consideration of industrial sources of cancer in favor of a victim-blaming approach. Likewise, Jesus Requena (1981) has documented how the existing social order is reproduced through the genre of crime drama, which typically associates all conflict with pathological individuals and develops its stories by setting in motion the regulatory mechanisms of society: curing, retraining, or outright repression.

The cumulative result of ideological depictions of the world in television is a saturation of the whole process of living by a hegemonic set of assumptions and values to the point where this constitutes what Raymond Williams (1977:110) has called a "sense of reality" for most people. Through television, a particular social point of view is universalized and legitimized by its reification of "standards for deciding what is, standards for deciding what can be, standards for deciding how one feels about it, standards for deciding what to do about it, and standards for deciding how to go about doing it" (Goodenough, 1971:22).

The purpose of this paper is not to produce more text-based ideological analysis, although there is an urgent need for the wide dissemination of the kind of demystified consciousness of mediated meaning that this criticism brings. Such criticism is already appearing with greater frequency in journals like *Screen, Media, Culture & Society, Ideology & Consciousness, Theory and Society, Jump Cut,* and *Social Text,* and occasionally in more traditional outlets. The objective here is rather to look beyond content and investigate the ideological dimensions of both the medium of television (its relationship to its spectators) and the predominant mode of representation utilized in television narrative. It is argued that in both of these, the weakness of identification between spectator and screen presents paradoxes and problems not yet addressed in the developing tradition of ideological theory (e.g., Althusser, 1971; Barth, 1976; Carlsnaes, 1981; Cohen, 1982; Curran, Gurevitch & Woollacott, 1979; Ellul, 1964; Fiske & Hartley, 1978; Gramsci, 1971; Gurevitch, Bennett, Curran & Woollacott, 1982; Hall, 1980; Laclau, 1977; Larrain, 1979; Mannheim, 1972; Parekh, 1982; Seliger, 1976; Veron, 1971).

In the first half of what follows, the evidence for viewers' indifference to the content of television is reviewed, and it is suggested that this detachment poses problems for theories of ideology which assume active engagement with the medium. In the latter half, the dominant mode of narration of television is compared with that of film. It is argued, first, that the roots of the peculiar pleasure afforded by screen media in this culture can be found in the spectator's concentration of psychic activity into a state of hyper-receptivity to the "world" of fiction, in response to the successful use of the narrative devices of classical realism. Futhermore, it is argued that the tradition of narrative realism dominating cinema has not been transferred wholesale to television. The implication of this is that the ideological critique of television should proceed along lines quite different from those evolving within film studies. The essay is heuristic in emphasis, culminating in questions rather than conclusions about the subtle connections between the ideological "power" of television and the "pleasure" which, in a culture of consumerism, acts as incentive to motivate the massive, voluntary use of a medium supposedly functioning as an agent of social control.

TELEVISION AS MEDIUM

The expansion of free time in industrialized countries since the beginning of this century has been accompanied by a large-scale technological revolution which "has transformed the world of free time as substantially as the technology of the Industrial Revolution transformed the world of work" (Sahin & Robinson, 1981:86). By far the most powerful force in reshaping the temporal structure of everyday life, usurping time formerly spent on existing forms of mass media as well as other free-time activities, is the technology of television. This has re-shaped the temporal landscape as radically as the automobile has reshaped the spatial landscapes of industrialized societies (Robinson, 1977). Yet the dominance of television in the world of leisure is itself enshrouded in ideological mists. Television-as-merely-entertainment, for instance, is not fully articulated as a doctrine but is widely believed in, and defended by, broad-casters whenever necessary. This posits that television is non-ideological "innocent fun" which is socially harmless and value-free. It is thought to lack a consistent point of view and operate outside the sociopolitical processes of the culture. Viewers, it is said, are given what they want, in the true spirit of cultural democracy. Television is a "mirror of reality," a position which is sometimes used as a defense against advocates of reduced violence in programming. Television is thought to provide free entertainment which is also effervescent, and therefore doesn't need serious criticism. Television is considered fair and objec-tive, its political neutrality maintained in a liberal-pluralist world by such checks and balances as the Fairness Doctrine and the Equal Time Rule. Finally, television viewing itself is legiti-mated as appropriate leisure activity, even when consumed in massive quantities. It is considered so appropriate, in fact, that nonviewing or nonpossession of a set is considered aberrant behavior, at best snobbish or elitist, at worst eccentric or so-cially deviant. In either case, nonviewing entails exclusion from the community which exists essentially through the shared experience of being television consumers (Dahlgren, 1981:301; Winn, 1977:214).

The pervasive belief in television as nonideological allows viewers to approach the set in an unguarded way, experiencing none of the resistance that would be evident if the viewing were presented as, say, "propaganda" or "education" or even as "an Academy Award-winning film." This unguardedness is rein-forced by the central fact of the viewing experience itself—program flow combined with program regularity—which al-lows for the uninterrupted processing of the inevitable social paradoxes transmitted through television, the sometimes jolt-ing juxtaposition of contradictory messages. For instance, an interview, telecast in New York City, March 26, 1983, with a Black South African pastor who had been tortured three times by his own government, appealing for a heightened American awareness of the international business props of the apartheid system, was interrupted by a "diamonds are forever" commercial from the South African deBeers Company. Such indiscriminate visual and thematic juxtapositions on television perform a normalizing function, the flow and regularity of its contents imparting a tone of indifference toward everything within its scope. This is in part a function of viewer habituation to "the constant rupturing and refocussing of attentional energy" in relation to the "perpetual dispersal of discourse" (Dahlgren, 1981:296). It promotes not only nonintervention in the sociopolitical environment (for instance, boycotting deBeers diamonds), but also the reabsorption of the viewer back into continued viewing. Commercials enhance the fragmentation effect by offering viewers a practical relief, knowledge that *is* relevant to daily life, a "time out" from programming that discourages the formation of participatory connections in viewers. Berger (1982) has noted a similar cycle of alienation and increased consumption among users of all-news radio, with the added generation of anxiety in the newsaholic.

How is viewer indifference to be interpreted? On the one hand, it can be understood within the context of critical theory as the standard ideological mechanism of naturalizing the status quo (Parekh, 1982:138), what Walter Cronkite called "the way it is," and obliterating any alternative realities. The problem for ideological theory, however, is the possibility that the sheer matter-of-factness of everything on television, its tendency to reduce all events to trivia, can promote generalized indifference and cynicism in the viewer. The desensitization and detachment of the spectator, emanating from the passive nature of television viewing, holds out the possibility that television, in continually announcing that it cannot be taken very seriously, weakens the ideological effect as the very point of reception in the spectator. This possibility warrants closer inspection.

One of the most glaring paradoxes emanating from the twentieth century transformation of the world of free time by the technology of leisure is the contrast between the level of television viewing evident in the United States and the degree of viewer dissatisfaction with television. Rather than having reached an asymptote with set saturation in the mid-1960s, television has steadily increased its share of free time right up to the present. At the same time, however, surveys show high levels of dissatisfaction with the medium. Sahin and Robinson

(1981), for instance, report that the average satisfaction rating for television among all social groups is below those for reading, evenings out, religion, and socializing. Television is not regarded as either "particularly enjoyable" or "necessary to one's daily life." It is the "most expendable" and the "least important" of daily activities. A recent National Association of Broadcasters' study (Roth, 1983) presents similar findings: viewing has increased over the last six years, the period of the study, but so have levels of dissatisfaction. Television has become less important and entertaining for all demographic groups and produces widespread guilt feelings about the amount of time it consumes.

One answer to the high viewing/low satisfaction paradox may lie in the peculiar nature of the pleasure derived from an activity that seems to involve viewers so minimally. Employing EEG analyses of Alpha and Beta brain waves, Krugman (1971:3, 8) has argued that television is indeed a "low involvement medium," perhaps "five times" less involving than print, and a form of "passive" reception in which huge quantities of information are "effortlessly transmitted into storage." He notes that television generates fewer spontaneous thoughts, fewer links to the content of the viewer's personal life, and "unformed and shapeless" responses. Chesebro (1984) cites more recent neurophysiological evidence, based on Positron Computer Tomography (PCT) that habitual mental response patterns can be socially conditioned (for instance, by the persistent use of any one medium as both source of information and dominant leisure activity). He goes on to suggest that from the repetitive use of certain mental patterns, such as ways of ordering space and time peculiar to each medium, "a self-sustaining and moral orientation toward reality," a particular world-view, may emerge. Similar media/world-view linkages, of course, have been argued previously by McLuhan (1966) and Innis (1950, 1951), though without empirical support.

Another factor affecting viewer involvement with television is the cultivation of a "personality" system on television, parallel with but standing in opposition to the "star" system of the film industry. Dahlgren (1981), for instance, examined the mechanisms whereby a viewer's passive relationship to news becomes one of static dependence through the intervention of the anchorperson, the Prime Knower, who "protects" the viewer from having to make sense of events, who buffers viewer confrontation with news stories by absorbing involvement to him or herself. Elimination of the Prime Knower, for example, would strip the news of a unifying subjectivity and force viewers to make sense of the news themselves, within the pluralism of subjectivity established by different newspersons, all of equal stature. This would focus attention on the *process* of newsgathering, of the putting together of one particular way of knowing the world rather than another, thus making that process—how the newsperson acquires knowledge of the event—opaque rather than transparent. The difference would be between politics-as-spectacle and politics-as-participation in the making of history.

Langer (1981) explored the systematic tendency of the television personality system to construct and foreground intimacy and immediacy, based on the ordinary, the everyday character who is "part of life" rather than "larger than life." This is in contrast with the emphasis of cinema's "star" system on the distanced, the exceptional, the idealized, the archetypal, to be contemplated and revered, standing outside the realm of the familiar and the routinized. What is popularly remembered in television is not the name of the "anonymous" actor but the name of the recurrent character in the series, even when recreated in a "spin-off" or encountered in the carefully orchestrated informality of a talk-show. Intimacy is further encouraged by the dominant convention of reliance on the close-up shot, which is thought to provide optimal conditions for disclosure of the privateness of character. Given the propensity of television for direct address and eye contact with the spectator (shunned in the classical Hollywood film mode of narration, calling attention to itself when the norm is occasionally broken), television "personalities" seem to be maintaining active, direct communication with viewers much of the time.

Television, then, seems to reduce the distance between itself and its viewers, weaving a space/time continuum in which spectator and personality share a common universe of experience. Its structure of intimacy creates even the illusion that the powerful members of our society (presidents, prime ministers, the rich and famous) disclose themselves to us in an intimate, familiar, amiable way. The ideological implications of this passage from actuality to representation through television, this masking of real gaps between different social groups through the creation of a "pseudo-gemeinschaft," are pursued by Langer. The question relevant to the line of inquiry being pursued here, however, is different. By diminishing the sense of social distance to "intimate" levels, television reduces the sense of power in society. But why does television viewing, as opposed to film viewing, seem to generate such little involvement in viewers, involvement which might be predicated on the pleasure presumably attached to the feelings of intimacy the medium supposedly generates? The answer may lie in more salient differences between film and television, particularly in their typical modes of narration, which will be explored in the next section. The question is central to the concern of this essay: how do the pleasures of television viewing play a role in the ideological effect of an imputedly powerful medium? If television is indeed a "plug-in drug" (Winn, 1977), distracting an indifferent, bored, and lethargic spectator with an audiovisual abundance "of small significance and no lasting consequence" (Dunn, 1983:44), is it actually debilitating the ideological effect, undermining its own much-vaunted technological power? On the other hand, if television has the power to reinforce a particular mental condition for literally hours at a time, robbing the spectator of energy, time, and interest in the sociopolitical milieu, can it be said to establish among heavy viewers an alienated world-view (albeit one based on a "pseudo-gemeinschaft" of "intimacy") with its own peculiar moral orientation? If this is the case, the ideological effect of television, then, is *not* to be found in the content of particular dramas, such as the dominant American medical ideology represented in *General Hospital*. The context will not have its effect because the spectator is too disengaged to respond effectively to such content. The ideological effect, instead, may be an habituated condition produced by prolonged exposure to the medium itself: the medium is the ideology. The question of spectator indifference, of vital interest to ideological theory, needs to be approached from another angle, a consideration of the dominant mode of representation in television drama.

TELEVISION AS NARRATIVE MODE

Criticism of the narrative media since at least the time of Brecht has been informed by an awareness of the means employed by classical narrative modes to mask the process of narration in favor of maximizing the involvement of the spectator in the imaginary time/space of the fictional world, with all its characters, landscapes, and events. The mode which continues to dominate our notions of representation today—intensifyiɳ̤ the presence of characters and their world by privileging plot linearity and motivational credibility, increasing the transparency of the narrative process by masking the novelistic mechanisms for producing meaning—is linked by Watt (1957) to the ascendency of the bourgeoisie and their literature in the eighteenth century. A similar process in cinema took place with the development of various codes for heightening cinema's power to absorb the spectator, for example, the development of the so-called Griffith codes of editing before 1920 (ellipsis, cutaways, cross-cutting, eye-line matching, etc.), three-dimensional lighting and composition in deep focus in the 1920s, lipsync sound in the 1930s, color in the 1950s. Noël Burch (1979) has sketched out the development of the classical realist mode of representation in the early American film industry. In its first ten years, film narrative was based on the folk art of the urban working classes of Europe and the United States, but as the cinema developed economically and generated the need for a new audience with more money and leisure at its disposal, the influence of bourgeois modes of representation (grounded in literature, painting, and theatre) made itself felt. The later development of such technical innovations as sound, 3-D, and Cinemascope was in response to the need for greater realism, though realist ideology held out against color until the arrival of color television (Buscombe, 1982:25).

The unconscious codes of realism are so naturalized and exercise such hegemonic control over Western film production today that one has to look far afield to discover alternative modes of representation in film. Some examples of these alternative views can be found among Navajos (Worth & Adair, 1972), Kpelles in Liberia or Bapostolos in Zambia (Bellman & Jules-Rosette, 1977), Japanese prior to the introduction of American films (Burch, 1979) or Americans themselves prior to 1910 (Burch, 1978/79). Alternative modes of visual presentation are today probably most accessible in the "art cinema," which, by accentuating the process of narration itself, dramatizes the hegemonic position of classical narrative codes. Fellini, Antonioni, Bergman, Godard, Lindsay Anderson, etcetera, subvert the authority of the central point of view by such devices as obscuring the locus of the narrative voice, subverting the straightforward drive of the cause-effect chain, or failing to bracket dream reality from nondream reality (Self, 1979). Realism is thus perceived as a mode of representation, not as *the* mode of representation.

Television offers very little to parallel the modernist aesthetic in film. The two media are what Christian Metz (1974) calls "neighboring languages," not identical ones. There are obvious differences. Television programming occupies a reduced part of the spectator's visual field and comes from a set that is a controllable possession, ready for use at any whim, within the familiar setting of everyday routine. In television, but not in film, the spectator is frequently addressed directly and held in eye contact by the performer (Heath & Skirrow, 1977). Television makes frequent use of sound that is not grounded in the fictional world which the spectator "enters"— theme tunes, background music, studio laughter, off-screen commentary (Nowell-Smith, 1978/79). Besides the fictional narrative mode of Hollywood film, television utilizes a wide variety of other modes, many of them calling attention to the technical apparatus itself, for instance, instant replay, slow motion, and freeze frame in televised sports.

By contrast, film viewing, in a calculated structuring of the spectator's time, leads away from domestic routine to a dark, unfamiliar theatre where the exceptional experience of viewing takes place with little possibility of social interaction, in front of a screen that dominates the field of vision, under the control of an invisible projectionist. In its drama, however, and in many of its documentaries, television obviously grows out of the same novelistic roots as film, the aesthetic tradition of building empathy between spectator and one or more characters in the fiction, though each medium favors a different way of building empathy. Much of recent film theory has been preoccupied with a consideration of the central filmic mechanism of identification. Edward Branigan (1975), for example, has identified the point-of-view structure favored in traditional Hollywood films as a code whereby we participate in characters' viewpoints and thereby experience all the elements of the fictional world contemporaneously with them. The various permutations of point-of-view shots follow the shifting narrative point of view of the filmic voice and therefore also enable us to know who is "speaking" (looking) at any one moment and from what viewpoint.

The resultant heightening of the imaginative identification established between spectator and screen, along with the obliteration of the mode of narration from the spectator's consciousness, seems to be the base of the pleasure derived from screen media. Laura Mulvey (1975) has identified the psychoanalytic phenomenon of scopophilia as the foundation of the peculiar pleasure derived from film viewing: the erotic pleasure of gazing at another person, which is related in Lacanian (1977) psychoanalytic theory to the narcissistic "mirror phase" in children's ego development. There are three different gazes in film: the camera as it records the pro-filmic event; the audience as it gazes at the final product on the screen; and the gaze of the characters at each other within the screen illusion. The conventions of the traditional narrative film deny the first (to eliminate intrusive camera presence) and the second (to prevent a Brechtian distancing awareness of viewing in the audience) and subordinate them to the third, so that imaginative identification is intensified. Without this, Mulvey claims, fictional reality could not achieve its ideological reality, obviousness, and truth.

Does television drama achieve the same intensity of identification? Two phenomena suggest that it does not: the general passivity of viewers, already explored, and the crucial difference between cinefiles and telefiles pointed out by John Caughie (1981). Quite differently from considerations of cinema, discussions of television seem to take place between people who can "see the seduction but *have not been seduced*" (1981:17). In classical film narrative, the identification established between the spectator's desire to see (scopophilia) and the gaze of a character within the fiction, displaces the spectator's identification from camera gaze to character gaze, thus giving the spectator a position as subject within the fictional world. The intensity of scopophilic pleasure is heightened by the continual relocation of our look within that world as we participate in the changing points of view of characters. Caughie (1981) suggests that the effect is not as common in television. The weakened emphasis on point of view produces greater distance between spectators and characters and more identification with the camera's (and director/author's) point of view. This renders problematic the notion of "intimacy" already discussed.

There is a double origin for this crucial difference between the rhetorical vocabulary of film and television. First, current notions of standard television practice have evolved from live, three-camera studio production based on continuous recording and vision mixing, a situation less likely than the single camera technology of film to highlight point-of-view shots in its technical vocabulary. "Freed from the fictional space, the spectator *watches* television (in a way quite different from the *look* in cinema) without being *lost* in it" (Caughie 1981:28). Of course, the smaller television image and the domestic conditions of viewing give the viewer the added sense of being in control of the drama, thereby further lessening voyeuristic pleasure. Second, television historically and professionally has affinities with radio, where the writer, and script, the *word*, is prominent, in contrast with film which developed its nascent visual codes in the total absence of sound. In television drama, the play of characters seems to be worked out through word and gesture more than through identification with character gaze, that is, television drama privileges the personal point of view of the author who is *showing* a fictional world. The result is the loss of a certain kind of visual and narrative pleasure provided by the rhetoric of film.

EMANCIPATORY TELEVISION

It is often suggested that emancipatory television, that is, television provoking "insight and awakening, leading to a transformation of thought and behavior" (Kellner, 1982:409) should reveal to viewers the actual mode of representation that it habitually uses. *Mary Hartman, Mary Hartman*, for instance, has been praised for laying bare the hidden practices in television's construction of reality. "Mary does for us the work of delayering metaphors, deciphering conventionally coded meanings and retracting the ideological content of seemingly neutral clichés" (de Lauretis, 1979:116). Like modernist films, such television programs become interventions into the process of naturalizing the world of representations, interrupting imaginary involvement, and evoking the active, critical, distanced viewing recommended by Brechtian aesthetics. Self-reflexivity or metarealism is emancipatory for Fiske and Hartley (1978:165) also, who see narrative realism as a kind of silent weapon in the extension of what amounts to bourgeois ideology over all other sections in society, whose power "resides in the appearance that its ideology isn't there and that its version of reality is true."

Does such metarealism in fact break the ideological spell of television content, by readjusting the balance between form and content? Does the alienating effect of undercutting the empathic power of imaginative involvement have the liberating role of enabling viewers to reflect on television and its ways of producing meaning? There are many reasons for believing that modern television, both as a medium and as a particular mode of representation, has diverged widely from realist film by greatly minimizing the possibilities for spectator engagement. Television viewing in general has an almost random quality, with viewers drifting in and out of the viewing experience over a period of time. People typically watch television as part of their engagement in other activities (housework, homework, etc.). Prolonged, intense involvement in the world of television images is radically undercut by the ten-minute reminders of the real mission of television in the form of commercial interruptions. It is also undercut by such self-reflexive techniques as those incorporated into the format of the *Eye Witness News* or the *David Letterman Show*, by the ironic, home-spun narration which dedramatizes every situation in *The Dukes of Hazzard*, by the parodies of television itself often incorporated into comedy shows, even by elements of self-derision in the ads. As Noël Burch (1982:32) points out, Brechtian distancing, the long-time hope of radical critics, has been co-opted by television. The predominant message of television is that none of it, no matter what it is, really matters. There is a "bland detachment . . . in which the repression in El Salvador is no more nor less involving than '*The Price is Right*' and in which even the most outspoken denunciation of, say, migrant workers' camps in Florida will be taken with the same bemused incredulity as the exploits of '*That's Incredible.*'" Burch suggests it represents a turning back of the clock to the early nickelodeon years of cinema, before it shifted from six-to-ten minute shorts, interrupted by songs or lantern-slides, to a format centered around films well over an hour long, which heralded the ascendency of cinema's ambition to build and intensify spectator engagement.

If this interpretation is correct, a number of important questions follow. Does the maintenance of relatively longer and uninterrupted dramas, for example, on the Public Broadcasting Service or on certain cable systems, make television a very different kind of ideological apparatus? What are the social and political implications of saying that nothing on television, neither an election campaign nor a presidential assassination, nor live coverage of a war, really *matters*? Was it always like this with television and if so, how do we evaluate such media platitudes as the role of television in ending the Vietnam War? Should there now be a radical divergence between the ideological critique of film and the ideological critique of television? Is this still true even in the face of technological changes in the medium of television which seem to bring it closer to film? (For instance, consider the uninterrupted projection of films, use of single-camera shooting in made-for-cable movies, enlargement of the screen, and the enhancement of picture resolution.) What is the relevance of ideological criticism of particular genres of television content in the context of profound spectator disengagement from the screen?

The answers to these questions hinge on a clarification of the concept of disengagement. This may also demand a reconceptualizing of ideology, at least as applied to television and how it helps to fashion individual consciousness. Antonio Gramsci's (1971) notion of state control of citizens through hegemony rather than coercion (i.e., through the ideological apparatuses of schools, trade unions, political parties, families, churches, media), for instance, is widely influential among theorists of ideology. Hegemony implies the active engagement of individuals with the ideology of the dominant sectors of society and therefore active cooperation in their own domination. Television today, however, may serve a different hegemonic function in American society by reducing the audience to a state of passive acquiescence. Parallels seem both pertinent and urgent between this and Wilhelm Reich's (1970, 1975, 1976) political-psychological theory of how social structure is reproduced in character structure, particularly his diagnosis of the submissive character structure that was formed in Germany in the 1930s within authoritarian and sexually repressed middle-class families—families that identified strongly with the Führer and the Party. The resurgence of the American New Right, with its combination of sexual repression and right-wing authoritarianism, would seem to make the reopening of Reich's psychological theory of ideology a valuable academic enterprise in these times.

FINAL THOUGHTS

This essay, as promised, has asked more questions than it has answered. Ideological criticism is a significant import to American media theory because it asks questions of media that previous paradigms have ignored. However, like all manipulatory theories of culture, its weakest link is its impoverished conceptualization of the construction of individual consciousness within the total ideological process. Much critical theory in the past has concentrated on what Fredric Jameson (1981:291) calls a "negative hermeneutic" function, that is, demystifying the instrumental function of cultural texts in the perpetuation and reproduction of a given power structure. He calls for the simultaneous exercise of a "positive hermeneutic," that is, a decipherment of the Utopian impulses released and managed by those same mass cultural texts within "a complex strategy of rhetorical persuasion in which substantial incentives are offered for ideological adherence." The suggestion here is that ideology implies a process of "compensatory exchange" in which the manipulated consumer is offered specific gratifications in return for his or her consent to passive acceptance of domination.

What is the nature of this exchange? Jameson (1981:287) speculates that if it is a process whereby "otherwise dangerous and protopolitical impulses" are "managed and defused, rechanneled and offered spurious objects," then it must be asked how "these same impulses—raw material on which the process works—are initially awakened within the very text that seeks to still them." The incentives, he suggests, are "collective-associational" or Utopian in nature: mythic visions of eternal life, of transfigured body, of preternatural sexual gratification, etcetera. However, it is possible that the incentives are more mundane: gratifications related to pressures encountered in the world of work (Blumler & Katz, 1975) or even the "competitive manoeuvres" of broadcasters to "grab and retain the largest chunk of the targeted audience for the longest period of time," by "closing off possible exits, whetting appetites for what is yet to come, and transforming television viewing into a continuous experience" (Sahin & Robinson, 1981:94). In further exploring the connections between the power and the pleasure of television, it remains to be seen whether critical theory must establish a rapprochement with myth analysis (see, e.g., Breen & Corcoran, 1982) or take the more traveled path of uses and gratifications theory.

REFERENCES

Altheide, D. (1976). *Creating Reality: How Television News Distorts Events*. Beverly Hills: Sage.

Althusser, L. (1971). *Lenin, Philosophy and Other Essays*. London: New Left Books.

Barth, H. (1976). *Truth and Ideology*. Berkeley: University of California Press.

Bellman, B. and B. Jules-Rosette (1977). *A Paradigm for Looking: Cross-Cultural Research in Visual Media*. Norwood, NJ: Ablex.

Berger, A. (1982). *Media Analysis Techniques*. Beverly Hills: Sage.

Blumler, J. and E. Katz (eds.) (1975). *The Uses of Mass Communications: Current Perspectives on Gratifications Research*. Beverly Hills: Sage.

Branigan, E. (1975). "Formal permutations of the point of view shot." *Screen* 16, 54–64.

Breen, M. and F. Corcoran (1982). "Myth in the television discourse." *Communication Monographs* 49, 127–136.

Burch, N. (1978/79). "Porter, or ambivalence?" *Screen* 19, 91–103.

—— (1979). *To the Distant Observer: Form and Meaning in the Japanese Cinema*. Berkeley: University of California Press.

—— (1982). "Narrativity/diegesis—thresholds, limits." *Screen*, 23, 16–33.

Burleson, B. R. and S. L. Kline (1979). "Habermas' theory of communication: a critical explanation." *Quarterly Journal of Speech* 65, 412–428.

Buscombe, E. (1982). Sound and color. *Jump Cut* 17, 23–25.

Cantor, M. G. (1980). *Prime-Time TV: Content and Control*. Beverly Hills: Sage.

Carey, J. (1979). "Mass communication research and cultural studies: an American view." in J. Curran, M. Gurevitch, and J. Woollacott (eds.) *Mass Communication and Society* (pp. 409–425). Beverly Hills: Sage.

Carlsnaes, W. (1981). *The Concept of Ideology and Political Analysis*. London: Greenwood Press.

Caughie, J. (1981). "Rhetoric, pleasure and art TV—dreams of leaving." *Screen* 22, 9–31.

Chesebro, J. (1984). "The media reality: epistemological functions of media in cultural systems." *Critical Studies in Mass Communication*, 1, 111–130.

Chibnall, S. (1977). *Law and Order News*. London: Tavistock.

Christians, C. G. and M. R. Real (1979). "Jacques Ellul's contribution to critical media theory." *Journal of Communication*, 29, 83–93.

Clarke, A. and I. Taylor (1980). "Vandals, pickets and muggers: television coverage of law and order in the 1979 election." *Screen Education* 36, 99–112.

Cohen, I. (1982). *Ideology and Consciousness*. New York: New York University Press.

Curran, J., M. Gurevitch, and J. Woollacott (eds.) (1979). *Mass Communication and Society*. Beverly Hills: Sage.

Dahlgren, P. (1981). "TV news as a social relation." *Media, Culture & Society* 3, 291–302.

de Lauretis, T. (1979). "A semiotic approach to television as ideological apparatus," in H. Newcomb (ed.) *Television: The Critical View* (2nd ed., pp. 107–117). New York: Oxford University Press.

Dunn, R. G. (1983). *Television, Consumption and the Commodity Form*. Paper presented at the fifth International Conference on Culture and Communication, Philadelphia, Pa.

Ellul, J. (1964). *The Technological Society*. New York: Knopf.

Fishman, M. (1978). "Crime waves as ideology." *Social Problems* 25, 531–543.

Fiske, J. and J. Hartley (1978). *Reading Television*. London: Methuen.

Gandy, O. (1982). *Beyond Agenda-Setting: Information Subsidies and Public Policy*. Norwood, NJ: Ablex.

Gans, H. (1979). *Deciding What's News*. New York: Pantheon.

Gitlin, T. (1980). *The Whole World is Watching*. Berkeley: University of California Press.

Glasgow Media Group. (1976). *Bad News.* London: Routledge & Kegan Paul.
—— (1980). *More Bad News.* London: Routledge & Kegan Paul.
—— (1982). *Really Bad News.* London: Writers & Readers.
Golding, P. and P. Elliott (1979). *Making the News.* London: Longman.
Goodenough, W. H. (1971). *Culture, Language and Society.* Reading, Mass.: Addison-Wesley.
Gramsci, A. (1971). *Selections from the Prison Noteboooks.* London: Lawrence & Wishart.
Gurevitch, M., T. Bennett, J. Curran, and J. Woollacott (eds.) (1982). *Culture, Society and the Media.* London: Methuen.
Hall, S. (1977). "Culture, media and the 'ideological effect,'" in J. Curran, M. Gurevitch, and J. Woollacott (eds.) *Mass communication and society* (pp. 315–348). Beverly Hills: Sage.
—— (1978). *Policing the Crisis: Mugging, the State, and Law and Order.* London: Macmillan.
—— (1980). *Culture, Media, Language.* London: Hutchinson.
Hartley, J. (1982). *Understanding News.* London: Methuen.
Heath, S. and G. Skirrow (1977). "Television–a world of action." *Screen* 18, 7–59ff.
Innis, H. (1950). *Empire and Communication.* Toronto: University of Toronto Press.
—— (1951). *The Bias of Communication.* Toronto: University of Toronto Press.
Jameson, F. (1981). *The Poilitical Unconscious.* Ithaca: Cornell University Press.
Kellner, D. (1981). "Network television and American society: introduction to a critical theory of television." *Theory and Society* 10, 31–62.
—— (1982). "TV, ideology and emancipatory popular culture," in H. Newcomb (ed.) *Television: The Critical View* (3rd ed., pp. 386–421). New York: Oxford University Press.
Knight, G. (1982). "'News and ideology." *Canadian Journal of Communication* 8, 96–112.
Knight, G. and T. Dean (1982). "Myth and the structure of news." *Journal of Communication* 32, 144–161.
Krugman, H. E. (1971). "Brain wave measures of media involvement." *Journal of Advertising Research* 11, 3–9.
Lacan, J. (1977). *Ecrits: A Selection.* New York: Norton.
Laclau, E. (1977). *Politics and Ideology in Marxist Theory.* London: New Left Books.
Langer, J. (1981). "Television's 'personality system.'" *Media, Culture & Society* 4, 351–365.
Larrain, J. (1979). *The Concept of Ideology.* London: Hutchinson.
Mannheim, K. (1972). *Ideology and Utopia: An Introduction to the Sociology of Knowledge.* London: Routledge & Kegan Paul.
McLuhan, M. (1966). *Understanding Media: The Extensions of Man.* New York: Signet.
Metz, C. (1974). *Film Language.* London: Oxford University Press.
Mulvey, L. (1975). "Visual pleasure and narrative cinema." *Screen* 16, 6–18.
Nowell-Smith, G. (1978/79). "Television—Football—The World." *Screen* 19, 45–60.
Parekh, B. (1982). *Marx's Theory of Ideology.* Baltimore: Johns Hopkins University Press.
Reich, W. (1970). *Mass Psychology of Fascism.* New York: Farrar, Strauss & Giraux.
—— (1975). *Sexual Revolution: Towards a Self-Regulating Character Structure.* New York: Simon & Schuster.
—— (1976). *Character Analysis.* New York: Simon & Schuster.

Requena, J. G. (1981). "Narrativity/discursivity in the American television film." *Screen* 22, 38–42.

Ricoeur, P. (1970). *Freud and Philosophy* (D. Savage, trans.). New Haven: Yale University Press.

Robinson, J. (1977). *How Americans Use Time*. New York: Praeger.

Roth, M. (1983). "U.S. public is jilting its own TV love." *Variety* (April 13) 1.

Sahin, H. and J. Robinson (1981). "Beyond the realm of necessity: television and the colonization of leisure." *Media, Culture & Society* 3, 85–95.

Schlesinger, P. (1978). *Putting "Reality" Together: BBC News*. London: Constable.

Self, R. (1979). "Systems of ambiguity in the art cinema." *Film Criticism* 4, 74–80.

Seliger, M. (1976). *Ideology and Politics*. London: George Allen & Unwin.

Tuchman, G. (1978). *Making News*. New York: Free Press.

Tumber, H. (1982). *Television and the Riots*. London: British Film Institute.

Van Poecke, L. (1980). "Gerbner's cultural indictors: the system is the message." in G. C. Wilhoit and H. de Bock (eds.) *Mass Communication Review Yearbook* (vol. 1, pp. 423–431). Beverly Hills: Sage.

Veron, E. (1971). "Ideology and social sciences: a communicational approach." *Semiotica* 3, 50–76.

Wander, P. (1983). "The ideological turn in modern criticism." *Central States Speech Journal* 34, 1–18.

Watt, I. (1957). *The Rise of the Novel*. London: Chatto & Windus.

Williams, R. (1977). *Marxism and Literature*. London: Oxford University Press.

Winn, M. (1977). *The Plug-in Drug*. New York: Viking.

Worth, S. and J. Adair (1972). *Through Navajo Eyes*. Bloomington: Indiana University Press.

Wren-Lewis, J. (1981). "The story of a riot: the television coverage of civil unrest in 1981." *Screen Education* 40, 15–33.

JOHN ELLIS

BROADCAST TV NARRATION

Commercial entertainment cinema is overwhelmingly a narrative fiction medium. Non-fiction films have always had a precarious place in the commercial cinema, and nowadays they are practically non-existent. Broadcast TV on the other hand carries large amounts of non-fiction: news, documentaries, announcements, weather forecasts, various kinds of segments that are purely televisual in their characteristic forms. It could be argued, therefore, that any model of televisual narration would have to give pride of place to this division of TV products between fiction and non-fiction. Whereas the classical narrative model, basically a fiction model, still underlies our assumptions about the entertainment film, it would seem that no such generalized conception of TV narration would be possible. In fact, this does not seem to be the case. Quite the reverse, the non-fiction and fiction modes of exposition of meanings seem to have converged within television, under the impulsion of the characteristic broadcast TV forms of the segment and the series, and the pervasive sense of the TV image as live. This has produced a distinctive regime of fictional narration on television which owes much to its non-fiction modes. After all, the first true use of the open-ended series format would seem to be the news bulletin, endlessly updating events and never synthesising them.

The mode of narration on television does not have to be divided into two distinct models, one appropriate to fiction, the other to non-fiction. Instead, one model seems to be enough, a model that is capable of inflection by fictional or non-fictional concerns. This explains the ease that television has long since had of producing programmes that are ambiguous in their status: the documentary-drama, or the drama-documentary, forms that seem to have existed in the late 1950s, at least on the BBC. The divisions between fiction and non-fiction exist at another level to that of narration; they are chiefly concerned with the origin of material used in the programme.

Any model of narration on broadcast TV therefore has to be based on the particular institutional and material nature of that television as we now know it. It depends on the conception of the broadcast output as that of segment following segment, segments which by no means always have any connection between them. It depends on the counterpart to this segmental process, the programme series with its distinctive forms of repetition and favoured forms of problematic. It depends on the conception of television as a casual, domestic form, watched without great intensity or continuity of attention. It assumes the ideology of television as a medium which transmits events as they happen, even though (especially in Britain) this is virtually never the case. It is worth repeating in this connection that, although the overwhelming mass of television output is recorded, it still carries a different sense of immediacy from the cinematic image. Broadcast TV is capable of adopting a filmic mode of narration as a kind of borrowing from an already established medium. This will almost always be announced as such: by the form of the TV movie (often a "pilot" for a series), or by the designation of a programme as a prestigious cultural event. This tends to mean that the program will not so much have been made on film as made within a cinematic mode of narration. In this sense, television acknowledges a certain inferiority to cinema. Cinema, for television, means the culturally respectable, the artistic text. The designation "film" for a TV transmission indicates that this transmission is to be viewed despite television; it is not to be segmented, interruptions in terms of advertisements, breaks for viewer attention "at home" are to be kept to a minimum. The "film" transmission on television will then proceed to construct a more cinematic narration. The vast majority of such events, indeed, are cinema films which have already been exhibited in a cinematic context. Cinema is currently not capable of a similar borrowing of broadcast TV forms, however: the colective exhibition of television material is still a novelty or an aberration.

Cinema narration has a strong internal dynamic, a movement from an initial equilibrium that is disrupted towards a new harmony that is the end of the fiction. Broadcast TV narration has a more dispersed narrational form: it is extensive rather than sequential. Its characteristic mode is not one of final closure or totalizing vision; rather, it offers a continuous refiguration of events. Like the news bulletin series, the broadcast TV narrative (fiction and nonfiction) is open-ended, providing a continuous update, a perpetual return to the present. Since closure and finality is not a central feature of TV narration (though it does occur in specific major ways), it follows that the hermetic nature of the cinema narrative, with its patterns of repetition and novelty, is also absent. Repetition in the TV narrative occurs at the level of the series: formats are repeated, situations return week after week. Each time there is novelty. The characters of the situation comedy encounter a new dilemma; the documentary reveals a new problem; the news gives us a fresh strike, a new government, another earthquake, the first panda born in captivity. This form of repetition is different from that offered by the classic cinema narrative, as it provides a kind of groundbase, a constant basis for events, rather than an economy of reuse directed towards a final totalisation.

The series is composed of segments. The recognition of the series format tends to hold segments together and to provide them with an element of continuity and narrative progression from one to the next. The segment form itself has a strong internal coherence. Certain forms of segments are freestanding: the spot advertisement and the item in the news bulletin are both examples. They occur alongside similar segments which have no connection with them except a similarity of class. Other segments, those in a documentary exposition of a particular situation, or a fictional depiction of characters, will have definite connections of a narrative kind. But again, the movement from event to event is not as concentrated and causal as it tends to be in classic cinema narration. Broadcast television's fictional segments tend to explore states and incidents in real time, avoiding the abbreviation that is characteristic of cinema. Hence a certain sense of intimacy in TV drama, a different pace and attention from entertainment cinema.

The segment is self-contained in TV production partly because of the fragmentary nature of much broadcast TV (especially if it carries spot advertising), but also because of the attention span that television assumes of its audience, and the fact that memory of the particular series in all its detail cannot be assumed. People switch on in the middle and get hooked; they miss an episode or two; someone phones up in the middle.

The TV production cannot be hermetic in the way that the film text is, otherwise the audience for a long-running soap opera like *Coronation Street* would now consist of half a dozen ageing addicts. The segment and the series are the repository of memory, and thus of the possibility of repetition and coherence.

The segment is a relatively self-contained scene which conveys an incident, a mood, or a particular meaning. Coherence is provided by a continuity of character through the segment, or, more occasionally, a continuity of place. Hence many fictional segments consist of conversations between two or three characters, an encounter which produces a particular mood (embarrassment, relief, anger, love-at-first-sight, insults, anxiety) and tends to deliver a particular meaning which is often encapsulated in a final line. The segment ends and, in conventional TV fiction, is succeeded by another which deals with a different set of (related) characters in a different place, or the same characters at a different time. There is a marked break between segments. The aspect of break, of end and beginning, tends to outweigh the aspect of continuity and consequence. The nonfiction segment tends to operate in the same way, though in the expository or investigatory documentary it is a series of fragments (interviews, stills, captions, studio presenters, reporter-to-camera in locations) which are held together as a segment by the fact that they all combine to deliver a particular message. Each segment then represents a "move" in the argument of the overall programme. In both drama and investigatory documentary, the segment is relatively self-contained and usually does not last longer than five minutes.

Being self-contained, the segment tends to exhaust its material, providing its own climax which is the culmination of the material of the segment. It is a characteristic of soap operas that they withhold the climactic revelation or action to the end of the segment and the end of the episode. This reaches a purely formal perfection with a series like *Crossroads* where the climactic revelation is followed directly by the credits (entering, emblematically, from every possible direction), and is then repeated as a kind of coda: two characters in frozen face-to-face confrontation with one delivering a line that summarises the previous segment. This process of climaxing directly followed by a break to other forms of segments (title sequences, advertisements, programme announcements, etc.) generates a series of segments in the next episode which effectively chart the repercussions of the climactic event. A series of conversations and actions exhaustively explores and, in the process, recapitulates the climactic action or revelation. The discovery of a husband's affair is followed by a rush of disconnected segments, ads and so on; a week's wait produces a series of conversations: wife to friend, children, neighbours; husband to lover, colleague; and perhaps even The Couple themselves. Each depicts a certain attitude and mood, produces subsidiary revelations, and mulls over the situation. These segments are self-exhausting: enough is said, done, and shown to convey a particular meaning. This completion and internal coherence means that movement from one segment to the next is a matter of succession rather than consequence.

This effect of the self-containedness of the segment is intensified, especially in fiction and observational documentary work, by the use of real time. Where cinema elides actions within a scene by cutting out "dead time" (a character's movement across a room that has no directly narrative function, for example), television tends to leave this "dead time" in. This stems directly fom the studio multiple camera technique, where events are staged in temporal sequence and picked up by a number of cameras one of whose images is selected at any one moment by the director. Where cinema stages events in a very fragmentary way (sometimes just a gesture, a look), television will stage much more like a theatrical scene. The result is that events unroll in real time for the audience, in the time that they took. A segment will tend to hold to temporal unity, especially if it is a conversation. This produces a sense of intimacy within the segment, and a sharp break between segments.

Not all segments hold to temporal unity, not all segments are so isolated from each other. It is quite simple for a segment to be organized around two locations and the journey between them made by a couple of characters. This will involve a great deal of compression and elision. It is also possible to produce effects of alternation and contrast between segments: the contrasting pastimes of two connected characters, or an anticipatory alternation between the tranquil life of one character and the arrival of another who will cause an upset. However, such effects do have to be marked, to be stressed so that they are visibly and audibly different from the normal neutral transition between segments. Hence the anticipatory alternation will be marked by a repeated and rapid movement between the two scenes together with a marked contrast on the level of the sound track. So it is with the beginning of the first episode of A

Bouquet of Barbed Wire. Peaceful scenes of Frank Finlay walking through the sunlit park back to his office are intercut with scenes of arrival at Victoria Station, crowds, train noises, doors slamming, station announcements. Discontinuity on the sound track indicates that this alternation is meaningful, that the arrival constitutes a disturbance. From the same series, examples abound of the segment structured around two locations and the journey between them. Here again, the sound track ensures that the continuity of the segment is recognised over its discontinuities of space and time. Dialogue overlaps: it is as though one conversation continues, with the same train of thought running through the segment.

These examples mark television's difficulty with connecting segments too closely. The normal movement between segments is one of vague simultaneity (meanwhile . . . meanwhile . . . a bit later). Where an event with narrative consequences does take place, several segments are required to work through those consequences and to recapitulate the event itself. There is far less concentration on the cumulative repetition and innovation of meanings than in the classic cinematic narration. The segment is coherent within itself, and may well contain its own echoes of dialogue and gesture. Apart from isolated examples of almost emblematic repetitions across TV narratives (a significant line of dialogue, for instance), this repetition is not characteristic of broadcast TV programmes.

The narrative movement between segments does not follow the cinematic pattern of a relatively rapid transition from event to event in causal sequence. The movement from event to event is more circumspect. This circumspection shows itself in two ways. The first is the multiplication of incidents whose consequences and conclusion are suspended. This is a characteristic of the TV action series like the cop saga *Starsky and Hutch*. Our heroes perpetually encounter fresh incidents, and equally often find themselves suspended in an ambiguous position at the end of a segment (cue for commercial break). The second form of circumspect movement from event to event is that characterised by the soap opera and the drama alike. Events are at a premium: when they occur they generate tidal waves of verbiage, of gossip, discussion, speculation, recrimination. Guilt, jealousy, worry, and an immense curiosity about people is generated by this form. The action series tends to generate car journeys, car chases, interrogations, and the segment that reveals the furtive goings-on that the action-heroes will head off.

In each form, the events that take place are anticipated. For the soap opera/drama, the deliciousness of the anticipation is worth in many instances more than the event itself. Speculation abounds; the event is perfunctory; the mulling over of the repercussions is extended. But it is a characteristic of the action series too that it carries few surprises. Its form of suspense is more incidental. Rather than proposing a central "whodunnit" problem, it is more characteristic to find the central mystery revealed fairly early in the programme. Suspense then becomes a serial affair: the heroes and villains become entangled in a series of different situations, each of which involves escape, chase, shoot-out, etcetera. Narration in the cinematic sense is relatively perfunctory. Little play is made with the fact that the solution to the "whodunnit" has been revealed to the audience before it has to the heroes. This differential knowledge and analytic attitude to the actions of the heroes, characteristic of a cinema director like Fritz Lang (who usually reveals the narrative enigma to the audience), is relatively absent. Instead, the narrative enigma (the aim of the heroes' quest) is incidental. It provides the ground for a series of relatively self-contained segments that deal with particular actions. These segments could be called "clinches": a struggle at close quarters (and also the standard term for an embrace between lovers in the entertainment cinema that thought mostly of such encounters as the male conquest of the female). The action series, then, breaks down into a series of clinches whose motivation is provided by a narrative enigma (a mystery) which more often than not is purely perfunctory. Some very elegant and accomplished uses of this form have been made, alongside the more automatic uses exemplified by a series like *Hawaii Five-O*. *The Rockford Files* produced a liberal-intellectual variant of the clinch. It became the encounter between the amiable Jim Rockford and a series of off-beat eccentrics, where the aspects of performance, milieu, and sparring conversation became the real pleasure of the series. Here, the cinematic genre of the *film noir* and private eye film provided a partial reference point. Another very cultish use of the clinch was *The Prisoner*, with Patrick McGoohan trapped within a series format from which he perpetually tried to escape. The essence of the series was that it was the same each week: the frustrated escape attempt and the frustrated search for some kind of explanation for the series format—who was keeping him prisoner and why. This generated a high degree of independence for each clinch action: it became the only comprehensible and explicable aspect of each episode.

Whereas in cinema this procedure would be intensely frustrating and ultimately pointless, the balance between enigma and clinch-incident in television is different. Clinches can carry the programme when the enigma is never resolved. It was enough to see McGoohan's attempts to enlist fellow inmates to help him escape and to see the doomed escape attempt. It was enough to see McGoohan's attempts to find the identity of "Number One," and to resist the intimidation of various sophisticated brainwashing techniques.

Broadcast TV characteristically has a slighter stress on the causal narrative chain of events than entertainment cinema. Instead, a more extensive mode operates: segments which are relatively self-contained, exploring a particular exchange between individuals, a conversation or an action-clinch. Movement from event to event is slower than in cinema, and particular incidents tend to proliferate and be explored in more detail. This tends to produce an emphasis on groups rather than individuals, on communities rather than couples. The core of a TV series is more often a family, a street, or a workplace than it is an individual. The kind of exploration of a relatively large group and their interrelations which the entertainment film rarely handles (*Written on the Wind* [1956] or *The Cobweb* [1955] being rare examples), is a common phenomenon on television. Similarly, the assurance with which a TV documentary is able to draw together, place, and relativise very disparate views is something that film documentaries produced before the era of television hardly dared attempt.

Groups of characters rarely appear all together in one segment. Arguments in expository documentaries are made by a series of relatively self-contained segmental "moves." The unifying principle behind these programmes is not as it is in cinema (significant patterns of repetition and innovation of meanings; narrative sequence; central problematic); it is the series which provides coherence between segments. The series provides the unity of a particular programme, pulling together segments into a sense of connection which enables a level of narrative progression to take place between them. The series is the major point of repetition in television, matching the innovation that takes place within each segment. This pattern of repetition and innovation is very different from the cinematic model. Where the cinematic form is a closed system which aims to reuse as much material as possible and to balance kinds of repetition and innovation against each other, the TV form is more open-ended. It is a pattern of repetition that is far more centred on the narrative problematic than in cinema. Cinema's single texts tend to inaugurate a novel problematic, a new story subject, for each film. The TV series repeats a problematic. It therefore provides no resolution of the problematic at the end of each episode, nor, often, even at the end of the run of a series. Hence again the reduction of onward narrative progression. The TV series proposes a problematic that is not resolved; narrative resolution takes place at a less fundamental level, at the level of the particular incidents (clinches, confrontations, conversations) that are offered each week (in the case of situation comedies) or between one week and the next (with the cliff-hanger serial ending). Fundamentally, the series implies the form of the dilemma rather than that of resolution and closure. This perhaps is the central contribution that broadcast TV has made to the long history of narrative forms and narrativised perception of the world.

The series is based on the repetition of a problematic. It repeats a situation, a situation which can be fictional or nonfictional. Hence the news series and the current affairs series both present a certain inquiring, fact-finding vision: the situation of reporters observing and collating information, then organizing it for presentation to an uninformed public. This is as much a situation as a father and son running a scrap business with a totter's horse and cart and a crowded London yard (*Steptoe and Son*). The news and current affairs series present a problematic of vision and of explanation. Specific characters encounter a specific set of circumstances every week. But across the specificity of the week's circumstances runs the generality of the same problematic: that of how to see, how to understand. The terms of the understanding are always specified by the program format. It will be "we go behind the scenes" (*Panorama*), "we ask the awkward questions" (*World in Action*), "we update and see how this affects London" (*The London Programme*), "we glance around" (*Nationwide*). In addition to these specific forms of understanding, there are the terms in which these understandings are cast: "moderate/extremist," "the housewife," "But surely you don't think that?" The role of presenter is fundamental to these operations. The characters who investigate and explain for us are a loose group remarkably similar to the cast of a soap opera: some are central, long-running figures (presenters, anchor-persons); others come and go (reporters). In some areas of current affairs, the soap opera aspect becomes more or less explicit. *Nationwide* and *That's Life* are specific examples. The series format constitutes a stable basis of repetition in the programme format, its cast of characters, and its particular kind of reporting attention. Novelty each edition is provided by the specific circumstances that these characters and their vision run up against. It is often explicit that the particular focus of attention for the characters is provided by outside forces over which they have no control, the world of current events. This world tends to be constituted as a place where problems occur. The political actions that the current events series is constituted to explain thus become a particular modality of action: they are problems, troubles, disturbances. The current events series provides a security against these disturbances. The result is that the political arena tends to be given the same status as the emotional problems encountered by soap opera characters. This is one effect of the series format, and one aspect of it.

The fictional series, too, repeats a basic problematic or situation week after week. Like the news and current affairs series, the situation comedy, the crime drama, and the hospital series all return to the stability of the basic dilemma at the end of the week's episode. There is no development at all across the series. The serial marks a long slow narrative movement towards a conclusion, but often that conclusion is tentative (allowing a second series) or incidental (the dispersion of the characters). The situation that provides the steady core is a state of permanent or semi-permanent relationships between a stable but antagonistic group of characters. This is most fully developed in the situation comedy. *Steptoe and Son* may well hate each other, but they also love each other, and Harold's repeated threats to leave his father were never serious. This is exactly the dilemma that situation comedy deals with: it presents conflicting forces or emotions that can never be resolved. Hence the series situation is highly suited to present a particular static vision of the family and of work relations. What is particularly marked about the situation series is that the characters lose all memory of the previous weeks' incidents. They never learn.

A kind of cross between the serial and the series has become increasingly popular on British television. In a light drama or a situation comedy like *Agony* a particular event is passed on from episode to episode, whilst the rest of the events are specific to one episode. Hence in *Agony* Maureen Lipmann's agony columnist is pregnant, and her pregnancy increases until the last episode is concerned with giving birth. However, everything else that occurs, the week's catastrophes and comic turns, take place within one episode which presents their resolution or expulsion from the programme. No memory remains of them next week.

Repetition across the series is one of problematic, of both characters and the situation (or dilemma) in which they find themselves. These situations provide a steady state to which audience and fiction return each week. Specific incidents are fed into this steady state, to provide fresh ammunition for our embattled family to fire at each other and the world, or for our reporters to look into and arrange for our inspection and concern. The incidental problems are solved, but the series format provides no real place for its own resolution. There is no final closure to the series' own recurring problematic. The run of a series ends without resolving its basic dilemma. This marks a basic difference between the cinema narrative and the TV series narrative. The film text aims for a final coherent totalising vision, which sets everything back into order. The series does not share this movement from stable state to stable state. The basic problematic of the series, with all its conflicts, is itself a stable state. The series works on a sense of perpetual tension between individuals, whose causes it routinely does not care to examine. These individuals encounter different incidents that do receive some kind of resolution each episode. Week by week, we choose to forget, as do the characters, the incidents of the week before. With the serial drama, the flow of events is much less: the serial works over its small ration of incidents; the series proposes more incidents but at the cost of forgetting them week by week. The soap opera comes between these two forms. It moves forward, a slow history always in the immediate present; characters remember, events are cumulative. The programme is ever-present, broadcast regularly throughout almost the whole year. It is massively composed of talk; conversation, speculation, confrontation, chat.

The TV series and serial form gathers together segments (both "fiction" and "non-fiction") to form patterns of repetition. These patterns of repetition pull segments together to constitute programmes. The repetition is of format or situation (of a basic problematic), and of characters (reporters, presenters, families, workmates). This particular series form of narration has a particular modality on television. Since television itself presents an immediacy at the level of the image and the experience of viewing, then the series tends to present itself as a kind of continuous update. This is explicit with the news and current affairs series. They bring us up to date with events here and there around the globe. Their movement is one of beginning in the immediate past and returning to the present. The current affairs presenter will tend to pose some rhetorical questions at the end of the programme: "Will the two sides sit down and talk through their differences?" (implication: they'd bloody well better). The soap opera does the same: an update on events followed by the cliff-hanging question. The series tends to do so too. The announcer's ritual before a situation comedy acknowledges this: "What are our (or your) favourite characters up to this week?" The same announcement could precede a news bulletin, or current affairs programme.

Perhaps exactly this remark couldn't precede news; the news bulletin and the current affairs program are filled with infuriating characters. Their regular cast is composed of stubborn individuals often beyond the TV consensus, acting without discernible motive, who should see reason. This feeling is the result of the series format working to create a continuous update. The updating takes place within a stable format of characters and reporting routines. This stable news reportage format comes to constitute normality, exactly as the family squabbles of *Till Death Us Do Part* or its imitator, *All in the Family*, constitute a normality. The routines are constant: particular events intrude episode by episode. These intrusions are incidental upsets. They are incidental because the basic problematic of the series (the situation, the news investigation procedure) remains unchanged by the episode-by-episode events. The series format therefore sets up a pattern of the normal or the everyday, which recurs more or less unaltered. This everyday is a dilemma between characters in the case of a fictional series, or a set of journalistic procedures in the case of news and current affairs. This normality then constitutes particular incidents as intrusions, upsets, or worries. In fiction, this tends to produce a view of family and work structures as unchanging and unchangeable, a stable core buffeted by outside forces. In news, this constitutes current events as bad news, as intrusions upon the peaceful life of the viewers at home and their surrogates, the reporters.

This, then, is the characteristic form of broadcast TV narration. The movement from event to event characteristic of cinematic narration is radically reduced in favour of the multiplication of incident, of action-clinch, and of conversation. These take place in relatively self-contained segments. Segments are bound together into programmes by the repetition device of the series. This constitutes a basic on-going problematic, which rarely receives a final resolution. This problematic has laid over it an episode-by-episode incident, often in the case of a fiction series an enigma whose solution is revealed very early to the audience. These incidents tend to constitute intrusions to the stable normality that is the series format. The characteristic form of series narration is that of the continuous update, returning to the present and leaving a question or a cliff-hanger for the future. Overall, it is a form of narration that lends itself to the exploration of incidents and their repercussions in terms of interpersonal psychology. It habitually deals with a larger number of characters than the cinematic narration, and can concern itself more with their interaction and nuances of behaviour. It is an extensive form rather than a consecutive one. Similar narrational forms can be found at the levels of fiction and of non-fiction. There is no real difference in narrational form between news and soap opera. The distinction is at another level: that of source of material.

This broadcast TV form of narration proposes itself to a particular kind of viewer, a viewer relaxing at home. It makes certain assumptions, more or less unwarranted, about this viewer, and proposes a particular kind of position or viewing for that viewer. This form of viewing attitude has the effect of sealing the consensus nature of broadcast TV.

RICK ALTMAN

TELEVISION SOUND

With the exception of a few lucid pages by John Ellis, critics have systematically steered clear of TV sound, preferring instead to dwell on narrative, industrial, or image-oriented concerns.[1] Yet a strong case can be made for the centrality of the sound track in the American commercial broadcast system and the other national systems that most resemble it. In order to develop this hypothesis I shall first need to subject two received notions of television criticism to careful scrutiny: the first is Raymond Williams's widely accepted notion of "flow"; the second is the well-known view that broadcast networks compete for viewers, with the ratings of the A. C. Nielsen Company charting their rate of success. The latter half of the paper will look closely at six specific roles of the sound track in American network television.

For Raymond Williams, "the central television experience [is] the fact of flow."[2] Declining to discriminate between television systems, Williams claims that "in all developed broadcasting systems the characteristic organization, and therefore the characteristic experience, is one of sequence or flow. This phenomenon, of planned flow, is then perhaps the defining characteristic of broadcasting, simultaneously as technology and as a cultural form."[3] Developing a teleological account which is surprisingly similar to Bazin's version of cinematic realism,[4] Williams proceeds to outline the seemingly necessary and natural development of flow in British and American broadcast television, stressing "a significant shift from the concept of sequence as programming to the concept of sequence as *flow*."[5] Reflecting ontologically, Williams eventually relates the notion of flow to "the television experience itself,"[6] as if the technology itself

---

were sufficient to assure a similarity of situations across cultures and industrial systems.

Now, the notion of flow has already proven to be extremely fertile for the analysis of American television. It is thus not the notion itself that I will critique, but the claim that it is characteristic of television in general. I will propose that the notion of flow is dependent on a specific cultural practice of television, that it cannot be properly understood without reference to the parallel notion of household flow, and that the sound track is specifically charged with mediating the relationship between these two flows. Williams himself lays the groundwork for this analysis when he recognizes significant differences between British and American practices, as well as between commercial and public systems. At every point, however, he is content to interpret those differences in terms of greater or lesser actualization of the medium's true nature. The British are "behind" the Americans, public television lags behind the commercial sector, but all are going in the same direction, because they all partake of the same technologically determined essence. Looked at from this vantage point, a nascent national broadcasting system providing one program per evening is simply not highly enough developed to support a fully operative flow, but give it time and eventually that flow will appear. But what of those broadcast or cable systems which, unlike the American and British industries on which Williams's analysis is so heavily dependent, impose and maintain programming restrictions which specifically preclude the development of a full-fledged flow?

Two alternative models are quite clear here. Either we explain the difference in level of flow by a difference in the stage of development of a particular television system, as Williams does, or we recognize the extent to which such differences in flow correspond to differences in function ascribed to television by a particular culture. Provisionally, I would suggest the following hypothesis: Flow replaces discrete programming to the extent that (1) competition for spectators is allowed to govern the broadcasting situation, and (2) television revenues increase with increased viewing. In short, flow is related not to the television experience itself—because there is no such single experience—but to the commodification of the spectator in a capitalist, free enterprise system. We thus find the lowest level of flow in Eastern bloc countries where programming is carefully controlled and dispensed in measured doses at appropriate

times like some cultural or political medicine. In heavily social-
ized Western European countries like France, where television
is produced and programmed by quasi-governmental, quasi-
independent organisms, the level of flow is somewhat higher,
but still clearly limited by state decisions. In Britain, which
began like France, but which has succumbed much more rapidly
to commercialism, the situation is still mixed, but as the two
BBC channels move toward increasing emulation of the two
commercial stations, and the system as a whole toward imitation of its American counterpart, the coefficient of flow grows
apace. Even within the United States, there is a radical difference in flow between networks, which compete openly and
directly for spectators, and thus foster a high level of flow, and
public channels or local access channels, which have a radically
different mission and thus an entirely different coefficient of
flow. But let a big-city public channel become overly aware of
its ratings (as in New York, Chicago, or Los Angeles), and the
flow begins to surface anew.

If flow is to be tied to profit motives and spectator commodification, it is hardly surprising to note that the countries with
the highest level of flow are also those with the most highly
developed ratings systems. Unlike the film industry, which sells
programming to audiences, commercial broadcast television
sells the audience, by units of a thousand, to advertisers. Just as
cinema spawned a complex industry devoted to evaluating the
quality and attractiveness of its product, so commercial television has needed a method of evaluating first the quantity and
then the quality of its product. Whereas cinema's secondary
industry concentrates on films themselves, and thus expresses
itself largely as newspaper and radio reviews, as Oscars and
other awards, television's evaluation service has been concerned with television's quite different product: the audience
itself. Like academic scholarship on television, distinct from the
more humanistic tradition surrounding cinema, the evaluation
of television audiences has been expressed almost exclusively in
numeric terms. Primary among evaluation devices are the ratings published by the A. C. Nielsen company. Now, there has
always been some controversy as to what Nielsen actually
measures. While Nielsen claims that their meter/diary combination provides a clear picture of the viewing audience, an
increasing number of studies have suggested that Nielsen's
model of attentive television viewing may need some revision.

Following up earlier studies by Robinson and Allen,[7] numerous portions of the 1972 Surgeon General's Report on Television and Social Behavior directly address the problem of viewer attentiveness to television programming.[8] Not surprisingly, Foulkes et al. found that eye contact dropped enormously when adolescent boys had an opportunity to enjoy alternative attractions such as games, books, and toys while watching television.[9] LoSciuto found that 34 percent of the programs listed in viewing diaries as "watched" were in fact intermittently watched or only overheard as the respondent engaged in other activities (in order of frequency: work, housework, eating, talking, reading, child care, sewing, personal care, hobbies, and schoolwork[10]). The most important of these studies, because the most accurate and complete, involved the videotaping of families who were also asked to respond to questionnaires about their viewing. Conducted by Bechtel et al., this study revealed that over half the time that families reported viewing, they were actually not viewing—even though the television might have been on.[11] Expressed as a percentage of the time the set was actually on, the figures are still striking: programs ranged from actually being watched while the set was on 55 percent (commercials) to only 76 percent (movies). This impressive study led the authors to the following conclusion: "Globally, the data point to an inseparable mixture of watching and nonwatching as a general style of television viewing behavior."[12] Indeed, the editor of volume four of the Surgeon General's Report, Jack Lyle, felt compelled to add an appendix to his introductory comments, reflecting on the continued tendency toward over-estimation of viewing time by commercial and academic studies alike. Attention time is not limited to eye contact time, he points out, but surveys continue to act as if it is.[13] Only recently have a few analyses corroborated Lyle's intuitions.[14]

The Nielsen ratings—as well as current studies on television aesthetics—have assumed active viewing as the exclusive model of spectatorship, yet there is a growing body of data suggesting that intermittent attention is in fact the dominant mode of television viewing. Now, this practice of intermittent spectatorship has important ramifications for programming decisions and for the construction of the sound track. Since network strategists aim not at increasing viewership, but at increasing ratings, and since those ratings count operating TV sets rather than viewers, the industry has a vested interest in keeping TV sets on even at a time when no viewers are seated in front of them.

But who leaves a set on when not solidly planted in front of it? This is precisely the point where the sound track begins to take on an active role. In order to help keep those sets operating even while all viewers are out of the room or paying little attention, the sound track must take on numerous, quite specific functions:

• The auditor must be convinced that the sound track provides sufficient plot or informational continuity even when the image is not visible. For example, it must be possible to follow the plot of a soap opera from the kitchen or the score of a football game while painting.

• There must be a sense that *anything really important* will be cued by the sound track. This notion grows in part out of the continued identification of TV programming with live presentation; it is at its height during all-day live coverage of such popular events as the Watergate hearings, election returns, or prolonged sporting events like the Olympics. As long as we can be assured of being called back for the important moments, then it remains worthwhile to keep the television on when we cannot remain within viewing distance.

• There must be recognizable continuity in the type of sound and material presented throughout individual programs or over succeeding programs. Radio stations recognize this by promising the same style of music and/or talk throughout the day. Television does it by sliding from one supposed women's concern to another throughout the day (at least until midafternoon, when the children's continuum starts) or from one sport to another on weekend afternoons. While this is mainly a negative criterion (if a break in continuity occurs, the television risks being turned off), it should be recognized that the whole system is predicated on negativity: the goal is not to get anyone to watch the television carefully (as in certain other countries and on my university channel), but to keep people from turning the television off (which is what Nielsen reports and thus what determines network income).

• The sound itself must provide desired information, events, or emotions from time to time during the flow—time of day, weather, school closings, news briefs, prize awards, emotional crises, and so forth. Even the straight news, sports, or film channels have solved this problem by scheduling updates on a more or less regular basis, or by interrupting one kind of program constantly with a short version of another. The CNN Headline News interspersed throughout the regular WTBS programming is the most obvious version of this syndrome, but the news briefs in the middle of the Olympic coverage or the Olympic updates in between standard network favorites are sufficient proof of the generalization of this practice. This principle is just as true of fictional programming as it is of real-life reporting. A program featuring silent images of skulduggery, heroism, fainting, true love, naked love, and the naked truth would still be lacking the audible evidence of these important occurrences that is needed to reassure the intermittent viewer of continued connection to the image and the excitement that it represents.

In short, with only one out of two switched-on televisions actually being watched (this is a rough average of the figures advanced by the various studies mentioned in the notes), the sound track becomes the major mode of mediation between what Williams calls "programming flow" and what I will term "household flow" (with, of course, the full understanding that this second flow can just as well occur in a bar, a student union, a fraternity house, a doctor's waiting room, or the break room of a factory or business[15]). Earlier, I suggested that the notion of flow is not a natural concomitant of television technology, but that it is rather the result of a particular consumption configuration. We now understand just what that rather enigmatic claim signifies: in a system where the audience is the ultimate commodity, and where the size of the audience is measured not by the number of persons actually watching the television, but instead by the number of sets turned on, television must organize itself in such a way as to harmonize with the household flow on which it depends. It does this by fragmenting itself into a large number of short segments which reflect the limited continuous viewing time of anyone caught up in the household flow; at the same time, renewed emphasis is laid on the message-carrying ability of the sound track, which alone remains in contact with the audience for fully half of the time that the set is on. Or, to put it in an entirely different way, we might say that the presence of flow is not so much dependent on competition between channels, as Williams claims,[16] but on *the competition with household flow*. In systems where programming flow is minimal, there is a similarly low interplay between the television and the household. In the many national systems where films occupy whole evenings of broadcast programming, unencumbered by intermissions or commercial breaks, the main relationship between the household flow and the television programming is not unlike that which exists between household flow and theatrical film exhibition: when it's time to watch the film, you leave the household behind.[17] Now, this is decidedly not the mode of television viewing in this country, for the development of programming flow is inseparably linked with the interpenetration of household flow and television programming,[18] a connection which is strongly supported by a tendency of measurement systems to confuse viewers with auditors. The most obvious result of this process is the investing of the sound track with a special responsibility, that of making sure that no potential auditor will turn off the set, thus assuring that the well-known over-reporting of viewing will continue to be the rule.

The remainder of this paper will be devoted to six important functions and techniques characteristic of the television sound track as it has developed in the flow of the American commercial network system.

Labeling

Where competition has led to a high level of flow, the typical television texture is that of the short segment. Now this is obviously true of commercials, *Good Morning America*, and the evening news, as well as variety shows, quiz programs, and the *Wide World of Sports*. It may not be quite as obvious in narrative fiction programming, but the same fragmentation is nevertheless operative. *Dallas* is organized not according to a novelistic hermeneutic, but around an intricate menu of topics which for some viewers are experienced by character (J.R., Bobby, Sue Ellen, Pam, Cliff, Miss Ellie, etc.), and for others by theme (sex, love, power, etc.). Because it is presented to us as "segmentation without closure," to quote Jane Feuer,[19] *Dallas* does not expect to subordinate all our attention to the linearity, directionality, and teleology of a goal-oriented plot. Instead, it recognizes from the start our desire to choose the objects of our attention on other grounds. Whereas the level of audience attention to a given Hollywood film scene may be roughly dependent on the importance of that scene for resolving the plot's dilemmas, attention to a given *Dallas* scene depends instead on the topic and characters present. In recognition of this difference, we might say that classical Hollywood narrative is in large part *goal-driven*, while attention to American television narrative is heavily *menu-driven*.

For the spectator firmly implanted in front of the television, the menu is made quite clear by the images. For the half of the audience whose eyes are not glued to the tube, however, the sound track must serve to *label* the menu items.

Italicizing

In *Visible Fictions*, John Ellis points out that "there is hardly any chance of catching a particular TV program 'tomorrow' or 'next week sometime' as there is with a cinema film."[20] Whether the events transmitted by television are live or not, the television experience itself is thus sensed as live by the home-viewing audience. Just as the camera has to be on-the-spot to record a live news event, so the potential spectator must make sure that her or his eyes are parked in front of the television when someting important happens—or risk missing it forever. Paradoxically, this is even more true of a canned fiction program than of a live news or sports program, for the latter may be covered in the late news, whereas Miss Ellie's reaction upon learning of Jock's death is lost forever to anyone who fails to return to the screen at the appropriate time. (It is worth pointing out here that, contrary to expectation, the much acclaimed practice of time-switching by VTR [video tape recording] does nothing to lessen this sense of potential loss, for time-switching is rarely used for those programs that are viewed intermittently, but instead for those programs that the viewer is dedicated to watching carefully from beginning to end.)

The characteristically irreversible exhibition situation of broadcast television provides a general link with a wider range of irreversible, unschedulable forms, all of which compensate for the inability to go back and see the same thing over again by ensuring a repetitious, quasi-ritual approximation of sameness in the next material to appear (oral epic and pastoral do this, as do the serial novel and the comic strip, as well as radio and television drama). Television programming itself thus takes on the attributes of irreversible reality. *We* cannot decide when to watch a particular type of programming, nor can we decide when a particular event will occur within a program. We can only be attentive to the programming on a more or less nonstop basis in order to make sure that we miss nothing, in the same way that a babysitter automatically monitors the reality of the house and children she/he has been given the responsibility for. It is precisely here that the italicizing function of the sound track takes over. We cannot always keep our eyes focused on the set, but we have learned to listen for certain sound cues which say: this is the part you've been waiting for, this is the exciting moment, this is the great play, this is the time when the program you are tuned to delivers up its basic stuff.

The news announcer speaks; his heightened objectivity requires a neutral image—nothing special, nothing unusual, no changes from minute to minute, from day to day, from month to month. But the sound changes constantly—*in fact it is for this very change that we are always there, listening,* even when we can't be viewing. But to what end are these verbal italics used? Uniformly, they serve to call me to the image, to let me know that something is happening that I dare not miss, in short something *spectacular.* The word is well chosen, because it reveals the extent to which the italicizing function of sound, unfaithful to its own medium, serves to identify that which is worth *looking at,* rather than just hearing. Television thus contributes directly to a notion of life in which daily events are hardly perceived; treated as life's uneventful, audible, continuous filler, our daily flow gains meaning only to the extent that it points to the spectacular, an event in which by definition I cannot participate, but which can give my life meaning through vision. By italicizing certain parts of each program, the sound track thus leads us back to the image, to the television set itself, and by so doing cements us permanently in an aesthetics and an ideology of the spectacular.

The Sound Hermeneutic

Sound has a hidden advantage over all other appeals, because in the Western world sound is always taken to be incomplete; it seems to call for identification with a visible object given as a sound source. Now, television has accustomed us to a high degree of return on our audiovisual investment; we are by now quite confident that television will show us the source of the sound, if only we rush in from the kitchen fast enough. We are used to the sense of wholeness that this arrangement assures.

When we hear a sound, we find its source on the screen, thus giving us a sense of presence, of resolution.

It is revealing to compare this situation to the common film arrangement. In an article in the *Cinema/Sound* volume of *Yale French Studies*[21], I have shown how off-screen sound, or, to be more precise, sound without a visible source (what Michel Chion calls acousmatic sound[22]), creates what I have termed a "sound hermeneutic": the sound asks the question "Where?" to which the image, upon identifying the source, eventually responds "Here!" In other words, the sound track initiates the so-called spectator's involvement, with the camera either complying or not with the spectator's desires. In television, however, the spectator/auditor takes the place of the camera in the sound hermeneutic. When the sound piques my curiosity, I can be nearly sure of satisfaction simply by turning my gaze to the screen. Instead of depending on the camera and the director, who may make me wait to see what is making that noise, I alone exercise control. By raising my eyes and glancing toward the screen I discover the sound source on my own, thus experiencing the wholeness that it implies. In passing, it is worth noting the ideological investment involved in this seeming liberty. Unlike film spectators, who take pleasure in being manipulated by the image-sound relationship (but who know that manipulation is taking place), television spectators are led to believe that they have power over the image, whereas in fact the labeling and italicizing that trigger the sound hermeneutic are carefully controlled and follow a prescribed path, thus creating for the TV subject an ideological positioning different from that of the cinema counterpart, one that the illusion of liberty manages to conceal even more fully.

Internal Audiences

When we hear the voice of a favorite star, we turn toward the screen to complete our sense of the star's presence. That star may be an actor, a political personality, a sports hero, or just a cute face in a commercial, someone who shares my accent and thus my regional or national origin, or simply the car I am thinking of buying. In all these cases, I have a reasonable degree of control over the kinds of sound I choose to follow to the screen. A far more common situation robs me of that power altogether: what I hear is not a mark of a particular visual presence on the screen but only a sign that someone else thinks that an important phenomenon is taking place on the screen. In fact, few techniques have a greater influence on television's overall inner dynamic than the nearly perpetual presence of the internal audience—in the image sometimes, but always on the sound track. Commonly, the sound track serves to editorialize even when it is matched with live images. What we call live sporting events are in fact live images accompanied by very few live sound effects, with the rest of the sound track devoted to voice-over commentary; even the short snatches of sync-sound dialogues are only relays from the announcer's speech, like direct quotation in a historical novel.

No matter how live the image, then, the sound continues to serve as presentation, as commentary, in short as audience to the image. Carefully carrying out its italicizing function, the sound serves a value-laden editing function, identifying better than the image itself the parts of the image that are sufficiently spectacular to merit closer attention by the intermittent viewer. The operative model for an understanding of television's audiovisual complex is thus not the one which would be appropriate to a truly live presentation of events. There it would be reasonable to expect that the viewer/auditor hears and sees both parts of the spectacle simultaneously. Quite the contrary, the TV viewer's vision of the live event is typically filtered through the sound track, speaking for an interposed interior audience. It is certainly not by chance that this is literally the arrangement preferred by most studio-shot television: the camera looks over the heads of the studio audience at the spectacle that they are consuming. Whether the sound track carries simultaneously recorded studio applause, or only an added laugh track, the sound is engineered in such a way as to convince us that the applause or laughter emanates from a spot closer to us than the spectacle itself. Indeed, it is striking to note how often newscasts and sports update programs, not to mention *Good Morning America* and other breakfast shows, include internal monitors, usually located behind the announcer, in such a way that the announcer has to look slightly away from the audience in order to see the on-screen monitor. In so doing, the announcer clearly establishes visually the general configuration constitutive of television's internal audience: in order to get to the promised images, we must look over, through, or with an internal spectator who may or may not be seen, but who is always heard, and who is always ready to tell us what we "need to know" about those images.

The most common internal audiences are well known and frequently used: the newscaster, the sports announcer, the studio audience (or its laugh track substitute), the stadium crowd, the users of advertised products. A more complex situation occurs in the increasingly frequent case of "location narratives" (as opposed to the "studio narratives" shot with an audience either actually present or implied by the sound track). Adult soaps or action shows, largely restricted to the later prime-time hours, as location narratives look and sound more like Hollywood films than any other TV products: with no announcer, no studio audience, and no satisfied consumers built into the sound track, it would seem that they alone of all television programming are utterly devoid of the influence of an internal audience. Far from it. First, these programs are often specifically built around a series of highly visible events and characters, for whom other characters serve as an internal audience. In *Dallas*, Ray and Donna constantly play the role of the show's "good conscience," existing more to provide a model moral reaction to J.R.'s shenanigans than to initiate their own activity. J.R.'s various bedmates—and especially Merrilee Stone—play the opposite role of gloating over his immorality. Poor pretty Afton is little more than a constant audience for Cliff Barnes and his ambitious ineptitude. Given its more ensemble-oriented style, *Hill Street Blues* does not single out a few objects of interest for the other secondary characters, but it does systematically construct nearly every important scene so as to provide an appropriate witness or two to react immediately to any important action.

When a program cannot comfortably provide an internal audience from among its own cast, or when greater intensity is needed, music provides the answer. In some ways, the music for location narratives would seem to take up where Hollywood leaves off, but we should not be fooled by this surface resemblance. To be sure, both are programmatic, but the path taken by TV music is far more commentative, far more likely to identify—usually just before it happens—even the slightest incident to the savvy listener in the next room. The movements of film music are long and general as compared to television's microcosmic attention to every high and low point. Just as the laugh track must guarantee a certain number of laughs per minute, so the music for a location narrative must provide a detailed road map for the housespouse trying to follow the program from the kitchen and unable to rush out for just anything. Though the method is different, the result is the same: the sound track provides an internal audience guiding the viewing choices of the external audience.

The Sound Advance

Lodged within the claims I have already made lies a significant contradiction. On the one hand, television tends toward live or "live-on-tape" presentation, with internal audiences reacting to internal spectacles in real time; on the other hand, television sound serves to call the intermittent viewer either to see the source of the sound or the reason for its emission. The problem is a simple one: how can the prospective viewer be sure of seeing the spectacle which has caused audience applause, when that applause has been caused by an activity which took place before the applause, and which may thus no longer be available to the external audience coming in from the kitchen or looking up from the daily paper? The image performs, the miked audience reacts, but by the time the TV audience looks, the spectacle may have disappeared. Logically, this is what should happen, but it is precisely what we do not find. For, in order to serve its own logic, network television commonly reverses the natural progression. The miked internal audience is made to react, drawing the external audience's attention, before the spectacle is revealed. On the surface of things, this arrangement sounds preposterous. How can the audience react to something it has not seen? It can't, and that's just the point: the internal audience must react to something that *we*, the external audience, have not yet seen. That is, there must be a delay between the time when the internal audience witnesses the relevant spectacle and the moment when that spectacle is revealed to the external audience. Now in studio recording, this is extremely simple. The most obvious expedient is simply to wave the "APPLAUSE" card in front of the audience just before the emcee appears. A similar result may be had from bringing the "star of our show" in from the side, in such a way that the studio audience sees and recognizes him or her before he/she is on screen. And what if a panelist were to fall over a microphone cord, releasing howls of spontaneous laughter from the studio audience? No problem, for as a television-trained actor, the panelist will undoubtedly remain on his or her keester for numerous seconds, mugging long enough to make sure that the camera—along with the home audience—has picked up the un-

graceful but nevertheless newsworthy pratfall. Through the
use of audience cue cards, clever set designs or mixing patterns,
programmatic music or instant replays, the intermittent viewer
has the time to be called to the set and witness the excitement,
thanks to the fact that the sound is followed, from the point of
view of the external audience, by the cause of which it is the
effect.

Now, what is the end result of this reversal? What earlier
looked like natural causality (objects make sounds) now takes
on a magical air (reaction produces action). Sound and image
are presented, as it were, backwards, transforming the casual
auditor into a spectator as well. The insertion of the auditor
into spectatorship, of household flow into television flow, thus
takes place through the reversal of accepted logical and temporal relationships between sound and image. The sound, which
is reaction, must be recast as prediction, so that the image, to
which I am being called, might instead seem to be made especially for me.

Discursification

Hollywood narrative film is heavily nondiscursive. It refuses to
recognize the presence of the viewer, making that viewer adopt
instead the stance of the voyeur, a stance that depends on a
level of attention that is dependable and continuous. With television the audience is not secure. Television competes with
surrounding objects of attention just as the products it advertises do; it is thus far more discursive as a whole, openly
interpellating, addressing the audience, and thus involving spectators in dialogue, enjoining them to look, to see, to partake of
that which is offered up for vision.

The use of sound to call the intermittent spectator back to
the set has wide-ranging effects on the discursivity of sound
and image alike. For the film spectator, Mamoulian's famous
dropped vase explosion in *Love Me Tonight* is a joke, an exaggeration, or a mismatch, but a similar sound event on television
would be a call to return to the set, a call to switch from sound
as *histoire* (the sound tells me what's happening) to sound as
discours (the sound tells me to look in order to find out what's
happening). In a similar way, American TV news has moved
increasingly toward the presentational, merging a primary level
composed of a neutral announcer image and a highly charged
presentational sound with a secondary level composed of a highly

charged image and tributary sound. The truth is thus recognized, paradoxically, as double: the announcer tells us the truth ("Today Mt. Elba erupted again, producing a lava flow which destroyed two villages, cut three roads, and took at least ten lives."), but that is a historic truth, an event which took place elsewhere involving others, and which thus does not involve me. But if I could see the events, if they could be reoriented from their historic position into a new slant where they would be played for me, then they would change form and function, becoming part of a discursive circuit. The deeper, paradoxical truth of our television is thus this discursification of the world. It is not so much that seeing is believing (an earlier assumption of TV audiences), but rather that images collected just for me give me a sensation that no flat, historical account could possibly give. And only their prior announcement by the sound track can make those images seem to be made just for me.

The instant replay is perhaps the ultimate and perfect example of this discursive syndrome. I'm in the kitchen getting a beer. Suddenly I hear cheering and an announcer losing his cool over the utter perfection of the throw and the acrobatic grace of the catch. Now, up until this point, the players have been playing to win, that is, for themselves, according to the rules, the objective, impersonal rules of the game. They may showboat from time to time for the stadium crowd or even for the telespectator, but when they are playing their actions must largely be aimed at disarming and defeating the opponent. But suddenly the crowd roars. I rush from the kitchen to catch the end of the play, but of course it is over, done, gone forever as a play. But the instant replay saves the day. It shows *me* exactly what *I* just came from the kitchen to see. With multiple cameras and variable slow motion, it seeks out the most extraordinary angle, or the one view that reveals the offensive interference that made the catch possible. The replay thus stands in the same relationship to the play as the process of representation has to the present. Formless, uninterpreted, lacking in direction, unvectorized, the present only takes on its meaning—its for-me-ness—in the process of re-presentation. The memory of television is thus not the memory of a whole game, but the combination of a certain liberty of circulation (beer, phone, john, newspaper, etc.) and the paradoxical knowledge that the game is summed up for me in the right shot at the right time.

Now, as often as not, no sound at all accompanies the instant replay, only a symbolic silence, for the sound has spent itself in calling the wandering spectator; by bringing a specially made image together at this specific time with a spectator especially desirous of seeing that very image, it has succeeded in involving both the spectator and the image in the discursive circuit which it—the sound—directs. On the one hand, the TV flow, on the other, the household flow. Only when the sound track reaches out to bring the two together do they fulfill their full mission. Charged with bringing me to the image, the sound track uses every weapon at its disposal: labeling, italicizing, the sound hermeneutic, internal audiences, the sound advance. But the ultimate argument, as well as the final goal, remains the notion, fostered continually by the sound track, that the TV image is manufactured and broadcast just for me, at precisely the time that I need it.[23]

NOTES

1. John Ellis, *Visible Fictions: Cinema, Television, Video* (London: Routledge & Kegan Paul, 1982), especially Chapter eight, "Broadcast TV as Sound and Image," pp. 127–44.
2. Raymond Williams, *Television: Technology and Cultural Form* (New York: Schocken, 1974), p. 95.
3. Ibid., p. 86.
4. For a critique of Bazin's approach to film history, see Jean-Louis Comolli, "Technique et idéologie: Caméra, perspective, profondeur de champ," *Cahiers du cinéma* (May–June, 1971), pp. 229, 230, 231, 233, 234–35, 241 ff.
5. Williams, p. 89.
6. Ibid., p. 94.
7. John P. Robinson, "Television and Leisure Time: Yesterday, Today and (Maybe) Tomorrow," *Public Opinion Quarterly* 33 (1969), pp. 210–22; C. L. Allen, "Photographing the TV Audience," *Journal of Advertising Research* 5 (March, 1968), pp. 2–8.
8. *Television and Social Behavior.* A Technical Report to the Surgeon General's Scientific Advisory Committee on Television and Social Behavior, eds. Eli A. Rubinstein, George A. Comstock, and John P. Murray (Washington, D.C.: U.S. Government Printing Office, 1971).
9. D. Foulkes, E. Belvedere, and T. Brubaker, "Televised Violence and Dream Content," in *Television and Social Behavior*, vol. 5, pp. 59–119.
10. Leonard A. LoSciuto, "A National Inventory of Television Viewing Behavior," in *Television and Social Behavior*, vol. 4, pp. 33–86.
11. Robert B. Bechtel, Clark Achelpohl, and Roger Akers, "Correlates Between Observed Behavior and Questionnaire Responses on Television Viewing," in *Television and Social Behavior*, vol. 4, pp. 274–344.
12. Bechtel et al., p. 298. It is important to note that this study includes as "watchers" numerous individuals who are simultaneously involved in other activities, thus suggesting a possible over-estimation of active viewers. The categories used are (1) Participating, actively responding to the TV set or to

others regarding content from the set; (2) Passively watching; (3) Simultaneous activity (eating, knitting, etc.) while looking at the screen; (4) Positioned to watch television but reading, talking, or attending to something other than television; (5) In the viewing area of the TV but positioned away from the set in a way that would require turning to see it; (6) Not in the room and unable to see the set or degree of impact of TV content. Categories 1–3 are considered "watching" while categories 4–6 are considered nonwatching. It is instructive to compare this approach to the more traditional categories offered by Jon Baggaley and Steve Duck, in *Dynamics of Television* (Westmead, England: Saxon House, 1976). Their *lowest* level of attention, "at which there is a totally passive involvement in the imagery's simply novelty value" (p. 68), corresponds to level two in the scheme of Bechtel et al., who list no less than *four* lower levels of attention.

13. Jack Lyle, "Television in Daily Life: Patterns of Use Overview," in *Television and Social Behavior*, vol. 4, pp. 26–28.

14. A convenient review of this literature is available in George Comstock, Steven Chaffee, Natan Katzman, Maxwell McCombs, and Donald Roberts, *Television and Human Behavior* (New York: Columbia University Press, 1978), pp. 141–72. In addition, see especially Helen Leslie Steeves and Lloyd R. Bostian, *Diary Survey of Wisconsin and Illinois Employed Women*. Bulletin 41 (Madison: University of Wisconsin-Extension, 1980). The data collected by this study, which suggests that working women view television without engaging in some simultaneous activity only 35.2 percent of their "viewing" time, serve as a base for a forthcoming article by Samuel L. Becker, H. Leslie Steeves, and Hyeon C. Choi, entitled "The Context of Media Use." See also the various reports of Television Audience Assessment, Inc., an alternative to Nielsen's, and Arbitron's Audimeter approach established by the Markle Foundation in 1979 with the help of the Ford Foundation. According to a preliminary report, 49 percent of the total audience surveyed reported additional activities during "viewing" time; 42 percent of those reported that they were distracted from viewing by their major additional activity, even though only prime-time viewing was surveyed. See Elizabeth J. Roberts and Peter J. Lemieux, *Audience Attitudes and Alternative Program Ratings: A Preliminary Study* (Cambridge, Mass.: Television Audience Assessment, 1981). Perhaps the best reflection of intermittent viewing from a fictional point of view is provided by Michael J. Arlen's short story "Good Morning," in *The View From Highway 1* (New York: Ballantine Books, 1976), pp. 13–19. Part of the historical context of early network strategies for promoting intermittent viewing patterns is provided by an unpublished paper by William Boddy [Boddy now teaches at Baruch College, City University of New York. ED.], "The Shining Center of the Home: Ontologies of Television in the 'Golden Age.'" Boddy points up the extent to which intermittent radio listening served as an early model for television spectatorship.

15. On television viewing outside the home, see the work of Dafna Lemish, "The Rules of Viewing Television in Public Places," *Journal of Broadcasting* 26 (Fall, 1982), pp. 757–82, and *Viewing Television in Public Places: An Ethnography*, Ph. D. dissertation, Ohio State University, 1982.

16. Williams, *Television*, p. 93.

17. Available cross-cultural data strongly support this claim. In *The Use of Time: Daily Activities of Urban and Suburban Populations in Twelve Countries*, ed. Alexander Szalai (The Hague: Mouton, 1972), Robinson and Converse report

the following figures, which I have regrouped into broad political/economical categories:

	Total minutes daily viewing	Viewing as primary activity	Viewing as secondary activity	Secondary activity as % of total minutes viewing
Eastern Europe	59	51	8	14
Western Europe	88	70	18	21
U.S.A.	129	92	37	29

Though these figures were collected in the late sixties, and thus call for updating, they clearly suggest a positive correlation between intermittent viewing and the American advertising-oriented, ratings-based model which Western Europe has resisted only in part. It should be noted that in the case of simultaneous activities not identified hierarchically by respondents, this survey classifies half of each activity as primary, half as secondary, thus assuring an *over-estimation* of viewing as a strictly primary activity. For information on data collection guidelines, see John P. Robinson, "Television and Leisure Time: Yesterday, Today, and (Maybe) Tomorrow," *Public Opinion Quarterly* 33 (Summer, 1969), pp. 210–22.

18. Just as I have argued against conflating all television systems into a single and undifferentiated "television experience," I would argue that American broadcast television must be broken down into appropriate time sectors, each corresponding to a different level of competition with household flow. As early as 1945, a CBS publication on *Television Audience Research* (New York: CBS, 1945) argued that "Television's daytime programs . . . can be constructed so that full attention will not be necessary for their enjoyment. Programs requiring full attention of eye and ear should be scheduled for evening hours when viewers feel entitled to entertainment and relaxation" (p. 6). The Allen study mentioned in note seven provides the following data broken down into daily time sectors:

	Total	Morning	Afternoon	Evening
Hours set in use per week	31.8	3.5	9.7	18.6
Nonviewing w/set in use	12.8	1.8	4.5	6.5
Nonviewing as % of set in use	40%	52%	47%	35%

The period with the lowest percentage of intermittent viewing thus corresponds both to the period of lowest competition with household flow (children in bed, housework done) and to the period characterized by the highest quotient of self-contained, goal-driven narrative programs. The daytime hours, which reveal a markedly higher percentage of intermittent viewing, are traditionally associated with female and children viewers. Szalai et al. report that viewing TV as a secondary activity is more than twice as frequent for American housewives (38%) as for employed men (18%). More recently, Roberts and Lemieux identified women aged 18–39 as the group least likely to give a program full attention (only 31% of women 18–39 remained in the room throughout a full program). What is shocking about these figures is the fact that Roberts and Lemieux conducted all surveys *in prime time only* (thus missing the periods of high intermittent viewing by women) and that Szalai et al. report that 36 percent of all TV viewing by *employed* women is secondary to some other activity—just 2 percent less than for housewives. These figures point to two related, but nevertheless separate phenomena in American broadcasting and its consumption:

1. Network programming choices are carefully correlated with household flow patterns, producing a coefficient of television flow which, while remaining high as compared to other national systems, decreases during evening hours.

2. Cultural patterns have created a substantially higher level of intermittent viewing for female adults than for male adults.

Both of these hypotheses call for further research, perhaps along the lines of Tania Modleski's "The Rhythms of Reception: Daytime Television and Women's Work," in *Regarding Television: Critical Approaches—An Anthology*, ed. E. Ann Kaplan (Frederick, Md: University Publications of America, 1983), pp. 67-75.

19. Jane Feuer, "The Concept of Live TV: Ontology as Ideology," in *Regarding Television*, pp. 15-16.
20. Ellis, *Visible Fictions*, p. 111.
21. Rick Altman, "Moving Lips: Cinema as Ventriloquism," in *Yale French Studies* 60 (1980), pp. 67-79.
22. Michel Chion, *La voix au cinéma* (Paris: Cahiers du Cinéma/Editions de l'Étoile, 1982).
23. I want to express my appreciation to Sam Becker, Eileen Meehan, and Paul Traudt, colleagues at the University of Iowa, who helped initiate me into the bibliography of what was for me a new field.

NICK BROWNE

THE POLITICAL ECONOMY OF
THE TELEVISION (SUPER) TEXT

THEORIZING TELEVISION

"Theorizing television," whatever that eventually might come to mean for the field of film, requires a radical reformulation of the questions and answers that compose contemporary film theory. This re-orientation of perspective and method is necessary because of differences between the two media themselves: in institutional form, program formats, economics, audiences, indeed, in the form of the discourse and in the practical and critical languages that have traditionally been associated with research and analysis in these domains. In contrast to the formalist definitions of "film" constructed by traditional film theory (with accent on its ontological status and aesthetic forms) or by contemporary film theory (through the notion of its language and codes), constituting American network television as an object of theoretical and critical study means characterizing the status and form of the television discourse specifically in relation to economic and social processes.

Culturally and historically, the replacement of film by television in the 1950s as the dominant form of American mass entertainment signified an important transformation of American life and culture. It altered the relation of the media, and of entertainment, to "culture" by substituting a system of continuous, "free" viewing for the theatrical system of discrete admissions on a pay-per-view basis. At the same time it restructured the contexts and modes of audience reception and behavior and indeed, its composition. Culturally, film and television came by the midfifties to define and occupy different

Reprinted from *Quarterly Review of Film Studies*, Vol. 9, No. 3, Summer 1984, with permission of author. Copyright © 1984.

social places and to exercise different entertainment and ideological functions for their audiences.

The fact that American broadcast television was constituted
in the image of commercial radio, to be received "free," at
home, by the general public definitively shaped the public policy
and critical discourses on it. Seldom, however, did discussion of
television conducted within the traditional effects paradigm
take the form of systematic social or economic analysis. Television, however, is an institution that mediates the relation of the
programming—its "texts"—to the social and economic world of
the audience in a mode altogether different from film, in ways
that call for systematic examination.

At present, two contemporary theoretical approaches to the
relation of television and society organize the emerging field of
television study—what we might call the ritualistic and the
ideological. The application of mythical or ritual models derived
from the analysis of primitive religious systems to postmodern,
Western consumer society and media (whether applied to program structure or to the audience's act of viewing) necessarily
misfigures the form and significance of the television discourse.
The Althusserian ideological approach to the analysis of the
relation of film and society—emphasizing the medium's role in
the reproduction of social relations—quickly reached the limits
of theoretical articulation of the problem of the *audience*." This
formulation provided only a general abstract conception of the
figure of the audience as "subject," one common to all social
institutions and specific to none, one that sustained a theory of
totalizing ideological discourse. Nowhere did Althusser provide
a place for the audience's differential positions and readings
according to different levels or instances of social position or
practice—for example, according to gender, class, ethnicity,
etcetera.

Under the aegis of "cultural studies," the ideological approach
to television has been moved decisively and systematically forward in the work of Stuart Hall and his associates in Birmingham, England.[1] Yet, the account of the television discourse that the Birmingham School provides is formulated on
the basis of the noncommercial British system. It is this "public
television" experience that has shaped the theoretical articulation of the relation of text and culture in Britain. The premise
of the American, advertiser-supported system is grounded in a
radically different relation between the form of the television
text and the processes of economy and culture. Contemporary

critical theory, in the American context, then, is in the position today of thinking the relation of media and society by theorizing the television discourse, the institution which supports it, the advertising that drives it, and the audience which consumes it, as elements in a general system.

With a view then to continuing and to renewing in a fresh context, discussion of the relation of the American network television institution to its public, I want to present a perspective on television that provides a necessary framework for any attempt to trace its social operations, meanings, and effects. Eric Barnouw's *The Sponsor* provides a crucial overview of the historical evolution of the relation between advertising and the television institution. I want to examine the *textual* and *cultural* implications of the economic foundation of American commercial television and to indicate the importance of re-contextualizing the problem of the figure of the television audience and the function assigned to it within a tradition of critical thought that has figured the medium's relation to its publics. By accenting the direct role of economy in shaping the form of American television texts, I mean to differentiate this approach from the British model, to underline the theoretical importance of linking economic and textual systems in a single model, and to insist on the framework of *political economy* as a powerful means of studying the complexity of their interrelations.

THE FORM AND GENEALOGY OF
THE TELEVISION "SUPERTEXT"

Considered as a business, television works on a basic exchange. For a fee, television delivers audiences, measured in thousands, to advertisers. That is, the business of television is showing ads to audiences. To attract viewers for the ads, the networks contract with program suppliers for the rights to distribute programs on their systems. Presently, the networks do not own such programs outright, but license rights to distribute them. The popularity of a program, its rating as measured by the Nielsen Television Index, determines the fee that an advertiser can be charged. Here is the way Nielsen advertises itself: "The Industry Standard for Buying, Selling, Planning, and Programming National Television."

Scheduling is the practice of selecting, placing, and coordinating programs with respect to each other for overall maximum

competitive business advantage. In general, though there are
changes from year to year, program positions through the day
and across the week have been codified and stabilized. Placement of a program with respect to the time of day, the day of
the week, in relation to what precedes it on the same network,
and what it plays against on the others, is the framework not
only of popularity, but, I submit, determines format and reception as well. The schedule determines the form of a particular
television program and conditions its relation to the audience.

Just as important, the position of programs in the television
schedule reflects and is determined by the work-structured
order of the real social world. The patterns of position and flow
imply the question of who is at home, and through complicated
social relays and temporal mediations, link television to the
modes, processes, and scheduling of production characteristic
of the general population. The temporality of television is organized—I am tempted to say like life—along several simultaneous registers: the order of the day, the week, the season,
the year. Television establishes its relation to the "real," not
only through codes of realistic representation, but through the
schedule, to the socially mediated order of the *workday* and the
workweek. In this way, television helps produce and render
"natural" the logic and rhythm of the social order.

The "television text" as a concept and as a practice is a unique
sort of discursive figure very different from the discrete unity
of film. Its phenomenology is one of flow, banality, distraction,
and transience; its semiotics complex, fragmentary, and heterogeneous. The limits of the text "proper" and its formal unity—
apt to be broken at any moment by an ad or a turn of the dial—
are suspect. Of course, the application of received methods of
textual analysis to particular programs, provided that they can
be separated from the flow and can be retrieved and held for
inspection, will yield a certain kind of result. Allied with generic, narrative, or even ideological analysis, the result of textual analysis of television programs can be generalized in accord
with the existing models provided by literary or film study. Yet,
the application of these methods or perspectives to the "television text" can only incompletely grasp its specificity of form,
force, and signification.

The television text, let us say, is a "supertext" that consists of
the particular program and all the introductory and interstitial
materials—chiefly announcements and ads—considered in its
specific position in the schedule. From the perspective of the

schedule, television study encounters, under a new, perhaps unfamiliar but insistent aspect, the long-standing difficulty in both literary and film studies of ascertaining and conceptualizing the relations of determination between the text and its relevant context. The most relevant context for the analysis of form and meaning of the "television text" consists of its relation to the schedule, that is, to the world of television, and second, of the relation of the schedule to the structure and economics of the workweek of the general population.

Advertising, and its attendant purpose and ideology, must be given its proper place as the central mediating discursive institution that links these two levels of textual determination. Advertising regulates the exchange between general processes of production and consumption—indeed, it is a discourse that *works* to articulate one with the other. In the early days of television, sponsors controlled the program "environment" by literally producing it through their advertising agencies. Today the network licenses programming from independent suppliers and sells time within and between those programs to advertisers. Within this system, the program must provide a suitable "environment" for the commercial message. Basically, advertisers' demand for viewers is the fundamental condition of a program occupying a particular slot in the schedule. The time sold to advertisers on U.S. television in 1982–83 was worth about $12 billion—more than three times the domestic theatrical box office.

Looked at broadly, we might say that the text of television, the *megatext*, as distinguished from the *supertext*, consists of everything that has appeared on television. No doubt this notion is unwieldy from a practical standpoint. However, linked to the concept of the *schedule*, it enables an enormously illuminating representative reduction of the scope and history of this comprehensive text. The history of the text of television can be made significantly available by a study of the logic and organization of the slots and formats that compose the framework of the television schedule. The schedule organizes the terms of television's disparate programming in the overall economy of the television world—achieving a profitable balance of news and entertainment, comedy and drama, talk and action, variety and monotony, games and indictments, movies and serial forms. The selection and arrangement of these program types, night by night, week by week, year by year, through the competitive strategies of the networks, compose the more or less orderly megatext of television. The schedule, we might say, *represents* the comprehensive text of television. The discursive unities, such as they are, of the single program, the genre, the series, are at the same time significantly dispersed and constrained by the strategies and determinations of the weekly schedule. An analysis of the schedule would allow us to identify the main lines of television programming—the rise and fall of genre, formats, personalities, the migrations and initiations of form—and to begin the process of charting the terms and contours of an institutional, as well as social, history of television. I mean then to put the analysis of the history, logic, and form of the schedule on the new agenda of contemporary television theory.

One of the central axes around which the form of the television schedule turns, from beginning to present, is the balance between freestanding, individual programs and the various forms of sequencing that we might call television *seriality*. Seriality in its various versions orders and regulates television programming—from daily news and talk shows through the typical weekly sequencing of prime-time entertainment programs. Indeed, serial form is the paradigmatic form of television programming and requires an analysis of its historical determinations and discursive functions.

Serial formats, sitcoms, variety and game shows—mostly borrowed from radio—were important to the television schedule in the early fifties. The development, and then elimination, of a new television form—the anthology drama—can serve as a way into the complicated problem of interpreting the dramatic form of television texts and the transformations of discursive authority by which they were sustained. Live dramas, sponsored by a number of major American corporations and originating from New York, were an important part of television up through the 1955–56 season. The circumstances which led to their replacement, and to the inauguration of serialized drama, indicate something of the function of seriality in the world of television.

Aesthetically, as Barnouw points out, the shift from anthology to serial form signaled a shift from dialogue to action, from intimate psychology to standardization of story and formularization of character type. Institutionally, serialization meant predictability and efficiency. The anthology approach, Barnouw argues, so dependent on New York writers with their codes of theatrical naturalism, resulted in a variable form often at odds in terms of topic and treatment with the interests of the sponsors. The displacement of an author-based dramatic form to a producer-based mode, organized around the conventions of formula, coincided with the industry's need for standardization and increased production capacity and offered the occasion for a realignment of network and sponsor interests. Moreover, film serials, as compared to *live* television, had specific advantages: flexibility of scheduling across time zones and the existence of texts which could generate an aftermarket through syndication. The stage was set in 1955 for a new relationship between network television and Hollywood film studios.

Early telefilm series were produced by small independents. However, by 1955, as Robert Vianello shows in "The Rise of the Telefilm and the Network Hegemony Over the Motion Picture Industry," television penetration was about 60 percent of U.S. households, advertising revenues were over $300 million, and costs of telefilm production had risen to $80 million annually. Network television moved to consolidate its position with respect to program suppliers and sponsors. In the competitive market for telefilm production, the networks instituted a policy of deficit financing—advancing only a percentage of the total cost of production, with the effect of giving a business advantage to large, well-capitalized enterprises that could afford to wait for profit from syndication. The major film companies—Hollywood—needed television in order to amortize studio costs in the post-Paramount period, and in the midfifties in fact entered the field in an intensive way. The networks sought in the same period to replace the sponsor-financed mode of program production with a system of selling spots, a system that tended to give television a distinctive, new, and more profitable institutional autonomy. The result was the introduction in 1955–56 of studio-produced serial dramas—like Warner's television Westerns—beginning the Majors' long-term investment in the serial form. By the midfifties, the film and television industries consolidated production arrangements which installed and secured the institutional place of serial form in television programming.

This industrial transformation led to a specific form of textual order sustained by a complex mode of discursive authority. Conventions of series formulae initiated and governed television form, but not in the same ways that film genres generated and governed film form. Television conventions arose from a specific and complex intra-institutional negotiation among four parties: the network, the movie studio as the producer *per se*, the advertisers, and the audience. In the end, the form of the television serial is determined by the networks' interest in reaching the mass audience in a way and through a medium determined by the purposes of advertisers.

In a sense, the network is basically a relay in a process of textualizing the interaction of audience and advertiser. The audience is active in the textual negotiation not directly by what it wants, but through the figure of what is wanted of it. Television is a discourse conducted in the name of the audience but—through the medium of money—it proceeds on the power of the corporation and the authority of the commodity. What drives and shapes television form is a set of manufactured objects that can efficiently be advertised on national television—chiefly, food, toiletries, cars, medicines, and soaps—products intimately linked to the ongoing biological and social maintenance of the subject and the family unit in time through the life cycle. The discursive authority, then, that generates and sustains television seriality is, in an extended sense, the complex, dispersed figure of the *network*, and as such is extended in space to the subjects that it addresses and is extended in time to cover the habitual, socially formulated, requirements of subject maintenance. Television's serial forms serve to continue the subject along the itinerary of habituated consumption.

THE MADE-FOR-TELEVISION MOVIE

The study of feature-length movies as they are deployed on prime-time network television offers a more contemporary perspective on the differences between the institutional and discursive relations of the two media. Specifically, it opens a perspective onto the form and function of a relatively stable format—that of the freestanding, autonomous program—in television schedules composed chiefly of serial forms, and it can serve as a window on the changing economic and cultural determinants of popular forms of feature-length dramatic entertainment. In this respect, movies continue the role of anthology drama in television's prime-time schedule.

The history of movies on network television is characterized by several rapid, significant transformations.[2] First introduced on the NBC network in 1961, the (theatrical) movie became part of the prime-time schedules of all three networks in 1965.

By 1968, a movie was scheduled each night of the week, and in 1973, the networks' movies competed head to head four nights a week. By the midsixties, with the depletion of the inventory of theatrical films and with Hollywood demanding higher and higher licensing fees, the networks implemented a counter-strategy—the made-for-television movie.

The Hollywood theatrical movie has a form determined by its intended release in theaters. It is characterized by a certain "theatrical" approach to story, casting, budget, look, etcetera. Television—network and later syndication—was the last stop in the domestic distribution chain for such a form of film. By contrast, the made-for-television movie is a form specific to television—it is conceived for and premiered on network television. That is, it is a new entertainment form designed for the particular requirements and audiences of network television. The introduction of the two-hour telemovie seemed, in part, to substitute for the older form, but in doing so served to reaffirm the continuing importance of the two-hour autonomous film experience in the television schedule.

Original production of made-for-television movies became feasible in the late sixties when, in relation to their power to draw an audience, they became cheaper than licensing theatrical films. The first regular television movie was introduced in 1966; two years later (1968) all three networks showed them; and in 1972, all three networks scheduled more original made-for-television movies (about 100) than theatrical films. The new format had quickly become a strategic programming tool in restructuring television's relations with movie studios, and at the same time had become an important part of networks' competition with each other. Within six seasons, the made-for-television movie became the dominant two-hour fictional entertainment form on television. Theatrical movies, though currently under pressure from pay television, have nevertheless maintained a strong position. In the 1982–83 season, the networks showed about 180 movies, 80 of them theatricals. Nielsen reported, in November 1982, that "feature films" (which include both theatricals and made-fors) were the most popular television fare (compared to "situation comedy," "adventure," etc.) and they attracted the highest numbers of women in two age categories especially important to advertisers: 18–34 and 35–54.[3]

As in previous years, theatrical films and made-for-television movies continue to play distinctly different roles in the prime-time network schedule and have established distinctly different relations to their audiences. During the 1982–83 season, approximately two-thirds of the theatrical movies played on a Friday, Saturday, or Sunday. Indeed, Sunday was the only day of the week where theatricals outnumbered made-fors. Five nights a week, made-fors outnumbered theatricals (basically, Thursday was not a movie night). Heaviest scheduling of made-fors was, in order, on Monday, Tuesday, and Wednesday, though Sunday was also strong. Movies, of any kind, figured least prominently on Thursday, Friday, and Saturday. The heaviest movie night (for any kind) was Sunday, followed by Monday. Moreover, movie types (genres) seem to have been scheduled in certain positions during the week: horror movies on Friday, Saturday, Sunday; biographies on Monday and Tuesday; fantasy on Sunday, etcetera.

The audiences for movies on television have distinct though variable demographic profiles. Though each network differs as to the composition of its general audience, and indeed as to the audience for its movies—and though audience composition for movies varies according to day of the week, program type, etcetera—we can say, nevertheless, that a general profile emerges. Chiefly, it is this: the network audience for theatrical movies is much more balanced by gender than is the audience for made-for-television movies. Within the adult network-viewing population (18+), the proportion of female to male viewers for theatrical films in the 1982–83 season was nearly equal; in marked contrast, the adult audience (18+) for made-for-television movies was distinctly female (on average, 52 percent of the made-fors audience was female [18+] and 34 percent male [18+]). Similarly, there were differences in the age mix of the audience for the two types of movies. Women made up a greater part of the "made-for" audience for all networks in all age categories; made-fors had a greater percentage of younger viewers (in the 18–54 category) than theatricals; theatricals had a greater percentage of their audience in the 55+ category, and older men watching theatrical movies outnumbered older women. In sum, there are distinct television audiences for different movie formats, and such differences are both adapted to and manipulated by the producers of the television supertext.

Women comprise, statistically, and perhaps culturally, the most important part of the audience for those movie forms designed specifically for television. Presumably, such an orientation toward women maximizes the size of the television world. Indeed, during the 1982–83 season, on an average, made-for-television movies drew larger ratings and audience share points than did theatrical films—typically an audience of 14 million households. The made-for-television movie is thus a program format that efficiently addresses and reaches commercially significant segments of the television audience, namely, the audience that uses products advertised on national television.

The made-for-television narratives fall into various genres (drama, comedy, crime-mystery, biography, etc.) though chiefly they are variants of the family melodrama. Of course, they have a particular inflection—focusing in the 1982–83 season on the dynamic, and the danger, of the dissolution of the domestic social unit—either the couple or the nuclear family. In this regard, the television movie relates, though in a different mode, and in specific dramatic ways, to the long tradition of family serial drama on television. In its most popular instances the format performs its social work by providing the audience flexible, dialectical terms with which to negotiate the tension between the advantages of personal freedom and the virtues of moral and familial restraint. As a format, in other words, it rests its economic viability on the representation of suffering and redemption in the family—that is, within the register and on the site of its reception.

To summarize then—the scheduling of movies on network television follows certain patterns: movies are distributed unevenly through the days of the week: theatricals and made-fors tend to be segregated and are clustered by sets in certain parts of the week, etcetera. These patterns indicate a distinctive strategy for organizing the week, and presumably the season as a whole, in ways that address the distinctive interests and preferences of the audience and its movement into and through the workweek. In general, by considering the transformation of the role of movies on television and the appearance of a new form specific to television, we can see the evolution of the links between program type, the pattern of its scheduling, the character of the television audience, and the advertiser's perception of new or significant agencies and aptitudes for extended consumption.

THE FORM OF TELEVISION'S DISCURSIVE ECONOMY

Practically, in order to construct an analytic framework for considering an "economy of the television supertext" in the way we have proposed, it is necessary to consider the formal and semiotic relation of the program proper to the series of ads interpolated into the structure of the program. It is one of the traditional commitments of network programming to try to secure a loyal flow of audience attention through the prime-time hours, warding off potential defections through strategies of continuity. How then can the effect of commercial interruptions be handled so as to maintain program and schedule flow? The problem becomes especially acute when we consider not only the abrupt breaks of narrative, but also the marked alteration of narrative voice, from third person in the program, to first-person address in the ad.

The discursive form of the television supertext, its mode of linking program and ad, works to effect a series of unifying symbolic exchanges at two levels. We might suppose at this early stage, for example, that program and ad are linked formally as question and answer and psychologically as lack and liquidation. In this "model," the story's problem and its resolution are answered, if only by implication, by the presentation of an interpolated microstory, an ad, in which a similar difficulty is resolved by an object. Though interruptive, the ad, in its role as agent of symbolic restitution for a lack in the narrative proper, constructs a kind of narrative pleasure that assures formal resolution and confers on the represented object the status of the good object.

More generally, at the second level, in "free" television the opportunity for viewing a television program is exchanged through a symbolic equation with the viewer's subjection to a call for consumption. That is, in "free" television, the general possibility of "entertainment" is exchanged for the willingness of the audience to be subjected to a view of something specific—the objects displayed in ads. Most viewers in America report that it is a fair price to pay. The literal circuit of exchange is closed when the viewer, through the relay of the represented object, purchases the actual object in whose price the invisible cost of the motivating ad is hidden. The actual commodity, then, is the ultimate referent of the television discourse. The discursive economy of the television supertext, in other words, actualizes a second exchange in another symbolic medium—money—in which the commodified object is treated as compensation for the effort of production in the day's work. In general, American television—however it presents itself—negotiates and justifies a particular linkage of sign and referent, money and commodity; ties the worlds of work and of entertainment together; and legitimates the social and economic order and the subject's relation to it, by interpolating the subject as a consumer freely and democratically participating in the free-market distribution of abundant social goods. Television presents and sustains consumption as an answer to the problems of everyday life. It articulates and, at the same time, dissolves the difference between the "supertext" and "supermarket."

Television's "textual economy" effects a current of *familiarity* between the television world—its personalities and formats—and the everydayness of the viewer's life. The circulation of a television star from a series to a made-for-television movie is a familiarizing device that extends and completes the self-determining power of the television institution, by inducing the audience to fully territorialize open slots in the schedule—slots that may previously, for example, have been occupied by theatrical films starring actors not otherwise visible on television. As a producer and distributor of feature-length drama, television is a powerful discursive institution that continuously works to construct the social imagination around suitable, recognizable, and familiar television personalities and narratives. In this it seeks to extend and complete the "world" of television. In this respect the displacement of theatrical movies by made-fors in the seventies is similar in function to the displacement of anthology drama by serial drama in the fifties.

The commercial development of television in the post-World War II years as a mechanism for reaching into the household represents a singularly significant moment in the development of American economy and culture. Through television, American business has represented, penetrated, and constructed the family with an eye to its aptitude for consumption and moved to complete its organization of the libidinal economy of the desiring and consuming subject. In the television age, consumption and social control have become linked. Television regulates the social order and offers a justification for it by inscribing the audience as consumer. The networks are one of the central mechanisms of modern consumption and of social discipline, working (as Foucault has suggested in other contexts) through the historical strategy of aligning and intermixing sexuality with the representation and consumption of objects. Television's serial and freestanding forms both repeat, though in different dramatic registers, the forms of everyday experience,

and have proved to be well suited to linking the consuming
subject with the system of production under multinational capitalism.

The specific project of a political economy of the television
megatext is to analyze the history and form of the schedule by
linking the world of television entertainment and the world of
work with the general mechanisms of circulation of capital and
commodity in Western industrialized societies. It is in this context that the analysis of serial forms, and their alternatives, in
the form of the schedule takes on particular significance. The
schedule, as it disposes and organizes the "supertext," is, let us
say, the chief institutional mediation between the worlds of
work and of entertainment. Modeling "television," then, along
the lines of the political economy of the television *megatext*
consists of elaborating a framework that links the statements
of social and psychical value specific to programs in diverse time
slots, and of particular audiences, to the processes of the
general economy. I have indicated schematically the centrality
of seriality, advertising, and of scheduling, to a comprehensive
account of the discursive order and social function of the television world.

It is in this general framework that a systematic approach to
television criticism could proceed—one that seeks to articulate
and explain the specific link between form, audience, schedule,
and mode of consumption. The description and analysis of the
political economy of the television megatext, in the sense
sketched here, coincides with one of the chief tasks of contemporary critical theory—analyzing and rethinking the relation of
economy, society, and television culture. So far as I can tell
now, a model of political economy alone provides the basis for
linking the form of programs to television's essential economic
function in the free-world supermarket.

NOTES

1. See, in particular, Michael Gurevitch et al., eds., *Culture, Society and the Media*
(London: Methuen, 1982) and Stuart Hall and Tony Jefferson, *Resistance
Through Rituals: Youth Subcultures in Post-War Britain* (London: Hutchinson,
1976).
2. See Douglas Gomery, "Television, Hollywood and the Development of

Movies Made-for-Television," in *Regarding Television: Critical Approaches*, ed. E. Ann Kaplan (Lanham, Md: University Publications of America, Inc., 1983).
3. This assessment of the audience is provided in the brochure, "The 1983 Nielsen Report on Television," A.C. Nielsen Co., 1983.

JOHN FISKE
AND JOHN HARTLEY

BARDIC TELEVISION

. . . The internal psychological state of the individual is not the prime determinant in the communication of television messages. These are decoded according to individually learned but culturally generated codes and conventions, which of course impose similar constraints of perception on the encoders of the messages. It seems, then, that television functions as a social ritual, overriding individual distinctions in which our culture engages, in order to communicate with its collective self (see Leach 1976, p. 45).

To encompass this notion, which requires that we concentrate on the messages and their language as much as on the institutions that produce them, and on the audience response as much as on the communicator's intentions, we have coined the idea of television as our own culture's *bard*. Television performs a "bardic function" for the culture at large and all the individually differentiated people who live in it. When we use the term *bard* it is to stress certain qualities common both to this multioriginated message and to more traditional bardic utterances. First, for example, the classically conceived bard functions as a *mediator of language*, one who composes out of the available linguistic resources of the culture a series of consciously structured messages which serve to communicate to the members of that culture a confirming, reinforcing version of themselves. The traditional bard rendered the central concerns of his day into verse. We must remember that television

renders our own everyday perceptions into an equally specialized, but less formal, language system.

Second, the structure of those messages is organized according to the needs of the *culture* for whose ears and eyes they are
intended, and not according to the internal demands of the
"text," nor of the individual communicator. Indeed the notion
of an individual author producing "his" text is a product of
literate culture. Barthes (1977) comments: "In ethnographic
societies the responsibility for a narrative is never assumed by a
person but by a mediator, shaman or relator whose 'performance'—the mastery of the narrative code—may possibly be
admired but never his 'genius.' The author is a modern figure, a
product of our society insofar as . . . it discovered the prestige
of the individual" (pp. 142–3). The real "authority" for both
bardic and television messages is the audience in whose language they are encoded.

Third, the bardic mediator occupies the *center* of its culture;
television is one of the most highly centralized institutions in
modern society. This is not only a result of commercial monopoly or government control, it is also a response to the culture's
felt need for a common center, to which the television message
always refers. Its centralization speaks to all members of our
highly fragmented society.

Fourth, the bardic voice is *oral*, not literate, providing a kind
of cementing or compensatory discourse for a culture which
otherwise places an enormous investment in the abstract, elaborated codes of literacy. These literate codes themselves provide a vast and wide-ranging—but easily avoided—cultural repertoire not appropriate to transmission by television.

Fifth, the bardic role is normally a positive and dynamic one.
It is to draw into its own central position both the audience
with which it communicates and the reality to which it refers.
We have tried to articulate this positive role by means of the
term *claw back*. The bardic mediator constantly strives to claw
back into a central focus the subject of its messages. This
inevitably means that some features of the subject are emphasized rather than others. For example, nature programs will
often stress the "like us-ness" of the animals filmed, finding in
their behavior metaphoric equivalences with our own culture's
way of organizing its affairs. It is this very characteristic of
claw back that enables the converse function also to be performed. If a subject *cannot* be clawed back into a socio-central
position the audience is left with the conclusion that some point

in their culture's response to reality is inadequate. The effect is to show, by means of this observed inadequacy, that some modification in attitudes or ideology will be required to meet the changed circumstances.

Sixth, the bardic function, appropriately, has to do with *myths*. . . . These are selected and combined into sequences that we have called *mythologies*. Since mythologies operate at the level of latent as opposed to manifest content, of connotation as opposed to denotation, their articulation does not have to be consciously apprehended by the viewer in order to have been successfully communicated.

In fact, mythologies can often be thought of in terms of a seventh characteristic shared by bardic television utterances and more traditional ones. They emerge as the *conventions* of seeing and knowing, the *a priori* assumptions about the nature of reality which most of the time a culture is content to leave unstated and unchallenged. It is in respect of this characteristic of its messages that we described the television medium as conventional earlier.

As Williams (1975) has pointed out in a slightly different context, conventions of this kind are not abstract, "they are profoundly worked and reworked in our actual living relationships. They are our ways of seeing and knowing, which every day we put into practice, and while the conventions hold, while the relationships hold, most practice confirms them" (pp. 15–16). Our "actual living relationships" are largely those which function through language, which are directed outside our "selves," and which we establish as members of a particular culture. One of the most potent vehicles by which these organizing conventions are "profoundly worked and reworked" is of course the television medium.

We suggest that the function performed by the television medium in its bardic role can be summarized as follows:

1. To *articulate* the main lines of the established cultural consensus about the nature of reality (and therefore the reality of nature).

2. To *implicate* the individual members of the culture into its dominant value-systems, by exchanging a status-enhancing message for the endorsement of that message's underlying ideology (as articulated in its mythology).

3. To *celebrate*, explain, interpret and justify the doings of the

culture's individual representatives in the world out-there; using the mythology of individuality to claw back such individuals from any mere eccentricity to a position of socio-centrality.

4. To *assure* the culture at large of its practical adequacy in the world by affirming and conforming its ideologies/mythologies in active engagement with the practical and potentially unpredictable world.

5. To *expose*, conversely, any practical inadequacies in the culture's sense of itself which might result from changed conditions in the world out-there, or from pressure within the culture for a reorientation in favor of a new ideological stance.

6. To *convince* the audience that their status and identity as individuals is guaranteed by the culture as a whole.

7. To *transmit* by these means a sense of cultural membership (security and involvement).

These seven functions are performed in all message sequences of the television discourse; successful *communication* takes place when the members of the audience "negotiate" their response to these functions with reference to their own peculiar circumstances. Just as the message is multi-originated, so the audience response is "multi-conscious"—it apprehends the various levels and orders of the discourse simultaneously and without confusion (see Bethell 1944, p. 29).

However, television's colossal output in fact only represents a selection from the more prolific utterances of language in general within our culture, and thus bears a metonymic relationship to that language. As a result its messages tend to assume the further characteristic that we have stressed, namely that of *socio-centrality*. The bardic mediator tends to articulate the negotiated central concerns of its culture, with only limited and often over-mediated references to the ideologies, beliefs, habits of thought and definitions of the situation which obtain in groups which are for one reason or another peripheral. Since one of the characteristics of western culture is that the societies concerned are class-divided, television responds with a predominance of messages which propagate and represent the dominant class ideology. Groups which can be recognized as having a culturally validated but subordinate identity, such as the young, blacks, women, rock-music fans, etc., will receive a greater or lesser amount of coverage according to their approximation to the mythology of the bourgeois.

RITUAL CONDENSATION

In anthropological terms this bardic function of the television medium corresponds to what is called *ritual condensation*. Ritual condensation is the result of projecting abstract ideas (good/bad) in manifest form on to the external world (where good/bad becomes white/black). Leach (1976, pp. 37–41) explains the process:

> By converting ideas, products of the mind (mentifacts), into material objects "out-there," we give them relative permanence, and in that permanent material form we can subject them to technical operations which are beyond the capacity of the mind acting by itself. It is the difference between carrying out mathematical calculations "in your head" and working things out with pencil and paper or on a calculating machine. (p. 37)

The projection of abstract ideas into material form is evident in such social activities as religious ritual. But the television medium also performs a similar function, when, for example, a program like *Ironside* converts abstract ideas about individual relationships between man and man, men and women, individuals and institutions, whites and blacks into concrete dramatic form. It is a ritual condensation of the dominant criteria for survival in modern complex society. Clearly in this condensed form individual relationships can be scrutinized by the society concerned, and any inappropriateness can be dealt with in the form of criticisms of the program. Hence *Ironside*'s ritual condensation of relationships is supplanted by *Kojak*'s, which is supplanted in turn by *Starsky and Hutch*. Each of these fictive police series presents a slightly different view of the appropriate way of behaving toward other people, and for a society which finds Starsky's boyish and physical friendship with Hutch appropriate, the paternal common sense of Ironside will emerge as old-fashioned.

The bardic function of ritual condensation occurs at what we have called the third order of signification, where the second-order myths cohere into sets or mythologies. To illustrate how this whole process manifests itself in the course of a single program, let us return to our *News at Ten* bulletin, broadcast in January 1976.

We have noted briefly how the mythology of the news can be discerned as an organizing principle beneath the first and second orders. In response, the myths appealed to in the second order cohere into two main categories: there are myths activated in this bulletin which deal with our apprehension of the macro-social or *secondary* social groups—institutional units such as the army, the government, the Department of Health, local authorities, trade unions. And there are myths dealing with *primary* social groups—the individual and domestic plane of the family, personal relationships and individual behavior. The relationships of the myths within each group, and particularly those between groups, set up a complex array of meanings at this third, ideological, order of signification, and it is in these relationships that we find the structure of the news—the form taken by its "conceptual movement."

Indeed, the relationship between the two main groups of myth is perceived as contradiction. The institutional mythology is presented in such a way as to produce a negative response in the audience: the mythology of the institutions is that although they are capable of decision, action, even glamour, they are at last ineffectual. Conversely, the mythology of individuals is presented in such a way as to affirm and confirm the primacy and adequacy of individual actions and relationships even when these may be operating on behalf of institutions. A man can be presented as adequate, even when he is a soldier in an army that is presented as inadequate and unable (ultimately) to cope.

However, there is an obvious sense in which a national news program must deal more extensively with institutions than with individuals. Individuals are generally presented as functions of their institutional status. There is thus a constant dialectical interaction between the two mythologies, whose contradictions generate a tension which needs to be resolved, and to which we shall return.

HERE IS THE NEWS

The news opens with Andrew Gardner, the newsreader, reporting a government decision to send an army group—the Special Air Service (SAS)—to resolve a macro-social problem in Northern Ireland. Peter Snow, the ITN defense correspondent, immediately personalizes the move:

> Mr. Wilson is taking a carefully calculated risk . . .

This is not merely because elite individuals can be metonymically representative of lesser mortals (see Galtang and Ruge

1973, p. 66), but also because the journalistic code takes account of the primacy of individuals; thus responding to and reaffirming the dialectic of the mythologies: what happens out-there is only a large-scale version of a generally available personal experience—a game of skill.

However, Snow's main task is to establish an identity for the then relatively unknown SAS, whose reality is in fact far from central to our culture, for it embodies many of the values that we consciously disown. But, says Snow, Mr. Wilson is

> putting into South Armagh the men who have the reputation, earned behind enemy lines in Indonesia, Malaya and other recent wars, for individual toughness, resourcefulness and endurance. They've been, not entirely of their own choosing, the under-cover men. The men whose presence has struck fear into the heart of the enemy.

The institution (the SAS) is defined in terms of the men, whose toughness, resourcefulness and endurance is *individual*. Furthermore, as a myth, the "reputation earned behind enemy lines" is common to many a movie or paperback: the commando/marine/"True Brit"/*Guns of Navarone/Green Berets* myth. Here all that changes is the signifier for this well-known myth. The SAS is now made to signify it, even though the notion of "enemy lines" is devoid of meaning in the Northern Ireland context.

Mr. Wilson, on behalf of the government, plays his game of skill by weighing up the mythic qualities and their likely effect, against what Snow calls the political "risk." When Snow comes to describe what the SAS will do, we are, as it were, taken behind the scenes at Battalion HQ, and initiated into the logistical minutiae of detailed planning:

> In the next day or two, probably a small group, maybe half a dozen, will fly across to Armagh to have a hard long look at the ground. Another small group will join one of the army regiments to liaise with them and watch how they go about their patrolling. All this will be reported back to SAS headquarters in Hereford, where a special squad of about fifty men—very much fewer than the whole of the SAS—will have been doing a period of intensive anti-IRA training. As soon as they're ready, they'll fly to Ulster. They'll be in full uniform, not disguised as civilians. That means SAS sandcolored berets, camouflage jackets, with perhaps a glimpse of those SAS parachute wings that every one of them wears. They'll be working in groups of four; a leader in his midthirties, a radio operator, a medical expert and an explosives expert. They'll be operating in the countryside, not the towns,

gathering intelligence by hiding up for long periods—they can last for weeks in one place on starvation rations—and laying ambushes near the border if necessary. They'll be gathering the information and then acting on it.

We are bombarded with very precise information about the SAS, even to the age of their squad leaders. An effect of busyness and purpose is thus created. But at the same time, the object of all this activity is systematically avoided. In every case the action is aborted into formulaic and negating phrases. The SAS will be taking a "hard long look at the ground," they'll be "liaising," "watching," "reporting," "training," "working," "operating," "gathering intelligence," "hiding up," "surviving," and finally—"acting." At all times Snow is careful not to suggest that the SAS will actually *do* any of the terrible things on which their reputation is based; anything, in short, which would render their presence effective, even though that presence, we are reminded, has by itself "struck fear into the heart of the enemy." As Snow closes his piece with the words

> that's why they, the SAS, believe that if anyone can find the killers who strike by stealth, they can,

we are driven by the way the message itself is constructed toward the response "but they can't." But successful or not, it is enough for Snow to have made the SAS a culturally identifiable unit.

This does not mean, of course, that the language of the news is necessarily articulating uncritical enthusiasm for established myths in order to create an artificial cultural consensus. Even in Peter Snow's discourse there is enough contradiction among the various responses triggered to negate much of the confident tone of effective expertise, as we have seen. In his effort to claw the potentially deviant SAS back into socio-centrality, Snow has to deflect adverse responses. The currently unwelcome associations of their undercover role are such that he has to work hard: "They've been, *not entirely of their own choosing*, the undercover men." They are available to "shoot it out"—but only *"if necessary"*—with IRA gunmen. And their relationship with the ordinary soldier, who is far more socio-central as one of "our lads," needs very careful handling:

> That is why the government is *making it clear tonight* that the Special Air Service will *not* be doing *anything very much out of the ordinary*, but *just* doing it *perhaps* a *bit* better, *because of their training*, than the *average* soldier is *able* to.

Here two positive myths about the army—the "commando" and the "our-lads" myths—collide with such force that the discourse seems to lose all momentum. It *cannot* disguise the contradictions it has raised.

The Irish themselves need no such careful handling. While Snow is clawing the SAS into the center, he is by a tacit converse action pushing the Irish as the actual or potential enemy in the opposite direction. Here the method is negative, unstated, but later in the bulletin it emerges as a positively articulated attempt to signify the Irish as culturally deviant. . . . For now it is sufficient to notice the paradoxical effect of Snow's successful attempt to bring the SAS into line with other culturally validated myths about the army. The British army's cultural function now is not to invade, conquer, win wars or even to be in the killing business at all. Its cultural function for the last generation has been to set a brave, well-trained, technological face upon defeat. The SAS has been identified by Snow with central myths more usually applied to commandos, and its men have been identified as regular—if slightly better than average—army troops. Hence, according to the terms of the institutional third order of mythology, they must inevitably but paradoxically prove ineffective. And the mythology becomes self-fulfilling as Snow associates the SAS with known army myths at the expense of effectiveness. Having watched this bulletin, members of our culture were no doubt prepared for the subsequent inability of the SAS to change the situation in Northern Ireland.

Interestingly, the second main news story also has a militaristic slant. It concerns the Anglo-Icelandic fishing dispute known as the Cod War. Once again the individual is celebrated, this time in the shape of Captain Robert Gerken of the navy frigate *Andromeda*. His vessel has been in collision with the Icelandic coastguard vessel *Thor*, and he radios his own account to ITN. We can perhaps "translate" the captain's report as it comes in:[1]

> . . . my assessment was that we were
> —*expert judgement*
> gonna have a collision
> —*but cool-headed (deadpan)*
> and therefore at that stage
> —*decision maker*
> I ordered
> —*leader*

emergency full ahead
—*crisis language (war-film myths)*
and put port, er, rudder, full port rudder
—*but precise*
to try and swing my stern away from her stem as it was coming
er into my, towards my stern . ...
—*personal responsibility for "my" ship, but no emotion towards the enemy*
—*"it."*

Note how neatly "it" is identified as the aggressor, despite the apparently analytical style of reporting. But once again this individual mythology is contradicted by the institutional mythology, which knows that Britain is eventually going to lose the Cod War. Again, history proved this bulletin absolutely right: Britain did indeed lose. The knowledge of ultimate defeat is inherent in the subsequent interview with a naval "expert," Captain John Cox, who is asked to "explain" the rammings. He does so by "showing" with authoritative-looking if somewhat mystifying diagrams, as well as explanations, that the various collisions are not caused by politics, or history, or Icelanders, but by fate:

Now *should* er der, an Icelandic gunboat try, as is common practice, to get round the stern of a frigate to get at a trawler, *it'll find itself* coming into the suction area, and as it comes in and tries to slow down to get round the stern, *you can see what's happened;* it *loses* all maneuverability *and at that stage collision is absolutely inevitable . . . Today's I don't understand, and nor does Captain Gerken. It* appeared that they were . . . both ships were on a steady course . . . and *then suddenly* er the gunboat *Thor* turned towards, and *had it not been for Captain Gerken* going full ahead and altering his wheel hard a-port it *would have,* the *Thor would have* hit the *Andromeda* or even further er forward, if I can put it that way, in an unprotected place, and *would may've* gone straight through the engine room and straight through the dining room *like a knife through butter.*

The second order myths of technological skill on the part of the British captain, and of individual adventure at sea are highly visible at the surface, but they are negated by the third order of mythology, which makes them reactive to an arbitrary fate—in the convincing guise of Icelandic skippers who do not have the British reluctance to initiate action. Captain Cox's catalogue of possible disasters in the conditional tense serves at once to demonstrate the skill of the captain in avoiding them, and the inability of the institution he represents—be that the navy or the government—actually to admit to carrying out the violence that an armed frigate intrinsically represents. However, determination to act is not the missing ingredient here. What prevents aggressiveness on the part of the frigate in this bulletin is our culture. The newsreader has to assure us at the outset that

> no one aboard either ship was hurt.

When the collisions are described, we are told that a "small" hole was "put" in the Icelandic ship. It does seem that in reality British aggression is possible, but there appears to be a kind of cultural embargo on reports about it. ITN had a reporter, Norman Rees, on board the Icelandic gunboat at the center of this encounter, and he is able to give an eyewitness report of the maneuvers:

> At one stage the *Andromeda* had sailed within feet of *us*, her warning sirens blaring . . . I *saw* the *Andromeda* approaching *us* at high speed from the stern of the gunboat. It overtook *us* with both vessels on a converging course.

But he is *unable* to "see" the actual collision:

> *According to Thor's skipper* . . . *he* dropped his engine speed and tried to turn away to avoid a collision. But *he claims* that the frigate herself turned at the last moment so that *Andromeda*'s stern *would* side-swipe the gunboat's bow. The *Thor*'s deck shook under the force of the collision . . .

Rees's eyewitness language changes abruptly into reporter language, even though he must have been able to observe the changes in direction of each ship just as well as the skipper. He avoids having to say "she hit us" or "we hit her" by the apparently dramatic "the *Thor*'s deck shook," but that phrase, describing the effect of the collision and not the collision itself, also paradoxically serves to mask intentional aggression on the part of the British frigate. Rees's apparent blindness is culturally determined, however, since his report articulates perfectly the journalistic codes of impartiality, even at the expense of his own observation. Even so, his report might still be suspect, because of his position among the (deviant) Icelanders, so the newsreader "balances" it by announcing that the frigate's captain will "describe *exactly* what happened."

The contradictory mythologies of individuals versus institutions develops throughout the bulletin. There follows a series of home affairs stories; the government is presented as ineffectual because of its inability to "get its figures right" in both a story about the junior doctors' dispute with the Department of Health and a story about cut-backs in mortgages granted by local government. In the first story, the individual alibi is provided by the doctors' leader on the one hand, who presents himself as a fair and patient man faced with insuperable idiocy, and by ITN's own home affairs correspondent on the other hand, who presents himself in an investigatory role—teasing out government figures from a deliberately confused tangle. This theme of bungling statistics is clearly imposed on the material by the ITN scriptwriters: it is perceived as newsworthy to the extent that it shows government inefficiency.

The advertisements sandwiched into the bulletin play a major and positive role in asserting the primacy of individual relationships and action, and it is significant that they foreground women, as the focal point of families, and as the practical copers-with-life. The first advertisement responds to the institutional problems of the economy (which have just been featured) with an appeal to self-help—a needlecraft manual which enables the buyer to save money by her own action. This is the individual antidote to the third-order failure (despite second-order appearances) of our cultural endeavors out-there.

This pattern is reiterated throughout the second half of the news which concentrates on the bungling this time of foreign governments. At the very end, the tailpiece (which in this case does indeed wag the dog), inverts the customary emphasis and celebrates directly and without an obvious institutional peg an individual success story:

> Here at home a man who a few years ago had no job and what he calls no prospects has been named shepherd of the year . . . He's Bill Graham who's thirty-nine and he lost his arm after a motorcycle accident in his twenties. Now he looks after more than 1000 sheep . . . He went to see his present employer without much hope of getting the job of assistant shepherd. But he did get it and now he's chief shepherd but he's refused to take a pay raise. He takes part in regular competitions an' he's well-known around the country . . .

The man is filmed with his sheepdog, to whom he gives priority over the interviewer. Rather than answer a question put directly to him he whistles up the dog. His reality takes precedence over that of the (institutional) interviewer. He embodies many of the second-order signs of the news as a whole. His economic position, like the culture's, was bleak. But by individual perseverance, even when both his luck and his natural attributes were truncated, he secured the means to survive, and went on to newsworthy success. He is fully involved in his society despite his lonely task—he competes and is well known and respected for his skills. He is an iconic representation of the "truth" of the mythology of the individual, and of its ultimate primacy over the mythology of the institution; a specific man who is at the same time a metonymic representative of his culture's values and a metaphor for individual success. In Bill Graham, all three orders of signification are presented simultaneously. He is a walking mythology.

It is no accident that after this tailpiece the same headlines that were read out in a grim-faced, serious manner at the opening of the bulletin can now be repeated—almost verbatim—in a cheerful, smiling tone. Bill Graham has single-handedly set the world to rights.

NOTES

1. We have transcribed all statements verbatim, since some apparently ungrammatical usage substantially modifies the meanings of messages. But without showing the corresponding visual images this transcription may appear to show unrehearsed interviewees, especially, at a disadvantage.

REFERENCES

Barthes, R. (1977) *Image-Music-Text*. London: Fontana.

Bethell, S. L. (1944) *Shakespeare and the Popular Dramatic Tradition*. St. Albans, Herts: Staples.

Galtang, J. and Ruge, M. (1973) "Structuring and Selecting News," in S. Cohen and J. Young (eds.) *The Manufacture of News*. London: Constable, pp. 62–72.

Leach, E. (1976) *Culture and Communication*. London: Cambridge University Press.

Williams, R. (1975) *Drama in a Dramatized Society*. London: Cambridge University Press.

HORACE NEWCOMB

TOWARD A TELEVISION AESTHETIC

Defining television as a form of popular art might lead one to ignore the complex social and cultural relationships surrounding it. In his book *Open to Criticism*, Robert Lewis Shayon, former television critic for *The Saturday Review*, warns against such a view.

> To gaze upon this dynamic complexity and to delimit one's attention to merely the aesthetic (or any other single aspect of it) is to indulge one's passion for precision and particularity (an undeniable right)—but in my view of criticism it is analogous to flicking a piece of lint off a seamless garment.
>
> The mass media are phenomena that transcend even the broad worlds of literature. They call for the discovery of new laws, new relationships, new insights into drama, ritual and mythology, into the engagement of minds in a context where psychological sensations are deliberately produced for nonimaginative ends, where audiences are created, cultivated and maintained for sale, where they are trained in nondiscrimination and hypnotized by the mechanical illusion of delight. When the symbols that swirl about the planet Earth are manufactured by artists who have placed their talents at the disposition of salesmen, criticism must at last acknowledge that "literature" has been transcended and that the dialectics of evolutionary action have brought the arts to a new level of practice and significance. [Boston, 1971, pp. 48–49]

Humanistic analysis, when used to explore aesthetic considerations in the popular arts such as television, can aid directly in that "discovery of new laws, new relationships, new insights into drama, ritual and mythology," which Shayon calls for. In doing so it is necessary to concentrate on the entertaining works themselves, rather than on the psychological effects of those works on and within the mass audience. In those areas the social scientific methodologies may be more capable of offering meaningful results. But we should also remember that most of the works we have dealt with are highly formulaic in nature, and if we think of formula, in John Cawelti's words, as "a model for the construction of artistic works which synthesizes several important cultural functions," then it is possible to see how the aesthetic point of view and the social scientific point of view might supplement one another in a fuller attempt to discover the total meaning of the mass media.

Television is a crucially important object of study not only because it is a new "form," a different "medium," but because it brings its massive audience into a direct relationship with particular sets of values and attitudes. In the previous chapter, where we examined works that are less formulaic, we should still be able to recognize the direct connection, in terms of both values and the techniques of presenting them, with more familiar television entertainment. In those newer shows, where the values may become more ambiguous, more individualized, we find an extension and a development of popular television rather than a distinct new form of presentation. The extension and development have demonstrated that even in the more complex series, popularity need not be sacrificed.

To the degree that the values and attitudes of all these shows are submerged in the contexts of dramatic presentation, the aesthetic understanding of television is crucial. We have looked closely at the formulas that most closely identify television entertainment. We have been able to see how those formulas affect what has been traditionally thought of as nondramatic entertainment or as factual information. We have determined some of the values presented in each of the formulas in terms of their embodiment in certain character types, patterns of action, and physical environment. In approaching an aesthetic understanding of TV the purpose should be the description and definition of the devices that work to make television one of the most popular arts. We should examine the common elements that enable television to be seen as something more than a transmission device for other forms. Three elements seem to be highly developed in this process and unite, in varying degree, other aspects of the television aesthetic. They are intimacy, continuity, and history.

The smallness of the television screen has always been its most noticeable physical feature. It means something that the art created for television appears on an object that can be part of one's living room, exist as furniture. It is significant that one can walk around the entire apparatus. Such smallness suits television for intimacy; its presence brings people into the viewer's home to act our dramas. But from the beginning, because the art was visual, it was most commonly compared to the movies. The attempts to marry old-style, theater-oriented movies with television are stylistic failures even though they have proven to be a financial success. Television is at its best when it offers us faces, reactions, explorations of emotions registered by human beings. The importance is not placed on the action, though that is certainly vital as stimulus. Rather, it is on the reaction to the action, to the human response.

An example of this technique is seen in episode twelve of Alistair Cooke's *America: A Personal History*. In order to demonstrate the splendor of a New England autumn, Cooke first offers us shots of expansive hillsides glowing with colored trees. But to make his point fully he holds a series of leaves in his hand. He stands in the middle of the forest and demonstrates with each leaf a later stage in the process from green to brown, stages in the process of death. The camera offers a full-screen shot of Cooke's hand portraying the single leaves. The importance of this scene, and for the series, is that Cooke insists on giving us a personal history. We are not so much concerned with the leaves themselves, but with the role they play in Cooke's memories of his early years in America. To make his point immediate, he makes sure that we see what he wants us to see about the autumnal color. The point about the process of death is his, not one that we would come to immediately, on our own, from viewing the leaves.

Commenting on the scene, Cooke praised his cameraman, Jim McMillan. It was McMillan, he said, who always insisted on "shooting for the box," or filming explicitly for television. Such filming is necessary in the series if Cooke's personal attitudes are to be fully expressed visually as well as in his own prose. (Alistair Cooke, concluding comments at a showing of episode twelve of *America: A Personal History* at the Maryland Institute College of Art, Baltimore, Maryland, April 1973)

Such use of technique is highly self-conscious. More popular television, however, has always used exactly the same sense of intimacy in a more unconscious fashion. It is this sense that has done much of the transforming of popular formulas into something special for television. As our descriptions have shown, the iconography of rooms is far more important to television than is that of exterior locations. Most of the content of situation comedies, for example, takes place in homes or in offices. Almost all that of domestic comedy takes place indoors, and problems of space often lead to or become the central focus of the show. Even when problems arise from "outdoor" conflicts—can Bud play football if his mother fears for his safety—are turned into problems that can be dealt with and solved within the confines of the living room or kitchen.

Mysteries often take us into the offices of detectives or policemen and into the apartments and hideouts of criminals. In some shows, such as *Ironside*, the redesigning of space in keeping with the needs of the character takes on special significance. Ironside requests and receives the top floor of the police headquarters building. In renovating that space he turns it not only into an office but into a home as well. His personal life is thereby defined by his physical relationship to his profession and to the idea of fighting crime. He inhabits the very building of protection. He resides over it in a godlike state that fits his relationship to the force. The fact that it is his home also fits him to serve as the father figure to the group of loyal associates and tempers the way in which he is seen by criminals and by audience. Similarly, his van becomes an even more confined space, also a home, but defined by his handicap. It is the symbol of his mobile identity as well as of his continued personal life.

Such observations would be unimportant were it not for the fact that as we become more intimately introduced to the environment of the detective we become equally involved with his personality. It is the character of the detective, as we have seen, that defines the quality of anticrime in his or her show. The minor eccentricities of each character, the private lives of the detectives, become one of the focal points of the series in which they appear. It is with the individual attitudes that the audience is concerned, and the crimes are defined as personal affronts to certain types of individuals.

Nowhere is this emphasis more important than in the Westerns. In the Western movie, panorama, movement, and environment are crucial to the very idea of the West. The films of John Ford or Anthony Mann consciously incorporate the meaning of the physical West into their plots. It may be that no audience could ever visually grasp the total expanse of land as depicted in full color, but this is part of the meaning of the West. The sense of being overwhelmed by the landscape helps to make clear the plight of the gunfighter, the farmer, the pioneer standing alone against the forces of evil.

On television this sense of expansiveness is meaningless. We can never sense the visual scope of the Ponderosa. The huge cattle herds that were supposed to form the central purpose for the drovers of *Rawhide* never appeared. In their place we were offered stock footage of cattle drives. A few cattle moved into the tiny square and looked, unfortunately, like a few cattle. The loneliness of the Kansas plains, in the same way, has never properly emerged as part of the concept of *Gunsmoke*.

What has emerged in place of the "sense" of the physical West is the adult Western. In this form, perfected by television, we concentrate on the crucial human problems of individuals. One or two drovers gathered by the campfire became the central image of *Rawhide*. The relationship among the group became the focus. Ben Cartwright and his family were soon involved in innumerable problems that rose out of their personal conflicts and the conflicts of those who entered their lives. Themes of love and rebellion, of human development and moral controversy, were common on the show until its demise. On *Have Gun—Will Travel* Paladin's business card was thrust into the entire television screen, defining the meaning of the show as no panoramic shot could. This importance of the enclosed image is made most clear in *Gunsmoke*. The opening shots of the original version concentrated on the face of Matt Dillon, caught in the dilemma of killing to preserve justice. The audience was aware of the personal meaning of his expression because it literally filled the screen, and the same sorts of theme have always dominated the program content. Even when landscape and chase become part of the plot, our attention is drawn to the intensely individual problems encountered, and the central issue becomes the relationships among individuals.

This physical sense of intimacy is clearly based in the economic necessities of television production. It is far more reasonable, given budgetary restraints, to film sequences within permanent studio sets than on location, even when the Western is the subject. But certainly the uses of intimacy are no longer exclusively based on that restriction. The soap operas, most financially restricted of all television productions, have developed the idea from the time when audiences were made to feel as if they were part of a neighborhood gossiping circle until today, when they are made to feel like probing psychiatrists. Similarly, made-for-television movies reflect this concern and

are often edited to heighten the sense of closeness. A greater
sense of the importance of this concept is found in those shows
and series that develop the idea of intimacy as a conceptual tool.
It becomes an object of study, a value to be held. In such cases
the union of form and content leads to a sense of excellence in
television drama.

The situation comedies such as *All in the Family, Maude, Sanford and Son*, and *M*A*S*H* have turned the usual aspects
of this formula into a world of great complexity. As we have
seen, their themes are often directed toward social commentary. The comments can succeed only because the audience
is aware of the tightly knit structures that hold the families
together. It is our intimate knowledge of their intimacy that
makes it possible. Objects, for example, that are no more than
cultural signs in some shows become invested with new meanings in the new shows. In the Bunker home a refrigerator, a
chair, a dining table, and the bathroom have become symbolic
objects, a direct development from their use as plot device in
more typical domestic comedy. They have become objects that
define a particular social class or group rather than the reflection of an idealized, generalized expression of cultural taste.
They are now things that belong to and define this particular
group of individuals. Similarly, our knowledge of the characters
goes beyond a formulaic response. Jim Anderson, of *Father
Knows Best*, was a type, his responses defined by cultural expectation. Archie Bunker is an individual. Each time we see
him lose a bit of his façade we realize that his apparently one-
dimensional character is the result of his choice, his own desire
to express himself to the world in this persona. With his guard
down we realize that he cares about his wife, in spite of the fact
that he treats her miserably most of the time.

In the mini-series of the BBC the technical aspects of this
sort of intimacy have been used to explore the idea itself and
have resulted in moments of great symbolic power. In the
adaptation of Henry James's *The Golden Bowl*, for example, we
begin with a novel crucially concerned with problems of intimacy. The series is then filled with scenes that develop the idea
visually. Such a sequence occurs during the days before Adam
Verver asks Charlotte to be his wife. Though he does not
realize it, Charlotte had at one time been the mistress of his
daughter's husband, the Prince. She is considerably younger
than Verver, and in order to establish a claim for her marriage,
he suggests that they spend time together, in the most deco-

rous manner, in his country home and in Brighton. In the midst of rooms filled with candles, furniture, paintings, and ornaments, the camera isolates them. Even in the huge ornate rooms they are bound together, the unit of our focus. One evening as Charlotte turns out the lamps, pools of light illuminate them, circled in the large dark rooms.

In one of the most crucial scenes of this sequence the camera moves along the outside of an elegant restaurant. Through the rain, through the windows, couples are framed at dining tables. A waiter arrives at Verver's table as the camera stops its tracking motion. The couple begins to laugh; we hear them faintly as if through the actual window. Then, apparently at Verver's request, the waiter reaches across the table and closes the drapes. We are shut out of the scene, and we realize how closely we have been involved in the "action." We are made more aware of private moments. In the closing scene of the episode the camera movement is repeated. This time, however, Charlotte has agreed to the marriage and the couple is celebrating. Again we are outside. But as the episode ends, we remain with Verver and Charlotte, participating in their lamplit laughter.

Finally, this same motif is used in another episode. Charlotte and the Prince have again become lovers. They meet for a last time, realizing that their secret is known. The camera frames their hands, meeting in a passionate grip. It is like an embrace and it fills the entire screen. Suddenly the camera pulls back and the two people are shown in an actual embrace. Again, suddenly, the camera zooms out and the couple is seen from outside the window. It is raining again, as it was in Brighton, and a rapid torrent of water floods over the window, blurring the picture in a powerful sexual image.

Clearly, in the adaptation of a novel so concerned with matters of intimacy, the attempt has been to convey that concern with a set of visual images. In *The Waltons*, however, we are reminded that this visual technique parallels a set of values that we have found operating in popular television throughout our survey of formulas. Intimacy, within the context of family, is a virtue, and when *The Waltons* uses specific techniques to make us aware of intimacy, it is to call our attention not to the form, but to the idea, of the show.

In that series each episode closes with a similar sequence. John Boy sits in his room writing in his journal. He has learned the requirement of solitude for his work, and his room has become a sacred space into which no one else intrudes. Other children in the family must share rooms, but he lives and works alone in this one. At the close of each story he narrates for us the meaning that he has drawn from the experience. We see him through a window as his voice comes over the visual track in the form of an interior monologue. As he continues to talk, the camera pulls back for a long shot of the house. It sits at the edge of the forest like a sheltered gathering place. It conveys the sense of warmth and protection, and even when there has been strain among the members of the family, we know that they have countered it as they counter their social and financial problems and that they will succeed. John Boy's window is lighted, usually the only one in the otherwise darkened home. As his speech ends, his light also goes out. We are left with the assurance of safety and love, as if we have been drawn by this calm ending into the family itself.

This sense of direct involvement can be enhanced by another factor in the television aesthetic, the idea of continuity. The sort of intimacy described here creates the possibility for a much stronger sense of audience involvement, a sense of becoming a part of the lives and actions of the characters they see. The usual episodic pattern of television only gives the illusion of continuity by offering series consisting of twenty-six individual units. The series may continue over a period of years, revolving around the actions of a set of regular characters. As pointed out, however, there is no sense of continuous involvement with these characters. They have no memory. They cannot change in response to events that occur within a weekly installment, and consequently they have no history. Each episode is self-contained with its own beginning and ending. With the exception of soap operas, television has not realized that the regular and repeated appearance of a continuing group of characters is one of its strongest techniques for the development of rich and textured dramatic presentations.

This lack of continuity leads to the central weakness of television, the lack of artistic probability. We have seen that many shows now deal with important subject matter. Because the shows conclude dramatically at the end of a single episode, and because the necessity for a popular response calls for an affirmative ending, we lose sight of the true complexity of many of the issues examined. This need not be the case, however, for we have seen two ways in which television can create a necessary sense of probability which can enhance the exploration of ideas and themes.

Probability in television may come in two major ways. The

first is the one with which we are most familiar. We see the same characters over and over each week. Often it is this factor that is most frustrating in its refusal to develop probability among the characters. But in a series such as *All in the Family* this becomes an advantage, for the Bunkers continually encounter new experiences. Though most of the episodes are thematically related to the idea of Archie's bigotry, we have seen in analysis some of the ways in which reactions are changed. Some of the shifts may be starkly bitter, a strong departure for television comedy. Similarly, the continual introduction of new characters who appear on a regular basis allows the world to grow around the central family. Even the slight shifts in more formulaic shows, such as *Owen Marshall* or *Marcus Welby*, aid in this direction when the characters appear on one another's shows. The appearance is of a world of multiple dimensions.

Another sort of probability is made possible by the creation of continued series. The soap operas provide the key to this understanding, and even though they are distorted by their own stereotypical views, the values of the shows are expressed far more clearly because of the continuous nature of the programming. Even with the distortions the shows offer a value system that may be closer to that of the viewer than he or she is likely to find in prime-time programming.

The BBC productions, however, adaptations of novels and original historical re-creations, offer a much more rounded sense of probability. As with historical fiction and movies, these productions are interpretations. Anyone who has watched the TV versions of the great novels is aware that choices and selections have been made in the adaptation of one medium to another. In both cases the result has been the creation of a new work of art. The central innovative factor in these productions has been their refusal to be dominated by the hour-long time slot. They do not end in a single episode. They range from the twenty-six episodes of *The Forsyte Saga* to three- or five-week adaptations of other novels. In this way we are allowed a far more extensive examination of motivation, character, and event than we are in the traditional television time period. The extension of time allows for a fuller development of the idea of intimacy, for we are allowed a broader as well as a deeper look at individuals. The use of narrators to deal with compressed time has been highly effective, especially in *The Search for the Nile*.

These factors indicate that the real relationship with other media lies not in movies or radio, but in the novel. Television, like the literary form, can offer a far greater sense of density. Details take on importance slowly, and within repeated patterns of action, rather than with the immediacy of other visual forms. It is this sense of density, built over a continuing period of time, that offers us a fuller sense of a world fully created by the artist.

Continuity, then, like intimacy, is a conceptual as well as a technical device. It, too, grows out of popular television and finds its fullest expression in the newer shows. The third factor that helps to define the aesthetic quality of television is also essential to its less sophisticated formulas, for we have seen from the very beginning how television has been dependent on the uses of history for much of its artistic definition.

The importance of history to the popular arts has been carefully dealt with by John Cawelti in an essay, "Mythical and Historical Consciousness in Popular Culture" (unpublished essay, 1971). The root of this distinction, which Cawelti takes from myth theorists such as Mircea Eliade, lies in the perception of time. In the mythical consciousness "time is multidimensional. Since mythical events exist in a sacred time which is different from ordinary time, they can be past and present and to come all at the same time." For modern man, however, history is unilinear and moves "from the past, through the present, and into the future."

Within the popular arts one can discover a similar distinction, and as an example might compare two types of Westerns. Resembling the mythical consciousness is the Lone Ranger. "Though from time to time the audience is reminded that the Lone Ranger brought law and order to the West, the advance of civilization plays a negligible role in the hero's adventure. . . . Instead . . . the manner of presenting the saga of the masked hero reflects the multi-dimentional time of the mythical consciousness" (ibid., p. 12). The contrasting example is Owen Wister's *The Virginian* in which ". . . The symbols and agents of advancing civilization play a primary role in the story. Indeed, they are commonly a major cause of the conflicts which involve the hero" (ibid.).

Another type of modification occurs among works that might be grouped within the mythical dimension. It is this form that depends most strongly on a sense of shared cultural values. At times as the values themselves begin to change there must be a shift in expression.

... to achieve the mythical sense in its traditional form, the writer must create and maintain a highly repetitive almost ritualistic pattern. This is one reason why series characters like Deadwood Dick, the Lone Ranger, and Hopalong Cassidy in regularly issued publications or weekly programs have been such a successful format for popular formulas. But the potency of such ritual-like repetitions depends on the persistence of underlying meanings. In ancient societies the fixed patterns of myth reflected continuity of values over many generations. In modern America, however, one generation's way of embodying the mythical pattern in cultural conventions tends to become the next generation's absurdities. [Ibid., p. 5]

It is the sort of shift in expression defined here that is most important for the television formulas we have examined. Shifts in underlying meanings occur more frequently than in the past, and instead of the changing patterns of generational attitudes it is almost as if America discovers new sets of values overnight. There seems to be little sense of value consensus. In spite of this, television manages to entertain vast numbers of viewers with patterns of action and with characters who seem familiar to the cultural consciousness.

Our analyses have shown, however, that there is little resemblance, in terms of underlying meaning, between the Western or the mystery as we know them on TV and the forms from which they emerge in literature, cinema, and radio. Similarly, the creation of special versions of families, of certain types of doctors and lawyers, indicates a type of formula that can cut across value distinctions and definitions that might have been embodied in these various formulas at one time.

The television formula requires that we use our contemporary historical concerns as subject matter. In part we deal with them in historical fashion, citing current facts and figures. But we also return these issues to an older time, or we create a character from an older time, so that they can be dealt with firmly, quickly, and within a system of sound and observable values. That vaguely defined "older time" becomes the mythical realm of television.

The 1973 season premier of *Gunsmoke* offered us all the trappings of the mythic and historical Western. There was a great deal of "on location" film (a common practice for season openers of the show, which then returns to the studio for most of the season) so that the environment created its sense of agency. The central plot involved the stealing of white women by Comancheros, and all the traditional villains, heroes, good and bad Indians appeared. The dual focus of the show, however, forced us to consider a thoroughly contemporary version of the problem. In one conflict we were concerned with the relationship of an orphaned child and a saloon girl. In the end the problems are resolved as the saloon girl gives up her own way of life in order to stay on a lonely ranch with the child and her grandfather. In another conflict we were concerned with the relationships of another orphan, a young man raised as a criminal by the Comanchero leader. In the end this young man must kill his surrogate father, escape with a haughty white girl, and be killed by her as he waits to ambush Marshal Dillon. In his dying words he says that he must have been a "damned fool" to believe that the girl loved him enough to overcome her class snobbery and go away with him. The ambiguity here forced us to admit the degree of goodness in the two outlaws and the saloon girl, to condemn racism in many versions, and to come to terms with the problems of the orphans in a particular social setting.

Although such generational and class conflicts could arise in any time and in any culture, they are framed so as to call attention to our own social problems. What has happened is that we have taken a contemporary concern and placed it, for very specific reasons, in an earlier time, a traditional formula. There the values and issues are more clearly defined. Certain modes of behavior, including violent behavior, are more permissible.

Detectives serve the same function. Ironside's fatherlike qualities aid in the solution of problems traditionally associated with the detective role. They also allow him to solve personal problems which appear to be large-scale versions of our own. Either by working out difficulties within his own "family team" or by working with the criminal or by working at the root cause of the crime, he serves as an appropriate authority figure for a society in which authority is both scarce and suspect.

In an even more striking television adaptation of history, we see families in domestic comedy behave as if they lived in an idealized nineteenth-century version of America. And our doctors and lawyers are easily associated with that same period. As if our time somehow mythically coexisted with that of an easier age, we create forms that speak in opposition to their contemporary settings. We turn our personal and social problems over to the characters who can solve them, magically, in the space of an enclosed hour. We have, in effect, created a new mythic pattern. It cuts across all the formulas with which we are familiar, transforming them and changing their force. Our own history is the one we see in these types, not the history common to the formula itself. Our history is all too familiar and perplexing, so to deal with it we have created the myth of television.

This aspect of television formula has enhanced the popularity of many widely viewed and accepted shows. Doubtless, one reason for the popularity of these successful series is the way in which they deal with contemporary problems in a self-conscious manner. They are highly "relevant" programs. They purport to question many issues. Such questioning is obviated, however, by the very structure of the shows. Always, the problems are solved. In most cases they are solved by the heroic qualities of the central characters. Whether the heroics take on the sterner aspects of frontier marshals or the gentler visage of kindly doctors, the questions that we take to our television stars are answered for us satisfactorily.

As with the other factors we can turn again to the newer shows to see the fuller development of the aesthetic sense of the use of history. With *The Waltons* it is possible to see a number of linked factors with the sense of history at the core. We are admitted to a tightly knit circle; we are intimately involved with a family, the central symbol of television. Because we share experiences with them, watch the children grow and deal specifically with the problems of growth and development, there is a enhanced by a sense of community, of place and character, developed by different aspects of the series.

The great power of the program, however, develops out of its historical setting, the America of the Great Depression of the 1930s. The show demonstrates that the Depression period now carries with it a sense of mythical time. Frozen in the memory of those who experienced it, and passed on to their children, it is crucial to a sense of American cultural history, popular as well as elite. Indeed, it is crucial in part because it is the period that determines many contemporary American values. Much of the power of the show rises out of the realization that time was much like our own—fragmented and frightening.

Like other mythical times, this period becomes, for television, a frame in which to examine our own problems. But the Depression does not yet have the qualities of the Western or detective story. Because it was a time of failure more than of success, it does not purport to offer heroic solutions to the problems. The solutions are those of "common" people, and we know that we will see the same characters in the following week and that they will have other problems of a variety not found in Westerns, mysteries, doctor and lawyer shows. Consequently there is little of the sense of a world made right by the power of the wise father. In the larger sense the continuing social context of the show, the unresolved Depression, brings to bear the feeling of a larger ill that cannot be corrected by strong, authoritative figures such as detectives and marshals.

The productions in the Masterpiece Theater series go a step further and refuse to offer firm final solutions to many problems confronted in the content of the shows. Many of the works raise complex moral and social issues. In many of them the central characters, far from serving as paternalistic guides and problemsolvers, die in the end. History is used here both to insulate the audience from the immediate impact of these unresolved issues and to demonstrate, at the same time, that the issues are universal, unbounded by history and defined by the fact that we are all human.

Finally, in shows such as *All in the Family* the mythical frame dissolves and the history we see is our own. Again, the sense of strong sense of continuity to the series. The continuity is that history is strong and is a crucial part of the show. Our sense of class and economic reality, the distinctions among groups of persons within American society, allows us to confront problems directly. To a degree the comic context replaces the comforting removal of a more remote time. But by breaking the frame of the typical situation or domestic comedy, by questioning the very premises on which television is built, these shows force the audience into some sort of evaluation of its own beliefs. Their consistently high ratings indicate that the television audience is ready to become involved in entertainment that allows at least some of its members a more immediate examination of values and attitudes than is allowed by more traditional forms.

The interrelationships among these shows, the historical and comparative relationships between simpler and more sophisticated versions of formulas, indicate that television is in the process of developing a range of artistic capabilities that belies the former one-dimensional definitions. The novel can offer entertainment from Horatio Alger to Herman Melville, mysteries from Spillane to Dostoevski. The cinema can range from Roy Rogers Westerns to *Cries and Whispers*. So, too, can television offer its multiple audiences art from the least questioning, most culturally insulated situation comedy to *All in the Family*, from *Adventures in Paradise* to *The Search for the Nile*, from *The Guiding Light* to *The Forsyte Saga*.

In the past one did not speak of any television programs as "art." The aesthetic viewpoint was ignored, at times excluded from the process of understanding and explaining the extraordinarily powerful economic, social, and psychological effects of television. But it should no longer be possible to discuss "violence on television" without recognizing the aesthetic structure within which that violence occurs. It should no longer be possible to categorize the audience in terms of social and cultural values without examining the artistic context of those values as presented on television.

Intimacy, continuity, and a special sense of history are not the sole defining aesthetic attributes in the broad world of televised entertainment. Like many of the popular arts, television is the expression of multiple talents. Good writing, fine acting, technical excellence, and the sure hand of directors and producers go into making the best of television. Similarly, production necessities, overtaxed writers, formulaic actors, and imitative directors and producers can contribute to the worst of it. But intimacy, continuity, and history are devices that help to distinguish how television can best bring its audience into an engagement with the content of the medium. It is precisely because the devices are value expressions themselves, and because the content of television is replete with values, judgments, and ideas deeply imbedded in our culture that we must continually offer new and supplementary ways of observing, describing, and defining it. In this manner we can better understand how television is different from other media. We can begin to understand how it has changed the style and content of popular entertainment into forms of its own, and we can examine the ways in which those forms have changed within television's own development. For more than three decades we have viewed television from many perspectives without having come to grips with what it is for most of its audience. TV is America's most popular art. Its artistic function can only grow and mature, and as it does, so must its popularity.

DAVID THORBURN

TELEVISION MELODRAMA

> I remember with what a smile of saying something daring and inacceptable John Erskine told an undergraduate class that some day we would understand that plot and melodrama were good things for a novel to have and that *Bleak House* was a very good novel indeed.—Lionel Trilling, *A Gathering of Fugitives*

Although much of what I say will touch significantly on the medium as a whole, I want to focus here on a single broad category of television programming—what *TV Guide* and the newspaper listings, with greater insight than they realize, designate as "melodrama." I believe that at its increasingly frequent best, this fundamental television genre so richly exploits the conventions of its medium as to be clearly distinguishable from its ancestors in the theater, in the novel, and in films. And I also believe, though this more extravagant corollary judgment can only be implied in my present argument, that television melodrama has been our culture's most characteristic aesthetic form, and one of its most complex and serious forms as well, for at least the past decade and probably longer.

Melo is the Greek word for music. The term *melodrama* is said to have originated as a neutral designation for a spoken dramatic text with a musical accompaniment or background, an offshoot or spin-off of opera. The term came into widespread use in England during the nineteenth century, when it was appropriated by theatrical entrepreneurs as a legal device to circumvent statutes that restricted the performances of legitimate drama to certain theaters. In current popular and (much) learned usage, *melodrama* is a resolutely pejorative term, also originating early in the last century, denoting a sentimental,

Reprinted from *Television as a Cultural Force*, ed. Douglass Cater and Richard Adler, by permission of Praeger Publishers, Aspen Institute Program on Communications and Society, and the author. Copyright © 1976 by David Thorburn.

artificially plotted drama that sacrifices characterization to extravagant incident, makes sensational appeals to the emotions of its audience, and ends on a happy or at least a morally reassuring note.

Neither the older, neutral nor the current, disparaging definitions are remotely adequate, however. The best recent writings on melodrama, drawing sustenance from a larger body of work concerned with popular culture in general, have begun to articulate a far more complex definition, one that plausibly refuses to restrict melodrama to the theater, and vigorously challenges long-cherished distinctions between high and low culture—even going so far as to question some of our primary assumptions about the nature and possibilities of art itself. In this emerging conception, melodrama must be understood to include not only popular trash composed by hack novelists and film-makers—Conrad's forgotten rival Stanley Weyman, for example; Jacqueline Susann; the director Richard Fleischer—but also such complex, though still widely accessible, art-works as the novels of Samuel Richardson and Dickens, or the films of Hitchcock and Kurosawa. What is crucial to this new definition, though, is not the actual attributes of melodrama itself, which remain essentially unchanged; nor the extension of melodrama's claims to prose fiction and film, which many readers and viewers have long accepted in any case. What is crucial is the way in which the old dispraised attributes of melodrama are understood, the contexts to which they are returned, the respectful scrutiny they are assumed to deserve.[1]

What does it signify, for example, to acknowledge that the structure of melodrama enacts a fantasy of reassurance, and that the happy or moralistic endings so characteristic of the form are reductive and arbitrary—a denial of our "real" world where events refuse to be coherent and where (as Nabokov austerely says) harm is the norm? The desperate or cunning or spirited stratagems by which this escape from reality is accomplished must still retain a fundamental interest. They must still instruct us, with whatever obliqueness, concerning the nature of that reality from which escape or respite has been sought. Consider the episode of the Cave of Montesinos in *Don Quixote*, in which the hero, no mean melodramatist himself, descends into a cavern to dream or conjure a pure vision of love and chivalry and returns with a tale in which a knight's heart is cut from his breast and salted to keep it fresh for his lady. This is an emblem, a crystallizing enactment, of the process whereby our freest, most necessary fantasies are anchored in the harsh, prosaic actualities of life. And Sancho's suspicious but also respectful and deeply attentive interrogation of Quixote's dream instructs us as to how we might profitably interrogate melodrama.

Again, consider the reassurance-structure of melodrama in relation to two other defining features of the form: its persistent and much-contemned habit of moral simplification and its lust for topicality, its hunger to engage or represent behavior and moral attitudes that belong to its particular day and time, especially behavior shocking or threatening to prevailing moral codes. When critics or viewers describe how television panders to its audience, these qualities of simplification and topicality are frequently cited in evidence. The audience wants to be titillated but also wants to be confirmed in its moral sloth, the argument goes, and so the melodramatist sells stories in which crime and criminals are absorbed into paradigms of moral conflict, into allegories of good and evil, in which the good almost always win. The trouble with such a view is not in what it describes, which is often accurate enough, but in its rush to judgment. Perhaps, as Roland Barthes proposes in his stunning essay on wrestling, we ought to learn to see such texts from the standpoint of the audience, whose pleasures in witnessing these spectacles of excess and grandiloquence may be deeper than we know, and whose intimate familiarity with such texts may lead them to perceive as complex aesthetic conventions what the traditional high culture sees only as simple stereotypes.[2]

Suppose that the reassuring conclusions and the moral allegorizing of melodrama are regarded in this way, as *conventions*, as "rules" of the genre in the same way that the iambic pentameter and the rimed couplet at the end of a sonnet are "rules" for that form. From this angle, these recurring features of melodrama can be perceived as the *enabling conditions* for an encounter with forbidden or deeply disturbing materials: not an escape into blindness or easy reassurance, but an instrument for seeing. And from this angle, melodrama becomes a peculiarly significant public forum, complicated and immensely enriched because its discourse is aesthetic and broadly popular: a forum or arena in which traditional ways of feeling and thinking are brought into continuous, strained relation with powerful intuitions of change and contingency.

This is the spirit in which I turn to television melodrama. In this category I include most made-for-television movies, the soap operas, and all the lawyers, cowboys, cops and docs, the fugitives and adventurers, the fraternal and filial comrades who have filled the prime hours of so many American nights for the last thirty years.[3] I have no wish to deny that these entertainments are market commodities first and last, imprisoned by rigid timetables and stereotyped formulas, compelled endlessly to imagine and reimagine as story and as performance the conventional wisdom, the lies and fantasies, and the muddled ambivalent values of our bourgeois industrial culture. These qualities are, in fact, the primary source of their interest for me, and of the complicated pleasures they uniquely offer.

Confined (but also nourished) by its own foreshortened history and by formal and thematic conventions whose origins are not so much aesthetic as economic, television melodrama is a derivative art, just now emerging from its infancy. It is effective more often in parts of stories than in their wholes, and in thrall to censoring pressures that limit its range. But like all true art, television melodrama is cunning, having discovered (or, more often, stumbled upon) strategies for using the constraints within which it must live.

Its essential artistic resource is the actor's performance, and one explanation—there are many others—for the disesteem in which television melodrama is held is that we have yet to articulate an adequate aesthetics for the art of performance. Far more decisively than the movie-actor, the television-actor creates and controls the meaning of what we see on the screen. In order to understand television drama, and in order to find authentic standards for judging it as art, we must learn to recognize and to value the discipline, energy, and intelligence that must be expended by the actor who succeeds in creating what we too casually call a *truthful* or *believable* performance. What happens when an actor's performance arouses our latent faculties of imaginative sympathy and moral judgment, when he causes us to acknowledge that what he is doing is true to the tangled potency of real experience, not simply impressive or clever, but *true*—what happens then is art.

It is important to be clear about what acting, especially television-acting, is or can be: nothing less than a reverent attentiveness to the pain and beauty in the lives of others, an attentiveness made accessible to us in a wonderfully instructive process wherein the performer's own impulses to self-assertion realize

themselves only by surrendering or yielding to the claims of the
character he wishes to portray. Richard Poirier, our best theorist of performance, puts the case as follows: "performance . . .
is an action which must go through passages that both impede
the action and give it form, much as a sculptor not only is
impelled to shape his material but is in turn shaped by it, his
impulse to mastery always chastened, sometimes made tender and possibly witty by the recalcitrance of what he is working on."[4]

Television has always challenged the actor. The medium's
reduced visual scale grants him a primacy unavailable in the
theater or in the movies, where an amplitude of things and
spaces offers competition for the eye's attention. Its elaborate,
enforced obedience to various formulas for plot and characterization virtually require him to recover from within himself and
from his broadly stereotyped assignment nuances of gesture,
inflection, and movement that will at least hint at individual or
idiosyncratic qualities. And despite our failure clearly to acknowledge this, the history of television as a dramatic medium
is, at the very least, a history of exceptional artistic accomplishment by actors. The performances in television melodrama
today are much richer than in the past, though there were
many remarkable performances even in the early days. The
greater freedom afforded to writers and actors is part of the
reason for this, but (as I will try to indicate shortly) the far
more decisive reason is the extraordinary sophistication the
genre has achieved.

Lacking access to even the most elementary scholarly resources—bibliographies, systematic collections of films or
tapes, even moderately reliable histories of the art—I can only
appeal to our (hopefully) common memory of the highly professional and serious acting regularly displayed in series such as
*Naked City, Twilight Zone, Route 66, Gunsmoke, The Defenders, Cade's
County, Stoney Burke, East Side, West Side, The Name of the Game*, and
others whose titles could be supplied by anyone who has
watched American television over the past twenty or twenty-
five years. Often the least promising dramatic formulas were
transformed by vivid and highly intelligent performances. I
remember with particular pleasure and respect, for example,
Steve McQueen's arresting portrayal of the callow bounty
hunter Josh Randall in the western series, *Wanted: Dead or
Alive*—the jittery lean grace of his physical movements, the
balked, dangerous tenderness registered by his voice and eyes

in his encounters with women; the mingling of deference and menace that always enlivened his dealings with older men, outlaws and sheriffs mainly, between whom this memorable boy-hero seemed fixed or caught, but willingly so. McQueen's subsequent apotheosis in the movies was obviously deserved, but I have often felt his performances on the large screen were less tensely intelligent, more self-indulgent than his brilliant early work in television.

If we could free ourselves from our ingrained expectations concerning dramatic form and from our reluctance to acknowledge that art is always a commodity of some kind, constrained by the technology necessary to its production and by the needs of the audience for which it is intended, then we might begin to see how ingeniously television melodrama contrives to nourish its basic resource—the actor—even as it surrenders to those economic pressures that seem most imprisoning.

Consider, for example, the ubiquitous commercials. They are so widely deplored that even those who think themselves friendly to the medium cannot restrain their outrage over such unambiguous evidence of the huckster's contempt for art's claim to continuity. Thus, a writer in the official journal of the National Academy of Television Arts and Sciences, meditating sadly on "the total absence" of serious television drama, refers in passing to "the horrors of continuous, brutal interruption."[5]

That commercials have shaped television melodrama decisively is obvious, of course. But, as with most of the limitations to which the genre is subjected, these enforced pauses are merely formal conventions. They are no more intrinsically hostile to art than the unities observed by the French neoclassical theater or the serial installments in which so many Victorian novels had to be written. Their essential effect has been the refinement of a segmented dramatic structure peculiarly suited to a formula-story whose ending is predictable—the doctor will save the patient, the cop will catch the criminal—and whose capacity to surprise or otherwise engage its audience must therefore depend largely on the localized vividness and potency of the smaller units or episodes that comprise the whole.

Television melodrama achieves this episodic or segmented vividness in several ways, but its most dependable and recurring strategy is to require its actors to display themselves intensely and energetically from the very beginning. In its most characteristic and most interesting form, television melodrama will contrive its separate units such that they will have substantial independent weight and interest, usually enacting in miniature the larger patterns and emotional rhythms of the whole drama. Thus, each segment will show us a character, or several characters, confronting some difficulty or other; the character's behavior and (especially) his emotional responses will intensify, then achieve some sort of climactic or resolving pitch at the commercial break; and this pattern will be repeated incrementally in subsequent segments.

To describe this characteristic structure is to clarify what those who complain of the genre's improbability never acknowledge: that television melodrama is in some respects an *operatic* rather than a conventionally dramatic form—a fact openly indicated by the term *soap opera*. No one goes to Italian opera expecting a realistic plot, and since applause for the important arias is an inflexible convention, no one expects such works to proceed without interruption. The pleasures of this kind of opera are largely (though not exclusively) the pleasures of the brilliant individual performance, and good operas in this tradition are those in which the composer has contrived roles which test as fully as possible the vocal capacities of the performers.

Similarly, good television melodramas are those in which an intricately formulaic plot conspires perfectly with the commercial interruptions to encourage a rich articulation of the separate parts of the work, and thus to call forth from the realistic actor the full energies of his performer's gifts. What is implausible in such works is the continual necessity for emotional display by the characters. In real life we are rarely called upon to feel so intensely, and never in such neatly escalating sequences. But the emotions dramatized by these improbable plots are not in themselves unreal, or at least they need not be—and television melodrama often becomes more truthful as it becomes more implausible.

As an example of this recurring paradox—it will be entirely familiar to any serious reader of Dickens—consider the following generically typical episode from the weekly series, *Medical Center*. An active middle-aged man falls victim to an aneurysm judged certain to kill him within a few years. This affliction being strategically located for dramatic use, the operation that could save his life may also leave him impotent—a fate nasty enough for anyone, but psychologically debilitating for this unlucky fellow who has divorced his first wife and married a much younger woman. The early scenes establish his fear of aging and his intensely physical relationship with his young wife with fine lucid economy. Now the plot elaborates further complications and develops new, related central centers of interest. His doctor—the series regular who is (sometimes) an arresting derivation of his television ancestors, Doctors Kildare and Ben Casey—is discovered to be a close, longtime friend whose involvement in the case is deeply personal. Confident of his surgeon's skills and much younger than his patient, the doctor is angrily unsympathetic to the older man's reluctance to save his life at the expense of his sexuality. Next, the rejected wife, brilliantly played by Barbara Rush, is introduced. She works—by a marvelous arbitrary coincidence—in the very hospital in which her ex-husband is being treated. There follows a complex scene in the hospital room in which the former wife acts out her tangled, deep feelings toward the man who has rejected her and toward the woman who has replaced her. In their tensely guarded repartee, the husband and ex-wife are shown to be bound to one another in a vulnerable knowingness made in decades of uneasy intimacy that no divorce can erase and that the new girl-wife must observe as an outsider. Later scenes require emotional confrontations—some of them equally subtle—between the doctor and each wife, between doctor and patient, between old wife and new.

These nearly mathematic symmetries conspire with still further plot complications to create a story that is implausible in the extreme. Though aneurysms are dangerous, they rarely threaten impotence. Though impotence is a real problem, few men are free to choose a short happy life of potency, and fewer still are surrounded in such crises by characters whose relations to them so fully articulate such a wide spectrum of human needs and attitudes. The test of such an arbitrary contrivance is not the plausibility of the whole but the accuracy and truthfulness of its parts, the extent to which its various strategies of artificial heightening permit an open enactment of feelings and desires that are only latent or diffused in the muddled incoherence of the real world. And although my argument does not depend on the success or failure of one or of one dozen specific melodramas—the genre's manifest complexity and its enormous popularity being sufficient to justify intensive and respectful study—I should say that the program just described was for me a serious aesthetic experience. I was caught by the persuasiveness of the actors' performances, and my sympathies were tested by the meanings those fine performances released.

The credibility of the young wife's reluctant, pained acknowledgement that a life without sex *would* be a crippled life; the authenticity of the husband's partly childish, partly admirable reverence for his carnal aliveness; and, especially, the complex genuineness of his ambivalent continuing bonds with his first wife—all this was there on the screen. Far from falsifying life, it quickened one's awareness of the burdens and costs of human relationships.

That the plots of nearly all current television melodramas tend, as in this episode of *Medical Center*, to be more artificially contrived than those of earlier years seems to me a measure not of the genre's unoriginality but of its maturity, its increasingly bold and self-conscious capacity to *use* formal requirements which it cannot in any case evade, and to exploit (rather than be exploited by) various formulas for characterization. Nearly all the better series melodramas of recent years, in fact, have resorted quite openly to what might be called a *multiplicity principle*: a principle of plotting or organization whereby a particular drama will draw not once or twice but many times upon the immense store of stories and situations created by the genre's brief but crowded history. The multiplicity principle allows not less but more reality to enter the genre. Where the old formulas had been developed exhaustively and singly through the whole of a story—that is how they became stereotypes—they are now treated elliptically in a plot that deploys many of them simultaneously. The familiar character-types and situations thus become more suggestive and less imprisoning. There is no pretense that a given character has been wholly "explained" by the plot, and the formula has the liberating effect of creating a premise or base on which the actor is free to build. By minimizing the need for long establishing or expository sequences, the multiplicity principle allows the story to leave aside the question of *how* these emotional entanglements were arrived at and to concentrate its energies on their credible and powerful present enactment.

These and other strategems—which result in richer, more plausible characterizations and also permit elegant variations of tone—are possible because television melodrama can rely confidently on one resource that is always essential to the vitality of any artform: an audience impressive not simply in its numbers but also in its genuine sophistication, its deep familiarity with the history and conventions of the genre. For so literate an audience, the smallest departure from conventional expectations can become meaningful, and this creates endless chances for surprise and nuanced variation, even for thematic subtlety.

In his instructive book on American films of the '40s and '50s, Michael Wood speaks nostalgically of his membership in "the universal movie audience" of that time. This audience of tens of millions was able to see the movies as a coherent world, "a country of familiar faces, . . . a system of assumptions and beliefs and preoccupations, a fund of often interchangeable plots, characters, patches of dialog, and sets." By relying on the audience's familiarity with other movies, Wood says, the films of that era constituted "a living tradition of the kind that literary critics always used to be mourning for."[6]

This description fits contemporary television even more closely than it does those earlier movies, since most members of the TV audience have lived through the whole history of the medium. They know its habits, its formulas, its stars and its recurring character actors with a confident, easy intimacy that may well be unique in the history of popular art. Moreover, television's capacity to make its history and evolution continuously available (even to younger members in its universal audience) is surely without precedent, for the system of reruns has now reached the point of transforming television into a continuous, living museum which displays for daily or weekly consumption texts from every stage of the medium's past.

Outsiders from the high culture who visit TV melodrama occasionally in order to issue their tedious reports about our cultural malaise are simply not seeing what the TV audience sees. They are especially blind to the complex allusiveness with which television melodrama uses its actors. For example, in a recent episode of the elegant *Columbo* series, Peter Falk's adventures occurred onboard a luxury liner and brought him into partnership with the captain of the ship, played by Patrick Macnee, the smooth British actor who starred in the popular spy series, *The Avengers*. The scenes between Falk and Macnee were continuously enlivened not simply by the different acting styles of the two performers but also by the attitudes toward heroism, moral authority, and aesthetic taste represented in the kinds of programs with which each star has been associated. The uneasy, comic partnership between these characters—Falk's grungy, American-ethnic slyness contrasting with, and finally mocking, Macnee's British public school elegance and fastidiousness—was further complicated by the presence in the show of the guest villain, played by yet another star of a successful TV series of a few years ago—Robert Vaughn of *The Man From U.N.C.L.E.* Vaughn's character had something of the sartorial, upper-class *elan* of Macnee's ship's master but, drawing on qualities established in his earlier TV role, was tougher, wholly American, more calculating, and ruthless. Macnee, of course, proved no match for Vaughn's unmannerly cunning, but Falk-Columbo succeeded in exposing him in a climax that expressed not only the show's usual fantasy of working-class intelligence overcoming aristocratic guile, but also the victory of American versions of popular entertainment over their British counterparts.

The aesthetic and human claims of most television melodrama would surely be much weakened, if not completely obliterated, on any other medium, and I have come to believe that the species of melodrama to be found on television today is a unique dramatic form, offering an especially persuasive resolution of the contradiction or tension that has been inherent in melodrama since the time of Euripides. As Peter Brooks reminds us in his provocative essay on the centrality of the melodramatic mode in romantic and modern culture, stage melodrama represents "a popular form of the tragic, exploiting similar emotions within the context of the ordinary." Melodrama is a "popular" form, we may say, both because it is favored by audiences and because it insists (or tries to insist) on the dignity and importance of the ordinary, usually bourgeois world of the theater-goer himself. The difficulty with this enterprise, of course, is the same for Arthur Miller in our own day as it was for Thomas Middleton in Jacobean London: displacing the action and characters from a mythic or heroically stylized world to an ordinary world—from Thebes to Brooklyn—involves a commitment to a kind of realism that is innately resistant to exactly those intense passionate enactments that the melodramatist wishes to invoke. Melodrama is thus always in conflict with itself, gesturing simultaneously toward ordinary reality *and* toward a moral and emotional heightening that is rarely encountered in the "real" world.

Although it can never be made to disappear, this conflict is minimized, or is capable of being minimized, by television—and in a way that is simply impossible in the live theater and that is nearly always less effective on the enlarged movie-screen. The melodramatic mode is peculiarly congenial to television, its inherent contradictions are less glaring and damaging there,

because the medium is uniquely hospitable to the spatial con-
finements of the theater and to the profound realistic intimacy
of the film.

Few would dispute the cinema's advantages over the theater
as realistic medium. As every serious film theorist begins by
reminding us, the camera's ability to record the dense multiplicity of the external world and to reveal character in all its outer
nuance and idiosyncrasy grants a visually authenticating power
to the medium that has no equivalent in the theater. Though
the stage owns advantages peculiar to it's character as a live
medium, it is clearly an artform more stylized, less visually
realistic than the film, and it tests its performers in a somewhat
different way. Perhaps the crucial difference is also the most
obvious one: the distance between the audience and the actor in
even the most intimate theatrical environment requires facial
and vocal gestures as well as bodily movements "broader" and
more excessive than those demanded by the camera, which can
achieve a lover's closeness to the performer.

The cinema's photographic realism is not, of course, an un-
mixed blessing. But it is incalculably valuable to melodrama
because, by encouraging understatement from its actors, it can
help to ratify extravagant or intense emotions that would seem
far less credible in the theater. And although television is the
dwarf child of the film, constrained and scaled down in a great
many ways, its very smallness can become an advantage to the
melodramatic imagination. This is so because if the cinema's
particularizing immediacy is friendly to melodrama, certain
other characteristics of the medium are hostile to it. The extended duration of most film, the camera's freedom of movement, the more-than-life-sized dimensions of the cinematic
image—all these create what has been called the film's mytho-
poeic tendency, its inevitable effect of magnification. Since the
natural domain of melodrama is indoors, in those ordinary and
enclosed spaces wherein most of us act out our deepest needs
and feelings—bedrooms, offices, courtrooms, hospitals—the reduced visual field of television is, or can be, far more nourishing
than the larger, naturally expansive movie-screen. And for the
kind of psychologically nuanced performance elicited by good
melodrama, the smaller television screen would seem even
more appropriate: perfectly adapted, in fact, to record those
intimately minute physical and vocal gestures on which the art
of the realistic actor depends, yet happily free of the cinema's
malicious (if often innocent) power to transform merely robust

nostrils into Brobdingnagian caverns, minor facial irregularities into craterous deformities.

Television's matchless respect for the idiosyncratic expressiveness of the ordinary human face and its unique hospitality to the confining spaces of our ordinary world are virtues exploited repeatedly in all the better melodramas. But perhaps they are given special decisiveness in *Kojak*, a classy police series whose gifted leading player has been previously consigned almost entirely to gangster parts, primarily (one supposes) because of the cinema's blindness to the uncosmetic beauty of his large bald head and generously irregular face. In its first two years particularly, before Savalas' character stiffened into the macho stereotype currently staring out upon us from magazine advertisements for razor blades and men's toiletries, *Kojak* was a genuine work of art, intricately designed to exploit its star's distinctively urban flamboyance, his gift for registering a long, modulated range of sarcastic vocal inflections and facial maneuvers, his talent for persuasive ranting. The show earned its general excellence not only because of Savalas' energetic performance, but also because its writers contrived supporting roles that complemented the central character with rare, individuating clarity, because the boldly artificial plotting in most episodes pressed toward the revelation of character rather than shoot-em-up action, and because, finally, the whole enterprise was forced into artfulness by the economic and technological environment that determined its life.

This last is at once the most decisive and most instructive fact about *Kojak*, as it is about television melodrama generally. Because *Kojak* is filmed in Hollywood on a restricted budget, the show must invoke New York elliptically, in ingenious process shots and in stock footage taken from the full-length (and much less impressive) television-movie that served as a pilot for the series. The writers for the program are thus driven to devise stories that will allow the principle characters to appear in confined locations that can be created on or near studio sound-stages—offices, interrogation rooms, dingy bars, city apartments, nondescript alleys, highway underpasses, all the neutral and enclosed spaces common to urban life generally. As a result, *Kojak* often succeeds in projecting a sense of the city that is more compelling and intelligent than that which is offered in many films and television movies filmed on location: its menacing closeness, its capacity to harbor and even to generate certain kinds of crime, its watchful, unsettling accuracy as a custodian of the lists and records and documents that open a track to the very center of our lives. *Kojak's* clear superiority to another, ostensibly more original and exotic police series, *Hawaii Five-O*, is good partial evidence for the liberating virtues of such confinement. This latter series is filmed on location at enormous expense and is often much concerned to give a flavor of Honolulu particularly. Yet it yields too easily to an obsession with scenic vistas and furious action sequences which threaten to transform the program into a mere travelogue and which always seem unnaturally confined by the reduced scale of the television screen.

That the characters in *Kojak* frequently press beyond the usual stereotypes is also partly a result of the show's inability to indulge in all the outdoor muscle-flexing, chasing, and shooting made possible by location filming. Savalas's Kojak especially is a richly individuated creation, his policeman's cunning a natural expression of his lifelong, intimate involvement in the very ecology of the city. A flamboyant, aggressive man, Kojak is continually engaged in a kind of joyful contest for recognition and even for mastery with the environment that surrounds him. The studio sets on which most of the action occurs, and the many close-up shots in each episode, reinforce and nurture these traits perfectly, for they help Savalas to work with real subtlety—to project not simply his character's impulse to define himself against the city's enclosures but also a wary, half-loving respect for such imprisonments, a sense indeed that they are the very instrument of his self-realization.

Kojak's expensive silk-lined suits and hats and the prancing vitality of his physical movements are merely the outer expressions of what is shown repeatedly to be an enterprise of personal fulfillment that depends mostly on force of intellect. His intelligence is not bookish—the son of a Greek immigrant, he never attended college—but it is genuine and powerfully self-defining because he must depend on his knowledge of the city in order to prevent a crime or catch a criminal. Proud of his superior mental quickness and urban knowingness, Kojak frequently behaves with the egotistical flair of a bold, demanding scholar, reveling in his ability to instruct subordinates in how many clues they have overlooked and even (in one episode) performing with histrionic brilliance as a teacher before a class of students at the police academy. Objecting to this series because it ratifies the stereotype of the super-cop is as silly as objecting to Sherlock Holmes on similar grounds. Like Holmes in many ways, Kojak is a man who realizes deeply private needs and inclinations in the doing of his work. Not law-and-order simplicities, but intelligence and self-realization are what *Kojak* celebrates. The genius of the series is to have conceived a character whose protrayal calls forth from Savalas exactly what his appearance and talents most suit him to do.

The distinction of *Kojak* in its first two seasons seems to me reasonably representative of the achievements of television melodrama in recent years. During the past season, I have seen dozens of programs—episodes of *Harry-O*, *Police Story*, *Baretta*, *Medical Center*, the now-defunct *Medical Story*, several made-for-TV movies, and portions at least of the new mini-series melo-dramas being developed by ABC—whose claims to attention were fully as strong as *Kojak's*. Their partial but genuine excel-lence constitutes an especially salutary reminder of the fact that art always thrives on restraints and prohibitions, indeed that it requires them if it is to survive at all. Like the Renais-sance sonnet or Racine's theater, television melodrama is al-ways most successful when it most fully embraces that which confines it, when *all* the limitations imposed upon it—including such requirements as the 60- or 90-minute time slot, the com-mercial interruptions, the small dimensions of the screen, even the consequences of low-budget filming—become instruments of use, conventions whose combined workings create unpre-tentious and spirited dramatic entertainments, works of popu-lar art that are engrossing, serious, and imaginative.

That such honorific adjectives are rarely applied to television melodrama, that we have effectively refused even to consider the genre in aesthetic terms is a cultural fact and, ultimately, a political fact almost as interesting as the art-works we have been ignoring. Perhaps because television melodrama is an au-thentically popular art—unlike rubber hamburgers, encounter-group theater or electric-kool-aid journalism—our understand-ing of it has been conditioned (if not thwarted entirely) by the enormous authority American high culture grants to avant-garde conceptions of the artist as an adversary figure in mortal conflict with his society. Our attitude toward the medium has been conditioned also by even more deeply ingrained assump-tions about the separate high dignity of aesthetic experience—an activity we are schooled to imagine as uncontaminated by the marketplace, usually at enmity with the everyday world, and dignified by the very rituals of payment and dress and travel and isolation variously required for its enjoyment. It is hard, in an atmosphere which accords art a special if not an openly subversive status, to think of television as an aesthetic medium, for scarcely another institution in American life is at once so familiarly *un*special and so profoundly a creature of the economic and technological genius of advanced industrial capitalism.

Almost everything that is said or written about television, and especially about television drama, is tainted by such prejudices; more often it is in utter servitude to them. And although television itself would no doubt benefit significantly if its nature were perceived and described more objectively, it is the larger culture—whose signature is daily and hourly to be found there—that would benefit far more.

In the introduction to *The Idea of a Theater*, Francis Fergusson reminds us that genuinely popular dramatic art is always powerfully conservative in certain ways, offering stories that insist on "their continuity with the common sense of the community." Hamlet could enjoin the players to hold a mirror up to nature, "to show . . . the very age and body of the time his form and pressure" because, Fergusson tells us, " the Elizabethan theater was itself a mirror which had been formed at the center of the culture of its time, and at the center of the life and awareness of the community." That we have no television Shakespeare is obvious enough, I guess. But we do already have our Thomas Kyds and our Chapmans. A Marlowe, even a Ben Jonson, is not inconceivable. It is time we noticed them.[7]

NOTES

1. The bibliography of serious recent work on melodrama is not overly intimidating, but some exciting and important work has been done. I list here only pieces that have directly influenced my present argument, and I refer the reader to their notes and bibliographies for a fuller survey of the scholarship. Earl F. Bargainnier summarizes recent definitions of melodrama and offers a short history of the genre as practiced by dramatists of the eighteenth and nineteenth centuries in "Melodrama as Formula," *Journal of Popular Culture*, 9 (Winter, 1975). John G. Cawelti's indispensable *Adventure, Mystery, and Romance* (Chicago, 1976) focuses closely and originally on melodrama at several points. Peter Brooks's "The Melodramatic Imagination," in *Romanticism: Vistas, Instances, Continuities*, ed. David Thorburn and Geoffrey Hartman (Cornell, 1973), boldly argues that melodrama is a primary literary and visionary mode in romantic and modern culture. Much recent Dickens criticism is helpful on melodrama, but see especially Robert Garis, *The Dickens*

Theatre (Oxford, 1965), and essays by Barbara Hardy, George H. Ford, and W. J. Harvey in the Dickens volume of the Twentieth-Century Views series, ed. Martin Price (Prentice-Hall, 1967). Melodrama's complex, even symbiotic linkages with the economic and social institutions of capitalist democracy are a continuing (if implicit) theme of Ian Watt's classic *The Rise of the Novel* (University of California Press, 1957), and of Leo Braudy's remarkable essay on Richardson, "Penetration and Impenetrability in Clarissa," in *New Approaches to Eighteenth-Century Literature*, ed. Phillip Harth (Columbia University Press, 1974).

2. Roland Barthes, "The World of Wrestling," in *Mythologies*, trans. Annette Lavers (Hill and Wang, 1972). I am grateful to Jo Anne Lee of the University of California, Santa Barbara, for making me see the connection between Barthes's notions and television drama.

3. I will not discuss soap opera directly, partly because its serial nature differentiates it in certain respects from the prime-time shows, and also because this interesting subgenre of TV melodrama has received some preliminary attention from others. See, for instance, Frederick L. Kaplan, "Intimacy and Conformity in American Soap Opera," *Journal of Popular Culture*, 9 (Winter, 1975); Renata Adler, "Afternoon Television: Unhappiness Enough and Time," *The New Yorker*, 47 (February 12, 1972); Marjorie Perloff, "Soap Bubbles," *The New Republic* (May 10, 1975); and the useful chapter on the soaps in Horace Newcomb's pioneering (if tentative) *TV, The Most Popular Art* (Anchor, 1974). Newcomb's book also contains sections on the prime-time shows I am calling melodramas. For an intelligent fan's impressions of soap opera, see Dan Wakefield's *All Her Children* (Doubleday, 1976).

4. Richard Poirier, *The Performing Self* (Oxford, 1971), p. xiv. I am deeply indebted to this crucial book, and to Poirier's later elaborations on this theory of performance in two pieces on ballet and another on Bette Midler (*The New Republic*, January 5, 1974; March 15, 1975; August 2 & 9, 1975).

5. John Houseman, "TV Drama in the U.S.A.," *Television Quarterly*, 10 (Summer, 1973), p. 12.

6. Michael Wood, *America in the Movies* (Basic Books, 1975), pp. 10–11.

7. Though they are not to be held accountable for the uses to which I have put their advice, the following friends have read earlier versions of this essay and have saved me from many errors: Sheridan Blau, Leo Braudy, John Cawelti, Peter Clecak, Howard Felperin, Richard Slotkin, Alan Stephens, and Eugene Waith.

CONTRIBUTORS

ROBERT C. ALLEN teaches radio-television-film at the University of North Carolina at Chapel Hill. He is the author of *Speaking of Soap Opera* (University of North Carolina Press), and co-author, with Douglas Gomery, of *Film History: Theory and Practice* (Knopf).

RICK ALTMAN teaches French and film studies at the University of Iowa. He is the author of *The Making of A Musical: Fiddler on the Roof* (Crown) and *The American Film Musical* (Indiana University Press).

CHRISTOPHER ANDERSON studies film and television at the University of Texas–Austin. He has published on the Jesse James film cycles in *Cinema Journal* and on television in *The Village Voice*.

DAVID BARKER teaches television production and television studies at Texas Christian University.

JONATHAN BLACK is a contributing editor for *Channels of Communication*.

WAYNE C. BOOTH is Pullman Professor of English at the University of Chicago. He is the author of many books, including *The Rhetoric of Fiction* and *The Limits of Pluralism* (University of Chicago Press).

NICK BROWNE teaches film and television studies at the University of California Los Angeles. He is the author of *The Rhetoric of Filmic Narration* (UMI Research Press) and of many articles on film.

MURIEL CANTOR teaches sociology at American University, Washington, D.C. She is the author of several books on television, most recently, with Suzanne Pingree, *The Soap Opera* (Sage Publications).

JAMES CHESEBRO teaches communication studies at Queens College of the City University of New York. He is the author of many articles on mass communication.

FARRELL CORCORAN teaches communication studies at Northern Illinois University. He is the author of articles on television, mass communication, and interpersonal communication.

JOHN ELLIS, author of *Visible Fictions* (Routledge and Keegan Paul), is an independent television producer and editor of the *Visions:Cinema* series for Britain's Channel 4.

MARTIN ESSLIN teaches drama at Stanford University. He is the author of many books on modern drama and of *The Age of Television* (Freeman).

JANE FEUER teaches film and television studies at the University of Pittsburgh. She is the author of *The Hollywood Musical* (Indiana University Press) and of essays on television.

JOHN FISKE teaches communication studies at Western Australia Institute of Technology. He is co-author *Reading Television* (Methuen) and editor of the Methuen series of communication texts.

TODD GITLIN teaches sociology and communication studies at the University of California-Berkeley. He is the author of several books on communications and politics and, most recently, of *Inside Prime Time* (Pantheon).

DOUGLAS GOMERY teaches film and television studies at the University of Maryland. He is the author of numerous articles on film and television history and industrial practice, and co-author, with Robert C. Allen, of *Film History: Theory and Practice* (Knopf).

JOHN HARTLEY teaches communication studies at Murdock University in Australia. He is the co-author of *Reading Television* (Methuen) and author of *Understanding News* (Methuen).

HAL HIMMELSTEIN teaches communication studies at Brooklyn College of the City University of New York. He is most recently the author of *Television Myth and the American Mind* (Praeger).

PAUL HIRSCH teaches sociology at the University of Chicago. He is the author of numerous articles on communication industries and on management practices in major corporations.

DOROTHY HOROWITZ studies communications at New York University.

WALTER KARP is author of several books on American life and politics, most recently of *The Center: A History and Guide to Rockefeller Center* (American Heritage Publishing Co.). He is a contributing editor for *Channels of Communication*.

ELIHU KATZ teaches sociology and communications studies and is director of the Institute for Communication Studies at Hebrew University, Jerusalem. He also teaches communication studies at the Annenberg School of Communication at the University of Southern California. He is the author of numerous books and articles on the sociology of communication.

DOUGLAS KELLNER teaches philosophy at the University of Texas–Austin. He is the author of many articles on television, cultural politics, and most recently of *Herbert Marcuse* (University of California Press).

MARSHA KINDER teaches film studies at the University of Southern California. She is co-author, with Beverly Houston, of *Self and Cinema:*

A Transformational Perspective (Redgrave) and *Close-up: A Critical Perspective on Film* (Harcourt Brace Jovanovich).

TAMAR LIEBES studies communication at Hebrew University, Jerusalem.

DAVID MARC teaches American Studies at Brown University. He is the author of *Demographic Vistas* (University of Pennsylvania Press) and numerous articles on television.

HORACE NEWCOMB teaches television and communication studies at the University of Texas-Austin. Most recently he is co-author, with Robert S. Alley, of *The Producer's Medium* (Oxford University Press).

JIMMIE REEVES teaches television and communication studies at Auburn University.

THOMAS SCHATZ teaches film and television studies at the University of Texas-Austin. He is the author of *Hollywood Genres* (Random House), *Old Hollywood/New Hollywood* (UMI Research Press), and numerous articles on film.

MICHAEL SCHUDSON teaches sociology and communication studies at the University of California-San Diego. He is the author of *Discovering the News* (Basic Books) and *Advertising: The Uneasy Persuasion* (Basic Books).

CATHY SCHWICTENBERG is a doctoral student at the University of Iowa. She has published several articles on television.

BERNARD TIMBERG teaches television studies and television production at Rutgers University—Newark. He is the co-editor, with John Lawrence of *Fair Use and Copyright* (Ablex).

DAVID THORBURN is Professor of Literature and Director of Film and Media Studies at MIT. He is the author of *Conrad's Romanticism* and a forthcoming book on television, *Story Machine*.